ENVIRONMENTAL PSYCHOLOGY

We do not own the Earth, we are merely borrowing it from our children.

—Amish saying

ENVIRONMENTAL PSYCHOLOGY
AN INTERDISCIPLINARY PERSPECTIVE

Russell Veitch
Bowling Green State University

Daniel Arkkelin
Valparaiso University

PRENTICE HALL, Englewood Cliffs, New Jersey 07632

Library of Congress Cataloging-in-Publication Data

VEITCH, RUSSELL.
    Environmental psychology : an interdisciplinary perspective /
RUSSELL VEITCH, DANIEL ARKKELIN.
    p. cm.
    Includes index.
    ISBN 0-13-282351-9
    1. Environmental psychology.   I. Arkkelin, Daniel.   II. Title.
    BF353.V45   1995
    155.9—dc20   94-37831

Acquistions editor: *Heidi Freund*
Project management and interior design: *Edie Riker*
Cover design: *Bruce Kenselaar*
Cover illustration: *Greg Claycamp*
Photo research: *Heidi Freund*
Buyer: *Tricia Kenny*
Editorial assistant: *Jennifer Fader*

Illustration credits: pp. 1, 16, 21, 52, 54, 75, 117, 149, 156, 160, 203, 205, 223, 255, 290, 315, 321, 411, Used with permission from Peg Randall Gardner, ms.-quotes fine-'tooning. p. 6 © 1981, p. 15 © 1985, p. 47 © 1977, by Sidney Harris-American Scientist Magazine. p. 8, Caterpillar Tractor Co. p. 29, Adapted from Russell & Ward (1982) with permission from the *Annual Review of Psychology*, Volume 33, © 1982 by Annual Reviews Inc. p. 50, Adapted with permission from Coombs, Dawes & Tversky (1970). p. 61, 140, 188, 193, 194, 429, 435, Courtesy of R. and J. Veitch. p. 92, Courtesy of Valparaiso University. p. 100, "Butterfly Curve" from *Adaptation-Level Theory: An Experimental and Systematic Approach to Behavior* by H. Helson. Copyright © by Harper & Row, Publishers, Inc. Reprinted by permission of HarperCollins Publishers. p. 101, From Russell & Pratt (1980). A description of the affective quality attributed to environments. *Journal of Personality and Social Psychology, 38*, 311–322. Copyright 1980 by the American Psychological Association. Adapted by permission. p. 125, 355, 372, AP/Wide World Photos. p. 128, NOAA. p. 128, Bermuda News Bureau. p. 134, From *Stressful Life Events and Their Contexts*, edited by Barbara Snell Dohrenwend and Bruce P. Dohrenwend. Copyright © 1984 by Rutgers, the State University. Reprinted by permission of Rutgers University Press. p. 158, UPI/Bettman. p. 237, © 1993 by Tom Cheney, reprinted with permission. p. 292, Irene Springer. p. 302, Federal Bureau of Prisons. p. 383, From the *Wall Street Journal*, with permission of Cartoon Features Syndicate.

 © 1995 by Prentice-Hall, Inc.
A Simon & Schuster Company
Englewood Cliffs, New Jersey 07632

Printed in the United States of America

10 9 8 7 6 5 4 3 2

ISBN   0-13-282351-9

Prentice-Hall International (UK) Limited, *London*
Prentice-Hall of Australia Pty. Limited, *Sydney*
Prentice-Hall Canada Inc., *Toronto*
Prentice-Hall Hispanoamericana, S.A., *Mexico*
Prentice-Hall of India Private Limited, *New Delhi*
Prentice-Hall of Japan, Inc., *Tokyo*
Simon & Schuster Asia Pte. Ltd., *Singapore*
Editora Prentice-Hall do Brasil, Ltda., *Rio de Janeiro*

Contents

Preface

Humans have only recently, yet painfully, become aware of the ways in which they to misuse and abuse the natural environment. They have also recently become more concerned with the ways in which the environment affects their own lives. We contaminate the air we breathe and pollute the rivers from which we draw our drinking water; we build energy-inefficient, dehumanizing buildings in which to live and hospitals which are unhealthy; our prisons promote crime and our schools retard learning. The recent emergence of the discipline of environmental psychology reflects the efforts of psychologists and other scientists to deal with these and many other issues in person/environment relationships. But, while we are gaining information daily, and while laudable steps are being taken to restore the balance between humans and the environment, these efforts must be increased if our planet is to remain habitable. This book was written to provide the reader with a comprehensive introduction to the new and growing field of environmental psychology and in the process increase understanding and awareness of person-environment relationships.

Issues in person-environment relationships are enormously complex and this complexity is reflected in the diversity of environmental psychology. Indeed, while the discipline emphasizes the individual in his/her relation to the environment (hence the "psychological" orientation), a host of social and physical forces also operate in this relationship. Thus, environmental psychology is inherently interdisciplinary, drawing from and contributing to other social sciences such as sociology, economics and political science, as well as other natural sciences such as meteorology, biology and chemistry. We have made a concerted effort to reflect this interdisciplinary orientation, incorporating theories and data from all of these disciplines as well as others such as architecture and law. Despite this interdisciplinary approach, the book is firmly anchored in psychology and includes comprehensive and up-to-date coverage of the extensive knowledge base contributed uniquely from our own discipline.

We believe that this dual focus makes this text appropriate for not only psychology students but also for students in all of the above disciplines. Indeed, it is our belief that this is the best way to contribute to the solutions of environmental problems and it is our hope that this book will be read by students from a variety of disciplines in environmental psychology courses as well as courses in related disciplines. To this end, the level of writing is easily accessible to the widest possible audience without doing injustice to the complexity and technical nature of the topics covered. We have endeavored to engage the student by providing a wide array of examples from readers' common experiences to illustrate concepts and to facilitate learning, enjoyment and appreciation of the discipline through personal application.

While examples permeate the entire text, some applications are highlighted in **"Time-Out"** exercises interspersed throughout each chapter. These sections invite the student to reflect on material presented in preceding sections and relate this to material in subsequent sections through personal application. This helps the reader to integrate information throughout the chapter in addition to providing a break from passive reading by encouraging active processing of the information. Other pedagogical aids include a chapter outline at the beginning of each chapter and chapter summaries and a listing of important terms at the end. Another feature that we believe renders the text useful as a research resource is that references in each chapter appear at the end of the chapter, rather than in a simple alphabetical listing of all references in an appendix.

The book is organized into three major sections. **PART I, "Basic Issues in Person-Environment Relationships,"** begins with a historical overview of the emergence of environmental psychology and a definition of the discipline in Chapter 1. Chapter 2 reviews important theories of environment-behavior relationships and introduces a unifying model which is continually referred to in subsequent chapters. Chapter 3 presents issues in research methods in environmental psychology, and Chapter 4 discusses the fundamental issues of environmental perception, cognition and evaluation. **PART II, "Effects of Environmental Stressors,"** begins with a comprehensive presentation of the concept of environmental stress in Chapter 5. The next two chapters discuss issues related to the atmospheric environment, beginning with a discussion of temperature, wind, sunshine and ion concentration in Chapter 6 and various types of chemical pollution in Chapter 7. Chapter 8 is devoted to a discussion of noise as an environmental stressor. This section concludes with a discussion of crowding, territoriality, privacy and personal space in Chapters 9 and 10. **PART III, "Applications of Environmental Psychology,"** includes discussions of institutional and residential design in Chapters 11 and 12, natural disasters and technological catastrophes in Chapter 13, and a consideration of economic, political and legal issues in the future of person-environment relationships in Chapter 14. The text concludes in Chapter 15 with a discussion of methods for changing environmental attitudes and behavior to preserve the environment for posterity.

While we recommend that Chapters one through five be covered first in a course to lay the groundwork for the rest of the material, the remaining chapters can be used in any order if the instructor chooses to depart from our organization. Further, the material in each chapter is self-contained, so the instructor can delete coverage of any particular chapter without concern for student understanding of others. Thus, the book is designed for flexibility of use, and we believe that it is appropriate for use as a primary text in both undergraduate and graduate environmental psychology courses as well as a supplementary text in courses in related disciplines.

This book has been a true "labor of love" reflecting both of our concern for enhancing person-environment relationships as well as promoting the science and application of the discipline of environmental psychology. The book has been in development for numerous years, and we would like to first express sincere appreciation to the hundreds of students who have given us useful feedback on various revisions as we "class-tested" them over the years. We also thank Susan Finnemore Brennan for her interest and encouragement in the initial stages of our work with Prentice Hall and especially to Heidi Freund, our managing editor who spent countless hours of her personal time helping us to bring the work to conclusion. Thanks are also due to Joan Polk and Jennifer Fader, editorial assistants at Prentice Hall, for their efforts, as well as to Edie Riker of East End Publishing Services for her professionalism in guiding the text through production. We also valued the helpful comments of several anonymous reviewers, and the book is improved considerably as a result of their careful and insightful feedback. We also thank Peg Randall Gardner, of ms.-quotes fine-'tooning, for her ability and willing efforts to illustrate many of our thoughts in original cartoon format. Last but not least, we thank our wives, Jan and Jan, and our children, Robin, Justin, Aaron, and Adam for their support, encouragement, patience and understanding of our inattention at times and our frequent abandonment of familial responsibilities while we worked on this labor of love. It is with far greater love that we dedicate this book to them.

Russell Veitch
Daniel Arkkelin

Introduction to Environmental Psychology

FIGURE 1-1 Only gradually have we become aware of the delicate balance between the quality of the environment and the quality of human life.

A DEFINITION OF ENVIRONMENTAL
    PSYCHOLOGY
THE ENVIRONMENT

CURRENT EVENTS INFLUENCING
    ENVIRONMENTAL PSYCHOLOGY
SUMMARY

Until relatively recently only a few scientists and perhaps fewer public officials were concerned with the influence of advancing technology, population growth, and urbanization on the quality of the environment and ultimately on the quality of human existence. Technological advances were hailed for making dramatic improvements in the quality of life and for facilitating the endless search for comfort and luxury, without appreciation of the effects these advances were having on the quality of the environment. The term *environment* was rarely mentioned in the media and few legislators were making any concerted efforts to pass laws to protect it. Gradually, though, we have become aware of the delicate balance between the quality of the environment and the quality of human life, and we have come to realize that this balance can be easily upset by human actions.

The dangers of acid rain, the fallibility of nuclear power plants, and the difficulties in handling and disposing of toxic chemicals are coming to be appreciated. Other stark realizations are also being confronted. Among these are that the pace of suburban sprawl and urban decay is quickening; the depletion of nonrenewable resources is an inevitability; and cheap energy is a thing of the past. Chemicals such as dioxin, formaldehyde, PCB (polychlorinated biphenyl), and sulfur dioxide, once found only in the lexicon of scientists, are becoming household words, and heretofore unknown places like Love Canal, Chernobyl, Bhopal, and Three Mile Island are making nearly everyone's list of places they would rather not be. The incredible capacity and propensity of humans to misuse and abuse the environment is now painfully apparent. Despite these seeming revelations, though, we have only begun to understand the human role in maintaining the health of the planet, to comprehend the effect of present actions on future outcomes, and to consider alternatives to environmentally destructive behaviors.

But begun we have, and today daily newspapers and the nightly news regularly report the abusive treatment received by our water, land, and air, as well as the rapid depletion of energy resources. Numerous local, state, and federal laws governing the use of our physical environment have been enacted and the Environmental Protection Agency (EPA) has been created. Steps are being taken to prevent massive oil spills at sea, to keep blast furnaces from belching ugly smoke and harmful particulates into the atmosphere, to preclude raw sewage and deadly chemicals from being discharged into water, and to forestall the accumulation of mountainous heaps of solid waste. Efforts are also being made to reduce energy consumption, to design buildings to promote human functioning, to plan for urban development, and to establish and preserve wilderness areas. The consciousness of the world has been so awakened that the first Earth Conference was held in Oxford, England, in 1988. In attendance were leading world scientists, as well as political and spiritual leaders, each in their own way, attempting to lay out a plan for Earth's survival (Vittachi, 1989).

Despite the accelerated efforts of scientists, engineers, political and spiritual leaders, and the general public, environmental problems are far from being solved. Without doubt there has been increased concern by humans for their environment, but the wherewithal to turn this concern into effective remediating actions has not always been available. In fact, there are those who claim that the environment has already received sufficient abuse to render the planet uninhabitable by the twenty-second century. They point with indignation to the number of species that have become extinct in the past 100 years, the desertification of once arable lands, the denuding of forests and eutrophication of waters caused by acid rain, and the increasing shroud of smog smothering more and more of the world's cities as evidence that the day of reckoning is approaching. They see the environment as a helpless pawn in the struggle between the haves and the have-nots. Usurpation of natural resources by the powerful and a desire to maintain them by the weak, they claim, has turned the environment into a battleground and the ultimate loser in this struggle.

There are those, of course, who just as emphatically point with pride to the great strides that have been made in alleviating human suffering and promoting human welfare in the areas of agriculture, medicine, and even design technology. If there is a problem, they claim human ingenuity will solve it. To them there is no energy shortage, only an extraction problem; there is no population problem, only an uneven distribution of the species; there is no toxic waste problem, only a few bugs to be worked out of the transportation and storage mechanisms.

Obviously, the jury is still out with respect to who is right in this debate. It is possible that technology will be made available to alleviate some of the pressure that humans are placing on the earth's resources. It is also possible that the destructive behavior of humans will change sufficiently to reverse the trend in environmental degradation. One thing for certain is that the debate is heating up. The convening of the United Nations Earth Summit in June 1992 in Rio de Janiero is ample evidence that more people are becoming aware of the situation.

Accompanying this recent heightened concern with human influences on the environment has been a resurgence of interest in the effect of the environment on human functioning. A multitude of biological, psychological, and social horrors have been augured given continued environmental degradation and unchecked population growth. Information is beginning to amass regarding the physiological, psychological, and behavioral effects of unwanted noise, air pollution, excessive temperatures, barometric pressure, building design, among other environmental factors. Short-term effects are being studied as well as long-term accumulative effects. Additionally, a growing literature suggests that some environmental conditions produce detrimental aftereffects in those exposed to them (i.e., the effects do not manifest themselves immediately, but rather show up much later after their causes have been removed). These, too, are being studied with renewed interest. Similarly, the potential to alter values, attitudes, and behavior vis-à-vis the environment is being explored.

The recent emergence of environmental psychology as a discipline signals a growing discontent with mere speculation and uninformed rhetoric (often emotional) and reflects the efforts of social, behavioral, and biological scientists (along with their colleagues in the design and engineering professions) to gain data-based answers to questions regarding human/environment interactions. This increased concern, coupled with increased research, has led to a substantiation of some popular opinions and to a refutation of others. This book

provides an introduction to what is currently known regarding person-environment relationships and invites the reader to think about, add to, and act upon
this information.

A DEFINITION OF ENVIRONMENTAL PSYCHOLOGY

Environmental psychology constitutes an area of inquiry that is rooted in
numerous disciplines. Biologists, geologists, psychologists, lawyers, geographers, economists, sociologists, chemists, physicists, historians, philosophers,
and all of their subdisciplines, and all of their engineering brethren share an
interest in understanding the complex, often delicate, set of relationships
between humans and their environments. While this understanding often is
sought for its own sake (the goal of basic research), it is probably safe to say that
most scientists get involved in the environmental sciences as a response to social
concerns. Its proponents, therefore, tend to focus on socially relevant problems
and to emphasize practical application of knowledge. They emphasize the interrelationship of environment and behavior—that is, they not only see the physical environment as influencing people's behavior but also see people as actively, though sometimes passively, influencing the environment. Because of this
multiplicity of origins, and because of its relative youth as a discipline, environmental psychology is still evolving. Any definition of the field must therefore
reflect its breadth and its changing nature, must include an acknowledgment of
its strong pull to application (while being careful not to dismiss the need for
basic research), and must stress the reciprocal relationship of organisms to their
environments. Environmental psychology could, therefore, be defined as *a behavioral science that investigates, with an eye toward enhancing, the interrelationships
between the physical environment and human behavior.*

Even though this definition includes the concerns expressed above, it
does not capture the richness of thinking of those involved in the discipline, nor
does it reveal the desire of its partisans to develop systemic and intersystemic
models of understanding. For example, environmental psychologists are interested in the various physiological, psychological, and behavioral processes by
which people respond to the complexities of their environment. Researchers in
the field therefore investigate questions that involve physiological content (e.g.,
changes in heart rate, endocrine functioning, Galvanic Skin Response, mortality), psychological content (e.g., spatial behavior patterns, mental images, environmental stress, attitude change, place satisfaction), and behavioral content
(e.g., altruism, aggression, performance). They are concerned with understanding human attitudes about, experiences within, and behaviors toward the environment, with an eye toward changing those attitudes and behaviors to promote
environmental preservation and to maximize human functioning. Furthermore,
they are likely to deal with this content from an interdisciplinary perspective;
that is, they might be concerned with meteorological, physical, geographical,
architectural, and/or ecological features of the environment that might have an
impact on its inhabitants. Without doubt these aspects are also of concern to

geologists, physicists, chemists, and biologists. The field of environmental psychology, however, attempts to deal with these concerns simultaneously to develop a systematic and integrated understanding of the interrelated processes governing organism/environment relationships.

Additionally, researchers in the field of environmental psychology are often simultaneously pulled toward both the resolution of practical problems and the formulation of broad-based integrative theory. Theoretical refinement often requires further (often nit-picking appearing) research, whereas practical concerns demand solutions to present problems. The environmental psychologist tends to deal with these facets simultaneously. For example, theoretical advances in our understanding of human responses to crowding can contribute to practical applications to prevent adverse reactions to high population density. Similarly, applied studies of "crowd control" techniques can help to refine theories accounting for responses to crowding. This interplay between basic and applied research will be considered in greater detail in Chapter 3 and will be noted throughout the present text.

It is clear that as a discipline the uniqueness of environmental psychology is found in its diversity. This diversity is manifest in terms of the disciplines that impact on it, in the research methods and tactics utilized within it, in the areas of human concern to which its findings are applied, and in the theories developed to account for its research findings. Given these various considerations, and the knowledge that any definition of the field of environmental psychology is subject to criticism and change, we will define environmental psychology as *a multidisciplinary behavioral science, both basic and applied in orientation, whose foci are the systematic interrelationships between the physical and social environments and individual human behavior and experience.*

THE ENVIRONMENT

The simplest expression of this definition is found in the work of psychologist Kurt Lewin (1951) who sometime ago made the following statement: "In principle it is everywhere accepted that behavior (B) is a function of the person (P) and the environment (E), $B = f(P,E)$ and that P and E in this formula are interdependent variables" (p. 25). However, as Wohlwill (1970) has noted: "the role of the environment has almost invariably referred to social or interpersonal influences, or else to effects presumed to be ascribable to the milieu in an altogether unspecified sense" (p. 304). And Saegert (1987), noting the lack of specificity for the term, has lamented that the social sciences tend to define the environment almost exclusively in terms of social transactions and institutions. Thus, although the term *environment* has been used for some time, it has remained vaguely defined, referring to an unspecified physical and social backdrop for behavior. And even when referring to nonsocial conditions the term *environment* has been used to apply to sets of conditions as diverse as the climatic conditions of a given geographic area, the cockpit of an airplane, the area surrounding a toxic waste site, the structure of large corporations, reward/punishment contin-

FIGURE 1-2 While meteorological, physical, geographical, architectural, and/or ecological features of the environment are of concern singly to geologists, physicists, chemists and biologists, the field of environmental psychology attempts to deal with these concerns simultaneously to develop a systematic and integrated understanding of the interrelated processes.

gencies, the design of nursery schools, the "turf" of street gangs, a church congregation, the temperature in experimental environmental chambers, and the size and placement of commodes in the residential bathroom, to name but a few.

It really should come as no surprise that the term *environment* lacks specificity. Among others, historians, biologists, architects, sociologists, economists, and psychologists have used the term idiosyncratically in defining variables of interest to their own discipline. Historians have sought the environmental *Zeitgeist*, biologists the *ecological niche*, architects the *design features* of the built environment, and economists the *ratio of supply to demand* to account for external influences on human behavior. We will return to the issue of environmental definition over and over again in the present text, and we will see that, whereas the term "environment" lacks specificity, it is nonetheless possible to be explicit regarding the assumptions that underlie its study.

The assumptions that we see as underlying all environmental science, independently of specific orientation, are as follows: (1) The earth is the only suitable habitat we have; (2) the earth's resources are limited; (3) the earth as a planet has been and continues to be profoundly affected by life; (4) the effects of land use by humans tend to be cumulative; and (5) sustained life on earth is a characteristic of ecosystems and not of individual organisms or populations. Implicit in these assumptions is a call not only for multidisciplinary but also interdisciplinary strategies, methods, and philosophical perspectives in perceiving, understanding, and maintaining the delicate relationships that exist between humans and their environments. In the following pages we will elaborate each of these assumptions.

The earth is the only suitable habitat we have, and its resources are limited. Throughout the history of the earth various forms of life have begun, evolved, prospered, and died out, with the present dominance by humans being a very

FIGURE 1-3 Some time ago Kurt Lewin (1951) made the following statement: "In principle it is everywhere accepted that behavior (B) is a function of the person (P) and the environment (E), $B = f(P,E)$ and that P and E in this formula are interdependent variables" (p. 25).

$$B = f\ (P,E = f\ \{B = f\ [P,\ E]...\})$$

B variables	P variables	E variables
Performance task perception	*Species* humans rats	*Pollutants* air-borne particulates noise temperature
Social aggression altruism	*Personality* authoritarianism locus of control	*Microenvironments* airplane cockpit classrooms
Physiological heart rate epinepherine secretion RAS activation	*Constitutional Differences* gender genetic make-up	*Macroenvironments* housing development nursing homes
Cultural differences child-rearing	*Cultural differences* perception	*Geoenvironments* weather conditions

A partial listing of some of the variables that have been researched by environmental psychologists. Note that Lewin's formulation $B = f(P, E)$ is embedded within itself to designate the reciprocal relations these variables have with one another.

FIGURE 1-4 Clearing forests not only affects the earth visually, but changes the amount of carbon dioxide in the atmosphere, the albedo of the earth's surface and hydrologic drainage patterns.

recent development. But, despite this current domination two fundamental truths must be faced: (1) Humans, too, will succumb to extinction either through geologic, meteorologic, or interstellar cataclysm, natural biological processes, internecine quarrels, or because the earth's resources will no longer support human life in its present form, and (2) although there may be other habitable islands in the cosmic sea, they are spaced at such great distances throughout the universe as to be virtually irrelevant to human survival. Notwithstanding these certainties, the earth is very important to those of us who are now living and to our children and to theirs. We must learn to live with the opportunities as well as the limitations the earth affords, with the inexorable fact that it is dynamic and changing. And, we must do so in a way that allows for continued human existence. The newly emerging area of environmental psychology holds the promise of providing information that will allow sustained human tenure on earth.

The earth as a planet has been profoundly affected by life. Human contributions to the visual landscape of the planet are everywhere: tall skyscrapers, intricate networks of highways and electrical lines, engineered lakes, and the vapor trails of high-flying jet planes are constant reminders of human presence. More subtle indicators are the changing quality of the chemical composition of the atmosphere, geologic changes in the earth's crust, engineering changes in hydrologic processes and chemical changes in the waters that cover the planet.

Clearing of forests, plowing of land, and black-topping of highways and parking lots not only affect the earth visually, but change the amount of carbon dioxide in the atmosphere, the light reflecting and absorbing characteristics of the earth's surface and hydrologic drainage patterns. These changes, in turn, influence the rate of heating and cooling and, therefore, the temperature of the earth and its atmosphere. Weather and climate are thus influenced by the presence of humans. It is hoped that a more thorough understanding of the ways in which humans influence earth's natural processes will lead to more intelligent and life-preserving behaviors on their part. Perhaps this text will add to that understanding.

The outcomes of land use by humans tend to be cumulative and therefore we have obligations to ourselves as well as to future generations to minimize their negative effects. A number of changes in the environment are brought about by human habitation; fall plowing, the development of sanitation systems, and the building of shelters are but just a few. These practices influence the earth immediately as well as having long-term impact. A dam built today not only supplies electrical energy for today's population but also influences the course of the waterways on which the dams are built, often in irreversible fashion. The inescapable conclusion of all this is that while humans have multiplied, their life's resources have shrunk, and there is every indication that this trend is continuing. For example, the same conditions that helped to create the Sahara are expanding it southward. Every year two to three more square miles are lost to the drought and sands. The Thar Desert of India is advancing at the rate of about one-half mile annually along its entire perimeter. We have an obligation to ourselves and to future generations to see that this trend is halted, if not reversed. An understanding of environmental psychology represents a start toward reversing these trends.

Sustained life on earth is a characteristic of ecosystems and not of individual organisms or populations. No single organism, population, or species is capable of both producing all its own food and completely recycling all of its own metabolic products. Green plants and light produce carbon dioxide, sugar and water; from sugar and inorganic compounds many organic compounds are manufactured including protein and woody tissue. But no plant can degrade the woody tissue developed in this fashion back to its inorganic compounds. This degradation requires other organisms such as bacteria and fungi. To complete the recycling of chemical elements from inorganic to organic and back to inorganic requires the use of several species. The smallest system capable of complete chemical recycling is known as an *ecosystem*. Humans are part of a very complex and delicately balanced ecosystem. Thus, to understand humans fully it is necessary to study them within the context of the ecosystems in which they survive. Environmental psychology is the field that attempts to develop an understanding of this interdependency.

It should be clear by now that to comprehend fully the relationship of humans to their environment the student of the environment should be aware of contributions from a large number of disciplines. *Environmental studies* by their very nature are the domain of a generalist with a strong interdisciplinary interest. All environmental problems must be looked at from numerous perspectives so that a clear and total picture can be put together from the many pieces.

CURRENT EVENTS INFLUENCING ENVIRONMENTAL PSYCHOLOGY

If present trends continue, the world will become increasingly crowded, more polluted (Leonard, 1986; Peterson, 1987), less stable ecologically (Manabe & Wetherald, 1986), and more vulnerable to disruption (World Commission on Environment and Development, 1987). Supplies of drinking water will diminish drastically, and despite greater material output, the world's people will become poorer than they are today (Postel, 1985, 1986, 1987). The forests of the world will become increasingly denuded as a result of the requirements of wood for building and burning (Bowander, 1987; Myers, 1984) and as a result of the increasing acidity of rainfall worldwide. Increases in arable land will be offset by the usurpation of land for dwelling sites and the desertification of lands resulting from overpopulation.

Population Trends

World population projections concur that, given current trends, our numbers will reach 10 billion by 2030 and 30 billion by the end of the twenty-first century. These numbers are close to the estimates of the carrying capacity of the entire earth. In some places on the globe, however, the carrying capacity has already been exceeded. Populations in sub-Saharan Africa and in the Himalayan regions of Asia have exceeded the capacity of the immediate area to sustain life. Overgrazing, fuelwood gathering, and destructive cropping practices have coalesced to cause a series of ecological transitions leading from open woodlands, to scrub, to fragile semiarid range, to worthless weeds, and finally to bare earth. Matters are made worse where animal dung and crop wastes must be burned for heating and cooking. Croplands are then deprived of organic materials, lose their ability to hold water, and become less fertile. In Bangladesh, Pakistan, and large parts of India, the efforts of large numbers of people to meet their basic needs have damaged the cropland, pasture, forests, and water supplies upon which their livelihood depends. Thus, the dramatic increase in world population has been an impetus for the emergence of environmental psychology.

Resource Depletion and Environmental Deterioration

Other examples of serious deterioration in the earth's basic resources can be found throughout the world, including the industrialized nations. Erosion of agricultural soil, salinization of highly productive irrigated farmland, deforestation, and lake acidification is becoming more prevalent in the United States, and extensive loss of tropical forests and more or less permanent soil degradation have occurred throughout much of the Amazon River Basin (McHale, 1979). The world's deserts now make up 800 million hectares and are increasing in size.

Regional water shortages and deteriorating water quality, already a problem in many parts of the world, are likely to worsen. Increases of 200 to 300 percent in the world water withdrawals are projected to occur in the next twenty years, with much of it being contaminated as a result of waterways being used to provide coolants and as waste transports. The potential for human conflict over the use of freshwater reservoirs is accented by the fact that of the 200 major river basins of the world, 148 are shared by two countries and 52 are shared by three to ten countries. Long-standing difficulties over the shared rivers of Plata (Brazil and Argentina), Euphrates (Syria and Iraq), and Ganges (Bangladesh and India) have the potential to intensify as the need for additional freshwater occurs. Thus, the depletion of natural resources essential for survival has been another factor influencing the development of environmental psychology.

The by-products of an industrialized, increasingly urbanized, and highly populated planet bring with them a host of problems. Chemical and human waste is being produced at rates faster than we can safely dispose of them; nonrenewable resources are being consumed at increasing rates; plans for reestablishing renewable resources are shortsighted, and the fate of our waterways, wildlife, climate, and perhaps the earth itself appears in jeopardy. The deterioration of the environment is thus another reason for the increased interest in environmental psychology.

Public Policy and the Environment

The problems in preserving the carrying capacity of the earth and sustaining the possibility of a decent life for human beings are indeed enormous and imminent, but they are just that—problems. Policy changes, coupled with government, business, and individual actions, can do much to alleviate many of them. Policies that mandate reforestation after cutting, that require detoxification of chemical by-products before disposal, and that involve judicious soil management have begun to be implemented. Interest in energy and material conservation is growing, industrial and household recycling is becoming more prevalent, and the need for family planning is becoming better understood. High-yield hybrids are continuously being introduced and methods for farming the seas are being developed. The need for reliable, scientific data upon which to base public policy has given a sense of urgency to the development of environmental psychology and has contributed to its growth as a discipline.

Human Behavior and the Environment

Encouraging as these policy developments are, they are far from adequate to meet the growing challenges of humankind. Needed changes go far beyond the responsibility of one nation, and new initiatives must be taken if worsening poverty, environmental degradation, and international conflict are to be averted. The solutions, if they exist, are complex and long-term and inextricably tied to the problems of poverty, injustice, and social conflict. The problems of the globe are human problems, many of which have been caused directly or indirectly by human presence. Advanced technology, while potentially a part of the solution to some of these problems, is also the cause of many of them. Because many of these problems are the result of human behavior, the psychologist, whose domain of interest is human behavior, has potentially a great deal to contribute in their resolution.

Environmental psychologists are very much attuned to the health of Mother Earth. They realize there are no quick fixes and that only through understanding and changing human behavior can there be any hope of maintaining a habitable planet—that is, even though psychologists recognize that many of the above problems are technological, they also emphasize that the source of these problems is human behavior. Equally important is their realization that without an understanding of the mechanisms and laws that govern the life-sustaining processes of the earth, there is no hope that any changes in human behaviors or policies will have any medicinal effects.

Note: Earlier in this chapter we said that we considered the present text to be an invitation to you, the reader, to "think about, add to, and act upon" the increasing knowledge you have regarding the relationship of humans to their environments. To assist you with this we will be providing "Time-Outs" throughout the text. These features will attempt to help you tie together material presented in the preceding sections, to reflect on this material, and to think about material in subsequent sections. What follows, then, is the first of these Time-Out sections.

TIME-OUT: Think for a moment about your principal place of residence. How has human occupation of this area changed it over the last ten years? Are there more or fewer trees? Are there more or fewer undomesticated animals? Has the number of houses increased or decreased? Do you have more or less space you can call your own? More or fewer places of solitude? Have there been changes that might be considered irreversible? What are they? How did these changes influence the ecology of this area? In what ways did they contribute to the quality of life for human inhabitants? Were the changes that you've noted planned or did they just happen? Earlier in the text it was suggested that if present trends continue, the world will become increasingly crowded, more polluted, less stable ecologically, and more vulnerable to disruption. Is there any evidence that the environment of your principal place of residence is contributing to this trend? If so, what is the evidence? If not, why do you think this is so?

Now think again about this environment. Only this time think not about how humans have modified it, but rather think about how this environment directs or modifies the behavior of its inhabitants. Are work and leisure times influenced by availability of public transportation or automobile traffic flow patterns? Was your interest in golf, tennis, swimming, the ballet, or roller skating enhanced by the availability of accessible facilities? Was the type of pet you had (or did not have) as a child influenced by the environment in which you lived? Is the extent to which you are likely to let a stranger into your house to use your phone influenced by the environment in which you live?

As you engage in this exercise it should become clear that very few environments escape human modifications—some moderate, but others extensive and irreversible. It should also become clear that our daily behaviors from the time we arise in the morning, through the routes we take to get to work, to the leisure-time activities in which we engage are often directed by environmental circumstances of which we are unaware or take for granted.

SUMMARY

Recently there has been a renewed interest in human/environment relations. Worldwide concern regarding equitable management of natural resources, absolute increases in population and increases in population density, and changing technologies with their subsequent demands for additional energy (as well as the problems they create as a by-product) have coalesced to fuel this rejuvenated interest. Thinkers in these and related areas have laid the groundwork for the development of some rudimentary theories to account for human/environment relations. It is to these theories that we will turn in the next chapter.

IMPORTANT CONCEPTS

defining environmental psychology
defining the "environment"

$B = f(P,E)$
influences on environmental psychology

REFERENCES

Bowander, B. (1987, Spring). Deforestation around urban centers in India. *Environmental Conservation*, 14(1).

Leonard, J. (1986, April). Hazardous wastes: The crisis spreads. *National Development*.

Lewin, K. (1951). *Field theory in social science*. New York: Harper.

Manabe, S., and Wetherald, R.J. (1984, May). Reductions in summer soil wetness induced by an increase in atmospheric carbon dioxide. *Science*.

McHale, M.C. (1979). *Children in the world*. Washington, D.C.: Population Reference Bureau, 30–34.

Myers, N. (1984). *The primary source: Tropical forests and our future*. New York: W.W. Norton & Co., Inc.

Peterson, C. (1987). Ozone depletion worsens: Hazards to research seen. *Washington Post,* October 28.

Postel, S. (1985, September). Conserving water: The untapped alternative. *Worldwatch Paper 67.* Washington, D.C.: Worldwatch Institute.

Postel, S. (1986, July). Altering the earth's chemistry: Assessing the risks. *Worldwatch Paper 71.* Washington, D.C.: Worldwatch Institute.

Postel, S. (1987, September). Defusing the toxic threats: Controlling pesticides and industrial waste. *Worldwatch Paper 74.* Washington, D.C.: Worldwatch Institute.

Saegert, S. (1987). Environmental psychology and social change. In D. Stokols & I. Altman (Eds.), *Handbook of environmental psychology.* New York: John Wiley.

Vittachi, A. (1989). *Earth conference one: Sharing a vision for our planet.* Boston: New Science Library.

Wohlwill, J.F. (1970). The emerging discipline of environmental psychology. *American Psychologist, 25,* 303–312.

World Commission on Environment and Development. (1987). *Our common future.* New York: Oxford University Press.

Theories in Environmental Psychology

2

FIGURE 2-1 The interdisciplinary nature of environmental psychology leads to difficulties in the systematic application of knowledge and in the development of well-articulated unifying theories.

In Chapter 1 it was noted that environmental psychology is an interdisciplinary field of study—that is, researchers in the area are based in various disciplines, and the observations from which they theorize and the data from which they draw conclusions have a multiplicity of origins. It would not be uncommon, for example, to find psychologists, anthropologists, sociologists, urban planners, architects, biologists, and physiologists all collecting data on, and attempting to understand, the impact of population density on behavior. Each may choose slightly different research designs, use slightly different methodologies, study different behaviors and perhaps even look at different species, but all would be concerned with the question of what happens to organisms singly, and in the aggregate, as their numbers increase without concurrent increases in the size of the environment housing them. Occasionally teams of researchers from diverse disciplines might even work together toward the understanding of some phenomenon. For example, researchers from the areas of medicine, psychology, engineering, and sociology have all studied the impact of the nuclear power plant accident at Three Mile Island.

THEORIES IN ENVIRONMENTAL PSYCHOLOGY

On the one hand, the interdisciplinary nature of environmental psychology is laudable in that various perspectives are brought to bear on a single phenomenon, leading, it is hoped, to fewer "tunnel-vision" theories, and to more generally applicable solutions. On the other hand, it is this very multiplicity that leads to difficulties in the systematic application of knowledge and in the development of well-articulated unifying theories.

FIGURE 2-2 Occasionally teams of researchers from diverse disciplines might even work together toward the understanding of some phenomenon.

Historical Influences

Thinking among environmental psychologists has been influenced by theories both within and outside of the discipline of psychology. Some of these theories are very broad in scope whereas others are more focused; some are lacking in empirical basis and others are more data-based. We will review a number of them to provide the context for a consideration of current theories of environment-behavior relationships. These perspectives include *geographical determinism, ecological biology, behaviorism,* and *Gestalt psychology.* See Moos (1976) for an in-depth discussion of these influences.

Some historians and some geographers have attempted to account for the rise and fall of entire civilizations on the basis of environmental characteristics. For example, Toynbee (1962) theorized that the environment (specifically, topography, climate, vegetation, availability of water, etc.) presents challenges to its inhabitants. Extreme environmental challenge leads to the destruction of a civilization, whereas too little challenge leads to stagnation of the culture. Thus, Toynbee proposed that an intermediate level of environmental challenge enhances the development of civilizations, and extremely diminished or excessive levels are debilitating. The notion of environmental challenge and behavioral response, although rooted in the thinking of such *geographical determinists,* appears often in one form or another in various theories in environmental psychology.

As one example Barry, Child, and Bacon (1959) have suggested that agricultural, non-nomadic cultures seem to emphasize responsibility, obedience, and compliance in their child-rearing practices, whereas nomadic cultures often emphasize independence and resourcefulness. These differences, they suggest, result from the fact that people who live and work together in organized non-mobile communities require more structured organization and therefore stress the importance of obedience and compliance. On the other hand, independence and resourcefulness are esteemed and inculcated by nomads in preparation to meet the changing and unpredictable demands of an environment confronted by a "roaming" people. Thus, the argument goes, the environment sets the stage for the development of cultures having the best chance of surviving it.

In a very real sense, this is no different from saying that ghetto culture cultivates a set of skills in its inhabitants that are best suited to survive the ghetto. Someone not skilled in the craft of street fighting, it can be argued, is not likely to survive the environment of the streets. We will see later in this text that some have carried this argument to the point of claiming that hospitals, prisons, and other institutional environments develop in their inhabitants characteristics that are ostensibly survival-oriented to these environments, yet turn out to be maladaptive in the larger environment.

The development of *ecological theories,* theories concerned with biological and sociological interdependence between organisms and their environment, has also significantly influenced thinking in environmental psychology. With the development of ecological science, organisms were no longer viewed as being separate from their environment, but were seen as integral to it. This notion of organism-environment reciprocity now appears in many current environment-behavior theories. The environment and its inhabitants are still often studied as separate components, but no one doubts their interdependency. These various components are seen as constituting a total system and changes in any single unit are assumed to change the nature of the entire system.

A third important influence on present thinking comes from the discipline of psychology and involves the reaction of *behaviorists* to the failure of personality theories to account fully for human behavior (see Mischel, 1968). It is now generally accepted that considering both the environmental context in which behavior occurs and person variables (i.e., personality, dispositions, attitudes, etc.) leads to more accurate predictions of behavior than does measurement of either alone. This interactionism is central to most current theories of environment-behavior relationships.

A fourth perspective, which developed primarily in Germany and concurrently with behaviorism was *Gestalt psychology*. Gestalt psychologists were more concerned with perception and cognition than with overt behavior. The most important principle of this body of work was that objects, persons, and settings are perceived as a whole, which is greater than the sum of the parts. From the Gestalt point of view, behavior is rooted in cognitive processes; it is determined not by stimuli, but from the perception of those stimuli. The Gestalt influence on environmental psychology can be seen primarily in the area of environmental cognition (i.e., explaining how people perceive, think about, and process environmental information).

The influence of each of these perspectives will be seen, and where appropriate elaborated upon, in the remainder of this text. However, as mentioned earlier, these approaches tend to be rather broad in scope and lacking in empirical referents. Each has its "focus of convenience," and no single perspective is satisfactory in accounting for the complexity of environment-behavior relationships. No "grand theory" exists that can incorporate the distinctive contributions of each of these influences on environmental psychology. This is so for at least four reasons: (1) There is not enough data available regarding environment-behavior relationships to lead to the kind of confidence needed for a unifying theory, (2) the relationships that researchers have looked at are highly varied, (3) the methods used are inconsistent, and (4) the ways in which variables have been measured have not always been compatible from one research setting to the next.

Despite the fact that well-articulated, all-encompassing theories are not available at this time, there are a number of "mini-theories," or mini-approaches, that have been used successfully in conceptualizing specific organism-environment relationships. Included in these are the *arousal* approach, the *stimulus load* approach, the *behavioral constraint* approach, the *adaptation level* approach, the *environmental stress* approach, and the *ecological* approach. Each of these is able to handle some, but not all, of the available data. Some are more useful in dealing with group behavior (the ecological approach), whereas others focus on the individual level of analysis (the stimulus load approach). Some find their greatest utility at the psychophysiological level (the stress approach); others are useful for accounting for individual differences (the adaptation level approach). Before turning to an orientation that attempts simultaneously to embrace aspects of many of these approaches, a brief description of each of these approaches will be provided.

Arousal Theories

Arousal theories have typically been concerned with the influence of arousal on performance. Generally, performance is maximized at intermediate levels of arousal but falls off as arousal is either increased or decreased. This relationship, sometimes referred to as an inverted-U relationship, has been shown to differ slightly depending on whether performance is measured on simple or complex tasks (see Figure 2-3) and is often referred to as the Yerkes-Dodson law. These relationships are consistent with other findings that humans tend to seek out intermediate levels of stimulation (Berlyne, 1974), and is reminiscent of Toynbee's assertion, referred to earlier, that cultures only develop in environments that provide intermediate challenges.

Performance changes that vary curvilinearly with temperature increases have been shown among women's apparel workers (Link & Pepler, 1970), gold miners (Wyndham, 1969), and in a variety of laboratory settings (Griffiths & Boyce, 1971; Pepler, 1963; Poulton & Kerslake, 1965; Provins, 1966; Provins & Bell, 1970). For a review of this literature see Bell (1981). One explanation for

FIGURE 2-3 The Yerkes-Dodson law. Performance is predicted to be optimal for both simple and complex tasks at intermediate levels of arousal. Arousal above that level leads to decrements in performance.

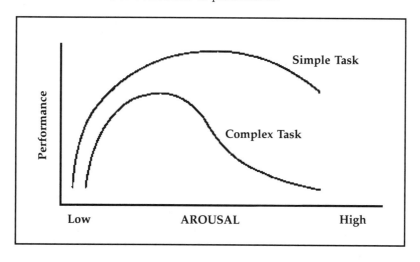

these findings is that increases in ambient temperature lead to increases in arousal levels. Initially, the higher arousal leads to performance enhancement, but as it increases further, overarousal occurs, causing performance decrements. Similarly, it has been shown that personal space invasions lead to increases in arousal (Middlemist, Knowles, & Matter, 1976) and to performance decrements (Evans & Howard, 1972; McBride, King, & James; 1965). Additionally, increases in noise level have been associated with changes in arousal and performance (see Evans & Cohen, 1987). Thus, a number of variables associated with arousal changes have been shown to be related to performance changes, and performance has consistently been curvilinearly related with arousal.

Other theorists utilizing an arousal perspective have featured physiological response to environmental stimulation. Changes in heart rate, blood pressure, respiration rate, galvanic skin response, and adrenaline secretion, among others, have been shown to occur with changes in the environment. Increased ambient temperature leads to blood vessel dilation, perspiration, increased heart rate, and in extreme conditions, lowered blood pressure and insufficient oxygen supplied to the brain. Personal space invasion has been linked to delayed onset and shorter duration of micturation for males. And exposure to noise alters blood pressure, heart rhythm, and the flow of gastric juices to the stomach.

Neurologists such as Hebb (1972) have linked arousal with increased activity of the reticular activating system of the brain. Still other theorists have equated arousal with changes in motor activity or with self-reports of arousal. Berlyne (1974) has, for example, characterized arousal as lying on a continuum anchored at one end by sleep and at the other by excitement, and Mehrabian and Russell (1974) have identified arousal as a major component in people's affective responses to their environment.

Independent of the orientation taken with respect to arousal, a number of consistencies are apparent: (1) Changes in arousal are associated with changes in the environment; (2) pleasant as well as unpleasant stimulation increases arousal—that is, room temperatures above 100 degrees Fahrenheit and loud, obnoxious noises influence arousal in ways similar to roller-coaster rides and passionate kisses; (3) changes in arousal lead people to seek information about their internal states (Schacter & Singer, 1962) as well as to seek information from others (Festinger, 1954); (4) people tend to evaluate moderate levels of arousal positively; and (5) often great expenditures of energy are utilized by individuals to bring the environment to a level of moderate stimulation.

Stimulus Load Theories

Central to stimulus load theories is the notion that humans have a limited capacity to process information. When inputs exceed that capacity, people tend to ignore some inputs and devote more attention to others (Cohen, 1978). These theories account for responses to environmental stimulation in terms of the organism's momentary capacity to attend to and deal with salient features of its milieu. Generally, stimuli most important to the task at hand are allocated as much attention as needed and less important stimuli are ignored.

For example, while driving during rush-hour traffic a great deal of attention is paid to the cars, trucks, buses, and road signs around us and less attention is paid to the commentator on the car radio, the kids in the back seat, and the clouds in the sky. If the less important stimuli tend to interfere with the task at hand, then ignoring them will enhance performance, (e.g., ignoring the children's fighting will make you a better and safer rush hour driver. If, however, the less important stimuli are important to the task at hand, then performance will not be optimal; for example, ignoring the road signs because you are attending to the more important trucks, cars, etc., may lead you thirty miles out of your way in getting home (Figure 2-4).

Sometimes the organism's capacity to deal with the environment is overtaxed or even depleted. When this occurs only the most important information is attended to, with all other information filtered out. Once attentional capacities have been depleted even small demands for attention can be draining. Thus, behavioral aftereffects including errors in judgment, decreased tolerance for frustration, ignoring others in need of help, and the like, can be accounted for by these theories. For example, the exhausted rush-hour driver eventually might reach the point where he or she doesn't notice the traffic light turn from red to green (or worse yet, from green to yellow to red), even though this is a very important stimulus. Additionally, decreased tolerance for frustration may lead to

FIGURE 2-4 While driving during rush hour traffic a great deal of attention is paid to the cars, trucks, buses, and road signs and less attention is paid to the commuter or the car radio, the kids in the back seat, and the clouds in the sky.

"laying on the horn" or "lane hopping" and motorists in the break-down lane may be ignored, if not looked upon with disdain.

Stimulus load theories are also able to account for behavioral effects in stimulus-deprived environments (e.g., certain behaviors occurring aboard submarines and in prisons). That is, this approach suggests that understimulation can be just as aversive as overstimulation. So-called cabin fever resulting from monotonous living conditions can also be seen as the result of understimulation. Wohlwill (1966) has argued that environments should be depicted in terms of measurements applied to the dimensions of *intensity, novelty, complexity, temporal variation, surprisingness,* and *incongruity*, all of which contribute to stimulus load. Subsequent behaviors can then be related to the stimulus properties of environments in systematic and comparable ways.

Behavior Constraint Theories

Behavior constraint theories focus on the real, or perceived, limitations imposed on the organism by the environment. According to these theories, the environment can prevent, interfere with, or limit the behaviors of its inhabitants (Rodin & Baum, 1978; Stokols, 1978). Friday afternoon rush-hour traffic interferes with rapid commuting; loud, intermittent noises limit effective communication; over-regimentation in hospitals can interfere with recovery, excessively high ambient temperatures prevent extreme physical exertion, and extremely cold temperatures limit finger dexterity. In a sense, these theories deal with situations where persons either actually lose some degree of control over their environment, or they perceive that they have.

Brehm and Brehm (1981) assert that when we feel that we have lost control over the environment, we first experience discomfort and then attempt to reassert our control. They label this phenomenon *psychological reactance*. If the rush-hour traffic interferes with getting home in a timely fashion, we may leave work early, or find alternate, less-congested routes. Loud, intermittent noises may be dealt with by removing their source or by changing environments. Extreme temperatures are handled by adjusting the thermostat. All that is needed is for individuals to perceive that they have lost some degree of control, or for that matter, to anticipate the loss of control, and reactance will occur. If repeated attempts to regain control are unsuccessful, *learned helplessness* may develop (Seligman, 1975). People begin to feel as though their behavior has no effect on the environment. They begin to believe they no longer control their own destiny, and that what happens to them is out of their personal control. These feelings can eventually lead to clinical depression, and in the most extreme form can lead people to give up on life, and to die.

On the opposite side of the coin, perceived control over one's environment (even when real control does not exist, or is not used) can alleviate the negative outcomes that the environment might otherwise bring about. Perceived control over noise (Glass & Singer, 1972), overcrowding (Langer & Saegert, 1977), and over one's daily affairs (Langer & Rodin, 1976) has been shown to influence in a positive manner a variety of behavioral responses. For example, residents of a nursing home who were given greater control over, and responsibility for their own well-being displayed enhanced mood and greater activity in comparison with residents who were not given control. Similarly, people who had control over the thermostats in their working and living environments reported fewer health complaints during the winter months than did those who did not have control. These results occurred despite the fact that they did not actually manipulate the thermostats and kept their environments at ambient temperatures similar to those without control (Veitch, 1976). Behavior constraint theories thus emphasize those factors (physical as well as psychological; real as well as imaginary) associated with the environment that limit human action.

Adaptation-Level Theories

Adaptation theories are similar to stimulus load theories in that an intermediate level of stimulation is postulated to optimize behavior. Excessive stimulation as well as too little stimulation is hypothesized to have deleterious effects on emotions and behaviors. Major proponents of this position include Helson (1964) and Wohlwill (1974). While all environmental psychologists emphasize the interrelationship of humans to their environment, adaptation-level theorists speak specifically of two processes that make up this relationship—the processes of adaptation and adjustment. Organisms either adapt (i.e., change their response to the environment) or they adjust, (i.e., change the environment with which they are interacting). Adaptation to decreases in ambient temperature include piloerection (hair on the body standing up or what is commonly called getting "goose pimples"), muscle rigidity, increased motor activity, vasoconstriction; adjustments include throwing another log on the fire or turning up the thermostat. Either process brings the organism back to an equilibrium with its environment.

Another value of this approach is that it recognizes individual differences in *adaptation level* (i.e., the level of stimulation/arousal that the individual has become accustomed to and expects or desires in a given environment). Thus, this approach is capable of explaining the different responses of two individuals to the same environment. For example, a boisterous party may be perceived as pleasant to a person high in need for sensation, but as overwhelming to the person who prefers a low level of sensation. By the same token, some people revel in the crowded atmosphere of last-minute Christmas shopping while others abhor the inconvenience of having two or more shoppers in the same store with them. These individual differences in adaptation level lead to quite different behaviors. The person high in need for sensation will seek out boisterous parties whereas the person preferring low levels of sensation would avoid them or seek out havens of solitude within them. We have all seen the "life of the party" and the "wallflower." Some of the differences in their behaviors can be ascribed to differences in their adaptation level.

Environmental-Stress Theories

Stress theories emphasize the mediating role of physiology, emotion, and cognition in the organism-environment interaction. Basically, environmental features are seen as impinging, through the senses, on the organism, causing a stress response to occur when environmental features exceed some optimal level. The organism then responds in such a way as to alleviate the stress. Part of the stress response is automatic. Initially there is an alarm reaction to the stressor, wherein various physiological processes are altered. Resistance then follows as the organism actively attempts to cope with the stressor. Finally, as coping resources are depleted, a state of exhaustion sets in (Selye, 1956).

Increasingly, though, psychologists have concerned themselves with additional aspects of the stress response. Lazarus (1966), for example, has focused on the appraisal process. According to him, people must cognitively appraise the environment as threatening before stress occurs and behaviors are affected. Our harried rush-hour driver of a few pages back would not, by this criterion, be stressed unless this individual appraised the traffic as threatening. Behavior would, thus, presumably not be affected. By the same token, if the traffic was what the driver was accustomed to, or had come to expect and desire, the situation would be within the individual's adaptation level as discussed above. Later we will deal with stress theories in great detail. For now, it is enough to say that stress theories provide a very powerful tool for studying person-environment relationships.

Ecological Theories

Central to the thinking of ecological theorists (Barker, 1963, 1968) is the notion of organism-environment fit. Environments are designed, or grow to accommodate, certain behaviors. *Behavior settings*, as Barker termed them, are evaluated in terms of the goodness of fit between the interdependent environmental features and the behaviors that take place. For example, a school yard, a church, a classroom, an office, or an entire business organization might be considered a behavioral setting; each would then be evaluated in terms of how suitable it is for the play behavior of children, how well it accommodates the religious sacraments, or how well it serves the functions of business.

While any number of behaviors can occur within any physical setting, cultural purpose is defined by the interdependency between *standing patterns of behavior* and the *physical milieu*. Standing patterns of behavior represent the collective behavior of the group rather than just individual behavior. The standing pattern of behavior in a classroom would include lecturing, listening, observing, sitting, taking notes, asking questions, and taking tests; the physical milieu of this behavior setting would include the room and such accoutrements as a lectern, chairs, chalkboard, microphone, overhead projector, and slide screen. Because this standing pattern of behavior occurs primarily in this behavior setting, social ecologists would suggest that knowing about the setting helps us predict what will occur in it. Once individuals making up this classroom leave this physical setting, most of the physical characteristics of the environment remain unchanged, but the behaviors likely will change dramatically. In other words, the students will move to a new physical milieu eliciting a different standing pattern of behavior.

Critical to Barker's thinking is the question of what happens when there are too few or too many individuals for maximum efficiency within a particular behavior setting. For example, what happens to students at small schools as opposed to students at large schools? Are there predictable differences in behaviors? Does the type of behaviors of participants from small churches differ from that of participants from large churches? Studies of these questions from a social ecological perspective led to theories of *undermanning* and *overmanning* (contemporary writers are more likely to use the gender-neutral terms *understaffing* and *overstaffing*) and are the topic of the book *Big School, Small School*, authored by Barker and Gump (1964).

According to these researchers (see Gump, 1987), as the number of individuals in a setting falls below some minimum, some or all of the inhabitants must take on more than their share of roles if the behavior setting is to be maintained. This condition is termed *understaffing*. The college roommate of one of your authors went to a very small high school, which in many ways exemplifies an understaffed setting. This roommate played football and, like most high-schoolers, played before fans on Friday night. Also, like most high schools, there was a high school band that performed at half-time. Your author's roommate, however, was also the best trumpet player in the school; so, at half-time while the rest of the football players were obtaining instructions as to what they should be doing the second half, he was out marching with the band. In understaffed settings inhabitants often have to assume a variety of roles.

If the number of participants in a setting exceeds the capacity for that setting, then the setting is considered *overstaffed*. Different strategies are brought into play when a setting is overstaffed than when it is understaffed. Too many swimmers waiting to get into the pool on a hot summer afternoon, commuters on the five o'clock train, football fans at the Super Bowl, and shoppers in department stores at Christmas time might all represent overstaffed settings. One obvious solution to overstaffing would be to increase the capacity of the physical setting, perhaps by enlarging it or by moving the setting. Another adaptive mechanism might be to control the entry of clients into the setting by forcing either stricter entrance requirements or through some sort of "funneling process." Still another mechanism would be to limit the amount of time participants can spend in the setting. This kind of regulatory mechanism is often seen at playground basketball games where teams are formed and wait to take on winners. Winners gain control of the court while the losers have to wait their turn to get on the court again.

Independent of whether a behavior setting is understaffed or overstaffed, the notion of social ecology has played an important part in the development of theories of environmental psychology. More will be said with regard to this theorizing later. For now, let it be said that in considering all of the theoretical approaches outlined here, the ecological approach is the broadest in its approach and most unique in its methods.

COMPARISON OF THEORIES

Each of these mini-theories has its benefits as well as its shortcomings. In this section we will briefly look at each. The *arousal, stimulus load*, and *adaptation level* approaches all share the advantage of the ability to incorporate a wide variety of physical and social environmental characteristics under the rubric of overall stimulation level. Thus, diverse factors such as noise, temperature extremes, room color, verbal information rate, and crowding can all be conceptualized as contributing to environmental stimulation level. Further, all three approaches are useful in predicting potential adverse responses when environmental stimulation deviates from some optimal level. The arousal approach is the most general in identifying physiological and affective mediators of environment-behavior relationships—that is, increases or decreases in stimulation produce corresponding changes in physiological and psychological arousal, which in turn produce predictable variations in behaviors such as task performance and aggression. The stimulus load approach is more specific, focusing on cognitive limitations in information-processing abilities, and yields predictions regarding the social/behavioral consequences of over/understimulation—excessive attentional demands have differential effects on performance of primary versus secondary tasks and the likelihood of attending to various social stimuli. The adaptation level approach is the most specific, predicting that the consequences of a particular stimulation level depends on the specific level to which a given individual has become adapted.

The generality-specificity dimension is a theoretical trade-off. The more general theories account for aggregate responses of large numbers of people to the same environmental conditions, but in doing so gloss over some potentially important individual differences in people's responses to those conditions. For example, while arousal theory might accurately predict worse performance, on the average, in noisy compared to quiet settings, there may be some individuals who, because of their adaptation level, might even perform better in the noisy setting. The more specific theories account for some of these individual differences, but in so doing are more limited in scope, thus creating difficulties in making inferences about what are generally optimal environmental conditions for most people. For example, adaptation-level theory could lead to as many predictions about performance level as there are people in the same level of noise. All three approaches have limitations regarding the reliability and validity of measures of their concepts. Thus, for example, measurements of physiological arousal (e.g., heart rate, galvanic skin response) and psychological arousal (e.g., self-reported emotional state) that are simultaneously obtained sometimes yield contradictory results. Also, systematic and valid measures of stimulus load and adaptation level are difficult to obtain. As a result, all three approaches have difficulty predicting what optimal stimulation levels are and exactly when these levels deviate significantly from optimum. This, in turn, limits the ability to predict behavioral responses to various stimulation levels.

The *stress approach* incorporates elements of all of the above. That is, stress can be characterized in terms of objective physical and social environmental conditions that deviate from some optimal level (e.g., a noisy and crowded subway) and are thus potentially disruptive to human functioning. Stress can also be conceptualized in terms of physiological responses (e.g., arousal and health), affective responses (e.g., subjective discomfort), and cognitive responses (e.g., appraisal) to environmental conditions. As such, this approach is also useful for accounting for the effects of a wide variety of objective environmental conditions on several important mediators of environment behavior relationships under the general construct of stress. The approach has the further advantage of predicting behavioral coping and the consequences of ineffective coping. Of course, this approach suffers from the same problems of measurement as those discussed above. For example, it can be difficult to determine objectively which conditions are stressful (e.g., heavy metal vs. jazz music), as well as individual differences in response to them (e.g., adolescents vs. their parents). Nonetheless, the stress approach has been widely used in environmental psychology, and as a result we have devoted an extensive discussion of this issue in Chapter 5.

The *behavioral constraint* approach is the most limited of all in scope, (i.e., it is primarily useful in situations where the perception of loss of control or threats to control are present). However, when such conditions do exist, the concepts of reactance and learned helplessness yield useful predictions of behavioral responses to such conditions. The *ecological* approach has the broadest scope with the concept of behavior setting, and as such is a useful descriptive approach to understanding the behaviors of large numbers of people in different settings. As discussed above, however, this generality limits the approach's ability to account for individual differences in the behavior setting. Another disadvantage is that its reliance on field observation methodology does not permit causal inferences regarding the determinants of behavior. However, the approach provides a distinctive perspective in emphasizing the reciprocity of environment-behavior relationships. In the remainder of this chapter we will describe a model of environment-behavior relationships which incorporates the best parts of these theories and attempts to minimize some of the more troublesome aspects of each of them.

A SLIGHT DIGRESSION: PUTTING THE "P" BACK INTO B=f(P,E)

Please recall from Chapter 1 Kurt Lewin's famous statement: "In principle it is everywhere accepted that behavior (B) is a function of the person (P) and the environment (E), B = f(P, E) and P and E in this formula are interdependent variables." Implicit in this statement is the theoretical issue of whether behavior is caused by the situation in which it occurs. The various theoretical perspectives we have looked at would seem to suggest that the situation does indeed

TIME-OUT: Imagine Jill, a college junior attending City University located in downtown Metropolis. She has a part-time job working at a hectic fast-food restaurant to support herself and pay tuition. She shares an old apartment in a suburb with two roommates. The apartment is located next to a railroad; it is small and has inconsistent heating. Jill commutes to City U three days a week. She always has trouble finding parking and frequently has to walk through a "seedy" neighborhood to get to campus. She is frequently late for classes and often has to run up several flights of stairs to be on time. Most of her classes are so large that she doesn't know any of her professors personally and she has only made casual acquaintances with her classmates. She sometimes feels overwhelmed by the amount of material covered in her courses and spends many a late night studying for what seems to be oppressive "exams from hell." Jill misses Small Town where she was raised and her close high school friends. Jill sometimes experiences headaches and stomach upsets for no apparent reason. She sometimes feels "alone in a crowd" and entertains thoughts of dropping out of school and returning to Small Town.

How would you assess Jill's life circumstances? What features of her physical and social environment influence the quality of her life? What might you infer about her personality and thought processes that may interact with her environment to influence her experiences? Can you apply the concepts of arousal, stimulus load, constraint, adaptation level, stress, and behavior setting to account for her thoughts, feelings, and behavior?

Do not worry if you are unable to answer all of these questions now. As you learn more about the discipline of environmental psychology and the effects of various environmental factors you will have a broader background with which to work. These issues will be dealt with throughout the remainder of the text. Further, as you study this text, you should learn many things that you can apply to your own life (some right away!) that can help you to understand how your physical and social environment affect you and how you can manage some of them to live a more fulfilling life.

influence behavior, either by arousing the organism, overloading or understimulating the organism's sensory system, constraining (or limiting the possibilities for) behavior, stressing the organism, exceeding its adaptation level, or by creating situations that are either understaffed or overstaffed. Common sense also tells us that the environment causes behavior. As people move from place to place their behavior changes accordingly. We behave differently at a rock concert than we do in church. We skate on ponds in the winter, but swim in them in the summer. We wear fewer clothes on public beaches than we do in any other public place. Thus some environments are more likely to bring about specific behaviors than are others. But what are the mechanisms creating this place-specificity? What are the psychological principles that can account for this causal relationship?

Lewin's statement "B = f(P, E)" assumes the environment exerts a powerful and direct causal influence on behavior. The organism (P) finds itself in an environment (E) and reacts to the affordances, constraints, arousal capabilities, etc., that are contained in that environment. The key word here is *reacts*. No mention of plans, goals, intentions, expectations, and the like are postulated. These factors are, however, undoubtedly what Lewin had in mind by including the "P" in his formula.

Another way of thinking about the place-specificity of behavior is to think of the environment as two places embedded in a third, and to impute to the organism the ability to think, plan, rehearse behaviors, and to have a mental map of the environment without actually being in it (see Figure 2-5.) The organism can concoct an image of an environment and "think-travel" through that environment without ever moving. An example might prove illustrative. As I sit here writing these words it is possible for me to form an image of a nearby restaurant where I plan to have lunch. Not only am I able to *see* the floor plan of the restaurant but I *know* how to get there from here and the best time of the day to go. I also *plan* to go there instead of a different restaurant that is more expensive. I have a fairly good idea of what is going to be on the menu, how long it will take to get served, and the quality of the food I'll be getting. In about an hour from now I will carry out this plan.

If, in an hour from now, you show up at the same restaurant you are likely to observe that not only am I eating, but that there is a substantial number of others in the same place and that we are all eating. You could conclude from this that the environment (restaurant) caused the behavior (eating), but you probably would be wrong. People rarely just find themselves in a choir and begin to sing, on a baseball field and begin to play, or in a bedroom and go to sleep. More often they go to certain places to carry out certain behaviors. We all ended up at the restaurant to eat; we did not eat because we ended up there. Typically we arrive at a place with considerable information about that place and with a plan in mind of what we will do there. We have certain expectations regarding the cultural purpose of the place, who will be there, the kind and degree of affect that will be elicited, the opportunities that will be afforded us

FIGURE 2-5 The environment can be represented as two places embedded within a third. In place one the person devises a plan to do something; s/he then travels to place two to do it, and finally the action is carried out in place two.

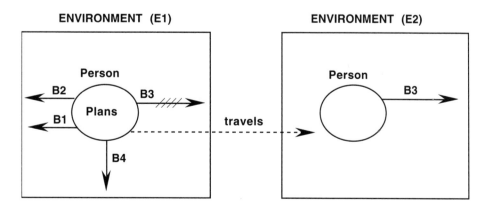

ENVIRONMENT (E1)   ENVIRONMENT (E2)

as well as the constraints that will be placed upon us. Further, we frequently make comparative judgments between images of two different instances of the same environmental setting (e.g., two different restaurants) and these judgments form the bases for our preferences and for seeking out one setting over another. The environment is more than an antecedent of behavior; it is a place of opportunity for a variety of possible futures. We often actively choose to enter certain environments because we know they will afford some desired outcome.

Figure 2-5 (fashioned on the work of Russell & Ward, 1982) is a graphic representation of the interrelatedness of persons and their environment. In Stage 1 person P in E1 (e.g., the living room) devises a plan to do something (e.g., go to the kitchen and get a glass of water). Person P then travels to the kitchen and assuming E2 (kitchen) is congruent with P's image of it, carries out his or her plan (i.e., getting glass of water). In Stage 2, P, having travelled to E2, forms a perception of this new environment and acts accordingly. This process is depicted in Figure 2-5. Before interpreting Figure 2-5, however, it is necessary to return to inspect and interpret Stage 1 further.

Planning and thinking must take place somewhere. It can occur, as in Figure 2-5, at a place remote from where the plan will be carried out or it can occur in the place being thought about (i.e., I could consider obtaining a glass of water while I'm in the kitchen). By the same token I can plan my meal before leaving for a restaurant or I can plan it after arriving. How much I can plan before arriving depends on how much knowledge I have before going, and how expeditiously I can carry out my plan depends on the degree of congruence between the image of the environment I have when concocting my plan and the properties of the environment once I arrive. If I devise my plan of action while in the environment where this action is to take place, then Stage 1 is not exited. The careful observer will note that in addition to the arrow labelled "travels" in Figure 2-5, there are two additional arrows emanating from P in Stage 1. These arrows serve to remind us that often we do plan courses of action while in the environment in which the action takes place. These actions, in turn, impact the environment in knowable ways. Person P in these, as in all circumstances, monitors the effects of his or her behavior and modifies plans or goals accordingly. In essence, when P plans an action and carries out that action in E1 his or her behavior alters the environment such that it can now be thought of as E2, and the words "alters to" can be substituted for "travels" in Figure 2-5.

Certainly this depiction of the causal links between environment and behavior is oversimplified. People sometimes do act first and think later; and they sometimes rationalize their behaviors on the basis of a post-hoc assessment of their circumstances. Nonetheless, people often plan their behaviors and do so with particular environments in mind. We don't just sleep anywhere at anytime; we plan to sleep (at night) in a particular place (in our bedroom). If we did not plan to eat but had to depend on food to be present to do so, many of us would starve to death. The notions of planning, of imaging, of travelling to environments which allow us to carry out our plans are very important concepts in the field of environmental psychology. They fall within the rhetoric of perception and of expectations, of attitudes and of beliefs, of stress and of adaptation level, of behavior setting and of cultural purpose, all of which could be classified under the general rubric of *environmental cognition* to be considered in more detail later. The bottom line of this slight digression, then, is that we must not forget the "P" in Kurt Lewin's formula, and we should treat this "P" as an active participant in its relations with the environment.

THE PRESENT FRAMEWORK

The present framework for understanding organism-environment relationships stems from a number of theoretical positions and data bases established within the domains of general and social psychology, as well as from the newly emerging area of environmental psychology, and attempts to bring them under the umbrella of a single model. The primary motif, however, is developed from theories emphasizing the affective components of the human experience, where overt behaviors, characterized as approach or avoidance responses, are seen as being mediated by the emotion-arousing properties of the environment. Specifically, environmental factors (e.g., density, personal space, noise, temperature, etc.) will be postulated to influence individual affective states, which in turn will be asserted to influence overt behavior. Table 2-1 lists summary statements of assumptions and assertions relevant to this guiding framework.

The environment consists of both physical and social variables existing in reciprocal relationships with behavior.   Attempts to understand human/environment relationships that have focused exclusively on either the human components or the environmental aspects have not met with great success. Humans are not only influenced by their environment, but through their behavior they also alter that environment. The altered environment in turn produces subtle changes in the environmental inhabitant and in its behaviors; these behaviors again produce subtle changes in the environment, and so on, indefinitely. For example, the classroom behaviors of teachers and students alike are influenced by such physical properties of the environment as room temperature, chalkboard space, windows (or the lack thereof), the arrangement of desks, available light, and ambient noise level. But the total classroom environment also includes social and demographic variables (e.g., the age and gender of classmates, the friendship groups, the type of activity being engaged in, and others). Each one of these factors, singly and collectively, influences the behavior that is enacted in this setting. By the same token, the resultant behavior changes the nature of that setting. For example, to enhance discussion, chairs may be moved, thus changing the environment; these changes may lead to changes in friendship groups or to a change in the ambient noise level. Teachers may now have to talk louder, perhaps also changing the tone of their voices, making them appear grumpy; this perception may in turn lead students to avoid the space around the teacher or may keep them from asking questions. Thus, the environment and its inhabitants never stay the same; each is constantly changing as a result of its interactions with the other. Any attempt to understand these relationships, there-

TABLE 2-1   Guiding Assumptions and Propositions

1a. The environment consists of both physical and social variables existing in reciprocal relationships with behavior.

1b. The physical and social environment can and should be characterized in terms of measurements applied to its salient characteristics.

2a. The environment, physical as well as social, typically exerts a steady-state influence on the behavior of its inhabitants.

2b. When the measured values of the environment's most salient characteristics undergo dramatic change, the environmental influence on behavior can no longer be characterized as steady-state.

2c. Disruptions from steady-state occur when present perceptions do not correspond to desired or expected levels of physical and social stimulation.

3. The influence exerted by the environment is indirect; i.e., the environment acts to influence people's emotional states, which in turn mediate their overt behavior.

4. Environment-evoked emotions are best depicted in terms of three distinct dimensions: pleasure-displeasure, degree of arousal, dominance-submissiveness.

5a. The environment-influenced behavior of the individual is dependent upon the extent and the configuration of the dimensions of emotions aroused.

5b. Behavior is goal directed, i.e., behavior in an environmental setting is performed to increase or decrease the pleasure, degree of arousal, or dominance elicited by changes in the environment in an attempt to return the environmental influence to steady-state.

6. When this goal-directed behavior is ineffective or when great expenditures of energy are required to maintain steady-state, the environment can be considered pathological and a disruptive influence on human functioning.

fore, requires a systematic approach emphasizing the bidirectional, often symbiotic, nature of this interaction.

The physical environment can and should be characterized in terms of measurement applied to its salient characteristics.   It is an obvious scientific advantage to be able to specify relationships between or among variables in precise mathematical terms. The symbolic representation of the effect x has on y is not as potentially ambiguous if x and y have properties that can be measured by agreed-upon and reliable techniques. Further, the symbolic representation of the effect can assume precise mathematical properties which permit greater precision in prediction. Thus, ambiguity in the discussion of the relationships between variables is reduced by precise measurement.

Statements like "high ambient temperatures may exert a detrimental influence on learning" carry global, but not precise, meaning. How "high" must the temperature be to exert this influence? Do variations in relative humidity combine with differences in temperature to produce different effects? Does the clothing the person is wearing moderate these effects? (Or for that matter, determine what temperature is designated as "high"?) Is length of time of exposure related to these effects? What is meant by the term "learning"? Does it mean something other than "performance"?

The essence of knowledge is that it is or can be precisely communicated. Without the application of agreed-upon measurement to the environment and its inhabitants, this type of precision in communication is impossible and knowledge is neither created nor shared. These notions will be discussed more fully in Chapter 3.

To be sure, complete agreement in the early stages of development in any science is not possible. There will be arguments as to whether the appropriate measure of noise, for example, is the "sone," the "phon," the "pNdB;" as to whether the "clo" is an appropriate scale for the insulative properties of clothing; or, whether pollution standards should be set with respect to measured health and behavioral changes or with respect to measurable changes in the chemical composition of the atmosphere. In spite of expected controversy, measures of such constructs as noise, insulative value, and pollution must be developed for knowledge to progress. For now, it is better to have several different measures (and disagreement) than it is to have no measures at all.

The environment, physical as well as social, typically exerts a steady-state influence on the behavior of its inhabitants. This assertion is not unlike the claim of Ittleson, Proshansky, Rivlin, and Winkel (1974) that the environment frequently operates below the level of awareness. The environment is seen as being taken for granted—we operate within an environmental context without paying much attention to it. "Normative" or "normal" behavior occurs in these circumstances. We behave in accordance with the cultural purpose of the setting. However, if the environment changes (or we change environments), we become aware of it because it is at that point that we must consciously begin to adapt or adjust (see assertion 2b and 5b in Table 2-1).

Roger Barker's (1968) notion of "behavior settings" is also congruent with this assertion. The arrangement of chairs at a table (Sommer, 1974) or desks in a classroom (Sanders, 1958), for example, have very powerful but nonconscious effects on their users; in a very real sense we inherit the use of space. Thus, the environment clearly influences our behavior even when its physical and social characteristics are within a normal range, but under these conditions we are typically unaware of that influence. Thus, you were probably not aware of the fact that your first day in the room in which this class meets, your behavior of note-taking vs. ballroom dancing was determined, in part, by the setting itself. Nor did you probably give much thought to the fact that you were dancing instead of taking notes the last time you attended a night club.

As you sit reading these pages your senses are being bombarded from a variety of sources. If you pause to listen you may hear, as I do, the whistle and rumble of a freight train some six blocks away, the ringing of a telephone four doors down the hall, the sound of footsteps out in the hall, the drone of a heating fan overhead, and sundry other sounds emanating from unknown sources. Switching senses, the smells of freshly brewed coffee, two-day-old cigarette smoke, Right Guard, and stale, musty, manuscripts take turns tugging at the nose. The chair in which I am sitting has become harder (perhaps yours has, too) as the *gluteus maximus* presses against it, and the cold of my left hand is now felt as it provides a resting place for my forehead. Looking up from these pages we may be confronted with a cacophony of sights varying in color, size, luminance, distance from the retina, etc. While engrossed in reading, however, we are virtually oblivious to these various sources of stimulation. The phone rings, unheard; the cigarette smoke goes undetected; and, except for occasional and minor shifts in our sitting position, the tactile stimulation provided by the chair goes unnoticed; that is, the environment is exerting a steady-state and unnoticed influence. Only when we consciously pause to note this stimulation does it exist in any meaningful sense.

When the measured values of the environment's most salient characteristics undergo dramatic change the environmental influence can no longer be characterized as steady-state. Helson's (1964) adaptation-level theory represents a general framework for the study of diverse responses to any set of stimuli varying along some dimension. Put briefly, Helson maintains that for any specified dimension of stimulus variation, individuals establish an adaptation level (AL; a preferred or expected level of stimulation), which determines their judgmental or evaluative response to a given stimulus located on that dimension. Deviations from AL in either direction (i.e., either increases or decreases in stimulation level) are evaluated positively within a certain range, but beyond these boundaries changes are experienced as "unpleasant."

When environmental-stimulus properties change to the extent that they have exceeded the AL boundaries, the individual experiences "unpleasantness," and the influence of the environment is no longer steady-state. It is only at this point that changes in the normative modes of behavior can be expected, that the regularized, routinized *behavioral-setting* influence begins to break down. The kinds of changes in behavior to be expected are considered under proposition 5b in Table 2-1.

If, as you sit reading these pages, your phone rings instead of the one four doors down the hall, or someone walks into the room wearing an unusual perfume (or no deodorant), or the room temperature increases to 85 degrees Fahrenheit or is reduced to 60 degrees Fahrenheit, or there is a knock on your door, then the environment no longer can be characterized as steady-state. Your response to the environment is now conscious and deliberate. You get up to answer the phone or the door; you look up to see who is wearing the unusual perfume; you open a window or turn up the thermostat (or put on or take off clothes) to return to a condition of thermal comfort. In other words, you become aware of your environment and begin adapting to it or making adjustments in it to achieve a new equilibrium.

Disruptions from steady-state occur when present perceptions do not correspond to desired or expected levels of physical and social stimulation. Disruptions in steady-state influence are brought about by the processes of sensation, perception, and cognition (the subjects of Chapter 4). Sensation involves those processes by which the world can be known to the perceiver. These processes typically involve the following modes: touch, smell, taste, vision, and hearing. We *know* silk by touching it, rotten eggs by smelling them, an orange by tasting it, and so forth. Environmental perception involves the initial gathering of information. It differs from sensation in that the perceiver is an active participant in the process whereas in sensation the perceiver is not. Ittleson (1978) distinguishes between more traditional perception, which he labels *object perception*, and *environmental perception*. In object perception, emphasis is placed on the properties of simple stimuli, such as color, depth, form, apparent movement, loudness, etc. In environmental perception, the emphasis is on larger entities, treated as wholes. In addition to the size and complexity of the stimulus, the two differ in that in the latter, participants often move around in and through the stimulus display and in fact become a part of it. Thus, the perceiver experiences the environment from multiple perspectives. Finally, in environmental perception the perceiver is often connected to the stimulus display by a clear goal or purpose—that is, the perceiver is in the environment to achieve some outcome. We go into a restaurant to obtain food, a swimming pool to cool off, and a theater to be entertained.

Environmental cognition involves further processing of information (e.g., storing, organizing, and recalling). It also involves appraisal processes. Is this environment good or bad, cold or hot, strong or weak? It includes the emotional impact of environments, attitudes toward environments, the preferences we have for some environments over others, and the categories we use to organize our knowledge about various settings. Through these various processes we appraise environments and compare them with mental images of what we desire or expect them to be. Most of the time, because we have planned well, environments are acceptable approximations of what we expect. Under these conditions the environment exerts a steady-state influence. Disruptions occur when we learn through these processes that present conditions do not correspond to our desired or expected levels of stimulation or are incapable of meeting the objectives of the plan with which we entered the situation.

The influence exerted by the environment is indirect; i.e., the environment acts to influence people's emotional states, which in turn mediate their overt behavior. One of the major assertions of Byrne and Clore's reinforcement-affect model of attraction (Byrne, 1971; Byrne & Clore, 1970; Clore & Byrne, 1974) as well as Mehrabian and Russell's (1974) framework is that a link exists between positive affect and such positive social interactions as interpersonal attraction and approach behaviors. Additionally, work by Baron and Bell also postulates emotion (affect) as a mediating link between the physical environment and aggressive behavior (e.g., Baron & Bell, 1976; Bell & Baron, 1976).

It has been shown that such diverse environmental conditions as temperature (Griffitt, 1970; Griffitt & Veitch, 1971), crowding (Baum & Valins, 1973; Griffitt & Veitch, 1971; Valins & Baum, 1973), noise (Bull, et al., 1972; Geen & O'Neil, 1969; Mathews & Cannon, 1975), air pollution (Rotton, Barry, Frey & Soler, 1976), and radio news broadcasts (Veitch, DeWood, & Bosko, 1977; Veitch & Griffitt, 1976) influence the affective state and interpersonal behaviors of individuals. If you feel annoyed by the phone ringing you might answer it in gruff tones, or not at all; if you are gladdened by the distraction you will probably answer with greater civility. If you like the smell of an unusual perfume, you are likely to strike up a pleasant conversation; if instead what you are confronted with is the smell of stale cigarettes and body odor, your disposition is likely to be less shining and your overt behaviors less positive.

A whole host of interpersonal behaviors might be negatively influenced by environmental conditions, but only to the extent that those environmental conditions elicit negative affective feelings, and conversely, behaviors might be positively influenced through their association with positive affective feelings. Indeed, studies of verbal as well as a wide range of nonverbal behaviors (Mehrabian, 1972) in social interaction situations have been shown to be related to the emotional states of the interactants. Put simply, how we *behave* is determined in part by how the environment makes us *feel*.

Environment-evoked emotions are best depicted in terms of three distinct dimensions: pleasure, arousal, and control. Researchers who study emotions and have attempted to categorize them have traditionally focused on facial expression of emotions and verbal self-reports. Those examining facial expression (e.g., Abelson and Sermat, 1962; Engen, Levy and Schlosberg, 1957, 1958; Gladstones, 1962; Schlosberg, 1954) have found pleasantness-unpleasantness and level of arousal to be two of the basic dimensions of emotions. Williams and Sundene (1965) and Osgood (1966) have likewise found evidence for these two plus a third characteristic resembling the potency factor of the Semantic Differential. Self-report measures of emotions, however, have typically yielded more dimensions than the three listed above (e.g., Izard, 1972; Nowlis, 1965) and have included such emotions as "stressed," "uncomfortable," "anxious," and "angry."

Mehrabian and Russell (1974) and Russell and Mehrabian (1977) have provided evidence to reconcile these two sets of research findings and have reported that the three dimensions of pleasure-displeasure, degree of arousal, and dominance-submissiveness constitute both the necessary and sufficient dimensions to describe all emotions. Results of their studies show that the larger number of dimensions obtained in verbal-report studies can be accounted for by these three dimensions. Thus, self-reports of emotions that employ different words (e.g., *joy* and *happiness*) may actually yield similar underlying configurations of pleasure, arousal, and dominance, which differ primarily in the intensity of affect. Further, differences between global emotional states can be best understood in terms of differences in the underlying configuration of these three dimensions. Thus, the best available evidence to date suggests that the emotional (affective) state of individuals can be adequately described by these three dimensions.

The environment-influenced behavior of the individual is dependent upon the extent and the configuration of the dimensions of the emotions aroused. In most of the studies to date where the emotional state of the individual is seen as a mediating factor for behavior, emotion has been conceptualized in a unidimensional manner (see assertion 3 in Table 2-1). Typically, the one dimension utilized has been pleasure-displeasure, although sometimes a variant of the dominance/submissiveness dimension has been used (e.g., studies of control, constraint, and reactance). However, researchers have seldom considered the interrelationships of these dimensions. The current framework attempts to utilize a multiple-dimension approach to emotion as a way of accounting for more of the reliable variance in the relationship between emotional states and overt behavior. As Mehrabian and Russell note, this approach has the advantage of integrating a variety of research findings dealing with the influence of a diversity of stimuli on the same three dimensions; for example, excessive noise, crowding, pollution all have similar effects on the degree of pleasure, arousal, and dominance a person experiences. This multidimensional description of emotion is not only important in theorizing but also in considering the effects of emotion on overt behaviors. We would expect different behaviors to ensue as a result of changes in the environment that elicited displeasure, high arousal, and submissiveness ("anxiety") from changes resulting in displeasure, high arousal, and dominance ("anger"). A teacher experiencing the former, for example, may attempt to "leave the field," whereas experiencing the latter may lead him or her to combat, or at the very least, to attempt to change the environment. Using earlier unidimensional conceptualizations (e.g., pleasure-displeasure) no differences in behavior would have been predicted. In short, the proposed framework calls for the simultaneous consideration of three major factors of emotions in an attempt to clarify some of the earlier research, which relied on a single factor.

Behavior is goal-directed; i.e., behavior resulting from environmental change is performed to return the environmental influence to steady-state. This proposition follows from 5a and 2b in Table 2-1, but the underlying assumption is that steady-state environments are preferred and actively sought (i.e., humans don't passively react to environmental stimulation, but rather attempt to alter their experiences to maintain a state of equilibrium). They do this by altering their evaluation, by altering the setting, or by changing settings altogether. This view is hardly new, and it provides the underpinnings of all homeostasis models of motivation and behavior. For example, Adaptation Level (AL) Theory (Helson, 1964) assumes that individuals have developed some frame of reference for evaluating a wide array of stimulus dimensions. Preferred stimulus values for a particular dimension, however, are narrow in range, and when the values deviate from this range, unpleasant feelings result.

In response to displeasure aroused by stimuli whose preferred values are exceeded (in either direction), the behaving organism attempts to decrease the unpleasantness. For example, the temperature of a particular environmental setting exceeding AL elicits discomfort. Simultaneously, degree of arousal and dominance-submissiveness will also be influenced. If the organism experiences great displeasure, high arousal, and high dominance, then aggressive behaviors may occur, which might be directed at removing the social source of that emotion. On the other hand, if displeasure is not felt, if the degree of arousal is low, or if submissiveness is felt, acquiescent behavior might occur. This could involve withdrawal to a different setting more conducive to the desired emotional configuration.

When goal-directed behavior is ineffective or when great expenditures of energy are required to maintain steady-state, the environment can be considered pathological and a disruptive influence on human functioning. What are the long-range effects of exposure to a given environment featured by a particular level of intensity, complexity, and incongruity of stimulation? According to AL theory, the individual's AL will be shifted to a value corresponding more nearly to that of the environment. This, of course, is what adaptation is. However adaptable humans may be, it is still possible that the range of environmental stimulation could be such that the energies expended in adaptation would have detrimental effects on the individual, or that the behavioral repertoire of the individual is too limited, thereby making adaptation impossible. It is under these conditions that the environment can be considered pathological. Evidence (to be detailed in later chapters) concerning the effects of prolonged exposure to noise (e.g., Glass & Singer, 1972; Weybrew, 1967) exemplify this state of affairs, as does the work of Calhoun (1962) who looked at the long-term effects of increased population density on social adaptive behaviors of Norway rats.

A MODEL OF ENVIRONMENT-BEHAVIOR RELATIONSHIPS

Figure 2-6 attempts to summarize components of the theories discussed earlier, as well as to incorporate important variables in a general model of environment-behavior relationships. Each box includes some examples of each of these variables. Reading from left to right, the *environment* influences *behavior* indirectly through the role of *moderator variables* (i.e., factors that increase or decrease the impact of the setting) and *mediator variables* (i.e., internal perceptual, cognitive, and affective processes in response to environmental conditions). The double arrows between these sets of variables and the two-way arrows within the sets indicate reciprocal relationships (i.e., the variables mutually influence one another). For example, the physical terrain can affect the type of activities and adaptation level of the environmental inhabitants, and the adaptation level of individuals can influence the kinds of activities engaged in, which in turn could affect the physical terrain. Similarly, the emotional state of the person can influence expectations, and the degree of control felt can influence goals. Thus, the physical environment exists in a dynamic and interactive relationship with the variables that moderate and mediate its effects on behavior.

The cognitive and affective responses result in *evaluative judgments* regarding the suitability of a setting (i.e., environment is judged to be either favorable or unfavorable). These judgments either result in behavior continuing as usual or efforts to restore equilibrium with the environment. Behaviors that are effective in restoring equilibrium return the environment to a steady-state influence and a continuation of normal behavior. These behaviors can have immediate or long-term effects on both the physical environment and the moderator and mediator variables, as indicated by the feedback arrows leading from behavior to these variables (Figure 2-6). Behavior that is ineffective in restoring equilibrium results in continued stress, and prolonged disequilibrium can result

FIGURE 2-6   A model for understanding Organism/Environment interaction.

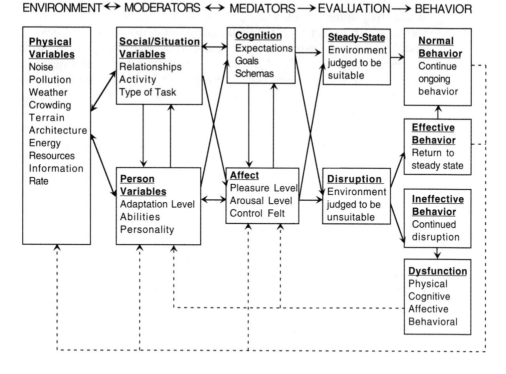

ENVIRONMENT ↔ MODERATORS ↔ MEDIATORS → EVALUATION → BEHAVIOR

in a variety of physical, psychological and behavioral impairments. These dys-functions can have immediate or long-term effects on the moderator and medi-ator variables, as indicated by the feedback arrows leading from dysfunction to these variables.

In sum, the physical environment (defined in terms of its measurable characteristics) and the environmental inhabitants (defined in terms of their observable, quantifiable characteristics) are depicted as separate but mutually interactive entities. They represent two components of the same system—each existing apart from the other but each deriving much of its identity from their coexistence. Bicycles can exist without riders and riders without bicycles, but it is the interaction of the two that provides the unique system, or process, of bicy-cle riding. It is also possible for environments to exist apart from some of its inhabitants and indeed for inhabitants to change environments, but it is the interaction of the two that provides meaning to each. Each responds to the other in an effort to maintain balance or homeostasis. The environment responds in terms of its carrying capacity, its physical and chemical makeup, for example; and, its inhabitants respond in terms of their ability to adapt or create adjust-ments. This reciprocity is represented by the double arrows between the envi-ronment and the person variables as well as the arrow returning from behavior to the environment (Figure 2-6).

The inhabitant, while typically unaware of the influence of the environment, is constantly on guard for changes in it. If no changes are occurring, and if the environment is providing the affordance deemed necessary and allowing the organism to carry out its plans, then the environment is judged to be benign and "business as usual" is conducted. The organism goes about the normal processes of living without undue attention paid to the setting in which these processes are being carried out. As long as the environment is not too noisy, too hot or too cold, too smelly, or the furniture too hard, the "business as usual" of reading these pages is conducted smoothly and is uninterrupted. The environment, however, can be judged to be disruptive of "business as usual." For instance, it may be too noisy or too hot. Remember that this judgment is brought about by not only the physical conditions of the environment, but also by the social/situational conditions, in addition to the personality and cognitive/affective responses of the individual. Thus, whether or not the setting is judged to be too noisy or hot will be determined by factors such as activity (e.g., resting or working), type of task (e.g., playing cards or studying), adaptation level (e.g., the temperature the individual is accustomed to), expectations (e.g., the setting is usually quieter), and emotional state (e.g., degree of pleasure felt). If the setting is judged to be too hot or too noisy, the environment and the inhabitant are no longer in a state of equilibrium, and the influence of the environment is no longer steady-state. Active compromises in the form of adaptation or adjustment must now be made.

In this model the kinds of compromises likely to be sought are those determined by the affective state of the individual—that is, the feelings engendered by the lack of equilibrium drive the organism to engage in behaviors to reattain it. The model draws heavily on the work of Mehrabian and Russell (1974) in which all affective states are seen as being comprised of three semi-independent dimensions. Thus, the particular responses are seen as being determined by the degree and configuration of pleasure, arousal, and control felt.

Some behaviors do return organism/environment relationships to a state of equilibrium and some do not. Unsuccessful behaviors lead first to changes in cognitive and affective responses (e.g., changed expectancies or intensified negative affect) and eventually to changes in the organism itself (e.g., physical or psychological disorders). These changes are represented by the arrow returning from dysfunction to person variables (Figure 2-6). Successful behaviors (i.e., those that bring present conditions to steady state) may have long-term detrimental effects on either the environment (e.g., nonrenewable resource depletion) or on its inhabitants (e.g., reduced frustration tolerance). These changes are represented by the arrows returning from normal behavior to the environment and to the moderating/mediating variables (Figure 2-6).

AN OVERSIMPLIFIED EXAMPLE

An example might be illustrative. If we were concerned with discerning the effect of noise on the study behaviors of adolescents, we might proceed in the following fashion. Objective physical characteristics of the environment that might influence study behaviors would be identified and either manipulated or controlled. All variables with the exception of "noise" would have to remain constant or be controlled for while the important parameters of "noise" would be free to vary within the limits of study and measurement. These important parameters would be identified in terms of characteristics capable of being measured. For example, we might want to consider the loudness level, the frequencies involved, the repetitiousness of the sound, its predictability and/or controllability, as well as other characteristics that identify the sound classified as noise. Having made such decisions, explication of the nature of the organism in a similar fashion would be done. For example, the individual's adaptation level, tolerance for frustration, coping skills, and current emotional state might be considered. Social/situational variables would also have to be considered (e.g., what the person is studying, whether or not others are present, and whom). Finally, cognitive variables such as goals need to be accounted for, such as whether the person desires to learn new material vs. simply review old material.

Assuming satisfaction with having been able to identify the most salient characteristics of the environment as well as those of the organism, let us now take the perspective of the organism (for illustrative purposes: the generalized adolescent) and consider the rest of the model. Based on past experience and the present use to which the environment is to be put, the adolescent might form one of two judgments. He or she might either conclude that the "noise" parameters are within the range that the person considers normal for studying the particular topic or that they are not. That is, this adolescent might decide that the noise from the overhead fan, the familiar 60-Hz hum of the fluorescent lights, the occasional footsteps in the hall, the infrequent and far-off sounds of fire and police sirens, and the sounds of rock music emanating from next door and permeating the paper-thin walls are within the range to be expected when it is time to study Introductory Calculus.

If this judgment is made, our student is likely to "crack the books" and to carry on with the "noise" exerting no apparent influence on study behavior (i.e., he or she will carry on "business as usual"). We, as observers, would then be led to conclude that for this type of individual the particular level of noise observed had no effect on study behavior. If, on the other hand, our student comes to the conclusion (not necessarily consciously) that the fan is too squeaky, the hum too steady, the footsteps too frequent, the sirens too shrill, or the music too loud, then he or she is likely to decide that the physical characteristics of the environment are outside his or her normal range for studying calculus, and a chain reaction of events brought on by environment-elicited feelings is likely to occur. Let us assume for the sake of illustration that the most upsetting aspect of the environment as we've described it for this individual is the loudness of the music coming from the next room. This "upset" can occur as a result of change in any one or combination of changes in the three underlying dimensions of emotion. Our student, could, for example, find him/herself in a heightened state of arousal, could feel that he or she has lost control vis-à-vis his environment, or there could be a change in the person's affective state in the direction of greater displeasure. The nature of the change in the emotional state will dictate the behaviors in which our student will now engage.

If the environment is extremely deviant from expectations it may, despite efforts to cope, lead to continued arousal, continued lack of control, and/or the maintenance of negative affect. In the short run, our student might not be able to complete his or her homework for calculus due tomorrow. Over a period of time this configuration of emotional state could result in physiological disorders such as stomach ulceration, feelings of learned helplessness sometimes referred to as demoralization, and/or affective disorders such as depression, free-floating anxiety, or others. Fortunately, it is rare that the environmental conditions are so extreme that they lead to that pattern of consequences. Most of the time the organism is either adaptable enough or clever enough to make appropriate adjustments in the environment to minimize any disruptive influences. Thus, coping behavior stems from the organism's ability to adapt (e.g., selectively attend to only certain cues in the environment, or habituate to potentially disruptive cues), or from its ability to change the environment to suit his or her preferences and needs at the time (i.e., adjustment).

Let us now return to our student who finds the loudness of the music interfering with his or her ability to study calculus. Because the music is coming from the neighboring room it would be safe to assume that our student would feel some loss of control. If it were the student's own stereo playing it would be very easy to take charge of the environment; one could turn down the volume, shut if off, or play a record or tape more to one's liking. However, since it is not one's own, none of these options are available and the student, therefore, does not have maximum control over the environment. Our student is probably also somewhat aroused, and this arousal probably has negative overtones to it. But, let us assume that the biggest change in the affective state of our student occurred on the dimension of control.

Given that such is the case, it would be predicted that his or her coping behavior would be directed at regaining control. If the coping response is an adaptive one, we might expect our student to reaffirm concentration abilities, "I'm not going to let that noise bother me; if I concentrate really hard on calculus I'll no longer hear the stereo." If the student chooses to engage in adjustment, several possibilities are available. The student can yell at the neighbor to turn down the stereo, he or she can wear earplugs; can turn on one's own stereo to mask the sounds of the neighbor's; or can, in the extreme, change environments altogether and trek to the library to study.

Either form of coping (adjustment or adaptation) is likely to be successful in the short run. Our student is likely to be able to regain control over the environment such that it is no longer disruptive to studying Introductory Calculus. (It should be noted that if our student had wanted to read the newspaper rather than study calculus, perhaps no coping strategies would have been necessary.) It is possible that these coping strategies can have residual aftereffects as well as cumulative or long-term effects. Changing the environment to fit the needs of the organism (if the change is irreversible) can lead to irreparable environmental damage, whereas the limits to adaptation may be reached in the form of loss of hearing, ulceration, etc., if the organism must constantly adapt to extreme environmental change. Our student could develop migraines as a result

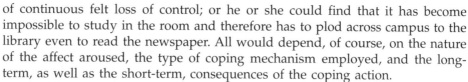

TIME OUT: Suppose you were interested in the effect of ambient temperature on the performance and health of workers at Expressway Trailers. You note that temperature shows a 15°F rise over the course of a daily shift. You also notice a curvilinear performance curve across the shift: i.e., productivity is low at the beginning of a shift, increases to a maximum about 4-1/2 hours into the shift, then slowly declines the remainder of the day. You further note that all workers consume more salt tablets and drink more water as the day progresses. The rest rooms are frequented more often and the time spent away from work stations increases for some workers but not for others as the shift wears on.

How would this information fit into the model for organism/environment interrelationships as detailed above? In a manner analogous to the "oversimplified example" provided, "walk" a worker through a shift, postulating the relationships of temperature to behavior at every step. Finally, think about the information you would need at every step along the way to add corroboration to the inferences you are making.

of continuous felt loss of control; or he or she could find that it has become impossible to study in the room and therefore has to plod across campus to the library even to read the newspaper. All would depend, of course, on the nature of the affect aroused, the type of coping mechanism employed, and the long-term, as well as the short-term, consequences of the coping action.

The preceding example is, of course, oversimplified and in no way exemplifies the precision that is required in the study of organism-environment relationships. The intent of the example is to provide the reader with a thumbnail sketch of the interrelatedness of the environment and organism, particularly as described from an emotion-as-mediator model. Much more detail will be provided later as specific aspects of these relationships are dealt with in the context of current and available data.

SUMMARY

Several mini-theories for conceptualizing the interrelationships of humans and their environments were presented. Among these approaches were the arousal approach, behavioral constraint theories, adaptation-level theory, the environmental stress approach, and Barker's ecological model. Each of these was evaluated and found to handle some data very well while falling short of accounting for other sets of data. The need for a more general model was accented and a model was presented, along with its underlying assumptions, for conceptualizing and understanding organism-milieu relationships. Direct tests of the model were not postulated, but it is hoped that the model will serve as a means of identifying and classifying information throughout the remainder of the text. In the next chapter the allowable methods for making scientific inferences will be discussed, and the procedures and techniques that are available to environmental psychologists will be elucidated.

REFERENCES

Abelson, R.P., & Sermat, V. (1962). Multidimensional scaling of facial expressions. *Journal of Experimental Psychology, 63,* 546–554.

Barker, R.G. (1963). On the nature of the environment. *Journal of Social Issues, 19,* 17–23.

Barker, R.G. (1968). *Ecological psychology: Concepts and methods for studying the environment of human behavior.* Stanford, Calif.: Stanford University Press.

Barker, R.G., & Gump, P.V. (1964). *Big school, small school.* Stanford, Calif.: Stanford University Press.

Baron, R.A., & Bell, P.A. (1976). Aggression and heat: The influence of ambient temperature, negative affect, and a cooling drink on physical aggression. *Journal of Personality and Social Psychology, 33,* 245–255.

Barry, H., Child, I., & Bacon, M. (1959). Relation of child rearing to subsistence economy. *American Anthropologist, 61,* 51–64.

Baum, A., & Valins, S. (1973). Residential environments, group size and crowding. *Proceedings of the 81st Annual Convention of the American Psychological Association,* 211–212.

Bell, P.A. (1981). Physiological, comfort, performance, and social effects of heat stress. *Journal of Social Issues, 37,* 71–94.

Bell, P.A., & Baron, R.A. (1976). Aggression and heat: The mediating role of negative affect. *Journal of Applied Social Psychology, 6,* 18–30.

Berlyne, D.E. (Ed.). (1974). *Studies in the new experimental aesthetics: Steps toward an objective psychology of aesthetic appreciation.* New York: Halsted Press.

Brehm, S.S., & Brehm, J.W. (1981). *Psychologica reactance: A theory of freedom and control.* New York: Academic Press.

Bull, A.J., Burbage, S.E., Crandall, J.E., Fletcher, C.I., Lloyd, J.T., Ravensberg, R.L., & Rocket, S.L. (1972). Effects of noise and intolerance of ambiguity upon attraction for similar and dissimilar others. *Journal of Social Psychology, 88,* 151–152.

Byrne, D. (1971). *The Attraction Paradigm.* New York: Academic Press.

Byrne, D., & Clore, G.L. (1970). A reinforcement model of evaluative processes. *Personality: An International Journal, 1,* 103–128.

Calhoun, J.B. (1962). Population density and social pathology. *Scientific American, 206,* 139–148.

Clore, G.L., & Byrne, D.A. (1974). A reinforcement-model of attraction. In T. L. Houston (Ed.), *Foundations of interpersonal attraction,* New York: Ballantine.

Cohen, S. (1978). Environmental load and the allocation of attention. In A. Baum, J.E. Singer, & S. Valins (Eds.), *Advances in environmental psychology* (Vol. 1). Hillsdale, N.J.: Erlbaum.

Engen, T., Levy, N., & Schlosberg, H. (1957). A new series of facial expressions. *American Psychologist, 12,* 264–266.

Engen, T., Levy, N., & Schlosberg, H. (1958). The dimensional analysis of a new series of facial expressions. *Journal of Experimental Psychology, 55,* 454–458.

Evans, G.W., & Cohen, S. (1987). Environmental Stress. In D. Stokols & I. Altman (Eds.), *Handbook of environmental psychology* (Vol. 1). New York: John Wiley.

Evans, G.W., & Howard, H.R.B. (1972). A methodological investigation of personal space. In W. J. Mitchell (Ed.), *Environmental design: Research and practice. Proceedings of EDRA3/AR8 conference.* Los Angeles: University of California Press.

Festinger, L. (1954). A theory of social comparison processes. *Human Relations, 7,* 117–140.

Geen, R.G., & O'Neil, E.C. (1969). Activation of cue elicited aggression by general arousal. *Journal of Personality and Social Psychology, 11,* 377–380.

Gladstones W.H. (1962). A multidimensional study of facial expression of emotion. *Australian Journal of Psychology, 14,* 95–100.

Glass, D.C., & Singer, J.E. (1972). *Urban stress.* New York: Academic Press.

Griffiths, I.D., & Boyce P.R. (1971). Performance and thermal comfort. *Ergonomics, 14,* 457–468.

Griffitt, W. (1970). Environmental effects on interpersonal affective behavior: Ambient effective temperature and attraction. *Journal of Personality and Social Psychology, 15,* 240–244.

Griffitt, W., & Veitch, R. (1971). Hot and crowded: Influences of population density and temperature on interpersonal affective behavior. *Journal of Personality and Social Psychology, 17,* 92–98.

Gump, P. (1987). School and classroom environments. In D. Stokols & I. Altman (Eds.), *Handbook of environmental psychology* (Vol. 1). New York: John Wiley.

Hebb, D. (1972). *Textbook of psychology* (3rd ed.). Philadelphia: Saunders.

Helson, H. (1964). *Adaptation-level theory.* New York: Harper & Row.

Ittleson, W.H. (1978). Environmental perception and urban experience. *Environment and Behavior, 10,* 193–213.

Ittleson, W.H., Proshansky, H.M., Rivlin, L.G., & Winkel, G.H. (1974). *An introduction to environmental psychology.* New York: Holt, Rinehart Winston.

Izard, C.E. (1972). *Patterns of emotions: A new analysis of anxiety and depression.* New York: Harper & Row.

Langer, E., & Saegert, S. (1977). Crowding and cognitive control. *Journal of Personality and Social Psychology, 35,* 175–182.

Lazarus, R. (1966). *Logical stress and the coping process.* New York: McGraw-Hill.

Link, J.M., & Pepler, R.D. (1970). Associated fluctuations in daily temperature, productivity and absenteeism. *ASHRAE Transactions, 76,* 326–337.

Mathews, K.E., & Cannon, L.K. (1975). Environmental noise level as a determinant of helping behavior. *Journal of Personality and Social Psychology, 32,* 571–577.

McBride, G., King, M.G., & James, S.W. (1965). Social proximity effects on galvanic skin responses in human adults. *Journal of Psychology, 61,* 153–157.

Mehrabian, A. (1972). *Nonverbal communication.* Chicago: Aldine-Atherton.

Mehrabian, A., & Russell, J.A. (1974). *An approach to environmental psychology.* Cambridge, Mass.: MIT Press.

Middlemist, R.D., Knowles, E.S., & Matter, C.F. (1976). Personal space invasions in the lavatory: Suggestive evidence for arousal. *Journal of Personality and Social Psychology, 33,* 541–546.

Mischel, W. (1968). *Personality and assessment.* New York: John Wiley.

Moos, R.M. (1976). *The human context: Environmental determinants of behavior.* New York: John Wiley.

Nowlis, V. (1965). Research with the mood adjective checklist. In S.S. Tomkins & C.E. Izard (Eds.), *Affect, cognition, and personality.* New York: Springer.

Osgood, C.E. (1966). Dimensionality of the semantic space for communication via facial expressions. *Scandanavian Journal of Psychology, 1,* 1–30.

Pepler, R.D. (1963). Performance and well-being in heat. In C.M. Herzfeld (Ed.), *Temperature: Its measurement and control in science* (Vol. 3, Pt. 3). New York: Reinhold.

Poulton, E.C., & Kerslake, M. (1965). Initial stimulating effect of work upon perceptual efficiency. *Aerospace Medicine, 36,* 29–32.

Provins, K.A. (1966). Environmental heat, body temperature, and behavior. *Journal of Psychology, 18,* 118–129.

Provins, K.A., & Bell, C.R. (1970). Effects of heat stress on the performance of two tasks running concurrently. *Journal of Experimental Psychology, 85,* 40–44.

Rodin, J., & Baum, A. (1978). Crowding and helplessness: Potential consequences of density and loss of control. In A. Baum & Y. Epstein (Eds.), *Human response to crowding.* Hillsdale, N.J.: Erlbaum.

Rotton, J., Barry, T., Frey, J., & Soler, E. (1976). Air pollution and interpersonal attraction. *Journal of Applied Social Psychology, 8,* 57–71.

Russell, J., & Mehrabian, A. (1977). Evidence for a three-factor theory of emotions. *Journal of Research in Personality, 11,* 273–286.

Russell, J.A., & Ward, L.M. (1982). Environmental psychology. *Annual Review of Psychology, 33,* 651–682.

Sanders, D.C. (1958). Innovations in elementary school classroom seating. *Bureau of Laboratory Schools Publication No. 10.* Austin: University of Texas Press.

Schacter, S., & Singer, J.E. (1962). Cognitive, social and physiological determinants of emotional states. *Psychological Review, 69,* 379–399.

Schlosberg, H. (1954). Three dimensions of emotion. *Psychological Review, 61,* 81–88.

Seligman, M.E.P. (1975). *Helplessness.* San Francisco: W.H. Freeman.

Selye, H. (1956). *The stress of life.* New York: McGraw-Hill.

Sommer, R. (1974). *Tight spaces: Hard architecture and how to humanize it.* Englewood Cliffs, N.J.: Prentice Hall.

Stokols, D. (1978). A typology of crowding experiences. In A. Baum & Y. Epstein (Eds.), *Human response to crowding.* Hillsdale, N.J.: Erlbaum.

Toynbee, A. (1962). *The study of history.* New York: Oxford University Press.

Valins, S., & Baum, A. (1973). Residential group size, social interaction and crowding. *Environment and Behavior, 5,* 421–440.

Veitch, R. (1976). *Temperature, thermostatic control, and perceived health.* Unpublished manuscript, Bowling Green State University, Bowling Green, Ohio.

Veitch, R., DeWood, R., & Bosko, K. (1977). Radio news broadcasts: Their affects on interpersonal helping. *Sociometry, 40*(4) 383–386.

Veitch, R., & Griffitt, W. (1976). Good news—bad news: Affective and interpersonal effects. *Journal of Applied Social Psychology, 6,* 69–75.

Weybrew, B.B. (1967). Patterns of psychological response to military stress. In M.H. Appley & R. Trumbull (Eds.), *Psychological stress.* New York: Appleton-Century Crofts.

Williams, F., & Sundene, B. (1965). Dimensions of recognition: Visual and vocal expression of emotion. *Audio Visual Communication Review, 13,* 44–52.

Wohlwill, J.F. (1966). The physical environment: A problem for a psychology of stimulation. *Journal of Social Issues, 22,* 29–38.

Wohlwill, J.F. (1974). Human response to levels of environmental stimulation. *Human Ecology, 2,* 127–147.

Wyndham, C. (1969). Adaptation to heat and cold. Environmental Research, 2, 442–469.

Research Methods in Environmental Psychology

3

FIGURE 3-1 To be scientific, data must be based on observations that are public and repeatable; they must be collected under highly specified conditions; and, they must stem from agreed upon definitions of constructs and agreed upon measurement procedures. While miracles might happen, they are not the stuff of which science is made.

In Chapter 1 environmental psychology was defined as a *multidisciplinary behavioral science, both basic and applied in orientation, whose foci are the systematic interrelationships between the physical and social environments and individual human behavior and experience.* The term science in this definition is used to denote both the end product of a special kind of activity or process, and the activity itself. In the first sense, it refers to the body of valid, reliable, and systematized information that researchers have accumulated, which forms the subject matter of the discipline, as, for example, in "the science of biology." In the second sense of the term, emphasis is on the means to this end, on the way in which information is obtained and systematized so that there is a reasonable guarantee of its acceptability. Inherent in the use of the term science is an insistence on operationism and a reliance on systematic and careful observation. Thus, environmental psychology can be thought of as an accumulating, specialized area of knowledge obtained by specific techniques with rigorous standards of acceptability.

To meet these standards of acceptability, environmental scientists engage in *research* and *experimentation*. These terms signify two important aspects of scientific inquiry. They imply, first, an active search for new facts, and, second, an attempt to order the facts into meaningful patterns. The former suggests empiricism and the latter theory-building. These processes involve making complex decisions involving such issues as defining key concepts, sampling subjects as well as conditions, measurement, scaling, instrumentation, design, and statistics. This chapter attempts to deal with these issues, occasionally noting problems faced by researchers in environmental psychology, and, wherever possible, suggesting possibilities for solving them.

THE GOALS OF SCIENCE

Scientific goals or objectives have been described in various ways, but common to all descriptions are the themes of *understanding*, *prediction*, and *control*. In this chapter we will deal with the meaning of these terms in some detail as well as with the procedures of science in general. We will also consider methodological issues more specific to environmental psychology. In doing so we will be developing the background necessary to evaluate research outcomes in the field and to set criteria for applying these findings to everyday situations.

Control

The goal of control is perhaps the easiest to articulate, yet most often misunderstood. Frequently, students complain that *control* smacks of totalitarianism, of a *big brother* mentality. "I don't want someone else controlling me," they'll say. These students are assuming that the scientist is seeking to *control* behavior, particularly that of other humans. This, however, is not necessarily what scientists mean when they speak of control. Rather, control to them often implies only the *control of variables*, control in the sense that the relevant variables can be *known* and *measured*. The environmental psychologist has *controlled* for temperature as an influence on behavior if accurate readings of temperature have been taken at appropriate times during data collection. The researcher has controlled for age as a determinant of behavior if the ages of the respondents have been ascertained.

Often, especially in the early stages of research or when it is important to provide exact predictions, the scientist may engage in *manipulating* the values of one or more variables **(independent variables)** and noting the effect of this manipulation on other variables **(dependent variables)**. For example, an environmental psychologist may carefully and systematically vary noise level and note the effect of this variation on performance; or, this individual may manipulate the concentration of atmospheric carbon monoxide and note resultant changes in human reaction time. Rather than wait for such conditions to occur naturally and noting their effect, the scientist creates the conditions and observes their effect. This is a more parsimonious use of time, and as long as the conditions created are not unlike those about which conclusions are to be drawn, the integrity of the scientific method remains intact.

Control need not involve *manipulation*, though, and should not be confused with it. Furthermore, manipulation is never seen as a goal, *per se*, but rather as a means to an end. In fact, control itself is always only a means to an end. Without control, functional relationships could not be established and science as a means of understanding would cease to exist. In a very real sense control is no more than the careful selection and measurement of presumed antecedent and causal influences on the phenomenon of interest.

Prediction

Prediction involves the anticipation of an event before it occurs. Being able to foretell the future based on information available in the present is a very useful ability in everyday life and is of the utmost importance in science. However, prediction does not represent the final step in developing scientific understanding. Humans could accurately predict some phenomena for centuries and yet were unable to adequately *explain* them. Primitive humans, no doubt, could predict with accuracy the rising and setting of the sun and the changing of the seasons, while understanding nothing about planetary rotation and orbits or the concept of a spherical earth. One of your authors can predict with a high degree of exactitude the behavior of his automobile given the manipulation of a few keys, knobs, and pedals. This precision, however, comes in the absence of an understanding of internal combustion processes, torque, friction, inertia, and other mechanical and physical principles.

In everyday circumstances, we often predict the behaviors of others. For example, it is a safe bet that if we order a Big Mac at a McDonald's restaurant, the employee will serve us a Big Mac, and, if we ask for one at a Wendy's, the employee there will not. Or, if we call someone a "no good, no account, lily-livered SOB," chances are that the person will not take kindly to us. This common sense, or "naive psychology" (Heider, 1958), allows us to predict behavior in a variety of settings. However, we should not feel that just because we are able to make a few correct predictions that we *understand* people scientifically or even satisfactorily. We often predict environmental events without any but a "because that's the way it is" understanding. For example, mood shifts in the direction of increased restlessness and irritability are predictably associated with periods of hot dry winds (see Chapter 6), but the reasons for the association are only now being investigated. One might say that the mood shifts occur because "that's just the way it is." However, an understanding of this phenomenon minimally requires knowledge of ionic valences, how they are produced, how they are adsorbed, and how they influence our biochemistry. Without such knowledge such predictions fall short of the goals of science.

Understanding

To articulate the role of understanding in science we must look at the roles of theory and data, and the interrelationship of the two. Figure 3-2 provides an idealized representation of these interrelationships. First, the assumption (formally known as *determinism*) is made that a knowable world exists—that is, it is assumed that events are not haphazard, but rather conform to a few basic, logically consistent principles of cause and effect. A *cognitive representation* of the world (often called a theory) is then developed in which events are categorized to form *constructs* and relationships among them postulated. Simultaneously, the

FIGURE 3-2 A model showing the interrelationships of data and theory, of hypotheses and measurement, of experimentation and interpretation.

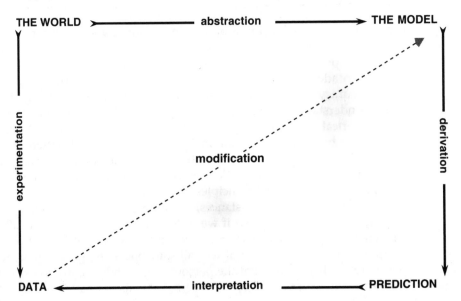

scientist continues to collect facts about the world. In Figure 3-2, this process is represented by the arrow leading from the world to data and labelled *experi-mentation*. This new information (data) often leads to changes in the model, as exemplified by the arrows labelled *modification.*

Data, however, are not collected in a value-free vacuum nor haphazardly. Data must be based on observations that are public and repeatable; they must be collected under highly specified conditions; and, they must stem from agreed-upon definitions of constructs and agreed-upon measurement procedures. If, for example, a scientist were interested in the effects of temperature on performance, the data collected would be determined by the interests and values of the scientist. Depending on whether that scientist were working on a government project whose concern was the effect of extreme cold on attentiveness among Air Force personnel in the Arctic, or on a project designed to determine the effect of high temperatures on worker output among gold miners in South Africa, the data would be very different.

The former might measure the number of errors of omission in detecting blips on a radar screen; the latter might measure tons of materials moved in an eight hour shift. Despite these differences, the two scientists and their projects would have a great deal in common: (1) Data would be collected using the same scale of measurement on the stimulus dimension, i.e., temperature in degrees centigrade or Fahrenheit; (2) this data could potentially be collected by other scientists with similar training; and (3) the data could be expected to be similar with repeated measurement.

If scientists have a well-articulated *model* of the world they are attempting to understand, a number of *predictions* regarding unknown aspects of this world are derivable. This process is typically labelled *hypothesis formation* or *derivation* (see Figure 3-2). These hypotheses are then tested (*interpreted*) against data collected from the world. If the hypothesis withstands the test of data, that is, yields accurate predictions, the scientist becomes increasingly confident that the model is an adequate, albeit tentative, representation of the world. If the data are at variance with these hypotheses derived from the model, the model may be modified or even rejected. Figure 3-2 provides a concise depiction of the process by which scientists come to an understanding of the world.

Derived hypotheses represent logical extensions of theories and typically are expressed in cause-effect terms, (e.g., X leads to or causes Y), or as relationships between variables (e.g., Y is a linear transformation of X). These statements are predictions about unknown events based on logical derivations from theory. For example, from atomic theory one could derive the hypothesis that by exposing to neutron radiation a known stable atom (uranium 235), a radioactive, unstable element with an atomic weight of 237 would result. Thus, the element neptunium was first logically deduced from a theory and then empirically created. From the model presented in Chapter 2 one could predict that if environmental characteristics are such that the organism feels controlled by them, then coping strategies will entail attempts to recover that lost control. In later chapters research will be presented that supports this prediction, and additional hypotheses derivable from this model will be suggested.

It is extremely advantageous to science if these hypotheses take the form of mathematical predictions, as in the example regarding atomic theory provided above. It should be apparent that if hypotheses can be formulated as mathematical relationships, and if data are collected under carefully controlled conditions with precise and agreed-upon measuring instruments, then it is possible to look for a match between our intellectual conceptualization of the world (the model or theory) and our measurement of that world (the mathematical description).

Thus, the scientific enterprise consists of collecting reliable and valid data under specifiable and measurable conditions and relating these data to one another in the form of mathematical functions. The scientific enterprise also consists of organizing events in convenient mental categories (constructs) and postulating logical relationships among them. In testing theories and in applying scientific knowledge, the scientist must engage in a rather sophisticated form of prognostication. Based on available data conforming to rigid criteria, predictions are made regarding as yet unattained data. In making predictions, the scientist must be mindful of the need for systematic and careful data collection. But above all, science aspires to a congruence between mental maps of the world (theories) and empirical descriptions of that same world (low-level empirical laws). This is what is meant by scientific understanding. The lack of congruence

FIGURE 3-3   The scientific enterprise consists of collecting reliable and valid data under specifiable and measurable conditions and relating these data to one another in the form of mathematical functions. Obviously this cartoon character is the victim of an illusory correlation.

TIME-OUT: A nomadic tribe of people travelled extensively throughout an area, settling for a period of time where food was available, and moving on when food sources diminished. The tribe made shelters out of whatever material was plentiful in the particular area they had settled—sometimes thatch huts were constructed, other times clay huts were made. Over time the tribe observed that "winters seemed milder" when they constructed clay abodes compared to thatch huts. They concluded that they could control the weather by selecting sites to settle on that allowed them to construct clay houses.

Analyze the above scenario in terms of the scientific method as discussed in this section. Were the tribesmen engaging in science? What causal relationships are implicit in their behavior? How did this thinking influence the hypotheses they developed, the subsequent data they collected, and their interpretation of the resulting evidence? What do you think are the important variables to be looked at? Design a study for these people that might help them sort out the relevant cause-effect relationships among pertinent variables.

---

is what drives the researcher to refine measurements, obtain additional data, and reconsider ways of explaining the phenomenon of interest.

CRITERIA FOR EVALUATING RESEARCH METHODS

To understand and evaluate research findings, a solid grasp of research methods is needed. Experimental design and instrumentation must be viewed as critically as any other part of an inquiry. Eddington (1939) succinctly captured the need for this form of analysis in his parable of the ichthyologist. It seems an ichthyologist interested in exploring ocean life used a fish net with a two-inch mesh; after a series of dippings and careful surveillance of his catch, he concluded that there is no fish in the ocean fewer than two inches long. Critics claimed that the net utilized was not sufficiently adapted to survey all ocean life and that the ichthyologist's conclusions were therefore suspect. The ichthyologist, undaunted, replied, "Anything uncatchable by my net is *ipso facto* outside the scope of ichthyological knowledge, and is not part of the kingdom of fishes . . . in short, what my net can't catch isn't fish" (pp. 16–17). There are several lessons to be learned from this hypothetical account, but foremost among them is that *the knowledge we gain and the inferences we make from that knowledge are inextricably tied to instrumentation and the process of data collection.*

Unfortunately, it is possible to conclude from a casual reading of journal articles in environmental psychology that there are as many different nets as there are fishers, and that these nets not only vary in the size of their mesh, but also in the quality of the materials from which they are made. But, despite the fact that there are many methods, the basic criteria for evaluating them can be

FIGURE 3-4 "Anything uncatchable by my net is outside the scope of ichthyological knowledge."

subsumed under the two broad categories of reliability and validity. It is to these criteria we turn next.

Reliability

First and foremost among the criteria utilized in evaluating the adequacy of research methodology, design, and instrumentality is *reliability*. Only when successive applications of measurement lead to highly similar values of the phenomenon being measured is the method of inquiry said to be reliable. But reliability also implies that the phenomenon is susceptible to measurement by *qualified others*. Thus, we have two related measures of consistency, intra-rater and inter-rater reliability.

Intra-rater reliability (sometimes labelled *internal consistency*) is a measure of consistency across time. Sometimes the time involved is as short as the time required to complete a single testing, as when one asks about the internal consistency of an attitude scale. In such cases *split-half* reliability coefficients are obtained. Responses to the first half of a testing session may be correlated with responses during the second half; or, the even-numbered responses might be correlated with the odd-numbered responses. If the scale has internal consistency those correlations should approach a value of +1.00 (although correlations as low as .70 are often acceptable). Sometimes researchers are interested in the consistency of measurement across longer periods of time. For example, it is assumed that intelligence is a rather stable characteristic of individuals, and therefore repeated measurement should lead to similar values throughout one's life. If our scale yields similar results across time it is said to display test-retest reliability. This type of intra-rater reliability is absolutely necessary for evaluating research designs which require repeated measurement of the dependent variable over time.

Inter-rater reliability, on the other hand, is obtained by correlating the values obtained from two ostensibly equivalent test forms or correlating the data obtained from two different data collectors. It is necessary to establish this type of reliability anytime there is more than one rater. This type of reliability is demonstrated when the correlations between scores obtained by two different raters, using the same instrument, approach +1.00. Unless the various raters agree on what is being measured and "how much" there is, the data have to be considered suspect. Without these two forms of consistency in research, any inquiry ceases to be scientifically meaningful.

Validity

The second criterion utilized in evaluating the adequacy of an inquiry involves *validity*. Validity is an index of the extent to which an experiment or experimental device measures what it is supposed to measure. If a test is designed to measure knowledge acquired, but is worded in such a way that the respondents do not know what is being asked of them, then the test does not have validity. Similarly, degrees centigrade, while a valid measure of temperature, is not a valid measure of distance. There are at least six components of validity to consider, each of which contributes to the overall validity of an experiment. These have been labelled *internal validity, external validity, construct validity, discriminant validity, convergent validity*, and *experiential realism* (Cook & Campbell, 1976; Patterson. 1977). Each is discussed in some detail below.

Internal Validity.   Internal validity is an index of the extent to which an experimental finding represents a *real finding*. If, in the course of data collection, two variables are found to be mathematically related to one another, it is important to know whether one caused the other, the two were both brought about by a third factor, or if the relationship can be accounted for in some other way. Internal validity is a reflection of the extent to which spurious variables can be ruled out as causes for change in the dependent variable. These spurious variables are often called *extraneous variables* because their effects are extraneous to the causal relationship of interest.

Suppose, for example, a researcher was interested in determining the relationship between noise and reading comprehension. To obtain samples for comparison the researcher chooses an inner-city school adjacent to an elevated commuter train line and a school located in the suburbs of a large metropolitan area. As a measure of reading comprehension, students in each of the schools read passages from two eighteenth-century novels, after which they write essays comparing the main characters. The essays are then turned over to a panel of high school English teachers who are told the nature of the study and apprised of the samples from which the essays came. These teachers are then told to evaluate the essays in terms of the students' comprehension of the passages.

This study would be deficient in internal validity for a number of reasons. Even if a relationship between *noise* and *reading comprehension* were found, it could not be known whether this relationship was due to differences in ambient noise level, differences in the samples chosen (e.g., age, socioeconomic status, ethnicity variables, etc.), self-fulfilling prophecies on the part of the English teachers doing the grading, or any number of other possible extraneous factors. Indeed, the above study suffers from many of the common threats to internal validity: (1) bias in the selection of subjects, (2) inaccurate measurement techniques, (3) rater bias, (4) differences in experimental procedures. Thus, we question internal validity when differences between groups can be explained by alternative variables instead of, or in addition to, the hypothesized variable (noise in the present example).

Luckily, a number of safeguards to internal validity are possible, and these should be considered before the implementation of any experiment. Among these are (1) piloting of measurement devices or using devices with known psychometric properties, (2) random assignment of subjects to experimental conditions, and (3) manipulation checks to see if respondents perceive the experiment in the way in which the experimenter intends.

Construct Validity. Construct validity is concerned with the extent to which the results of a study can be used to draw conclusions about a model or a theory. In short, construct validity is the extent to which the *things* being manipulated and/or measured in the experiment are an adequate representation of the *things* represented in the theory. As an example, in the hypothetical study regarding noise level and reading comprehension, the experimenter assumes that the grades assigned by high school English teachers adequately measure *reading comprehension*. To the extent that these grades are consistent with what is generally thought of as reading comprehension, then that part of the study would have high construct validity. The researchers in this hypothetical example would have to make two additional inquiries to determine if their measurement was consistent with their theoretical constructs. These inquiries revolve about the notions of *convergent validity* and *discriminant validity*. If an instrument is a valid measure of a construct (e.g., reading comprehension), then it should correlate highly with other valid measures of that construct. Indeed, if varying measurements of the same construct show a high degree of correlation, the instruments are said to display convergent validity. They *converge* on the same construct. In our example, if the teachers' evaluation of the written essays correlated highly with, say, a multiple-choice questionnaire over the reading materials or an oral examination of reading comprehension, these measures could be said to display convergent validity.

While many investigators are content with establishing convergent validity, Campbell and Fiske (1959) have made a case for establishing discriminant validity as well. Clearly, two measures of the same construct may be highly correlated—that is, have convergent validity—but the basis for the correlation may be the same constant error rather than the *true* score. To eliminate this possibility it must be shown that when the same method or the same instrument is used to measure different variables, different results are obtained. That is, to have discriminant validity, an instrument must be measuring the construct of interest and no other. The instrument must *discriminate* between its measurement of that construct and other unrelated constructs. In the previous example, the teachers' rating of the essays must be a reflection of reading comprehension and not the raters' biases, the students' IQ, the respondents' socioeconomic status, or other factors.

External Validity. External validity refers to the extent to which results obtained in one setting can be generalized to other settings or contexts. Context refers to subject populations, environmental settings, times, cultures, etc. External validity tends to be low when the setting of data collection is not representative of the setting of research application. Thus, external validity depends on the extent to which the data collection context mirrors the real world. External validity is particularly important in environmental psychology where the results sought have direct, immediate applications. However, if one's concerns are with the development of an organism/environment interaction theory, concerns for external validity may often be temporarily relaxed for the sake of internal and construct validity. Put another way, if one is attempting to identify basic processes without regard to their application in specific settings, internal validity is more important than external validity. In our example, we would want to know the extent to which any relationship between noise and reading comprehension found in our selected samples would generalize beyond these two samples. If we could show that the same relationships hold across settings, socioeconomic classes, and age groups, our findings could be said to exhibit external validity.

Experiential Realism. A final criterion for evaluating data-collection procedures has been termed experiential realism (Patterson, 1977). Here the impact that experimental conditions have on respondents and the extent to which that impact represents events that occur in *real life* are featured. Sometimes called *mundane realism*, this criterion refers to whether subjects' experiences in the data-collection setting reflect what they experience in day-to-day living. Thus, experiential realism is related to external validity. Experiential realism is high to the extent that variables are not manipulated, represent the real world, and their measurement is nonreactive and nonobtrusive. If data collection interferes with ongoing processes and/or the processes are observed under nonrealistic or artificial conditions, then experiential realism is low. Thus, experiential realism concerns questions regarding how *typical* the experiment is; for example, do the experimenter and the respondent believe that the data being collected are representative of behavior that would occur in the absence of such data collection, or has the procedure interfered with naturally occurring processes? Are the high school students who were writing essays, based on their reading of two eighteenth-century novels, behaving differently from how they normally would because they knew they were part of a study? To the extent that their behavior was affected by the data-collection process, the study can be said to exhibit low experiential realism due to "demand characteristics" of the study.

Brief Summary

The term *science* carries with it a double meaning. In one sense it denotes a body of knowledge that has been derived by a particular method, and in the second sense it refers to the method itself. All science stems from careful, systematic, reliable, valid, measured observations. These observations are the basis for establishing functional relationships between events in the form of mathematical equations. On the other hand, these same observations are organized conceptually to form the basis for theories. Logical extension of theories (hypotheses) are then compared with the data. It is this reliance on empirical fact that makes the scientific enterprise more dispassionate than any other mode of inquiry, and it is the comparison of data with theory that makes the scientific enterprise the only known self-correcting model of inquiry.

The goals of any science include understanding, prediction, and control, and the goals of environmental psychology are no exception. To meet these goals environmental psychologists utilize operationism and measurement. These processes, however, are not applied haphazardly; to meet the rigorous demands of the scientific method, both operationism and measurement must be well thought out and systematically applied.

Although it is uncontested that observation forms the basis for science, and that this observation must meet rigid criteria of acceptability to be admissible as scientific, the techniques of measurement and manipulation of variables appropriate to the relationships being investigated are not always clear. Both the size of the net and the kind of net being cast are matters of concern.

This analysis of the scientific method is fairly accurate if one is considering only what is known as basic research. Slightly different goals, procedures, and methods are utilized when the scientist is engaging in applied research. As is apparent in the definition of environmental psychology, much of what environmental psychologists do can be considered applied research, a more thorough account of this enterprise is necessary. Therefore, after considering the types of research methods, instrumentation techniques, and measurement devices that environmental psychologists have at their disposal, a description of applied research will be provided and a comparison of applied and basic research will be developed.

TIME-OUT: The following experiment was conducted on the effects of crowding on performance: Ten subjects were asked to categorize and then collate a collection of papers on a table placed next to a window at the side of a lounge area; they were also asked to add a series of single-digit numbers while seated in the adjacent lounge on comfortable furniture. A second group of twenty subjects were seated at desks in a windowless classroom and solved finger mazes and anagrams. The researcher found that the performance of the latter group was "poor," while that of the former was "good." The experimenter concluded that crowding inhibits performance.

How many problems are you able to identify in this study (make reference to concepts such as internal/external validity, operationism, measurement, and experiential realism). How would you conduct this study to eliminate some of these problems?

RESEARCH METHODS IN ENVIRONMENTAL PSYCHOLOGY

The methods, procedures, and measurement devices utilized by a researcher depend on the questions being asked, the availability of previous data, the accessibility of the data source, the psychometric properties of available measurement devices, the desirability of manipulation, and the ethical considerations surrounding subjects' rights. Despite the almost infinite variety of methods derivable from permuting these and other considerations, they can all be classified within three major types: laboratory experimentation, field correlational studies, and field experimentation.

Laboratory Experimentation

If the researcher is concerned primarily with establishing a high level of internal validity, the laboratory experiment is usually the method of choice. This method allows the experimenter to systematically manipulate assumed causal variables under carefully controlled conditions designed to eliminate the influence of extraneous variables, and to assess the effects of this manipulation on outcome variables. In this way the outcomes of data collection are logically attributable only to those variables that have been manipulated by the experimenter. This method of research also generally involves the random assignment of subjects to experimental conditions. *Random assignment* means that each subject has an equal opportunity of being in each experimental condition, thus ensuring that subjects comprising one condition have a very good chance of collectively resembling the subjects comprising every other condition of the experiment. In this way, individual variations in the subjects themselves can be ruled out as a reason for differences in experimental outcomes, and greater confidence can be placed in the inference that outcomes are due to manipulations of the independent variables.

Although laboratory research increases confidence that observed outcomes are due to independent variable manipulations, researchers must remain skeptical of the limits of these relationships. Experimenters cannot be certain that these outcomes would occur in the multivariate complexity existing outside the laboratory setting. In other words, a trade-off often exists between internal and external validity; an increase in internal validity tends also to reduce external validity. Later in this text we will see that laboratory experiments designed to assess the relationship between density and interpersonal behaviors do not always lead to the same conclusions as data collected by other methods.

Field Correlational Studies

If the goal of research is to establish a high degree of external validity, investigators are likely to use a variation of the field correlational method. Studies utilizing this method are designed to provide information about the relationship among naturally occurring real-world events unencumbered by the influence of data collection. The field correlational studies we report in this text generally involve either naturalistic observation or survey research techniques. These methods of data gathering are discussed in detail later.

No matter which method is used, though, the inferences that investigators legitimately can draw differ from those that can be made when using laboratory experimentation. With laboratory experimentation, inferences regarding causation (within a pre-established margin of error) are appropriate. When correlational techniques are used, no such inferences are possible—it can only be known that two or more variables are *associated* with one another. For example, it is possible to determine that population density is associated with various indices of social pathology by utilizing correlational methods, but one cannot conclude that population density *causes* social pathology. It may be that both are caused by a third factor such as lack of education or poverty.

It is impossible to draw clear causal inferences because studies of this sort lack internal validity, yet it is clear that the associations are not confined to artificially circumscribed boundaries predetermined by the experimenter. Put simply, laboratory studies maximize internal validity while eschewing external validity, and field correlational studies maximize external validity but often lack internal validity.

Field Experimentation

If researchers want to balance the internal validity achievable through laboratory experimentation with the external validity achievable through field correlational studies, they may employ a hybrid method known as the field experiment. Here experimenters systematically manipulate some proposed causal antecedents while simultaneously permitting presumed extraneous variables to operate in their naturally occurring setting. Some degree of control is lost, but, at the same time, much of the naturalness of the field correlational method is retained. Hence, the researchers have control over variables, maintain some degree of external validity, and retain much of the experiential realism needed for good research. For example, a researcher might systematically manipulate temperature in a subway car under different levels of density to assess the effects of these variables on the likelihood that passengers would pick up a letter "accidentally" dropped by the experimenter.

FIGURE 3-5 The effects of environmental prompts are often tested using the field experimentation approach.

In developing a scientific understanding of a phenomenon, the scientist must not only develop theories and carefully observe phenomena of interest, but also must determine the best method for testing theories and for making observations. The methods available are myriad, and as we have seen, there is no single right or wrong method because each method has certain advantages and limitations. In the final analysis, the investigator must make clear the goals of a specific piece of research and then select the method that has the best chance of achieving those goals. In the long run the best strategy is probably to utilize a variety of methods to study a problem. The results of these methods will then converge to give a clearer picture of the interrelationships among variables.

MEASUREMENT TECHNIQUES

To be scientific, observations must meet severe criteria. They must be public and repeatable; they must be capable of being plotted against a scale of measurement; and they must meet certain standards of reliability and validity. Despite these seemingly stringent rules of acceptability, however, there exist many measurement techniques capable of providing data for the scientific grist mill. It is to these various techniques that we now turn our attention with special consideration given those techniques that are easily devised, administered, scored, and interpreted.

Self-Report Measures

The most frequently utilized method of collecting data about individuals is self-report. In self-reports, people are asked to provide information concerning their opinions, beliefs, behaviors, attitudes, and feelings to the investigators. Self-report procedures include such varying techniques as questionnaires, interviews, and rating scales, all of which are discussed in some detail below. These procedures share one common trait—all involve information in which subjects provide their own interpretation. For example, a question might ask "How often do you recycle?" with the respondent given the following alternatives with which to answer: "never," "seldom," "often," "always." You will note there is no actual observation of recycling behavior; the respondent is allowed to interpret what is meant by recycling; and, the respondent determines what frequencies are associated with each of the descriptors. As a result, self-report measures are subject to two separate sources of bias, one stemming from the investigator, and one from the subject's interpretation of the investigator's goal.

Other problems arise when nonstandardized self-report measures are used to meet the needs of a specific study. For example, not all researchers in a given content area use the same self-report form, and this makes it difficult to compare research from one laboratory or research setting to the next. Second, if subjects are given the opportunity to label their responses in a multiple-choice format, they are likely to choose one of the labels that is provided by the experimenter, when they may have described their behavior very differently if constructing their own labels. This, of course, is the problem of *reactance* (see section on the reactive nature of self-report measure later in this chapter).

Questionnaires

Questionnaires are represented by a wide range of self-report paper-and-pencil techniques. Items are generally formulated as questions and may call for factual responses (asking for age, gender, and other traits) as well as attitudinal responses (emotions, values, and beliefs). Sometimes items take the form of statements to which respondents indicate their degree of agreement/disagreement, and sometimes respondents are asked to select from a list of descriptors those words that best describe their position.

Several reasons exist for using a questionnaire for data collection. First, questionnaires are easy to produce, administer, understand, distribute, and collate. Additionally, they can be given to a large number of subjects at the same time, and respondent anonymity is easily provided. For these reasons questionnaires make it easy for investigators to study a number of inter-related variables simultaneously, to get information from a large number of respondents, to sample responses over rather long periods of time, and, to do so efficiently and relatively inexpensively.

Questionnaires, like all forms of self-report, can be either standardized or nonstandardized. Standardized questionnaires have been pretested and have known psychometric properties (e.g., reliability and validity). Nonstandardized questionnaires are rarely pre-assessed in terms of their reliability. We do not know how consistently they elicit similar answers, nor do we know anything of their validity. These measures are typically designed for the immediate research project and usually are not conceived as potentially applicable to other contexts. Thus, the researcher usually decides on the dimensions for which information is needed and then designs or constructs questionnaires to elicit the necessary data. Throughout this text we will be discussing a number of studies that have relied on questionnaire data. Where appropriate, we will be returning to issues of reliability and validity as they pertain to the interpretations of these studies.

The Interview

The second form of self-report is the interview. Interviews can vary in terms of their formality and the kinds of questions they ask. Cannell and Kahn (1968) have referred to the interview as "a two person conversation, initiated by the interviewer, and focused by him on content specified by research objectives of systematic description, prediction or explanation" (p. 527). In a sense, the interview is a dialogue designed to obtain quantifiable information. Viewed in this way, the interview process becomes much more than mere conversation and, as Cannell and Kahn (1968) have suggested, entails at least the following five discrete steps: (1) creating or selecting an interview schedule (a set of questions, statements, pictures, or other stimuli to evoke responses) and a set of rules or procedures for using this schedule; (2) conducting the interview (that is, evoking the responses or events that are to be classified); (3) recording these responses (by means of paper-and-pencil notes, electronic equipment, or other devices); (4) creating a numerical code (a scale or other system of numbers into which the recorded responses are to be translated and a set of rules for making the translations); (5) coding the interview responses (p. 531). The end product of the interview, it is hoped, will be data that has met the requirements of scientific admissibility detailed earlier in this chapter.

Rating Scales

A final form of self-report measure utilized by the environmental psychologist is the rating scale. Rating scales come in a variety of formats, including the checklist, bipolar verbal descriptions, and nonverbal descriptive scales. The respondent, independent of format, is asked to provide the researcher with a description or a rating of the phenomenon of interest. This could be a rating of the respondent's emotional state, a description of the environment, or of other people in the environment. For a detailed description of the development of these forms of measurement, see Fishbein and Ajzen (1975).

THE REACTIVE NATURE OF SELF-REPORT MEASURES

Any measurement that allows respondents to know that they are being measured or the object of concern to a researcher has the potential of being reactive, (i.e., the measurements may be influenced by the very process of measuring). Reactance occurs for a number of reasons. One very common reason is *evaluation apprehension*. Respondents are concerned with appearing normal and therefore respond as they believe *normal* people would respond and not necessarily as they would usually respond. A second source of reactance occurs when the subject chooses a role to play. Any of several roles may be adopted. For instance, a respondent (the *faithful subject*) may choose to attempt to help the researcher: "This must be what they want and therefore I'll give them this information." In direct opposition is the *belligerent subject*: "I'll show those hot shots; I'll screw up their data for them." A third role may be that of the *self-serving subject*: "If I respond in this way, maybe we'll get things done my way around here."

In addition to these roles, respondents may bring with them a *response set* (a predetermined style of responding that occurs independently of the question being asked.) Among these consistent sources of error is the *social acceptability* set, where subjects respond in a way that they feel will meet with social approval. Some subjects have a penchant for choosing strong statements over moderate ones; others for choosing middle-of-the-road responses. Some subjects enter the research setting with an acquiescent set (a tendency to pick positive over negative statements), others tend to select the left side or the right side of the page, or always choose the last alternative.

Still another source of reactance is the measurement itself. This is particularly true of pre-to-post designs in which the initial measurement itself changes the nature of the response or changes how the individual views the environment. The best example of this kind of reactivity is the Hawthorne studies referred to by Roethlisberger and Dickson (1939) where it was shown that changes in behavior could be accounted for by the fact that people knew their behavior was being observed rather than the changes in the environment that were introduced. Environmental psychologists attempting to assess the effects of altered environments have to be very careful of this source of bias so as not to falsely conclude effects where none exist.

Finally, a fifth source of error, *experimenter bias*, resides in the researcher. The researcher may beg the question from the outset without realizing it. For example, we will see in Chapter 7 that only 2 percent of the citizens of the United States (in answering an open-ended questionnaire) mention air pollution as being a major problem. However, if the question is asked directly: "Is air pollution a problem in your area?" 75 to 80 percent of all respondents agree that it is. So, depending on how the question is asked, very different data are obtained.

Asked in the first format, the answers would lead to the conclusion that only 2 percent of the population think air pollution is a problem, whereas asked in the latter fashion the answers would lead to the conclusion that almost 80 percent believe that air pollution is a problem.

There are several other difficulties that reside within the researcher. Among these are that researchers increase their skill in interviewing or in administering test scales over time; they simply get better at what they are doing so that later data is not psychometrically equivalent to earlier data. Second, the researcher gains rapport with respondents over time (or in some instances antagonizes them) so the latter part of an interview or questionnaire is likely to give different kinds of data from the earlier part of the session. Additionally, the experimenter (as well as the respondent) may become bored or grow fatigued as a result of the process.

All of these things lead to measurement that is in part truly reflective of the underlying construct being measured but also a reaction by the respondent to the measurement process itself. These, of course, are the threats to internal validity referred to earlier in this chapter. All researchers should, therefore, take these various factors into consideration and try to set up the investigative process so that much of the reactance can be eliminated and only true scores obtained.

OTHER MEASURES

We have seen that the use of self-report measures can bias or cover up the effect that a researcher wishes to study. As a means of diminishing this effect, various nonreactive, nonobtrusive measures have been developed. These measures consist of either direct or indirect observations of behavior (how individuals actually perform rather than how they would like to perform, think they should perform, or think they have performed). Observational techniques are second only to the questionnaires in frequency of usage by environmental psychologists.

To satisfy the rigors of scientific inquiry, observational techniques must be systematic, public, repeatable, quantifiable, reliable, and valid. In a sense, observational techniques are very much like interview techniques. The procedures for both involve: (1) researchers creating or selecting a schedule (a set of behaviors they are looking for, or the specified times they will be observing), and establishing a set of rules or procedures for utilizing this schedule; (2) making observations at specified times; or (3) numerically coding behaviors with a predetermined set of rules for making such translations; and (4) recording responses, either by means of paper-and-pencil notes, electronic equipment, or some other device.

Depending on the goals of a particular piece of research, the environmental psychologist is likely to choose one of three specific kinds of observations: *The behavior setting, the behavior specimen, or behavior mapping*. The particular method is chosen by the researcher on the basis of his or her particular emphasis. In the *behavior setting*, for example, the emphasis is on the environ-

FIGURE 3-6 Interviewers have to be careful not to let their own opinions guide the responses of the interviewee. (Drawing by Weber, 1975, *The New Yorker Magazine, Inc.*)

"That's the worst set of opinions I've heard in my entire life."

ment; periodic observations are made within a single environmental setting and observations are recorded, (i.e., what is going on at this particular point in time in this environmental setting?). Invariances across time are then looked for and differences between settings are compared.

With the *behavior specimen*, the emphasis is on the person in the environment. Continuous observation is made of a given individual as he or she moves through various environments, and variations in behavior are then attributed to variations in the environments that the respondent experiences. *Behavior mapping* is a combination of these. Here, the researcher records *what* occurs *where* and by *whom*. As one might guess, behavior-mapping techniques are much more comprehensive than the former two techniques, but much more difficult to utilize.

Researchers have a variety of *instrumentation* available to them. For example, the environmental psychologist may choose to use still photographs, time-lapse photography, or video and audio-taping. Environmental researchers are also likely to use various electrodermal tests including galvanic skin response, Palmer Sweat Index, respiratory and cardiac rates, etc. Various biochemical tests including urinalysis or blood analysis can be used depending upon the nature of the inquiry. In some instances, particularly when animals other than humans are being utilized, biopsies and histological examinations are appropriate.

All of these forms of instrumentation are, of course, direct measures of behavior or the direct result of an environmental agent. In addition, the environmental psychologist has available a number of indirect, unobtrusive measures of organism-environment interaction. For example, the environmental psychologist may use, as anthropologists often do, a measure of erosion (the extent to which things are worn away) to make inferences about behavior. If one wanted to see which museum exhibits were being utilized most, one might look at the floor tiles to see how they are worn away.

Those exhibits showing more wear on the tiles around them are probably being viewed more than those where the tile is still shiny or not worn. If one is planning pathways between buildings, it might be wise to let pedestrian traffic take its course, and then put the sidewalks in where the grass is worn most from people walking—the wearing away of the grass is a reliable indicator of how people are using the space between buildings. A similar measure is one of accretion, or examining things that are accumulated. For instance, large numbers of nose smudges on the glass of a museum exhibit indicate that the object is presently being viewed a great deal. As another example, janitors have known for some time that they can determine the intimate details of their clientele by studying their garbage.

FIGURE 3-7 You can sometimes determine intimate details of people's lives by carefully examining their garbage. (Courtesy of Bob Zumph)

TIME-OUT: Assume you have been commissioned to study the relationship between "crowding" and "aggression." Design a laboratory study in which you will manipulate crowding and measure aggression. What would be your operational definitions of these variables? What measurements would you make? What sources of bias would be important to avoid?

Redesign the projects as a field study. What types of observations would you make? When and where would you make them? Do your operational definitions change? Could relevant information be obtained on this relationship by the use of running records? If so, what might that information be and what would be your source of that information? Compare the data that you would get by utilizing these two techniques. Do they answer the same questions or only similar questions?

Environmental psychologists also have available what are called *running records*: the ongoing records of society. This includes such information as deaths, births, marriages, voting records, judicial records, etc. In addition to these continuous records, episodic records are available to researchers, like sales records, personal documents, or records of the amount of money taken in by parking meters at various times during the day. Webb, Campbell, Schwartz, and Sechrest (1966) suggested that water pressure would be a good indirect measure of TV viewing habits. If one observes the drop in water pressure and graphs these times against the times that commercials are shown on the various networks, an indirect measure of the networks that people are watching at a particular time can be obtained.

APPLIED VERSUS BASIC RESEARCH

In contrast to the older and more firmly established sciences, it appears necessary in environmental psychology to spend more time defending the rationale as well as the content of one's research endeavors. There appears to be an inordinate amount of conversation, if not downright name-calling, regarding the methods and goals of this fledgling area. There are those who claim that nothing can be learned about environment/organism interrelationships if the relationship is studied in the lab. To them the lab does not constitute a *real* environment and therefore any data collected under these conditions would be pertinent only to these conditions (a problem in external validity). Others claim that the larger environment is far too complex to be studied simultaneously in its entirety, and that it must be therefore broken down into smaller components and various aspects must be looked at in isolation and one at a time (a problem in internal validity).

Much of this internecine bickering over the types of methods to be used and the types of questions our research should be addressing boils down to a failure to distinguish differences as well as similarities in applied and basic research. It is often the case that applied research is criticized because it does not meet the criteria for good basic research, and basic research is condemned because it does not have immediate applied value to questions begging for quick answers. There are those who feel that basic research is too far removed from life as it is lived, that scientists ought to be primarily concerned with the improvement of society and not in the scientific analysis of some minor, perhaps trivial, aspect of behavior. Legislators, taxpayers, and even a number of scientists would like to see developed in the social sciences the technological equivalents of moon landings, laser beams, and nuclear weapons.

In later chapters we will report on researchers studying the effect of noise on performance by having subjects listen to a tape-recorded cacophony of sounds including a typewriter, people speaking in a foreign language, and white noise—this is hardly the stuff of which most of our environments are made. We will see researchers studying the effect of *population density* by exposing "too many people in a too small room" for brief durations of time—this hardly approximates the living conditions of Calcutta. We will see researchers asking subjects to breathe air with certain concentrations of carbon dioxide and then measuring their reaction times—this hardly approximates the conditions of the Los Angeles commuter on freeways heading home in the late afternoon.

On the other hand, we will find that some researchers have found that they can reduce littering by providing prompts to keep an area clean, but if asked why the prompts work, or how they might work better, or more efficiently, or more cheaply, they might be hard-pressed to give an answer. We will find that some physical designers have been able to design interior spaces that are aesthetically pleasing and perhaps even able to increase productivity, but if asked if that same design would work elsewhere, they could give no definitive answer. We will see that it is easy enough to get people to comply with reduced indoor temperatures in the winter time, but despite their compliance, certain groups report living healthier lives, while others feel their health has been compromised. These are the things of which real life is made, but without basic research to complement it, we may consistently find ourselves in the position of having to re-invent the wheel.

Cures for cancer are not found because scientists don't want to find them; they are not found because scientists simply do not have enough basic knowledge. To understand the effect of noise in the workplace, and the effect it might have on performance, it is first necessary to understand the important parameters of noise. What is bringing about any detrimental effects: the loudness level, pitch, timbre, predictability, controllability? Key breakthroughs in the development of moon-landings, laser beams, and nuclear weapons had to await very important basic research discoveries in metallurgy and rocket propulsion, in the interaction of molecules with microwaves and in the bombardment of atomic nuclei with neutrons using such artificial means as wind tunnels and cyclotrons. These latter conditions are also hardly the stuff of which the real world is made, but they are the stuff from which we can isolate important features of the real world.

Having said all this, it is probably clear that your present authors feel that it is possible, even necessary, to engage in both kinds of research without arousing the cry that "My research is better than your research; the real road to salvation is the one I am pursuing, and if you were smart you'd be following my lead; share my values and do as I do." As someone once said, "there is enough sand on the beaches of scientific discovery for us all to build the castles of our choosing; and, that it is a far better enterprise to be building our own than it is to be kicking down those of others." The only important reason for making a distinction between the two types of research activities is so that you will apply the correct criteria for evaluating the outcomes of the enterprise. But, of course, this is easier said than done.

Applied research constitutes the utilization of scientific methods, procedures, and concepts for the express purpose of solving a problem or answering a question posed in the world of everyday life. Basic research, on the other hand, is primarily an intellectual undertaking that aims toward a conceptual explanation of given phenomenon or phenomena. An applied problem might be to develop an alloy with which rockets could be made so that they would be able to withstand the extreme temperatures generated by re-entering the earth's atmosphere. Basic research might include the study of ionic bonding, or of molecular sharing of electrons, or the like, which may or may not have a direct bearing on rocket re-entry. Applied research might involve ways of capturing and housing California condors and imprinting them to Andean condors, so they might develop new habitats and thus be saved from extinction. Basic research might involve the effect of DDT on the development of eggs among all avian species, or on the migratory flight patterns of various species of birds, or on the role of heredity and learning on the eating and nesting habits of certain wildlife. The important distinction is that in applied research there is a problem (e.g., a crisis) whose solution is dependent on immediate additional knowledge, and researchers are not concerned with whether that knowledge generalizes beyond the immediate situation or not; in basic research the emphasis is on obtaining knowledge that is generalizable to a wide array of situations, and if that knowledge has some immediate application, that is fine, but not necessary.

Because of this, applied research quite often involves the study of the phenomenon in its naturally occurring setting. The questions that are asked and the solutions being sought are enmeshed in the complexities of the everyday world. Saving the condor involves studying it in its natural habitat, replete with diminished territorial range, fewer prey, DDT-infested croplands, etc. If it is impossible to study the phenomenon in its naturally occurring state (e.g., rocket re-entry) then real-life situations are simulated as closely as possible. On the other hand, in basic research there is often a deliberate suspension of interest in real-life problems, and therefore accurate reproductions of the world outside the laboratory are not sought, nor are they deemed necessary. The goal of basic research is to develop and articulate a model of the world that would operate with all other things being equal. And while the social sciences are often criticized for this tactic, very few persons second-guess their counterparts in the other sciences: Cloud chambers, sterile tissue cultures, temperatures of absolute zero, unadulterated chemicals and numerous other oddities are hardly representative of the "real" world.

Earlier in the chapter we discussed the roles of laws and theories in scientific understanding. One goal of basic research is the discovery of these laws and the articulation of these theories. Applied research, by its very nature, is not likely to lead to generalizable laws—its scope of investigation is typically and purposefully too narrow, and for the same reason, it is not likely, in any meaningful way, to extend or to articulate theory. Saving the condor may or may not tell us much about bird life in general; developing an alloy to withstand re-entry temperatures may or may not tell us much about ionic bonding, or the nature of subatomic particles. On the other hand knowing something about subatomic particles might lead to the development of an appropriate alloy, or understanding the migratory habits of birds; or the effect of DDT on egg production might have a significant impact on saving not only the condor but also other birds.

In the final analysis, what we have is an environment that is confusing and often threatening. Any system that attempts to bring order out of this chaos is both anxiety reducing and potentially necessary for the survival of the species. These order-bringing systems can be highly situation specific or they can be more general in nature. If a tornado is imminent, a situation-specific action system is likely to have greater survival value; if Mother Earth is to withstand the ravages of an often unappreciative progeny, then perhaps a more general conceptualization is required. The real issue then becomes not whether scientists are engaged in applied or basic research, but how well they move back and forth between the two.

Throughout the remainder of this text a great deal of research will be presented. This research, like all information you read or hear, should be viewed with a critical eye. You should be careful, however, to evaluate the research in the light of what the researcher was trying to do and not by what you would have liked for him or her to do. Basic research should be evaluated in terms of how well it adds to our conceptualization of a given phenomenon; applied research should be evaluated in terms of how well it has provided a solution to a particular problem posed in the everyday world.

TIME-OUT: Return to the question of the relationship between crowding and aggression. Think of examples of basic research that could be conducted on this issue. How is this research likely to be carried out? What role would theory play in this research? Now think of examples of applied research on this issue. How and where might this research be conducted? Would the results of these studies solve specific problems? Which of the studies that you thought of seem the most worthwhile to you? Why?

SUMMARY

The environmental psychologist has a variety of methods, techniques, and instrumentation available that allow for the collection of scientifically admissible data. The particular method and kind of instrumentation utilized, however, will depend on the nature of the question being asked by the researcher, the availability of previous data, the accessibility of the data source, the psychometric properties of available measurement devices, the desirability of using manipulation, and, of course, ethical considerations surrounding the subject's rights.

This collection of information is often utilized to develop precise mathematical descriptions of relationships within the organism-milieu system, and to develop theoretical models (intellectual conceptualizations) of that system. Assuming high reliability and validity, congruence is sought between the mathematical description and theoretical predictions. Incongruence leads to additional research and refinements in observation.

The researcher in environmental psychology is often caught in the quandary of whether to be doing basic research (i.e., extending the data base regarding theoretically meaningful questions and attempting to further articulate that theory) or whether to be engaged in applied research (i.e., solving some of the problems that have occurred as a result of humankind's inability to adapt to environmental demands or to making irreversible and deleterious adjustments to an already over-taxed environment). The two horns of this dilemma, it has been shown, can be reconciled if the researcher is willing and creative enough to move back and forth through these two types of research enterprises.

IMPORTANT CONCEPTS

goals of science
scientific method
observation
theoretical-empirical linkage
inter-rater reliability
intra-rater reliability
split-half reliability
test-retest reliability
equivalent forms reliability
internal validity
external validity
construct validity
convergent validity

divergent validity
lab/experimental research
field/correlational research
field experiment
self-report measures
evaluation apprehension
subject reactance/bias
experimenter bias
unobtrusive measures
archival research
applied research
basic research

REFERENCES

Campbell, D.J., & Fiske, D.W. (1959). Convergent and discriminant validation by the multitrait-multimethod matrix. *Psychological Bulletin, 56,* 81–105.

Cannell, C.F., & Kahn, R.L. (1968). Interviewing. In G. Lindsey & E. Aronson (Eds.), *The handbook of social psychology,* (Vol. 1, Chap. 15) (2nd ed.). Reading, Mass.: Addison-Wesley.

Cook, T., & Campbell, D. (1976). The design and conduct of quasi-experiments in field settings. In M. Dunnette (Ed.), *Handbook of industrial and organizational research.* New York: Rand McNally.

Coombs, C.H., Dawes, R.M. & Tversky, A. (1970). *Mathematical psychology: An elementary introduction.* Englewood Cliffs, NJ: Prentice-Hall.

Eddington, A.S. (1939). *The philosophy of physical science.* Cambridge: Cambridge University Press.

Fishbein, M., & Ajzen, I. (1975). *Belief, attitude, intention, and behavior: An introduction to theory and research.* Reading, Mass.: Addison-Wesley.

Heider, F. (1958). *The psychology of interpersonal relations.* New York: John Wiley.

Patterson, A.H. (1977). Methodological developments in environment-behavior research. In D. Stokols (Ed.), *Perspectives on environment and behavior.* New York: Plenum.

Roethlisberger, F.J., & Dickson, W.J. (1939). *Management and the worker.* Cambridge, Mass.: Harvard University Press.

Webb, E.J., Campbell, D.T., Schwartz, R.D. & Sechrest, L. (1966). *Unobtrusive measures: Nonreactive research in the social sciences.* Chicago: Rand McNally.

Environmental Perception, Cognition, and Attitudes

4

FIGURE 4-1 The same objective environmental conditions can result in very different subjective perceptions.

erception is one of the most basic and fundamental psychological processes in which humans engage. The process begins the moment we are born, if not before, and continues to play a central role in our daily lives thereafter. It is the process by which sensory impressions of stimuli in the environment are translated into mental representations, and, therefore, it is the first step in processing information from the world around us. Perception is the basis of our evaluations of, attitudes toward, and behavioral responses to that world (see Figure 2-6). Accordingly, an understanding of environment-behavior relationships requires a detailed consideration of perception.

This chapter will begin with a discussion of the basic processes of sensation and perception, after which several influential theories of environmental perception are examined. The way in which knowledge about the environment is developed and organized, (i.e., the processes of environmental cognition) is also considered, and affective and evaluative responses as mediators of behavior are discussed. Finally, because cognitive, affective, and behavioral responses to the environment can all be incorporated in the concept of attitude, this chapter concludes with a consideration of the processes of environmental attitude formation and the relationship between attitudes and behavior.

ELEMENTARY PSYCHOPHYSICS

To begin to understand the process of perception, it is necessary to know something about psychophysics (i.e., to be familiar with the processes of *detection*, *recognition*, *discrimination*, and *scaling*). In dealing effectively with the environment a number of questions have to be answered: "Is there anything out there?" (detection); "What is it?" (recognition); "Is this stimulus different from that one?" (discrimination); and finally "How much of it is there?" (scaling). These questions are basic to the processes of sensation and perception and were the subject of much early research in psychology.

Stimulus Detection

The most basic task for any sensory system is to detect the presence of energy changes in the environment. These changes may be in electromagnetic energy (light), mechanical energy (sound, touch, movement, muscle tension), chemical energy (taste, smell), or thermal energy (heat). Detection centers around the question of how much of a change from a zero energy level is necessary for the organism to realize its presence (i.e., How loud must a noise be to be heard? What concentration must a chemical be to be tasted or smelled? What pressure must be exerted on the skin to be felt?). Considerable early research in psychology was, therefore, concerned with establishing the *absolute threshold* of a variety of stimuli, or the level of intensity above which the presence of a stimulus could be detected, and below which individuals were unable to detect its presence.

Detection is obviously necessary for survival. Unless we could detect extremely high or low ambient temperatures, chemicals in the gases we inhale, or pressure exerted on the surface of our bodies, we would be unable to protect ourselves from extreme temperatures, noxious (if not debilitating or lethal) gases lingering in the atmosphere, and hydraulic pressure. Thus, it is not surprising that a great deal of early research in perception was directed at understanding how variations in the intensity of *physical* stimuli are *psychologically* detected—hence, the term *psychophysics*.

Stimulus Recognition

Assuming that sufficient energy is present to render a stimulus detectable, organisms must determine what the stimulus is. Is it something that has been encountered before? Is it recognizable? Thus, *recognition* is the second phase of the perception process. Everyday detection and recognition problems are usually achieved quickly and easily, since familiar stimuli are very strong (making detection easy), and contain enough information that they pose no problem for recognition. For example, noises are usually loud and unique enough, odors

TIME-OUT: The multifarious nature of detection and recognition only emerges in complex, novel, or degraded stimulus situations. One of your authors, on a recent camping trip in northern Ontario, found himself in just such a situation. Having awakened in the middle of the night and having crawled out of the tent to take care of necessary bodily functions, he was confronted with a world of darkness and shadows. Having seen a black bear foraging in the area earlier in the day, a sharp eye was kept for movement and an ear was bent for sounds as he moved some distance from the tent. Various twigs snapped, leaves rustled in the wind, loons in the distance sent ominous vocalizations, and the waves of the nearby lake lapped upon the shore. The faint smells of a burned-out campfire and fried walleye wafted through the air, and the prick of pine needles stung bare feet.

In retrospect, detection was keen and recognition easy. At the time, however, he was certain that the rustling leaves and snapping twigs were caused by the movement of big, strong, and no doubt starving bears; that the waves licking the shore was the tongue of the bear lapping up water; that the campfire smells were so strong that they had probably attracted every bear within thirty miles; that the loon was crying death screams as it was soon to become bear supper; and a particular human (in the form of yours truly) would be the next target for this marauding behemoth. Obviously, in this environment of unfamiliar and degraded stimuli, detection was acute but recognition was suboptimal.

Take a moment to think back on experiences that you have had that are similar to the one just described. Perhaps one occurred while you were walking in a dark alley or on a street in a strange city; perhaps while lying in bed in a strange house. What aspects of stimulus detection and recognition were illustrated by your experience? How long did it take you to resolve the problem of stimulus recognition? What factors contributed to your solution? How do you account for the relationships between detection and recognition in this experience?

strong and distinct enough, and objects illuminated and large enough, so that we have no trouble in detecting and recognizing them.

To recognize and identify a stimulus is one of the major tasks that the perceptual system must perform. The difficulty of this task depends on the novelty of the context, the number of alternatives available, and various "perceptual sets" that the observer takes into the perceiving situation. In the above example, the context was novel and a very strong set had been established earlier in the day by the sighting of a lone bear. Thus, while the ability to detect was high, recognition was poor. We will have more to say about this in our discussion of the perception of various environmental stressors in Chapter 5.

Stimulus Discrimination

An interior decorator glances at some strips of cloth and then at a living room couch, shakes her head and mutters to herself, "Not quite the same." She takes out a few more and compares them to the couch in the same way. Eventually, she looks up at her client and says, "There, a perfect match." The interior decorator is engaged in solving the problem of discrimination. Is this stimulus different from that one? In our interactions with the environment we must constantly be dealing with this problem.

In addition to being concerned with absolute thresholds, early psychophysical research concentrated on the concept of the *just noticeable difference threshold* (JND). The JND was defined as the increase in intensity of a stimulus above its original level required for a person to notice a difference in the level of intensity. In fact, one of the first "laws" discovered in psychology is known as Weber's law, which states that high-intensity stimuli require a proportionally larger increase to produce a JND than do low-intensity stimuli. For example, a 90-decibel tone would require a much greater increase in volume to be noticeably louder than would be required to produce a JND following a 40-decibel tone. Likewise, a small temperature change from 75 degrees Fahrenheit would be detected while the same change from 95 degrees would not.

In Chapter 2 we discussed the notions of steady-state influence and adaptation level. Steady-state influence is maintained as long as the stimulus conditions remain within the organism's adaptation level; once outside that range, the influence is no longer steady-state. Organisms must continually determine if the environmental stimulation is still within the level of established adaptability, or whether it has changed enough that something has to be done about it (i.e., is adaptation or adjustment required?). This obviously involves the process of stimulus discrimination. If the organism perceives that the environment has exceeded the range of adaptability, it must then muster defenses or resources to bring the relationship back to steady-state. But how much in the way of resources is needed? This question can only be answered by knowing the magnitude of the change from steady-state. This is the fourth problem in psychophysics, the problem of scaling.

Stimulus Scaling

Scaling is no different from the problem of measurement encountered in Chapter 3. All organisms, including humans, must engage in a kind of measurement. They must determine that this light is twice as bright as that one, or that there is enough smoke in this room to indicate that a dangerous fire is burning. The magnitude of the stimulus, as scaled by the perceiver, thus determines the magnitude of the response deemed necessary to deal with it.

The process of stimulus scaling, however, is more sophisticated than the previous examples suggest, and is the least understood. Nonetheless, as the above examples illustrate, it is an extremely important process for effective commerce with the environment, and we shall see in later chapters that many crucial environmental issues could be framed in terms of scaling. For example, whether an individual considers airport noise as stressful is a matter of how intense the individual considers the noise to be. Also, whether a person believes that adequate measures have been taken to control air pollution can be understood in terms of the individual's perception of the magnitude of the problem.

Making sense of our world is a very complex process, and central to this process are the interrelated problems of stimulus detection, recognition, discrimination, and scaling. Each of these is the subject of a great deal of research whose details are beyond the scope of the present text. From here on we will deal with the perception of "macrostimuli" and will show less concern with the problems of psychophysics and unidimensional stimulation.

PERCEPTION

When we think of perception we usually think first of visual perception. This is probably because we gather so much information from the environment via this sensory system. With the exception of listening to speech, the vast majority of our everyday activity is guided by vision. Vision guides our motor behavior (getting us from here to there while avoiding running into things on the way), providing us with information concerning what is out there and where it is. Through the mediation of photographs, television, newspapers, books, and magazines, vision provides information about what is going on beyond the grasp of our immediate senses. We can know about the cold of Antarctica, the heat of the Sahara, or the crowdedness of Calcutta, without ever having been there. Additionally, much of our interpersonal behavior is guided by the visual information we receive. Our judgments of the emotional states of others (and ourselves, for that matter), and our intentions, likes, and dislikes, are determined in good part by what we see. No wonder we rely so heavily on our sense of vision to inform us of the world that we inhabit! There is an old adage that "seeing is believing," and when it comes to conflicting cross-modal information, we do indeed tend to believe our eyes over the other senses (Freides, 1974).

Despite this great reliance on vision, perception is more than just sensory input to the visual system. Often we must depend on other systems when interacting with the environment. For example, we cannot see heat, so we must depend on thermal receptors on the skin's surface to warn of the dangers of placing the hand on a stove; we cannot see natural gas and must depend on olfactory cues and odorous additives to warn of a gas leak in the home; we cannot see the Civil Defense siren warning of an impending tornado, and therefore must rely on our sense of hearing. But perception of the environment is even more than the summation of all these sensory inputs. It involves labelling, describing, and attaching meaning to the world around us. Perception, in addition to being sensory, is also highly cognitive.

Cognitive Bases of Perception

All environments carry a set of meanings acquired through their specific physical, social, cultural, aesthetic, and economic attributes. These meanings are extracted from the environment by the perceiver in terms of his or her own attitudes, beliefs, values, and physical limitations. We may admire an apple orchard in spring for its floral beauty and its aromatic fragrance, while simultaneously realizing its worth in terms of the honey that will be produced by bees from its nectar and the apples to be harvested in the fall. Additionally, we may see the orchard as symbolic of the economic power of its owner, his or her ability to buy and sell, and ultimately the political influence that person is likely to exert in the community. Finally, we may see it as representing the outcome of years of research in the development of hybrid apples. We perceive all of these meanings and respond to them in some degree as the sight and smell of the spring blossoms reaches our eyes and noses.

Our assessment of the environment is achieved within the context of three broad but not always congruent ways of viewing the world. First, we develop attitudes as a result of living within a *culture*, and these attitudes determine, in part, whether we see a sea of white fragrant apple blossoms or whether we see the raw materials from which bees will make hundreds of pounds of honey. Our contemporary perceptions are thus conditioned by forces that have shaped us and the culture in which we reside. To this extent, we perceive the present through the eyes of the past. We also perceive and assess our environment in terms of our immediate *needs and preferences*. This viewpoint represents that of the functionalist, who views nature as being subject to human exploitation, limited only by technological ability. Finally, we observe and recognize the environment in terms of its and our *future*. Not only is the question of "What's in it for me?" asked, but also, "What effect will my presence and interaction have on the environment being viewed?" If trees are seen only in terms of the apples they will produce and care is not taken to preserve them, soon there will be no apples and eventually no trees. This view of the environment is much like the ecologist's view outlined in Chapter 2, and we will return to a discussion of this perspective in Chapter 14.

Humans are cognitive beings and thus define and give meaning to environments with respect to their role in them. How environments should look and be used, what other people should be involved, what activities should go on in them, and what they stand for symbolically are all determined in great part by the viewer. However, there is a regularity and consistency of perception within physical settings over time and space, because perceptions are tightly interwoven with the fabric of the social, organizational, and cultural systems that circumscribe the everyday life of all humans. In Chapter 2, we described the environment as "typically neutral." In the present context we should take that phrase to mean that within a given social, cultural, and organizational climate, an environment typically has agreed-upon meaning. This meaning is easily ascertained and usually judged to be nonendangering. In Lewin's (1951) terms the environment has a "cultural purpose."

Contextual and Social Bases of Perception

It is important to emphasize that perception is contextual. Cultural, social, gender, and individual differences all influence what we do and do not see in our environment (see Figure 4-2). For example, Deregowski (1980) has shown that relatively isolated and uneducated African observers have difficulty seeing depth in two-dimensional pictures; Segall, Campbell & Herskovits (1966) have shown that urban groups are more susceptible to some perceptual illusions than are rural groups; and, Turnbull (1961) has noted the inability to maintain size constancy at varying distances among the Bambuti of Africa. Numerous studies show that adults who grow up with exposure to only one language have difficulty in discriminating certain non-native linguistic contrasts (Strange & Jenkins, 1978), and gender differences in perception have been found in vision, taste, tac-

FIGURE 4-2 Figures commonly recognized as being in motion by Western observers, but not necessarily by non-Western observers.

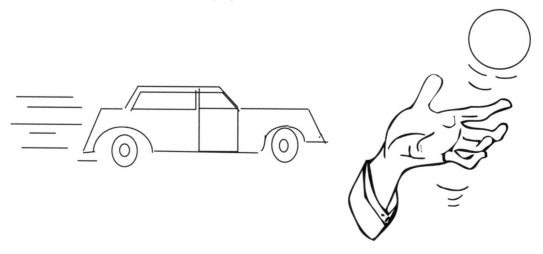

tile sensitivity, hearing, olfaction, and visual-spatial ability (Ippolitov, 1973; Linn & Peterson, 1986; McGuinness, 1976; Money, 1965; Weinstein & Sersen, 1961). Additionally, age and occupational differences have been shown to account for variations in perception (McGuinness & Pribram, 1979; Yuille, 1983).

Thus, perception is not simply a matter of the individual responding to sensations created by energy from stimuli impinging on the sensory organs. Rather, this process is embedded in a cultural context, and various social factors have been demonstrated to produce differences in the ways two individuals will perceive the same stimulus. Individual differences in backgrounds, experiences, values, and purposes can have a profound influence on the end result of the processing of information from the world around us. These differences, however, do not detract from the fact that perception is a fundamental psychological process in which all humans engage.

Complex Perceptual Processes

The exercise below illustrates the complexity of processes taken for granted and engaged in almost automatically when perceiving individual stimuli in the environment. As indicated, such processes are extremely important, and psychologists have exerted considerable effort to understand them. However, the primary concern of environmental psychologists is understanding how people perceive molar aspects of the environment. That is, in addition to understand-

TIME-OUT: Despite the pervasiveness of the perception process in our experience and interactions with our environment, we perform this important function without conscious thought most of the time. In fact, as you read the words in the preceding paragraphs, you were probably not aware of the complex processes by which you transformed the lines on the page into meaningful ideas. To begin with, you started with a specific purpose that directed your attention to the page while you simultaneously screened out the myriad other stimuli impinging on your senses at the time (e.g., the inviting eyes of the person depicted on the poster on your wall, or the irritating sounds of rock music emanating through the walls of your neighbor's room).

After your eyes translated the light waves reflected off the paper into neural energy and your sensory pathways transmitted a series of electrical impulses to your higher brain centers, you began an active process of organizing and interpreting the input, matching the present patterns of sensations with images of previous inputs. To the extent that the words and phrases were coherent and you recognized them, you achieved a match, resulting in the perception and comprehension of the meaning of the paragraphs.

Why do you think people respond to "special effects" in science-fiction movies (e.g., the Star Wars series) with such awe? Or consider people's first responses to such stimuli as the Rocky Mountains, a Picasso painting, or even a new apartment building. Think of these reactions in terms of sensory processes and the "matching" process in the comparison of images of previous perceptions with current sensory impressions. What does this suggest regarding the complexity of perceptual processes?

ing how discrete stimuli or objects are perceived, environmental psychologists attempt to understand the processes by which whole environments are perceived. In a sense, they are interested in the forest, not just the individual trees. Further, since it is important to account for the relationships among the perceptual, cognitive, and evaluative processes that affect experience and determine behavior, discussion of these processes will follow. Although highly interdependent, they will be discussed separately, making note of their interrelationships where appropriate.

THEORIES OF ENVIRONMENTAL PERCEPTION

Gestalt Theory

Much research and theory exist regarding basic processes involved in perception. Among the earliest and most significant contributors to this area was a group of German psychologists working within a framework known as *Gestalt* theory (e.g., Koffka, 1935; Kohler, 1929). These theorists emphasized the active role of the brain in searching for meaning in stimuli. The term Gestalt means "good form" and Gestalt theorists proposed that the brain is organized in such a way as to construct meaning from stimuli, and even to impose meaning where it might not appear to exist objectively in order to achieve this "good form." In the first *Time-Out* of this chapter many stimuli were erroneously identified and interpreted to maintain the Gestalt that there were bears present in the campground. As a final illustration, it is not uncommon for students, when proofreading their term papers, to "read" words that do not exist on the paper. The sentence "The bear climbed up tree" might be read, "The bear climbed up *the* tree."

A second characteristic of the Gestalt approach is its *holistic* orientation (i.e., the assumption that the perceptual process must be understood in its entirety rather than broken down into discrete elements). This assumption is often expressed in the statement that in perception, "the whole is greater than the sum of the parts." A number of principles of perceptual organization, including proximity, similarity, and closure, were developed by these theorists, and they illustrate the manner in which the brain actively organizes sensory inputs to perceive meaningful perceptual relationships. Another illustration of the tendency to impose meaning on sensory inputs is the principle of *size constancy*, in which changes in the size of the retinal image of an object are interpreted as changes in distance rather than changes in the size of the object. In this case, the brain is actually "overriding" sensory inputs to maintain a Gestalt.

Functionalism

A theoretical orientation that differs from the previous approach views perception as a much more direct process that involves less mediation by higher brain centers to perceive meaning in the environment. It is argued that meaning already exists in the environment, and that our sensory mechanisms are "prewired" to respond to meaningful aspects of our environment. This approach is related to ecological biology, which studies organisms' adaptation to their environment (see Chapter 2). For example, the concept of an *ecological niche* refers to the instinctive tendency observed in animals to seek out that area of their environment which affords them the greatest chance of survival. Gibson (1979) applied this notion to human perception. She suggests that humans are innately endowed with the ability to perceive those aspects of our environment that have *functional value* for them. Thus, according to this view, an infant should be born with the ability to perceive its mother's face, since this stimulus has obvious survival value.

Gibson proposed the concept of the perception of *affordances*—that is, invariant properties of objects that afford adaptation to the environment. These affordances are discovered by the organism as a result of active commerce with the environment, and they have survival value. The same object often offers different affordances for different species. For example, a tree affords food to the termite, shade to the dog, and building material to the carpenter. There is evidence that at least some innate perceptual response tendencies exist in humans. Gibson and Walk (1960) employed a device known as a "visual cliff," which creates the impression of a sharp drop on a solid glass surface, to demonstrate that the ability to perceive depth is innate. Human infants show a reluctance to approach the "cliff" as soon as they are able to crawl (i.e., before they have had experience with falling). Additionally, researchers have demonstrated that newborn infants exhibit a marked tendency to spend more time looking at pictures of human faces than pictures of nonhuman objects. Both of these perceptual abilities have clear survival value (the former to avoid the dangers of falling, and the latter to recognize the source of sustenance), so it should not be surprising that we are born with these tendencies.

In Gibson's view, all the information necessary for environmental perception is directly contained in the physical energy impinging on the sense organs. Often, though, the sensory input from the environment is overwhelming in terms of amount, intensity, or duration. Thus, we are not always able to direct our attention to the most informative information. This view, like that of Brunswik (to be discussed later), is embedded in an information-processing perspective (i.e., the utilization of information from the environment requires more than simply responding to or interpreting sensory excitation). By actively exploring the world over time and space the individual is able to extract invariant properties and thus obtain a progressively more accurate picture of what the environment is really like. Unlike Brunswik, though, who believes that the information contained in stimuli is probabilistic, Gibson asserts that the information is absolute; only the processing of this information is subject to error or inexperience.

Learning Theory

Much research on human perception concerns the role of *experience* in perceptual development. From this perspective, our perceptions are not innately determined, but rather we must learn to perceive critical aspects of our environment.

For example, the principle of size constancy referred to above is not seen as an inborn perceptual ability, but one that develops only through the experience of seeing many objects from a variety of distances. Gradually the infant learns that the objects are not growing or shrinking, but remaining a constant size regardless of their distance. This happens despite the fact that the retinal images, and thus the neural impulses sent to the brain, vary dramatically.

Learning theorists propose that an important result of experience and learning in perception is the development of *assumptions* about the world around us. These assumptions facilitate our interactions with the environment because they save us time and effort in coping with new stimuli. That is, we do not have to approach new situations as though we had never encountered them before. We assume that many elements of the situation are similar to those of situations that we have previously experienced. Thus, we bring to the present situation learned assumptions in the form of *expectancies* about what is likely to happen. These expectancies are usually correct, making for easy processing of information and adaptive functioning. In these ways, learning theories are not unlike those of the functionalists.

Our assumptions, however, can sometimes be misleading, resulting in misperceptions or illusions (e.g., Ames, 1951). The research described above regarding contextual and social bases of perception supports the role of experience in the development of perceptual expectancies. For example, cross-cultural comparisons of susceptibility of particular illusions indicate that experiences with different kinds of environments are related to differences in susceptibility. Allport & Pettigrew (1957) demonstrated that children in *curvilinear* cultures (i.e., primitive African cultures where dwellings are round rather than rectilinear) are less susceptible to illusions dependent on the perception of lines and angles such as the trapezoid illusion, and as mentioned earlier, urbanites are more susceptible to the Mueller-Lyer illusion than are rural inhabitants. Also, in a study referred to earlier, it was shown that even size constancy is related to the experiences that individuals have had viewing the same object from varying distances (Turnbull, 1961).

Probabilistic Functionalism

Earlier we noted that at any given moment vast amounts of stimuli simultaneously impinge on our senses. In fact, even in relatively calm environments, more stimuli are present than our perceptual systems have the capacity to process. Given the complexity of environments, the goal stated earlier that environmental psychologists must account for the processes by which molar environments are perceived is an exceedingly difficult one to achieve. Therefore, one of the most important learning theories of perception, and potentially the most fruitful for environmental psychology, is Brunswik's lens model (1956, 1969). Brunswik's approach provides a model for mathematically describing individuals' perceptual processes when making judgments in response to molar environments containing multiple stimulus dimensions.

FIGURE 4-3 Brunswik's probabilistic theory illustrates one way of relating the information available from the environment to the way the individual perceives the environment.

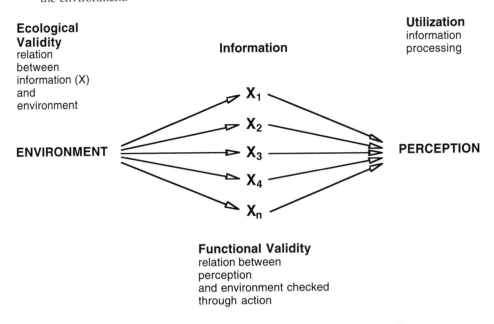

Ecological Validity
relation between information (X) and environment

Information

Utilization
information processing

ENVIRONMENT

X_1
X_2
X_3
X_4
X_n

PERCEPTION

Functional Validity
relation between perception and environment checked through action

Brunswik argues that complex stimulus patterns are processed as though through a "lens" (see Figure 4-3), where the scattered stimuli are "focused" into a single perception of the environment. In this way we manage to reduce the complexity of our environment by filtering the various available stimuli through the lens, discounting or ignoring some perceptual cues while emphasizing others. We do this not only to simplify judgmental tasks, but because we learn from experience that some sensory information is misleading (in Brunswik's terms, they are lacking in *ecological validity*), and other cues are of minimal value, (i.e., of low ecological validity) in correctly perceiving the true state of the environment. Given the ambiguities and inconsistencies present in environments, people assign probabilities to the various cues in the attempt to achieve a perception that "mirrors" the true environment. Sensory cues that are assigned high probabilities are assumed to possess high ecological validity, and are given more weight (i.e., they are attended to more closely than cues assigned low probabilities). Through continued experience in the environment, we learn whether or not our perceptions are appropriate. When we do not achieve a match between our perceptions and the world (i.e., our perceptions are inaccurate), we alter the probability weights assigned to the different cues.

This approach is of value not only because it provides an elegant conceptual model for describing the processes by which we perceive complex environments and change our perceptions through learning, but also because it permits researchers to describe these processes in precise mathematical terms. Although the statistical techniques employed are beyond the scope of this book, researchers can derive "weighting values" that correspond to the probabilities that the perceiver assigns to various stimulus cues. Further, the researcher can vary the stimuli and their levels to assess changes in subjects' perceptions. The model can also be applied to study the accuracy of environmental perception, as well as individual differences. For example, we shall see in a later chapter that the general public relies heavily on certain cues in perceiving the presence of air pollution (e.g., the sight of smog). These cues, however, are far less *ecologically valid* than the presence of other cues (e.g., the presence of automobiles, in predicting actual pollution levels). Finally, Craik & Appleyard (1980) have suggested that Brunswik's lens model may provide the methodology needed to account for the interrelationships among environmental perception, cognition, and evaluation that we noted earlier.

The perception of a wide array of stimulus dimensions in the environment is important for information processing and acquiring knowledge about the environment. Such knowledge is essential for our survival and adaptive functioning. Formation of mental images of the settings in which we live involves the process of *environmental cognition*, and this process is closely linked to that of *environmental evaluation*. We now turn to these two processes.

TIME-OUT: Think about the first day you arrived on campus. Unless you had been on campus on several previous occasions, you probably had difficulty finding your way around your dormitory, let alone finding your way around campus. While that may not have caused you to experience any particular anguish as long as you were able to find the cafeteria and restroom, you probably felt a little apprehensive about how you were going to get to all the places you had to be in order to attend orientation meetings, register for classes, and get to social events without being late. This apprehension may have turned to frustration when even the campus map was not all that helpful for getting you back and forth. The frustration may have turned to actual fear on the first day of classes when you discovered that you had three successive classes in three different buildings!

As the first semester progressed, what features of the campus caught your attention, and how did this help you find your way around? Compare your experience in the first semester to that of the second semester. What changes in your thoughts, feelings, and behaviors did you experience? Explain these in terms of the model of environment-behavior relations discussed in Chapter 2.

ENVIRONMENTAL COGNITION

The term, *cognition*, refers to thought processes. Thus, environmental cognition concerns thinking about the environment (i.e., the ways in which individuals process information and organize their knowledge about characteristics of their environment). Also of interest is how this knowledge is acquired, or learned, as well as how individuals differ in their knowledge of the environment. Finally, environmental cognition concerns how variations in the environment affect the ability to understand the setting. For example, important differences in knowledge clearly exist between familiar versus novel environments. We will consider novel environments first.

Responses to Novel Environments

In Chapter 2 it was asserted that from the participant's point of view, the environment is typically neutral and enters into awareness only when it deviates from some adaptation level. Your first few days on campus can be thought of as a non-neutral situation, one that from your perspective at the time deviated from the norm and made you self-consciously aware of your new surroundings. Ittleson, Proshansky, Rivlin, & Winkel (1974) claim that in situations of this kind, six different but interrelated types of responses occur: *affect, orientation, categorization, systemization, manipulation, encoding.* While in the following paragraphs we will discuss each of these in the order just presented, these responses are probably not made serially. In fact, each tends to blend with the other as we attempt to bring the environment and ourselves into a state of equilibrium.

Affect.   The nature of our *affective* response to new environments will depend on many factors, some of which will be discussed later in this chapter. At a minimum, the affect will consist of a heightened degree of awareness and arousal (see Chapters 2 and 5) occasioned by the need to know, predict, and therefore to feel in control of and secure in an unknown setting. Aside from this general reaction, a number of other feelings may emerge because of the particular characteristics of a new setting. Discovering that the tennis courts are close to the dorm may lead to happiness, whereas finding that you live adjacent to the cemetery might lead to fear and trepidation. The thought of long walks to the library through a grove of oak trees might conjure romantic images and feelings of love, or graven images of rapists and muggers, leading to fear and anxiety. Such affective responses, both general and specific, may govern the direction that subsequent relations with the environment will take. First impressions (feelings) about places can and do have enduring consequences.

Orientation.   Individuals in a new setting actively seek to find their place, their "niche." This is primarily a cognitive process and to use a slang expression involves "scoping out" a place. You probably asked yourself on those first days: Where, relative to my dorm, is the dining hall, the recreation center, the library? Where do you go to buy books, to get athletic tickets, to pay parking fees? Which dorm is the one that your cousin Fred lives in? Ittleson, et al. (1974) describe the process of finding answers to questions such as these as *orientation.* Orientation, in short, expresses a person's desire to "know where one is" physically in relation to the total milieu. Here we see the beginning of environmental cognition, with the individual actively attempting to identify the location of important stimuli in the new environment in relation to where one is at.

Categorization.   In new situations, though, a person does more than just orient; he or she also *categorizes*. The individual evaluates the new environment and imposes his or her own unique meaning to various aspects of it. Not only do people ask where they can get a pizza, but they also ask where to find the best or the cheapest pizza. To which pizzerias do you take dates, and which are primarily solo? Knowing where there is a "pizza joint" is not half as useful as knowing where there is one where you can get pizzas that are tasty, cheap, and will bring you the accolades of your date. Categorization is therefore the process of extending the meaning of the environment by functionally relating its various aspects to one's own needs, predispositions, and values. Thus, categorization represents a more sophisticated understanding of the environment than simple orientation, in that the individual now knows several instances of stimuli in a particular category and is able to distinguish among them in terms of their relative utility to the satisfaction of one's needs.

Systemization.   It is difficult to say where categorization leaves off and systemization begins, but at some point individuals organize their environments into more meaningful and more complex structures. They know, for example, the best time to go to the library, not only in terms of when it is the quietest, but also when it is easiest to find a place to park, or when the most helpful librarians are working, or when the latest issue of *Sports Illustrated* arrives.

Manipulation.   Out of such systemization, individuals achieve a sense of order and understanding; they not only know the new setting but they can predict it and make it work to their benefit. If people have ordered their environment, they usually can manipulate it or control it to their advantage. If the cheapest pizza parlor in town is closed, they know how to get to the second cheapest, or know their options with respect to having Chinese or Mexican food instead.

Encoding.   Finally, to communicate with others and to form mental maps of new environments, people must agree on what the component parts of the environment are called. This naming is called *encoding*; it permits us to do our systemizing and manipulating cognitively, by simply thinking about our environment. Encoding represents the highest level of understanding about the environment, because the individual is no longer tied to concrete perceptions of the setting. People can function more effectively with this knowledge, and can also communicate with others about using shared symbols. Encoding allows us to "think-travel" through environments (see Figure 2-5) and to prepare us for changes in our interrelationships with our environments. We will return to these notions in the next section of this chapter.

Of course the reason for your difficulties that first day you arrived on campus is that you didn't know the names of the buildings, nor their locations relative to one another. You had not yet had time to categorize or systematize the campus environment. And although there was an encoding schema in place, you were not, at that time, privy to it. Environmental cognition refers to knowledge about the environment, and the purpose of this example is to illustrate the importance of environmental cognition to the individual in performing such seemingly simple actions as getting from one place to another. Without an understanding of spatial relationships between objects of importance in the environment, we would not only be lost, but we would be literally paralyzed, unable to function in the setting. These mental representations of the environment are referred to as *cognitive maps*. The processes of perception, learning, and memory are all involved in the study of spatial cognition. We will now discuss the characteristics of cognitive maps, some factors affecting their development, and the functions that such environmental cognitions serve.

Characteristics of Cognitive Maps

A common approach to studying spatial cognition is to ask people to draw "sketch maps" of environments. Research indicates that sketch maps are a reliable method of data collection (Blades, 1990). Lynch (1960) conducted one of the first comprehensive studies of the nature of cognitive maps when he asked residents of three American cities (Boston, Los Angeles, and Jersey City) to draw maps of their city environments. He analyzed these drawings for commonalities in the features of people's mental images of their cities. This resulted in the identification of five major characteristics: (1) *paths*: major arteries of traffic flow through the city (e.g., Main Street); (2) *edges*: major lines (either natural or built) that divide areas of the city or delimit the boundaries (e.g., river); (3) *districts*: large sections of the city that have a distinct identity (e.g., "Chinatown"); (4) *nodes*: points of intersection of major arteries (e.g., the corner of Twelfth Street and Vine); and (5) *landmarks*: architecturally unique structures that can be seen from a distance and can be used as reference points (e.g., a tall building).

Thus, the objective physical setting comes to be represented as "cognitive space," organized and structured mentally in terms of distinct "regions" of the environment. According to the "anchor-point" hypothesis (Couclelis,

---

TIME-OUT: Take a few minutes to draw a map of your college campus. Make it as accurate and detailed as possible. Ask a friend to do the same. Compare the two, looking for commonalities and indicating characteristics such as paths, edges, districts, nodes, or landmarks. Next draw a map of the city or nearest city to your campus. Compare both your campus and city maps to published ones. Check for accuracy and detail. On which dimensions did your maps differ? What factors could account for these differences?

Golledge, Gale, & Tobler, 1987) the regionalization and hierarchical organization of cognitive space is brought about by the active role of salient cues in the environment. For example, primary nodes or other reference points "anchor" distinct regions in cognitive space. These components or reference points provide the "skeleton" of the individual's map. As we shall see, the degree and accuracy of the detail of the remainder of the map is a function of both aspects of the environment and individual differences.

Factors Affecting Cognitive Maps

Environmental Differences. Environments differ from one another in the ease with which people are able to develop cognitive maps of them. Lynch (1960) coined the term *legibility* to refer to the extent to which the spatial arrangement of a city facilitates a clear and unified image in the minds of its inhabitants. For example, Boston provides a clear center, the Boston Common, around which people organize their cognitive maps. On the other hand, Los Angeles does not appear to have any central core, but sprawls out in all directions, which inhibits an organized mental representation. Similarly, Warren, Rossano, and Wear (1990) suggested that errors in building floor-plan maps can be understood in terms of variations in salience of building features. Milgram and his associates (Milgram, Greenwald, Kessler, McKenna, & Waters, 1972) argued that recognizable areas of an environment are important for developing accurate cognitive maps. They proposed the following formula for predicting the recognizability of an area:

$$R = f(C \times D).$$

This formula is read, "The recognizability of an area (R) is determined by its centrality to population flow (C) and its architectural or social distinctiveness (D)." Thus, environments that have structures that stand out (such as a hilltop church) and are frequently passed by people facilitate a clear picture of the setting in the minds of the inhabitants (see Figure 4-4).

Both of these environmental differences can be understood in terms of the "anchor-point" hypothesis in spatial cognition. That is, salient, objective physical cues in the environment facilitate the accurate organization of cognitive space, and the absence of such reference points inhibits accuracy.

Errors in Cognitive Maps. The physical characteristics of a setting are not the only determinants of the accuracy and detail of cognitive maps. People are prone to a number of cognitive errors in the process of developing cognitive maps. Downs & Stea (1973) point out that most of us form *incomplete* maps, leaving out both minor and major details; we tend to *distort* our maps, by placing some areas closer together than they actually are and others farther apart than they actually are; and, we sometimes *augment* our maps by including elements that do not actually exist. Further, we often *give undue prominence* to areas of the environ-

Figure 4-4 A hill-top church located on a major pathway contributes to cognitive map formation due to recognizability.

ment that are personally meaningful or important to us. For example, Saarinen (1973) asked students from different countries to draw maps of the world. He found that the students tended to draw their own countries in the center of the map, drawing them larger than countries that are actually larger than their own. More recently, Herman, Miller, & Shiraki (1987) demonstrated distortions in distance judgments in relation to the affect associated with different environmental locations. College freshmen who were asked to choose their four most-liked and four least-liked campus locations subsequently underestimated distances to the locations associated with positive affect to a greater degree than they did to the places associated with negative affect. Other recent studies have demonstrated errors in estimations of the differences in elevation between locations (Garling, Book, Lindberg, & Arce, 1990) and memory for turns of varying angularity encountered during pathway traversal (Sadalla & Montello, 1989).

　　The above errors are most likely due to limitations in human spatial cognitive abilities, rather than to objective environmental characteristics. As with any kind of information-processing task, the accuracy of our spatial knowledge of the environment is unlikely to ever be complete, and some tasks are easier than others. For example, Teske & Balser (1986) asked individuals to identify various destinations in a city and their strategic ordering (i.e., plan itineraries), and Veitch & O'Connor (1987) asked students to do the same on their college campus. Subjects found planning itineraries more difficult, because this requires a higher-level cognitive organization. That is, while the former task requires knowledge only of the route from point A to B, the latter also requires knowledge of the route from B to C and the interrelationships among A, B, and C. Moeser (1988) has suggested such "survey maps" do not automatically develop in complex environments. She reported that student nurses failed to form survey maps of a hospital with a unique configuration, even after traversing it for two years. Further, these students performed worse on objective measures of cognitive mapping than did a control group of "naive" college students who were first asked to memorize the floor plans of the building.

Finally, Stanton (1986) investigated the relationship between "socio-spatial neighborhood" (the perception of a street network without continuous boundaries) and the experience of "homeground" (defined as the mental form and geographical extent of those places that evoke a feeling of being near home). She reported that only residents of city blocks that were no more than 460 feet long were able to think of their homeground as an experiential network, concluding that there may be a mental time limit to such cognitions. Thus, these studies all suggest that general cognitive limitations of information processing are involved in spatial cognition as in any other type of complex task, and these limitations are a major source of errors in cognitive maps.

Individual Differences. Investigators have also suggested that some people seem to be better at forming cognitive maps than others. For example, gender differences have been reported. Appleyard (1970) reported that the cognitive maps of men are generally more accurate than are those of women. More recently, Ward, Newcombe, & Overton (1986) examined how men and women gave directions from maps that had been memorized. Male subjects exhibited higher levels of cognitive organization, such as using more mileage estimates and cardinal directions (i.e., east, west, north, and south) and made fewer errors of commission or omission than did female subjects. Antes, McBride, & Collins (1988) reported that distance judgments of women were more affected by a change in travel paths through a city occasioned by the construction of a new connecting street than were men. They suggested that women based their judgments on inferences from travel paths, while men approached the task in a more spatial manner. Orleans & Schmidt (1972) reported that women's maps were more detailed for the home and neighborhood than were those of men, whereas men's cognitive maps were more comprehensive and complete for the larger surrounding environment. Finally, some investigators have reported socioeconomic differences, suggesting that the cognitive maps of people low in socioeconomic status are also less complete and accurate than are those individuals of higher socioeconomic status (Goodchild, 1974; Orleans, 1973).

Note that the individual differences listed above may not be due to differences in ability, but rather to differences in *familiarity*. That is, there is much evidence that people draw more detailed and accurate maps of areas with which they have had more experience (and thus are more familiar to them) than areas where they have spent little time (e.g., Appleyard, 1970; Evans, 1980; Holahan & Dobrowolny, 1978; Moore, 1974). Of course, it stands to reason that we would have better images of settings that are familiar to us than of unfamiliar places. Indeed, some of the studies on errors in cognitive maps discussed earlier also indicated that the extent of error can be moderated by experience. For example, the study by Herman et al. (1987) indicated that the estimations of distances to campus locations associated with positive and negative affect were not significantly different for upperclassmen. Teske & Balser (1986) reported that subjects who lived closest to the city where they were asked to identify locations and plan itineraries performed at a higher level on these tasks than did subjects who had less contact with the city. Finally, Fridgen (1987) asked travelers who stopped at a travel information center in Michigan to indicate which parts of Michigan they perceived to be tourism and recreation areas. Subjects familiar with the state differentiated more regions along the coast, whereas less familiar subjects perceived more regions to be present in the southeastern urban portion of the state.

Moreover, typically there are differences in *mobility* among the groups discussed above (i.e., in opportunity for travel through the setting). Thus, for example, if a husband works and the wife stays at home, it is not surprising that the husband would develop a better cognitive map of areas beyond the immediate neighborhood while the wife would develop a more detailed map of the local environment. Similarly, people of higher socioeconomic status have much greater mobility to gain experience in the larger environment than do individuals of lower socioeconomic status. These suggestions are supported by the research of investigators who have controlled for mobility (e.g., Appleyard, 1976; Karan, Bladen, & Singh, 1980; Maurer & Baxter, 1972). While the individual differences reported above could be due to inherent differences in spatial ability, this seems unlikely to be the major reason. A study by Pearson and Ialongo (1986) measured spatial ability and environmental knowledge independently. Spatial ability accounted for only 14 percent of the variance in environmental knowledge. Thus, learning brought about by relevant experience in an environment is likely to be a more important determinant of the accuracy of cognitive maps than are the individual or cultural differences discussed above.

Developmental Aspects of Environmental Cognition. A number of changes occur in environmental cognition as children mature and as adults become familiar with a new place. Two essential features of such cognitive growth are the increasing *differentiation* and *abstractness* in cognitive representations of the environment, and the increasing ability to conceive of the environment from different topographical perspectives. The first of these is illustrated by a progressive shift from enactive to iconic to symbolic representation of the environment and coincide with Piaget's developmental stages: sensorimotor, preoperational, concrete-operational, and formal-operational (Flavell, 1977). The latter is illustrated by a shift from an egocentric spatial reference (possible only with respect to one's own bodily position), to a fixed spatial reference (possible with respect to some fixed object or direction), to a coordinated system of reference (spatial reference possible with respect to a system of polar coordinates such as the cardinal directions of east-west or north-south). These trends represent progressive increases in the complexity and sophistication of the cognitive styles and sets for organizing and interpreting environmental information (Leff, 1978). These trends also correspond to the stages of responses to novel environments discussed above.

In addition, Hart & Moore (1973) posit that as adults or children become more familiar with a new environment, their topographical representations tend to shift from a *route* to a *survey* orientation (i.e., places will be first conceived in terms of paths from point to point and eventually mental maps will be formed that embody an awareness of broad areas and their interrelationships). Various researchers have found support for this notion (Gould, 1973; Gould & White, 1974; Leiser & Zilbershatz, 1989). Finally, a number of investigators are beginning to look at the role of affect in the determination of mental maps. Such structural elements as paths, nodes, landmarks, edges, and districts may require considerations of social and personal meaning to account for their inclusions in people's mental maps (see also our earlier discussion of Herman, et al., 1987, regarding affect and distance judgments).

TIME-OUT: Assume that Wednesday is very busy for you. You have to be in a professor's office by 7:30 A.M. for a research meeting; then you have a class across campus at 9:30 A.M. You also have a committee meeting in the Administration Building at 10:30; next, you have to mail some bills at the post office and deposit your paycheck so the checks for the bills won't bounce. You have another class from 1:30 to 2:30 P.M. and another meeting at 2:30. Assuming that the meeting takes no longer than usual, you should have plenty of time to pick up your friend and go to soccer practice. You should be able to do that since you've done it before, usually with enough time left over to have lunch, shoot the breeze with your roommate, and do some research at the library. This series of activities may not seem to be a miraculous feat, but it would simply not be possible without a mental representation of the environment. Further, you probably find these tasks much easier to do now than you did the first week you were on campus. Now you know where the bank and post office are, where your meetings are held, and where soccer practice takes place. You also know the best roads to get to these places and how much time it takes to get from one place to the other.

Think back to the previous TIME-OUT in which you were asked to relive your first day on campus. Now think about a typical day this past week as you made your way to the various places you had to be that day. Is your present experience similar to that described above? What can account for the differences between your present and first experience on campus? Think in terms of errors in cognitive maps and the role such mental images play in our mobility in novel vs. familiar environments.

Functions of Cognitive Maps

The above exercise reiterates the importance of cognitive maps for our very ability to move around in our environments. It also illustrates that cognitive maps serve the important function of facilitating the ease of *adapting* to our environments. That is, life would be much more difficult if, because I had to wander around in circles trying to find my way from the post office to the bank, I didn't have time to both post my bills and deposit my paycheck. Thus, perhaps the most important function of cognitive maps is their adaptive value. Kaplan (1973) suggested that the ability of prehistoric humans to develop cognitive maps had a crucial survival value in a hostile world. How do I get from where I am to the safety of my cave and where, relative to where I am now, did I hide those ostrich eggs I found the other day? These are the kinds of questions that primitive humans must have asked themselves—the answers to which must have required some sort of cognitive map.

Downs & Stea (1977) discuss the role of cognitive maps in *problem solving* (i.e., in helping us make decisions about where things that we need are and how to get them). This function is also illustrated in the above example, in that I used my cognitive map to solve the problem of where I needed to go in relation to the amount of time I had available between classes. Thus, maps facilitate coping strategies involved in planning our daily lives.

Finally, cognitive maps also serve the important social function of *communication*. While we all develop our own idiosyncratic maps of the environment, we also learn certain *shared symbols* (Strauss, 1961) that allow us to communicate with others about the same physical environment. It is this system of symbols that permits the out-of-towners to navigate their way to a place in response to the statement "turn left at the second intersection, then make a right at the first stop sign and look for the carry-out store." These shared symbols also help us to decide whether to visit a particular city in the first place. For example, we might tell a European friend planning to visit the United States to be sure to include New York, the "Big Apple," on the itinerary, but forget Cleveland, the "Mistake by the Lake" (see Table 4-1, by Downs & Stea, 1977). Both the development and the use of shared symbols to communicate with others about the environment depend on the encoding processes discussed earlier.

Thus far we have considered the important and interrelated processes of environmental perception and cognition. We have seen that the ability to form mental images of our environment is closely related to the ability to perceive and interpret the spatial components of the setting, and that both of these processes are strongly influenced by our learning experiences in the environment. In the next section of this chapter we turn our attention to the processes by which we arrive at an evaluation of a particular setting. Again we will see that perception and cognition are important determinants of environmental evaluation, and that all of these processes interact to determine our behavior in the environment.

TABLE 4-1   Symbols and Nicknames for Cities and Countries

Nicknames for Cities

Detroit: the Motor City
Cleveland: the Mistake by the Lake
Chicago: the Windy City
New York: the Big Apple, Fun City, Sin City
Boston: Beantown
Pittsburgh: the Steel City
Milwaukee: the Beer Capital of the World
Philadelphia: the City of Brotherly love
St. Louis: the Gateway to the West

Graphic Symbols for Cities

Seattle: the Space Needle
St. Louis: the Gateway Arch
Washington, DC: the Capitol, the Washington Monument
San Francisco: the Golden Gate Bridge
New York: the Empire State Building, the Statue of Liberty
Philadelphia: the Liberty Bell
Copenhagen: the Little Mermaid Statue
Paris: the Arc de Triomphe, the Eifel Tower
Athens: the Parthenon, the Acropolis
London: Big Ben, the Tower of London
Venice: canals, gondolas
Sydney: the Harbor Bridge

Graphic Symbols for Countries

Italy: the Coliseum, the Leaning Tower of Pisa
The Netherlands: tulips, barges, canals, clogs, windmills
India: the Taj Mahal
Egypt: the Sphinx
Switzerland: the Alps, skiing, chalets

From Downs and Stea (1977). Adapted with permission.

Environmental Evaluation

The question of how we come to evaluate an environment favorably or unfavorably is a complex one, yet it is an important one for predicting behavior. At a very general level, people prefer and approach environments they evaluate favorably and avoid environments they evaluate negatively. Environmental psychologists have dealt with the first question using a variety of operational definitions. For example, a favorable evaluation could be viewed as a preference for certain configurations of stimuli in some environments over that of other environments, a cognitive judgment of beauty, or as a positive affective reaction to the environment. Each of these approaches has led to the identification of different, though related, aspects of the physical environment as determinants of evaluative responses. The answer to the question "What aspects of the environment lead to a favorable evaluation?" is going to depend on the answer to the question "What is meant by a favorable evaluation?" Consideration of each of these approaches, as well as their implications for the relationship between environmental evaluation and behavior, follows.

Environmental Preference: Would you rather be here or there?   Kaplan (1975) developed a model for predicting preferences of some environments over others. This model provides a link between environmental cognition and evaluation, in that it assumes an important dimension of environmental preference to be the informational content of those environments. For example, Kaplan (1979) suggested that one basis for preferences is the ability of the individual to "make sense" out of the environment and the extent to which the environment involves the individual by motivating him or her to try to comprehend it. Kaplan & Kaplan (1978) identified four important factors influencing our preferences: coherence, legibility, complexity, and mystery. *Coherence* and *legibility* refer to the degree to which the elements of a setting are organized (i.e., "fit together") in an orderly fashion, and the ease with which the individual can process and categorize the elements of the setting. Both of these factors contribute to the ability to make sense out of the environment. People prefer environments high in coherence and legibility to those low on these dimensions. The factors influencing involvement with the environment are *complexity* (the number and variety of elements) and *mystery* (the degree to which the setting has hidden information that captures the viewer's imagination). As with the first two factors, greater degrees of complexity and mystery produce a preference for a setting. Kaplan (1987) has recently argued for a biological basis to such preferences (i.e., there is a survival value to preferring environments that offer informational advantages over others). The Kaplans' recent research points to the importance of *mystery* in predicting landscape preferences (Kaplan, Kaplan, & Brown, 1989), but others have applied their model to predict preferences for urban environments (Herzog, 1989) and interiors (Scott, 1989).

Environmental Aesthetics: Is beauty in the eye of the beholder?   Apart from the intuitive appeal of the notion that *beauty* is a subjective and relative concept, psychologists have attempted to identify objective dimensions of environments that lead to judgments of their aesthetic appeal. The assumption is that although there may indeed be individual differences in judgments of beauty, it is still possible to identify commonalities in what most people consider to be beautiful. For example, most people consider the Grand Canyon to be beautiful and a junk yard to be ugly. By researching a variety of settings, it is possible to identify dimensions along which different environments judged to be beautiful are similar.

Berlyne (1960) conducted one of the first important series of studies along these lines. He identified four basic *collative properties* of environments—

that is, characteristics of the environment that cause us to compare present settings to previous settings we have encountered: (1) *complexity* refers to the degree of variety in the elements of the environment, (2) *novelty* is the extent to which stimuli not previously encountered or noticed are present, (3) *incongruity* concerns the extent to which the environment contains stimuli that do not seem to "go together" harmoniously, and (4) *surprisingness* refers to the environment that contains elements that we do not expect to be present. In subsequent research, Berlyne (1974) argued that aesthetic judgments are most positive for environments at intermediate levels of each of these dimensions. That is, according to Berlyne, we judge either too much or too little complexity, novelty, incongruity, and surprisingness as detracting from the beauty of a setting. This finding falls in line with the notion of adaptation levels and behavior in response to environments that deviate from that level, as outlined in Chapter 2. However, Wohlwill (1976) has suggested that this curvilinear relationship holds only for the dimension of complexity, and that judgments of beauty increase monotonically with increases in novelty and surprisingness, as well as with decreases in incongruity. Only additional empirical studies using a broad range of environments varying on these dimensions will tell us who is right.

Berlyne (1974) attempted to relate collative properties to exploratory behaviors in a setting. He distinguished between *specific* and *diversive* exploration. Specific exploration increases as the level of uncertainty in the environment increases. Presumably, uncertainty creates arousal, which leads to specific exploration to identify the source of the arousal. Berlyne proposed that the pleasantness of a setting is greatest at intermediate levels of uncertainty, and that diversive exploration occurs when uncertainty-arousal levels are low. In other words, when the collative properties of an environment are at low levels, we feel understimulated or bored, and we search the environment for ways to increase our arousal level.

There has been a recent upsurge in research on environmental aesthetics. These studies have ranged from development of reliable and valid measures of scenic beauty (e.g., Ribe, 1988; Ruddell, Gramann, Rudis, & Westphal, 1989) to cross-cultural comparisons in aesthetic judgments (e.g., Hull & Revell, 1989; Wong, 1990). Others have argued for the value of studying environmental aesthetics in architectural design (e.g., Broadbent, 1989; Stamps, 1989). Finally, Bourassa (1990) has recently proposed a paradigm for landscape aesthetics that integrates biological, cultural, and personal modes of aesthetic experience.

Affective Bases of Environmental Evaluation

Working within the framework of Helson's (1964) Adaptation Level Theory, Wohlwill (1966) proposed that our affective responses to environments are determined by the degree of discrepancy between current levels of stimulation and the adaptation level (i.e., the level of stimulation we have become accustomed to). Wohlwill proposed the *butterfly curve hypothesis* predicting a curvilinear relationship between positive affect and discrepancies resulting in either increases

FIGURE 4-5   Change in affective response to stimuli as a function of extent of deviation from adaptation level (After Helson, 1964).

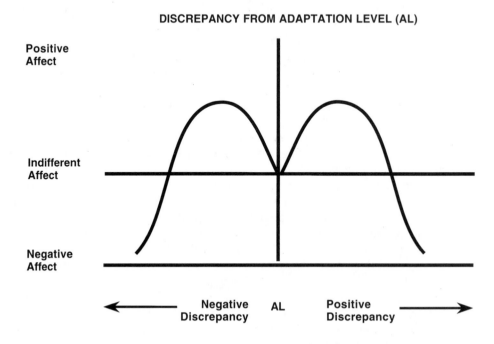

or decreases in arousal from adaptation level (see Figure 4-5). That is, we view moderate increases or decreases in stimulation from adaption level as pleasant. However, extreme deviations in either direction result in negative affect. This approach is useful in accounting for individual differences in evaluations of a setting. Individual differences in adaption level result from living in different environments, leading to what might be called the "one person's ceiling is another person's floor" effect. That is, the same environment might be perceived as overstimulating to one person while understimulating to another. For example, a person raised in a small rural town in Iowa might perceive a city of 20,000 people overwhelming, while the same city might be perceived as boring to a person raised in Chicago. Note, however, that both individuals would experience negative affect, because the discrepancies from their adaptation levels are extreme, even though in different directions.

The work of Mehrabian & Russell (1974) has added considerably to our understanding of the relationship among stimulation levels, arousal, and positive/negative affective responses to environments. Further, their model accounts for the relationship between these variables and behavior. Mehrabian and Russell propose the concept of *information rate* to define environmental stimulation level. Information rate refers to the average amount of information impinging on the senses per unit of time. This concept can be used to integrate the various dimensions of environmental stimulation discussed above, such as complexity, novelty, incongruity, surprisingness, mystery, and coherence, in that all of these dimensions contribute to the information rate of a setting. Mehrabian & Russell

(1974) present a great deal of research demonstrating that arousal is a direct correlate of information rate, and that approach behaviors in an environment (i.e., seeking out or desiring to remain in a setting) are greatest for intermediate levels of arousal.

However, Mehrabian and Russell suggest that the curvilinear relationship between approach and arousal is moderated by the degree of pleasure a person experiences. Specifically, this relationship appears to hold only when pleasure is at an intermediate level. When pleasure is extremely high, approach behaviors strengthen with either increases or decreases in arousal, and when pleasure is extremely low, both increases and decreases in arousal lead to avoidance behaviors.

These ideas have been extended by Russell & Pratt (1980), who proposed a model of emotional reactions to environments in which arousal and pleasure are viewed as independent dimensions. This is illustrated in Figure 4-6. As can be seen, the model depicts all possible combinations of pleasure and arousal. Thus, environments high in arousal can be perceived as pleasant (i.e.,"exciting" settings, such as a football game), as can environments low in arousal (i.e.,"relaxing" settings, as a picnic in the park). Note that we are likely to engage in approach behaviors to both types of environments. The same can be said of avoidance behaviors to unpleasant environments high in arousal

FIGURE 4-6 Circular ordering of eight terms to describe the emotional quality of environments (from Russell and Pratt, 1980).

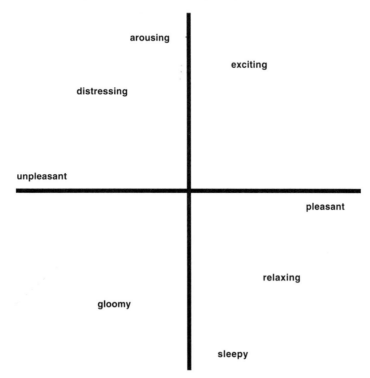

("distressing" settings, such as a final exam) and low in arousal ("gloomy" settings, such as a funeral). This *circumplex model* has been recently demonstrated to reliably differentiate between people's experiences in and preferences for suburban parks (Hull & Harvey, 1989).

We have seen that environmental perception and cognition influence our evaluative and affective responses to a setting. The relationships between these processes can be difficult to grasp. A useful model for describing these relationships has been proposed by Purcell (1986). Referred to as a *schema discrepancy model*, ongoing environmental experience is posited to result from a matching process between currently available environmental characteristics and a representation stored in memory of the gist of previous similar experiences (called a "schema," which is based on prototypical examples). Purcell proposes that affective responses occur when there is a mismatch, or discrepancy, between the attributes of a current instance and the attributes of the schematic prototype. He reports results consistent with this model in an experiment in which subjects were shown slides of churches and were asked to judge how good an example of a church each slide was. Note that this model is quite consistent with the model of environment-behavior relationships presented in Chapter 2. This latter model further predicts that our behaviors in a setting are likely to be influenced by these cognitive and affective responses. We turn now to a consideration of a concept that incorporates all of these issues: environmental attitudes.

ENVIRONMENTAL ATTITUDES

The relationships among the processes of environmental perception, cognition, and evaluation as well as their effects on behavior can be best summarized in the notion of environmental attitudes. An attitude is typically defined as consisting of a *cognitive component, an affective component, and a behavioral component.* That is, an attitude involves the way we think about, feel about, and behave toward an object. Consider, for example, your attitude toward the city of Chicago. Your attitude about this environment includes your thoughts about Chicago (e.g., cognitions about its size, traffic and pollution levels; things to see and do there), your feelings about Chicago (e.g., excitement, anxiety, fear), and your behavior vis-à-vis Chicago (e.g., you may plan a trip there to watch the Bears, or you may plan a trip so as to bypass Chicago altogether).

Thus far in this chapter we have discussed the processes by which we perceive our environment and how these perceptual processes are involved in developing our cognition or understanding of the environment. These are the processes by which the cognitive component of an attitude is formed. In the following sections we will discuss the particular characteristics of cognitions that have implications for one's overall attitude toward the environment. We have also discussed the role of perception and cognition in the formation of favorable or unfavorable evaluations of the environment, as well as the relationships between environmental characteristics and emotional responses to a setting. These evaluative and emotional responses constitute the affective component of

TIME-OUT: Visit four distinctly different settings on your campus: (1) a place you really enjoy and where you spend a lot of time, (2) a place you enjoy, but where you do not spend a lot of time, (3) a place you really do not enjoy, and avoid whenever possible, and (4) a place you neither enjoy nor dislike in which you spend moderate amounts of time. Make three copies of the Mehrabian-Russell scale of pleasure, arousal, and dominance (see Mehrabian & Russell, 1974) and complete it in each setting. Compute your scores on this scale and compare them between settings. What aspects of the settings account for differences in pleasure, arousal, and dominance you reported? Relate these differences to aesthetic and affective bases of environmental evaluation.

an environmental attitude. In the following sections we shall also discuss theories regarding the processes by which this component is formed. We also discussed earlier how environmentally induced affective states mediate approach-avoidance behaviors. Approach-avoidance behaviors constitute one category of the behavioral component of environmental attitudes, but we shall also see that attitudes have other behavioral implications besides approach-avoidance. We will conclude our discussion of environmental attitudes with a consideration of attitude-behavior consistency.

Environmental Attitude Formation

Social psychologists have devoted considerable time and effort toward understanding the processes by which attitudes are formed. We will consider environmental attitude formation as a special case of the general process by which any attitude is formed. Most explanations of attitude development invoke learning principles such as classical conditioning, operant conditioning, and observational learning. Each of these principles will be discussed below, but we will first consider two important cognitive foundations of attitudes: beliefs and values.

Beliefs and Values. Daryl Bem (1970) has suggested that beliefs constitute the cognitive "building blocks" of attitudes. Bem distinguished between *primitive beliefs* and *higher-order beliefs*. Primitive beliefs are nonconscious (i.e., they are accepted as givens, and are seldom consciously questioned). Primitive beliefs are either based on direct experience (e.g., the belief in the validity of our sense impressions) or on external authority (e.g., the belief that if Mommy says so, it must be true). The processes of sensation and perception discussed earlier are involved in the development of primitive beliefs. Because we have faith in our sensory impressions, if something smells or tastes bad, we will hold a negative attitude toward that thing. Alternatively, if Mommy tells us that we will get sick if we eat something, since we believe (at least as young children) that "Mommy is always right and never lies," we will also develop a negative attitude toward that thing. These primitive beliefs usually serve us well. Indeed, as we discussed earlier in this chapter, we would be immobilized if we could not trust our senses, and young children might end up eating something poisonous if they could not trust Mommy. However, our perceptions and beliefs based on sense impressions are not always correct, and we learn later in life that Mommy can be wrong and is even capable of lying!

Of greater importance to the present discussion is the notion of *higher-order beliefs*. According to Bem (who is always right and never lies), these beliefs involve the insertion of a conscious premise in the thought process of arriving at the belief. Thus, a belief can be thought of as a conclusion to a syllogism. For example, if I believe that air pollution leads to respiratory illness, it is unlikely that I arrived at that belief through direct experience or because Mommy said so. Rather, it is more probable that I heard a newscast reporting the results of a study conducted by the office of the Surgeon General warning of the health hazards of air pollution. Thus, the belief that air pollution is hazardous to one's health is itself based upon several other beliefs, such as the belief in the accuracy of the newscast, the trustworthiness of the Surgeon General, and the validity of the research itself.

This analysis suggests that the cognitive component of attitudes can be quite complex, sometimes exhibiting great depth (i.e., many premises all leading to the same conclusion) as well as breadth (i.e., many syllogisms all leading to the same conclusion). To complicate matters further, although the language of syllogisms, premises, and conclusions suggests that the process of arriving at higher-order beliefs is inherently logical and rational, this is not necessarily the case. Bem invokes the idea of *psychologic* to account for irrational beliefs that are nonetheless internally consistent in the individual's cognitive structures. Further, it is possible to believe that something is bad for you but still evaluate the thing favorably. For example, I may know that smoking is bad for me, but simultaneously enjoy it (or alternatively, I may believe that exercise is good, but I may hate it anyway!).

Despite the cognitive complexity or potential irrationality of attitudes, the evaluative component of an attitude is usually quite simple: The person either likes or dislikes the attitude object. We will soon discuss the affective basis of this evaluation, but first a word should be said about the cognitive foundation of evaluation: *values*. Values can be defined as basic preferences for certain end states (see Rokeach, 1968). For example, *equality* is a value referring to an end state such as equal opportunity. Values serve as the functional basis for attitudes. That is, holding a particular attitude is a means for attaining a preferred end state. Thus, a person who strongly values equality is likely to be in favor of civil rights legislation. Similarly, if one values clean air, then that person is likely to evaluate actions to control pollution favorably. Indeed, Neuman (1986) has reported that values pertaining to environmental quality are positively related to beliefs about the efficacy and necessity of conservation and actual conservation behavior.

Affective Bases of Attitudes. As mentioned at the beginning of this section, most social psychologists believe that the affective component of an attitude is learned. One important theory of attitude formation was discussed in Chapter

2: The Byrne-Clore reinforcement-affect model (Byrne, 1971; Byrne & Clore, 1970). This model is based on principles of *classical conditioning*. Specifically, if an affectively "neutral" stimulus (called a *conditioned stimulus*) is paired with a stimulus that does elicit an affective response (called an *unconditioned stimulus*), then the previously neutral stimulus will acquire the same ability to produce the response. The affective response to the unconditioned stimulus is referred to as an *unconditioned response*, because it occurs unconditionally (i.e., without the organism having to learn the response). The acquired response is called a *conditioned response*, because the organism must be conditioned to make the response in the presence of that stimulus (i.e., the organism must "learn" the response through association).

This model can be readily applied to the conditioning of the affective component of environmental attitudes (see Figure 4-7). As discussed in Chapter 2, environments are typically neutral in their effect on behavior (i.e., we usually

FIGURE 4-7 Conditioning of the affective component of environmental attitudes.

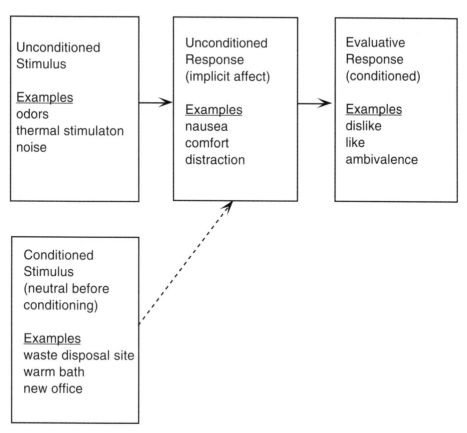

do not think about the environment if the stimulation levels are within some optimal range). However, if some quality of the environment changes to deviate from the optimal stimulation level, a negative affective response automatically occurs. Through association, the entire environment comes to elicit the same negative affect. For example, when you first encountered your dormitory room, your affective response to the desk in the room (the "conditioned stimulus") was likely to have been neutral. However, if when you sat down to study at the desk, your neighbor turned rock music (the "unconditioned stimulus") on his or her stereo at full volume, you may have experienced negative affect (the "unconditioned response"). If this happened repeatedly, you would develop a negative affective response to your desk (the "conditioned response"). Further, through a phenomenon known as *stimulus generalization*, you might come to experience a generalized negative affective response to your entire room. Thus, not only would you come to avoid studying at your desk, but you might even come to avoid your room altogether.

Behavioral Bases of Attitudes.   Another important way in which attitudes are learned is through the process of *operant conditioning* (Skinner, 1938). According to this model of learning, any behavior that is followed by a pleasant consequence (i.e., *positive reinforcement*) will increase in frequency. Behaviors that lead to unpleasant consequences (i.e., *punishment*) will become *extinguished*, that is, they will not be repeated. The expression of a particular attitude is a form of behavior, and can therefore be operantly conditioned as any other behavior. Thus, we learn to express attitudes that lead to favorable consequences for us, and we avoid attitudes that pose aversive consequences. For example, attitudes toward a "windfall profits tax" on oil during an energy crunch could be predicted according to the potential consequences of being in favor of or opposed to the tax. If the tax dollars were earmarked for highway construction projects, individuals likely to benefit from these projects would be expected to be in favor of the tax. On the other hand, oil company executives would be likely to oppose the legislation, since they would stand to lose money as a result of the tax.

A considerable amount of research supports this notion. For example, Van Der Pligt, Eiser, & Spears (1986a, 1986b) reported that attitudes toward the building of a nuclear power plant in one's locality are related to differential evaluations of the perceived cost and benefits to the differing sides on the issue, as well as the perceived importance of the potential consequences. Pro-nuclear groups were more optimistic about and attached greater value to the possible economic benefits, whereas anti-nuclear groups were more pessimistic about the risks and attached greater value to the dangers of building and operating the station. As we shall see in Chapter 14, many environmental attitudes can be understood in terms of the social, political, and economic consequences of those attitudes. Similar results were reported by Napier, Carter, & Bryant (1986) regarding perceptions of the impact of a reservoir on the local environment. Finally, Jackson (1986) reported that participants of "appreciative" activities (e.g., cross-country skiing, hiking) had stronger pro-environmental attitudes than did participants of "consumptive" activities (hunting, fishing) or "mechanized" activities (snowmobiling, trail biking). Clearly, the attitude held by any of the above groups can be understood in terms of the potential rewards or costs of consequences of these attitudes.

Social Bases of Attitudes. Another important way in which attitudes are formed is through observation of other people's expression of attitudes and the consequences of their attitudes. The process of learning via observation of a model's behavior is known as *social learning,* and the means by which we are influenced by the consequences of the model's behavior is known as *vicarious conditioning* (Bandura, 1974). Thus, if an individual observes another person expressing a particular attitude, and also observes that the attitude led to favorable consequences, then the individual will imitate the model's behavior in anticipation of incurring the same favorable consequences. For example, if a person who works for an oil company observes a co-worker express opposition to a windfall profits tax, and the co-worker is praised by the boss, then the individual is likely to imitate this opposition in anticipation of also gaining the boss's approval.

Another way in which social influences can impact attitudes is through the dynamics of interpersonal processes. Put simply, if my friends have pro-environmental attitudes, and I enjoy my friends' company, then I am likely to adopt similar attitudes. Manzo & Weinstein (1987) studied differences in active and nonactive members of the Sierra Club and reported significant differences in commitment to environmental protection as a function of club-related friendships. Thus, friends tend mutually to reinforce attitudes toward the environment.

Attitudes and Behavior

A major assumption of research on attitude formation is that attitudes mediate behaviors which are consistent with those attitudes. Thus, if I hold an attitude favoring energy conservation, it would be expected that this attitude would mediate behaviors such as walking instead of driving to work, or turning my thermostat down during the winter and up during the summer. Although this may seem like an obvious and reasonable assumption, in recent years research has led social psychologists to question the degree to which attitudes do, indeed, reliably predict behavior (e.g., Wicker, 1969). These studies have suggested that there is much less consistency between measured attitudes and subsequent behaviors than had previously been assumed.

Attitude-Behavior Consistency. The major principle of *consistency theories* of attitude-behavior relationships (see Festinger, 1957) is that people strive to maintain logical consistency between cognitions about their attitudes and cognitions about relevant behaviors in which they engage. Thus, if a person has the opinion that air pollution should be brought under control, a logically consistent behavior would be to vote for measures requiring utility companies to install pollution-control equipment in energy plants. However, if this person knows

---

TIME-OUT: Think about your attitude regarding some environmental issue (e.g., nuclear energy). List the factors that influenced you in arriving at this attitude. Analyze these influences in terms of cognitive, affective, social, and behavioral determinants of attitude formation. Which determinant in your list had the greatest impact on your attitude? If a proposal was put forth to construct a nuclear facility in your area, would you vote for it? What role would your attitude play in determining your vote?

---

that he or she voted against such a measure, the perceived attitude-behavior inconsistency would create a state of *cognitive discomfort*, which would motivate the individual to attempt to restore consistency. This would be accomplished either by changing the attitude (e.g., deciding that pollution control is not as important as controlling the costs of energy production), or by changing the behavior (e.g., by voting in favor of the next such measure). More will be said about attitude/behavior change in Chapter 15, but for now the main point is that consistency theories imply that attitudes should reliably predict relevant behaviors that would be consistent with those attitudes.

The fact that the research mentioned above suggests that there is frequently a lack of consistency between attitudes and behavior might seem to raise a considerable theoretical problem, as well as the practical question of whether there is any value in attempting to predict behavior from attitudes at all. Fortunately, Ajzen & Fishbein (1977) have developed a theory of attitude-behavior relationships that helps to clarify when this relationship will or will not hold. Ajzen & Fishbein propose that attitudes can, at best, yield good predictions of classes of behaviors, but are not necessarily predictive of specific behaviors. For example, energy conservation is a class of behaviors consisting of a variety of different specific actions, such as walking rather than driving, turning down the thermostat, switching off lights when leaving a room, using energy-efficient appliances, etc. If we measured a person's overall attitude toward energy conservation, we might find that a favorable attitude toward this issue may predict all, many, or perhaps only a few of the specific behaviors in this class. However, Ajzen & Fishbein have shown that a *behavioral index* consisting of a combined score of measurements of all individual behaviors can, indeed, be accurately predicted from the overall attitude. Evidence supporting this assertion was provided in a study by Gill, Crosby, & Taylor (1986), in which consumer behavior on container deposit (bottle) bills in California and Colorado demonstrated that "ecological concern," measured as a global attitude, was mediated by more specific attitudinal, normative, and behavioral intention variables.

The Reasoned Action Model. Another clarification of attitude-behavior relationships is suggested by Ajzen and Fishbein's Reasoned Action Model of attitudes and behaviors (see Figure 4-8). They argue that decisions to engage in particular behaviors are made by the individual reasoning about the potential

FIGURE 4-8　Another clarification of attitude behavior relationships suggested by Fishbein and Ajzen's (1977) "Reasoned Action Model" of behavior.

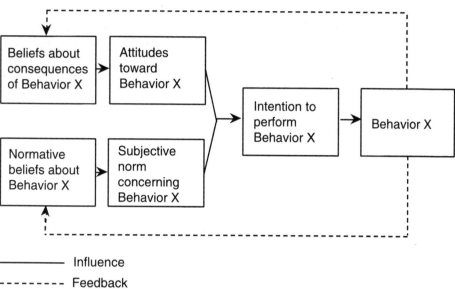

——————— Influence

- - - - - - - - Feedback

outcome of the behavior (i.e., judgments of how good/bad and likely/unlikely the outcome would be, called the *behavioral attitude*) and thoughts about social pressure to engage in the behavior (i.e., judgments about whether others think we should/should not engage in the behavior and our motivation to comply with their expectations, called the *subjective norm*). The behavioral attitude and subjective norm combine to determine the *intention* to perform the behavior or to avoid the behavior. Thus, an important implication of this model is that attitudes are too far removed from the actual behavior to provide reliable prediction. That is, attitudes affect behavior indirectly via intentions and jointly with the subjective norm. This model has been recently applied to understanding the relationships among beliefs, attitudes, and behavioral intentions toward nuclear energy vs. coal in the production of electricity (Verplanken, 1989).

Attitude-behavior inconsistency would actually be predicted by this model if the behavioral attitude and subjective norm were in conflict, and if the subjective norm were stronger than the behavioral attitude. Thus, I may negatively evaluate the outcome of turning my thermostat down during the winter months (i.e., it will make me cold), but I may intend to do it anyway if people who are important to me pressure me to do it (and if I am more concerned about living up to their expectations than I am about my personal comfort). In this case, a measure of my intention to turn my thermostat down would have accurately predicted my behavior, whereas a measure of my attitude would have led to an erroneous prediction. We will also return to a discussion of this model in Chapter 15, where we will discuss the factors influencing the consistency between intentions to engage in environmentally constructive behaviors and the actual behaviors that are needed to protect the environment.

We have seen in this section that attitudes are not always predictive of specific behaviors, but if appropriate measures are taken, attitudes can be shown to be at least indirectly related to behavior. Also, attitudes and behaviors may in some instances be consistent with one another, but this is not necessarily always the case. Thus, the question should not be whether or not attitudes reliably predict behavior, but, rather, under what conditions attitudes will be consistent with behaviors. For example, attitudes that are salient in the person's cognitive structures, that are strongly held, and that are stable over time generally are very predictive of behaviors, whereas attitudes low in salience, strength, and stability are poor predictors of behavior. Finally, it was also pointed out that attitudes can predict general classes of behaviors, but may not be very predictive of individual actions within a behavioral category.

ENVIRONMENTAL PERCEPTION, COGNITION, AND BEHAVIOR

In this chapter we discussed the processes by which we perceive our environment and how these perceptual processes are involved in developing our cognition or understanding of the environment. We also considered the role of perception and cognition in the formation of favorable or unfavorable evaluations of the environment. Finally, we discussed the relationships between environmental characteristics and emotional responses to a setting, as well as how affective states mediate approach-avoidance behaviors. All of these factors combine to determine our attitude toward the environment. These relationships have been demonstrated empirically in two recent studies (Arkkelin, 1988; Milan, Arkkelin, Veitch, & O'Connor, 1989). Subjects were asked to visit three very different settings on a college campus: a spacious two-story campus chapel, a comfortable dining area in the student union, and a small classroom in an old building. They completed measures of perceived environmental aesthetic quality, affective responses, and a measure of approach-avoidance behavior in each setting. Positive correlations were obtained among all three variables. That is, environments that were perceived as aesthetically pleasing were associated with both positive affective responses and approach behaviors. This pattern of relationships also corresponds to the model of environment-behavior relationships presented in Chapter 2. We seek out those environments that afford an optimal affective experience based upon our perceptions of current environmental conditions compared to optimal or desired levels of these characteristics.

Further, we have seen that attitudes have other behavioral implications besides approach-avoidance. For example, our attitudes toward the environment will influence such behaviors as energy use, littering, and voting for measures to deal with air pollution. In Chapters 14 and 15 we will discuss some of these issues in the context of how environmental attitudes are related to the use and abuse of our environment, as well as how to best bring about attitude change to encourage environmentally constructive behavior.

SUMMARY

Perception of the environment and our place in it is necessary for individual survival. This understanding stems from, but is not limited to, the reception of energy emitted by environmental objects and events impinging on the various sense organs. The sensory systems detect the presence of energy changes and turn this information over to higher-cognitive processes. The energy change is then recognized and mental measurement begins, first on a rank-order scale (i.e., is this greater or less than some other amount of energy?) and later on more sophisticated scales (e.g., the water is too cold to swim in, or the noise is loud enough to require ear protection). But while these are ordinarily problems of psychophysics, they are nonetheless affected by our attitudes, values, and expectations regarding the environment.

Our first response to environmental change is probably an affective one. Knowing that there has been an energy shift, we probably ask how this change makes us feel. Is my arousal level lower or higher? Do I feel as though I am in control of my present circumstances or do I feel that I am being controlled? How would I rate my present feelings along some positive to negative dimension? Am I required to make a response to the environmental change? How much of a response is required and what kind of response could it be?

Through continued interaction with our environment we learn the answers to the above questions and establish some guidelines (adaptation levels) for when responses on our part are required. If our perception of a given environment is within the individually established guidelines, homeostasis exists in the person/environment relationship; if it is outside of those guidelines, we engage in a number of processes that can be categorized as either adaptations or adjustments to re-establish homeostatic conditions. With the passage of time the perception of our environment becomes more dependent on cognitive processes and less on purely sensory processes. These cognitive processes primarily involve the development of mental images of the environment through experience. Environmental evaluation is related to the processing of information about the environment as well as affective responses to a setting, and is generally predictive of approach-avoidance behaviors.

The concept of environmental attitude summarizes the cognitive, affective, and behavioral responses to a setting. Although attitudes and behaviors are not always consistent, predictable behavioral adaptations or adjustments typically result when environmental characteristics deviate from the optimal level. These adaptations or adjustments are typically minor, but occasionally major changes are required. When this is so, radical modifications in either the environment or in the organism take place. This is known as a situation of stress and will be the topic of the next chapter.

IMPORTANT CONCEPTS

perception
stimulus detection
absolute threshold
psychophysics
stimulus recognition
stimulus discrimination
just noticeable difference threshold
stimulus scaling
constructivist theory
Gestalt theory
functionalism
learning theory
probabilistic functionalism
Brunswik's lens model
environmental cognition
orienting, categorizing, systemizing, encoding
cognitive maps, paths, edges, districts, nodes, landmarks
legibility
$R = f (C \times D)$
environmental evaluation
coherence, complexity, mystery

environmental preference
environmental aesthetics
    collative properties
butterfly curve hypothesis
specific vs diversive exploration
information rate
environmental attitudes
beliefs and values
    primitive beliefs
    higher-order beliefs
    psychologic
classical conditioning
stimulus generalization
operant conditioning
social learning
vicarious conditioning
consistency theories
cognitive discomfort
behavioral index
behavioral attitude
subjective norm

REFERENCES

Allport, G.W., & Pettigrew, T.F. (1957). Cultural influence on the perception of movement: The trapezoid illusion among the Zulus. *Journal of Abnormal and Social Psychology, 55,* 104–113.

Ajzen, I., & Fishbein, M. (1977). Attitude-behavior relations: A theoretical analysis and review of empirical research. *Psychological Bulletin, 84,* 888–918.

Ames, A., Jr. (1951). Visual perception and the rotating trapezoid window. *Psychological Monographs, 65*(7), (Whole No. 324).

Antes, J.R., McBride, J., & Collins, D. (1988). The effect of a new city traffic route on the cognitive maps of its residents. *Environment and Behavior, 20*(1), 75–91.

Appleyard, D. (1970). Styles and methods of structuring a city. *Environment and Behavior, 2,* 100–118.

Appleyard, D. (1976). *Planning a pluralistic city.* Cambridge, Mass.: MIT Press.

Arkkelin, D. (1988). *Cognitive, affective and behavioral responses to three different environments.* Paper presented at the Annual Meeting of the Midwestern Psychological Association, Chicago.

Bandura, A. (1974). Analysis of modeling process. In A. Bandura (Ed.), *Modeling: Conflicting theories.* New York: Lieber-Atherton.

Bem, D. (1970). *Beliefs, attitudes and human affairs.* Belmont, Calif.: Brooks/Cole.

Berlyne, D.E. (1960). *Conflict, arousal, and curiosity.* New York: McGraw-Hill.

Berlyne, D.E. (1974). *Studies in the new experimental aesthetics: Steps towards an objective psychology of aesthetic appreciation.* New York: Halsted Press.

Blades, M. (1990). The reliability of data collected from sketch maps. *Journal of Environmental Psychology, 10*(4), 327–339.

Bourassa, S.C. (1990). A paradigm for landscape aesthetics. Conference of the Association of American Geographers (1990, Toronto, Canada). *Environment and Behavior, 22*(6), 787–812.

Broadbent, G. (1989). Are environmental aesthetics worth studying? *Journal of Architectural and Planning Research, 6*(4), 356–359.

Brunswik, E. (1956). *Perception as a representative design of psychological experiments.* Berkeley: University of California Press.

Brunswik, E. (1969). The conceptual framework of psychology. In O. Neurath, R. Carnap, & C. Morris (Eds.), *Foundation of the unity of science: Toward an international encyclopedia of unified science.* Chicago: University of Chicago Press.

Byrne, D. (1971). *The attraction paradigm.* New York: Academic Press.

Byrne, D., & Clore, G.L. (1970). A reinforcement model of evaluation responses. *Personality: An International Journal, 1,* 103–128.

Couclelis, H., Golledge, R.G., Gale, N., & Tobler, W. (1987). Exploring the anchor-point hypothesis of spatial cognition. *Journal of Environmental Psychology, 7*(2), 99–122.

Craik, K.K., & Appleyard D. (1980). Streets of San Francisco: Brunswik's lens model applied to urban inference and assessment. *Journal of Social Issues, 36,* 72–85.

Deregowski, J.B. (1980). *Illusions, patterns and pictures: A cross-cultural perspective.* London: Academic Press.

Downs, R.M., & Stea, D. (1973). Cognitive maps and spatial behavior: Process and products. In R.M. Downs & D. Stea (Eds.), *Image and environment: Cognitive mapping and spatial behavior.* Chicago: Aldine.

Downs, R.M., & Stea, D. (1977). *Maps in minds: Reflections on cognition mapping.* New York: Harper & Row.

Evans, G.W. (1980). Environmental cognition. *Psychological Bulletin, 88,* 259–287.

Festinger, L.A. (1957). *A theory of cognitive dissonance.* Evanston, Ill.: Row-Peterson.

Flavell, J.H. (1977). *Cognitive development.* New York: Prentice Hall.

Freides, D. (1974). Human information processing and sensory modality: Cross modal functions, information complexity, memory and deficit. *Psychological Bulletin, 81,* 284–310.

Fridgen, J.D. (1987). Use of cognitive maps to determine perceived tourism regions. *Leisure Sciences, 9*(2), 101–117.

Garling, T., Book, A., Lindberg, E., & Arce, C. (1990). Is evaluation encoded in cognitive maps? *Journal of Environmnental Psychology, 10*(4), 341–351.

Gibson, J.J. (1979). *The ecological approach to visual perception.* Boston: Houghton Mifflin.

Gibson, E.J., & Walk, R. (1960). The "visual cliff." *Scientific American, 202,* 64–71.

Gill, J.D., Crosby, L.A., & Taylor, J.R. (1986). Ecological concern, attitudes and social norms in voting behavior. *Public Opinion Quarterly, 50*(4), 537–554.

Goodchild, B. (1974). Class differences in environmental perception. *Urban Studies, 11,* 59–79.

Gould, P.R. (1973). On mental maps. In R.M. Downs & D. Stea (Eds.), *Image and environment: Cognitive mapping and spatial behavior.* Chicago: Aldine.

Gould, P.R., & White, R. (1974). *Mental maps.* New York: Penguin.

Hart, R.A., & Moore, G.T. (1973). The development of spatial cognition: review. In R.M. Downs & D. Stea (Eds.), *Image and environment: Cognitive mapping and spatial behavior.* Chicago: Aldine.

Helson, H. (1964). *Adaptation-level theory: An experimental and systematic approach to behavior.* New York: Harper & Row.

Herman, J.F., Miller, B.S., & Shiraki, J.H. (1987). The influence of affective associations on the development of cognitive maps of large environments. *Journal of Environmental Psychology, 7*(2), 80–98.

Herzog, T. (1989). A cognitive analysis of preference for urban nature. *Journal of Environmental Psychology, 9*(1), 27–43.

Holahan, C.J., & Dobrowolny, M.B. (1978). Cognition and behavioral correlates of the spatial environment: An interactional analysis. *Environment and Behavior, 10,* 317–344.

Hudson, W. (1962). Pictorial perception and educational adaptation in Africa. *Psychologica, Africana, 9,* 266–239.

Hull, R.B., & Harvey, A. (1989). Explaining the emotion people experience in suburban parks. *Environment and Behavior, 21*(3), 323–345.

Hull, R.B., & Revell, G. (1989). Cross-cultural comparison of landscape scenic beauty evaluations: A case study in Bali. *Journal of Environmental Psychology, 9*(3), 177–191.

Ippolitov, F.W. (1973). Interanyalyzer differences in the sensitivity-strength parameter for vision, hearing and cutaneous modalities. In V.D. Pebylitsyn & J.A. Gray (Eds.), *Biological basis of individual behavior.* New York: Academic Press.

Ittleson, W.H., Proshansky, H.M., Rivlin, L.G., & Winkel, G.H. (1974). *An introduction to environmental psychology.* New York: Holt, Rinehart & Winston.

Jackson, E.L. (1986). Outdoor recreation participation and attitudes to the environment. *Leisure Studies, 5*(1), 1–23.

Kaplan, S. (1973). Cognitive maps in perception and thought. In R.M. Downs & D. Stea (Eds.), *Image and environment: Cognitive mapping and spatial behavior.* Chicago: Aldine.

Kaplan, S. (1975). An informal model for the prediction of preference. In E.H. Zube, R.O. Brush, & J.G. Fabos (Eds.), *Landscape assessment.* Stroudsburg, Pa.: Dowden, Hutchinson and Ross.

Kaplan, S. (1979). Perception and landscape: Conceptions and misconceptions. In G. Elsner & R. Smardon (Technical Coordinators), *USDA Forest Service Report PSW-35.* Berkeley, California.

Kaplan, S. (1987). Aesthetics, affect, and cognition: Environmental preference from an evolutionary perspective. *Environment and Behavior, 19,* 3–32.

Kaplan, S., & Kaplan, R. (1978). *Humanscape: Environments for people.* North Scituate, Mass.: Duxbury.

Kaplan, R., Kaplan, S., & Brown, T. (1989). Environmental preference: A comparison of four domains of predictors. *Environment and Behavior, 21*(5), 509–530.

Karan, P.P., Bladen, W.A., & Singh, G. (1980). Slum dwellers' and squatters' images of the city. *Environment and Behavior, 12,* 81–100.

Koffka, K. (1935). *Principles of gestalt psychology.* New York: Harcourt, Brace and World.

Kohler, W. (1929). *Gestalt psychology.* New York: Liveright.

Leff, H.L. (1978). *Experience, environment, and human potentials.* New York: Oxford University Press.

Leiser, D., & Zilbershatz, A. (1989). The traveller. A computational model of spatial network learning. *Environment and Behavior, 21*(4), 435–463.

Lewin, K. (1951). *Field theory in social science.* New York: Harper.

Linn, M.C., & Peterson, A.C. (1986). Meta-analysis of gender differences in spatial ability. In J. Hyde & M. Linn (Eds.), *The psychology of gender: Advances through meta-analysis.* Baltimore: Johns Hopkins University Press.

Lynch, K. (1960). *The image of the city.* Cambridge, Mass.: MIT Press.

Manzo, L.C., & Weinstein, N.D. (1987). Behavioral commitment to environmental protection: A study of active and nonactive members of the Sierra Club. *Environment and Behavior, 19*(6), 673–694.

Maurer, R., & Baxter, J.C. (1972). Image of the neighborhood and city among black anglo and Mexican children. *Environment and Behavior, 4,* 351–388.

McGuinness, D. (1976). Away from a unisex psychology: Individual differences in visual sensory and perceptual processes. *Perception, 5,* 279–294.

McGuinness, D., & Pribram, K. (1979). The origins of sensory bias in the development of gender differences in perception and cognition. In M. Bortner (Ed.), *Cognitive growth and development.* New York: Brunner/Mazel.

Mehrabian, A., & Russell, J. A. (1974). *An approach to environmental psychology.* Cambridge, Mass.: MIT Press.

Milan, L., Arkkelin, D., Veitch, R., & O'Connor, R. (1989). *Cognition and affect on predictors of behavioral responses to different environments.* Paper presented at the Annual Meeting of the Midwestern Psychological Association, Chicago.

Milgram, S., Greenwald, J., Kessler, S., McKenna, W., & Waters, J. (1972). A psychological map of New York City. *American Scientist, 60,* 194–200.

Moeser, S.D. (1988). Cognitive mapping in a complex building. *Environment and Behavior, 29*(1), 21–49.

Money, J. (1965). *Sex research: New developments.* New York: Holt, Rinehart & Winston.

Moore, G.T. (1974). Developmental variations between and within individuals in the cognitive representation of large-scale spatial environments. *Man-Environment Systems, 4,* 55–57.

Napier, T.L., Carter, M.L., & Bryant, E.G. (1986). Local perceptions of reservoir impacts: A test of vested interests. *American Journal of Community Psychology, 14*(1), 17–37.

Neuman, K. (1986). Personal values and commitment to energy conservation. *Environment and Behavior, 18*(1), 53–74.

Orleans, P. (1973). Differential cognition of urban residents: Effects of social class on mapping. In R.M. Downs, & D. Stea (Eds.), *Image and environment: Cognitive mapping and spatial behavior.* Chicago: Aldine.

Orleans, P., & Schmidt, S. (1972). Mapping the city: Environmental cognition of urban residents. In W. Mitchell (Ed.), *EDRA 3.* Los Angeles, University of California Press.

Pearson, J.L., & Ialongo, N.S. (1986). The relationship between spatial ability and environmental knowledge. *Journal of Environmental Psychology, 6*(4), 299–403.

Purcell, A.T. (1986). Environmental perception and affect: A schema discrepancy model. *Environment and Behavior, 18*(1), 3–30.

Ribe, R.G. (1988). Getting the Scenic Beauty Estimation method to a ratio scale: A simple revision to assess positive and negative landscapes. Nineteenth Annual Conference of the Environmetnal Design Research Association (1988, Pomona, California). *Environmental Design Research Association,* 19-41-47.

Rokeach, M. (1968). *Beliefs, attitudes, and values.* San Francisco: Jossey-Bass.

Ruddell, E.J., Gramann, J.H., Rudis, V.A., & Westphal, J.M. (1989). The psychological utility of visual penetration in near-view forest scenic-beauty models. *Environment and Behavior, 21*(4), 393–412.

Russell, J.N., & Pratt, G. (1980). A description of the affective quality attributed to environments. *Journal of Personality and Social Psychology, 38,* 311–322.

Saarinen, T.F. (1973). Student views of the world. In R.M. Downs & D. Stea (Eds.), *Image and environment: Cognitive mapping and spatial behavior.* Chicago: Aldine.

Sadalla, E.K., & Montello, D.R. (1989). Remembering changes in direction. *Environment and Behavior, 21*(3), 346–363.

Scott, S.B. (1989). Preference, mystery and visual attributes of interiors: A study of relationships. *Dissertation Abstracts, 50*(11), 3386.

Segall, M.H., Campbell, D.T., & Herskovits, M.J. (1966). *The influence of culture on visual perception.* Indianapolis: Bobbs-Merrill.

Skinner, B.F. (1938). *The behavior of organisms.* New York: Appleton-Century-Crofts.

Stamps, A.E. (1989). Are environmental aesthetics worth studying? *Journal of Architectural and Planning Research, 6*(4), 344–356.

Stanton, B.H. (1986). The incidence of home grounds and experiential networks: Some implications. *Environment and Behavior, 18*(3), 299–329.

Strauss, A. (1961). *Images of the American city.* New York: Free Press.

Teske, J.A., & Balser, D.P. (1986). Levels of organization in urban navigation. *Journal of Environmental Psychology, 6*(4), 305–327.

Turnbull, C.M. (1961). Some observations regarding the experiences and behaviors of Bambuti pygmies. *American Journal of Psychology, 74,* 304–308.

Van der Plight, J., Eiser, J.R., & Spears, R. (1986a). Attitudes toward nuclear energy: Familiarity and salience. *Environment and Behavior, 18*(1), 75–93.

Van der Plight, J., Eiser, J.R., & Spears, R. (1986b). Construction of a nuclear power station in one's locality: Attitudes and salience. *Basic and Applied Social Psychology, 7*(1), 1–15.

Veitch, R., & O'Connor, R. (1987). *Identifying campus locations spatially and functionally: Cognitive maps do not always help.* Unpublished manuscript, Bowling Green State University, Bowling Green, Ohio.

Verplanken, B. (1989). Involvement and need for cognition as moderators of beliefs-attitude-intention consistency. *British Journal of Social Psychology, 28*(2), 115–122.

Ward, S.L., Newcombe, N., & Overton, W.F. (1986). Turn left at the church or three miles north: A study of direction giving and sex differences. *Environment and Behavior, 18*(2), 192–213.

Warren, D.H., Rossano, M.J., & Wear, T.D. (1990). Perception of map–environment correspondence: The roles of features and alignment. *Ecological Psychology, 2*(2), 131–150.

Weinstein, S., & Sersen, E.A. (1961). Tactual sensitivity as a function of handedness and laterality. *Journal of Comparative and Physiological Psychology, 54,* 665–669.

Wicker, A.W. (1969). Attitudes vs. actions: The relationship of verbal and overt behavioral responses to attitude objects. *Journal of Social Issues, 25,* 41–78.

Wohlwill, J.F. (1966). The physical environment: A problem for a psychology of stimulation. *Journal of Social Issues, 22,* 29–38.

Wohlwill, J.F. (1976). Environmental aesthetics: The human environment as a source of affect. In I. Altman & J. F. Wohlwill (Eds.), *Human behavior and environment: Advances in theory and research* (Vol. 1). New York: Plenum.

Wong, K.K. (1990). Scenic quality and cognitive structures of urban environments: The role of scene attributes and respondent characteristics. *Dissertation Abstracts International, 51*(5), 4269.

Yuille, J. (1983). Research and teaching with police: A Canadian example. *International Review of Applied Psychology, 33*(1), 5–23.

Environmental Stress

5

FIGURE 5-1 Humans are incredibly adaptable; when not satisfied with their lot, they have the intelligence and ingenuity to create new things.

Humans are incredibly adaptable; when not satisfied with their lot, they have the intelligence and ingenuity to create new things, to adapt to what is available, and even to adjust or alter their living environment to make it more congenial. But this flexibility is daily being challenged. Forces from within the species (e.g., violent crimes, war, acts of terrorism, and genocide), widespread natural catastrophes (e.g., famines, floods, droughts, earthquakes, and volcanic eruptions), and ever-increasing and dangerous technological developments (e.g., faster automobiles, increasing numbers of aircraft attempting to occupy the same air corridors, escalating numbers of chemicals, and the proliferation of nuclear devices) are coalescing to test the limits of human adaptability. Additionally, interpersonal forces demanding more material goods and greater and more efficient provision of services are increasingly straining limited physical and human resources. In the process of developing technology and modifying the environment to make it serve the goals of comfort and luxury, a world has been created that is itself potentially lethal. Air, water, and noise pollution, accelerating energy consumption, pressures toward excessive work, and an increased tempo of life are but a few manifestations of these forces. Thus, over and over again in the course of daily living, we witness threats to human adaptability, feel pressure for increased ingenuity to provide protection from external forces, and struggle to reconcile material possessions with individual desires. The operation of these forces is inextricably tied to what has commonly come to be labelled *stress*.

But what exactly is stress? Personal accounts of stress, scales for measuring it, instructions for coping with it, and personality tests to see how well one can endure it have found their way into print and are supplemented by TV and radio accounts featuring self-proclaimed "experts" in its early detection and management. Hardly a week goes by when we are not reminded by some talk show host and "enlightened guest" that we are living in a stressful world. Often we are told that if we would only follow the exercise program, the dietetic regime, or the religious practices of the "guest of the day" our stress would dissipate and we could live normal, happy lives.

Although these claims have dubious value, a potentially robust way to understand the interrelationships between environment and behavior might be to consider the role of stress on human functioning. In this regard, the concept of stress has been helpful in specifying environmental characteristics that interfere with human functioning, that create physiological or psychological discomfort, and that lead to ill health (Evans & Cohen, 1987).

DEFINING STRESS:
THEORETICAL PERSPECTIVES

Stress has been defined as a state that occurs when people are faced with demands from the environment that require them to change in some way. Most researchers agree with this definition. What they do not agree on is whether stress is the demand itself or the person's response to that demand.

Response-Based Definitions of Stress

Some theorists have argued for a response-based definition of the term. Stress, they argue, should be defined in terms of some change from base rate in the number or intensity of some specified response. Response candidates have included psychophysiological measures like galvanic skin response, heart rate, blood pressure, and such corresponding psychological manifestations as anxiety, loss of individual control, and lowered self-esteem. In this sense stress can be defined in terms of "blood pressure above some threshold," or "change in heart rate greater than some specified minimum," or "anxiety scores exceeding some predetermined cut-off." A major problem with this approach is that these same responses occur as a result of very different stimuli (e.g., heart rate may increase as a result of physical exercise, viewing a horror movie, riding a roller coaster, or waiting for a blind date). Likewise the psychological manifestations of anxiety, loss of felt control, and lowered self-esteem have myriad antecedents. But, while the immediate responses may be similar, the enduring effects resulting from these various sources are likely to be highly variable (e.g., the anxiety felt as a result of going on a blind date is not likely to have the same long-term repercussions as the anxiety resulting from impending layoffs at one's place of employment). A definition of stress featuring only the "immediate" response component of the *stimulus-organism-response* system will, therefore, inevitably prove inadequate.

Stimulus-Based Definitions of Stress

Other theorists have argued for a stimulus-based definition of stress. They argue for a taxonomy of environmental events based on their covariation with systemic, psychological, and/or social disturbance, and include such events as noise, air, and water pollution, population density, odors, loss of loved ones, and changes in life style. The emphasis here is on environmental events that impact on any of several response systems either immediately or as a result of prolonged exposure. A stressful environment, for example, is one where noise level exceeds some specified decibel (dB) level, or where the carbon dioxide concentration equals or exceeds some agreed-upon value, or where environmental occupants exceed some number. In subsequent chapters we will discuss the effects of these types of environmental stressors in great detail. In the meantime, it can be seen that a major problem with this view is that any stimulus may or may not be disturbing (stressful) depending on the personality of the individuals involved, the situation in which the event occurs, other competing behaviors, and the rewards and costs involved in dealing with the event. For example, a loud stereo can be enjoyable at a party, but very disturbing (stressful) if you are preparing for final exams; likewise, both high population density and isolation can be stressful or enjoyable depending on the amount of contact desired. Thus, it can be seen that nomothetic approaches to defining stress only in terms of the stressor also run into difficulty.

Stress as Cause and Effect

From the preceding discussion it is clear that it is possible to think of stress as both something that is happening to a person and the person's response to what's happening. It involves environmental and psychological events, the interpretation of these events, and behavioral as well as physiological responding. Noisy environments, for example, may be related to physiological, psychological, and behavioral changes in those exposed to the noise. These responses, in turn, may change the nature and interpretation of the noise itself (i.e., noise changes neural activity in the reticular activating system, which subsequently changes the organism's perception of the noise; this altered perception, in turn, influences reticular activating system activity, and so on). Stress, therefore, is neither the stimulus nor the response; it is a process involving both, and, as a process, it influences the ways in which environmental events are attended to, interpreted, responded to, and changed. It is also the process within which the responder also is likely to be changed.

While the specification of just what stress is has yet to be fully articulated, it is clear that such a thing actually exists, and it appears to involve physiological, psychological, and behavioral responding. It is also clear that at times it may even play a broader role by affecting human social systems (see Chapter 13). Confronted by environmental events which pose threat, challenge or danger, organisms respond physiologically, psychologically, and behaviorally. These responses not only are helpful in meeting the demands of the changing environment, but may even alter that environment, making it more benign (not always without cost to the organism). Monat and Lazarus (1977) have defined stress as any event in which environmental demands and/or internal demands (physiological or psychological) tax or exceed the adaptive resources of the individual, his or her tissue system, or the social system of which one is a part. (cf. Cohen, Evans, Stokols, & Krantz, 1986; Singer, 1980). Within this definition, change becomes stressful only when it strains the coping capacities of the entire organism/environment system to adapt to the change. This definition encompasses aspects of both the stimulus and the response, and includes the organism as an active participant in the process. It is therefore consistent with definitions utilized by most current researchers and is the one that will be used when referring to stress throughout the remainder of this text.

In discussing the model of environment-behavior in Chapter 2, we emphasized the importance of perception in understanding the relationship of organism to environment. We suggested that most of the time the environment is perceived as falling within the organism's "window of adaptability" and therefore the influence of the environment can be characterized as steady-state. The above definition of stress presupposes that this is not always the case, that states of disequilibrium can occur, and that sometimes this disequilibrium "taxes or exceeds the adaptive resources" of the entire organism/environment system. Fundamental to dealing with this state of affairs is the ability to evaluate the environment in terms of the demands that are being made, and to assess the self with respect to the resources available to deal with these demands. This process is known as *appraisal* and will be turned to next.

Appraisal

One's perception of the environment as well as one's attitudes toward the source of stress will mediate the individual's response to it. If we believe that a stressor will cause us no permanent harm, our response will likely be less extreme than if it carries the threat of lasting harm. Also, if our attitudes are strongly in favor of something that is potentially harmful, we may appraise the threats as less alarming. Individuals who believe that nearby airports are an economic asset to the community are less concerned with the noise generated by planes taking off and landing than are people who do not perceive such benefits. There are three basic types of assessments made with regard to potential stressors. We can assess the environmental event as posing a challenge or constituting a threat, or we can assess it in terms of the damage it has already done. While we have separated these appraisals for the sake of exposition, it is likely that all three take place in response to most environmental stressors.

Harm or loss assessments typically involve analysis of damage that has already been done. The properties of a sudden event such as a tornado may predispose people toward such appraisal because damage is done very quickly and people are more concerned with the immediate consequences than the possibility of more. Bereavement is also likely to reflect a harm-loss evaluation in the wake of the loss of a loved one, although when a loved one has been chronically ill for an extended period of time, bereavement may also occur in anticipation of loss. In addition to the actual loss of a loved one, we may be concerned with demands that will occur after death. Concern over these types of demands can be interpreted as challenges or as threats, that is, "Let's get on with life," or, "How will I get on with life?"

Threat appraisals are concerned with future dangers. If a tornado is sighted, it may initially be appraised as a threat and subsequently be appraised as something else. The stress of moving away to college, of learning to live with a roommate, and similar events is largely anticipatory as a student prepares to start school. Likewise, waiting to take an exam may be more stressful than taking it or even failing it. The ability to foresee problems and anticipate difficulties allows us to solve them or prevent their occurrence. At the same time, though, it may lead to the perception of threat and, thus, anticipatory stress.

Challenge appraisals focus not on the harm or potential harm of the event, but on the possibility of overcoming the stressor. Some stressors may be beyond our ability to cope, but we all have a range of events with which we are confident of our ability to cope successfully. Stressors that are evaluated as challenges fall within this hypothetical range. The event may be seen as potentially harmful, but we feel that we can prevent the harm from occurring. A person may have just lost his or her job because of a plant relocation. This stress can be seen as threatening (how are we going to make ends meet; how will we survive?) or as challenging (what else can I do to make a living; how can I make the best of a bad situation?). The magnitude of the stressor, our estimates of our coping resources, and our styles of coping with problems all determine whether an event is seen as challenging or threatening. Among the primary psychological variables that affect these appraisals are our attitudes toward the source of stress. These attitudes may act to moderate or intensify our reactions to stressors.

In summary, if we perceive our immediate environment as challenging or threatening to equilibrium and, if the perceived demands of that environment tax or exceed our ability to satisfy or alter those demands, then stress occurs. Coping behaviors are selected to relieve that stress, and secondary appraisals are made to determine the efficacy of those selections. Before looking at the characteristics of environments and the predispositions of organisms that lead to stress, a brief description of the physiological and psychological processes involved is necessary. It is to these systems that we turn next.

PHYSIOLOGY OF STRESS

Although the causes of stress are many and varied and can be either pleasant (e.g., a passionate kiss) or unpleasant (e.g., an electric shock), they all demand adaptation. This adaptation invariably involves the activities of various hormones and numerous biological systems including the hypothalamus, cerebral cortex, reticular formation, limbic system, and autonomic nervous system. Regardless of its ultimate expression, the stress response is initially activated by alerting the organism to environmental change and readying it for action. This process is generally labelled *arousal*.

Arousal

In the core of the hindbrain and extending upward to the midbrain and forebrain is a network of neurons known as the *reticular formation*. This network of nerve fibers, with cell bodies in the interior of the brain stem and axons projecting throughout the higher brain center, is referred to as the reticular activating system (RAS). The basic functions of these neural branches are twofold. First, they screen information on its way to the higher centers in the brain, blocking irrelevant information and allowing relevant information to pass upward where it can be processed and acted upon. Second, the RAS has the job of *alerting* the cerebral cortex. According to Beck (1983) the reticular system works "something like a fire alarm that gets people into action but does not really say where the fire is" (p. 104). Through this system the organism is made vigilant and aware of what is happening in the environment, and is made ready for action. Included in this readiness are "increased metabolism of carbohydrates to produce more glucose and the release of fatty acids for greater energy, higher heart rate and oxygen consumption, constriction of blood flow to peripheral areas of the body with greater supply to the skeletal muscles, kidneys and brain" (Evans & Cohen, 1987; p. 576). This increased readiness, coupled with appropriate information about bodily needs and environmental demands, plays an important role in determining the ultimate expression of behavior.

The capacity of sensory stimulation to guide behavior is poor, however, when arousal is either very high or very low. With very low arousal, the sensory message does not get through; with very high arousal it is likely that too many messages get through and prevent the organism from responding selectively to appropriate stimuli. The latter presumably is what happens when people "lose their heads" in an emergency and to soldiers who panic under enemy fire. Thus, an intermediate level of arousal produces optimal functioning (see Figure 2-1). What constitutes low, high, and intermediate arousal, however, varies as a function of a number of constitutional and psychological characteristics. For some people a ride on a double-loop roller coaster is not all that arousing, whereas for others the merry-go-round provides more than enough arousal.

When the RAS is damaged the organism becomes comatose and is unresponsive to stimulation. Additionally, drugs such as amphetamines increase RAS activity, whereas barbiturates depress it. Thus, arousal is partially neurochemical, and partially subjectively determined. What is becoming increasingly clear is that arousal is related to stress and is the mechanism by which the organism is alerted to changes in bodily needs and environmental demands. Ultimately, if one is to understand the role of the external environment in influencing human behavior, one needs to understand the arousal-producing properties of that environment. An understanding of how that arousal gets translated into goal-directed behaviors is also required. This translation process will be considered when we look directly at "coping," but first a formal model that incorporates the arousal dimension and known as the *general adaptation syndrome* will be examined.

General Adaptation Syndrome (GAS)

Hans Selye (1976) has extensively studied the body's reaction during stress and has postulated that it occurs in three major phases: the *alarm reaction*, the *stage of resistance*, and the *stage of exhaustion*. In response to any stressor, either physical or psychological, the hypothalamus is activated, mediating the secretion of large amounts of ACTH by the pituitary. This ACTH, in turn, stimulates the adrenal cortex to secrete increased amounts of adrenal corticoids. In general, these hormones activate the organism (as discussed in the previous section) allowing it to deal more adequately with its environment. This phase is called the *alarm reaction*.

In the second stage the organism recovers from the initial stress and begins to attempt to cope with the situation, mobilizing the body physically as well as psychologically to meet the demands of the environment. The organism, in a sense, is resisting the demands of the situation This stage was, therefore, labelled by Selye as the *stage of resistance*. If the organism is unsuccessful in its attempts to cope, or if the stress persists, the *stage of exhaustion* is reached. At this stage the adrenal gland can no longer respond to the stress by secreting adrenal corticoids and the organism has exhausted its ability to cope with the stressor.

Later in this text we will see how the stress of overpopulation is related to increased adrenal activity and to adrenal hypertrophy; we will also see how this has an inhibiting effect on gonadal functioning resulting in a decline in reproductive fitness, and ultimately to a decline in population and population density. Evans and Cohen (1987) suggest that chronic exposure to a variety of environmental and/or social psychological conditions can in and of themselves be stressful, that the process of coping with them can be stressful, and that the energy available for dealing with these conditions is limited. Thus, like Selye, they suggest that prolonged stress will eventually deplete the individual's adaptive resources. Both approaches imply that stress produces a physical "wear and tear" on the system, and when coping abilities are exhausted, the individual becomes vulnerable to a variety of physical and psychological disorders. For further discussion and a comparison of the psychological and physiological models of stress see Baum, Singer, & Baum (1981), Cohen, Evans, Stokols, & Krantz (1986), and Evans & Cohen (1987).

PSYCHOLOGY OF STRESS

There is growing awareness of the importance of psychological factors (i.e., cognitive and emotional processes) in response to the environment. Additionally, such factors as beliefs, attitudes, and perceptual sets may, themselves, act as threats For these reasons, researchers concerned with understanding stress are increasingly considering the impact of psychological variables and are incorporating them into stress theories as both mediators of physical stressors and as stressors in their own right (Frankenhaeuser, 1978; Kasl & Cobb, 1970; Lazarus, 1966).

Primary Appraisal: The Perception of Threat

Acknowledging the role of cognitive processes in stress suggests one reason for our susceptibility to it. We not only respond to dangers or threats that have materialized, but are influenced by our anticipation of them and by symbols of dangers experienced previously (Wolfe & Goodell, 1968). Thus, a situation in which stress has been experienced (e.g., a dentist's office) may be symbolic of danger to us and we may experience stress in anticipation of danger when we are there (e.g., we may have increased blood pressure or perspiration simply while waiting for a friend at the dentist's office). Similarly, an event that has never occurred or may never occur may elicit stress. Living near a nuclear power plant or a toxic waste disposal site may engender stress in residents independent of whether either has ever precipitated imminent danger. In a study of the decontamination procedures at Three Mile Island, for example, stress levels were higher just before radioactive gases were released into the atmosphere than while the releases were actually occurring (Baum et al., 1980). Additionally, Veitch and colleagues (Stang & Veitch, 1985; Veitch, Stang, & Conley, 1985) have shown that merely living near a chemical waste disposal site can lead to levels of chronic stress nearing those that are experienced by individuals in the aftermath of actual technological and natural disasters.

Studies of anticipated crowding suggest that individuals experience stress when expecting to be crowded even if the crowding never actually materializes (Baum & Greenberg, 1975). Furthermore, Spacapan and Cohen (1983) have shown that subjects expecting to experience a cold stressor exhibit as strong a stress response as subjects actually exposed to it. Psychological perspectives on stress, therefore, emphasize the role of interpretation or appraisal of potential stressors. When an event threatens harm or loss, or when internal

FIGURE 5-2 In a study of decontamination procedures at Three Mile Island, stress levels were higher just before radioactive gases were released into the atmosphere than while releases were actually occurring.

demands challenge or surpass one's ability to adapt to them, the event or its demands are likely to result in an interpretation of stress.

Appraisal of potential stressors depend on a number of factors including attitudes toward the source of noxious stimulation, prior experience with it, knowledge of how to cope with it or knowledge of its consequences, and evaluation of its apparent costs. If, for example, residents of Onaga, Kansas, hear on the radio that a tornado watch has been issued for their area, the appraisal of this news will depend on their attitudes toward tornadoes, previous experience with them, the preparations they have made to cope with them, and the likely magnitude of the costs to be incurred should they actually be hit by one. When exposed to potentially stressful situations or events, we appraise the setting or the event and make judgments about how threatening it is. After a situation is judged to be threatening and stressful (i.e., the environment possesses the possibility of potential loss, of danger, or merely represents a challenge), *secondary appraisals* are made. No longer concerned with assessment of danger, attention is turned to the dangers or benefits of different modes of coping with these threats. In a sense this is the psychological equivalent to the physiological "resistance stage" of the GAS. Later in this chapter we will look at specific moderators of the stress response.

Secondary Appraisal: Selecting Coping Behaviors and Evaluating Their Effectiveness

The perception of danger motivates a search for coping responses that will reduce this threat. Thus, one's response to a situation will depend on two kinds of appraisal. First, an interpretation of the situation and a consideration of its potential threat is made (i.e., primary appraisal); second, response choices to ameliorate the situation are considered (i.e., secondary appraisal). By weighing the costs and benefits of these choices, a coping strategy is selected. Coping involves both action-oriented and intrapsychic efforts to manage environmental and internal demands, and conflicts among them, which tax or exceed a person's resources—that is, the individual masters, tolerates, or reduces the effects of environmental and internal demands. These actions are the end product of secondary appraisal, and if they are successful they bring the organism back into equilibrium with its environment.

An individual exposed to a stressor attempts to "prevent, avoid or control emotional stress" (Pearlin & Schooler, 1978, p. 3). This is indeed what coping is. It is a response to environmental or internal demands. Before such a response can be made, the individual must determine the resources available for making such a response, including social variables (i.e., the interpersonal network of which the individual is a part, including friends, relatives, fellow workers, neighbors, etc.), psychological resources (i.e., the personality characteristics that people draw upon to help them withstand the stressor), and constitutional resources (i.e., genetic strengths and vulnerabilities, state of health, etc.). Having assessed one's resources, a coping response is chosen, carried out, and its success evaluated.

TIME-OUT: Reflect on a time when you were feeling well and working well. You felt healthy and fit; you had no difficulty making deadlines and others appraised your performance in glowing terms. Now consider the life circumstances that might have contributed to these feelings. Examine these circumstances in terms of the presence or absence of major life events, daily hassles, cataclysmic events, and ambient stressors.

By contrast, now consider a time when you were not feeling well and your work was a bit shoddy. You constantly seemed to be behind schedule and others appraised your work as subpar. Again consider your life circumstances at that time in your life. Are there any differences in the two sets of circumstances? If there are, are some of them attributable to the environment (e.g., more or less noise, hotter or cooler temperatures, more or fewer roommates, more or less sunshine, etc.)?

Assess your choice of coping behaviors in these two situations. Were they the same? If not, why not? What effects do you believe these stresssors and your coping behaviors had on your physiological and psychological stress response systems?

RESEARCHING STRESS: THE ENVIRONMENTAL CONTEXT

Organisms, including humans, undergo stress in the context of the greater environment of which they are a part. At any given moment the environment/organism system can be in a state of equilibrium on some dimensions, but in disequilibrium with respect to others. It is therefore important to be able to identify potential sources of stress and to determine the levels of those sources likely to lead to disequilibrium.

Measuring Stressors: Qualitative Differences

Knowing the source of stress is important because a number of properties unique to the stressor can shape the appraisals made or the effects it may have. First, it is obvious that while some events are threatening to almost no one (a cool ocean breeze, for example) and some are threatening to almost everyone affected (a tornado), most events carry a range of potential problems, some or all of which will be appraised as stressful under some conditions, but not stressful under other conditions (a summer thunderstorm). Second, it is equally obvious that some sources of stress are ever-present and chronic (e.g., living near a toxic waste disposal site, or near a rail line or freeway) while others are recurring and acute (e.g., living on a floodplain, or an earthquake fault). Third, stressors can vary with respect to their predictability (the noise of the 3:15 A.M. freight train would be highly predictable, but the next nuclear power plant failure would not be), and controllability (while I might be able to control the ambient temperature of my office by a turn of the thermostat, I have no control over the path taken by a tornado).

Evans and Cohen (1987) have compiled a typology of stressors. Their compilation is useful in that it allows distinctions to be drawn along several

FIGURE 5-3 Some events are threatening to almost everyone affected and some are threatening to almost no one.

major dimensions, including how long the stressor persists, the magnitude of response required by the stressor, and the number of people affected.

Daily Hassles. The category that includes some of the most chronic environmental stressors has been labelled *daily hassles*. These are present during most of our daily lives and include such conditions as job dissatisfaction (Frankenheuser & Gardell, 1976; Kahn & French, 1970), neighborhood problems (Harburg, Erfrut, Chaperi, Hauenstein, Schull, & Schork, 1973), crowding (Langer & Saegert, 1977), and noise (Glass & Singer, 1972). We have all been confronted by automobiles that won't start on cold mornings, buses that run late, toasters that burn bread, bosses who demand too much in too little time, and neighbors who party too much or too late. Such is the stuff of life. These petty annoyances constitute the daily hassles and can be stressful. Individually they tax us little, but collectively and accumulatively they affect behavioral as well as psychological and physiological responding.

Cataclysmic Events. A second category represents those stressors whose sudden and powerful impact are more or less universal in eliciting a response, and which demand a great deal of effort for effective coping. These stressors, labelled *cataclysmic events*, will be dealt with in greater detail in Chapter 13. Examples include war, natural disasters, and nuclear accidents. These events are unpredictable and powerful and generally affect all who are touched by them. The accident at Three Mile Island, the eruption of Mount St. Helen, a plane crash, the heat wave in the American Southwest, the flooding in Missouri, as well as more common events like tornadoes, hurricanes, and other natural disasters, can be considered in this category of stressors (Baum, et al., 1980; Pennebaker & Newtson, 1983).

Major personal life events. A third group of stressors include those events powerful enough to individually challenge our adaptive abilities. These events include illness, death, or significant loss (psychological or economic). The label attached to this type of stressor is *major personal life events*. See Table 5-1 for a partial listing of some common stressors. The distinction here is important because coping with cataclysmic events entails sharing loss with numerous others, whereas loss sustained by the latter involves only a few people. Further, McGrath (1970), Schacter (1959), and Cobb (1976) have identified affiliative and social comparative behavior as a reasonable means for coping with and understanding the effects of stress; hence, the number of people affected by the stressor may play a critical role in dealing with it. While the old adage that misery loves company may or may not be true, it is most often true that the greater numbers of people who share in the stress of personal life events, the easier they are to deal with.

Ambient stressors. A final class of stressors has been labelled *ambient stressors* and include such environmental background conditions as work overload, poverty, family conflicts, and air pollution. They represent the relatively continuous, stable, and intractable conditions of the environment (Cambell, 1983).

TABLE 5-1   A Partial Listing of Some Common Stressors

Listed below are a number of events that sometimes bring change in the lives of those who experience them and that necessitate social readjustment.

Marriage	Detention in jail or comparable institution
Death of spouse	Major change in sleeping habits
Death of close family member	Major change in eating habits
Foreclosure on mortgage or loan	Death of a close friend
Outstanding personal achievement	Minor law violation
Male: wife/girlfriend pregnant	Female: pregnancy
Changed work situation	New job
Major change in living conditions	Sexual difficulties
Trouble with employer	Trouble with in-laws
Major change in financial status	Major change in closeness of family
Gaining a new family member	Change in residence
Marital separation from mate	Major change in church activities
Marital reconciliation with mate	Being fired from job
Borrowing more than $10,000	Borrowing less than $10,000
Male: girlfriend having abortion	Female: having abortion
Major personal illness or injury	Major change in social activities
Divorce	Serious injury or illness to close friend
Retirement from work	Son or daughter leaving home
Ending of formal schooling	Separation from spouse
Engagement	Breaking up with boy/girlfriend
Leaving home for the first time	Reconciliation with boy/girlfriend

Source: Holmes, T. H., & Rahe, R. H. (1967) The Social Readjustment Rating Scale. *Journal of Psychosomatic Research, 11,* 213–218.

These stressors may go unnoticed until they interfere with some important goal or directly threaten one's health. People habituate to rather than actively attempt to confront these stressors. For example, it is often easier to live with family problems than to seek professional help or dissolve the relationship; it may be easier to breathe polluted air than to take measures to clean it up or to move.

Measuring Stressors: Quantitative Differences

A number of easily recognizable qualitative differences exist among these categories of stressors and these have been alluded to in the above paragraphs. However, there are also a number of quantifiable dimensions among and within these categories that can be expected to lead to differential responding and therefore need to be considered. Consequently, we now turn our attention to such variables as intensity, duration, rate, and controllability. Furthermore, we will suggest some ways in which these variables might be measured as well as their possible relationships to behavior.

Intensity.   Intensity of the stressor refers in some sense to the "power" of the stimulus. Intensity can be "measured," for example, in terms of the magnitude or frequency (loudness or pitch) of sound, the concentration (parts per million) of a pollutant, the velocity of the wind, or the temperature or relative humidity of the atmosphere. It can also be measured in terms of its physical effects; for example, the number of homes destroyed in a flood, the number of persons killed by a tornado, the number of victims hospitalized as a result of a nuclear accident, or the number of birth defects resulting from water contamination.

It is generally assumed that the greater the intensity of the stressor, the greater the resulting stress response. And while this may be a warranted assumption, much more research needs to be done to determine if the functional relationship between intensity of the stressor and magnitude of the stress response is exponential, linear, curvilinear, or perhaps even some form of step function. Throughout the remainder of this text we will, where the data allow, suggest the probable form of these functions.

Duration.   Independent of the intensity of the stressor is its impact with regard to time. The immediate presence of a tornado, for example, is relatively short (perhaps only a few minutes), but its intensity is great. On the other hand, an airborne pollutant (such as asbestos) might have a low concentration, yet be ever-present. Duration and intensity, it can be seen, are independent dimensions. All other things being equal, we can expect stressors of long duration to have a greater effect on the stress response than stressors of short duration. However, the accumulative effect of low-level stressors over long periods of time may result in deceptively severe consequences. Any consideration of the potential effects of an identified stressor, therefore, has to take into account both the duration of the stressor and its intensity.

Rate.   While some stressors occur but once, many are recurring. Their periodicity can be regular or irregular, predictable or unpredictable, and short-phased or long-phased. For example, residents of a floodplain may expect that flooding will occur, but only in the spring of the year (perhaps on average once in ten years). This stressor is thus irregular and therefore unpredictable, with a relatively long phase. By comparison, the 3:15 A.M. freight train that rumbles past your apartment, alerting cars at the nearby corner with its silence-piercing whistle, is regular (3:15 every morning) and therefore predictable and has a short phase (every 24 hours).

While very little empirical data has accumulated with respect to the influence of phase length on the stress response, there is some evidence to suggest that both regularity and predictability lead to increases in the stress of anticipation, but can also lead to decreases in overall stress by allowing for the careful selection of coping strategies (e.g., adaptation or habituation).

Controllability.   Stressors vary with respect to the degree of control humans have over them. It is possible to exert some control over the temperature of our indoor environments, over the noise level of our offices, and even over the traffic we have to drive in. We do this by turning the thermostat either up or down, by putting sound-damping or sound-absorbing equipment in our offices and by choosing the times of the day and the routes to take to avoid traffic. It is not possible to exert control over other stressors. We cannot stop a hurricane; we cannot prevent an earthquake. There are still other stressors where it is possible, theoretically, to exert control, but practically we are unable to (e.g., the loud stereo in the adjacent apartment, or the litter in the streets below). Researchers have shown that the lack of control over environmental stressors where it is possible to have it can exacerbate the stress response.

In our discussion of environmental stressors throughout this text we will again and again be looking at potential stressors in terms of their intensity, duration, rate, predictability, and controllability, and we will be calling for additional means of measuring these characteristics.

Measuring Stress: The Immediate Response

Physiological and Somatic Responses.   The most common measures of stress allow inferences about emotional states by assessing physiological reactivity. This has been done directly by measuring levels of catecholamines (e.g., adrenaline, noradrenaline) and corticosteroids in the blood or urine (e.g., Frankenhaeuser, 1978), and indirectly by measuring systematic reactions caused by increased levels of these hormones (e.g., Ax, 1953). Increased cardiovascular reactivity (i.e., faster heart rate, higher blood pressure), muscle potential changes, and skin conductance measures have also been used to show the effects of acute stress.

These somatic correlates of stress are important for a number of reasons. First, increased catecholamine and corticosteroid secretion is associated with a wide range of other physiological responses, such as the aforementioned changes in heart rate, blood pressure, breathing, muscle potential, and other autonomic functions. Prolonged or sudden elevation of circulating catecholamines may damage body tissue. Catecholamines also appear to affect cognitive and emotional functioning, and elevated levels of epinephrine or norepinephrine in the blood may affect our mood and behavior.

Cannon (1929, 1931) suggested that adrenaline has a salutary effect on adaptation; by arousing the organism, adrenaline provides a biological advantage to the organism, enabling it to respond more rapidly to danger. When we are extremely frightened we experience an arousal that, although possibly uncomfortable, readies us to act against the thing that scares us. Thus, stress-related increases in catecholamines may facilitate adaptive behavior. In fact, studies have shown superior performance on tasks following epinephrine infusion (Frankenhaeuser, Jarpe, & Mattell, 1961). However, arousal has also been associated with impaired performance on complex tasks (cf. Evans, 1978). In any event, it is clear that arousal influences behavior.

Measuring Stress: The Long-Term Response

Stress and Illness.   Studies of stress and illness provide additional evidence of the negative effects of stress. While illness traditionally has been viewed as a biological phenomenon, there seem to be diseases that do not fit within a strict biomedical model (i.e., they do not appear to be the result of specific physiological dysfunction or an invasion by some foreign substance). Diseases of *life style*, such as heart disease, seem to be related to patterns of coping that characterize behavior. Hypertension, heart disease, and the like are not contagious; they do not seem to be caused by germs, microbes, or other simple infection-causing mechanisms. Rather, they develop over a person's lifetime and are contributed to by a number of factors including responses to stress.

Dohrenwend & Dohrenwend (1981) have conceptualized the possible processes whereby stress induces adverse health changes (see Figure 5-4). In this figure, Model A contains no intervening processes. Rather, it postulates a simple and direct effect of stressful events on health. It further suggests that the effects of stressful life events are cumulative, thus accounting for studies of extreme situations, such as combat or incarceration in concentration camps. Other severe stresses over which an individual has no control, such as the death of a loved one, are also accounted for by this model. This model is called the *victimization hypothesis*. Model B, the *stress-strain hypothesis*, postulates that psychophysiological strain mediates the impact of life events on subsequent health and illness. Evidence in support of this hypothesis comes from studies that show that if the effects of symptoms of psychophysiological straining are eliminated, correlations of stressful life events scores and measures of illness are significantly reduced (Bloom, 1985). This model is most closely related to the conceptualization of stress in this text.

Model C, the *vulnerability hypothesis*, suggests that there are preexisting personal dispositions and social conditions which moderate the causal relation between stressful life events and health. It is this model that suggests to researchers a search for such mediating factors as the strength of social support systems, optimism, locus of control, etc. Model D, by contrast, postulates that personal dispositions and social conditions make independent causal contributions to the occurrence of pathology. This model suggest that personality variables and/or social conditions are a potential source of added burden to the individual in the precipitation of illness and is thus called the *added burden hypothesis*. Model E proposes that transitory life events have no role in precipitating illness, but rather that stable personal characteristics and social conditions by themselves cause adverse health changes. This model is called the *chronic burden hypothesis*. Finally, Model F portrays stressful life events as exacerbating already existent health disorders. It is called the *event proneness hypothesis* because stressful life events are thought to characterize individuals who are already ill.

Research on the relationships between stress and illness has been conducted in several settings and at different levels. Early research, for example, considered the stress of the mass bombings of London during World War II, and the stress associated with the German concentration camps. Many survivors of these brutalities showed relatively permanent adjustment problems. Others showed elevated blood pressures during initial exposure, greater physical illness later, and a greater incidence of premature or sudden death than did people their age who did not undergo the stressful experience.

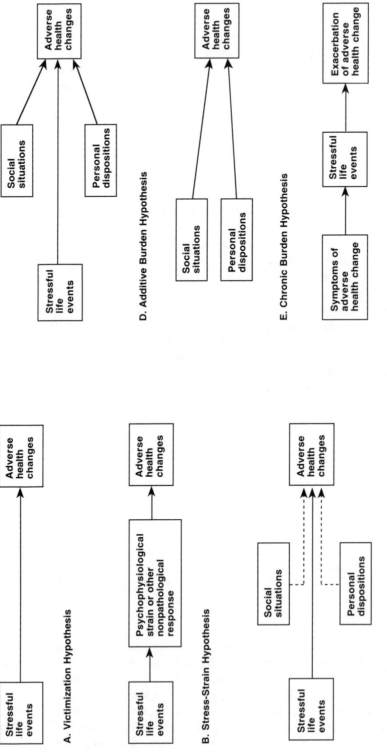

FIGURE 5-4 Six hypotheses about the life stress process.
From Dohrenwend, B.S., and Dohrenwend, B.P. (eds.), *Stressful Life Events and Their Contexts.* Neale Watson Academic Publications, Inc. (1981).

Other studies (Reynolds, 1974; Warheit, 1974) reveal dramatic examples of stress-related illness and death. Research conducted at the space center at Cape Kennedy during the last years of this country's moon program considered base employees who monitored moon missions from the ground. Increased rates of alcoholism and divorce were observed as pressure to complete the mission increased. More seriously, there was a spontaneous increase in sudden deaths among the relatively young workers. These deaths, presumably caused by heart failure, were nearly 50 percent more frequent than the average for that age group. The sudden deaths peaked as the space program was being phased out and, as Eliot and Buell (1979) note, "was most notable during the year when space employees were fired more often than rockets."

Research on stress and the human immune system has revealed some extremely interesting findings. The immune system manufactures antibodies to fight against invasions of bacteria, viruses, allergens, and even cancerous cells. Evidence suggests that functioning of the immune system is impaired while a person is experiencing stress, thus leaving the individual more vulnerable to disease (Jemmott & Locke, 1984). One study involving college students found that secretions of immunoglobulin (an antibody that fights against upper respiratory infections) were lower when the students were under stress (during midterm and final exams). Their rate of respiratory infection also was up during these same periods (Jemmott, Borysenko, McClelland, Chapman, Meyer, & Benson, 1983). Higher stress levels have also been shown to be related to low T-lymphocyte responsiveness (Zautra, Okun, Robinson, Lee, Roth, & Emmanual, 1989) and to a greater spread of cancer through the lymph nodes (Morris, Greer, Pettingale, & Watson, 1981).

Generally speaking, illness as a function of stress is a result of the stress response more than it is a part of it. If stress is sufficiently prolonged, repeated long enough, or severe enough to resist adaptation, illnesses such as Selye's diseases of adaptation are more likely. To some extent, these are directly caused by the continuous high level of physiological responding characteristic of stress. This is analogous to a car's engine continuously racing at high RPMs. Eventually, this overactivity will cause engine breakdown. Chronically elevated levels of catecholamines, blood pressure, or gastric acid can cause a number of diseases. Reduced efficacy of the immune system can cause or exacerbate others. The important point is that the stress process can predispose an organism to illness or death.

Measuring Stress: Psychological Assessment

Psychological Measures.   Psychological measurement of the stress response has focused on various psychiatric symptoms and has utilized a variety of standard psychiatric symptom inventories. The common denominator among the various scales seems to be the extent to which respondents perceive themselves to be in an intractable situation marked by negative affect and a degree of uncertainty. Among the more widely used psychological measures of stress are the Hopkins

Symptom Checklist, a self-report measure incorporating the dimensions of obsessive-compulsiveness, hostility, depression, somatization, and anxiety (see, for example, Derogatis, Rickels, & Rock, 1976), the State-Trait Anxiety Inventory (see Spielberger, 1972), the Demoralization Scale (see Dohrewend, Dohrewend, Kasl, & Warheit, 1980), and the Life Experience Scale (see Sarason, Johnson, & Siegel, 1978).

These scales, collectively, reflect distress arising from perceptions of bodily dysfunction. Complaints focus on cardiovascular, gastrointestinal, and respiratory systems with such manifestations as headaches, pain and discomfort localized in gross musculature. They also tap such behaviors and feelings as restlessness, nervousness, free-floating anxiety, panic, aggression, rage, and resentment. Thoughts, impulses, and actions that are experienced as unremitting and irresistible but are simultaneously ego-alien and unwanted are also assessed. Finally, some attempt is made to have respondents identify the sources of their feelings and the impact that each of these sources may have.

Measures of Coping.   The level of stress a person experiences and the extent to which deleterious effects occur as a result of exposure to a stressor will depend, in part, on how well the individual copes with the stressor. The theoretical literature (e.g., Lazarus & Folkman, 1984) as well as the practitioner literature (Switzer, 1979) acknowledge this. Empirical studies, however, are rare, owing in great part to a lack of scales with known psychometric properties or verified construct validity. At a conceptual level it is possible to think of coping as taking one or more of several forms, each focusing on some aspect of the stress situation. For example, individuals can engage in behaviors that attempt to alter the situation (in a cold environment the individual can change the thermostat setting, go to another room, put on another layer of clothing), they can attempt to manage or reduce the emotional distress (they can focus on the energy they are saving, they can convince themselves that colder environments are healthier), or they can attempt to manage the symptoms of stress by relaxation or diet or exercise. Scales that tap into these modes of dealing with stress are, at best, in the formative stage (see Latack, 1986).

Rather than focusing on scales that are intended to measure coping strategies, a second way of dealing with these issues is to consider the side effects of coping independent of the particular strategy being used. It is to these side effects that we next turn.

Behavioral Coping Responses.   As already noted, stress can cause both cognitive deficits and improved performance. Cognitive deficits may in turn be caused by behavioral strategies that are used for coping—the person exposed to loud noise may "tune out" or narrow his or her field of attention (Cohen, 1978; Deutsch, 1964). But the same behavior may render us unable to concentrate or unwilling to put effort into a task (e.g., Glass & Singer, 1972). As exposure to stress increases, the adaptive reserves are depleted, causing aftereffects and reductions of subsequent coping ability. Evidence for the existence of poststressor effects comes from a number of sources, including research on the effects of noise (e.g., Glass & Singer, 1972; Rotton, Oszewski, Charleton, & Soler, 1978; Sherrod & Downs, 1974; Sherrod, Hage, Halpern, & Moore, 1977), crowding (Evans, 1979; Sherrod, 1974), and electric shock (Glass, Singer, Leonard, Krantz, Cohen, & Cummings, 1973).

Aftereffects that occur after exposure to a stressor include decreases in cognitive functioning and tolerance for frustration, increased aggressiveness, helplessness, decreased sensitivity to others, and withdrawal (Cohen, 1980). These postexposure consequences appear to be affected by perception of control during exposure to the stressor, with fewer aftereffects following experiences in which participants felt that they had control. One explanation for this is that aftereffects are related to the amount of effort expended in coping with a stressor. Because perceived control appears to ease the difficulties posed by a stressor, it should reduce the effort needed to adapt, and therefore reduce aftereffects. Thus, costs of adaptation may be reflected by aftereffects, and we should be careful to look for them even when people seem to have successfully coped with a stressor.

MODERATORS OF THE STRESS RESPONSE

The extent to which a stressor produces adverse effects has been shown to be moderated by attitudes toward the stressor, perceived control over it, the general level of fitness of the individual, as well as by the support system that the individual has available. As these factors will increase or decrease a stressor's impact, we turn now to a discussion of them.

Attitudes Toward the Source of Stress

As mentioned earlier, responses to stressors are necessarily related to the way in which a stressor is perceived. Attitudes toward the source of the stress are important psychological factors and act as filtering devices that moderate perception of the stressor. For example, high levels of noise are generally recognized as potent environmental stressors (Glass & Singer, 1972). Although noise levels in areas surrounding airports are highly correlated with noise annoyance reported by residential groups in these areas, the relationship between noise exposure and individual ratings of annoyance is generally not strong (Wilson 1963). Tracor, Inc. (1971) found that individual annoyance ratings were more highly correlated with several attitudinal measures than they were with the various indices of physical exposure to noise. In a number of studies, attitudinal measures account for up to a third of the variance in response to noise, and that the addition of attitudinal measures increases the predictability of annoyance to between 58 percent and 65 percent (Leonard & Borsky, 1973; Tracor, Inc., 1971).

There is even some evidence that manipulating attitudes changes people's evaluation of their environment (Cederlof, Honsson, & Sorenson, 1967). Fear of nearby airplane crashes seems to be the single most powerful predictor of individual annoyance in response to airport noise. Attitudes toward nuclear power are also related to its perceived costs and benefits. In a survey of residents in Truesdale County, Tennessee, where Tennessee Valley Authority officials planned to construct a nuclear power plant, it was found that supporters of the plant felt economic benefits would be more likely to result than did opponents of the plant. Opponents rated the disruptive effects of population growth and hazards to safety and environment as more likely than did supporters. The same process appears to have been active at Three Mile Island. Evaluation, thus, is a function of the balance between perceived benefit and cost. To the extent that cost is weighed heavily, attitudes may become more negative (see Chapters 4 and 14) and heightened stress is likely to occur.

Control

Perceived control is another powerful psychological mediator of stress, providing a sense of being able to cope effectively, to predict events, and to determine consequences before they happen. Glass and Singer (1972) considered the effects of perceived controllability and predictability in their studies of stress due to noise and found that predictable or controllable noise exacted smaller costs in adaptation. The perception that the noise might be accurately anticipated or even turned off, if desired, facilitated adaptation with minimal aftereffects. Subsequently, Sherrod (1974) found the same relationship for stress due to crowding, and Rodin, Solomon, and Metcalf (1978) found that providing control reduced crowding stress.

A study by Staub, Tursky, and Schwartz (1971) has some relevance here. Subjects who were given perceived control over shocks reported less discomfort than did subjects who did not control the intensity or administration of the shock. This was so even though all subjects actually received the same number and intensity of shocks and the "control" subjects did not actually exercise their control. The perception of control seemed to affect perception of the stressor used in this study. Similarly, Veitch (1976) found that residents of northwest Ohio who had individual control over the thermostat settings in their homes and apartments reported fewer ill effects of reduced residential temperatures in the winter months than those who did not have such control. Finally, evidence from Phifer (1990) suggests that such symptomology as gastrointestinal disorders, headaches, and susceptibility to infectious diseases is enhanced, if not caused by, inability to control environmental stressors.

Somewhat more direct evidence of control influencing appraisal of stressors comes from the growing literature on cognitive control. By providing subjects with information about a stressor prior to their exposure to it, researchers have been able to reduce the threat appraisal made when the stressor is experienced. Some studies have considered medical settings and have found that the stress of surgery or of unusual medical procedures can be reduced by providing patients with accurate expectations of what they will feel (e.g., Johnson, 1973, 1984; Johnson & Leventhal, 1974; Taylor & Clark, 1986). By giving normative information about sensations to patients, researchers have provided them with "road maps" telling them what they may expect. As a result, when these sensations are experienced they will not be appraised as abnormal or frightening. Other studies have found that accurate expectations also reduce crowding stress (Baum, Fisher, & Solomon, 1981; Langer & Saegert, 1977). Inaccurate or violated expectations of crowding result in some negative responses (Greenberg & Baum, 1979).

Patient well-being and the effectiveness of medical treatment can also be improved by giving patients some choice in their treatment program (Miller & Mangan, 1983; Mendonca & Brehm, 1983). It would appear that providing patients with preparatory information or with some choice about the treatment they will receive can increase their feelings of control, self-confidence, and motivation and thus improve the effectiveness with which they deal with certain types of stressors. There is evidence, however, that shows that sometimes distraction and emotional disengagement may be more adequate coping strategies than the attention, involvement, and sense of personal responsibility provided by increased control. Carey and Burish (1988) have shown that distraction helps cancer patients undergoing chemotherapy from focusing on a variety of psychological side effects. Ludwick-Rosenthal and Neufeld (1988) suggest that the benefits of control must be balanced against its potential costs, and Ward, Leventhal, and Love (1988) caution that the short-term benefits of avoidance and denial must be weighed against their potential for long-term damage. Obviously, there is no universally beneficial treatment approach.

As a general rule, though, it can be said that to the extent that people have either real or perceived control over environmental stressors or are provided with accurate expectations (real or perceived) regarding those environmental events, the resultant stress will be reduced either in the appraisal stage of the stress process or in the coping stage. Any condition of the environment or information with respect to it that increases the person's sense of personal control should have a salutary effect on the stress response and should be sought after and developed where possible.

The Hardy Personality

Two additional factors that moderate the effects of stressors are the general level of fitness and the personality of the individual involved. Generally, the more one exercises, the greater one's physical fitness (endurance, strength, and maintenance of good physical condition), the less the chances for illness (Roth, Wiebe, Fillingim, & Shay, 1989). In addition to the physiological system being in "better shape" to withstand stress, it has been suggested that those individuals who are fit experience less cognitive and physiological arousal when confronting stress (McGilley & Holmes, 1988).

Often coupled with good physical fitness is a psychological factor involving a sense of commitment, the perception of difficult situations as challenges and opportunities, and the belief that one has control over one's life. This

FIGURE 5-5 Generally, the greater one's physical fitness the less debilitating are stressful situations.

factor has been labelled *hardiness* (Kobasa, 1979), and is related to what Zimmerman (1990) has called *learned hopefulness*: knowing how to solve problems paired with a sense of control. Contrada (1989) has shown that persons fitting the description of being "hardy" tend not to be overwhelmed by difficult situations; rather, they are spurred on to seek solutions, to be constructive. As a result, they experience less stress, contract fewer illnesses, and have lower blood pressure. Less hardy, more pessimistic individuals, on the other hand, report more symptoms of illness after experiencing stressful events (Scheier & Carver, 1987) and die at earlier ages (Peterson, Seligman, & Vaillant, 1988).

Social Support

In Chapter 13 we will discuss at length the role of social support in helping people to cope with natural disasters and technological catastrophes. For now we will content ourselves with providing a few suggestions as to why social support networks might be expected to ameliorate the effects of stressful events. The most obvious way in which a social support network operates is that "many hands make light the work." Clearly, it there are more people working on "cleaning up" the effects of a tornado, each individual person has less of the burden on his or her shoulders. Cohen and Ashbey-Wills (1985) suggest that social networks operate in two ways. First, people who have social support are generally healthier to begin with, and second, when confronted by a stressful event, others in the network can act as a buffer providing comfort and encouragement and, if necessary, food and money (Pilisuk, Boylan, & Acredolo, 1987). Additionally, others in an interpersonal network provide opportunities for self-disclosure (Pennebaker, Hughes, & O'Heron, 1987), expressing emotion (Pennebaker & Beall, 1986), and problem solving (Costanza, Derlaga, & Winstead, 1988), all of which allow individuals to more effectively cope with stress.

The Relaxation Response

Just as stress can be thought of as a nonspecific response by the body to any demand that is made upon it, there is growing evidence that there is an anti-stress response, a relaxation response (Benson, 1975). Benson finds that in this response muscle tension decreases, cortical activity decreases, heart rate and blood pressure decrease, and breathing slows. The stimuli needed to produce this response, according to Benson, include a quiet environment, closed eyes, a comfortable body position, and a repetitive mental device. The first three factors lower afferent input to the nervous system, while the fourth lowers the internal stimulation to the nervous system. These conditions allow the body to reach a low level of arousal and to recuperate from stress. Benson suggests that these four conditions are met by most traditional and religious techniques of meditation and prayer, and further asserts that in addition to whatever spiritual function they may serve, such techniques directly promote recuperation from stress. Transcendental meditation, biofeedback techniques, some forms of verbal self feedback, and certain group experiences also appear to share these qualities and may account, in part, for their success in dealing with stress.

THE ROLE OF STRESS IN UNDERSTANDING ORGANISM-ENVIRONMENT RELATIONSHIPS

Stress is characterized as a process that unfolds as we encounter a stressor, become aware of its danger, mobilize our efforts to cope with it, engage in confronting it, and succeed or fail in adapting to it. This process follows a logical sequence (see Figure 5-6). The danger posed by a stressor is evaluated; strategies are selected to cope with it; the body mobilizes itself psychologically as well as physiologically to combat the stressor; and the coping is put into action. If coping behavior is successful, adaptation is achieved, and the effects of the stress diminish. If coping is unsuccessful, stress persists, physiological arousal and psychological arousal are not reduced, and pathological end states (gastrointestinal disorders, cardiac malfunction, psychological disorders, etc.) are made increasingly likely.

All of this should sound repetitive with the model for understanding organism/environment relationships detailed in Chapter 2. While most of the time the organism operates in equilibrium with its environment (i.e., is not

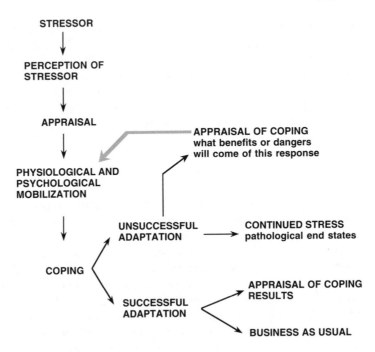

FIGURE 5-6 The stress response including secondary appraisal processes (fashioned after Monat & Lazarus, 1977).

stressed by it), there are times when the relationship is stressed. Indeed, stress can be thought of as "disequilibrium." There are times when either the environment presents too great a challenge or the organism has depleted its coping capabilities, or both. It is at these times when the relationship is in disequilibrium. Whether or not this disequilibrium occurs depends on a number of physical, psychological, and physiological processes, not the least of which is the process of perception as described in Chapter 4 and the affective processes as described in the present chapter.

Throughout the remainder of this text we will be looking at elements of the environment that, other things being equal, can influence these processes to create disequilibrium or promote equilibrium in the organism/environment relationship. We will see, for example, how sound under certain conditions can be perceived as noise and how this perception in turn influences psychological and physiological responding to the source of that noise. Similarly, we will look at other environmental elements including atmospheric conditions, population density, architectural design, and technological developments. In short, there are many aspects of the environment that may act to produce stress. We will attempt to elucidate the conditions when this is likely to occur and to discern those individuals who are most likely to be affected. Finally, we will attempt to suggest ways of preventing either stress or its adverse effects, assuming it cannot be avoided.

TIME-OUT: Remember Jill? We met her in a *Time-Out* back in Chapter 2. She's the small-town girl now sharing an apartment next to the railroad in the suburbs and commuting to City University. Go back and read about her to see if you can identify sources of stress in her life. Specifically, analyze her life experiences in terms of the concepts and measures presented in the present chapter. What do you think the short-term effects of these stressors might be? What about the long-term effects?

How might you conduct a study to determine the effects of these stressors on behavior, generally. Identify your independent and dependent variables, operationalize them in terms of how you would measure them. How would you test for the reliability of your data? for the validity of your measurements? Finally, what do you think this data would look like, and how would it contribute to our understanding of the role of stress in understanding environment/organism relationships?

SUMMARY

Stress is a term that has entered common nomenclature in the past two decades. Numerous accounts of stress have found their way into print, and newspaper and magazine articles stressing instructions for coping with stress and featuring personality tests to see how well individuals can stand it dot the newsstands. Often these accounts go beyond the pale of what is scientifically known regarding the processes involved in stress production and management.

Recent research makes it clear, though, that stress does indeed exist, that it is not just a catchy term used to account for the unaccountable. It is also clear that stress involves the interaction of physical, psychological, physiological, and behavioral systems, and it therefore must be considered in relational terms. Furthermore, it is becoming ever clearer that our understanding of organism/environment relationships is enhanced when stress is thought of as a mediator among these systems.

In the next chapter we will look at the atmospheric environment and will show how, at times, extremes in temperature and/or humidity, wind, available sunshine, and ion concentration can influence human performance and feelings of well-being. We will further show how these interrelationships can be understood by utilizing the stress construct.

IMPORTANT CONCEPTS

stress as response, stimulus
primary appraisal
secondary appraisal
arousal
reticular activating system (RAS)

major personal life events
ambient stressors
catecholamines
corticosteroids
victimization hypothesis

general adaptation syndrome (GAS)
  alarm reaction
  stage of resistance
  stage of exhaustion
daily hassles
cataclysmic events

stress-strain hypothesis
vulnerability hypothesis
added burden hypothesis
chronic burden hypothesis
event proneness hypothesis
control

REFERENCES

Ax, A.F. (1953). The physiological differentiation between fear and anger in humans. *Psychosomatic Medicine, 15*, 433–442.

Baum, A., Fisher, J.D., & Solomon, S. (1981) Type of information, familiarity, and the reduction of crowding stress. *Journal of Personality and Social Psychology, 40*, 11–23.

Baum, A., Gatchel, R., Streufert, S., Baum, C.S., Fleming, R., & Singer, J.E. (1980). *Psychological stress for alternatives of decontamination of TMI-2 reactor building atmosphere.* U.S. Nuclear Regulatory Commission (NUREG/CR-1584).

Baum, A., & Greenberg, C.I. (1975). Waiting for a crowd: The behavioral and perceptual effects of anticipated crowding. *Journal of Personality and Social Psychology, 32*, 667–671.

Baum, A., Singer, J.E., & Baum, C.S. (1981). Stress and the environment. *Journal of Social Issues, 37*, 4–35.

Beck, R.C. (1983). *Motivation: Theories and principles* (2nd ed.). Englewood Cliffs, N.J.: Prentice Hall.

Benson, H. (1975). *The relaxation response.* New York: Morrow.

Bloom, B.L. (1985). *Stressful life event theory and research: Implications for primary prevention.* Rockville, Md: National Institute of Mental Health.

Campbell, J.M. (1983). Ambient stressors. *Environment and Behavior, 15*, 355–380.

Cannon, W.B. (1929). *Bodily changes in pain, hunger, fear, and rage.* Boston: Branford.

Cannon, W.B. (1931). Studies in the conditions of activity in the endocrine organs. XXVII. Evidence that the medulliadrenal secretion is not continuous. *Journal of Physiology, 98*, 447–452.

Carey, M.P., & Burish, T.G. (1988). Etiology and treatment of the psychological side effects associated with cancer chemotherapy: A critical review and discussion. *Psychological Bulletin, 104*, 307–325.

Cederlof, R., Honsson, E., & Sorenson, S. (1967). On the influence of attitudes toward the source of annoyance reactions to noise: A field experiment. *Nordisk Hygiensk Tidskrift, 48*, 46–55.

Cobb, S. (1976). Social support as a moderator of life stress. *Psychosomatic Medicine, 38*, 300–314.

Cohen, S. (1978). Environmental load and the allocation of attention. In A. Baum, J.E. Singer, & S. Valins (Eds.), *Advances in environmental psychology* (Vol.1). Hillsdale, N.J.: Erlbaum.

Cohen, S. (1980). Aftereffects of stress on human performance and social behavior: A review of research and theory. *Psychological Bulletin, 87*, 578–604.

Cohen, S., & Ashby-Wills, T. (1985). Stress, social support, and the buffering hypothesis. *Psychological Bulletin, 98*, 310–357.

Cohen, S., Evans, G.W., Stokols, D., & Krantz, D.S. (1986). *Behavior, health and environmental stress,* New York: Plenum.

Contrada, R.J. (1989). Type A behavior, personality hardiness, and cardiovascular responses to stress. *Journal of Personality and Social Psychology, 57*, 895–903.

Costanza, R.S., Derlaga, V.J., & Winstead, B.A. (1988). Positive and negative forms of social support: Effects of conversation topics on coping with stress among same-sex friends. *Journal of Experimental Social Psychology, 24*, 182–193.

Derogatis, L.R., Rickels, K., & Rock, A.F. (1976). SCL-90 and MMPI-Step in validation of a new self-report scale. *British Journal of Psychiatry, 128*, 280–289.

Deutsch, C.P. (1964). Auditory discrimination and learning: Social factors. *The Merrill-Palmer Quarterly in Behavior and Development, 10*, 277–296.

Dohrenwend, B.S., & Dohrenwend, B.F. (1981). *Stressful life events and their contexts.* New York: Prodist.

Dohrenwend, B.P., Dohrenwend, B.S., Kasl, S.V.,

& Warheit, G.J. (1980, October) *Report of the Task Group on Behavioral Effects to the President's Commission on the Accident at Three Mile Island.* Washington, D.C.

Evans, G.W. (1978). Human spatial behavior: The arousal model. In A. Baum & Y. Epstein (Eds.), *Human response to crowding.* Hillsdale, N.J.: Erlbaum.

Evans, G.W. (1979). Behavioral and physiological consequences of crowding in humans. *Journal of Applied Social Psychology, 9,* 27–46.

Evans, G.W., & Cohen, S. (1987). Environmental stress. In D. Stokols & I. Altman (Eds.), *Handbook of environmental psychology* (Vol. l). New York: John Wiley.

Frankenhaeuser, M. (1978). *Coping with job stress: A psychobiological approach.* Report from the Department of Psychology, University of Stockholm, 532.

Frankenhaeuser, M., Jarpe, G., & Mattel, G. (1961). Effects of intravenous infusions of adrenaline and noradrenaline on certain psychological functions. *Acta Physiologica Scandanavia, 51,* 175–186.

Glass, D.C., & Singer, J.E. (1972). *Urban stress.* New York: Academic Press.

Glass, D.C., Singer, J.E., Leonard, H.S., Krantz, D., Cohen, S., & Cummings, H. (1973). Perceived control of aversive stimulation and the reduction of stress responses. *Journal of Personality, 41,* 577–595.

Greenberg, C.I., & Baum, A. (1979). A compensatory response to anticipated densities. *Journal of Applied Social Psychology, 9,* 1–12.

Harburg, E., Erfrut, J.C., Chaperi, C., Hauenstein, L.S., Schull, W.J., & Schork, M.A. (1973). Socioecological stressor areas and black-white blood pressure. *Journal of Chronic Diseases, 26,* 595–611.

Holmes, T.H., & Rahe, R.H. (1967). The social readjustment rating scale. *Journal of Psychosomatic Research, 11,* 213–218.

Jemmott, J.B., III, Borysenko, M., McClelland, D.C., Chapman, R., Meyer, D., & Benson, H. (1983). Academic stress, power motivation, and decrease in salivary secretory immunoglobulin A secretion rate. *Lancet, 1,* 1400–1402.

Jemmott, J.B., III, & Locke, S.E. (1984). Psychosocial factors, immunologic mediation, and human susceptibility to infectious diseases: How much do we know? *Psychological Bulletin, 85,* 78–101.

Johnson, J.E. (1973). Effects of accurate expectations about sensations on the sensory and distress components of pain. *Journal of Personality and Social Psychology, 27,* 261–275.

Johnson, J.E., (1984). Psychological interventions and coping with surgery. In A. Baum, S.E. Taylor, & J.E. Singer (Eds.), *Handbook of psychology and health* (Vol. 4, pp. 167–187). Hillsdale, N.J.: Erlbaum.

Johnson, J.E., & Leventhal, H. (1974). Effects of accurate expectations and behavioral instructions on reactions during a noxious medical examination. *Journal of Personality and Social Psychology, 29,* 710–718.

Kasl, S.V., & Cobb, S. (1970). Blood pressure changes in men undergoing job loss: A preliminary report. *Psychosomatic Medicine, 32,* 19–38.

Kobasa, S.C. (1979). Stressful life events, personality, and health: An inquiry into hardiness. *Journal of Personality and Social Psychology, 37,* 1–11.

Langer, E., & Saegert, S. (1977). Crowding and cognitive control. *Journal of Personality and Social Psychology, 35,* 175–182.

Latack, J.C. (1986). Coping with job stress: Measures and future directions for scale development. *Journal of Applied Psychology, 71,* 377–385.

Lazarus, R. (1966). *Psychological stress and the coping process.* New York: McGraw-Hill.

Lazarus, R.S., & Folkman, S. (1984). *Stress, appraisal, and coping.* New York: Springer-Verlag.

Leonard, S., & Borsky, P.N. (1973). A causal model for relating noise exposure, psychosocial variables and aircraft noise and aircraft noise annoyance. In W. Ward (Ed.), *Proceedings of the International Congress on Noise as a Public Health Problem.* Washington, D.C.: Environmental Protection Agency.

Ludwick-Rosenthal, R., & Neufeld, R.W.J. (1988). Stress management during noxious medical procedures: An evaluative review of outcome studies. *Psychological Bulletin, 104,* 326–342.

McGilley, B.M., & Holmes, D.S. (1988). Aerobic fitness and response to psychological stress. *Journal of Research in Personality, 22,* 129–139.

McGrath, J.E. (1970). *Social and psychological factors in stress.* New York: Holt, Rinehart & Winston.

Mendonca, P.J., & Brehm, S.S. (1983). Effects of choice on behavioral treatment of overweight children. *Journal of Social and Clinical Psychology, 1,* 343–358.

Miller, S.M., & Mangan, C.E. (1983). Interacting effects of information and coping style in adapting to gynecologic stress: Should the doctor tell all? *Journal of Personality and Social Psychology, 45*, 223–236.

Monat, A., & Lazarus, R. (1977). *Stress and coping: An anthology.* New York: Columbia University Press.

Morris, T. , Greer, S., Pettingale, K.W., & Watson, M. (1981). Patterns of expression of anger and their psychological correlates in women with breast cancer. *Journal of Psychosomatic Research, 25*, 111–117.

Pearlin, L.I., & Schooler, C. (1978). The stress of coping. *Journal of Health and Social Behavior, 19*, 2–21.

Pennebaker, J.W., & Beall, S. (1986). Confronting a traumatic event: Toward an understanding of inhibition and disease. *Journal of Abnormal Psychology, 95*, 274–281.

Pennebaker, J.W., Hughes, C.F., & O'Heron, R.C. (1987). The psychophysiology of confession: Linking inhibitory and psychosomatic processes. *Journal of Personality and Social Psychology, 52*, 781–793.

Pennebaker, J.W. & Newtson, D. (1983). Observation of a unique event: The psychological impact of the Mount Saint Helens's volcano. In H.T. Reiss (Ed.), *Naturalistic approaches to studying social interaction. New directions for methodology of social and behavioral science* (No. 15). San Francisco: Jossey-Bass.

Peterson, C., Seligman, M.E.P., & Vaillant, G. (1988). Pessimistic explanatory style is a risk factor for physical illness: A thirty-five-year longitudinal study. *Journal of Personality and Social Psychology, 55*, 23–27.

Phifer, J.F. (1990). Psychological distress and somatic symptoms after natural disasters: Differential vulnerability among older adults. *Psychology and Aging, 5* (3), 412–420.

Pilisuk, M., Boylan, R., & Acredolo, C. (1987). Social support, life stress, and subsequent medical care utilization. *Health Psychology, 6*, 273–288.

Reynolds, R.C. (1974). Community and occupational influences in stress at Cape Kennedy: Relationships to heart disease. In R.S. Eliot (Ed.), *Stress and the heart.* Mt. Kisko, N.Y.: Future.

Rodin, J., Solomon, S., & Metcalf, J. (1978). Role of control in mediating perceptions of density. *Journal of Personality and Social Psychology, 36*, 989–999.

Roth, D.L., Wiebe, D.J., Fillingim, R.B., & Shay, K.A. (1989). Life events, fitness, hardiness, and health: A simultaneous analysis of proposed stress-resistance effects. *Journal of Personality and Social Psychology, 57*, 136–142.

Rotton, J., Oszewski, D., Charleton, M., & Soler, E. (1978). Loud speech, conglomerate noise, and behavior after-effects. *Journal of Applied Psychology, 63*, 360–365.

Sarason, I.G., Johnson, J.H., & Siegel, J.M. (1978). Assessing the impact of life changes: development of the life experiences survey. *Journal of Consulting and Clinical Psychology, 46*, 932–946.

Schacter, S. (1959). *The psychology of affiliation.* Stanford, California: Stanford University Press.

Scheier, M.F., & Carver, C.S. (1987). Dispositional optimism and physical well-being: The influence of generalized outcome expectancies on health. *Journal of Personality, 55*, 169–210.

Selye, H. (1976). *The stress of life.* New York: McGraw-Hill.

Sherrod, D.R. (1974). Crowding, perceived control and behavioral aftereffects. *Journal of Applied Social Psychology, 4*, 171–186.

Sherrod, D.R., & Downs, R. (1974). Environmental determinants of altruism: The effects of stimulus overload and perceived control on helping. *Journal of Experimental Social Psychology, 10*, 468–479.

Sherrod, D.R., Hage, J., Halpern, P.L., & Moore, B.S. (1977). Effects of personal causation and perceived control on responses to an aversive environment: The more control the better. *Journal of Experimental and Social Psychology, 13*, 14–27.

Singer, J.E. (1980). Traditions of stress research: Integrated comments. In E. Sarason & C.O. Spielberger (Eds.), *Stress and anxiety* (Vol. 7). Washington, D.C.: Hemisphere Press.

Spacapan, S. & Cohen, S. (1983). Effects and aftereffects of stressor expectations. *Journal of Personality and Social Psychology, 45*, 1243–1254.

Spielberger, C.D. (1972). Anxiety as an emotional state. In C.D. Spielberger (Ed.), *Anxiety: Current trends in theory and research* (Vol 1). New York: Academic Press.

Stang, S., & Veitch, R. (1985, May). *Anticipatory stress in a potentially toxic environment.* Paper presented at the annual meeting of the Midwestern Psychological Association.

Staub, E., Tursky, B., & Schwartz, G.E. (1971). Self-control and predictability: Their effects of reactions to aversive stimulation. *Journal of Personality and Social Psychology, 18*, 157–162.

Switzer, L. (1979). Gelusil, jogging and gin: How executive educators deal with stress. *Executive Educator, 1,* 27–29.

Taylor, S.E., & Clark, L.F. (1986). Does information improve adjustment to noxious medical procedures? In M.J. Saks & L. Saxe (Eds.), *Advances in applied social psychology* (Vol. 3, pp. 1–28). Hillsdale, N.J.: Erlbaum.

Tracor, Inc. (1971). Community reaction to aircraft noise. (Vol.1) (NASA Report CR-1761). Washington, D.C.: National Aeronautics and Space Administration.

Veitch, R. (1976). *Temperature, thermostatic control, and perceived health.* Unpublished manuscript, Bowling Green State University, Bowling Green, Ohio.

Veitch, R., Stang, S., & Conley, L. (1985). *Stress and technological catastrophes: What are the relationships?* Unpublished document provided to the Northern Ohioans for the Protection of the Environment (NOPE).

Ward, S.E., Leventhal, H., & Love, R. (1988). Repression revisited: Tactics used in coping with a severe health threat. *Personality and Social Psychology Bulletin, 14,* 735–746.

Warheit, G.J. (1974). Occupation: A key factor in stress at the Manned Space Center. In R.S. Eliot (Ed.), *Stress and the heart.* Mt. Kisco, N.Y.: Future.

Wilson, A.H. (1963). *Noise: Final Report of the Committee on the Problem of Noise (Cmnd. 2056).* London: Her Majesty's Stationery Office.

Wolfe, S., & Goodell, H. (1968). *Stress and disease* (2nd ed.). Springfield, Ill.: Chas C Thomas.

Zautra, A.J., Okun, M.A., Robinson, S.E., Lee, D., Roth, S,H., & Emmanual, J. (1989). Life stress and lymphocyte alterations among patients with rheumatoid arthritis. *Health Psychology, 8*(1), 1–14.

Zimmerman, M.A. (1990). Toward a theory of learned hopefulness: A structural model and analysis of participation and empowerment. *Journal of Research in Personality, 24,* 71–86.

The Atmospheric Environment I

Temperature, Humidity, Sunshine, Wind, and Ion Concentration

FIGURE 6-1 Physically, weather can give you a headache or a heart palpitation.

Without doubt, the atmospheric environment includes some of the most conspicuous and seemingly capricious environmental variables in human life. Conditions of ambient temperature, rainfall, humidity, barometric pressure, sunshine, cloud cover, wind chill, and pollution are ever-present and ever-changing. Indeed, a significant segment of the morning and evening news is set aside for the delivery of meteorological information, and often our days are planned on the basis of what is said on these broadcasts. Shall I go to work? to the ball park? on a picnic? Should I take my umbrella? my coat? my sunglasses? Aside from planning our days based on what the weather forecaster has to say, we tend to view atmospheric conditions as constituting hazards at worst ("Hurricane Herkimer, with winds of 140 mph, is approaching the port of New Orleans and can be expected to blow ashore by midday tomorrow"), and as forming idyllic settings at best ("Tomorrow's temperature will be in the mid-70s with a relative humidity of 20 percent; we will have mostly sunny skies and winds out of the southwest at 5 to 10 mph"). Almost a half century ago, though, Berke and Wilson (1951) wrote: " Physically, weather can give you a headache or a heart palpitation; it can send you to the hospital with appendicitis. On the mental side, weather can interfere with your speed in adding up income tax returns; it can set off a crime wave. . .it can raise or lower your IQ." (p. 3). Whether or not the effects of weather are as dramatic as Berke and Wilson suggest, it is widely assumed that atmospheric conditions do influence our physical, emotional, and intellectual states, and in turn, our everyday behaviors.

One of the most popular notions regarding the role of weather in determining behavior is that high ambient temperatures (heat discomfort) causes social aggression (Harries & Stadler, 1983). Archival and field studies tend to bear out this belief, revealing that increases in temperature are often positively and monotonically related to aggression as defined by certain types of violent crimes, for example, rape and murder (Anderson, 1987; Anderson & Anderson, 1984; Perry & Simpson, 1987; Rotton & Frey, 1984), and milder forms of social aggression like horn-honking by motorists (Kenrick & MacFarlane, 1986). Laboratory studies, on the other hand (see Baron, 1978), suggest that the relationship is curvilinear rather than monotonic. These latter studies show that with increased temperatures aggression increases, but that with still further increases in temperature, aggression tends to dissipate.

Other common beliefs regarding weather variables are that gray skies lead to psychological depression, hot, dry winds negatively influence rational judgment, low barometric pressure induces memory deficits, and so on. Despite these widely held beliefs, though, there is little systematic research either to vindicate or refute them. The major reason for this scarcity of evidence may be that research in this area is fraught with methodological difficulties. Rotton (1986) has argued that research regarding the effects of climate and weather on behavior has been hampered by the search for single-factor explanations and proffers a redux determinism model that systematically includes sociocultural as well as climatic variables. These multivariate models, he attests, account for more of the variance in a variety of dependent variables than do univariate models, and clear up seemingly anomalous findings. Rohles (1967), whose specific area of interest is thermal comfort, has referred to the field as a "bucket of worms." He lists a total of 18 physical, organismic, and interactive variables that must be taken into account in any single study on thermal comfort. Each of these variables is independent or semi-independent and must be explicitly controlled. In even a simple study that assumed only two levels of each of these variables, a complete factorial design with 10 subjects per condition would require the utilization of 2,621,440 subjects. The "bucket of worms" becomes even more unmanageable as designs approach real-life proportions.

One way to begin making sense of some of these relationships would be to identify precisely the range of the atmospheric environment of interest. In this regard Bates (1966) has distinguished three levels of atmospheric environment: microclimate, ecoclimate, and geoclimate. The *microclimate* refers to the relatively thin layer of atmosphere immediately surrounding the body (the air between one's skin and one's clothing), whereas the *ecoclimate* refers to the climate of the working and living environment (e.g., a home, office, the beach, the inside of an automobile), and the *geoclimate* refers to atmospheric conditions covering wide geographical areas (e.g., the average rainfall in June in the American Midwest, a high pressure front extending from the Rockies to the Ohio River Basin). Put another way, microclimates and ecoclimates refer to those atmospheric conditions that are readily available through our senses, whereas the only practical way we can know the condition of the geoclimate is to consult the Weather Bureau, the Environmental Protection Agency, or some other keeper of records. But while these distinctions are simple enough to make, their independent and specific effects on human behavior may not be so easily discernable. This chapter and the next will deal specifically with the atmospheric variables that constitute our ecoclimate, bearing in mind that often micro- and geo-climatic variables cannot be ruled out as moderating some of the reported effects.

Temperature, humidity, sunlight, barometric pressure, air movement, concentration of airborne particles, gaseous composition of inhaled air, ion concentration, and radiation are all readily identifiable atmospheric conditions. We are well aware of some of them; we take note of changes in temperature, humidity, and wind, and are mindful of their effects. (If the temperature exceeds 85°F, or the humidity is in excess of 75 percent, or the wind is blowing at more than 20 mph, I will not play tennis; if the windchill outdoors exceeds −40°F, I refuse to leave the warmth of my living room.) Other aspects of our ecoclimate are less salient and their effects more subtle. For example, we do not easily perceive variations in ion concentration or radiation, so any changes in these are likely to go unnoticed and any effects are likely to be more insidious. At any given moment the influence of the ecoclimate on human functioning is a result of the combined effects of many variables. For the sake of clearer exposition and in keeping with a great deal of the research in this area, we will deal with these variables one at a time. Occasionally, though, researchers have looked simultaneously at more than one variable, and when this has been done it will be noted.

TIME-OUT: How does the weather influence your behavior? One way to find out might be to keep a *weather and behavior* diary. For some predetermined number of days, say 14, you could keep track of weather conditions (do it the same time every day). You could, for example, watch the noon or evening news each day and record temperature, relative humidity, barometric pressure, wind speeds and degree of cloudiness. You might decide that you'd like to relate this information to your affective state. If so, you would want an assessment of that each day as well (Mehrabian and Russell's [1974] Semantic Differential formatted scale would be appropriate). You could also record any asocial, antisocial, or pro-social behavior you had engaged in during the previous hour.

At the end of the 14-day period, you could inspect your diary to see if any meaningful consistencies appeared. For example, were you more or less happy when the sun was shining? More or less antisocial when temperatures were high, etc.? Based on your diary and the conclusions you've made, could you now design a research study that would allow you to make causal inferences regarding the effect of weather on behavior?

AMBIENT TEMPERATURE

High Temperature

The relationship between ambient temperature and human functioning is extremely complex, particularly within the range of temperatures a person normally experiences in living and working environments (approximately 55°F–95°F). However, extreme temperatures (those that produce changes in body temperature) have a fairly predictable impact. For example, a body (core) temperature of 101.8°F in most cases coincides with the onset of heat exhaustion and deteriorated functioning, while hand skin temperatures below 60°F interferes with fine motor coordination of the fingers. The tolerance limits of extreme temperatures are related to a number of factors, including the ability to sense temperature, loss of heat by regulatory perspiration, the evaporation of perspiration as a result of air flow across the surface of the body, and the movement of heat from the core of the body to the skin surface via blood flow. Extreme temperatures are therefore tolerated for varying amounts of time. For example, temperatures of 180°F have been tolerated by lightly clothed men at rest for periods of about 50 minutes (ASHRAE Transactions, 1977), despite the fact that pain receptors at the skin surface are triggered at temperatures of about 110°F.

As ambient temperature climbs, core body temperature rises, blood vessels dilate, with more blood flowing to the surface to be cooled. With added blood at the surface, the skin looks pink and the body begins to perspire. Heart rate increases (even more so if the person is working). Evaporation of the perspiration cools the surface of the body and the blood flowing at the surface. Continued exposure to high ambient temperature, though, can lead to reduced blood volume resulting from perspiring, and thus to insufficient blood to fill the dilated blood vessels. Blood pressure consequently falls, the brain receives insufficient oxygen, and the person faints. If blood circulation can be maintained, core body temperature continues to rise. The person may then become delirious, have convulsions, and eventually become comatose. Ultimately, of course, exposure to exceedingly high ambient temperature for prolonged periods of time leads to death.

Individuals living in the hot/dry environment of deserts often have to adapt to the alternating heat of day and cold of night (Suedfeld, 1987). These high-temperature and low-humidity conditions are often accompanied by sparse vegetation leading to low availability of food (Hanna & Brown, 1983) and precious little shade, making sunburning a problem. Water supplies are often limited, and this, coupled with excessive sweating, leads to problems associated with dehydration and electrolyte depletion. In contrast, people living in hot/humid environments often have natural leaf canopies and increased cloud cover to protect them from solar radiation, but the high humidity makes perspiring less effective in maintaining core body temperature (Suedfeld, 1987). Thus, we see that temperature effects are nearly always moderated by humidity conditions. Fortunately, such extreme climatological conditions are rare and affect relatively few individuals.

Low Temperature

In contrast, surface temperature of the extremities is frequently the critical factor for tolerance of low temperatures. One of the first responses to cold ambient temperature is vasoconstriction and thus lessened blood flow to the body surface. With this decreased blood flow to the extremities there is a commensurate drop in surface temperature, leading to increased discomfort and decreased motor efficiency. Hand skin temperatures of 68°F lead people to report discomfort, and 41°F, pain. Identical reports occur for foot surface temperatures at approximately 71°F and 45°F. Exposure to cold ambient temperatures over prolonged periods of time can lead to chronic inflammatory swellings (*chilblains*) or even slow healing ulcerations (frostbite). As ambient temperature falls, so does core body temperature. Heat production is enhanced by tensing the muscles and maintained through piloerection and decreased flow of blood to the surface of the body. Shivering is eventually replaced by permanent muscular rigidity. Once core temperature has fallen to about 90°F, heart irregularities begin to appear, blood pressure falls, and the individual becomes confused and eventually loses consciousness. Death from heart failure usually occurs by the time core temperature has fallen to 75°F (Kazantizis, 1967).

Residents of polar environments not only must adapt to extremely cold temperatures but also to low food productivity of the terrestrial ecosystem, extended periods of both light and dark, and the inherent dangers of working on snow and ice (Moran, 1979). Body energy expenditure is very high because of the excessive clothing, the high winds, and the sheer difficulty of traveling through snow. In fact, residents of polar climates expend nearly twice the energy that would be required for the same actions in more temperate climates (Suedfeld, 1987). Retinal damage from the sun reflecting off the ever-present ice, hypothermia, and frostbite are not uncommon. Injuries sustained on the rugged terrain are an ever-present danger, and disruption of circadian biorythms and sleep disturbances, due to extended periods of light and dark, are frequent (Condon, 1983). Additionally, some diseases of nutrition are more likely in these environments (see Zimmerman, 1985).

Individuals living in natural high altitude environments not only have extremely cold temperatures to contend with but also hypoxia, dehydration, and radiation exposure. Adaptation takes place by increasing efficiency of oxygen flow and changes in body weight. Glucose metabolism and other biochemical alterations have been reported to occur at altitudes as low as 6,300 meters (West, 1984). While it is important that we understand these effects and be prepared to ameliorate them, it should be kept in mind that they are rare.

Most naturally occurring extremes in temperatures have associated with them other confounding factors that make it difficult to draw causal inferences. Among these factors, we have already noted humidity, sunshine, altitude, wind, terrain, vegetation, and diet. In today's world, though, many of us spend much of our time in climate-controlled environments. For these reasons we will now turn our attention to research which involves the effect of indoor temperature (and its various moderating variables) on human functioning.

Indoor Temperature

It has been shown that extremes in ambient temperature can have serious effects for those exposed to them, but what are the effects of ambient temperature on human functioning within the range of 55°F–95°F? What is the maximum comfortable temperature possible? What temperatures lead to increased cognitive or motor task performance? These questions are not so easily answered. For example, cross-cultural differences in preferred ambient temperature have been reported. Early in this century Yaglou and Drinker (1929) reported that the English preferred building temperatures of 8°F lower than Americans. Rohles (1975) has reported that even among Americans the ambient temperature considered comfortable has changed over time. In 1924 an indoor temperature of 64°F was considered comfortable; by 1929 this had increased to 66°F, to 68°F in 1950, to 71°F in 1960, and to 76°F in 1972. As a final example of these differences, the McQuarrie Islanders report feeling comfortable indoors irrespective of temperature (MacPherson, 1973). Obviously, there is more to thermal comfort than just temperature.

Thermal Comfort

Thermal comfort has been defined as "that condition of mind which expresses satisfaction with the thermal environment" (ASHRAE Handbook of Fundamentals, 1967). In this way, thermal comfort may be viewed as a combination of a "feelings state" and an evaluation of the environment in terms of satisfaction or dissatisfaction. Of course, this feelings state is likely to be affected by activity level, clothing worn, and by temperature and humidity.

Over the years numerous criteria for thermal comfort have been developed. These criteria have typically specified a range of ambient temperature and air humidity levels within which some arbitrary percentage of the occupants of an indoor environment will report feeling comfortable. The KSU-ASHRAE Comfort Envelope (Rohles, 1973) represents an attempt to specify the thermal environment within which humans are comfortable. These "comfort zones" are empirically derived in experiments where ambient temperature and relative humidity are independently manipulated and subjects report their degree of comfort/discomfort. Applying this method, thermal comfort reports have been shown to be affected by relative humidity, by clothing, and by activity level.

The limiting effects of *relative humidity* (RH) on thermal comfort (at any particular ambient temperature) are clearly illustrated in the results of the Kansas State study from which the KSU-ASHRAE Comfort Envelope was derived (Rohles, 1975). The findings suggest that relative humidity is an important determinant of people's affective response to thermal conditions, appearing to have approximately one-eighth of the impact that ambient temperature has on thermal comfort.

The impact of *clothing* needs to be considered anytime one is studying thermal comfort (Rohles, Woods, & Nevins, 1973). As would be expected, subjects wearing lighter clothing report feeling cool at somewhat higher temperatures. The role of clothing, particularly its insulative properties, in maintaining thermal comfort has been summed up neatly by the Chinese. They describe the weather in terms of the number of suits required for thermal comfort. Moderate weather is a "one suit" day, a "two suit" day is a little cooler, and a "twelve suit" day is bitterly cold (Winslow & Herrington, 1949).

Activity level is another determinant of thermal comfort (McNall, Jaax, & Rohles, 1967). The greater the activity level, the cooler the ambient temperature required to maintain thermal comfort. If all the other factors influencing thermal comfort are held constant and activity level alone is manipulated, several results occur: As activity level increases, thermal comfort is obtained at cooler temperatures; as activity level decreases, thermal comfort is more difficult to obtain even at warm temperatures, and discomfort is highly probable at cool temperatures.

A few of the many factors influencing thermal comfort have been described. It is apparent that ambient temperature, while exerting a large influence, is just one of many factors influencing thermal comfort. The way one reaches a state of thermal comfort can occur in a wide variety of ways. In fact, groups of people across time and cultures have achieved thermal comfort at differing ambient temperatures by varying these other factors. It may be argued that in different time periods, people held differing expectations as to the adaptive behavior (e.g., adjusting temperature, relative humidity, and/or clothing) appropriate for maintaining thermal comfort. Therefore, while ambient temperatures have varied, thermal comfort was maintained by adjustment along other comfort-moderating dimensions.

FIGURE 6-2 The Chinese describe weather in terms of the number of layers of clothing required to maintain thermal comfort.

In summary, extreme ambient temperatures in either direction can be debilitating; if the ecoclimate is too hot, humans can succumb to heat exhaustion, and if it is too cold, to hypothermia. However, lengthy exposure to these extremes is rare, and when exposures of short duration are necessary, precautions (mostly in the form of protective clothing) can be taken to eliminate these effects. Humans report feeling comfortable within a narrow band of indoor temperature. However, this narrow band has changed over time, is cross-culturally variable, and is influenced by relative humidity, clothing, and amount and type of activity engaged in by the respondent. Various studies have examined the effect of moderate temperature on performance, social behaviors, and health. It is to these studies that we now turn.

Ambient Temperature and Task Performance

The role of ambient temperature in moderating sensory, cognitive and motor processes has been investigated. These studies reveal that visual acuity can be adversely affected by increased temperatures (Hohnsbein, Piekarski, Kampmann, & Noack, 1984) even with increased background luminance, and that visual decrements occur within 30 minutes of exposure (Hohnsbein, Piekarski, & Kampmann, 1983). Other studies have shown cognitive deficits resulting from increased temperatures (Curley & Hawkins, 1983; Fine & Kobrick, 1987; Hancock, 1986a, 1986b; Kobrick & Sleeper, 1986; Sharma, Sridiharan, Pichan, & Panwar, 1986). These cognitive deficits often take the form of deteriorated vigilance and ability to attend, errors of omission, longer response latencies, and difficulties in response acquisition. A number of performance variables have also been shown to be affected by temperature changes (Meese, Lewis, Wyon, & Kok, 1984; Ramsey, Burford, Beshir, & Jensen, 1983; Riley & Cochran, 1984). However, Hancock (1986a), after a careful review of the literature involving temperature and human performance, has concluded that individuals who are skillful at a task are better able to withstand the effects of temperature exposure than their unskilled counterparts.

Other laboratory studies concerning the influence of ambient temperature on such performance variables as vigilance, memory, ability to carry out mathematical calculations, and reaction time have been conducted. Provins and his associates are responsible for much of this research (e.g., Bell, Provins, & Hiorns, 1964; Provins, 1966; Provins & Bell, 1970), but other noteworthy studies include those of Griffiths and Boyce (1971), Pepler and Warner (1968), Poulton and Kerslake, (1965), and Wilkinson, Fox, Goldsmith, Hampton, and Lewis (1964). With respect to temperatures at the upper end of the moderate zone (85°–90°F) the studies have led to equivocal results. Some have found temperatures to have a detrimental effect on performance, others determined that temperature had no effect, and some have even found increases in temperature lead to performance enhancement. But even these findings have to be tempered; the best performance does not occur at the same temperature for all individuals (Rohles, 1974; Wilkinson, 1974).

Additional research in such varied environments as tropical combat zones (Adam, 1967), elementary school classrooms (Aucliems, 1972; Dexter, 1900), steelmills (Crockford, 1967; Hill, 1967), and a gold mine (Wyndham, 1969) has shown temperature to exert an effect on task performance, but these effects can be radically reduced or eliminated by using *acclimatized* respondents. That is, if humans are given the opportunity to adapt to temperatures in the moderate to extreme range, these temperatures no longer exert an effect. It is safe to say that whether increased temperatures lead to performance increments or to performance decrements will depend on the arousal changes brought about by the temperature variations and whether the task to be completed is simple or complex, and well learned or novel (see Figure 2-3).

Ambient Temperature and Social Behavior

Our language reveals folklore about the relationships between temperature and social behavior. We talk about people being "hot under the collar" or "hot and bothered"; some people are "hot-headed," "hot-blooded,"or "hot-tempered." Sometimes others do things that "make my blood boil." Other times people are "cold and cunning" or perhaps "cool and aloof"; we sometimes tell others to "be cool" or to "cool it," and sometimes they give us the "cold shoulder." "Happiness is a warm puppy," and sometimes people are "warm and loving." Inherent in this use of language is a curvilinear relationship between temperature and social behaviors. The terms "cold-blooded" or "hot-blooded" imply negative social tendencies, whereas being cool and being warm connote more positive interpersonal relations. But what do scientific investigations tell us about the relationship between temperature and social behaviors? (Figure 6-3.)

Most individuals exposed to moderately high ambient temperatures report discomfort, as do individuals exposed to moderately cool temperatures. Such individuals might also report being irritable and may find others to be disagreeable (Griffitt, 1970). Studies conducted by Robert Baron and his colleagues (Baron, 1972; Baron & Bell, 1975; Baron & Lawton, 1972; Bell & Baron, 1976, 1977) lead to the conclusion that there is a critical range of uncomfortably warm ambient temperatures which facilitate aggressive responding in humans but, unlike folklore would suggest, it is the more moderate temperatures that are associated with antisocial behaviors. Extremely high temperatures reduce aggression (perhaps because of the debilitating effects of the heat), as do extremely cold temperatures (perhaps by reducing arousal); but moderately

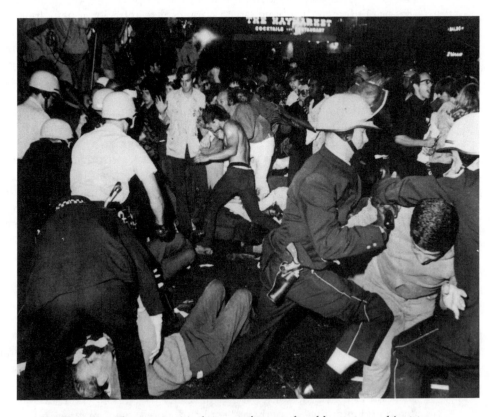

FIGURE 6-3 There is a critical range of uncomfortably warm ambient temperatures which facilitate aggressive responding in humans but, unlike folklore would suggest, it is the more moderate temperatures which are associated with antisocial behaviors.

warm and moderately cool temperatures facilitate aggression (Bell & Baron, 1977). The relationship between temperature and aggression does seem to be curvilinear, at least when considering indoor temperatures and laboratory settings. Other evidence, however, suggests that in the world outside the laboratory, the relationship between temperature and antisocial behavior is monotonic (e.g., Anderson, 1987; Kenrick & McFarlane, 1986; Perry & Simpson, 1987). Furthermore, calls for police assistance change predictably and linearly with changing temperatures (Le Beau & Langworthy, 1986).

Ambient Temperature and Health

After the first oil embargo of 1973 people became more conscious of energy and energy use. Our concern over energy consumption, because of our reliance on the automobile in the United States, was first reflected in the increased use of smaller cars and car pooling, but individually and collectively we soon realized that a significant amount of the money spent on energy goes for heating and cooling indoor environments. It became apparent that energy, and thus money, could be saved if thermostats were turned up in the summer (thus cooling units would come on only during extremely warm conditions) and turned down in the winter (heating units would not operate until reduced temperatures were achieved). While a great many people engaged in "thermostat conservation" many others refused, often citing health reasons for their refusal (Veitch, 1976). Cooler indoor temperatures in the winter months (i.e., 66°F) were seen as leading to more frequent and more severe colds, a greater probability of contracting influenza and pneumonia, and to an overall reduction in feelings of well-being. But just what are the effects of indoor temperatures in the range 60° to 80°F?

Numerous attempts have been made to determine the relationship between the occurrence of illness and the vagaries of the weather and indeed some relationships have been reported. However, the correlations that have been found may be indirect and do not necessarily imply a causal relationship between the two phenomena. Despite the questionable validity of the available data, it is still safe to expect differences in illnesses coinciding with ordinary seasonal changes. For example, minor respiratory infections such as colds and sore throats tend to predominate in the fall and winter, while other diseases such as intestinal infections (e.g., dysentery and typhoid fever), and some insect-transmitted diseases, (e.g., encephalitis or endemic typhus) occur more frequently in the summer.

Respiratory diseases are perhaps the most common illnesses and therefore the most likely targets for research. It has been estimated that the number of respiratory illnesses occurring in the United States each year is somewhere in the neighborhood of 250 million to more than one billion accounting for a loss of more than 14 million work-days annually. It is a real practical concern, therefore, to understand the relationship between temperature and respiratory ailments.

FIGURE 6-4 A significant amount of the money spent on energy goes for heating and cooling our indoor environments.

The common cold as an upper respiratory infection has been linked to indoor atmosphere, particularly in schools (Gelperin, 1973; Green, 1974). However, it is not safe to conclude that variations in the incidence of this disease are clearly or even singularly the result of temperature. For example, other factors such as sunlight, humidity, and population density all influence viral and bacterial survival and, thus, the infectivity of diseases. It has been shown, for example, that the infectivity of cholera, meningitis, poliomyelitis, and smallpox is influenced by humidity. High humidity tends to favor the spread of cholera and poliomyelitis. Thus seasonal changes in environmental conditions may produce seasonal changes in the spread of communicable diseases. However, Gelperin (1973) has indicated that there are also seasonal changes in human physiology and that these changes may be as important to the seasonal patterns of disease as are the environmental changes themselves. It is possible that these seasonal changes would occur independently of changes in temperature. Thus, temperature alone never tells the whole story.

In studies where indoor relative humidity has been manipulated, increases in relative humidity have produced significant reductions in respiratory illnesses in the winter. Raising the relative humidity from 10 to 20 percent above that in a nonhumidified space reduced absenteeism and the recurrence of upper respiratory infections (Gelperin, 1973). However, one must again recall that humidity is not only a very important component in changing viral and bacterial survival rates and, thus, infectivity, but also that it influences many physiological functions. So whether the increased humidity is producing its effect on the infected organism, on the infecting organism, or both, is not clear.

Temperature extremes, again in combination with humidity, have also been shown to have an adverse effect on cardiovascular systems. Individuals with heart diseases are extremely sensitive to high temperature and particularly to moist heat (Burch & De Pasquale, 1962). Coronary heart disease and anginal symptoms are more frequent with both cold and hot temperatures. Respiratory diseases frequently increase in number and grow more severe in extremely cold weather. However, no increase in these diseases has been noted with extreme heat. In a study by Holland (1961) in which the relationship of acute respiratory illness and temperature was studied with the effects of seasonal trends removed, a negative correlation between acute respiratory illness and ambient temperature was found.

While it can be seen that indoor temperature, particularly when combined with humidity, does have an effect on the survival rate of various bacteria and viruses and perhaps even on the physiology of humans, there is no information that would suggest adverse health effects as a result of maintaining indoor temperatures in the 60° to 80°F range. As we have seen, low temperature alone has no known direct effect on the transfer of communicable diseases, and therefore indoor winter temperatures as low as 60°F should have no effect on the likelihood of infection with the common cold, influenza, or pneumonia. In fact, the growth of bacteria and viruses is actually inhibited at these lower temperatures, and therefore, all other things being equal, minor reductions in the incidence of these diseases in the winter months might be expected with indoor temperatures reduced to about 60°F.

These generalizations apply to most normal, healthy individuals of all age groups. However, very young infants who have not fully developed their thermal regulatory mechanisms should be treated with caution if exposed to cooler temperatures. Parents should take special care in seeing that infants are adequately clothed and adequately sheltered from ambient temperatures as low as 60°F. The elderly, especially those over 70, should also be protected against prolonged exposure to cold. Many elderly people take a much longer time to adapt to temperature changes due to the physiological changes which occur as a result of increasing age. For them, even mildly cool temperatures (i.e., within the 60°–65°F range) can trigger accidental hypothermia.

The symptoms of hypothyroidism, certain peripheral vascular disorders, arthritis, angina pectoris, and diabetes mellitus are aggravated by reduced environmental temperatures. Individuals with these particular ailments should take precautions when exposed to lower temperatures for extended periods of time. However, the majority of individuals can cope quite easily and without great discomfort to indoor temperatures as low as 60°F, particularly if proper clothing is worn. Further, there is no evidence to indicate that setting the thermostat at 80°F in the summer is going to affect the physical health of individuals of any age. We will return to these issues in Chapter 15.

TIME-OUT: If you were on a team of environmental engineers who were asked to establish the parameters of living space which would promote human welfare and functioning, what range of values for temperature would you recommend? Would the range of temperatures you set for comfort be at odds with those promoting health? Would healthful temperatures also be productive temperatures? Would the range of temperatures you set for leisure-time activities be the same as those for work activities? In setting these temperatures, have you made sure to consider humidity and air flow across the body as moderators? Does your engineered environment resemble a "bucket of worms" as expressed by Rohles?

By now it should be clear that these parameters can only be set by considering the type of space being thermally controlled and the kinds of activities to go on there and the population who will be utilizing it. Therefore, now be more specific and set these parameters for your home environment. What are they and how have you arrived at these values?

THE EFFECT OF SUNLIGHT ON PHYSIOLOGY AND BEHAVIOR

When we think of the role of light in our lives we generally think of vision and certainly our ability to see depends on the quality and quantity of the illumination around us. That we can see at all depends on light waves of various frequencies being reflected off surfaces and impinging on the retina of the eye. But anyone who has ever had a sunburn knows that light can effect our bodies in other ways as well. Anecdotally we talk about "bringing a ray of sunshine" into people's lives and about people as having "sunny dispositions." We "put on a sunshine face" when we are happy and things "look cloudy" in our moments of despair. Our use of such language reflects the belief that sunshine is related to moods. But just how light can affect us is only beginning to be understood and appreciated by scientists. Until very recently scientists were concerned with only the ability of sunshine to stimulate the production of vitamin D. We are now beginning to learn that sunlight can be as important to our health and well-being as the food we eat and the air we breathe. Indeed, new information is being generated that shows that sunshine helps to regulate our biological rhythms, damage or repair our genetic material, change our moods, improve our productivity, and can even be used to treat such diseases as jaundice in newborns and some forms of depression and leukemia.

Light Dimensions

Any thorough study of the biological effects of light must be conducted with at least three dimensions of light in mind: (1) the *intensity* of the light, (2) the *timing* and *exposure* to the light or sunshine, and (3) the *spectrum* of the lighting provided. The importance of considering *intensity* can be seen in the study of the role of light in regulating our biological rhythms. Until very few years ago many scientists did not realize that light had any effect on the production of hormones (other than in vitamin D synthesis) in human beings, even though such a fact had been clearly demonstrated in lower animals. It was only when researchers began to experiment with high intensity, full-spectrum light that clear effects of light and human hormones could be observed in the laboratory. (See, for example, the work of Rosenthal and his colleagues, 1984, 1985, 1986a, 1986b.) Likewise, the *timing* and *duration* of exposure to light (that is, how often, when, and for how long) is critical for understanding how light affects our bodies. Whether we get sunburned or suntanned at the beach depends not only on how intense the light is but also how long we spend under it, the time of day, our skin type, and our degree of pre-exposure. Other less apparent effects of light are also dependent on timing. One of the most exciting areas of recent research is the discovery that certain people experience a psychological depression every winter, apparently as a result of insufficient light during shorter periods of daylight during that season. It now appears this condition is related to sunlight and can be successfully corrected by artificially extending the "daylight" period for these patients. Similarly, properly timed exposures to light have been shown to ameliorate some of the unpleasant effects of jet lag, the desynchronization of body rhythms experienced by people who fly across time zones. We will deal with these effects in more detail later in this chapter.

A third important aspect of light is *spectrum*. Natural sunlight filtered through the atmosphere delivers a consistent spectrum ranging from the shorter invisible wavelengths of the ultraviolet through the visible frequencies and the longer wavelengths of the infrared. Different parts of this spectrum have been shown to have different effects on the body. The ultraviolet rays, for example, are involved in vitamin D synthesis, in tanning, and in bactericidal effects. The visible portion of the spectrum is involved in vision and is most likely involved in setting our biological clock. The portion used in treating infant jaundice is the visible blue portion of the spectrum. The longer infrared wavelengths have a role in relieving muscle soreness. The ability of researchers to analyze the effects of light in terms of *intensity*, *timing*, and *spectrum* has led to many exciting developments in our understanding and in the control of sunlight on our health.

The Role of the Pineal Gland

The most important organ in the coordination of body rhythms to the cycles of external light and darkness appears to be the pineal gland. The process begins, however, with light falling on the retina of the eye, but unlike the visual system, which responds to patterns of light by interpreting them as meaningful images, the system that controls biological rhythms responds to the amount and timing of incoming light. This internal clock sends information to the pineal gland via the suprachiasmatic nucleus (SCN) located in the hypothalamus of the midbrain.

Nerve impulses from the eye go directly to this brain center. From the SCN further nerve impulses are generated that travel by an indirect route through the spinal cord to the pineal gland where they are converted to chemical signals in the form of hormones. These hormones then travel through the bloodstream to act on a variety of tissues and organs.

The pineal produces a number of chemical products, but the one that has been most thoroughly studied is the hormone *melatonin*. This hormone is manufactured and released into the bloodstream only during hours of darkness. It is hypothesized that an animal's internal sense of the length of the day, crucial to the timing of such seasonal behaviors as mating and hibernation, is then calculated by the body on the basis of changing melatonin levels. Different species use this melatonin clock in a similar way to keep track of the relative lengths of the day and night, but each species' response to the information provided by melatonin varies as seen in the different breeding behaviors of different species. Sheep, for example, take the melatonin signals of the shortening days to begin their mating activity, while Syrian hamsters go out of their breeding season as the days shorten in autumn (Bittman, Dempsey, & Karsch, 1983; Carter & Goldman, 1983; Lincoln, 1983).

Human Rhythms

What about humans? We certainly have many bodily functions that follow daily cycles—for example, body temperature, hormone levels, sleeping, and wakefulness. But, as a species, we don't seem to exhibit many behaviors that follow seasonal cycles such as hibernation or seasonal breeding, though psychiatrists have long been aware that some persons seem to be particularly sensitive to the changing of the seasons. During the shorter days of winter in the temperate latitudes, these people feel chronically tired and sad, they sleep too much and they eat too much, especially carbohydrates (Zifferblatt, Curtis, & Pinsky, 1980; Zahorska-Markiewicz, 1980). This condition has been labelled *Seasonal Affective Disorder* (SAD) and its dependence on the seasons seems clear. With the coming days of spring and summer this "funk" lifts, and SAD sufferers are able to resume their normal lives.

For the past several years Dr. Norman Rosenthal and his colleagues have been treating SAD patients with a specially tailored experimental light regimen. They have found that by artificially extending the length of their days by a few hours during the winter they have been able, in many cases, to reverse the symptoms of this disorder. This extension of "daylight" time is accomplished by exposing patients to high levels of artificial sunlight. The light induces an antidepressant effect that is often evident after just two to four days of treatment. It is thus faster acting than any other antidepressant medication now in use and does not have the poetential for adverse side effects that accompany some medications.

BENEFICIAL AND HARMFUL EFFECTS OF LIGHT

Even people whose bodily rhythms are not chronically at odds with their environment can, under certain conditions, suffer certain disturbances. Workers who change shifts often experience the discomfort of jumbled cycles as do jet travelers who cross many time zones. The symptoms of this modern malady, called jet lag, varies from person to person, but can include headaches, sleep disturbances, digestive disorders, fatigue, and general malaise. These symptoms can last until all the desynchronized rhythms have fallen back in step, which sometimes takes up to two weeks. The process of readjustment can be speeded up by the same kind of light exposure techniques used with seasonal depressions.

Jet travel, however, is not the only aspect of modern life that is proven a mixed blessing to our health. The industrial revolution that began our modern era when it swept across modern Europe and North America brought with it a disease called *rickets*. This disease typically affected small children in crowded cities leaving them with bowed, weak and deformed leg joints, knuckle-like projections along their rib cages, and deformities of the pelvis. For centuries the cause of this crippling condition remained a mystery and it was not until the early 1900s that researchers demonstrated that rickets resulted directly from a deficiency of vitamin D and indirectly from the lack of exposure to sunlight.

Vitamin D is normally produced in the skin when natural ultraviolet is absorbed by a special molecule in the skin. This sets off a series of chemical events resulting in the production of the active form of vitamin D. This hormone then facilitates the absorption of calcium by the intestine and the uptake and release of calcium by the skeleton. Without a continuing supply in the diet or regular exposure to appropriate ultraviolet light the body's store can become rapidly depleted. After only two or three weeks of lacking light in the ultraviolet range humans begin to show a decrease in their body's stores of vitamin D, leading to inadequate absorption of calcium in their intestine.

Fortunately it takes very little exposure to sunlight to ensure adequate production of vitamin D in most people, only about 15 minutes of noontime sunlight on the face and backs of the hand. Researchers have found that the ability of the skin to synthesize vitamin D, however, declines with age, and low vitamin D levels exacerbate a condition known as *osteoporosis* in which bone mass, especially calcium, is decreased and bones become porous and fragile. Vitamin D deficiency therefore is a risk factor of broken hips among the elderly and especially among elderly women.

It is now known that the elderly can receive special benefit from light but so too can the very youngest among us. The first important role of visible light in medicine was its use in treating *jaundice* in premature babies. Normally when red blood cells die, a yellowish compound called *bilirubin* is released. But for some reason when bilirubin is not excreted normally it can accumulate in the bloodstream, giving the skin a characteristic yellow tinge of jaundice. Jaundice is a common symptom in newborn infants particularly in those born premature and whose liver has not matured sufficiently to break down the bilirubin (McDonagh & Lightner, 1985). As many as 10 to 20 percent of premature babies have an excess of bilirubin in their bloodstreams. The situation is potentially dangerous because bilirubin is capable of entering the brain, causing a condition known as *kernicterus*, in which irreversible nerve damage can occur leading to mental and motor retardation and even to death. Thus, when bilirubin levels are high in the bloodstreams of newborns, doctors want to lower them quickly. In the past the only means to this end was to perform an exchange transfusion, completely replacing the jaundiced blood of the infant with blood from a compatible healthy donor. Unfortunately, this procedure carries considerable risks, resulting in death in approximately 1 percent of the cases. In the late 1950s it was discovered that bilirubin can be bleached out by light. Newborns whose cribs had been placed near an open window showed less evidence of jaundice than those exposed to less light. Since then, phototherapy, utilizing the blue end of the visible light spectrum, has been used in selected cases of neonatal jaundice. Phototherapy it would now appear is a highly efficient means to handling jaundice babies and appears to be completely safe. In fact, in selected newborns this therapy can be effectively carried out in the home (Ellis, 1985).

As we have seen, the interaction of light with our bodies are many and complex; some can be harmful while others can protect us and still others repair damage that has already been done. The ultraviolet portion of the spectrum provides a good example. Light in this region is needed for the body to synthesize vitamin D. Too much ultraviolet, however, can result in sunburn, perhaps even cancer, while the same light in milder doses can induce tanning and the production of melanin, which protects against sunburn (Wolken, 1986). A less obvious but perhaps more important example of the two-sided nature of light has recently been investigated. It has been shown that ultraviolet light can cause "dimerization" of certain parts of the DNA molecules. That is, parts of the molecules that are not normally linked together can, when exposed to ultraviolet light, hook up together, causing the DNA to malfunction, possibly leading to the beginnings of cancerous conditions. But just as light can cause damage, it can also fight it. To begin with, tanning can protect against DNA damage. Tanning of the skin is produced by the activation of the skin pigment called *melanin*, and this pigment absorbs potentially harmful ultraviolet rays. Light in the ultraviolet range can actually be absorbed by certain DNA dimers, breaking them apart and thus repairing the damaged molecules. Further, there is some evidence that light in the ultraviolet range activates special enzymes which help unlink DNA dimers. Natural sunlight, therefore, cannot be neatly divided into separate narrow bands of the spectrum where one portion of the spectrum causes damage and another portion of the spectrum corrects that damage, although this is sometimes the case. Sometimes particular portions of the spectrum will cause certain forms of damage but will also have other healing effects (Morison, 1984; Wurtman, Baum, & Potts, 1985).

Finally, recent research has shown that certain drugs in combination with ultraviolet light can be used in therapy for such diseases as psoriasis, bitiligo, and certain types of skin cancer (Wolken, 1986). In this treatment patients are first given an oral dose of particular drugs. Their blood is then shunted through a transferring tube and exposed to light falling within a particular spectrum. It then reenters circulation. The drug activated by the light attacks the cancerous white cells because they are dividing more rapidly than are the healthy cells.

In conclusion, light can have a wide range of biological effects apart from its obvious role in making vision possible. But even then, visual properties turn out to have subtle effects on our well-being and productivity. Norman Rosenthal and his colleagues have shown that although humans are not regarded as seasonal creatures that there is ample evidence to show that seasonal rhythms do occur in a variety of human phenomena, including rates of birth, growth, suicide, and death from natural causes. There is also extensive evidence that shows seasonal variations in weight of humans, with a tendency to increase weight in the fall and winter and to lose weight most easily in the spring and summer (for a review see Attarzadeh, 1983). Humans also show seasonal changes in food choices, with starches and whole milk showing increases over protein and skim milk in the fall and winter months (Zahorska-Markiewicz, 1980; Zifferblatt, et al., 1980). Some individuals show an exaggerated behavioral response to the seasons. For these individuals, behavioral response to seasonal changes reaches such a degree of severity that it impairs functioning both at work and in their interpersonal relations. Many of them become nonmotivated and tend to withdraw from others during the fall and winter months. In contrast, during the spring and summer their energy levels, degree of motivation, and tendency to interact with others is often higher than normal. Their winter state frequently meets clinical criteria for depression whereas their spring and summer state often meets criteria for hypomania (Spitzer, Endicott, & Robins, 1978). This, of course, is what has come to be labelled SAD.

While these individuals represent rare instances of severe effects of sunshine and weather on behavior, there are many more instances of minor effects that the weather plays on human beings. We know, for example, of some 44 conditions, including blood pressure changes, migraine headaches, and mood shifts that correlate with the weather (Rosen, 1985). For example, temperature, humidity, snow, rain, clouds, haze, sunrises, and sunsets influence our moods. Undoubtedly you have at times felt great just because it was sunny, or grumpy simply because it was cloudy. Current research suggests that your mood today may even be associated with weather conditions that occurred yesterday or the day before and that a common cold today may have begun with the weather two to four days previous (Rosen, 1985). Finally, we have not even begun to consider the potential effects of the changes in the amount and type of light the earth is currently receiving owing to changes in atmospheric conditions from pollution.

TIME-OUT: Earlier it was suggested that a *weather and behavior* diary be kept to provide information regarding how weather conditions are associated with mood and behavior. Fourteen consecutive days were recommended to allow for fluctuations in conditions. Changes in ambient temperature were emphasized at that time. You might now reconsider your diary entries while emphasizing sunshine and cloud cover as the independent variables of interest. If you were to carry out this little project for an extended period of time (across several seasons) the number of hours of daylight available would show considerable change and with it perhaps seasonal changes in your emotional state and in your social behaviors. While it is extremely unlikely that changes similar to those of persons suffering from SAD will show up, it is possible that minor variations in your behaviors are predictably associated with variations in day/night hours resulting from seasonal changes.

WIND AS AN ENVIRONMENTAL DETERMINANT OF BEHAVIOR

Put simply, wind refers to the movement of air parallel to the earth's surface. It can vary in terms of speed and turbulence, with winds formed in tornadoes and hurricanes easily reaching speeds in excess of 80 mph. There are few areas in the country that escape the presence of wind, but there are some areas likely to be exposed to either more frequent (the Midwest) or more severe (the southwestern tornado belt) winds than others. Anyone who has had to work in a windy setting, or for that matter had to walk against a severe wind, knows how discomforting and often debilitating the wind can be. But how is it that we come to perceive the wind? How do we know when it is blowing, or how discomforting or debilitating it is likely to be?

While the body has specialized sensory receptors for detecting light, color, sound, odors, and even temperature differentials, there are no receptors designed specifically for wind detection. Humans must, therefore, rely on several modes of sensory input to detect the presence of wind. If you are not directly in the wind but looking, perhaps, out a window, the most important cue to the wind and its speed is the perception of movement of other environmental objects. The sight of leaves moving, a flag flying, debris tumbling along the ground are visual evidence of a wind; the violence of their movements hints at the speed of that wind. If you are unprotected in the wind, the most salient cue comes from the pressure receptors of the skin; the more pressure felt, the more intense the wind. Muscular effort in resisting the wind is a third cue to its force, and the intensity and frequency of the sound of the air moving past the ears is a fourth.

Sir Francis Beaufort developed one of the first known indexes for evaluating the wind in terms of human behavior (Penwarden, 1973). This scale ranges from 0 to 12 with 0 indicating calm, 5 being the upper limits of agreeable wind on land, 9 indicating winds so strong that people can be blown over by gusts and slight structural damage occurs, and 12 hurricane force. These scale values have counterparts in miles per hour of approximately 0, 19–24, 47–55 and 93–136 mph respectively. Since Beaufort, a number of researchers have called for more precise scales of wind effects and a few have been forthcoming (Penwarden, 1973). Perhaps the most rigorous scale to date involves the development of a body heat loss index which takes into account not only the windspeed across the surface of the body but also the moisture content and the temperature of that wind. It's not just the heat, nor just the humidity, but the airflow across the body as well. This is commonly referred to as "wind chill."

Behavioral and Emotional Effects of Wind

A colleague of one of the authors prides himself in having adapted to the Midwest summers. He has developed avocational interests in tennis and in sailing. If the summer's day is calm he plays tennis; if the wind is blowing he sails; if it's raining he works. Few people's behavior, however, is so predictable, and very little systematic research has been conducted to date on the specific behavioral effects of wind. However, Poulton, Hunt, Mumford, and Poulton (1975) report a rather intriguing series of studies in which female human subjects were exposed to winds of 9 or 20 mph, which varied in degrees of turbulence. Air temperature and humidity (65°–70°F and 70–85%) were held relatively constant across conditions. The higher speed winds in comparison with those of lesser speeds interfered with subjects walking a straight path, increased the amount of time required to don articles of clothing (raincoat, scarf), increased subjects' blinking, interfered with a cognitive task (word recognition), and led to reports of increased discomfort and perceived windiness. In summarizing these effects, it is safe to suggest that winds influence affective states, and can influence some kinds of performance as well. Anyone who has played tennis in the wind knows how performance can be affected by the wind and is probably most envious of the colleague with the catamaran. Further, that person knows that his or her "feelings state" while playing tennis is affected (often very negatively) by the wind.

Sommers and Moos (1976) report a number of effects that are associated with the hot, dry winds of the Foehn, Bora, Sharav, Chinook, and Santa Anas. For example, it is common for residents of the plains area adjacent to the mountains from which the warm, dry Foehn and Chinook winds descend, to attribute depression, nervousness, pain, irritation, and even traffic accidents to the wind. Rim (1975) evaluated the performance of two groups of individuals. He found that those tested during periods of hot desert wind (the Sharav of Israel) scored higher on neuroticism and extroversion and lower in I.Q. than those tested at other times. As early as 1900, Dexter reported a relationship between poor classroom behavior and the wind, and as recently as 1978, researchers (Banzinger & Owens, 1978) have reported correlational evidence for a relationship between wind speed and mortality rates, felonies, and delinquency. In the Near East some governments forgive criminal acts that are committed during periods of "disturbing winds" and some surgeons will operate only in an emergency, believing that such times are particularly inauspicious (Leiber, 1978).

As these studies are primarily correlational it is impossible to attribute these effects directly to the wind. Indeed, other factors typically covarying with changes in wind speed are temperature, atmospheric air pressure, relative humidity, and ion concentration. Any one or several of these variables might account for the perceived effects. Whichever one or combination is the crucial variable, it is probably safe to assume that these weather conditions influence human behavior through attentional processes (perceived change in environmental conditions), a heightened degree of arousal, and a loss of perceived control.

As a final comment it should be noted that tall buildings in our urban centers exacerbate the effect of natural wind. For example, if a wind strikes a relatively tall building the winds are typically deflected straight down. If the building then has an open passageway at ground level the winds rush through it causing a "wind tunnel." Natural winds of 15 to 20 miles an hour can easily exceed 40 mph in these tunnels depending on the size of the building and the passageway. Most urban centers are thus becoming high wind areas as a result of architectural design rather than meteorological shifts. If the wind does have deleterious effects on human performance and emotional functioning, we would be wise to *design out* of our cities these new and often treacherous wind accelerators.

FIGURE 6-5 The wind can influence human behavior through attentional processes, a heightened degree of arousal, and perceived loss of control. (Courtesy of Bob Zumph)

ION CONCENTRATION

Atmospheric ion formation begins when the energy produced by radioactive elements in the soil or the cosmic rays entering the atmosphere causes a gaseous molecule to lose an electron. This freed electron then attaches to an adjacent molecule, resulting in this new molecule having a net negative charge and the original having a positive charge. Water vapor, oxygen, and hydrogen molecules cluster around these charged particles to form small air ions (Kreuger & Siegel, 1978). These positively and negatively charged ions are nearly equal in numbers in the earth's atmosphere (although there is a slightly larger number of positive particles) so that the net effect is a nearly neutral electrical atmosphere. There are, however, meteorological and geophysical processes that result in local disturbances of this equilibrium. For example, a preponderance of positive ions is associated with the movement of such warm, dry air masses as the Santa Anas of Southern California, the Sharav of Israel, the Chinook of Canada, and the Foehn of Central Europe (Sulman & Pfeifer, 1964). This excess of positive ions has also been known to occur in large self-contained buildings or work spaces that are climatized by artificial heating and cooling procedures, and in areas of higher-than-normal air pollution. Conversely, excesses of negative ions are associated with the presence of moving water—for example, immediately after a rainstorm, near waterfalls or fountains, at the site of streams (Hansell, 1961).

Soyka and Edmonds (1978) report that early observers of atmospheric effects noted that air electricity (as it was then called) influenced the rate of plant growth and speculated that it might also have an effect on humans. As early as 1775, Fr. Gian Battista Baccaria noted that artificial electricity had the same effect on plant growth as did atmospheric electricity. Recent speculation, along with research surrounding the possible effects of differential atmospheric ion concentration, has departed from plant growth and turned to human behaviors and emotions. Assael, Pfeifer, and Sulman (1974) provide evidence for a moderate to strong association between positive ionic concentration and human irritability, depression, tension, insomnia, and migraines. People in areas frequented by the Santa Anas, Foehns, Sharavs, and Chinooks commonly explain bad moods and strange behaviors on "the wind," or more remotely, on the differential ion concentration associated with the wind.

Falkenberg and Kirk (1977) investigated the effects of air ionization on the acquisition of avoidance responses. Rats that were trained in the presence of negative ions were superior in performance to those trained in the presence of positive ions. Lambert and Olivereau (1980), also utilizing rats, found both short- and long-term memory impairment resulting from positive ion concentrations, but did not find an enhancement for negative ions.

Because of its possible benevolent side effects, however, the influence of negative ions has been more widely claimed, even if not more thoroughly researched. Among the positive effects claimed to be associated with breathing air containing more negative than positive ions are improved cognitive functioning, increased attentional posture, improved working capacity, faster rate of healing, greater endurance and efficiency, and more positive mood states (Finley, 1981; Sullivan, 1981; Voisinet, 1978). Unfortunately, most of these claims have not withstood the rigors of empirical scrutiny, and studies which refute the claims are equal or greater in number than those that provide vindication (Buckalew & Rizzuto, 1984; Charry, 1977; Charry & Hawkinshire, 1981; Duffee & Koontz, 1965; Falkenberg & Kirk, 1977; Gavalas-Medici & Day-Masdaleno, 1976; Hawkins & Barber, 1978; Tom, Poole, Galla, & Berrier, 1981). Many of these studies suffer one or more of the problems associated with internal validity, and the equivocation in results should therefore be expected. Indeed, Kreuger and Reed (1976) cite the uneven quality of research and faulty experimental procedures as major nemeses to understanding ion effects.

A series of studies by Robert A. Baron and his colleagues (Baron, Russell, & Arms, 1985; Baron, 1987a, 1987b) have attempted to account for some of these discrepancies. By utilizing the same procedures for generating ions and by maintaining similar concentrations across several experiments, cross-study comparisons can be made. Results of these several studies suggest that high concentrations of negative ions intensify interpersonal attraction through increments in physiological arousal, as measured by systolic and diastolic blood pressure (Baron, 1987b). Additionally, subjective reports of psychological arousal are influenced by ion concentration, but these reports are unrelated to performance measures. These findings lead to the conclusion that the impact of negative ions on overt behavior are mediated by physiological but not psychological arousal. This finding, coupled with the fact that increased negative ion concentrations do not exert uniformly positive influence on performance, suggests that the effect of increasing negative ionic concentration is to increase arousal level, which then impacts on overt behavior. In the light of Zajonc's (1980) theory of social facilitation, dominant, well-learned, and simple tasks should be enhanced under conditions of increased ionization, whereas subordinate, poorly learned, and complex tasks should be handled less expeditiously. Further, these effects should be more pronounced for individuals varying on certain individual difference dimensions (e.g., TypeA/Type B personalities, gender, etc.). These effects are just the sort reported by Baron and colleagues, (Baron, 1987a, 1987b; Baron et al., 1985).

A separate line of research (not without problems of its own) has searched for relationships between cortical neurohormones (particularly serotonin) and ion concentration (Frey, 1967; Gilbert, 1973; Tal, Pfeifer, & Sulman, 1976). Korentsky (1976) has looked at the relationship of serotonin to the control of affective states, body temperature, and sensory perception, whereas Ray (1978) related the increased serotonin brought about by positive ion concentration to the slowing or stopping of certain behaviors. Giannini, Castellani, and Dvoredsky (1983) have offered case study evidence for the existence of a "seratonin irritation" syndrome (an anxiety state associated with cation environments, serum serotonin, and decreased urinary 5-hydroxyindoleacetic acid). Because their report involves a limited number of cases (5), these results should be viewed skeptically. Obviously, much more research is needed before any definite statements concerning the effects of differential ion concentration on human performance and well-being can be made. The potential positive application of this research, however, makes it imperative that this research be done soon.

TIME-OUT: The design and siting of buildings can have a dramatic effect on the presence and impact of both winds and ionic concentration. For example, tall buildings can accelerate normal wind speeds and thus exacerbate their negative effects, and large self-contained buildings that are artificially heated and/or cooled lead to excesses of positive ion concentration. Additionally, design and siting determines the extent to which sunlight can be used to heat buildings (see Chapters 11, 12, and 13), and provide added luminance to work spaces.

Given these potential negative as well as positive effects resulting from careful design and siting procedures, begin developing a list of recommendations for building planners. Where and how should buildings be sited to take advantage of natural light? to avoid increasing the negative effects of wind? to cut down on positive ion concentrations? What are the potential side effects of these decisions on heating and maintenance cost? on durability? on the environment? Add to this list of recommendations as you continue to read this text. Consider such variables as noise, pollution, social interaction, special user groups, etc.

SUMMARY

Atmospheric conditions of temperature, humidity, sunshine, wind, and ion concentration have been shown to influence human performance and well-being. The exact nature and limits of this influence, however, has yet to be determined. Research in this area has been slow to make progress because the variables of concern are seldom independent, the nature of their interdependency is not as yet determined, and because humans are so capable of adaptation that they often acclimate (habituate to a single stimulus dimension) or become acclimatized (adapt to a multitude of conditions) vis-à-vis their atmospheric environment. In the short run, this adaptation is, of course, very beneficial, however, the potential cumulative effects and aftereffects of exposure to the vagaries of the weather are only now beginning to be considered.

IMPORTANT CONCEPTS

microclimate
ecoclimate
geoclimate
ambient temperature
thermal comfort
heat collapse, exhaustion, stroke
chillblains, hypothermia
task performance
sunlight
    (intensity, SCN timing and exposure,
    spectrum)

pineal gland
melatonin
Seasonal Affective Disorder (SAD)
vitamin D
jaundice
melanin
wind
ion concentration

REFERENCES

Adam, J.M. (1967). Military problems of air transport and tropical service. In C.N. Davies, P.R. Davis, & F.H. Tryer (Eds.), *The effects of abnormal physical conditions at work*. London: E. & S. Livingstone.

Anderson, C.A. (1987). Temperature and aggression: Effects on quarterly, yearly, and city rates of violent and nonviolent crime. *Journal of Personality and Social Psychology, 52*(6), 1161–1173.

Anderson, C.A., & Anderson, D.C. (1984). Ambient temperature and violent crime: Tests of the linear and curvilinear hypotheses. *Journal of Personality and Social Psychology, 46*, 91–97.

Armstrong, C. (1961). Atmospheric conditions and the spread of poliomyelitis. *American Journal of Public Health, 51*.

Ashrae *Handbook of fundamentals* (1967). New York: American Society of Heating, Refrigerating, and Air-conditioning Engineers, Inc.

Ashrae *Transactions*. (1977). New York: American Society of Heating, Refrigerating, and Air-conditioning Engineers, Inc.

Assael, M., Pfeifer, Y., & Sulman, F. G. (1974). Influence of artificial air ionization on the human electroencephalogram. *International Journal of Biometeorology, 18*, 306–312.

Attarzadeh, F. (1983). Seasonal variation in stature and body weight. *International Journal of Orthodonics, 21*(4), 3–12.

Aucliems, A. (1972). Some observed relationships between the atmospheric environment and mental work. *Environmental Research, 5*, 217–240.

Banzinger, G., & Owens, K. (1978). Geophysical variables and behavior: II. Weather features as predictors of local social indicators of maladaptation in two non-urban areas. *Psychological Reports, 43*, 427–434.

Baron, R.A. (1972). Aggression as a function of ambient temperature and prior anger arousal. *Journal of Personality and Social Psychology, 21*, 183–189.

Baron, R.A. (1978). Aggression and heat: The "long hot summer" revisited. In A. Baum, S. Valins, & J.E. Singer (Eds.), *Advances in environmental research* (Vol.1, pp.186–207). Hillsdale, N.J.: Erlbaum.

Baron, R. A. (1987a). Effects of negative ions on cognitive performance. *Journal of Applied Psychology, 72*(1), 131–137.

Baron, R. A. (1987b). Effects of negative ions on

interpersonal attraction: Evidence for intensification. *Journal of Personality and Social Psychology, 52*(3), 547–553.

Baron, R.A., & Bell, P.A. (1975). Aggression and heat: Mediating effects of prior provocation and exposure to an aggressive model. *Journal of Personality and Social Psychology, 31*, 825–832.

Baron, R.A., & Lawton, S.F. (1972). Environmental influences on aggression: The facilitation of modeling effects by high ambient temperatures. *Psychonomic Science, 26*, 80–83.

Baron, R.A., Russell, G.W., & Arms, R.L. (1985). Negative ions and behavior: Impact on mood, memory, and aggression among Type A and Type B persons. *Journal of Personality and Social Psychology, 48*, 746–754.

Bates, M. (1966). The role of weather in human behavior. In W. Sewall (Ed.), *Human dimensions of weather modification*. Chicago: University of Chicago Press.

Bell, C.R., Provins, K.A., & Hiorns, R.F. (1964). Visual and auditory vigilance during exposure to hot and humid conditions. "Ergonomics, 7, 279–288.

Bell, P.A., & Baron, R.A. (1976). Aggression and heat: The mediating role of negative affect. *Journal of Applied Social Psychology, 6*, 18–30.

Bell, P.A., & Baron, R.A. (1977). Aggression and ambient temperature: The facilitating and inhibiting effects of hot and cold environments. *Bulletin of the Psychonomic Society, 9*, 443–445.

Berke, J., & Wilson, V. (1951). *Watch out for the weather*. New York: Viking.

Bittman, E.L., Dempsey, R.J., & Karsch, F.J. (1983). Pineal melatonin secretion drives the reproduction response to day length in ewes. *Endocrinology, 113*, 2276–2283.

Buckalew, L.W., & Rizzuto, A.P. (1984). Negative air ion effects on human performance and physiological condition. *Aviation, Space, and Environmental Medicine, 55*(8), 731–734.

Burch, G.E., & DePasquale, N.P. (1962). *Hot climates, man and his heart*. Springfield, Ill.: Chas. C Thomas.

Carter, D.S., & Goldman, B.D. (1983). Antigonadal effects of timed melatonin infusion in pinealectomized male Dungarian hamsters (*Phodopus sungorus sungorus*): Duration is the critical parameter. *Endocrinology, 113*(6), 1261.

Charry, J.M. (1977). Meteorology and behavior: The effects of positive air ions on human performance, physiology and mood. Dissertation Abstracts *International, 37,* 4751.

Charry, J.M., & Hawkinshire, F.B.W. (1981). Effects of atmospheric electricity on some substrates of disordered social behavior. *Journal of Personality and Social Psychology, 41,* 185–197.

Condon, R.G. (1983). Seasonal photoperiodism, activity rhythms, and disease susceptibility in the central Canadian Arctic. *Arctic Anthropology, 20,* 33–48.

Crockford, G.W. (1967). Heat problems and protective clothing in iron and steel works. In C.N. Davies, P.R. Davis, & F.H. Tyler (Eds.), *The effects of abnormal physical conditions at work.* London: E.& S. Livingstone.

Curley, M.D., & Hawkins, R.N. (1983). Cognitive performance during a heat acclimatization regimen. *Aviation, Space, and Environmental Medicine, 54*(8), 709–713.

Dexter, E. (1900). School deportment and the weather. *Educational Review, 19,* 160–162.

Duffee, R.A., & Koontz, R.H. (1965). Behavioral effects of ionized air on rats. *Psychophysiology, 1,* 347–359.

Ellis, J. (1985). Home phototherapy for newborn jaundice. *Birth, 12* (Suppl. 3), 15–17.

Falkenberg, V., & Kirk, R.E. (1977). Effects of ionized air on early acquisition of Sidman avoidance behavior in rats. *Psychological Reports, 41,* 1071–1074.

Fine, B.J., & Kobrick, J.L. (1987). Effect of heat and chemical protective clothing on cognitive performance. *Aviation, Space, and Environmental Medicine, 58*(2), 149–154.

Finley, L.S. (1981). *Get ionized: Discovery of happy making generators provide proof that negatives attract. Washington Post,* July 11.

Frey, A.H. (1967). Modification of the conditioned emotional response by treatment with small negative air ions. *Journal of Comparative and Physiological Psychology, 63,* 121–125.

Gavalas-Medici, R., & Day-Masdaleno, S.R. (1976). Extremely low frequency, weak electric fields affect schedule controlled behavior of monkeys. *Nature, 261,* 258–259.

Gelperin, A. (1973). Humidification and upper respiratory infection incidence. *Heating, Piping and Air Conditioning, 45,* 3.

Giannini, A.J., Castellani, S., & Dvoredsky, A.C. (1983). Anxiety state: Relationship to atmospheric cations and serotonin. *Journal of Clinical Psychiatry, 44*(7), 262–264.

Gilbert, G.O. (1973). Effects of negative air ions upon emotionality and brain serotonin level in isolated rats. *International Journal of Biometeorology, 17,* 267–275.

Griffiths, I.D., & Boyce, P.R. (1971). Performance and thermal comfort. *Ergonomics, 14,* 457–468.

Griffitt, W. (1970). Environmental effects on interpersonal affective behavior: Ambient effective temperature and attraction. *Journal of Personality and Social Psychology, 15,* 240–244.

Hancock, P.A. (1986a). The effect of skill on performance under an environmental stressor. *Aviation, Space, and Environmental Medicine, 57*(1), 59–64.

Hancock, P.A. (1986b). Sustained attention under thermal stress. *Psychological Bulletin, 99*(2), 263–281.

Hanna, J.M., & Brown, D.E. (1983). Human heat tolerance: An anthropological perspective. *Annual Review of Anthropology, 12,* 259–284.

Hansell, C.W. (1961). An attempt to define ionization of the air. *Proceedings of the International Conference on Ionization of the Air.* Philadelphia: Franklin Institute, I-J, 1–10.

Harries, K.D., & Stadler, S.J. (1983) Determinism revisited: Assault and heat stress in Dallas, 1980. *Environmental Behavior, 15*(2), 235–256.

Hawkins, L.H., & Barber, T. (1978). Air ions and human performance. *Ergonomics, 21,* 273–278.

Hill, J.W. (1967). Applied problems of hot work in the glass industry. In C.N. Davies, P.R. Davis, & F.H. Tyler (Eds.), *The effects of abnormal physical conditions at work.* London: E. & S. Livingstone.

Hohnsbein, J., Piekarski, C., & Kampmann, B. (1983). Influence of high ambient temperature and humidity on visual sensitivity. *Ergonomics, 26*(9), 905–911.

Hohnsbein, J., Piekarski, C., Kampman, B., & Noack, T. (1984). Effects of heat on visual acuity. *Ergonomics, 27*(12), 1239–1246.

Holland, W.W. (1961). Influence of the weather on respiratory and heart disease. *Lancet, 2,* xx–xx.

Jordan, W.S. (1967). Etiology of the acute infectious respiratory diseases. *Archives of Environmental Health, 14.*

Kazantizis, G. (1967). Hypothermia. In C.N. Davis, P.R. Davis, & F.H. Tryor, (Eds.), *The effects of abnormal physical conditions at work.* Edinburgh: Livingstone.

Kenrick, D.T., & MacFarlane, S.W. (1986) Ambient temperature and horn honking: A field study of the heat/aggression relationship. *Environment and behavior, 18*(2), 179–191.

Kobrick, J.L., & Sleeper, L.A. (1986). Effect of wearing chemical protective clothing in the heat on signal detection over the visual field. *Aviation, Space, and Environmental Medicine, 57*(2), 144–148.

Kornetsky, C. (1976). *Pharmacology: Drugs affecting behavior.* New York: John Wiley.

Kreuger, A.P., & Reed, E.J. (1976). Biological impact of small air ions. *Science, 193,* 1209–1213.

Kreuger, A.P., & Siegel, S. (1978). Ions in the air. *Human Nature, 1,* 46–72.

Lambert, J.F., & Olivereau, J.M. (1980). Single-trial passive avoidance learning by rats treated with ionized air. *Psychological Reports, 47,* 1323–1330.

LeBeau, J.L., & Langworthy, R.H. (1986). The linkages between routine activities, weather, and calls for police services. *Journal of Police Science and Administration, 14*(2), 137–145.

Leiber, A.L. (1978). The lunar effect. Garden City, N.Y.: Anchor Press/Doubleday.

Lincoln, G.E. (1983). Photoperiodism: Melatonin as a seasonal home cure, a commercial story. *Nature,* (London) 302:755.

MacPherson, R.K. (1973). Thermal stress and comfort. *Ergonomics, 16*(5), 611–623.

McDonagh, A.F., & Lightner, D.A. (1985). "Like a shrivelled blood orange"—Bilirubin, jaundice and phototherapy. *Pediatrics, 75*(3), 443–455.

McNall, P.E., Jaax, J., & Rohles, F.H. (1967). Thermal comfort (thermally neutral) conditions for three levels of activity. *ASHRAE Transactions, 73*(I), 3.1–3.13.

Meese, G.B., Lewis, M.I., Wyon, D.P., & Kok, R. (1984). A laboratory study of the effects of moderate thermal stress on the performance of factory workers. *Ergonomics, 27*(1), 19–43.

Mehrabian, A., & Russell, J.A. (1974). *An approach to environmental psychology.* Cambridge, Mass.: MIT Press.

Moran, E.F. (1979). *Human adaptability: An introduction to ecological anthropology.* North Scituate, Mass.: Duxbury.

Morison, W.L. (1984). Photoimmunology. *Photochemistry and Photobiology: An International Journal, 40,* 781–787.

Olivereau, J.M. (1976). Atmospheric ionization and its effects on animals and man. *Annee Psychologique, 76,* 283–291.

Penwarden, A.D. (1973). Acceptable wind speeds in towns. *Building Science, 8,* 259–267.

Pepler, R.D., & Warner, R.E. (1968). Temperature and learning: An experimental study. *ASHRAE Transactions, 74,* 211–219.

Perry, J.P., & Simpson, M.E., (1987). Violent crimes in a city: Environmental determinants. *Environment and Behavior, 19,* 77–90.

Poulton, E.C., Hunt, F.C.R., Mumford, J.C., & Poulton, J. (1975). Mechanical disturbance produced by steady and gusty winds of moderate strength: Skilled performance and semantic assessments. *Ergonomics, 18,* 651–673.

Poulton, E.C., & Kerslake, M. (1965). Initial stimulating effect of warmth upon perceptual efficiency. *Aerospace Medicine, 36,* 29–32.

Provins, K.A. (1966). Environmental heat, body temperature, and behavior. *Australian Journal of Psychology, 18,* 118–129.

Provins, K.A., & Bell, C.R. (1970). Effects of heat stress on the performance of two tasks running concurrently. *Journal of Experimental Psychology, 85,* 40–44.

Ramsey, J.D., Burford, C.L., Beshir, M.Y., & Jensen, R.C. (1983). Effects of workplace thermal conditions on safe work behavior. *Journal of Safety Research, 14*(3), 105–114.

Ray, O. (1978). *Drugs, society, and human behavior* (2nd ed.). Saint Louis, Mo.: C.V. Mosby.

Riley, M.W., & Cochran, D.J. (1984). Dexterity performance and reduced ambient temperature. *Human Factors, 26*(2), 207–214.

Rim, Y. (1975). Psychological test performance of different personality types on Sharav days in artificial air ionization. *International Journal of Biometeorology, 21,* 337–340.

Rohles, F. (1967). Environmental psychology. *Psychology Today, 1,* 54–63.

Rohles, F.H. (1973, May). *The revised modal comfort envelope: Description, validation, and application of a new tool for studying thermal comfort.* Paper presented at ASHRAE Spring Conference Regina, Saskatchewan, Canada.

Rohles, F.H. (1974). The modal comfort envelope and its use in current standards. *Human Factors, 16*(3), 314–322.

Rohles, F.H. (1975). Humidity, human factors and the energy shortage. *ASHRAE Transactions, 81*(1), 38–40.

Rohles, F.H., Woods, J.E., & Nevins, R.G. (1973, May). *The influence of clothing and temperature on sedentary comfort.* Paper presented at the ASHRAE Spring Conference, Regina, Saskatchewan, Canada.

Rosen, S. (1985). The weather: Windy and grouchy. *The Catholic Digest*, 94–97.

Rosenthal, N.E., Sack, D.E., Gillin, J.C., Lewy, A.J., Goodwin, F.K., Davenport, Y., Mueller, P.S., Newsome, D.A., & Wehr, T.A. (1984). Seasonal affect disorder. *Archives of General Psychiatry*, 41, 72–80.

Rosenthal, N.E., Sack, D.E., Carpenter, C.J., Parry, B.L., Mendelson, W.B., & Wehr, T.A. (1985). Antidepressant effects of light in seasonal affective disorder. *American Journal of Psychiatry*, 142(2), 163–170.

Rosenthal, N.E., Carpenter, C.J., James S.P., Parry, B.L., Rogers, S.L.B., & Wehr, T.A. (1986a). Seasonal affect disorder in children and adolescents. *American Journal of Psychiatry*, 143(3), 356–358.

Rosenthal, N.E., Genhart, M., Jacobsen, F.M., & Skwerer, R.G. (1986b, June). *Disturbances of appetite and weight regulation in seasonal affective disorder.* Paper presented at Conference on Human Obesity, the New York Academy of Sciences.

Rotton, J. (1986). Determinism redux: Climate and cultural correlates of violence. *Environment and Behavior*, 18(3), 346–368.

Rotton, J., & Frey, J. (1984). Psychological costs of air pollution: Atmospheric conditions, seasonal trends and psychiatric emergencies. *Population and Environment: Behavioral and Social Issues*, 7(1), 3–16.

Sharma, V.M., Sridiharan, K., Pichan, G., & Panwar, M.R. (1986). Influence of heat-stress induced dehydration on mental functions. *Ergonomics*, 29(6), 791–799.

Sommers, P. , & Moos, R. (1976). The weather and human behavior. In R.H. Moos (Ed.), *The human context: Environmental determinants of behavior.* New York: John Wiley.

Soyka, F., & Edmonds, A. (1978). *The ion effect.* New York: Bantam.

Spitzer, R.L., Endicott, J., & Robins, E. (1978). Research diagnostic criteria: Rationale and reliability. *Archives of General Psychology*, 35, 773–782.

Suedfeld, P. (1987). Extreme and unusual environments. In D. Stokols & I. Altman (Eds.), *Handbook of environmental psychology.* New York: John Wiley.

Sullivan, W. (1981). Ions created by the winds may prompt changes in emotional states. *New York Times*, October 6.

Sulman, F.G., & Pfeifer, Y. (1964). Effects of hot, dry desert winds (Sharav, Hamsin) on the metabolism of hormones and minerals. *Harokeach Haivi*, 10, 401–404.

Tal, E., Pfeifer, Y. , & Sulman, F.G. (1976). Effects of air ionization on blood serotonin in vitro. *Experientia*, 32, 326–327.

Tom, G., Poole, M.F., Galla, J., & Berrier, J. (1981). The influence of negative air ions on human performance and mood. *Human Factors*, 23(5), 633–636.

Veitch R. (1976). *Temperature, thermostatic control and perceived health.* Unpublished manuscript, Bowling Green State University, Bowling Green, Ohio.

Voisinet, R. (1978). Ionization as a socially useful technology in a co-evolving man-environment system. *Journal of Environmental Sciences*, 21, 28–29.

West, J.B. (1984). Human physiology at extreme altitudes at Mount Everest. *Science*, 223, 784–788.

Wilkinson, R.T. (1974). Individual differences in response to the environment, *Ergonomics*, 17, 745–756.

Wilkinson, R.T., Fox, R.H., Goldsmith, R., Hampton, I.F., & Lewis, H.E. (1964). Psychological and physical responses to raised body temperature. *Journal of Applied Physiology*, 29, 287–292.

Winslow, C.E., & Harrington, L.D. (1949). *Temperature and human life.* Princeton, N.J.: Princeton University Press.

Wolken, J.J. (1986). *Light and life processes.* New York: Van Nostrand Reinhold.

Wurtman, R.J., Baum, M.J., & Potts, J.T. Jr. (Eds.) (1985). The medical and biological effects of light. *New York Academy of Science Annual*, 453.

Wyndham, G., (1969). Adaptation to heat and cold. *Environmental Research*, 2, 442–469.

Yaglou, C.P., & Drinker, P. (1929). The summer comfort zone: Climate and clothing. *ASHRAE Transactions*, 35.

Zahorska-Markiewicz, B. (1980). Weight reduction and seasonal variation. *International Journal of Obesity*, 4, 136–143.

Zajonc, R.B. (1980). Compresence. In P.B. Paulus (Ed.), *Psychology of group influence.* Hillsdale, N.J.: Erlbaum.

Zifferblatt, S.M., Curtis, C.S., & Pinsky, J.C. (1980). Understanding food habits. *Journal of the American Dietetic Association*, 76, 9–14.

Zimmerman, M.R. (1985). Paleopathology in Alaskan mummies. *American Scientist*, 73, 20–25.

The Atmospheric Environment II

Chemical Pollution

7

FIGURE 7-1 Pollution of all sorts will not go away simply because we want it to. Concerted individual, industrial and physical efforts must be expended to curb pollution. (Drawing by O'Brien, ©1972 The New Yorker Magazine, Inc.)

In Chapter 2 the relationship between living organisms and their environments was described as one of mutual interdependence. Understanding this relationship, it was noted, requires an understanding of both the organism and its environment. When defined in terms of human existence, however, the *environment* includes situations as specific as an airplane cockpit, as mundane as the residential bathroom, and as compact as the sleeping quarters of spacecraft. Thus, measurement of the environment is always subject to the interests and idiosyncrasies of the investigator. In its largest scale, the study of the terrestrial environment is the study of the biosphere, reaching from the depths of the oceans to the summits of the tallest mountains. But, any attempt to understand the mutual interdependency of organisms with their life-supporting environments requires understanding of the environment extending even beyond these limits (e.g., recent concerns center on the ozone layer miles above the earth's surface and the protective function it serves for humans and other animals). However atomistic the level of analysis begins, the need for information expands to the point where an understanding of atmospheric and geologic processes are eventually necessary.

The atmosphere consists of a layer of gas molecules held close to the earth's surface by gravity. This layer consists of approximately 78 percent nitrogen, 21 percent oxygen, 0.9 percent argon, and 0.03 percent carbon dioxide. There are also a number of minor elements in trace amounts including methane, ozone, hydrogen sulfide, carbon monoxide, the oxides of nitrogen and sulfur, hydrocarbons, and dust particles. Additionally, water vapor exists throughout the atmosphere in varying concentrations. These *chemical* properties of the atmosphere remain relatively constant; *physical* properties, however, change rapidly and continually and, in fact, are relatively unstable. The basic elements that make up the earth's atmosphere tend to circulate, to mix readily, and to be transported over the surface of the earth easily. When the lower atmosphere is heated by radiant energy reflecting off the surface of the earth, this warm air rises, expanding and cooling as it does so; winds are then produced as the cooler surface air is drawn in to replace the rising warmer air. These winds are the major transportation vehicle for elements in the lower atmosphere, keeping some pollutants from building up to dangerous levels while simultaneously spreading pollution throughout the biosphere.

With air quality indices now being provided as a regular part of the nightly news and the successful merchandising of bottled water, we are all becoming increasingly aware that the air we breathe may not be as healthful, and the water we drink may not be as pure as we'd like it to be (i.e., the biosphere is changing, and not for the better). Coupled with this awareness is the knowledge that many harmful substances find their way into the biosphere as a result of seemingly benign everyday behaviors (exhausts from automobiles, smoke billowing from the chimney of the family-room fireplace, and hydrofluorides emanating from aerosol spray cans). Even the convenience of taking out fast-food hamburgers in insulating packages contributes to both air pollution and solid waste, a fact that has led some of the major fast-food franchises to begin phasing out the use of containers made from *chlorofluorocarbons*, more commonly known as CFCs (World Environment Report, 1987).

TIME-OUT: Consider the ways you may be inadvertently and unthinkingly (but yet directly), contributing to atmospheric pollution. Do you own and operate an automobile? If you do, you are adding carbon monoxide, nitrous, and sulfuric oxides and various particulates to the atmosphere. Do you smoke tobaco? If so, you are increasing the atmospheric levels of 4,720 different compounds, some of which are know to be carcinogens or are implicated in cardiovascular disorders. Burning leaves, operating an inefficient furnace, using aerosol sprays, and utilizing various chemical cleaners and solvents also contribute directly to atmospheric pollution. Indirect complicity also takes many forms. Using energy-inefficient appliances, buying products in excessively packaged form, not car pooling, using CFC products, are but a few.

List those activities that you engage in each day that you feel might add to air pollution. Now list alternative behaviors that would contribute less. Compare the benefits as well as the costs of engaging in these alternative behaviors.

The ill-effects of air pollution are often dramatized by recounting severe episodes of acute pollution (e.g., the sulfuric acid mist of the Meuse Valley of Belgium in 1930; the Donora, Pennsylvania, industrial sulfur dioxide emissions of 1948; the killer smog of London in 1952; and the hydrogen sulfide leak in Poza Rica, Mexico in 1950). Deaths (sometimes reaching into the thousands) from these episodes occurred most frequently in the elderly and those predisposed to pulmonary-cardiovascular problems. What is now being learned is that the more insidious effects of prolonged exposure to these same pollutants in less concentrated form may be just as harmful in the long run.

Among the common pollutants now thought to produce maladaptations in human functioning and changes in the ecology of the biosphere are carbon monoxide, carbon dioxide, sulfur dioxide, nitrogen dioxide, formaldehyde, various hydrocarbons, the photoelectric pollutants, and particulate matter. Any attempt to understand the problems posed by these pollutants must necessarily involve an understanding of how they are produced, and the effects they have on individual living organisms, on entire species, and on the ecosystem of which the species is a component. Additionally, knowledge of how pollutants are transported and the means by which they are to be disposed of must be understood. Finally, ultimate concern must be with the effects on humans. Chemical pollutants have myriad origins, various modes of transport, and each has its own special effects. All are, nonetheless, spread throughout the biosphere by air and by water.

Almost every part of the human body is affected by some pollutant. Lead and mercury, for example, primarily affect neural tissue, arsenic affects the skin, carbon monoxide the lungs, and chlorinated hydrocarbons concentrate in fatty tissue (Waldbott, 1978). Similarly, the effects of pollutants on wildlife have been documented for many aspects of the life cycle. Arsenic, asbestos, cadmium, fluoride, hydrogen sulfide, the nitrogen oxides, the sulfur oxides, and vanadium all influence the abundance rates of wildlife. Fluoride, some particulates, and the sulfur oxides influence the distribution of populations throughout the ecosystem. Arsenic, lead, the photochemicals, and some oxidants affect fertility. Arsenic, asbestos, beryllium, boron, hydrogen sulfide, and lead, among others, influence mortality; finally, changes in growth rates have been shown to be affected by such pollutants as borium, hydrochloric acid, lead, and the nitrogen and sulfur oxides (Newman, 1980).

Both the number and the volume of manufactured chemicals have increased in the past 40 years. In the United States alone, the annual production of synthetic organic chemicals (those containing carbon) has risen from 6.7 million metric tons to 102 million (U.S. International Trade Commission, 1986). With the increase in new products from plastics to pesticides to birth control pills to synthetic fibers, there are some 70,000 chemicals presently in everyday use ("The Quest for Chemical Safety," 1985) with 500 to 1,000 new ones added annually (Schodell, 1985). This expanding use of chemicals only increases the difficulties in disposal and increases the likelihood of lethal exposure.

TWO CASE HISTORIES

Minamata Bay

Before looking specifically at the health and psychological effects of various common pollutants, two case histories will prove informative. Over a period of several years in the 1950s an ailment peculiar to the families of fishermen in the coastal town of Minamata, Japan, occurred. Early symptoms included fatigue, irritability, headaches, numbness in arms and legs, and difficulty in swallowing. Subsequently, more severe symptoms involving the sensory organs began to develop. Vision became blurred and visual fields restricted; some people experienced hearing loss and some lost muscular coordination. A great many complained of a metallic taste in their mouths, their gums became inflamed, and many suffered from diarrhea. Eventually, 43 people died, 111 were severely disabled, and 19 babies were born with congenital defects. Of those affected, all lived relatively close to one another and all relied very heavily on fish taken from the Minamata Bay for food.

An examination of the problem showed that a plastics factory near the bay had used the element mercury in its production processes; by-products were released into water which flowed into Minamata Bay. What was not realized immediately was that the industrial processes involved in manufacturing the plastic converted inorganic mercury into the much more toxic organic methyl mercury. Inorganic mercury does not pass through cell membranes readily, although if taken internally it will damage the intestinal lining and potentially damage liver and kidneys. Methyl mercury, on the other hand, readily passes through cell membranes and is easily transported by the red blood cells throughout the body, entering and then destroying brain cells (Waldbott, 1978). Additionally, organic methyl mercury enters the food chain much faster. For example, fish absorb methyl mercury from water 100 times faster than they absorb inorganic mercury. Methyl mercury is also retained as much as two to five times longer than inorganic mercury (Patrick, Binetti, & Halterman, 1981). The normal amount of mercury in humans is about 5 parts per billion, and it is estimated that 50 parts per billion is the maximum safe level. At 10 times that amount, or 500 parts per billion, symptoms such as fatigue, irritability, headaches, and numbness begin to appear. In some of the affected fishermen of Minamata the concentration of mercury had reached 1,300 parts per billion.

Love Canal

A second example comes from an incident that occurred in 1976 in upstate New York near Niagara Falls, now familiarly known as Love Canal. The first concerns expressed by residents were that trees, vegetables, and flowers in the area began to discolor and die; rubber on children's tennis shoes and on bicycle tires began disintegrating at a faster than normal rate; and, the neighborhood dogs developed sores on their noses that would not heal (Janerick, et al., 1981). This residential community had been built on the site of a chemical dump, originally a channel dug in the 1890s. This channel was to have provided a transportation route between industrial centers in and around Niagara Falls, but that attempt was abandoned and the ditch was unused for a number of years. From the 1920s to the 1950s the ditch was used as a landfill, and in that period more than 80 different chemicals were dumped there. In 1953 the company that was dumping the chemicals donated the land to the city of Niagara Falls. Some 200 homes and an elementary school were built.

In addition to worn tennis shoes and sore noses, a number of other more serious phenomena occurred. A higher than average miscarriage rate was noted, there was a large number of blood and liver abnormalities diagnosed, and the rate of birth defects was higher than expected. Even today, experts admit that they know little about the impact of the chemicals dumped into the canal. However, a number of these substances, including dioxin, benzene, dichlorethylene, and chloroform, are now suspected of being carcinogenic.

Several lessons can be learned from these two illustrations. First, our society is producing chemicals at a much faster rate than we can determine their environmental and health impact. Second, we have not identified appropriate means for the disposal of many chemicals. Third, individuals seem to differ in their response to exposure to various pollutants (e.g., some fishermen of Minamata and some residents of Love Canal were affected more than others). Fourth, some pollutants may have a threshold (i.e., we may be able to withstand penetration of a pollutant up to a point with no measurable symptoms, then upon reaching a certain concentration severe symptoms rapidly appear). The fifth lesson gleaned from these two incidents is that some effects are reversible (some of the fishermen in Minamata, for example, recovered when the mercury-filled fish were removed from their diet), but some are not. Sixth, the chemical form of a pollutant has a great effect on its toxicity: The inorganic mercury, although toxic, was not nearly as hazardous as the organic methyl mercury. And finally, a pollutant and its effects can be changed markedly by ecological and biological processes. The mercury changed in the plastic factory from inorganic to organic mercury. In the fish it was found in low concentrations; as it passed through the food chain and reached humans it built up to levels that, for some at least, became lethal. For a general idea regarding the known effects of some major pollutants see Figure 7-2.

With this general introduction in mind, let us now turn our attention to some major pollutants and consider their impact on the world in which we live, including the short- and long-term effects on human health and behavior. Whole volumes have been written documenting the effects of various atmospheric pollutants. In this chapter, we will deal with just a few common pollutants. The choice of which to look at was made on the basis of abundance, commonness, ubiquity, and ease of remediation, given changes in public policy and personal values.

CARBON DIOXIDE (CO_2)

Carbon dioxide (CO_2) is a colorless, tasteless, nontoxic gas. It is exhaled by all animals as a product of metabolism and it is absorbed by plants as part of the process of photosynthesis. Carbon dioxide and water are the basic products of the combustion of all hydrocarbons including all fossil fuels and wood. The amounts produced annually by exhalation and combustion are immense, and the only possible means of disposal is to discharge it into the atmosphere. The atmospheric CO_2 content is therefore very large, in the neighborhood of 332 parts per million (ppm), and is increasing at the rate of around 5 percent every 20 years (Barney, 1980). The possibility of the "greenhouse" effect caused by the increased carbon dioxide concentration in the atmosphere is reason for concern. In a greenhouse, shortwave solar radiation (i.e., light from the sun) passes through the glass and is re-radiated as infrared, longwave heat radiation. The heat radiated upward is then trapped inside the greenhouse by the glass, which is impenetrable by the longer waves. Carbon dioxide in the atmosphere acts in much the same way as the glass. It permits solar radiation to pass through to the earth's surface, then intercepts some of the heat radiated upward from the surface toward space and redirects it back toward the surface. With increasing amounts of carbon dioxide in the atmosphere, the balance between the incoming and outgoing radiation can be maintained only with an increase in surface and lower atmospheric temperatures.

Projections are not sufficiently precise to permit accurate calculations of how much carbon dioxide will accumulate in the atmosphere in the coming decades. Nonetheless, increases can be expected. In fact, one of the major points of discussion during the UN Earth Summit in Rio de Janiero in 1992 was a resolution to reduce carbon dioxide emission levels to those of 1990 by the year 2000. The United States came under fire for not supporting this resolution. Industrial emissions as well as deforestation and increased fossil fuel combustion are projected to increase in the coming decades, each of which will act to increase significantly the amount of CO_2 in the atmosphere. Based on a geo-

FIGURE 7-2   The sites of effects of some major pollutants in humans. (From G.L. Waldbott, 1978. *Health Effects of Environment Pollutants*. St. Louis: C.V. Mosby.)

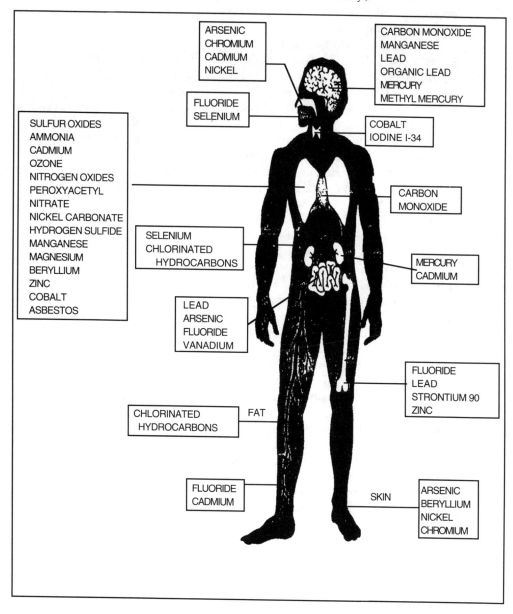

physical study by the National Academy of Sciences (Geophysics Study Committee, 1977) it is projected that even a doubling of carbon dioxide in the atmosphere will bring about a 2°–3°C rise in the air temperature of the lower atmosphere at the middle latitudes, and up to a 7 percent increase in average precipitation. These changes will not be distributed evenly though, as some regions will be wetter, others drier (MacCracken & Kulka, 1985; Manabe &

Wetherald, 1986). The temperature rise will be greater by a factor of 3 or 4 in the polar regions (Geophysics Study Committee, 1977). The increase in carbon dioxide anticipated in the next 40 to 50 years might lead to an increase in the global mean air temperature of more than 8°C (Brown, et al., 1988).

The effects on life systems of an atmospheric increase in the concentration of carbon dioxide are at this time largely unknown. In smaller controlled environments, an increase in the amount of the intake of carbon dioxide in the atmosphere leads to a proportional increase in the intake of carbon dioxide by plants, and thus leads to much faster growth. On a worldwide scale, greater absorption of carbon dioxide by the oceans occurs as the concentration of carbon dioxide in the atmosphere increases. However, it is unknown exactly how much more carbon dioxide the oceans are able to absorb without having detrimental effects on marine life, both plant and animal. It is possible that there are additional absorption pockets yet to be discovered, but whether the total ecosystem is adaptive enough to maintain equilibrium with substantial increases in carbon dioxide is at this time unknown.

Very little work has been done on the physiological or the behavioral effects of increased carbon dioxide intake by humans. It is known that carbon dioxide is a stimulant to the brain mechanisms that control breathing. If carbon dioxide levels increase, individuals reflexively breathe more rapidly. In fact, during some forms of surgery, especially if there is a danger of the breathing process stopping, carbon dioxide is deliberately added to the oxygen being inhaled to aid in stimulating the breathing process. Hyperventilation during smog alerts is thus a common occurrence.

It is obvious that if carbon dioxide is substituted for oxygen, detrimental effects, including hypoxia, will occur. However, assuming that the concentrations of oxygen remain unchanged while carbon dioxide increases, the physiological effects are unclear. In a study by Weitzman, Keeney, and Luriator (1969) humans exposed to continuous low-level concentrations of carbon dioxide showed a decrease in night visual acuity and a loss of green-color sensitivity. It is probably safe to assume that any effect carbon dioxide does have on human functioning probably occurs as a result of combination with other pollutants such as carbon monoxide. In fact, most research to date on pollution and human behavior (particularly performance behavior) has involved the study of carbon monoxide.

CARBON MONOXIDE (CO)

Much of the carbon monoxide (CO) in the atmosphere results from the incomplete burning of substances containing carbon. In the normal process of respiration, humans and other animals breathe in air from the atmosphere. The oxygen from this air unites with the hemoglobin in the red blood cells to produce oxyhemoglobin. The air is deoxygenated, with the residue being expired through respiration. Most oxygen in the blood is transported in the form of oxyhemoglobin. When an individual breathes air containing carbon monoxide, however, the carbon monoxide unites with the hemoglobin to produce carboxyhemoglobin. Thus, when the blood contains carboxyhemoglobin, it contains proportionally less oxyhemoglobin, and body tissues, including muscles and brain cells, receive less oxygen and can, therefore, be expected to perform in less than optimal ways. Important indicators of high levels of carboxyhemoglobin in the blood are bright red fingertips and lips.

Exposure to carbon monoxide over extended periods of time can cause health problems. For example, minimal exposure levels have been shown to lead to visual and hearing impairment, Parkinsonism, epilepsy, headache, fatigue, memory disturbances, and even retardation or psychotic symptoms. In one of the first studies performed to determine the effects of low-level concentrations of carbon monoxide, McFarland, Roughton, Halperin and Niven (1944) found that the visual threshold for a flash of light was influenced by the percentage of oxyhemoglobin in the blood, and thus influenced indirectly by the intake of carbon monoxide through breathing. In a follow-up study, Halperin, McFarland, Niven and Roughton (1959) found that when a person stops breathing carbon monoxide the amounts of carboxyhemoglobin in the blood fall very slowly, with the visual threshold lagging behind the reduction in carboxyhemoglobin. Thus, the effect is not only immediate but also long lasting. Additional studies on the influence of carbon monoxide by Beard and Wertheim (1967) have indicated that individuals show a decrement in their ability to make time-interval discrimination judgments and that reaction time, manual dexterity, and attentiveness are adversely affected by exposure to carbon monoxide (Breisacher, 1971).

Field studies have also demonstrated sensory-perceptual impairments, decreased ability to concentrate, and memory deficits in people living in heavily polluted areas compared to controls living in unpolluted areas (Arochova, Knotrova, Lipkova, & Liska, 1988; Bullinger, 1989). Additionally, there is some research that suggests that breathing the carbon monoxide contributed by automobile traffic may impair driving ability enough to increase the frequency of automobile accidents (Chovin, 1967; Lewis, Baddeley, Bonham, & Lovett, 1970; Moureu, 1964). Finally, Horvath, Dahms, and O'Hanlon (1971) have found performance decrements on information-processing tasks for subjects breathing polluted air containing moderate levels of carbon monoxide. When levels of carboxyhemoglobin get above 5 percent of all hemoglobin, increased cardiac output occurs, there is impaired oxidative metabolism of the cardiac muscle, and perhaps even structural changes in the heart and brain take place. Finally, an exposure of less than 0.1 percent carbon monoxide for several hours can result in death. The accidental death of tennis star Vitas Gerulaitis, by carbon monoxide poisoning points to the need to have carbon monoxide detectors installed in homes.

THE SULFUR AND NITROGEN OXIDES (SO_2 and NO_2)

About 45 percent of the sulfur oxides found in the atmosphere are the result of anthropogenic emissions stemming from the combustion of fossil fuels. An additional fractional percentage results from other industrial processes including the smelting of various ores. The most direct health effect of the sulfur oxides on humans is irritation of the respiratory system, with potential diminished lung functioning. The sulfur oxides are particularly aggravating to people with asth-

FIGURE 7-3 Breathing carbon monoxide contributed by automobile traffic may impair driving ability enough to increase the frequency of automobile accidents.

ma or other chronic respiratory problems. Any direct psychological or behavioral effects of the sulfur oxides are at this time largely unknown and unresearched. Much more is known about the indirect effects of these emissions into the biosphere, and it is to these effects that we now turn.

Fossil fuels and many ores contain sulfur. This sulfur is converted to sulfur dioxide during the combustion of fuels and the smelting of ores. The nitrogen oxides are also produced during these and any other high-temperature process. Sulfur and nitrogen oxides, once released into the atmosphere, combine with water to form *sulfuric* and *nitric acid*, respectively.

It is estimated that over 27 million metric tons of sulfur oxide and an additional 20 million metric tons of nitrogen oxide are released yearly into the atmosphere in the United States. Of this nitrogen discharge, 29 percent results from the combustion of fossil fuels at power plants, whereas 44 percent is released from transportation-related sources (Postel, 1986). Subsequently, much of this effluent combines with water in the atmosphere and forms *acid rain*. Acid rain, in turn, moves with the wind away from the source and spreads widely, so that the effects of the effluent are not necessarily produced at the source of the pollution.

Not too many years ago it was believed that acid rain was primarily a European problem. However, acid rainfall has spread from a relatively small area in the United States to nearly all of eastern North America. The major known effect of acid rain is to upset the ecosystem of land and water; the impact is particularly severe on freshwater lakes. It is also known that some soils are sensitive to acid rain: Many nutrients are leached out by the acid, and therefore plant productivity is adversely affected. Acid rain not only affects forests, lakes, and farm crops, but it has also been shown to leach exposed rock, particularly the soft, easily eroded rocks. Acid rain has also damaged buildings by eroding building material and/or affecting paint. Rock types such as marble and lime-stone are particularly susceptible because they dissolve in weak acids. Obviously, much more research is needed to provide valuable data on air pollution and the meteorological patterns that contribute to acid rain.

OZONE (O_3)

At the upper levels of the atmosphere, ozone plays an important protective role by absorbing harmful ultraviolet rays from the sun. Mounting evidence suggests that human-made chemicals (primarily CFCs used in aerosol propellants and refrigerants) are creating an "ozone hole" above the North and South Poles by destroying huge quantities of ozone. Continued ozone depletion is predicted to have serious consequences, most notably a drastic increase in skin cancer produced by ultraviolet sun rays (see Chapter 5).

At the lower atmospheric levels, ozone is a secondary pollutant derived primarily from the reactions of nitrogen dioxide and oxygen in sunlight. The concentrations in the atmosphere depend a great deal on reactions occurring in the lower atmosphere, which involve hydrocarbons and thus, indirectly, automobile exhaust. Ozone in increasing concentrations is toxic; in less concentrated form it leads to nose and throat irritations, fatigue, and in some instances a lack of coordination. Again, the psychological effects are not well known, the long-term behavioral effects have been virtually untested, and the cumulative health effects have not, to date, been studied.

Breathing ozone in concentrations of 3 ppm for several hours has been shown to lead to hemorrhaging and edema in human lung tissue and to death in rats and mice. In similar concentrations, structural damage has occurred and fibrous tissue was formed in the lungs of rabbits. In varying concentrations ozone has been shown to affect enzyme production and composition. These changes are thought to play a role in aging, with increased ozone inhalation leading to a speeding of the aging process.

TOBACCO SMOKE AS A POLLUTANT

In a discussion of strategies for assessing the toxicology of indoor air pollutants, Lewtas (1989) listed tobacco smoke as the number-one contributor to indoor air pollution. In response to increased public concern regarding the

---

TIME-OUT: In the two centuries since the dawn of the Industrial Revolution humans have altered the basic chemical cycles that had evolved over many millennia. There is a fixed supply of the six elements (carbon, oxygen, nitrogen, hydrogen, phosphorus, and sulfur) that comprise 95 percent of the mass of all living matter on earth. Life therefore depends on their efficient cycling through a process known as biogeochemical cycling. For example, in the past 130 years the combustion of fossil fuels has released 185 billion tons of carbon into the atmosphere, with current amounts equal to 53 times those of 1860. Figures for the other elements are equally impressive.

What might you, as an individual, do to bring these biogeochemical cycling processes back into equilibrium? Visit a nearby industrial plant and find out what the operators are doing to control industrial emissions. Find out from your automobile dealership the differences in the amounts of harmful emissions that are discharged by a well-tuned auto as compared to one out-of-tune.

---

effects of involuntary exposure to tobacco smoke, on October 29, 1987, the United States Senate, by a vote of 84 to 10, passed a law forbidding smoking on all commercial airline flights of 90 minutes or less. Numerous states and municipalities have passed similar legislation restricting cigarette, cigar, and pipe smoking to designated areas in their respective government office buildings. Some municipalities have gone a step further, banning smoking in other designated public places as well, including restaurants. Much of the impetus to this legislation is provided by studies showing that second-hand or "sidestream" inhalation of tobacco smoke may have long-term effects similar to, and perhaps more detrimental than, "mainstream" inhalation (mainstream smoke is smoke that the smoker inhales directly during puffing; sidestream smoke is smoke emitted from a smoldering cigarette into the ambient air). The long-term effects of tobacco smoke inhalation have been the subject of a number of separate reports of the Surgeon General of the United States (U.S. Department of Health, Education, and Welfare, 1982, 1983, 1984, 1985, 1986, 1988, 1989, 1990). These reports have focused on the relationship of smoke inhalation and cancer, cardiovascular disease, chronic obtrusive lung disease, cancer and chronic lung disease in the workplace, and nicotine addiction. Additional volumes have reported the effects of involuntary smoking and the health benefits of smoking cessation.

The smoke generated by a burning cigarette represents a very dense aerosol containing a number of particulates (collectively known as tar) and vapors including nitrogen, oxygen, carbon dioxide, and carbon monoxide (Brunnemann & Hoffmann, 1982; Dube & Green, 1982). In smaller concentrations a total of 4,720 compounds have been identified in cigarette smoke (Dube & Green, 1982). Nitrates in tobacco smoke serve as precursors to the development of hydrogen cyanide (HCN), nitric oxide (NO), nitrous oxide (N_2O), and nitrogen dioxide (NO_2).

Cigarette smoking has been identified as a major cause of coronary heart disease and as the major cause of lung cancer in the United States. Cigarette smoking is also the major cause of laryngeal cancer in the United States. Cigar and pipe smokers put themselves at similar risk to cigarette smokers in the development of this type of cancer. Cigarette smoking has also been shown to be a major cause of cancers of the oral cavity, esophageal cancer, and as a contributing factor in bladder cancer, kidney cancer, pancreatic cancer, stomach cancer, and uterine cervix cancer. Finally, it has been reported by the Surgeon General (U.S. Department of Health, Education, and Welfare, 1984) that more than 60,000 Americans die in a single year owing to chronic obstructive respiratory conditions (chronic bronchitis, emphysema, chronic obstructive lung disease, and allied conditions) related to smoking.

Sidestream Smoke versus Mainstream Smoke

Involuntary smoking is defined as the exposure of nonsmokers to tobacco combustion products from the smoking of others. Reasonable analyses of the health effects of passive smoking or involuntary smoking require not only some knowledge of the constituents of tobacco smoke but also some quantification of tobacco smoke exposure. Tobacco smoke in the environment is derived from two major sources, mainstream smoke and sidestream smoke. Mainstream smoke enters the environment after having first been drawn through the cigarette, which filters some of the active constituents. The smoke is then filtered by the smoker's own lungs and exhaled. Sidestream smoke arises from the burning end of the cigarette and enters directly into the environment. Differences in the combustion temperature, the degree of filtration, and the amount of tobacco consumed all lead to marked differences in the concentration of the constituents of mainstream smoke and sidestream smoke. Indeed, many potentially toxic-gas-phase constituents are present in higher concentrations in sidestream smoke than in mainstream smoke.

Nearly 85 percent of the smoke in any room containing smokers results from sidestream smoke. Therefore, both active and passive smokers may be similarly exposed to sidestream smoke whereas only smokers are exposed to mainstream smoke. In two recent epidemiological studies an increased risk in lung cancer in nonsmoking wives of smoking husbands has been found. Further, increases in heart rate and both systolic and diastolic blood pressure of elementary school children who are exposed to sidestream smoke have been reported (Report of the Surgeon General, U.S. Department of Health, Education, and Welfare, 1984). Although currently available evidence is not sufficient to conclude that passive or involuntary smoking causes lung cancer in nonsmokers, the evidence does raise concern about a possible serious health problem. Further, some studies have suggested that high levels of involuntary smoke exposure might produce small changes in pulmonary function in normal subjects. Children of smoking parents have an increased prevalence of reported respiratory systems and have an increased frequency of bronchitis and pneumonia early in life (Report of the Surgeon General, 1984).

A general conclusion that can be reached is that while the nature of the association between sidestream smoke and pulmonocardiovascular diseases and cancer are unresolved, they do raise concern that involuntary smoking may pose a threat to the nonsmoker. Any health risk resulting from involuntary smoke exposure is a serious public health concern because of the large numbers of non-smokers in the population who are potentially and involuntarily exposed. There-fore, for the purpose of preventative medicine, prudence dictates that nonsmok-ers avoid exposure to second-hand tobacco smoke to the extent possible.

Social Effects of Tobacco Smoke

Increasingly, individuals are seeing cigarette smoke as a pollutant and as a health hazard. For example, smoking was first linked to lung cancer over 50 years ago, but in 1954 fewer than half of the adults (41 percent) thought that smoking was one of the causes of cancer. By 1987 this proportion increased to between 87 to 95 percent (Report of the Surgeon General, U.S. Department of Health, Education, and Welfare, 1989). Likewise, the proportion of the adult public who believe a causal relationship exists between smoking and the risk of heart disease has increased from about 40 percent to near 80 percent in the last 25 years (Report of the Surgeon General, U.S. Department of Health, Education, and Welfare, 1989).

Bleda and Sandman (1977) have found that nonsmokers expressed less liking for a person who smoked in their presence than for the same person when he or she did not smoke. Additionally, subjects have given more "hostile" eval-uations of a researcher in a study when someone in the room had smoked, even if it was not the experimenter (Zillmann, Baron, & Tamborini, 1981). Volunteers have administered higher levels of aversive noise to another person when they were exposed to cigarette smoke (Jones & Bogat, 1978) and people have fled public benches in a shopping mall faster after their personal space was invaded if the invader smoked (Bleda & Bleda, 1978).

It has become quite clear that tobacco smoke, either in mainstream or sidestream form, constitutes a health problem in that it has an effect on pul-monocardiovascular performance as well as acting as a known carcinogen. Given that over 50 million Americans still smoke, cigarette smoke may be one of the most insidious pollutants of the atmosphere today, and oddly enough may be the one form of pollution most easily rectifiable.

Best evidence would suggest that tobacco smoke as a pollutant could be obliterated and that the risk of pulmonocardiovascular diseases, chronic obtru-sive lung disease, and a variety of cancers would also be decreased in involun-tary as well as voluntary smokers if smokers would stop completely. In fact, the Surgeon General (U.S. Department of Health, Education, and Welfare, 1990) emphatically states that the health benefits of smoking cessation far exceed any associated risks of weight gain (5 pounds on the average), or any psychological effects that may occur as a result of quitting. It would appear that the two most common excuses for not quitting are just that, excuses.

FIGURE 7-4 Increasingly individuals are seeing cigarette smoke as a pollutant and as a health hazard.

TIME-OUT: As this is being written the U.S. Congress is again considering raising the federal tax on cigarettes. Proponents argue that since cigarette smoking costs the American taxpayer an excess of $20 billion a year that the recovery of some of this through additional taxes is justified. What do you think of this proposal? Should these additional monies, if the law is passed, be put in a special health care fund or in the general coffers? How do your representatives in Congress feel about this legislation?

What are the major stumbling blocks to getting such legislation passed?

If you were interested in establishing a "smoke-free" environment how might you go about it? Start first with your place of work, or your dorm, or apartment building. What kinds of obstacles do you anticipate running into? What kinds of moral and ethical issues arise? Are these obstacles and issues any different from those involved in attempts to reduce industrial pollutants?

PARTICULATES

About 11 percent of all particulates in the atmosphere are anthropogenic in origin. Of that, roughly 51 percent come from industrial processes. The health effects of particulates stem from several mechanisms, including the fact that they can become lodged in the lungs and thus interfere with the proper functioning of the respiratory tract. Additionally, various toxic gases are either absorbed or adsorbed on or in these particles. The importance of particulate matter in the atmosphere is just beginning to be appreciated. Sources such as automobiles, home gas heaters, and power plants burn fossil fuels and release very small primary particulates. When these particles are exhausted they have a diameter of about 0.1 micron, but these particles can grow under certain conditions and inhibit visibility. More important, dust that enters the lungs may lodge there and have chronic effects on respiration. Certain materials such as asbestos are particularly dangerous in this way. Dust can also be deposited on the surface of green plants and interfere with absorption of carbon dioxide and the release of oxygen and water, thus interfering with photosynthesis. The relative size and toxicity of particulates and their influence on human health and welfare are only beginning to be studied.

Particulate accumulations are also the result of natural geophysical occurrences such as volcanoes and soil erosion. The effects of this particulate matter on climate and on human health vary. The shape, size, color, electromagnetic and chemical properties, and distribution into the atmosphere determine how they will influence solar and terrestrial radiation, how they will influence the formation of clouds and rainfall, whether they will affect the surface temperature of the earth, and in general, how they will affect the quality of the

FIGURE 7-5 The importance of particulate matter in the atmosphere is just beginning to be appreciated.

air for both plant and animal life. Naturally produced particulates tend to have a more widespread effect than do those produced by human activity. For example, volcanic activity injects particulates high into the atmosphere, where they tend to reflect much more of the solar radiation than do particles generated by human activity. Volcanic particles are known to have been carried completely around the world, and they have also been known to remain in the atmosphere for up to three years. These heavy clouds of dust and ash may suppress cloud formation, block off incoming solar radiation, and decrease the probability of precipitation. Thus, particulates could be implicated as a cause of drought.

FORMALDEHYDE (HCOH)

Formaldehyde is used in manufacturing particle board, plywood, paper, home insulation, material polymers and resins, leather, agricultural products, permanent press fabrics, preservatives, embalming fluids, drugs, and cosmetics. About 7 billion pounds of the chemical are produced each year. In fact, formaldehyde ranks as the twenty-sixth largest volume chemical produced in the United States. About 1.4 million people are exposed to formaldehyde in the workplace, and 11 million people breathe vapors in their homes due to construction materials and insulation. Formaldehyde levels in urban air frequently range about 0.1 ppm, and concentrations of more than 8 ppm have been measured in the workplace and in homes insulated with urea formaldehyde foam (Perera & Petito, 1982).

Formaldehyde enters the body via inhalation, ingestion, or skin absorption (Greisimer, 1982). Upon entering the body, it is thought that a rapid conversion to formate occurs and that combination with tissue constituents is likely (McMartin, Martin-Amato, Makar, & Tophly, 1979). Reaction with these basic tissue elements is of particular concern, because formaldehyde reacts with nitrogen compounds and these compounds are the very building blocks of life (DNA, RNA, proteins, and amino acids). The effect of these reactions has not as yet been fully determined.

Grafstrom, Fronace, Autrup, Lechner, and Harris (1983) used cultured human bronchial cells, both epithelial and fibroblastic, to study DNA damage and cell toxicity caused by formaldehyde. They found that the chemical damaged human DNA, inhibited DNA repair, and increased the susceptibility of the cell to X-ray damage. These findings are significant because they involved human cells of the respiratory tract (i.e., cells that are the most likely candidates for damage since most people come in to contact with formaldehyde via inhalation).

Acute effects of formaldehyde include eye, nose, and throat irritation, sneezing, shortness of breath, sleeplessness, nausea, and excess phlegm (Greisimer, 1982). Chronic effects include genetic abnormalities. Auerbach, Moutschen-Dahmen, and Moutschen (1977) clearly demonstrated that ingested formaldehyde causes gene mutation and chromosome aberrations in drosophila and other organisms, including bacteria. Goldmacher and Thilly (1983) showed that formaldehyde, above 4 ppm concentration is mutagenic, for cultured human cells. Levy, Nocentini, and Billardon (1983) have shown that formalde-hyde in these chromosome aberrations increased with increasing concentrations of formaldehyde in human fibroblast cell cultures. Kreiger and Garry (1983) found that formaldehyde induced cytotoxicity and sister chromatid exchanges in human lymphocyte cell cultures.

Epidemiological studies are perhaps the most important in determining the health risks of formaldehyde. Unfortunately, they are also the most difficult to assess owing to the many sources of confounding and the questionable valid-ity of particular methodologies. Nevertheless, many acute and chronic health effects have been reported as being related to formaldehyde exposure. In addi-tion to the effects discussed previously, chronic coughs, asthma, airway obstruc-tion, bronchitis, pharyngitis, menstrual and reproductive disorders, and even cancer have been documented as "formaldehyde caused" (Greisimer, 1982).

Most of the epidemiological studies are of a cross-sectional design and thus disallow the determination of order of events. Additionally, many of the studies lack appropriate controls and environmental measurement. However, independent reports of respiratory tract disorders and dermatitis among persons in a variety of work settings overwhelmingly indicate that formaldehyde is at least a contributor to these problems. A second survey of residents of homes insulated with urea formaldehyde foam evaluated the acute effects of living in such an environment. Unfortunately, it did not include air monitoring in the homes (Thun, Lakat, & Altman, 1982). A 1983 study (Walrath & Fraumeni, 1983) provides some additional data. In this study, reasons for mortality among New York State morticians were assessed. Investigators found that mortality was ele-vated for cancers of the skin, brain, and kidney as well as the colon. Mortality was also high for arteriosclerotic heart disease.

No data are presently available concerning the possibility of formalde-hyde having direct psychological effects on humans. Exposure to some organic chemicals—for example, methyl mercury—has resulted in direct psychological impairment. No such data exist for formaldehyde. It is wrong, however, to dis-count any psychological effects on the basis of the absence of data. A family liv-ing in a urea-formaldehyde-foam-insulated house may well be affected psycho-logically by reports that formaldehyde inhaled in amounts as small as 2 parts per million causes cancer in rats; or, an individual working in a plywood facto-ry, or a mortician, or perhaps even a biological scientist, all of whom are exposed to formaldehyde being used as a preservative, may be concerned about their health. In Chapter 5 we suggested that anticipatory stress may be equally or more harmful than the actual stress of environmental conditions. Individuals such as those described above may experience high levels of anticipatory stress with the psychological effect of the exposure being indirect and more damaging than first might have been suspected.

A large number of other chemicals (some quite common and abundant, others more limited in quantity) are being produced daily, either to promote human welfare or as a by-product of other industrial processes. Included among these are various pesticides and biocides, the polychlorinated biphenols, dioxin, and even the various food additives and supplements found on our grocer's shelf and druggist's counter. These chemicals may indeed be serving the goals of comfort, luxury, and longevity, or they may be leading us down a one-way street to oblivion. Only more research and time will reveal the answers.

PUBLIC REACTION TO POLLUTION

As we have seen, a number of chemicals are being released into and transported through the atmosphere or waterways and are exerting detrimental effects on the biosphere, the ecosystem, or humankind. What are the public attitudes toward such degradation of the biosphere? DeGroot (1967) summarizes from eight studies concerning the public attitudes concerning air pollution. Specifically, when subjects are asked whether air pollution is a problem, 50 percent generally respond that it is. However, few ever report complaining to public agencies and most see other neighborhoods as being more polluted than their own. Specifically, in a survey of the residents of Buffalo, New York, in 1962, DeGroot and Samuels (1962) showed that 43 percent of the 460 respondents thought that air pollution was a serious problem in that area, but few reported making any complaints to public agencies. Similarly, Medalia and Finkner (1965) in a study of the Clarkston, Washington, area showed that 85 percent of those who lived in the vicinity of a Kraft mill, even though they were subjected to tarnished house paint, reduced visibility, and malodor from the mill, still described Clarkston as an "excellent place to live." When asked specifically about air pollution, 78 percent responded that it was a problem; only 2 percent had ever registered a complaint with a public agency. Medalia (1964) asked residents of the Clarkston area to rank from most to least severe the negative effects of the pulp mill. They were ranked as follows: dust in the air, eye irritation, nose irritation, haze or cough, bad smells. When asked specifically whether they considered the air to be polluted, most did; however, those individuals of higher socioeconomic status were more likely to report a greater perception of air pollution than those of lower socioeconomic status.

Crowe (1968) found that most individuals respond to air pollution as a nuisance; that is, people typically cite odor and reduced visibility as reasons for concern, yet few ever perceive pollution in health-related terms. In fact, perception of air pollution is primarily determined by the nuisance value, as opposed to the other, perhaps more important, cues. In detecting particulate pollution, it is quite easy to observe dust on clothing, pitting of paints, coughing, congestion, and other signs. A great deal of the nonparticulate pollution, however, is perceived in terms of smell and of visual acuity. This is unfortunate because, as already noted, carbon monoxide is both an odorless and colorless pollutant. One difficulty arising from the fact that our perception of pollution is determined by smell and visual acuity is that it directs attention to the effects of air pollution and away from specific causes such as factories and automobiles.

Because much harmful pollution is not detectable by smell or visibility, how can the average individual detect air pollution? Well, one obvious way is to provide training in the causes of air pollution. In a study done by Hummel,

Loomis, and Herbert (1975), it was found that experts used the presence of automobiles as their primary cue in detecting pollution. As automobiles account for
nearly 50 percent of urban pollution, it makes sense to use automobile concentration as an indicator of pollution in that area. In the same study, it was found
that nonexperts tended to use visibility as a cue more than experts did. Further
work by Hummel (1977) suggests that instructing the public in the use of such
cues as the presence of automobiles is indeed potentially useful. Other cues that
might be used as predictors of air pollution are the absence of rain, and the
presence of tall buildings that tend to block winds, stop-and-go traffic, and
smokestacks.

PSYCHOLOGICAL STRESS: THE HIDDEN HAZARD IN POLLUTION

Environmental science was given its first public acknowledgment with the publication of Rachel Carson's *Silent Spring* (1962). Since then many others have
warned of the dangerous acts perpetrated on Mother Earth in the name of
progress. Biologists and those interested in environmental medicine have also
recognized the impact that a changing environment can have on the physiological functioning and other biological processes of living organisms. Possible biological consequences are being enumerated daily and their probabilities of
occurrence are being established. Only in the past 10 years or so, however, has
there been any attempt to understand the human psychological impact of environmental adjustments.

In Chapter 5 the role of stress in adaptation was dealt with in some
detail. Central to the concept of stress is the appraisal process. Humans first
appraise their environment in terms of whether it is stressful or not; then, if
judged to be stressful, they determine the kind of stress (challenge, threat, etc.)
that is there, and finally appraise their resources for dealing with it. In light of
DeGroot's work (1967) that showed that only 2 percent of the population of
highly polluted areas ever feel that pollution is a problem burdensome enough
to complain to officials, it should come as no surprise that psychologists have
been remiss in studying pollution as a source of stress.

Recent investigations, however, have shown that various pollutants and
the attending lack of information regarding their potential harm can indeed be
psychologically stressing. The eventual controlled release of radioactive gases at
Three Mile Island and the chemical caldron at Love Canal come to mind. Lack
of information, misinformation, low predictability, and low levels of personal
control coalesce to render psychological stress an inevitable outcome of certain
forms of pollution. Residents at Three Mile Island evidenced symptoms of acute
stress including heightened anxiety, demoralization, and somatic complaints
(Baum, Fleming, & Davidson, 1983; Baum, Gatchel, & Schaeffer, 1982; Bromet,
1980). Furthermore, Biela (1987) demonstrated that for nature-related workers
(foresters), the very awareness of the degeneration of their job environment due
to industrial pollution is a very powerful stressor affecting them. Finally, recent
studies have shown that merely living near a toxic waste disposal site, even if

no leakage has been proven to have occurred, can be highly psychologically stressful (Stang & Veitch, 1985; Veitch, Stang, & Conley, 1985). These studies will be dealt with further in Chapter 13.

Pollution alters the environment, potentially irreversibly. This alteration in turn affects the quality of human life, often initially for the better. Time and/or additional amounts of the pollutant are likely to render the initial positive effects void and the new environment less predictable and perhaps less hospitable. Much more needs to be known about the eventual effects of the by-products of our modern technological world. Much more needs to be known before our knowledge will do us any good in reversing potentially catastrophic trends.

SUMMARY

Increasing population and advancing technology have altered and will continue to alter the biosphere. In "conquering" the world around us it has become possible to, and increasingly likely that we will destroy it. In Chapter 2 a model was presented which postulated that a precarious equilibrium is maintained between organisms and their environments via the processes of adaptation and adjustment. Humans, with their superior intellect and less-than-perfect ability to adapt, have often opted for the adjustment mechanism (i.e., change the environment to restore homeostasis). These changes, however, are not without their aftereffects. Burning fossil fuels to maintain thermal comfort changes the carbon dioxide concentration of the immediate environment and perhaps eventually the entire biosphere; insulating homes with urea formaldehyde foam helps maintain thermal comfort while cutting down on fossil fuel combustion, but increases the amount of formaldehyde in the immediate environs. In the process of manufacturing other products to maintain comfortable, if not luxurious, equilibrium other dangerous by-products are formed. PCBs are formed as a result of electrical transformer production; atomic waste is a by-product of electrical generation by nuclear power plants; sulfur and nitrogen oxides are the result of manufacturing and internal combustion processes. Carbon monoxide, the hydrofluorides, and many particulates are the result of human attempts to make the interaction with the environment less disagreeable.

The short-term effect of these adjustments is to bring the environment into equilibrium with the needs of its human inhabitants. Thermal comfort is maintained; travel is made possible; night vision through the use of electrical power is taken for granted; and food is produced, preserved, and prepared as a result of adjustments made to the environment. But while the short-term adjustments are first lauded as progress, and later taken for granted, interest in the long-term effects of continued adjustment has only just begun. Scientists, and very recently the public, have begun to consider the possible consequences of continued environmental degradation. Further research and public education is needed to halt or reverse some of the potentially lethal effects of the proliferation of chemical pollution.

IMPORTANT CONCEPTS

air pollution
Minamata Bay
Love Canal
carbon dioxide
   greenhouse effect
carbon monoxide
sulfur oxides
nitrogen oxides

ozone
tobacco smoke
sidestream smoke
cardiovascular disease
chronic obstructive lung disease
particulates
formaldehyde
acid rain

REFERENCES

Arochova, O., Kontrova, J., Lipkova, V., & Liska, J. (1988). Effect of toxic atmosphere emissions on cognitive performance by children. *Studia Psychologia*, 30(2), 101–114.

Auerbach, C., Moutschen-Dahmen, M., & Moutschen, J. (1977). Genetics and cytogenetical effect of formaldehyde and related compounds. *Mutation Research*, 39, 317–362.

Barney, G.O. (1980). *The global 2000 report to the president of the U.S.* New York: Pergamon Press.

Baum, A., Fleming, R., & Davidson, L.M. (1983). Natural disaster and technological catastrophe. *Environment and Behavior*, 26, 333–354.

Baum, A., Gatchel, R.J., & Schaeffer, M.A. (1982). Emotional, behavioral and physiological effects of chronic stress at Three Mile Island. *Journal of Consulting and Clinical Psychology*, 51(4), 565–572.

Beard, R.R., & Wertheim, G.A. (1967). Behavioral impairment associated with small doses of carbon monoxide. *American Journal of Public Health*, 57, 2012–2022.

Biela, A. (1987). Job stress in foresters employed in a heavily polluted area. *Polish Psychological Bulletin*, 18(3), 169–175.

Bleda, P., & Bleda, S. (1978). Effects of sex and smoking on reactions to spatial invasion at a shopping mall. *Journal of Social Psychology*, 104, 311–312.

Bleda, P.R., & Sandman, P.H. (1977). In smoke's way: Socioemotional reactions to another's smoking. *Journal of Applied Psychology*, 62, 452–458.

Breisacher, P. (1971). Neuropsychological effects of air pollution. *American Behavioral Scientist*, 14, 837–864.

Bromet, E. (1980). *Preliminary report on the mental health of Three Mile Island residents.* Pittsburgh, Pa.: Western Psychiatric Institute, University of Pittsburgh.

Brown, L.R., Chandler, W.U., Durning, A., Flavin, C., Heise, L., Jacobson, J., et al. (1988). *State of the World 1988.* A Worldwatch Institure Report on Progress Toward a Sustainable Society. New York: W.W. Norton & Co., Inc.

Brunnemann, K.D., & Hoffman, D. (1982). The pH of Tobacco smoke. *Food and Cosmetics Toxicology*, 12(1):115–124.

Bullinger, M. (1989). Psychological effects of air pollution on healthy residents: A time-series approach. *Journal of Environmental Psychology*, 9(2), 103–118.

Carson, R. (1962). *Silent spring.* Boston: Houghton Mifflin.

Chovin, P. (1967). Carbon monoxide: Analysis of exhaust gas investigations in Paris. *Environmental Research*, 1, 198–216.

Crowe, M.J. (1968). Toward a "definitional model" of public perceptions of air pollution. *Journal of the Air Pollution Control Association*, 18, 154–157.

DeGroot, I. (1967). Trends in public attitudes toward air pollution. *Journal of the Air Pollution Control Association*, 17, 679–681.

DeGroot, I., & Samuels, S. (1962). *People and air pollution: A study of attitudes in Buffalo, New York.* Interdepartmental Report of the New York State Department of Health Air Pollution Control Board, Buffalo.

Dube, M.F., & Green, C.R. (1982). Methods of collection of smoke for analytical purposes. *Advances in Tobacco Science: Formation, Analysis and Composition of Tobacco Smoke*, 8:42–102.

Geophysics Study Committee. (1977). *Energy and climate.* Washington, D.C.: National Academy of Sciences.

Goldmacher, V.S., & Thilly, W.G. (1983). Formaldehyde is mutagenic for cultured human cells. *Mutation Research, 116,* 417–22.

Grafstrom, R.C., Fronace, A.J., Autrup, H., Lechner, J.F., & Harris, C.C. (1983). Formaldehyde damage to DNA inhibition of DNA repair in human bronchial cells. *Science, 220,* 216–218.

Greisimer, R.A. (chairman). (1982). Report of the Federal Panel on Formaldehyde. *Environmental Health Perspectives, 43,* 139–168.

Halperin, M.H., McFarland, R.A., Niven, J.I., & Roughton, F.J.W. (1959). The time course of the effects of carbon monoxide on visual thresholds. *Journal of Physiology, 146,* 583–593.

Horvath, S.M., Dahms, T.E., & O'Hanlon, J.F. (1971). Carbon monoxide and human vigilance: A deleterious effects of present urban concentration. *Archives of Environmental Health, 21,* 343–347.

Hummel, C.F. (1977). *Effects of induced cognitive sets in viewing air pollution scenes.* Unpublished doctoral dissertation, Colorado State University, Ft. Collins, Colo.

Hummel, C.G., Loomis, R.J., & Herbert, J.A. (1975). *Effects of city labels and cue utilization on air pollution judgments* (Working Papers in Environmental-Social Psychology, No. 1). Unpublished material, Colorado State University, Ft. Collins, Colo.

Janerick, D.T., Burnett, W.S., Feck, G., Hoff, M., Nasca, P., Polednak, A.P., et al. (1981). Cancer incidence in the Love Canal area. *Science, 212,* 1404–1407.

Jones, J.W., & Bogat, G.A. (1978). Air pollution and human aggression. *Psychological Reports, 43,* 721–722.

Kreiger, R.A., & Garry, V.A. (1983). Formaldehyde-induced cytotoxicity and sister-chromatid exchanges in human lymphocyte cultures. *Mutation Research, 120,* 51–55.

Levy, S., Nocentini, S., & Billardon, C. (1983). Induction of cytogentic effects in human fibroblast cultures after exposure to formaldehyde or x-rays. *Mutation Research, 119,* 309–317.

Lewis, J., Baddeley, A.D., Bonham, K.G., and Lovett, D. (1970). Traffic pollution and mental efficiency. *Nature, 225,* 96.

Lewtas, J. (1989). Toxicology of complex mixtures of indoor air pollutants. *Annual Review of Pharmacology & Toxicology, 29,* 415–439.

MacCracken, M.C., and Kulka, G.J. (1985) Detecting the climatic effects of carbon dioxide: Volume summary. In Michael C. MacCracken & Frederick M. Luther (Eds.), *Detecting the climatic effects of increasing carbon dioxide.* Washington, D.C.: U.S. Government Printing Office.

Manabe, S., & Wetherald, R.T. (1986, May) Reductions in summer soil wetness induced by an increase in atmospheric carbon dioxide. *Science, 232,* pp. 626–628.

McFarland, R.A., Roughton, F.U., Halperin, M.H., & Niven, J.I. (1944). The effects of monoxide and altitude on visual thresholds. *Journal of Aviation Medicine, 16,* 381–394.

McMartin, K.E., Martin-Amat, G., Makar, A.B., & Tephly, R.R. (1979). Lack of role for formaldehyde in methanol poisoning in the monkey. *Biochemical Pharmacology, 28,* 645–649.

Medalia, N.Z. (1964). Air pollution as a socio-environmental health problem: A survey report. *Journal of Health and Human Behavior 5,* 154–165.

Medalia, N.Z., & Finkner, A.L. (1965). Community perception of air quality: An opinion study in Clarkston, Washington. Cincinnati: U.S. Public Health Services Publication, 999–10.

Moureu, H. (1964). Carbon monoxide as a test for air pollution in Paris due to motor vehicle traffic. *Proceedings of the Royal Society of Medicine, 57,* 1015–1020.

Newman, J.R. (1980). *Effects of air emissions on wildlife resources.* U.S. Fish and Wildlife Biological Service Program, National Power Plant Team. FWS/OBS-80/40. Washington, D.C.: U.S. Fish and Wildlife Services.

Patrick, R., Binetti, V.P., & Halterman, S.G. (1981). Acid lakes from natural and anthropogenic causes. *Science, 211,* 446–448.

Perera, F., & Petito, C. (1982). Formaldehyde: A question of cancer policy? *Science, 206,* 1285–1291.

Postel, S. (1986). Altering the earth's chemistry: Assessing the risks. *Worldwatch Paper 71,* Washington, D.C.: Worldwatch Institute.

Schodell, M. (1985, October). Risky Business. *Science '85.*

Stang, S., & Veitch, R. (1985, May). *Anticipatory stress in a potentially toxic environment.* Paper presented at the annual meeting of the Midwestern Psychological Association.

"The Quest for Chemical Safety," (1985, May). *International Register of Potentially Toxic Chemicals Bulletin.*

Thun, M.J., Lakat, M.F., & Altman, R. (1982). Symptom survey of residents of homes insulated with urea-formaldehyde foam. *Environmental Research*, 29:320–34.

U.S. Department of Health, Education, and Welfare. (1982) *The health consequences of smoking: Cancer. A report of the Surgeon General.* U.S. Department of Health and Human Services, Public Health Service, Office on Smoking and Health. DHHS Publication No. (PHS) 82-50179.

U.S. Department of Health, Education, and Welfare. (1983) *The health consequences of smoking: Cardiovascular disease. A report of the Surgeon General.* U.S. Department of Health and Human Services, Public Health Service, Office on Smoking and Health. DHHS Publication No. (PHS) 84-50204.

U.S. Department of Health, Education, and Welfare. (1984) *The health consequences of smoking: Chronic obstructive lung disease. A report of the Surgeon General.* U.S. Department of Health and Human Services, Public Health Service, Office on Smoking and Health. DHHS Publication No. (PHS) 84-50205.

U.S. Department of Health, Education, and Welfare. (1985) *The health consequences of smoking: Cancer. and chronic lung disease in the workplace. A report of the Surgeon General.* U.S. Department of Health and Human Services, Public Health Service, Office on Smoking and Health. DHHS Publication No. (PHS) 82-50179.

U.S. Department of Health, Education, and Welfare. (1986) *The health consequences of involuntary smoking: A report of the Surgeon General.* U.S. Department of Health and Human Services, Public Health Service, Centers for Disease Control, Center for Health Promotion and Education, Office on Smoking and Health. DHHS Publication No. (CDC) 87-8398.

U.S. Department of Health, Education, and Welfare. (1988) *The health consequences of smoking: Nicotine addiction A report of the Surgeon General.* U.S. Department of Health and Human Services, Public Health Service, Centers for Disease Control, Center for Health Promotion and Education, Office on Smoking and Health. DHHS Publication No. (CDC) 88-8406.

U.S. Department of Health, Education, and Welfare. (1989) *The health consequences of smoking: 25 Years of progress A report of the Surgeon General.* U.S. Department of Health and Human Services, Public Health Service, Centers for Disease Control, Center for Chronic Disease Prevention and Health Promotion, Office on Smoking and Health. DHHS Publication No. (CDC) 89-8411.

U.S. Department of Health, Education, and Welfare. (1990) *The health benefits of smoking cessation: A report of the Surgeon General.* U.S. Department of Health and Human Services, Public Health Service, Centers for Disease Control, Center for Chronic Disease Prevention and Health Promotion, Office on Smoking and Health. DHHS Publication No. (CDC) 90-8416.

U.S. International Trade Commission, (1986). *Synthetic organic chemicals: United States production and sales 1985.* Washington, D.C.: U.S. Government Printing Office.

Veitch, R., Stang, S., & Conley, L. (1985). *Stress and technological catastrophies: What are the relationships?* Unpublished document provided to the Northern Ohioians for the Protection of the Environment (NOPE).

Waldbott, G.L. (1978). *Health effects of environmental pollutants* (2nd ed.). St. Louis, Mo.: C.V. Mosby.

Walrath, J., & Fraumeni, J.F. (1983). Mortality patterns among embalmers. *Cancer*, 31, 407–411.

Weitzman, D.C., Kenney, J.A., & Luriator, S.M. (1969). *Effects on vision of repeated exposure to carbon monoxide.* Groton, Conn.: Naval Submarine Medical Research Laboratory, 10.

World Environment Report. (1987). "'Mac' Backs CFC Attack," August 20.

Zillmann, D., Baron, R.A., & Tamborini, R. (1981) Social costs of smoking: Effects of tobacco smoke on hostile behavior. *Journal of Applied Social Psychology*, 11, 548–561.

Noise

The Ubiquitous Pollutant

8

FIGURE 8-1 Noise, simply defined, is unwanted sound.

In Chapter 4 we stated that humans depend very heavily on their sense of vision to develop internal conceptions of their external environment. In fact, vision for most humans is their most important sense, enabling them to visualize unseen environments, to make plans regarding future environments, and to orient themselves with respect to their current environment. The second most important sensory system for obtaining information about the environment, though, is the auditory system. We obtain a great deal of information about the environment by conversing with others, listening to TV and radio broadcasts, and by being attuned to the sounds stemming from various aspects of the environment. We hear the sounds of the storm warning siren before the arrival of the storm, the honking of the on-coming automobile before we turn our head to notice it coming at us, and the chirping of the birds visually hidden in the nearby treetops. As a species, we have even developed a number of elaborate acoustical forms of communication we call language by which various vocal utterances can be strung together to transmit meaningful information.

While visual information comes to us in the form of reflected electromagnetic energy travelling at a speed of approximately 186,000 miles per second, sounds (irrespective of their source) reach our ears via elastic waves in an air medium at a rate of about 1,100 feet per second. As the succession of compressions and expansions that disturb the normal density of the medium in which they are created reach the ear they are transformed into mechanical energy in the middle ear, transmitted as hydraulic energy in the inner ear, and converted to electrical impulses along the auditory nerve. These electrical impulses reach the brain and are interpreted as sound. All of this is necessary for effective acoustical intercourse with the environment. But deficiencies in the hearing apparati can develop, or ambient levels of sound can be such that effective commerce is rendered impossible. In fact, anything that interferes with the transmittal or reception of acoustical information has to be considered less than satisfactory. Noise, therefore, can be considered a pollutant, a potential deterrent to normal interactions with one's environment and a possible source of stress.

NOISE

Noise is different from the pollutants we have discussed in the previous two chapters. Indeed, although most people consider noise a nuisance, we do not normally think of it as a pollutant. Perhaps this is because noise, unlike other pollutants, is almost totally anthropogenic, is seldom lethal, most of its major consequences occur only after long exposure, and these consequences tend to be cumulative and chronic rather than immediate and acute. Nonetheless, noise has been the subject of a great deal of research and is discussed here in some detail. In the following pages, we will concern ourselves with defining noise, measuring it, and examining its effects on physiological functioning, task performance, and social behavior. We will also be looking at individual differences that appear to moderate these effects and at special environments where noise may be particularly debilitating.

FIGURE 8-2 Noise is almost totally anthropogenic.

The simplest and most common definition of noise is that it is *unwanted* sound. To the student studying calculus in Chapter 2 the rock music from nextdoor was noise, although the neighbor next door may have found the sound relaxing. During his childhood in Wisconsin, one of the authors deemed the sound of a cock pheasant at 5:30 A.M. unwanted (and therefore noise), although the same sound today would be welcomed at any hour. Hammer mills, pneumatic drills, jet aircraft, semi-trucks, automobiles and even computer keyboards, video games and small children generate sound, and any of these can be considered a source of noise if the sound they create is found undesirable and thus unwanted. Inherent in the concept of noise, then, is a psychological component. To partially answer an old philosophical question, the tree crashing in the forest may or may not create a sound when there is no one there to hear it, but it does not create noise unless there is someone there to declare it *unwanted*.

Sound of any sort has physical components, including wavelength frequency, wavelength amplitude, and wavelength purity. Each component produces different physiological effects that interact to bring about various psychological effects. Physiologically, sound is produced by the changes in the air pressure of molecules at the eardrums. The number of times the wave goes through a complete *cycle* in a standard unit of time (usually one second) determines the frequency of the sound. Frequency, the number of cycles per second, is usually expressed in units called a Hertz (Hz), and is perceived psychologically as *pitch*. The regularity or symmetry of a sound wave pattern is known as *timbre* or *tonal quality*. Single-frequency sounds are rare (unless one is using a tuning fork). Those sounds that consist of a few frequencies are known as *narrow band* and those that are made up of a wide range of frequencies as *wide band* (clever, eh?). A very wide range of unpatterned frequencies is called *white noise*. The normal ear is capable of perceiving frequencies and combinations of frequencies as low as 20 Hz and as high as 20,000 Hz.

Sound waves also vary with respect to their height or *amplitude*. This characteristic is perceived psychologically as loudness (i.e., the greater the amplitude, the louder the sound). Physically, amplitude is related to the amount of pressure or energy in the sound wave, and is often called sound intensity. Absolute levels of intensity detectable by the human ear vary by 1 trillion to 1 (Konz, 1973). The smallest pressure distinguishable is about 0.0002 dynes per square centimeter, called a *microbar*. A dyne is equal to the force that imparts to a mass of one gram an acceleration of one centimeter per second. A scale of measurement that includes the lowest detectable intensity (0.0002 microbars) to one causing pain (1,000 microbars) would be very awkward to work with, so a less cumbersome scale has been developed. This scale is a logarithmic function of the microbar, and its units are expressed in *decibels* (dB). This unit of noise intensity, however, causes considerable confusion among the general public because it is not on a linear scale. For example, a tenfold increase in intensity as expressed in microbars results in a twofold increase in dB if our starting point is 0.002 microbars (i.e., 0.002 microbars equals 20 dB, and 0.02 microbars equals 40 dB). However the next tenfold increase in microbars (i.e., from 0.02 to 0.2 microbars) results in only a 50 percent increase in dB (i.e., from 40 to 60 dB). For a more complete table of equivalents see Table 8-1.

There are some additional complications. The human ear is more sensitive to sound at some frequencies than it is at others. Thus, to the perceiver an 80-dB sound at 800 Hz is not equal in psychological loudness to an 80-dB sound at 2,400 Hz. Two additional units of loudness have thus been developed, the

TABLE 8-1   Decibel Equivalents of Microbars

Sound Pressure in Microbars	Equivalent decibels
0.0002	0.0
0.002	20.0
0.02	40.0
0.2	60.0
2.0	80.0
20.0	100.0
200.0	120.0
2000.0	140.0

more common of which is the *phon*. The phon equates loudness at other frequencies with the sound pressure level of a 1,000-Hz tone. Thus, 60 dB at 1,000-Hz equals 60 phons, but 60 phons at 100 Hz will require an intensity of 68 dB. To determine the phon level of a given sound, subjects are asked to adjust a 1,000-Hz tone until it and the test tone appear to be of equal loudness. The dB level of the 1,000 Hz tone at the point of apparent equal loudness is then considered to be the phon level of the test sound.

To summarize this point, psychological perceptions of sounds vary in their timbre, pitch, and loudness. These three characteristics are related to the physical properties of wave symmetry, wavelength, and wave amplitude. The physical properties of sound influence various anatomical structures and physiological processes in the auditory system. The vibrations produced by fluctuating air pressure is translated into neural impulses, which eventually reach the temporal lobe via the auditory nerve. The code that allows an organism to perceive these neural impulses and interpret them in terms of their psychological qualities, however, has not as yet been determined. (For a schematic representation of the auditory mechanisms responsible for translating the mechanical energy emanating from the sound source to the psychologically interpreted sound, see Figure 8.3).

FIGURE 8-3 A schematic representation of the auditory mechanisms responsible for translating the mechanical energy emanating from a sound source to the psychologically interpreted sound.

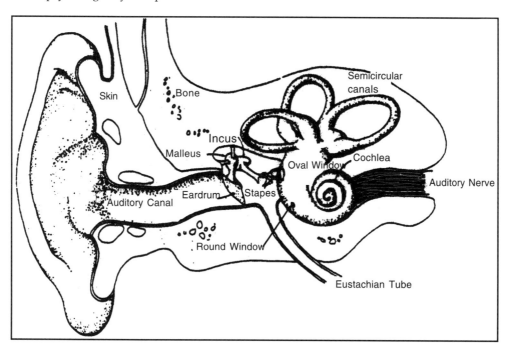

TIME-OUT: When we think of noise we usually think of loudness level—the greater the loudness level the greater the noise. But as we have seen noise is as much a psychological phenomenon as it is a physical one. Try this: Obtain several different kinds of recordings. Perhaps some heavy metal, big band, polka, classical, country and western, etc. Play each of these at the same volume (elevated) on your stereo. Do they all sound equally noisy? If not, which is noisier for you? Now try the same thing with several of your friends, with your parents, with your grandparents. Do they all provide the same noise ratings that you did? Perhaps instead of getting "noise ratings" you could ask how irritable or how pleasant your subjects find the sound. Maybe you could have your subjects work on math problems while listening or perhaps try to carry on a telephone conversation. Are noise ratings correlated with either performance scores or communication decrements?

If you wanted to be more systematic in this study, you obviously would have to take decibel readings to see how loud each was. You would also have to control for pitch and timbre as these influence the perception of sound. What other possible influences would you either have to control for or measure so that you would be able to attribute performance changes to sound level or noise perception?

SOURCES OF NOISE

Because noise is any unwanted sound, it has the potential for displaying an almost unlimited number of characteristics. The most lilting of melodies, the most babbling of brooks, the quietest of pins dropping could all, at one time or another, be perceived as noise by someone. Noise can come from anything that makes a sound, because noise is in the perception of the hearer and not in the sound itself. In spite of the highly idiosyncratic nature of our definition of noise, there are a number of sound sources and a number of settings for the perception of sound in which there is general agreement that the sound(s) constitute noise. Among the sources of sound that are agreed upon as creating noise are the motorized equipment used in the manufacturing and construction trades, transportation vehicles like cars, trucks, trains, and planes, and gatherings of people at, for example, a rock concert, the neighborhood bar, or a Saturday night BYOB party.

NOISE IN THE WORKPLACE

It is estimated that more than half of the production workers in the United States labor in settings where the noise level is so high that hearing loss is likely, and perhaps as many as 5 million workers are exposed to levels above the 90 dB which is legally permissible. Among the noisiest of work settings are construction sites where the din created by pneumatic drills and high horsepower engines may create noise levels as high as 100 dB. At this level even co-workers standing only one yard apart may have to shout to be heard. Others in high-noise occupations include miners, aircraft mechanics, and millers. Even such seemingly sedentary and innocuous work settings as a business office have machinery that can bring the noise level up to prohibitive levels. Certainly these noise levels have their effects on human functioning.

EFFECTS OF NOISE IN THE WORKPLACE

Konz (1973) suggests that noise abatement can be carried out if management makes a concerted effort to do so. It is unlikely that the effort will be made, however, unless the noise interferes with efficiency or is shown to be perilous to those exposed to it. For these and other reasons, it is important to know what the effects of noise in the workplace are. Productivity, comfort, and health are all affected, to a certain extent, by noise in the workplace. What the effect is likely to be and when it is likely to occur is related to factors like the loudness, pitch, band width, predictability, and controllability of the noise and the age, gender, and exposure duration of the perceiver as well as the person's attitudes regarding the source of the noise.

Health Effects

Rosen (1970) describes the involuntary human reactions to loud noises: "The blood vessels constrict, the skin pales, the pupils dilate, the eyes close, one winces, holds the breath, and the voluntary and involuntary muscles tense. Gastric secretion diminishes and the diastolic pressure increases. Adrenalin is suddenly injected into the bloodstream, which increases neuro-muscular tension, nervousness, irritability and anxiety" (p. 57). This involuntary response to loud noise is typical of a variety of stress responses and is physiologically triggered by stimulation of the auditory nerve by sound. The response occurs in humans while they are awake, asleep, under anesthesia, and even after the cerebral hemispheres have been removed (Ward, 1953). Humans can adapt to loud noises, and such habituation can provide short-lasting protection against subsequent exposure. However, chronic overstimulation has potentially pathological consequences; a level of stimulation greater than the optimum can result in the so-called diseases of adaptation (Dubos, 1965; Seyle, 1956; Wolf, 1968).

Perhaps the clearest associations between exposure to occupational noise and the diseases of adaptation have been made by the National Academy of Sciences (1981), which says noise has contributed to various neurologic and gastrointestinal problems. For example, ulcers appear to be more prevalent among workers exposed to occupational noise than among those not exposed (Jerkova & Kremorova, 1970).

Noise has also been associated with a number of cardiovascular problems. Ponomarenko (1966) has found that adolescents exposed to a constant

1,000 to 2,000 Hz, 85 dB industrial noise showed a decrease in systolic blood pressure and an increase in diastolic blood pressure, as well as increases in pulse rate, systolic index, diastolic and cardiac cycle time, and in reaction times to light and sound. Ising and Melchert (1980) report that workers who wear hearing protectors exhibit lower blood pressures and lower levels of norepinephrine in their urine than do those who wear no protectors. Additionally, Darner (1966) has shown that when exposed to repetitive audible sound pulses, the heart rates of workers tend to synchronize with those sound pulses. Workers exposed to repetitive rates higher than the normal heart rate appear to have their heart rate fixed (in synchrony) at those higher rates. Rates can be returned to normal by resynchronizing the beat with slower pulsing sounds, but this resynchronization takes longer than that required initially to bring about the abnormality.

Finally, measures of heart rate, heart rate variability, and blood pressure were obtained from university students during a 55-minute vigilance task (Carter & Beh, 1989). The task was carried out under quiet conditions or under one of three conditions of intermittent noise. Intermittent noise significantly increased diastolic and mean blood pressure and heart rate variability. Heart rate, itself, though, increased significantly only for those receiving unpredictable intermittent noise. In this study none of the subjects showed any habituation effects over the nearly one hour of testing.

In summary, noise can create a stress response in humans, affecting the endocrine, nervous, digestive, and cardiovascular systems. Adaptation and habituation can occur, but prolonged exposure may lead to any of the diseases of adaptation, including digestive and cardiovascular problems. The evidence for noise as a pathogenic agent, however, is inconclusive (Cohen, Glass, & Phillips, 1977). That is, the direct link from noise to pathology has yet to be established, and while correlational studies have linked noise to reports of acute and chronic illness (Cameron, Robertson, & Zaks, 1972) and with the increased use of sleeping pills and physician calls (Grandjean, Graf, Lauber, Meier, & Muller, 1973), we should remember that correlations do not prove a causal link.

Hearing Loss

In a 1972 survey by the Environmental Protection Agency (USEPA, 1972), it was estimated that nearly 3 million Americans suffered from noise-induced hearing loss. By 1991 this estimate had grown to nearly 10 million or fully one-third of all individuals suffering hearing loss (Select Commitee on Children, Youth and Families, 1991). The usual index for hearing loss is the number of decibels above normal threshold for a given frequency that is required to reach a new threshold because when a hearing loss occurs at a given frequency, an increase in the amplitude of that sound is needed before the person can hear it. Hearing loss typically results from damage to the tiny hair cells of the cochlea of the inner ear (see Figure 8-3). Although the assault on the cochlea may be brought about by loud noises, in some cases hearing loss is totally unrelated to ambient noise level. Studies have shown that oxygen deprivation and certain drugs such as quinine and ototic-mycins can cause high-frequency hearing loss (Lenhardt, 1970), and there is the possibility that other drugs might interact with noise to bring about increased hearing loss. In fact, in separate studies, hearing loss in noisy environments has been associated with various industrial solvents (Bergstrom & Nystrom, 1986) and with carbon disulfide (Morata, 1989).

Extremely loud noises (150 dB or more) can rupture the ear drum, and prolonged exposure to less intense noises (90 to 120 dB) can cause permanent damage to other parts of the inner ear. Thus, workers who are exposed to those levels continuously (miners, construction workers, etc.) can, without protection, expect to sustain hearing loss as a result of noise-induced damage to the ear. Progressive noise-induced hearing loss occurs through continuous exposure to sound levels above 80 db over an eight-hour day. The first loss of hearing is to the high-frequency sounds of speech. The first sounds lost to the nerve-deaf are, therefore, the fricative consonants *f, s, th, ch,* and *sh.* Sufferers of nerve-deafness often have difficulty differentiating the words *sick, thick, flick,* and *chick.* As hearing loss becomes worse, the explosive consonants *b, t, p, t, k, g,* and *d* become increasingly difficult to discriminate. After a time, speech communication is rendered impossible.

Comfort Effects

The most obvious comfort effect of noise in the workplace is that speech communication is impaired and normal conversations are impossible. Workers must increase the degree of concentration to obtain any meaning from the speech of others, and subtle nuances in inflection, intonation, and enunciation become nonexistent. Comfort decreases, while fatigue and annoyance increase. Often the only respite from the noise is earplugs or earmuffs, which only make speech communication more difficult. All told, there is little that is comfortable or that can be made comfortable about a noisy work environment.

Productivity Effects

Few studies show direct deleterious effects of noise on productivity in the workplace (K.D. Kryter, 1970). Even where performance effects have been found (e.g., Kovigin & Mikheyev, 1965) the causal link to noise is tenuous at best. As Kryter points out, changes in noise level also influence employee morale, communication effectiveness, and fatigue; any one or combination of those may have a moderating influence on performance. Indeed, perhaps the most serious problem created by noise in the workplace is that it interferes with effective communication (MacKenzie, 1975; Nemacek & Grandjean, 1973). Interestingly, loud background conversation is more disruptive to performance than background noise of similar loudness but nonconversational in nature (Olszewski, Rotton, & Soler, 1976). This is so because the inner ear has difficulty discriminating among simultaneous presentations of a number of auditory signals. When loud conversations are presented simultaneously the listener has difficulty attending to any one of them in attempting to glean meaning from the environment. A great deal of attention is required to *unmask* these simultaneous signals, thus impairing performance.

Difficulty in hearing is related not only to amplitude, frequency, and masking but also to the time spent in the noisy environment (Acton, 1970) and to the distance between the communicator and the listener (Beranek, 1957). Even in a noisy environment we can communicate more easily as we become acclimated to it. Also, it is obviously easier to hear and understand a communicator if the distance from the listener is not great.

In regard to many workplaces, then, loud noises have been shown to lead to a number of physiological responses. However, acclimatization or habituation appears to occur, and no lasting health effects can be linked directly to the noise itself. Recent evidence does suggest, however, that gastrointestinal disorders might be the direct result of noise showing up as an accumulated effect. Hearing loss is a definite health-related problem, but one for which precautions can be taken. The discomfort felt by those subjected to noise is more psychological than physiological; noise is a nuisance and interferes with normal conversation. Field studies of noise in the workplace have not conclusively shown that noise interferes with productivity or efficiency on the job. As we will see in the next section, however, the noise can have residual and cumulative effects not only on health but perhaps on comfort and productivity as well.

NOISE REDUCTION IN THE WORKPLACE

In an article appearing in the *Bulletin–Association of Operative Millers*, Stephen Konz (1973) provides a number of recommendations for noise abatement in the workplace. The procedures are listed under four basic headings: (1) Plan ahead, (2) Modify the noise source, (3) Modify the sound waves, (4) Provide personal protection.

Plan Ahead

Among the things that can be done to reduce noise during production start-up is substituting less noisy for more noisy processes. For example, welding is quieter than riveting, compression riveting is quieter than pneumatic riveting, and high-strength bolts are quieter than either of the other two. Certain types and sizes of equipment are quieter than others. For example, squirrel cage fans are quieter than propeller-type, and belt drives are quieter than pneumatic tools. At start-up, manufacturers can purchase quieter equipment in deference to noisier equipment. It is also possible to choose and use quieter construction materials—wood block floors are quieter than concrete, for instance, or mechanical transmission of remote vibration can be reduced by the addition of expansion joints, flexible coupling, or the separation of facilities. If chutes are used, they could be made of plastic or wood, which is quieter than metal. Double doors and double walls can be used to separate noisy areas from other areas. And finally, if construction design will allow, workers can be separated from noise-producing equipment.

Modify the Noise Source

Konz (1973) notes that attempts to reduce noise should always start with the loudest noise first. We have seen that decibels do not increase linearly; hence, three noise sources of 90, 95, and 101 dB would combine to 102 dB. If the 90 dB source were completely eliminated, the 95 and 101 would still add up to 102 dB. Thus, eliminating the 90-dB source in this instance does absolutely nothing to reduce sound levels. Of course, the loudness of the noise is only one parameter contributing to the experience of annoyance and therefore is only one of several characteristics of noise that might require modification. Additional variables that contribute to the psychological experience of annoyance as well as to performance include noise as a generator of rattles (Schomer & Averbuch, 1989), vibration (Landstrom & Lofstedt, 1987), and reverberation (Harris & Reitz, 1985). Measures should, therefore, be taken to reduce the impact of these variables wherever possible.

Among strategies for modifying the noise source Konz recommends (a) reducing the driving force: sharpen tools, tighten screws and bolts, lubricate, replace worn-out parts; (b) reducing the response of vibrating surfaces: use stiffeners and perforated material where possible, employ damping materials; (c) changing the direction of the source: for directional noise, point the source away from people; and (d) minimizing air velocity and turbulence: cutting air velocity in half can reduce noise levels by 15 dB.

Modify the Sound Waves

Noise should be confined as much as possible to the immediate area where the noise is created, and when possible sound-absorbing materials should be placed between the noise source and workers. A much more ingenious means of combatting noise has become available with the development of high-speed computer microprocessors. Essentially this involves producing sounds that are the mirror image of those whose effects are to be eliminated. Like the waves in the ocean, sound travels through the air in waves. If the peak of one wave combines with the valley of another wave of the same strength, they cancel each other out. This noise cancellation is relatively easy if the noise can be predicted and is essentially repetitive, such as the drone of a high-speed fan or even the engine

---

TIME-OUT: Think about the environments in which you live and work. Are they noisy? Are you subjected to noise levels that may be harmful? Is this subjection to noise voluntary or involuntary? If you were concerned with reducing the noise level in these environments, what steps might you take? (Remember that noise levels are not additive.)

How would reducing these noise levels influence your everyday behavior? How much of this change in behavior might be attributed to your "exerting control" as opposed to reduction in sound levels?

---

noise of an automobile. Unexpected noises, or nonrepetitive noises, are harder to cancel out because they must first be picked up by a microphone and analyzed by a digital signal processor before a mirror image can be generated to cancel the sound. The technology to do this is now available and is being introduced into some industries to cut down on industrial noise, in some headphones for airplane pilots to make it easier for them to hear over cockpit noise, and in some automobiles to help eliminate engine noise.

Personal Protection

Two important keys to personal protection are time and equipment. Higher noise levels can be tolerated if exposure times are short; thus exposure time should be as short as possible. When total time cannot be shortened, the exposure should be intermittent; when workers must labor near noisy sources, earplugs and/or earmuffs should be utilized.

NOISE IN THE LABORATORY

Laboratory studies have generally found that significant and consistent increases in physiological arousal do not occur for noises below 60 to 65 dB. Beyond that level, however, definite arousal changes are noted, and at levels exceeding 130 dB, pain is often reported (K.D. Kryter, 1970). Additionally, noise by itself has been shown to have little or no effect on one's ability to carry out mental and psychomotor tasks ranging from boring and simple to interesting and complex. These results hold for college-aged as well as older-age men and women (Glass & Singer, 1972). On the other hand, it has been shown that noise can impair performance under highly specified conditions (Nagar & Pandey, 1987; Harcum, 1987; Britton & Delay, 1989). For example, performance degradations have been noted when individuals are asked to work on two tasks simultaneously or when they are asked to maintain continuous vigilance on a tracking task (Glass & Singer, 1972). The latter results are most likely to occur when the noise is experienced as *unpredictable* and/or *uncontrollable*. These findings show the importance of cognitive factors in determining the effects of noise on behavior, although the preponderance of data would indicate that humans are able to carry out a variety of cognitive and psychomotor tasks in the presence of rather intense noise with little or no decrement in performance capabilities (Arnoult, Gillfillan, & Voorhees, 1986; Koelega, Brinkman, & Bergman, 1986; Smith & Broadbent, 1985).

Further, Glass and Singer (1972) have shown that the small decrements in performance that occasionally occur can be minimized if the person subjected to the noise has control over its termination, even if the person does not exercise that control. Exposure to loud and uncontrollable noise in one study, however, led to a substantial increase in the number of negative trait words recalled, an increase in tension, and a worsening of mood (Willner & Neiva, 1986). This memory bias for negative aspects of the task is suggested to be qualitatively similar to that found in clinically depressed patients.

But while the majority of research shows no decrements in performance as the result of noise, other research suggests that sudden, loud, unpredictable, momentary noise can be distracting and leads to immediate, but soon rectified, errors of concentration or vigilance (Broadbent, 1954; Woodhead, 1964). Auble and Britton (1958) assert that the effects of noise can be mediated by the subjects' anxiety level, and Corcoran (1962) has shown that noise actually has a facilitative effect for individuals who have been sleep-deprived.

Perhaps the most important insight that comes from the laboratory research (especially that of Glass and Singer and associates) is that noise has more than just immediate effects on performance, and that the important effects may be insidious and require the passage of time to be detectable. For example, Glass, Singer, and Friedman (1969) found that tolerance for frustration, quality of proofreading performance, and ability to resolve cognitive conflict were all impaired following exposure to high-intensity noise (108 dB) providing that the noise was unpredictable and uncontrollable. These effects occurred despite the fact that the degree of adaptation shown for subjects exposed to the noise was comparable to an appropriate control group. Thus, the aftereffects of noise may be more deleterious than the effects brought about during actual response to the noise, especially if the noise is unpredictable and/or uncontrollable. In a more recent study, Sherrod, Hage, Halpern, and Moore (1977) manipulated the *degree of control* over noise. Some subjects had control over its onset, others had control over stopping the noise, and a third group could control both its start and its termination. Results of this study indicate that the aftereffects on a puzzle-solving (tolerance for frustration) task diminished as a function of the amount of perceived control. Additionally, noise has been shown to interact with level of illumination in the determination of performance on both manual dexterity and speed and efficiency tasks (Bhattacharya, Tripathi, & Kashyap, 1989).

Hartley and his colleagues (Hartley Boultwood, & Dunne, 1987; Hartley, Dunne, Schwartz, & Brown, 1986) have shown noise to influence different problem-solving strategies differentially. Noise benefitted verbal, but hindered spatial strategies for subjects asked to verify the truth/falsity of sentences used as picture descriptions. Consistent results were obtained when subjects were asked to solve a Rubik's cube, given either spatial or verbal instructions. Finally, in his review of the literature, Smith (1989) emphasized the importance of considering the nature of the task being performed in noise studies. It is therefore important to specify the exact conditions where noise is expected to have an effect and the exact kinds of effects that might occur. Obviously more research is needed.

Thus, we have seen that laboratory studies lead to results similar to those found in the field-correlational research of the workplace regarding performance during exposure to noisy conditions. However, unlike fieldwork, lab research indicates that these results can be modified. For example, noise perceived as uncontrollable or unpredictable is likely to lead to performance decrements, particularly on vigilance-type tasks (and on tasks requiring communication among co-workers). Also, the laboratory research suggests the need for testing individuals for effects not only during response to noise, but after the noise has been terminated. Indeed, some of the strongest effects for noise-induced task performance impairments are aftereffects.

NOISE IN THE LIVING ENVIRONMENT

As suggested earlier, noise can come from any source that makes a sound as long as the sound is evaluated as unwanted. The dripping faucet that was not bad enough to fix during the daylight hours becomes a noisy distraction at night when you're trying to get to sleep. The "yip" of your new Irish setter is a source of pleasure in the afternoon when he has flushed his first partridge, but is annoying when he has treed a cat at three o'clock in the morning. But sounds from some sources like autos, trains, and buses are subject to less interpretation, and are generally agreed upon as noise. The existence of noise at potentially harmful levels has been documented as resulting from automobiles and buses (Lawson & Walters, 1974), from rail traffic (Raloff, 1982), and from aircraft (Burrows & Zamarin, 1972; McClean & Tarnopolsky, 1977). Transportation noise is particularly disturbing because it is ever-present in large urban areas, it is uncontrollable, it is usually loud, and in the case of sonic booms, unpredictable. Ambient noise levels in apartments near rail systems can reach the 80 to 100 dB range, and the noise levels in third-floor apartments near the freeways in the Los Angeles area have been recorded at 90 dB.

Add to these noises the sounds of everyday living—stereos, vacuum cleaners, doors slamming, the neighbors' voices, and others—and the modern urban dweller is confronted with a cacophony of sounds continuous in presence and increasing in intensity. Walters (1968) reviewed a study done by the Bell system, and reported that experts have estimated a 1-dB increase in urban noise level annually for the years 1948 to 1968. This translates, you will recall from our earlier discussion, to a thousandfold increase in intensity over that period of time. We have no reason to believe that this trend has abated in the past 20 years. Indeed, we have every reason to believe it has increased.

But just what are the effects of this increased intensity of noise to which we are all being constantly exposed? Generally speaking, noisy environments,

FIGURE 8-4 College and high school students often expose themselves to yet another high intensity sound: loud music. (FUNKY WINKERBEAN by Tom Batiu Field Enterprises, Inc., 1972. Reprinted with special permission of North America Syndicate.)

in comparison to noise-abated ones, have been shown to lead to more tension and uncertainty and to talking faster (Ward & Suedfeld, 1973). A noisy environment has been reported to lead to a greater arrest rate, a decreased likelihood of caring for the area surrounding one's apartment, and to increased truancy for a group of apartment dwellers (Damon, 1977); and it has led to less informal interaction among neighbors (Appleyard & Lintell, 1972). Finally, high ambient noise levels have been related to school performance (Cohen, Evans, Krantz, & Stokols, 1980) and to elevated blood pressure (Cohen et al., 1980; Knipschild, 1980). And, although we might expect noise to have a detrimental effect on sleep, recent evidence (Thiessen, 1988) suggests that its impact may be negligible.

College and high school students often choose to expose themselves to yet another high-intensity sound: loud music. Lebo and Oliphant (1968) have found that persons in bars and nightclubs featuring live music often expose themselves to sound in the 110 to 120 dB range for periods in excess of one and one-half hours. Consequently, as many as 60 percent of 18- to 19-year-olds now show a substantial noise-induced hearing loss. Danenberg, Loos-Cosgrove, and LoVerde (1987) report as much as a 5 dB pure-tone air-conduction threshold shift for teens, as well as adults, attending a live rock-music concert. A majority of these individuals also reported *tinnitus*, and in a subgroup tested three days after the concert, most had not fully recovered to pre-exposure thresholds. Further, Ayres and Hughes (1986) have shown that visual acuity is impaired by the presence of loud music but not by loud noise. They suggest that the momentary peak levels in music may play a role in disrupting vestibular-ocular control. Other potential effects of this and related noise include the following: headaches, irritability, insomnia, reduction in sexual desire, and loss of appetite.

A growing number of teenagers as well as younger children around the world are exposing themselves to potentially dangerous sound levels in yet another manner. Portable radios, tape players, and compact disc players with headphones are becoming increasingly popular. It is estimated that as many as 80 percent of children in middle-class elementary schools in the United States own or use personal stereos at least occasionally (Clark, 1991). This figure compares with approximately 37 percent of school children in England (Bradley, Fortnum, & Coles, 1987) and 87 percent in Hong Kong (Wong, Van Hasselt, Tang, & Yiu, 1990). Most of these devices are capable of producing sound levels in the ear in excess of 100 dB sound pressure level. Such levels are capable of producing noise-induced hearing loss, and evidence suggests that when played at the listener's preferred volume, they do indeed produce hearing loss (Catalano & Levin, 1985; Lee, Senders, Gantz, & Otto, 1985; Rice, Rossi, & Olina, 1987).

Abey-Wickerama, a'Brook, Gattoni and Herridge (1969) compared psychiatric admission rates for high and low noise areas around Heathrow Airport in London and found higher admission rates for the high noise area. These results have been challenged by Chowns (1970), who argued that these two areas represented populations that varied on more dimensions than simply ambient noise level. Subsequent research with improved methodology (Herridge, 1974; Herridge & Low-Beer, 1973) has led to results similar to, though weaker than, the Abey-Wickerama et al., findings. Finally, D.D. Kryter (1990) has recently concluded that aircraft noise is significantly and positively related to rates of admission to psychiatric hospitals (i.e., the stress associated with airport noise is sufficient to contribute to health disorders requiring admission to hospitals for psychiatric care). Of course, all residents living near airports do not experience psychiatric symptoms. There is some evidence, though, that everyday errors such as forgetting appointments, dropping things, confusing right and left when giving directions, etc., are more likely to occur in those exposed to high levels of airport noise than in those who are not exposed (Smith & Stansfeld, 1986).

Studies on airport noise have shown that adverse public reaction to noise can be averted by sending positive information regarding the economic value of the airport and other relevant facts to nearby residents who are likely

---

TIME-OUT: Do you own a portable radio/cassette, CD player with headphones? How often do you listen to it? What do you listen to? for what length of time? at what volume? Do you think that using it has influenced your ability to hear? If so, how? If not, how do you know? Have you had a hearing test recently to find out?

Try this. Develop a survey questionnaire by which you can ask naive respondents questions akin to those posed above. You might look for age or gender differences in their responses. You might even see if you can get a local audiologist to test your subjects for hearing loss to see if more frequent users, or users of a particular ilk, are more or less likely to show hearing impairment.

Remember, though, that the data you will be getting is correlational, and therefore you will not be able to draw causal inferences.

to be affected by the noise. Resident perceptions of individual control in airport planning and management significantly influence their annoyance with noise and their opinions about noise-management policies. The greater the perceived control, the less annoyance is expressed and the greater the satisfaction with noise management-policies (Jue, Shumaker, & Evans, 1984). In a review of the literature on airport noise in which noise level, various respondent-related variables, and culture were considered, Job (1988) concludes that sensitivity to noise and attitudes toward it account for more variation in noise reactions than does actual noise exposure. Thus, the more informed that residents are regarding the positive economic impact of an airport, and the more control they feel they are able to exert in the decision-making process, the less annoyed they report being with the inevitable noise of low-flying aircraft. But Pretemon (1968) has shown that despite people's ability to be favorably influenced by cognitive intervention, most are willing to pay extra dollars in rent for guaranteed quiet.

There is increasing evidence that noise may influence the course of pregnancy in humans, lead to increased miscarriages, decrease the number of viable young, and raise the number of birth defects of various kinds. Interestingly, noise appears to stimulate the ovaries to accelerate the development and release of ova, but the blood supply to the eggs and later to the developing embryo is poorer than normal. Work with animals other than humans has shown that exposure to noise increases susceptibility to certain bacterial and viral infections. Furthermore, noise alters blood pressure, the rhythm of the the heart, the flow of the gastric acids to the stomach and, as anyone who has been exposed to noise can attest, it can cause headaches and increased irritability and nervousness.

Obviously, high ambient noise levels are discomforting, and occasionally these levels may lead to serious individual complications (e.g., hearing loss, psychiatric admission, headaches, fatigue, and other symptoms). But are there more subtle effects of noise on social behaviors? Aside from the fact that high levels of noise can trigger communication breakdowns which may in turn lead to interpersonal difficulties, are there other consequences influencing the way in which we meet, greet, and interact with our fellow beings? With this question in mind, we will now turn to laboratory and experimental work on the relationship of noise to attraction, altruism, and aggression.

NOISE AND SOCIAL BEHAVIOR

Any noise that interferes with effective communication can be seen as negatively influencing interpersonal behavior. If that noise is also stressful, overly annoying, interferes with one's attention processes, or in any way constrains behavior, then its effect will be exacerbated. Griffitt (1970) suggested that any of a whole host of environmental conditions act to influence our attraction to others. The only requirement is that those others be contiguous with the environmental condition, and that the environmental condition be evaluated negatively. In this respect, then, we would expect noise to have a dampening effect on our liking for others. Bull and co-workers (1972) found potential support for this hypothesis for men but not women, and Mathews, Canon, and Alexander (1974) reported increased comfortable interpersonal distancing with noise elevated to levels of only 80 dB. Finally, Siegel and Steele (1979) and Siegel (1980) showed that often the positivity-negativity of responses to others is not affected by noise, but by the time taken to make judgments of others. Noise often leads to premature and more extreme responses (i.e., to a judgment with narrowed focus and extreme results). It is probably safe to say that whatever the underlying mechanism (arousal, narrowed attention, negative feelings in general) noise does nothing to increase our liking for others, and often leads to dislike.

Research on the relationship between noise and aggression and noise and helping has been more fertile, both in numbers and in the nonequivocality of the findings. Generalizing from a series of studies (Geen & O'Neal, 1969; Donnerstein & Wilson, 1976; Konecni, 1975) we can state flatly that there is no evidence to suggest that increased noise causes increased aggression, but rather that noise serves to facilitate aggression in those already predisposed to act aggressively (e.g., those who have been angered). Additionally, if individuals can exert some degree of control over the noise, even the facilitative effects disappear (cf. Glass & Singer, 1972). Additionally, if the noise is from an uncontrollable source, both aggression and physiological arousal increases (Geen & McCown, 1984).

Several studies have shown that noise produces a negative effect on helping behavior (see, for example, Mathews & Canon, 1975; and Page, 1977). Based on an urban field study in roadwork environments Moser (1988) suggests that helping responses are negatively influenced by reduced attentiveness in noisy environments as well as an unwillingness (often refusal) to engage in verbal interaction. One study, however, has found that under very specific conditions, noise might lead to an increase in helping (Yinon & Bizman, 1980). The most promising explanation for these findings is that noise can act to cause negative feelings, which in turn mediate avoidance or retaliatory behavior vis-à-vis others in the environment.

In summary, noise (particularly if it is unpredictable or uncontrollable and intense enough) will lead to less harmonious interpersonal behaviors. The specific processes that mediate this relationship, however, are not well understood, and additional research is sorely needed.

INDIVIDUAL DIFFERENCES IN RESPONSE TO NOISE

Earlier in this chapter we said that the simplest and most widely used definition of noise was that it was "unwanted sound," and we suggested that because of this what constitutes noise is necessarily idiosyncratically determined. Despite this, it may be possible to identify individual difference variables related either to the definition of sound as noise, or to the effects of being exposed to various conditions of noise. In this regard researchers have determined that such individual characteristics as introversion/extroversion (Geen, McCown, & Broyles, 1985), TypeA/TypeB personality (Moch, 1984), internal/external locus of control (Collins-Eiland, Dansereau, Brooks, & Holley, 1986), residential crowding experience (Nagar, Pandey, & Paulus, 1988), previous noise experience (Hambrick-Dixon, 1986), gender (Hambrick-Dixon, 1988; Holding & Baker, 1987; Koelega et al., 1986), and noise sensitivity (Iwata, 1984; Stansfeld, Clark, Jenkins, & Tarnopolsky, 1985a, 1985b) all appear to moderate the effects of noise.

For example, when noise of low intensity was given to introverts performing a vigilance task, an impairment in detection rates across trials was noted, whereas for high-intensity noise, introverts showed a decline in detection rates. On the other hand, extroverts responded to low-intensity noise by showing a slight decrease in detection rates but showed an impairment in detection rates for high-intensity noise (Geen et al., 1985). TypeA in comparison with TypeB individuals appear to deny the aversive aspects of noise or simply ignore the acoustic environment when asked to perform complex cognitive tasks (Moch, 1984). Internal locus of control individuals appear to behave much like TypeA's as evidenced by their superior performance in comparison with externals in noisy environments and their inferior performance in no noise conditions (Collins-Eiland et al. 1986).

There is no universal pattern of effects for gender, but rather gender seems to interact with other variables such as time of day and intensity (Holding & Baker, 1987; Smith, 1985). Finally, high noise-sensitive individuals, while not differing in auditory threshold from low noise-sensitive individuals living in high aircraft noise environments, show consistently lower heart rates (Stansfeld et al., 1985b) and exhibit more psychiatric symptoms. Additionally, they have higher neuroticism scores and display a greater reactivity to other sensory stimuli (Stansfeld et al., 1985a).

NOISE IN SCHOOLS AND HOSPITALS

Given what we know regarding the effects of noise on cognitive performance and its relationship to the stress response, it would make sense that researchers look at the influence of noise in schools and hospitals, specifically. They have; and we will turn to that research now. DeJoy (1983), in reviewing over 30 articles in the literature concerning children's susceptibility to noise with respect to academic performance and cognitive development, concluded that deficiencies in reading achievement and cognitive task performance are due directly or indirectly to noise interfering with speech. May and Brackett (1987) pointed out that hearing-impaired students have a specially difficult time in school environments, with acoustic distortion resulting from noise, reverberation, and distance. Furthermore, Soyer and Houdet (1986) suggested that most, if not all, schools are inadequately acoustically designed for the avoidance of noise-induced fatigue.

The importance of individual differences in response to noise cannot be overstated. For example, Christie and Glickman (1980) and Hykin (1984) have shown in two separate samples (first to fifth graders and college students) that girls perform better and boys worse in quiet conditions, but boys better and girls worse in noisy conditions. Also Zentall (1983) has shown that, at least for simple tasks, performance is enhanced by noise for hyperactive children, but degraded for autistic ones.

As with the earlier work of Glass and Singer (1972) it has been found that aftereffects for children may be more important than concurrent effects (Cohen & Weinstein, 1982). This could occur for at least four reasons. First, noise in the classroom could interfere with communication, and thus students may fail to understand instructions, resulting in poor performance. Second, noise might interfere with the student's development of strategies for processing information. Third, if the noise is uncontrollable, the student's sense of self-efficacy (important to learning and performance) may be undermined. Fourth, the arousal created by the noise may carry over to other settings and interfere with performance.

In summary, noise does appear to have a detrimental effect on classroom performance. This effect, however, is moderated by individual differences, the type of task involved, and the nature of the noise. Further, these effects appear to be greater postexposure than they are during exposure to noise.

Health care providers have recently begun to consider the role of ambient stressors in the prognosis of hospitalized patients. Of particular concern are intensive care units (ICUs) and critical care units (CCUs) where patients may be particularly vulnerable to such factors as continuous lighting, crowding, unpleasant odors, disturbing or painful touch, and noise (Baker, 1984). These stressors, added to the inherent stress of patients' diseased state, the pain they may be enduring, and the fear they may be experiencing, make ICU and CCU patients particularly susceptible to environment induced stress. Baker (1984) concluded that the intensity and frequency of noise may contribute to the individual patient's feelings of well-being, but these effects are moderated by such factors as whether the persons making the noise are concerned about the patient's welfare, whether the patient has a feeling related to a particular noise source, and whether the patient has control over it.

Snyder-Halpern (1985) suggests that the noise inherent in CCUs interferes with normal sleep and thus with patient recovery rate. Further, Topf (1985a; 1989) has shown that hospital noise not only affects the patients but also the nursing staff. Several studies, though, have shown that these effects can be ameliorated by providing patients with greater control over ambient noise (Topf, 1985b), or by providing them with training in progressive muscle relaxation (Griffin, Myers, Kopelke, & Walker, 1988).

Thus, noise can be considered to be just one of several ambient stressors inherent in the hospital environment. Although noise may have some effect on sleep it does not appear to be sufficient to prolong recovery. Further, as with many stressors, its effects are ameliorated by providing some degree of control over it.

FIGURE 8-5 Health care providers have recently begun to consider the role of ambient stressors in the prognosis of hospitalized patients.

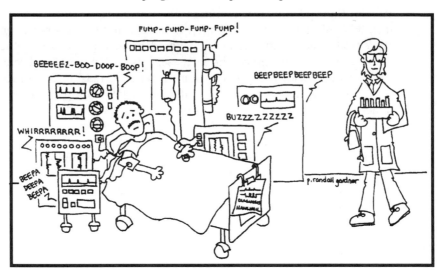

NOISE AND THE LAW

Various estimates have been made regarding the number of workers who are exposed, as a result of their occupations, to extremely noisy work conditions. Some estimates indicate that over half of American production workers may be exposed to noise levels so high that hearing loss is likely (i.e., they are exposed to intermittent noise equal to or exceeding 80 dB) and that perhaps as many as 5 million workers are exposed to levels in excess of the legally permissible 90 dB. Various state and federal laws have been passed to protect workers from being exposed to levels of noise constituting a health hazard. By 1965, thirty-five states had passed legislation making hearing loss compensable, and in 1968 the Walsh-Healy Public Contracts Act was passed. This act states that any firm which has government contracts of $10,000 or more must limit noise in the work environment to 90 dB. Finally, almost every city of any size has passed noise ordinances in an attempt to curtail excessive noise.

In 1972, congress voted to give the EPA the power to set stringent standards for noise from all new products, and these controls extend to construction, transportation equipment, motors, and engines. All new power equipment must now clearly label the expected dB output so that users may take whatever precautions are necessary. A number of cases are presently pending regarding whether penalties for damages will be assessed on industries that are exposing workers to noises above EPA standards and on airports whose operations bring the ambient noise of the surrounding community to uncomfortable, if not health-affecting, levels.

SUMMARY

We can think of unwanted sounds like unwanted chemicals as a pollutant. In fact, this pollutant has been shown to have a number of physiological and psychological effects that can be considered unhealthy. As with other pollutants, ambient noise levels are on the increase. It has been estimated that in the major cities of the world, the ambient noise level is increasing by approximately 1dB per year. With no programs of abatement, cities would be unlivable and residents would be totally nerve-deaf by the year 2000.

Aside from its physiological effects, noise can interfere with effective interpersonal communication, making it more likely that civil disruption will occur and the quality of life will be diminished. Recognizing the handwriting on the wall, legislation has been passed at various levels of government to provide some abatement. Despite these attempts, noise levels in cities continue to rise, and additional legislation and enforcement are both needed.

IMPORTANT CONCEPTS

sound
noise
   frequency, Hertz
   timbre
narrow band
wide band
white noise

dyne
decibels
   phon
hearing loss
noise reduction
noise predictability
noise controllability
legal noise limits

REFERENCES

Abey-Wickerama, I., a'Brook, M.F., Gattoni, F.E.G., & Herridge, C.F. (1969). Mental hospital admission and aircraft noise, *Lancet, 2* (7633), 1275–1277.

Acton, W.I. (1970). Speech intelligibility in a background noise and noise-induced hearing loss. *Ergonomics, 13*, 546–554.

Appleyard, D., & Lintell, N. (1972). The environmental quality of streets. The resident's viewpoint. *Journal of American Institute of Planners, 38*, 84–101.

Arnoult, M.D., Gillfillan, L.G., & Voorhees, J. W. (1986). Annoyingness of aircraft noise in relation to cognitive activity. *Perceptual and Motor Skills, 63*(2, Pt. 1), 599–616.

Auble, D., & Britton, N. (1958). Anxiety as a factor influencing routine performance under auditory stimuli. *Journal of General Psychology, 58*, 111–114.

Ayres, T.J., & Hughes, P. (1986). Visual acuity with noise and music at 107 dbA. *Journal of Auditory Research, 26*(1), 65–74.

Baker, C.F. (1984). Sensory overload and noise in the ICU: Sources of environmental stress. *Critical Care Quarterly, 6*(4), 66–80.

Beranek, L.L. (1957). Revised criteria for noise in buildings. *Noise Control, 3*, 19–26.

Bergstrom, B., & Nystrom, B. (1986). Development of hearing loss during long-term exposure to occupational noise: A 20-year follow-up study. *Scandinavian Audiology, 15*(4), 227–234.

Bhattacharya, S.K., Tripathi, S.R., & Kashyap, S.K. (1989). The combined effects of noise and illumination on the performance efficiency of visual search and neuromotor task components. *Journal of Human Ergology, 18*(1), 41–51.

Bradley, R., Fortnum, H., & Coles, R. (1987).

Research note: Patterns of exposure of school-children to amplified music. *British Journal of Audiology, 21,* 119–125.

Britton, L.A., & Delay, E.R. (1989). Effects of noise on a simple visual attentional task. *Perceptual and Motor Skills, 68*(3), 875–878.

Broadbent, D.E. (1954). Some effects of noise on visual performance. *Quarterly Journal of Experimental Psychology, 6,* 1–5.

Bull, A.J., Burbage, S.E., Crandall, J.E., Fletcher, C.I., Lloyd, J.T., Ravenberg, R.L., & Rockett, S.L. (1972). Effects of noise and intolerance of ambiguity upon attraction for similar and dissimilar others. *Journal of Social Psychology, 88,* 151–152.

Burrows, A.A., & Zamarin, D.M. (1972). Aircraft noise and the community: Some recent survey findings. *Aerospace Medicine, 43,* 27–33.

Cameron, P., Robertson, D., & Zaks, J. (1972). Sound pollution, noise pollution, and health: Community parameters. *Journal of Applied Psychology, 56,* 67–74.

Carter, N.L., & Beh, H.C. (1989). The effect of intermittent noise on cardiovascular functioning during vigilance task performance. *Psychophysiology, 26*(5), 548–559.

Catalano, P.J., & Levin, S.M. (1985). Noise-induced hearing loss and portable radios with headphones, *International Journal of Pediatric Otorhinolaryngology, 9,* 59–67.

Chowns, R.H. (1970). Mental hospital admissions and aircraft noise. *Lancet, 1* (7644), 467.

Christie, D.J., & Glickman, C.D. (1980). The effects of classroom noise on children: Evidence for sex differences. *Psychology in the Schools, 17,* 405–408.

Clark, W.W. (1991). Noise exposure from leisure activities: A review. *Journal of the Acoustical Society of America, 90,* 175–181.

Cohen, S., Glass, D.C., & Phillips, S. (1977). Environment and health. In H.E. Freeman, S. Levine, & L.G, Reeder (Eds.), *Handbook of medical sociology.* Englewood Cliffs, N.J.: Prentice Hall.

Cohen, S., Evans, G.W., Krantz, D.S., & Stokols, D. (1980). Physiological, motivational and cognitive effects of air craft noise on children: Moving from the laboratory to the field. *American Psychologist, 35,* 231–243.

Cohen, S., & Weinstein, N. (1982). Nonauditory effects of noise on behavior and health. In G.W. Evans (Ed.), *Environmental stress.* New York: Cambridge University Press.

Collins-Eiland, K., Dansereau, D.F., Brooks, L.W., & Holley, C.D. (1986). Effects of conversational noise, locus of control, and field dependence/independence on the performance of academic tasks. *Contemporary Educational Psychology, 11*(2), 139–149.

Corcoran, D.W.J. (1962). Noise and loss of sleep. *Quarterly Journal of Experimental Psychology, 14,* 178–182.

Damon, A. (1977). The residential environment health and behavior. Simple research opportunities, strategies, and some findings in the Solomon Islands and Boston, Massachusetts. In L.E. Hinckle, Jr., & W.C. Loring (Eds.), *The extent of the man-made environment on health and behavior.* Atlanta: Center for Disease Control, U.S. Public Health Service.

Darner, C.L. (1966). Sound pulses and the heart. *Journal of the Acoustical Society of America, 39,* 414–416.

Danenberg, M.A., Loos-Cosgrove, M. & LoVerde, M. (1987). Temporary hearing loss and rock music. *Language, Speech, and Hearing Services in Schools, 18*(3), 267–274.

DeJoy, D.M. (1983). Environmental noise and children: Review of recent findings. *Journal of Auditory Research, 23*(3), 181–194.

Donnerstein, E., & Wilson, D.W. (1976). Effects of noise and perceived control on ongoing and subsequent aggressive behavior. *Journal of Personality and Social Psychology, 34,* 774–781.

Dubos, R. (1965). *Man adapting.* New Haven, Conn.: Yale University Press.

Geen, R.G., & McCown, E.J. (1984). Effects of noise and attack on aggression and physiological arousal. *Motivation and Emotion, 8*(3), 231–241.

Geen, R.G., McCown, E.J., & Broyles, J.W. (1985). Effects of noise on sensitivity of introverts and extraverts to signals in a vigilance task. *Personality and Individual Differences, 6*(2), 237–241.

Geen, R.G., & O'Neal, E.C. (1969). Activation of cue-elicited aggression by general arousal. *Journal of Personality and Social Psychology, 11,* 289–292.

Glass, D.C., & Singer, J.E. (1972). *Urban stress.* New York: Academic Press.

Glass, D.C., Singer, J.E., & Friedman, L.W. (1969). Psychic cost of adaptation to an environmental stressor. *Journal of Personality and Social Psychology, 12,* 200–210.

Grandjean, E., Graf, P., Lauber, A., Meier, H.P., &

Muller, R. (1973). A survey on aircraft noise in Switzerland. In W.D. Ward (Ed.), *Proceedings of the International Congress on Noise as a Public Health Problem*. Washington, D.C.: U.S. Government Printing Office.

Griffin, J.P., Myers, S., Kopelke, C., & Walker, D. (1988). The effects of progressive muscular relaxation on subjectively reported disturbance due to hospital noise. *Behavioral Medicine, 14*(1), 37–42.

Griffitt, W. (1970). Environmental effects on interpersonal affective behavior: Ambient effective temperature and attraction. *Journal of Personality and Social Psychology, 15*, 240–244.

Hambrick-Dixon, P.J. (1986). Effects of experimentally imposed noise on task performance of black children attending day-care centers near elevated subway trains. *Developmental Psychology, 22*(2), 259–264.

Hambrick-Dixon, P.J. (1988). The effect of elevated subway train noise over time on black children's visual vigilance performance. *Journal of Environmental Psychology, 8*(4), 299–314.

Harcum, E.R. (1987). Disturbance ratings for relevant and irrelevant noise during performance of a cognitive task. *Perceptual and Motor Skills, 65*(1), 333–334.

Harris, R.W., & Reitz, M.L. (1985). Effects of room reverberation and noise on speech discrimination by the elderly. *Audiology, 24*(5), 319–324.

Hartley, L.R., Boultwood, B., & Dunne, M.P. (1987). Noise and verbal or spatial solutions of Rubik's cube. *Ergonomics, 30*(3), 503–509.

Hartley, L., Dunne, M., Schwartz, S., & Brown, J. (1986). Effect of noise on cognitive strategies in a sentence verification task. *Ergonomics, 29*(4), 607–617.

Herridge, C.F. (1974). Aircraft noise and mental health. *Journal of Psychomotor Research, 18*, 239–243.

Herridge, C.F., & Low-Beer, L. (1973). Observation of the effects of aircraft noise near Heathrow Airport on mental health. In W.D. Ward (Ed.), *Proceedings of the International Congress on Noise as a Public Health Problem*. Washington, D.C.: U.S. Government Printing Office.

Holding, D.H. & Baker, M.A. (1987). Toward meaningful noise research. *Journal of General Psychology, 114*(4), 395–410.

Hykin, S. (1984). *The effects of classroom noise on adults: Evidence for sex differences*. Unpublished master's thesis, University of Victoria, Victoria, British Columbia.

Ising, H., & Melchert, H.U. (1980). Endocrine and cardiovascular effects of noise. In J.V. Tobias, G. Jansen & W.D. Ware (Eds.) *Noise as a public health problem. Proceedings of the Third International Congress*. ASHA Report No. 10, Rockville, Md.: American Speech and Hearing Association.

Iwata, O. (1984). The relationship of noise sensitivity to health and personality. *Japanese Psychological Research, 26*(2), 75–81.

Jerkova, H., & Kremorova, B. (1970). Observation of the effect of noise on the general health of workers in large engineering factories; attempt at evaluation. *Pracovni Lekarstvi 17*, 147–148.

Job, R.F. (1988). Community response to noise: A review of factors influencing the relationship between noise exposure and reaction. *Journal of the Acoustical Society of America, 83*(3), 991–1001.

Jue, G.M., Shumaker, S.A., & Evans, G.W. (1984). Community opinion concerning airport noise–abatement alternatives. *Journal of Environmental Psychology, 4*(4), 337-345.

Knipschild, P.G. (1980). Aircraft noise and hypertension: In J.V. Tobias, G. Jansen, & W.D. Ware (Eds.), *Noise as a public health problem: Proceedings of the Third International Congress* (ASHA Report No. 10). Rockville, Md.: American Speech and Hearing Association.

Koelega, H.S., Brinkman, J.A., & Bergman, H. (1986). No effect of noise on vigilance performance? *Human Factors, 28*(5), 581–593.

Konecni, V. (1975). The mediation of aggressive behavior: Arousal level vs. anger and cognitive labeling. *Journal of Personality and Social Psychology, 32*, 706–712.

Konz, S. (1973). Noise abatement and control. *Bulletin–Association of Operative Millers*, 3417–3423.

Kovrigan, S.D., & Mikheyev, A.P. (1965). The effect of noise level on working efficiency. *Report N65-28297*. Joint Publications Research Service, Washington, D.C.

Kryter, D.D. (1990). Aircraft noise and social factors in psychiatric hospital admission rates: A re-examination of some data. *Psychological Medicine, 20*(2), 395–411.

Kryter, K.D. (1970). *The effects of noise on man*. New York: Academic Press.

Landstrom, U., & Lofstedt, P. (1987). Noise, vibration and changes in wakefulness during helicopter flight. *Aviation, Space, and Environmental Medicine, 58*(2), 109–118.

Lawson, B.R., & Walters, D. (1974). The effects of a new motorway on an established residential area. In D. Canter & T. Lee (Eds.), *Psychology and the built environment.* New York: John Wiley.

Lebo, C.P., & Oliphant, K.P. (1968). Music as a source of acoustic trauma. *Laryngoscope, 78,* 1211–1218.

Lee, P.C., Senders, C.W., Gantz, B.J., & Otto, S.R. (1985). Transient sensorineural hearing loss after overuse of portable headphone cassette radios *Otorhinolaryngology, Head and Neck Surgery, 93,* 623–625.

Lenhardt, D. (1970). Die Berufsschaden des Ohres. *Arch Orhen-Nasen Kehlkoptheilk 185,* 11, 1965 as noted in K.D. Kryter. *The effects of noise on man.* New York: Academic Press.

MacKenzie, S.T. (1975). *Noise and office work: Employee and employer concerns.* Ithaca: New York State School of Industrial and Labor Relations, Cornell University.

Mathews, K.E., Jr., & Canon, L.K. (1975). Environmental noise level as a determinant of helping behavior. *Journal of Personality and Social Psychology, 32,* 571–577.

Mathews, K.E., Canon, L.K., & Alexander, K. (1974). The influence of level of empathy and ambient noise on the body buffer zone. *Proceedings of the American Psychological Association Division of Personality and Social Psychology, 1,* 367–370.

May, J., & Brackett, D. (1987). Adapting the classroom environment. *Hearing Rehabilitation Quarterly, 12*(2), 7–9, 14–15.

McClean, E.K., & Tarnopolsky, A. (1977). Noise, discomfort and mental health: A review of the socio-medical implications of disturbance by noise. *Psychological Medicine, 7,* 19–62.

Moch, A. (1984). Type A and Type B behaviour patterns, task type and sensitivity to noise. *Psychological Medicine, 14*(3), 643–646.

Morata, T. (1989). Study of the effects of simultaneous exposure to noise and carbon disulfide on workers' hearing. *Scandinavian Audiology, 18*(1), 53–58.

Moser, G. (1988). Urban stress and helping behavior: Effects of environmental overload and noise on behavior. *Journal of Environmental Psychology, 8*(4), 287–298.

Nagar, D., & Pandey, J. (1987). Affect and performance on cognitive task as a function of crowding and noise. *Journal of Applied Social Psychology, 17*(2), 147.

Nagar, D., Pandey, J., & Paulus, P.B. (1988). The effects of residential crowding experience on reactivity to laboratory crowding and noise. *Journal of Applied Social Psychology, 18*(16), 1423–1442.

National Academy of Sciences. (1981). *The effect on human health from long-term exposure to noise (Report of Working Group 81).* Washington, D.C.: National Academy Press.

Nemacek, J., & Grandjean, E. (1973). Results of an ergometric investigation of large space offices. *Human Factors, 15,* 111–124.

Olszewski, D.A., Rotton, J., & Soler, E.A. (1976, May). *Conversation, conglomerate noise, and behavioral after-effects.* Paper presented at the meeting of the Midwestern Psychological Association, Chicago.

Page, R.A. (1977). Noise and helping behavior. *Environment and Behavior, 9,* 559–572.

Ponomarenko, I.J. (1966). The effect of constant high frequency noise on certain physiological functions in adolescents. *Hygiene and Sanitation, 31,* 188–193.

Pretemon, D.R. (1968). How much does noise bother apartment dwellers? *Architectural Record, 143,* 155–156.

Raloff, J. (1982). Occupational noise—The subtle pollutant. *Science News, 121*(21), 347–350.

Rice, C.G., Rossi, G., & Olina, M. (1987). Damage risk from personal casette players. *British Journal of Audiology, 21,* 279–288.

Rosen, S. (1970). Noise, hearing and cardiovascular function. In B.L. Welch & A.S. Welch (Eds.), *Physiological effects of noise.* New York: Plenum.

Schomer, P.D., & Averbuch, A. (1989). Indoor human response to blast sounds that generate rattles. *Journal of the Acoustical Society of America, 86*(2), 665–673.

Select Committee on Children, Youth and Families (1991). Turn it down: Effects of noise on hearing loss in children and youth. Hearing before the Select Committee on Children, Youth and Families in the House of Representatives, July 22, 1991, Washington, D.C.: U.S. Government Printing Office.

Seyle, H. (1956). *The stress of life.* New York: McGraw-Hill.

Sherrod, D.R., Hage, J., Halpern, P.L., & Moore, B.S. (1977). Effects of personal causation and perceived control on responses to an aversive environment: The more control the better. *Journal of Experimental Social Psychology, 13,* 14–27.

Siegel, J.M. (1980). Environmental distortion and interpersonal judgments. *British Journal of Social and Clinical Psychology, 19,* 23–32.

Siegel, J.M., & Steele, C.M. (1979). Noise level and social discrimination. *Personality and Social Psychology Bulletin, 5,* 95–99.

Smith, A. (1989). A review of the effects of noise on human performance. *Scandinavian Journal of Psychology, 30*(3), 185–206.

Smith, A.P. (1985). The effects of different types of noise on semantic processing and syntactic reasoning. *Acta Psychologica, 58*(3), 263–273.

Smith, A.P., & Broadbent, D.E. (1985). The effect of noise on the naming of colors and reading of colour names. *Acta Psychologica, 58*(3), 275–285.

Smith, A.P., & Stansfeld, S. (1986). Aircraft noise exposure, noise sensitivity and everyday errors. *Environment and Behavior, 18*(2), 214–226.

Snyder-Halpern, R. (1985). The effect of critical care unit noise on patient sleep cycles. *Critical Care Quarterly, 7*(4), 41–51.

Soyer, M., & Houdet, C. (1986). Reduction of acoustic annoyance in school dining halls. *Journal of Auditory Research, 26*(3), 191–196.

Stansfeld, S.A., Clark, C.R., Jenkins, L.M., & Tarnopolsky, A. (1985a). Sensitivity to noise in a community sample: I. Measurement of psychiatric disorder and personality. *Psychological Medicine, 15*(2), 243–254.

Stansfeld, S.A., Clark, C.R., Jenkins, L.M., & Tarnopolsky, A. (1985b). Sensitivity to noise in a community sample: II. Measurement of psychophysiological indices. *Psychological Medicine, 15*(2), 255–263.

Thiessen, G.J. (1988). Effect of traffic noise on the cyclical nature of sleep. *Journal of the Acoustical Society of America, 84*(5), 1741–1743.

Topf, M. (1985a). Personal and environmental predictors of patient disturbance due to hospital noise. *Journal of Applied Psychology, 70*(1), 22–28.

Topf, M. (1985b). Noise induced stress in hospital patients: Coping and nonauditory health outcomes. *Journal of Human Stress, 11*(3), 125–134.

Topf, M. (1989). Sensitivity to noise, personality hardiness, and noise-induced stress in critical care nurses. *Environment and Behavior, 21*(6), 717–733.

U.S. Environmental Protection Agency (1972). *Report to the President and Congress on Noise, December 1971.* Washington, D.C.: U.S. Government Printing Office.

Walters, S. (1968). Sound and the psyche. *Mechanical Engineering,* 40–41.

Ward, A.A. (1953). Central nervous system effects. *BENOX REPORT: An exploratory study of the biological effects of noise.* The University of Chicago, 73–80.

Ward, L.M., & Suedfeld, P. (1973). Human responses to highway noise. *Environmental Research, 6,* 306–326.

Willner, P., & Neiva, J. (1986). Brief exposure to uncontrollable but not to controllable noise biases the retrieval of information from memory. *British Journal of Clinical Psychology, 25*(2), 93–100.

Wolf, H. (1968). *Stress and disease,* (2nd ed.). Springfield Ill.: Chas. C Thomas.

Wong, T.W., Van Hasselt, C.A., Tang, L.S., & Yiu, P.C. (1990). The use of personal cassette players among youth and its effects on hearing. *Public Health, 4,* 327–330.

Woodhead, M.M. (1964). Visual searching in intermittent noise. *Journal of Sound Vibration, 1,* 157–161

Yinon, Y., & Bizman, A. (1980). Noise, success, and failure as determinants of helping behavior. *Personality and Social Psychology Bulletin, 6,* 125–130.

Zentall, S.S. (1983). Learning environments: A review of physical and temporal factors. *Exceptional Education Quarterly, 4,* 90–115.

Population Density, Urbanization, and Crowding

9

"Excuse me, sir, I am prepared to make you a rather attractive offer for your square."

FIGURE 9-1 Increasing population and increasing urbanization combine to bring about dramatic rises in population concentration. (Drawing by Weber, ©1971 The New Yorker Magazine, Inc.)

URBANIZATION
CROWDING
SUMMARY

The human population of 6000 B.C. is estimated to have been about 5 million people. By A.D. 1650 our numbers reached 500 million and in the succeeding two hundred years we had doubled our numbers to 1 billion. In 80 years, by 1930, we had doubled them again. The current rate of population doubling is approximately 35 years (Ehrlich, 1968); that is, at current growth rates, we can expect the number of human beings inhabiting the earth to double every 35 years and to quadruple within the expected life span of any given individual. Put differently, the world's population of humans is currently growing (total births minus total deaths) by an average of over 100,000 people per day (that's approximately one new city of Chicago each month). By the year 2030, barring unforeseen catastrophe, the number of humans vying for space on our planet will exceed 10 billion. Thus, humans are remarkably prolific procreators, and it could be argued that reproducing is one of the things they do best! (See Figure 9-2.) Carried to the absurd, Isaac Asimov tells us that, at present rates of increase, in 6700 years all the matter in the universe will have been converted to human flesh by unchecked fecundity. Such a geometric explosion of population (Asimov's preposterous projections aside) elicits rather frightening, and highly probable, scenarios with respect to the quality of life in the future. Obviously there are limits to population growth, and the rate of acceleration has begun to slow down, but whether this acceleration can be halted or perhaps even reversed in time for our planet to remain habitable is a much debated question.

At the same time that our absolute numbers are growing, there has been a trend toward urbanization. Rather than spreading ourselves evenly over the surface of the earth we have tended to concentrate our numbers into limited geographical areas. The number of cities with populations in excess of 100,000 has quadrupled in the last 20 years and is expected to quadruple again in the next 20 years. In the United States alone, 70 percent of our citizens live on only 2 percent of the habitable land. These two trends (increasing numbers and increasing urbanization) combine to bring about dramatic rises in population concentration. The effects of these increases are only beginning to be considered worthy of investigation. Furthermore, these trends are magnified in the developing countries (i.e., third world countries show not only faster rates of population increase but also accelerated rates of urbanization). In light of the fact that third-world countries do not have a highly sophisticated agri-economy upon which to build up an urban population, these figures are especially disconcerting.

This unmistakable, worldwide, positively accelerating trend toward urbanization has led a number of scholars to claim that in today's world the major problems of society are urban ones, and that coping with urbanization constitutes the major behaviors of modern humans. Personal anonymity, lack of privacy, crowding, feelings of powerlessness, a pull between monotony and overstimulation, traffic, pollution, and other problems that are either created or aggravated by increasing population concentrations are twentieth-century problems with which the inhabitants of Planet Earth may not be ready to cope. Those who have looked to the future predict a world in flux and one quite different from the world we now inhabit. Increases in starvation, pollution, communicable diseases, physical malfunctions, and slums are but a few of the physical

FIGURE 9-2 World human population size from 8000 B.C. to A.D. 2000.

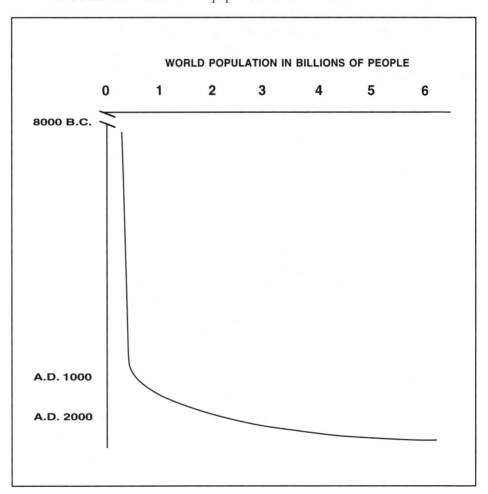

effects predicted to be influenced by increased population concentrations. Poorer physical and mental health facilities and an increase in crimes and civil disturbances are listed among the social problems, and such psychological effects as increases in drug and alcohol abuse, greater family disorganization, withdrawal, aggression, and decreased quality of life are also foreseen.

Clearly, this is a rather alarming and dismal picture of the future brought on by unchecked population growth. But is this mere speculation, the rantings of doomsdayers, or do these projections have some basis in fact? Predicting the effects of population growth is perhaps one of the most central and fundamental issues in the field of environmental psychology, and in this chapter we will attempt to provide some tentative conclusions from the research on this issue. We will first review some of the research on the effects of urbanization, and then we will consider the related question of how humans respond to high levels of population density (i.e., the study of "crowding").

URBANIZATION

As noted in the chapter's introduction, the majority of our population lives in or near large cities. Thus, it is not surprising that considerable effort has been expended toward describing and understanding the experience of urban life. In this section we will discuss the physical, social, and psychological effects of urbanization.

Physical Effects

The unchecked physical expansion of cities has created what some have called *urban sprawl*. This term refers to a random, and sometimes unseemly, spreading out of the city-proper in all directions. This often results in business and industrial areas bordering or surrounding residential and recreational areas of the city. One consequence of such random growth is the difficulty in maintaining an efficient and effective public transportation system, with the paths of industrial, business, and residential traffic criss-crossing.

Apart from the bewilderment created for "out-of-towners" trying to find their way around the city, the noise and traffic can disrupt the daily lives of inner-city residents (see Chapter 8 regarding the effects of noise on apartment dwellers near freeways). Those who can afford it relocate and move to the suburbs on the outskirts of the cities. The inner-city neighborhoods tend to deteriorate and become overcrowded—creating slums, or ghettoes. Problems of disease, crime, and race relations become inevitable results of inner-city life. The flight of the wealthy to the suburbs, together with the growth of *super malls* and shopping centers in the suburbs, leads to the economic decline of the inner city. Finally, the dramatic population increase in the suburbs creates the same problems that the suburbanites were originally attempting to avoid. Little wonder, given such a vicious circle of events, that so many cities today are in a state of crisis!

In addition to the effects of urban sprawl on the life and vitality of the city-proper, a number of broader environmental problems have been created by increased urbanization. Many of these were discussed earlier in the chapters on climate and pollution, and more will be dealt with in later chapters on energy use and environmental attitudes. Clearly, problems such as garbage, sewage, and industrial waste disposal, energy shortages, air and noise pollution have their seeds in urbanization, and they are growing every day. While the roots of environmental problems rapidly extend to the rural areas of our country (and others), they remain firmly planted in the urban centers. Fortunately, public concern for these problems has grown in the last decade, and steps are being taken

FIGURE 9-3 Cities are not only randomly spreading out in all directions but they are "spreading" upward as well.

to improve them. Nonetheless, steady increases in population concentrations in urban areas continue to aggravate the problems and impede efforts to eliminate them. Finally, while researchers have only recently begun to investigate the causes and solutions of physical environmental problems resulting from urbanization, they have been even slower to study the effects of urban life on human beings. Some research has been done, however, and it is to this that we turn next.

Theories of Urban Effects

The large number of variables potentially affecting the city-dweller makes it difficult to achieve a simple conceptualization of the effects of urban life on individual and social behavior. Some possible negative effects of living in a city have been determined and accounted for by a variety of theoretical constructs, many of which were discussed in Chapter 2. For example, Glass and Singer (1972) have studied the influence of particular physical *stressors* (e.g., noise) on performance and mental health. Wohlwill's *adaptation-level* theory (1976) proposes that humans function best at intermediate levels of arousal. This latter approach accounts for negative effects of city life by asserting that the excessive stimulation level in the urban environment produces over-arousal. A related approach suggested by Milgram (1970) is that the quantity and rate of stimulation that urbanites are exposed to exceeds their systems' capacity, resulting in *information overload*. Proshansky, Ittleson, and Rivlin (1970) suggest that the demands of city life limit an individual's freedom, leading to *behavioral constraints* that can produce the feeling of loss of control over one's life. Finally, Barker (1968) argues that cities are *overmanned* environments, where the number of inhabitants exceeds the system's capacity to provide meaningful roles for its denizens. This lack of well-defined roles, in fact, produces feelings of marginality and alienation.

While the various theoretical positions outlined above highlight slightly different aspects of the urban experience, each can be integrated in the model presented in Chapter 2. To the extent that the configurations of physical and social variables present in the urban environment are perceived by the individual as being outside an optimal range, displeasure, heightened arousal, and loss of control are experienced. This then leads to coping behaviors designed to return the individual to an optimal range of pleasure, arousal, and dominance. If these efforts are successful, the individual functions without behavioral disturbance. Unsuccessful coping leads to the various negative effects discussed above. But while most of the research on urban life has dealt with these negative effects, some theorists have proposed beneficial results of city life.

Urban-Rural Comparisons

A number of studies have compared differences in the incidence of physical and psychological disorders in urban and rural environments. Interestingly, the results of these studies do not reveal uniformly worse physical and/or mental health in cities in comparison with rural areas. It is perhaps not surprising that there is a higher rate of respiratory diseases in cities, since these ailments are closely linked to air pollution. Although common depictions of city life suggest a greater presence of stress, Hay and Wantman (1969) report only minimal differences in the incidence of stress-related illnesses such as heart disease and hypertension, and some researchers have even reported a lower incidence of other physical ailments in urban areas in comparison with rural areas (Srole, 1972). Similarly, while alcoholism and drug addiction have been reported to be more common in urban than rural areas (Trice, 1966), Dohrenwend and Dohrenwend (1972) have reported that the incidence of psychoses is higher in rural areas than in cities. Thus, the city does not seem to be a consistently *pathological* environment when compared with rural areas.

Social-Behavioral Effects

Differences between urban and rural settings have been reported in the occurrence of *affiliation*, *prosocial*, and *antisocial* behavior. Studies have indicated that urbanites are less affiliative toward strangers than are people in rural areas (e.g., McCauley, Coleman, & DeFusco, 1977; Milgram, 1977; Newman & McCauley, 1977). Urbanites tend to avoid eye contact with strangers and are less likely to reciprocate friendly gestures than are rural-dwellers. While studying prosocial behavior, several researchers have reported that urbanites are less likely to help a stranger (Gelfand, Hartman, Walder, & Page, 1973; Korte & Kerr, 1975; Milgram, 1970, 1977). However, it does not follow that urbanites are inherently less friendly and helpful than people in rural areas. These differences could be explained simply in terms of the urbanites paying less attention to other people, perhaps as a means of coping with excessive stimulation (see Moser, 1988).

Finally, regarding antisocial behavior, clear differences have been reported between urban and rural areas in the incidence of crime (Carlstam & Levy, 1971; Fischer, 1976; Zimbardo, 1969), with rural areas definitely being safer than cities. While this may seem obvious, the reasons for greater crime rates in cities are not wholly understood. Zimbardo (1969) proposed the concept of *deindividuation* to explain the high crime rate in cities. The inhibitions against antisocial behavior, such as the fear of getting caught and being humiliated before the community, are less effective in a city than in a small town. Owing to the large number of people in the city, individuals may feel more anonymous and thus less concerned about what other people in the community think about them. Theories of overmanning could also account for high crime rates in cities. Given that there are many more people than there are jobs, unemployment is higher in cities, leading the unemployed to resort to crime to "make a living."

Beneficial Effects

As mentioned earlier, much of the research comparing urban and rural life has sought to identify the negative effects of urbanization on the city-dweller. This negative image of the city was underscored in a study by Melton and Hargrove (1987) in which rural scenes were substantially more likely than urban scenes to be described in pleasant terms. Rural inhabitants were more likely to be perceived as friendly, and purposeless activity was commonly attributed to urban populations. While there certainly seems to be some ill effects of city life, some theorists (e.g., Freedman, 1975) have argued that much of this research starts with a biased and pessimistic assumption that cities are bad. That this assumption may not be valid is suggested by a Gallup survey (*Gallup Opinion Index*, 1973) in which the majority of the respondents indicated that they preferred to live near a city. Thus, although it is common for people to extol the joys of life "in the country," cities still have an attraction to most people. Among the obvious advantages of the city are greater entertainment and cultural opportunities, in addition to specialized medical facilities. Furthermore, the results of some studies show that rural areas are not necessarily perceived as *utopias* (e.g., Krupat, Guild, & Miller, 1977). Finally, some theorists (e.g., Proshansky, 1976) have suggested that life in the city makes an individual more versatile and adaptable and gives a broader perspective on life than is afforded by a rural existence.

At this point you may be wondering about the status of the questions raised at the beginning of this chapter concerning the relationship between the rapid increase in population density and the prospects for the quality of life in the future. We have discussed some physical environmental problems associated with urbanization, but the potential social and psychological effects of heightened population concentrations seem to be less clear. So if you have concluded that "the jury is still out" regarding the predictions discussed earlier, you are right. Human beings are remarkably adaptable, and whether increased population density leads to deleterious effects is still under debate. One line of inquiry receiving increased attention deals with the fundamental issue of how humans respond to high levels of physical density (i.e., the study of crowding). This research has attempted to identify basic human responses to density rather than to take the *molar* approach as exemplified by the research on urban life reviewed above. In the remainder of this chapter, we will discuss three major approaches to this issue: *animal studies* of crowding, *correlation/survey* studies of human crowding, and *human experimental* studies. We will conclude with a consideration of recent research on crowding in the home, neighborhood, and recreational settings. In the process, we hope to shed some light on how best to conceptualize the experience and consequences of crowding for the individual.

CROWDING

Animal Studies of Crowding

Two major lines of research exist with respect to animal studies. The first involves *naturally occurring* population cycles and the second involves *experimentally controlled* population concentrations. Two notable examples of the study of naturally occurring cycles are the lemmings' "march to the sea" (Dubos, 1965) and the (Sika) deer die-off on James Island (Christian, Flyger, & Davis, 1960). The Norwegian lemmings are small rodents resembling the field mouse but having short tails and fur-covered feet. They live primarily in the Scandinavian mountain regions. About every three or four years they appear to migrate (march) to the sea, with many of them drowning as an end result. Scandinavian mythology contends that the lemming ritual begins with the search for a home and ends in a deliberate attempt to commit suicide, explaining the phenomenon as a biologically pre-programmed and orderly way to limit their numbers. Closer inspection of the "march," however, has revealed that the movement is not orderly at all, but rather a wild frenzy. This helter-skelter activity quite accidentally results in large numbers of the lemmings reaching the sea and thus drowning. It now appears that these prolific reproducers reach considerable numbers every three to four years and that this increased population (and thus population density) acts to influence brain and adrenal functioning, which in turn is overtly manifested in nondirected activity.

Christian, Flyger, and Davis (1960) have observed similar abnormal adrenal functioning in a herd of deer and have suggested the stress resulting from increased population density as a causal agent. In 1916 four or five deer were released on James Island in the Chesapeake Bay off the coast of Maryland. By 1955 this small herd had grown to 280 to 300 deer (approximately one per acre). In 1958 over half of the herd died, and by 1960 it had been reduced to 80 members. The herd stabilized at the threshold of 80 members. During this time, Christian's group was performing detailed histological examinations of the deer's adrenal glands, thymus, spleen, thyroid, gonads, kidney, liver, heart, lungs, and other tissue. The carcasses were found to be in excellent shape throughout. All had shiny coats, well-developed muscles, healthy fat deposits between the muscles, and other indicators of good health. The only abnormal finding was an increase in the size of the adrenal glands. In the most severe case the adrenal glands were found to be 10 times the size of base rate samples. From

FIGURE 9-4 What at first may appear to be deliberate and premeditated behavior may turn out to be random activity resulting from density-induced adrenal malfunctions.

"And based on a random sampling of the lemming population, these figures clearly indicate that the time has come for us to rush headlong into the sea."

these and other data, infection, starvation, and illness were ruled out as causes for the dramatic two year die-off. Overactive adrenal functioning was inferred on the basis of the enlargement, and increased stress due to crowding was proclaimed as the cause of this increased endocrine activity.

Perhaps the most dramatic and well-known of the animal studies involving *experimentally* controlled population concentrations is the research conducted by Calhoun (1962). Calhoun provided his animals (in this case, Norway rats) with a luxurious environment. Food and water were provided *ad lib* and nesting materials were always available. In fact, the only limitation on the environment was space. The rat populations were free to grow, but the space that housed them remained the same. As time passed the rats segregated themselves, with the more dominant animals laying claim to the more spacious areas while simultaneously limiting their members. The remaining members had to eat, sleep, and raise their young in more highly concentrated areas of this finite human-made universe. Calhoun called this area a *behavioral sink*.

Those animals that inhabited the behavioral sink began to exhibit behavioral as well as physiological pathologies. For example, nest building among females was incomplete or poorly managed: Pups were left on their own, and unguarded; nursing behavior was disrupted. Among the juvenile males, pansexualism was practiced and incidents of cannibalism were detected; aggressive behavior was heightened among some and withdrawal behavior among others. Infant mortality increased, as did the number of aborted pregnancies. Among the physiological pathologies discovered were tumors of the mammary and sex glands in females and abnormal kidneys, livers, and adrenal glands in both sexes. The search for association between rates of pathology and population density in humans was no doubt guided by the work of Calhoun. Indeed, the pathologies suggested by Calhoun (i.e., morbidity, mortality, fertility, ineffectual parenting, and psychiatric disturbance) or their manifestations (i.e., incidence of infectious diseases, juvenile delinquency, adult crime, and others) have all been linked, though not always successfully, to increasing human population concentrations.

Additional effects of increased population concentrations have been reported subsequent to Calhoun's seminal work. For example, it has been shown that population density leads to the production of fewer sperm by males, to later onset of estrus, less frequent and shorter duration estrus, and consequently less frequent births and smaller litters (Crow & Mirsikowa, 1931; Snyder, 1966; 1968) among females. There is also evidence for an increase in alcohol consumption and performance decrements on complex tasks (Goeckner, Greenough, & Maier, 1974) for rats raised under high-density conditions.

Effects similar to these have been found for such diverse animals as swine, chickens, cattle, and elephants in addition to other rodents (Greenburg, 1969; Hafez, 1962; Marsden, 1972; Theissen, 1966). However, caution must be exercised in generalizing these results to humans. First, it is quite likely that the behavior of animals other than humans is more biologically determined and less dependent on learning and cultural inputs (Swanson, 1973). Second, humans usually find respites, if only briefly, from high-density situations, whereas in the animal studies no escapes were possible (Evans, 1979). Finally, humans have shown themselves to be more capable of adaptation and adjustment than any other animals.

Despite the fact that it is always difficult and often misleading to generalize the findings of animal research to humans, the animal research is of extreme value in our attempts to understand human behavior. Indeed, the use of animals as a source of hypotheses about human behavior is the only way some questions can be logically and ethically addressed. For example, if we are concerned with the effects of increased population concentrations over several generations, it is more sensible to use animals that bear young more quickly than humans. Second, if the effects are thought to be even remotely hazardous, it would be unethical to subject humans to those conditions. Third, with modern telemetry equipment and the miniaturization of sensing devices it is quite easy to study behavioral and physiological responses without disturbing the processes that are being monitored. Aside from the ethical issues involved, the greater cognitive capacities of humans do not allow for such clean monitoring. Work with humans has been done, however, and it is to this research that we now turn.

Human Correlational/Survey Studies

Most early work on the influence of population concentration among humans centered on its relationship to crime, mental illness, and other indices of social upheaval and disorganization. Crime statistics show that a disproportionate number of violent crimes are committed in our most densely populated cities and that indicators of mental illness worsen as people move from rural areas, to urban areas, to the inner city of large metropolitan areas. The prospect of increased population concentration acting as the cause of these and other effects is both pessimistic and alluring: pessimistic because of the two undeniable trends stated at the beginning of this chapter, alluring because human effects could then be accounted for by the same mechanisms that account for effects on other animals. Because of this lure, a number of investigators have turned to demographic, often archival, studies to explore the effect of increased population concentrations on human behavior.

Defining Density. Investigators have utilized various measures of population concentration, and for the most part have been indiscriminate in using the terms *crowding* and *density* to refer to these measures. Where the distinction has been made, there remains no consensus as to the *appropriate* measure of density. Schmitt (1957), for example, assessed the relationship between five semi-independent measures of density and adult crime and juvenile delinquency. Of the following five measures—(1) average household size, (2) proportion of married couples without their own home, (3) proportion of dwelling units in structures with four or more living units, (4) population per acre, and (5) percentage of occupied dwellings with 1.51 or more persons per room—only the last two showed strong positive relationships with delinquency and adult crime. In subsequent work Schmitt (1966) has distinguished between *inside density* and *outside density*. That is, Schmitt noted the difference between the number of people per unit of living space and the number of people in the larger community (e.g., persons per acre). Others have made similar distinctions (see, for example, Galle, Gove, & McPherson, 1972; Jacobs, 1961; Zlutnick & Altman, 1972). The importance of these contrasts becomes apparent when the following possibilities are considered: low inside–low outside (suburbs); high inside–high outside (urban ghettoes, barrios, and others); low inside–high outside (luxury inner city apartments and condominiums); high inside–low outside (rural farm areas). Using only inside density as a predictor one would have to presume the effects of density to be the same in the urban ghettoes as in the rural farm areas, whereas using outside density would lead to predictions of luxury apartment dwellers and ghetto residents showing similar effects. These predictions are, of course, absurd and underscore the need for careful delineation of the term *density*.

A second difficulty that the preceding possibilities illuminate is the differences in socioeconomic, ethnic, and social structure variables that are likely to exist among the four areas. It is possible that these variables may be related to degenerative or pathological effects independent of population concentration, but owing to their naturally occurring co-variation with density, the cause gets misplaced. More recent studies have therefore been somewhat more explicit in the density measures being utilized and have *controlled* for the possible confounds of social structure variables. For example, in a study by Galle, Gove, and McPherson (1972) persons per acre was shown to be positively related to public assistance rate, juvenile delinquency, and the rate of admission to mental hospitals. However, when the authors controlled for social class and ethnicity these correlations disappeared. Thus, density appeared to be unrelated to social disorganization when social class and ethnic variables were considered. Galle's group, not content with such a simple conclusion, reanalyzed their data. In the subsequent analysis, density was defined differentially as (1) the number of residential structures per acre, (2) the number of living units per structure, (3) the number of residents per living unit, and (4) the number of persons per room. Utilizing multiple correlation techniques, they showed that the combined effects of the four measures of density correlated significantly with each pathology with class and ethnicity being controlled. The most important contribution to the various pathologies was the number of persons per room, with the exception of admissions to mental hospitals. The percentage of people living alone and the number of persons per living unit were the best predictors of this last pathology. However, Kellett (1989) has recently argued that density is an inadequate concept to investigate the relationship between health and housing.

The Density/Crowding Distinction.   A major conceptual breakthrough resulting from these and other data is that most theorists now agree that the physical state of high density is not the same as the psychological experience of crowding (Altman, 1975; Loo, 1973; Proshansky et. al., 1970; Stokols, 1972a, 1972b, 1976) and that these two must be differentially defined. Daniel Stokols (1972a) noted the confusion regarding the terms *density* and *crowding*, especially as their use is reflected in research concerning humans. He states that as a result of this confusion many writers use the two terms interchangeably and tend to view crowding in terms of spatial considerations alone, deplete of social and personal dimensions, which may interact with those spatial factors to mediate the experience of crowding. Density is a *physical* condition involving space limitations, whereas crowding is an *experiential state* determined by perceptions of restrictiveness when exposed to spatial limitations. Thus, Stokols proposes that density is a *necessary* but not *sufficient* condition for crowding. As Stokols views it, the potential inconveniences of limited space such as the restriction of movement, the preclusion of privacy, and other disadvantages of space limitation must reach some degree of saliency and be viewed as aversive before people experience crowding.

For example, Desor (1972) has defined crowding in terms of excessive stimulation from social sources; Zlutnick and Altman (1972) have defined crowding in terms of an individual's inability to adequately control interactions with others; Van Staden (1984) emphasized perception of large numbers of people, spatial restriction, and an aversive experience of the situation as relevant components of the crowding construct. In this regard crowding may be thought of as a psychological concept referring to a subjective experience, which may or may not be adequately reflected by population density measures such as the amount of physical space per person or number of people per unit of living space. In short, there seems to be general agreement that high density is seldom a sufficient and probably never a necessary condition for the experience of crowding.

As important as this conceptual breakthrough is, a complete understanding will elude researchers unless the physical state of density is carefully elucidated and the psychological state of crowding is properly operationalized. For example, population per unit of land (areal density) is a composite of several levels of land use: net residential average, structures per residential area, dwellings per structure, rooms per dwelling, and persons per room (Carnahan, Gove, & Galle, 1974). Density is therefore highly complex, and its components are likely to vary independently of each other. With this realization it is obvious that neighborhoods may have the same population density and yet be quite different from one another. For example, one neighborhood may have large portions of its land being used for industrial or commercial purposes rather than residential purpose, and thus have low population density, whereas a second neighborhood may have equally low density because its residential area is comprised of detached single family dwellings located on spacious suburban lots. Obviously, density does not mean the same thing in these two instances.

Operationalizing the psychological construct *crowding* has proven to be difficult, and the present state of development of the correlational/survey approach appears to rest on finding associations between one or more measures of density and one or more archival measures of pathology. The inability to control for a host of important extraneous social/situational variables has also limited definitive conclusions about the effects of density.

For these reasons many environmental psychologists turned to the laboratory to achieve greater control over antecedent physical and social parameters of crowding, as well as more valid measurement of the construct. For example, Arkkelin, Veitch, Kruempel, & Christensen (1982) developed a simulation technique that permitted the manipulation of the two physical components of density (the number of people present and interpersonal distance) independently of one another. They concluded that the interaction of interpersonal distance with a social/situational variables (e.g., gender, acquaintance, activity) was a more important determinant of subjective discomfort than was the absolute number of people present in a setting. They further determined that the aversive experience of *crowding* could be characterized as an affective state of displeasure, heightened arousal, and lack of control. In the following section we will review other studies that have systematically manipulated density and measured affective and social-behavioral responses.

Human Experimental Studies

As discussed previously in this chapter, conducting carefully controlled experimental studies of the effects of population density on human behavior involves many difficulties. Nonetheless, a number of studies have been conducted and reported. Some research has utilized rather interesting, but naturally occurring, high-density situations like prisons, commuter trains, playgrounds, and shopping centers. Others have purposely manipulated either numbers of persons within a setting while holding setting size constant (i.e., manipulated *social density*) or have maintained the same number of respondents while manipulating the setting size available to them (i.e., manipulated *spatial density*; see, for example, Loo, 1972; McGrew, 1970; Pedersen, 1983; Saegert, 1973, 1974). In keeping with the previous chapters, we will look at what is known about the effects of density on physiological processes, on task performance, and on such social affective behaviors as attraction, altruism, and aggression.

Physiological Reactions.   One of the first researchers to report on the physiological effects of density was D'Atri (1975). He observed the blood pressure levels of inmates in a prison who were confined to either single or double occupancy cells and found those inmates in the latter cells to exhibit higher levels. Paulus, McCain, and Cox (1978) have also found blood pressure to be positively related to increased density, and McCain, Cox, and Paulus (1976) have reported that inmates in high-occupancy dormitory settings complain more of illness than do those in lower-density cell blocks. This finding may occur as a result of real illness brought on by physiological disturbances or by a desire on the part of the inmate to be taken from the high-density dormitory to the lower-density infirmary. In either case, the differential density seems to be the reason for the discrepancy in the number of complaints. Aiello, DeRisi, Epstein, and Karlin (1977) have shown density to be related to increased skin conductance; Fleming, Baum, and Weiss (1987) reported elevations in urinary catecholamines under conditions of high social density; and Heshka and Pylypuk (1975) have reported increased adrenocortical activity in males as a result of high social density.

Other indirect evidence that density may influence physiological processes is reported by Baron, Mandel, Adams, and Griffen (1976) and by Dean, Pugh, and Gunderson (1978). The former researchers found that students who lived in dormitories of high social density frequented the Student Health Center more often than those in low social density dormitories, and Dean and his colleagues found that illnesses among enlisted navy personnel were positively correlated with both social and spatial density. Based on these and other data, most researchers in the field have concluded that the physiological and health effects of increasing density are strongly influenced by the individual and by social coping mechanisms that people have learned to use in dealing with these situations. (For a more detailed discussion of these issues see Chapter 10.)

Task Performance. Early research on the effects of density on task performance utilized relatively simple tasks like psychomotor tasks, problem solving, or anagram solving in laboratory contexts where subjects either knew or could easily discern the interests and hypotheses of the experimenter. These studies failed to demonstrate any consistently reliable effects, positive or deleterious, of density on performance (Freedman, Klevansky, & Ehrlich, 1971; Freedman, Levy, Buchanan, & Price, 1972; Rawls, Trego, McGaffey, & Rawls, 1972; Stokols, Rall, Pinner, & Schopler, 1973). More recent laboratory studies, as well as some small-scale field experiments, however, have shown that under some circumstances density can adversely affect task performance. Performance decrements as a result of increases in either spatial or social density have been reported for tasks that are sufficiently complex or require a high rate of information processing (Bray, Kerr, & Atkin, 1978; Evans, 1979; Paulus, Annis, Seta, Schkade, & Matthews, 1976; Paulus & Matthews, 1980). Additionally, performance impairments are, as might be expected, reported for situations in which people must interact with one another in the process of carrying out their task (Heller, Groff, & Solomon, 1977), particularly if the presence of others impedes required locomotion.

Saegert, Mackintosh, and West (1975) found support in an interesting and provocative field study for the notion of increased density leading to performance decrements. Saegert and her colleagues tested subjects in a socially dense department store and in a busy railway terminal. Among the tasks subjects were asked to perform was to provide a *cognitive map* (see Chapter 4) of their environment. The researchers concluded that tasks which involved knowledge and/or manipulation of their environments were impeded by increased density. The fact that increasing density is accompanied by a corresponding decrease in the clarity of one's mental image and knowledge of the immediate environment may also explain the findings of Glassman, Burkhart, Grant, and Vallery (1978) and Karlin, Rosen, and Epstein (1979). These researchers showed that social density was related to grades attained in two separate university settings. Additionally, Karlin et al. (1979) showed that once conditions of high social density removed (i.e., students were reassigned to less crowded quarters) grades improved significantly. Thus, increased density may *overload* one's information-processing ability, resulting in impaired performance on tasks that require higher-level cognitive skills.

TIME-OUT: Think about times when you have not performed at your best when there were a lot of other people around (e.g., giving an oral presentation before a large group). What aspects of their presence inhibited your performance? Do you recall your emotional state at the time? Were the members of the audience distracting? Compare this to participating in an informal discussion in a small seminar. Finally, can you think of times when the presence of a large number of people not only did not disturb you, but actually resulted in an elevation in your mood and performance? What factors contributed to the differences in your experience and behavior?

Social-Affective Responses

It is not difficult for any of us to recall situations of high density that have made us feel uncomfortable. Crowded elevators, bargain basement sales, the first day of classes in a large lecture hall, bus depots and airport terminals where we are hurrying to make connections are but a few. Without much difficulty we could probably also recall occasions when this discomfort has led to feelings of tenseness, anxiety, or even anger. On the other hand, parties, rock concerts, and crowds at athletic contests also represent situations of high density that may have evoked very different, perhaps even very positive, feelings. Hence, our feelings are obviously related not only to density but to the circumstances under which density occurs.

Freedman (1975) proposed a *density-intensity* model to account for these seemingly contradictory responses to high density. Freedman argues that increases in density serve to intensify the prevailing affective state induced by social/situational variables. More recently, Duckitt (1983) obtained measures of both positive and negative affect in relation to different degrees of household crowding. He reported an association between increased density and elevations of negative affect, but no reduction in positive affect. Thus, perhaps instead of asking simply whether or not people respond aversively to high density, it would be better to ask *under what conditions* high density is likely to elicit negative affect.

Support for this fairly straightforward conclusion comes from a number of studies including those by Griffitt and Veitch (1971), Baxter and Deanovich (1970), Smith and Haythorn (1972), Stokols et al. (1973), Evans (1975), Sundstrom (1975), and McClelland and Auslander (1978). What may not be so evident at first (unless the findings are being carefully considered in light of the model presented in Chapter 2) is that these differential feeling states are likely to lead to quite diverse social behaviors. Hence, a number of studies have looked at the effects of density on such social behaviors as attraction, altruism, and aggression.

Attraction. The first laboratory study to show that interpersonal attraction (liking) is reduced under conditions of high social density was conducted by William Griffitt and Russell Veitch (1971) at Kansas State University. Subjects in that experiment were exposed to one of two conditions of social density and one of two levels of ambient temperature. After being given time to become inured to these conditions, participants were asked to make evaluations of strangers and to indicate their degree of probable liking for them. Subjects who were exposed to the high-density conditions gave significantly more negative evaluations and expressed a lower degree of probable liking than did those exposed to low-density conditions. Similar results have been obtained by numerous researchers, with some finding these effects for males but not for female respondents (see, for example, Epstein & Karlin, 1975).

Additionally, a number of laboratory and field setting studies have shown a relationship between density and such attraction-related responses as eye contact, sociableness, visiting behavior, talkativeness, and intimacy. For example, early research by Hutt and Vaizey (1966) revealed that as the number of children in an experimental play setting increased, the amount of interaction among them decreased. Simultaneously, they exhibited greater social withdrawal. Baum and his associates (Baum, Harpin, & Valins, 1975; Baum & Valins, 1977; Valins & Baum, 1973) have found similar results with dormitory-housed students. Those students living in more socially dense dormitories were discovered to be less talkative, less sociable, and less group oriented than those from more sparsely populated settings.

Eye contact, often an indicator of positive interpersonal relations, was found to decrease as a function of density in a quasi-laboratory study (Baum & Greenberg, 1975). This finding, incidentally, has been confirmed in a very different setting by McCauley, Coleman, and DeFusco (1977), and by Newman and McCauley (1977). Finally, if it is assumed that liking is related to one's willingness to discuss intimate topics, then Sundstrom (1975) has produced additional evidence for an inverse relationship between density and liking. He found a decrease in the willingness to discuss intimate topics as the number of others in an interview situation increased. The evidence is fairly clear, then, that increases in density stand a very good chance of leading to decreases in liking. But before leaping to overwhelming conclusions, recall the positive feelings you may have had at your last socially dense party.

Altruism.   If density is inversely related to liking, one might also expect it to be inversely related to our willingness to lend a hand, to provide assistance, or to be charitable to our fellow humans. This proposition presumes that liking does indeed increase the likelihood of persons engaging in helping behavior. Studies attempting to test this notion increased dramatically after the murder of a young woman in New York City occurred in a densely populated area in full view of many witnesses and after repeated pleas for help (for a detailed account see Rosenthal, 1964). Social scientists began questioning the generality of this kind of occurrence and speculated as to the reasons why it might happen. One plausible explanation was that the high-density neighborhood somehow led to a social callousness that would not be engendered in low-density areas.

The laboratory and field studies conducted on altruism in the last 20 years are too numerous to detail here. However, the results, contrary to speculation, indicate generally that density is not directly related to helping behavior. Rather, density conditions act indirectly, depending on other factors, to increase or decrease helping. Wohlwill (1976) has shown that the environment is an important source of affect, and Holahan (1977) suggests that decreased helping behavior in densely populated areas is based on the fear for personal safety engendered in some socially dense areas. If there were no reason for fearing personal safety, presumably no decreases in helping would be apparent. This explanation is consistent with the findings of Alice Isen and her associates (Isen, 1970; Isen, Clark, & Schwartz, 1976; Isen & Levin, 1972) and by Veitch, DeWood, and Bosko (1977), who have shown helping behavior to be positively related to positive mood states. Finally, rural and urban differences in helping behavior (Gelfand et al., 1973; Korte & Kerr, 1975; Milgram, 1970) and the equally often reported lack of differences (Forbes & Gromoll, 1971; Korte, Ypma, & Toppen, 1975; Weiner, 1976) may be explained in terms of attentional processes associated with differences in density or by differential time available to provide help given the variable pace of the respective life styles.

Aggression. It might be expected that if differential density leads to diverse emotional responses, then to the extent that aggression is related to mood, aggression might be expected to vary as a function of density. Research to date indicated that this causal chain of events is either not entirely accurate or not fully articulated or appreciated. Most studies, however, have not independently and simultaneously considered all three variables; hence, this inferential chain is difficult to realize. For example, early research in the relationship between density and aggression utilized school children in a play setting (Ginsburg, Pollman, Wanson, & Hope, 1977; Hutt & Vaizey, 1966) and found the two to be related; however, no measure of affect was taken. Two other studies with children showed no effects (Loo, 1972; Price, 1971), but again no measures of affect were taken. It is likely that the critical variable (i.e., differential affect) may not have been present in any of these studies. This conclusion is strengthened by the finding that autistically withdrawn children (emotional stabiles) showed no effect for changes in density in the Hutt and Vaizey (1966) study.

As noted earlier, density does not automatically lead to a specific emotional response. For this reason, and following the above logic, aggressive responses would be expected only to the extent that density elicits negatively toned affective responses. This elicitation results not only from the density of the environment but by the personal and social conditions of the setting. For example, Rohe and Patterson (1974) have found that high density leads to aggression in children when the play situation does not provide ample toys for each. As long as there are plenty of toys to go around, increases in density did not affect children's aggressive behavior. Thus, it is likely that density, like temperature (see Chapter 6), acts only to moderate aggressive responses and is not the direct cause of them.

Crowding in Everyday Settings

Researchers have increasingly moved out of the laboratory to study crowding in commonly experienced settings such as the residence, neighborhoods, and recreational areas. In the following section we will review some of this research, and will conclude with a comparison of these studies with those discussed in the previous sections.

The Residence. Sweaney, Inman, Wallinga, and Dias (1986) reported a significant relationship between increasing household density and feelings of crowding in children. As noted earlier, Duckitt (1983) reported an association between increased household density and negative affect. However, he reported that the relationship was nonlinear, with increasing density associated with a sharp initial rise, followed by a flattening out of the curve. Further, Gabe and Williams (1986) reported that residential dissatisfaction was associated with both high and low density. These inconsistent findings have also been reported examining the ubiquitous residence hall on university campuses. For example, Hughey (1983) reported that occupants of rooms accommodating three students in space designed for only two people had lower self-esteem than did occupants of two-person rooms. However, Ronchi and Sparacino (1982) compared residents of triple vs. single occupancy rooms, and reported no differences in either judged pleasantness or arousal level. Measures of blood pressure indicated a tendency for *higher* blood pressure levels in residents of single rooms.

These contradictory results could be due to differences in methodologies and in definitions of density and crowding, or they could simply mean that there is no consistent relationship between residential density and crowding. It is possible, however, that the differential results are mediated by social variables. An illustrative study in this regard was conducted by Wenz (1984). Data were obtained on household density, loneliness, and suicide ideation. Wenz reported that *both* loneliness and density were associated with suicide ideation. He argued that density bears only a *distal* relationship to suicide ideation (i.e., it is not density level *per se*, but the quality and quantity of social interaction and the nature of separation between people that may be "pathological"). Wenz concluded that household density may simply aggravate or accelerate—not cause or motivate—preexisting suicidal tendencies. Also, Neil and Jones (1988) studied the impact of environmental stressors on psychological health in remote "boom" communities in Australia and reported that most of the variance could be explained by loneliness. Thus, it is possible that *either* high or low density produces adverse effects, a point to which we will return in Chapter 10 regarding territoriality and privacy.

Many people have questioned whether responses to density are culture-specific. For example, there are clear differences in objective population density in the United States compared to China. Could it be that individuals in these countries differ in their responses to density? Gillis, Richard, and Hagan (1986) did report cross-cultural differences, with Asians being more tolerant of high density and British respondents being less adaptable, with Southern Europeans somewhere in between these two. Churchman and Ginsberg (1984) reported that the negative image and experience of "high-rise" housing prevalent in our culture did not emerge in responses of such residents in Israel.

These differences could be due to varying adaptation levels across cultures developed by lifelong exposure to different population densities. However, we must be careful of overgeneralization. Chalsa Loo and her colleagues (Loo, 1986; Loo & Ong, 1984) have challenged the belief that the Chinese hold different attitudes toward crowding than the larger U.S. population. In surveys of residents of San Francisco's Chinatown area, these researchers reported a relationship between high population density/commercial development and lowered neighborhood satisfaction and between increased building density and lesser feelings of safety. Their respondents generally evaluated crowding as undesirable, and their results indicate that prolonged exposure to high density breeds dislike for crowding in a primary environment (i.e., the home) more than in a secondary environment (i.e., the neighborhood). Similarly, Homma (1990) reported that the Japanese also view crowding as a negative experience.

Recreational Areas.   An increasing number of Americans are visiting our country's national parks each year. Ironically, many people visit such parks in order to appreciate the natural environment away from the "rush of the crowd." This trend has led some to suggest that limitations should be placed on the number of visitors to recreational areas. Because of this concern, researchers have recently begun to examine perceptions of and reactions to density in these settings. Westover and Collins (1987) interviewed urban park visitors and reported that the most important predictor of perceived crowding was, indeed, the actual number of visitors on a daily basis. Burrus-Bammel and Bammel (1986) reported a negative correlation between the daily number of users at a visitors' center and the average duration of visit. Thus, these studies suggest that perception of density is related to feeling crowded, and people spend less time in recreational areas as the number of users increase.

However, other researchers have argued that the relationship between density and the wilderness experience is complex, and decisions to limit capacities should not be made simply on perceived crowding. For example, Bultena, Field, Womble, and Albrecht (1981) interviewed hikers at Mount McKinley National Park about their expectations and preferences for sights of other parties, number of parties seen daily, and trip satisfaction. Reported crowding was a function of preferences and frequency of contacts, but perceived crowding was unrelated to overall trip satisfaction. Similarly, Shelby, Heberlein, Vaske, and Alfano (1983) reported that people engaged in three different recreational activities felt more crowded when the number of encounters exceeded expectations or preferences, which were better predictors of crowding than was the absolute number of encounters. These authors suggest that crowding could be reduced by providing information that makes expectations realistic and allows visitors to select densities.

Absher and Lee (1981) challenged the commonsense notion that crowding in backcountry settings is dependent on the sheer number of people. They reported that when personal and experiential motives were statistically controlled, the effect of social density on perceived crowding was nonsignificant. They argued for a complex formulation of crowding that incorporates normative, motivational, and social organizational aspects. Manning (1985) has also argued for a normative conceptualization of crowding in outdoor recreation, suggesting that crowding norms are influenced by visitor characteristics, characteristics of those encountered, and situational variables. Support for this assertion was provided by Gramann and Burdge (1984). They reported that objective density was unrelated to crowding perception, but perceived crowding was positively related both to the probability that physical movement was restrained and the probability of exposure to threatening behavior of others. West (1981) reported only a weak relationship between perceived crowding in backcountry campers and the desire to further limit established carrying capacities. Westover (1989) demonstrated that perceived crowding resulted from a dynamic process influenced by site image, subjective interpretation of objective reality, and constant reassessment of site conditions' salience to individual goals.

Thus, just as we saw in correlational research on pathologies associated with high density, and laboratory research on social, affective, and behavioral effects of density, research in naturalistic environments such as the home, neighborhood, and parks has also yielded inconsistent results. Hence, the answer to the question of whether or not humans respond aversively to high density must be a qualified one. Yes, high density can have detrimental effects *given the presence of certain social conditions*. In their absence, however, it is unlikely that density will have any significant direct effect on human responses.

SUMMARY

We have discussed the physical effects of urbanization on the environment and have reviewed some evidence of social and psychological effects on urban dwellers. We have also seen rather compelling evidence of deleterious physical and social effects of excessive population density in animals. Because of the problems of generalizing the results of animal research to humans, however, this evidence can only be viewed as suggesting the possibility of similar adverse effects in humans. Humans are much more capable of adaptation or adjustments that could minimize any negative effects of high density. More importantly, humans are incredibly complex organisms and, as we have seen from the correlational studies, their behavior is determined by an extremely complicated web of social-situational variables independent of density *per se*. Even those studies finding correlations between density and pathology suffer from serious methodological flaws apart from the general problem of not being able to draw cause-effect conclusions from correlational data. For example, the confounding of social structure variables such as socioeconomic status and dwelling type seriously limits the internal validity of naturalistic studies of human responses to density.

Perhaps a more important problem has been the absence of a reliable, agreed-upon measure of population density. While at first the construct would appear to be easily defined and measured, it becomes considerably more confusing when we consider such distinctions as "inside" vs. "outside" density. Finally, the major problem with the measures that have been used is that they were made independently of the individuals' perception of density. As mentioned earlier, researchers have frequently used the terms *density* and *crowding* interchangeably, perhaps assuming that objectively-defined physical density invariably produces the experience of crowding. As we have seen in this chapter, this is probably a false assumption, and we are still left with the question of whether or not humans react negatively to high population concentrations. The distinction between objective density and the subjective perception and evaluation of that density is crucial in understanding and predicting behavioral responses to density. We have seen in settings ranging from the laboratory to the home, the neighborhood, the city and recreation areas that a variety of positive and negative responses to objective density depend on the individual, social, and situational parameters of that density.

In the next chapter we will examine three very important aspects of community life. We will attempt to show how these factors may help to determine when density will lead to the subjective experience of crowding and when we can expect this experience to have negative effects on physiological, task-related, and social behaviors. The three factors to be discussed in the next chapter are *territoriality, personal space,* and *privacy.*

IMPORTANT CONCEPTS

exponential growth
urbanization
urban-rural comparisons
affiliation
prosocial/antisocial behavior
deindividuation
Sika deer/Norwegian lemmings
adrenal functioning

behavioral sink
inside density
outside density
spatial density
social density
density-crowding distinction
density-intensity model

REFERENCES

Absher, J.D., & Lee, R.G. (1981). Density as an incomplete cause of crowding in backcountry settings. *Leisure Sciences, 4*(3), 231–247.

Aiello, J.R., DeRisi, D., Epstein, Y., & Karlin, R. (1977). Crowding and the role of interpersonal distance preference. *Sociometry, 40,* 271–282.

Altman, I. (1975). *The environment and social behavior.* Monterey, Calif.: Brooks/Cole.

Arkkelin, D., Veitch, R., Kruempel, S., & Christensen, C. (1982). *An explication of affective responses to physical and social conditions of group density.* Paper presented at the annual meeting of the Midwestern Psychological Association, Minneapolis.

Barker, R.G. (1968). Ecological psychology: Concepts and methods for studying the environ-

ment of human behavior. Stanford, Calif.: Stanford University Press.

Baron, R.M., Mandel, D.R., Adams, C.A., & Griffen, L.M. (1976). Effects of social density in university residential environments. *Journal of Personality and Social Psychology, 34,* 434–446.

Baum, A., & Greenberg, C.I. (1975). Waiting for a crowd: The behavioral and perceptual effects of anticipated crowding. *Journal of Personality and Social Psychology, 32,* 667–671.

Baum, A., Harpin, R.E., & Valins, S. (1975). The role of group phenomena in the experience of crowding. *Environment and Behavior, 7,* 185–198.

Baum, A., & Valins, S. (1977). *Architecture and social behavior: Psychological studies in social density.* Hillsdale, NJ: Erlbaum.

Baxter, J.C., & Deanovich, B.S. (1970). Anxiety-arousing effects of inappropriate crowding. *Journal of Consulting and Clinical Psychology, 35,* 174–178.

Bray, R.M., Kerr, N.L., & Atkin, R.S. (1978). Effects of group size, problem difficulty, and sex on group performance and member reactions. *Journal of Personality and Social Psychology, 36,* 1224–1240.

Bultena, G., Field, D.R., Womble, P., & Albrecht, D. (1981). Closing the gates: A study of back-country use-limitation at Mount McKinley National Park. *Leisure Sciences, 4*(3), 249–267.

Burrus-Bammel, L.L., & Bammel, G. (1986). Visiting patterns and effects of density at a visitors' center. *Journal of Environmental Education, 18*(1), 7–10.

Calhoun, J.B. (1962). Population density and social pathology. *Scientific American, 206,* 139–148.

Carlstam, G., & Levy, L. (1971). *Urban conglomerate, as psychosocial human stressors.* Report to the Swedish Preparatory Committee for the United Nations Conference on Human Environment, Stockholm.

Carnahan, D.W., Gove, W., & Galle, D.R. (1974). Urbanization, population levels and overcrowding. *Social Forces, 53,* 52–72.

Christian, J.J., Flyger, V., & Davis, P.C. (1960). "Factors in the mass mortality of a herd of Sika deer, *Cercus nippon. Chesapeake Science, 1,* 79–95.

Churchman, A., & Ginsberg, Y. (1984). The image and experience of high-rise housing in Israel. *Journal of Environmental Psychology, 4*(1), 27–41.

Crow, F.A. & Mirsikowa, L. (1931). Effects of density on adult mouse populations. *Biologia Generalis, 7,* 239–250.

D'Atri, D.A. (1975). Psychophysiological responses to crowding. *Environment and Behavior, 7,* 237–252.

Dean, L.M., Pugh, W.M., & Gunderson, E.K. (1978). The behavioral effects of crowding: Definitions and methods. *Environment and Behavior, 10,* 419–432.

Desor, J.A. (1972). Toward a psychological theory of crowding. *Journal of Personality and Social Psychology, 21,* 79–89.

Dohrenwend, B.S., & Dohrenwend, B.P. (1972). Psychiatric disorder in urban settings. In G. Caplan (Ed.), *American handbook of psychiatry* (Vol. 3, rev. ed). New York: Basic Books.

Dubos, R. (1965). *Man adapting.* New Haven, Conn.: Yale University Press.

Duckitt, J.H. (1983). Household crowding and psychological well-being in a South African couloured community. *Journal of Social Psychology, 121*(2) 231–238.

Ehrlich, R. (1968). *The population bomb.* New York: Ballantine.

Epstein Y.M., & Karlin, R.A. (1975). Effects of acute experimental crowding. *Journal of Applied Social Psychology, 5,* 34–53.

Evans, G.W. (1975). *Behavioral and physiological consequences of crowding in humans.* Unpublished doctoral dissertation, University of Massachusetts, Amherst.

Evans, G.W. (1979). Crowding and human performance. *Journal of Applied Social Psychology, 9,* 27–46.

Fischer, C.S. (1976). *The urban experience.* New York: Harcourt Brace Jovanovich.

Fleming, I. Baum, A., & Weiss, L. (1987). Social density and perceived control as mediators of crowding stress in high-density residential neighborhoods. *Journal of Personality and Social Psychology, 52*(5), 899–906.

Forbes, G., & Gromoll, H. (1971). The lost letter technique as a measure of social variables: Some exploratory findings. *Social Forces, 50,* 113–115.

Freedman, J.L. (1975). *Crowding and behavior.* San Francisco: W.H. Freeman.

Freedman, J.L., Klevansky, S., & Ehrlich, P.I. (1971). The effect of crowding on human task performance. *Journal of Applied Social Psychology, 1,* 7–26.

Freedman, J.L., Levy, A., Buchanan, R.W., & Price, J. (1972). Crowding and human aggressiveness. *Journal of Experimental Social Psychology, 8,* 528–548.

Gabe, J., & Williams, P. (1986). Is space bad for your health? The relationship between crowding in the home and emotional distress in women. *Sociology of Health and Illness, 8*(4), 351–371.

Galle, O.R., Gove, W.R., & McPherson, J.M. (1972). Population density and pathology: What are the relationships for man? *Science, 176,* 23–30.

Gallup Opinion Index. (1973). Princeton, N.J.: American Institute of Public Opinion, No. 102.

Gelfand, D.M., Hartman, D.P., Walder, P., & Page, B. (1973). Who reports shoplifters? A field-experimental study. *Journal of Personality and Social Psychology, 25,* 276–285.

Gillis, A.R., Richard, M.A., & Hagan, J. (1986). Ethnic susceptibility to crowding: An empirical analysis. *Environment and Behavior, 18*(6), 683–706.

Ginsburg, H.J., Pollman, V.A., Wanson, M.S., & Hope, M.L. (1977). Variation of aggressive interaction among male elementary school children as a function of changes in spatial density. *Environmental Psychology and Nonverbal Behavior, 2,* 67–75.

Glass, D.C., & Singer, J.E. (1972). Behavioral aftereffects of unpredictable and uncontrollable aversive events. *American Scientist, 80,* 457–465.

Glassman, J.B., Burkhart, B.R., Grant, R.D., & Vallery, G.G. (1978). Density, expectation, and extended task performance: An experiment in the natural environment. *Environment and Behavior, 10,* 299–316.

Goeckner, D., Greenough, W., & Maier, S. (1974). Escape learning deficit after overcrowding rearing in rats: Test of a helplessness hypothesis. *Bulletin of the Psychonomic Society, 3,* 54–57.

Gramann, J.H., & Burdge, R. J. (1984). Crowding perception determinants at intensively developed outdoor recreation sites. *Leisure Sciences, 6*(2), 167–186.

Greenburg, G. (1969). *The effects of ambient temperature and population density on aggression in two strains of mice.* Unpublished doctoral dissertation, Kansas State University.

Griffitt, W., & Veitch, R. (1971). Hot and crowded: Influences of population density and temperature on interpersonal affective behavior. *Journal of Personality and Social Psychology, 17,* 92–98.

Hafez, E.S.E. (Ed.). (1962). *The behavior of domestic animals.* Baltimore: Williams & Wilkins.

Hay, D.G., & Wantman, M.J. (1969). *Selected chronic diseases: Estimates of prevalence and of physicians services.* New York: Center for Social Research, Graduate Center, City University of New York.

Heller, J.F., Groff, B.D., & Solomon, S.H. (1977). Toward an understanding of crowding: The role of physical interaction. *Journal of Personality and Social Psychology, 35,* 183–190.

Heshka, S., & Pylypuk, A. (1975, June). *Human crowding and adrenocortical activity.* Paper presented at the meeting of the Canadian Psychological Association, Quebec.

Holahan, C.J. (1977). Urban-rural differences in judged appropriateness of altruistic responses: Personal vs. situational effects. *Sociometry, 40,* 378–382.

Homma, M. (1990). A Japanese perspective on crowding: How well have the Japanese adjusted to high density? *Psychologia: An International Journal of Psychology in the Orient, 33*(2), 128–137.

Hughey, A.W. (1983). Effects of living accommodations of high proximity on the self-perceptions of college students residing in university housing facilities. *Psychological Reports, 53*(3), 1013–1014.

Hutt, C., & Vaizey, M.J. (1966). Differential effects of group density on social behavior. *Nature, 209,* 1371–1372.

Isen, A.M. (1970). Success, failure, attention and reactions to others: The warm glow of success. *Journal of Personality and Social Psychology, 15,* 294–301.

Isen, A.M., Clark, M., & Schwartz, M.F. (1976). Duration of the effect of feeling good on helping: "Footprints on the sands of time." *Journal of Personality and Social Psychology, 34,* 385–393.

Isen, A.M., & Levin, P.F. (1972). The effect of feeling good on helping: Cookies and kindness. *Journal of Personality and Social Psychology, 21,* 384–388.

Jacobs, J. (1961). *The death and life of great American cities.* New York: Random House.

Karlin, R.A., Rosen, L.S., & Epstein, Y.M. (1979). Three into two doesn't go: A follow-up on the effects of overcrowded dormitory rooms. *Personality and Social Psychology Bulletin, 5,* 391–395.

Kellett, J. (1989). Health and housing. *Journal of Psychosomatic Research, 33*(3), 255–268.

Korte, C., & Kerr, N. (1975). Responses to altruistic opportunities under urban and rural conditions. *Journal of Social Psychology, 95,* 183–184.

Korte, C., Ypma, I., & Toppen, A. (1975). Helpfulness in Dutch society as a function of urbanization and environmental input level. *Journal of Personality and Social Psychology, 32,* 996–1003.

Krupat, E., Guild, W., & Miller, M. (1977). *Characteristics of large and medium sized cities, and smaller towns.* Unpublished manuscript, Boston College.

Loo, C. (1986). Neighborhood satisfaction and safety: A study of a low-income ethnic area. *Environment and Behavior, 18*(1), 109–131.

Loo, C., & Ong, P. (1984). Crowding perceptions, attitudes and consequences among the Chinese. *Environment and Behavior, 16*(1), 55–87.

Loo, C.M. (1972). The effect of spatial density on the social behavior of children. *Journal of Applied Social Psychology, 2,* 372–381.

Loo, C.M. (1973). Important issues in researching the effects of crowding on humans. *Representative Research in Social Psychology, 4,* 219–227.

Manning, R.E. (1985). Crowding norms in backcountry settings: A review and synthesis. *Journal of Leisure Research, 17*(2), 75–89.

Marsden, H.M. (1972). Crowding and animal behavior. In J.F. Wohlwill & D.H. Carson (Eds.), *Environment and the social sciences: Perspectives and applications.* Washington, D.C.: American Psychological Association.

McCain, G., Cox, V.C., & Paulus, P.B. (1976). The relationship between illness complaints and degree of crowding in a prison environment. *Environment and Behavior, 8,* 283–290.

McCauley, C., Coleman, G., & DeFusco, P. (1977). Commuters' eye contact with strangers in city and suburban train stations: Evidence of short-term adaptation to interpersonal overload in the city. *Environmental Psychology and Nonverbal Behavior, 2,* 215–225.

McClelland, L., & Auslander, N. (1978). Perceptions of crowding and pleasantness in public settings. *Environment and Behavior, 10,* 535–554.

McGrew, P.L. (1970). Social and spatial density effects on spacing behavior in preschool children. *Journal of Child Psychology and Psychiatry, 11,* 197–205.

Melton, G.B., & Hargrove, D.S. (1987). Perceptions of rural and urban communities. *Journal of Rural Community Psychology, 8*(2), 3–13.

Milgram, S. (1970). The experience of living in cities. *Science, 167,* 1461–1468.

Milgram, S. (1977). *The individual in a social world: Essays and experiments.* Reading, Mass.: Addison-Wesley.

Moser, G. (1988). Urban stress and helping behavior: Effects of environmental overload and noise on behavior. *Journal of Environmental Psychology, 8*(4), 287–298.

Neil, C C., & Jones, J.A. (1988). Environmental stressors and mental health in remote resource boom communities. *Australian & New Zealand Journal of Sociology, 24*(3), 437–458.

Newman, J., & McCauley, C. (1977). Eye contact with strangers in city, suburb and small town. *Environment and Behavior, 9,* 547–559.

Pederson, D.M. (1983). Perception of spatial and social density. *Perceptual and Motor Skills, 57*(1), 223–226.

Paulus, P.B., Annis, A.B., Seta, J.J., Schkade, J.K., & Matthews, R.W. (1976). Density does affect task performance. *Journal of Personality and Social Psychology, 34,* 248–253.

Paulus, P.B., & Matthews, R.W. (1980). When density affects task performance. *Personality and Social Psychology Bulletin, 6,* 119–124.

Paulus, P.B., McCain, G., & Cox, V. C. (1978). Death rates, psychiatric commitments, blood pressure, and perceived crowding as a function of institutional crowding. *Environmental Psychology and Nonverbal Behavior, 3,* 107–116.

Price, J.L. (1971). *The effects of crowding on the social behavior of children.* Unpublished doctoral dissertation, Columbia University.

Proshansky, H.M. (1976). Environmental psychology and the real world. *Amercian Psychologist, 31,* 303–310.

Proshansky, H.M., Ittelson, W.H., & Rivlin, L.G. (1970). The influence of the physical environment on the behavior: Some basic assumptions. In H.M. Proshansky, W.H. Ittelson, & L.G. Rivlin (Eds.), *Environmental psychology: Man and his physical settings.* New York: Holt, Rinehart & Winston.

Rawls, J.R., Trego, R.E., McGaffey, C.N., & Rawls, D.J. (1972). Personal space as a predictor of performance under close working conditions. *Journal of Social Psychology, 86,* 261–267.

Rohe, W., & Patterson, A.H. (1974). *The effects of varied levels of resources and density on behavior in a day care center.* Paper presented at annual meeting of Environmental Design Research Association, Milwaukee.

Ronchi, D., & Sparacino, J. (1982). Density of dormitory living and stress: Mediating effects of sex, self-monitoring, and environmental affective qualities. *Perceptual and Motor Skills, 55*(3), 759–770.

Rosenthal, A.M. (1964). *Thirty-eight witnesses.* New York: McGraw-Hill.

Saegert, S. (1973). Crowding: Cognitive overload and behavioral constraint. In W.F.E. Preiser (Ed.), *Environmental design research.* Stroudsburg, Pa.: Dowden, Hutchinson & Ross.

Saegert, S. (1974). *Effects of spatial and social density on arousal, mood, and social orientation.* Unpublished doctoral dissertation, University of Michigan, Ann Arbor.

Saegert, S., Mackintosh, E., & West, S. (1975). Two studies of crowding in urban public spaces. *Environment and Behavior, 7,* 159–184.

Schmitt, R.C. (1957). Density, delinquency and crime in Honolulu. *Sociology and Social Research, 41*, 274–276.

Schmitt, R.C. (1966). Density, health and social disorganization. *Journal of the American Institute of Planners, 32*, 38–40.

Shelby, B., Heberlein, T.A., Vaske, J.J., & Alfano, G. (1983). Expectations, preferences and feeling crowded in recreation activities. *Leisure Sciences, 6*(1), 1–14.

Smith, S., & Haythorn, W.W. (1972). The effects of compatibility, crowding, group size, and leadership seniority on stress, anxiety, hostility, and annoyance in isolated groups. *Journal of Personality and Social Psychology, 22*, 67–69.

Snyder, R.C. (1966). Fertility and reproduction performance of grouped male mice. In K. Benirschke (Ed.), *Symposium on comparative aspects of reproductive behavior.* Berlin: Springer.

Snyder, R.C. (1968). Reproduction and population pressures. In E. Stellar and J.M. Spragne (Eds.), *Progress in physiological psychology.* New York: Academic Press.

Srole, L. (1972). Urbanization and mental health: Some reformulations. *American Scientist, 60*, 576–589.

Stokols, D. (1972a). On the distinction between density and crowding: Some implications for future research. *Psychological Review, 79*, 275–278.

Stokols, D. (1972b). A social psychological model of human crowding phenomena. *American Institute of Planners Journal, 38*, 72–83.

Stokols, D. (1976). The experience of crowding in primary and secondary environments. *Environment and Behavior, 8*, 49–86.

Stokols, D., Rall, M., Pinner, B., & Schopler, J. (1973). Physical, social, and personal determinants of the perception of crowding. *Environment and Behavior, 5*, 87–117.

Sundstrom, E. (1975). An experimental study of crowding: Effects of room size, intrusion, and goal-blocking on nonverbal behaviors, self-disclosure, and self-reported stress. *Journal of Personality and Social Psychology, 32*, 645–654.

Swanson, C.D. (1973). *The natural history of man.* Englewood Cliffs, N.J.: Prentice-Hall.

Sweaney, A.L., Inman, M.A., Wallinga, C.R., & Dias, S. (1986). The perceptions of pre-school children and their families' social climate in relation to household crowding. *Children's Environments Quarterly, 3*(4), 10–15.

Theissen, D.D. (1966). Role of physical injury in the physiological effects of population density in mice. *Journal of Comparative and Physiological Psychology, 1962*, 322–324.

Trice, H.M. (1966). *Alcoholism in America.* New York: McGraw-Hill.

Valins, S., & Baum, A. (1973). Residential group size, social interaction and crowding. *Environment and Behavior, 5*, 421–440.

Van Staden, F.J. (1984). Urban early adolescents, crowding and the neighborhood experience: A preliminary investigation. *Journal of Environmental Psychology, 4*(2), 97–118.

Veitch, R., DeWood, R., & Bosko, K. (1977). Radio news broadcasts: Their effects on interpersonal helping. *Sociometry, 40*, 383–386.

Weiner, F.H. (1976). Altruism, ambiance, and action: The effects of rural and urban rearing on helping behavior. *Journal of Personality and Social Psychology, 34*, 112–124.

Wenz, F.V. (1984). Household crowding, loneliness and suicide ideation. *Psychology: A Quarterly Journal of Human Behavior, 21*(2), 25–29.

West, P.C. (1981). Perceived crowding and attitudes toward limiting use in backcountry recreation areas. *Leisure Sciences, 4*(4), 419–425.

Westover, T.N. (1989). Perceived crowding in recreational settings: An environment-behavior model. *Environment and Behavior, 21*(3), 258–276.

Westover, T.N. & Collins, J.R. (1987). Perceived crowding in recreation settings: An urban case study. *Leisure Sciences, 9*(2), 87–99.

Wohlwill, J.F. (1976). Environmental aesthetics: The environment as a source of affect. In I. Altman & J.F. Wohlwill (Eds.), *Human behavior and environment: Advances in theory and research* (Vol. I). New York: Plenum.

Zimbardo, P.G. (1969). The human choice: Individuation, reason and order vs. deindividuation, impulse and chaos. In W.J. Arnold & D. Levin (Eds.), *Nebraska symposium on motivation.* Lincoln: University of Nebraska Press.

Zlutnick, S., & Altman, I. (1972). Crowding and human behavior. In J.F. Wohlwill & D.H. Carson (Eds.), *Environment and the social sciences: Perspectives and applications.* Washington, D.C.: American Psychological Association.

Territoriality, Privacy, and Personal Space

10

FIGURE 10-1 Territorial behavior has been observed in animals and humans.

TERRITORIALITY
PRIVACY
PERSONAL SPACE
SUMMARY

We are all familiar with the various ways in which animals "stake out their turf" (i.e., establish the spatial boundaries of areas that they have claimed for their own). Many people have observed with amusement (some with disgust) the unique manner in which a dog deposits his odoriferous markers on the boundaries of his territory. Similarly, we have all seen (and, unfortunately, postal carriers frequently experience) the dog's reaction when an uninvited "guest" dares to intrude upon his sanctuary by stepping over that invisible, but well-demarcated olfactory line.

In this chapter we will review some of the research on territoriality in animals. However, as in the previous chapter where we discussed the studies of population concentrations in animals, we will do so with an eye to what this research can tell us regarding territoriality in humans. Also as noted in the last chapter, while animal studies can be helpful in understanding human behavior, generalizations are limited by the differential influence of instincts and learning on animal and human behavior.

Thus, while the example given above is a rather straightforward illustration of animal territoriality, human territorial behavior is often far more complex and certainly less obvious. Territoriality is only one of the many ways in which humans use and respond to spatial aspects of the environment. The study of person-environment spatial relationships is known as *proxemics*, and includes issues such as *territoriality*, *personal space*, and *crowding*. All three of these topics concern the factors influencing the ways humans position themselves vis-à-vis others in the social and physical environment.

TIME-OUT: To illustrate the variety and subtlety of spatial usage in humans, we invite you to reflect on common experiences that you have had that involve (perhaps unconsciously) the use and regulation of space in everyday life. For example, think back to your childhood clubhouse on which you posted the forbidding warning: KEEP OUT! or NO GIRLS/BOYS ALLOWED! Do you remember clinging tightly to your mother's coat while walking around a big and strange shopping mall? Contrast that behavior to the distance that you tried to keep from your Aunt Mathilda the first time she came to visit, as well as the revulsion you experienced when this strange woman immediately smothered you with kisses! Perhaps more recently you recall your disgust at the person with the bad breath who insisted on standing so close behind you in line at the grocery store, or your uneasiness as the stranger in the bus station sat down next to you when there were other seats available.

What did you think of the person who rudely "butted in line" in front of you after you had been waiting half an hour to get in to see *Forrest Gump*? When you go to a class, do you avoid sitting in the front row? How about the annoyance you felt when you last went to class to find someone else sitting in "your" seat? Contrast that to how you felt upon returning to your dorm room to discover that your roommate had invited one of your not-so-well-liked acquaintances in to play cards. How did your feelings then differ from the time you entered your room to discover that you were intruding upon a passionate embrace between your roommate and his or her beloved? Finally, perhaps you were outraged when the Soviet Union invaded Afghanistan, but were you just as mortified when the United States marched on Iraq? How do those two situations differ, and are there any similarities between them and U.S. involvement in Haiti?

These are just a few examples of the vast number of ways people use and react to physical space in their environment. In the following sections we will discuss the theories and research of environmental psychologists and other social scientists on animal and human spatial regulation. We will begin with a discussion of animal and human *territoriality*. Then we will consider a central concept in understanding humans' use of space: privacy. Finally, we will review some of the considerable amount of research on the concept of *personal space*. Along the way we hope to provide some insights regarding some of the questions about human responses to crowding that were raised in the previous chapter.

TERRITORIALITY

The concept of territoriality is most commonly used to refer to the consistencies in the ways in which humans and other animals govern the space around them—that is, the manner in which they regulate the distance between themselves and others of the same species. It is a recently developed concept first described by Howard (1948) and popularized by Ardrey (1966) in *The Territorial Imperative*. Territoriality is usually defined as behavior by which an organism characteristically lays claim to an area and defends it against intrusion by members of his or her own species. While there are similarities between territoriality in humans and animals, there are also some important differences that we will point out in our discussion.

Animal Territoriality

Given that there are consistencies in the ways organisms regulate the distance between themselves and other members of the same species, as well as the way in which they regulate the distances between themselves and members of other species, what is the nature of these regularities? Hediger (1950) has identified a number of them and has indicated that they are used in one form or another by most animals. With regard to *interspecies* spacing, he has described what he terms *flight distance* and *critical distance*. Flight distance refers to that distance which an organism will allow a potential enemy to approach before it flees, whereas critical distance is that narrow zone separating flight distance from attack distance. Depending upon the size of the organism, the size of the intruder, and situational variables such as having offspring nearby, organisms of one species will allow members of another species to approach them within specifiable limits and will then flee. If the intruder then minimizes that distance (i.e., encroaches upon the critical distance), the intruded upon is likely to stop fleeing and turn to attack.

With respect to *intraspecies* regulation, Hediger has used the terms *personal distance* and *social distance* in describing the normal spacing that noncontact animals maintain between themselves and their fellows. These distances can be seen as setting the limits of spatial regulation, with personal distance referring to the minimum spacing allowed and social distance as the maximum distance preferred. Personal distance serves to facilitate smooth functioning of the group, such as the maintenance of dominance hierarchies, whereas social distance serves to protect the group. According to Hall (1966), social distance is not simply the distance at which an animal will lose contact with his or her group—that is, the distance at which it can no longer see, hear, or smell the group—it is rather a "psychological distance," one at which the animal apparently begins to feel anxious when its limits are exceeded. We can think of it as a hidden bond that contains the group.

The above discussion suggests that territoriality in animals serves a regulatory function in the social organization and behavior among members of a species, as well as a protective function between species. Hediger (1961) suggests examples of social regulation, including feeding, mating, and rearing of young. Burt (1943) describes territory as the protective part of the geographical area over which the animal normally travels.

It is important to note the *instinctive* basis of territoriality in animals. For example, the demarcations of the boundaries of animal territories are often olfactory, as noted in the example at the beginning of this chapter. Because olfaction is a chemically based sense, it is clear that the dog's *territorial markers* consist of chemicals emanating from its urine. The receptor cells in the olfactory sense of other dogs respond to these chemicals and trigger an instinctive avoidance response. These instinctive responses are frequently called *fixed action patterns* (FAP) by ethologists, in that the responses are automatically elicited by triggering stimuli in the environment and occur independently of experience or learning. Thus, for example, even a dog raised in isolation will exhibit an avoidance response to the smell of another dog's urine. Another well-known example of an FAP of territorial behavior is the aggression of the male stickleback fish during mating season. During this time, the underside of the male becomes bright red. This color serves as a trigger stimulus that elicits an automatic attack response from the male toward any other male that enters its mating territory, and even males raised in isolation exhibit this behavior when presented with another male stickleback—in fact, they will even attack an inanimate object painted red! Thus, territoriality is clearly genetically based in animals, with the most common manifestation being the aggessive defense of the organism's "home turf." Some theorists propose that territorial behavior is a basic drive in animals that serves the purpose of controlling population size (e.g., Wynne-Edwards, 1962) and reducing unnecessary competition for resources such as food (e.g., Eibl-Eibesfeldt, 1970).

Territoriality in Humans versus Animals

Some researchers (e.g., Ardrey, 1966; Lorenz, 1966) have proposed that territoriality in humans is also instinctive, and they have suggested this as a major cause of humans' frequent aggressiveness toward themselves and other species.

This might seem to be a reasonable proposal in that one does not have to look hard to find compelling evidence of territorial behavior in humans—witness, for example, the prevalence of locks on doors, fences, and No Trespassing signs in our culture alone. Daily news reports certainly document humans' propensity to stake out and defend territory with a vengeance that shocks the sensibilities (c.f. the current conditions in Somalia). However, it is important to recognize that these types of behavior can be just as well accounted for in terms of learning, and the bulk of evidence regarding most human behaviors indicates minimal, if any, effects of instincts when compared with the role of sociocultural influences. Further, apart from questions of whether or not there is an instinctive basis to human territoriality, important differences exist between the territorial behavior of humans and animals.

Altman (1975) discusses a number of these distinctions. Within territorial groups, animals take on a very limited number of roles (e.g., mate, parent, leader), whereas most humans assume a wide diversity of social roles, resulting in a much greater complexity of territorial grouping in humans than in animals. Additionally, the social spheres themselves among animals are small in comparison to, say, the social spheres of a nation. The geographical complexity of human territories is another distinguishing characteristic. Altman notes that the geographical area of an animal's territory is restricted by the animal's size, mobility, food requirements, and life span, whereas the location(s), the size, and the diversity of a human's territory are limited by no such restrictions, and in many cases are passed on to the next generation.

Although territorial behavior serves an organizing and protective function in both humans and animals by preventing contact, the means by which this preventive function is accomplished differ markedly. For example, as discussed above, territorial boundaries in animals are most commonly marked by *physical* indicators, such as urination and glandular secretions, whereas humans rely heavily on *symbolic* markers, such as signs and personal possessions.

Perhaps the most important difference between human and animal territoriality is in the territorial behavior itself. Altman emphasizes the *reactive* nature of animal territoriality. As we saw in our earlier discussion, animals respond reflexively (i.e., instinctively), and in very predictable ways, to intrusions of their territories. Human territorial behavior is, by far, less rigid and less predictable. For example, while animals automatically defend against invasions of their territory, humans often invite others into their territory. On the other hand, while animal territorial aggression typically occurs between individuals and involves simple occupation of space, it more frequently occurs between groups in humans and often involves ideologies as well as physical space. As an illustration of the symbolic nature of group territoriality in humans, it was once noted that invasion of one's own country by another nation is labelled "aggression," while invasion of another country by one's own nation is labelled "patriotism"! Finally, a sadly ironic distinction between animal and human territoriality is that animals can only occupy an enemy's territory, while humans have the capacity to destroy their enemy's territory. Altman succinctly captures these behavioral differences: "Thus, human-response repertoires seem to be richer, more variable, and more complex than animal territorial responses. . . . People seem to have a very subtle and sensitively gradated response repertoire in relation to territory, involving complex blends of verbal, nonverbal, and environmentally related behaviors" (p. 109). It is to this complex human territorial behavior that we turn next.

Types of Human Territoriality

Altman (1975) describes three kinds of territories that humans differentiate: *primary*, *secondary*, and *public*. These correspond to the centrality of the territory to one's personal life, the degree of ownership and perceived control of the area, and the relative permanence of duration or occupancy.

    Primary territories (e.g., a home) are owned exclusively by the occupant(s) for a relatively permanent duration of time, and they are perceived as under the total control of the owner. This means that they are "off limits" to the outsider unless invited in by the owner; intrusions without permission are viewed as an extremely serious matter (in fact, in our culture such invasions are illegal), and the occupant usually actively attempts to ward off the intruder. Recall earlier that we asked you to reflect on how you would feel to return to your dorm room to find that your roommate had invited in to play cards a person you dislike. Imagine what your reaction would be if you discovered this disliked person playing cards alone in your room!

    Primary territories are often thought of as an extension of the self, with one's self-identity and self-esteem being closely linked to the area (e.g., often people purchase houses or cars that are bigger than they need simply for the status or prestige that goes with ownership). Occupants of primary territories establish clear boundary markers, such as shrubs, fences, and name plates, and they personalize them with decorations and objects that are expressions of one's identity, attitudes, and values. Witness, for example, the variety of posters with which college students are fond of plastering their room walls! These and other personal possessions are typically seen as more than mere decorations; they are intended to "make a statement" about the owner's personality to all those who see them.

    Although *secondary* territories are based on some degree of *perceived ownership*, the rights to these areas are not exclusive to the occupant; the person does not have complete control over the area, and the duration of occupancy is usually temporary. Examples of secondary territories include the desk that a student usually sits at in a classroom, a favorite study carrel in the library, or one's regular barstool in a local tavern. Altman (1975) refers to these as *semipublic* areas and sees them as the bridge between the total control over primary territories and the almost complete lack of control over public territories. Use of secondary territories is regulated by informal or unspoken rules and norms, and violations or intrusions are often not actively defended against by the owner. Thus, while you might be annoyed when someone else sits in your seat in a classroom, you are probably not likely to ask the intruder to move. This is not to say that you would not engage in a variety of subtle non-verbal behaviors to communicate your displeasure with the inconsiderate oaf, such as glaring at him or her, huffing, or noisily placing your books down on the next desk! In fact, occasionally secondary territories are defended against invasions in a not-so-subtle fashion, such as by making insulting or threatening statements to the intruder, or actively attempting to "make life difficult" for intruders by getting in their way.

Public territories are free-access areas, in that everyone has equal right to them. Examples include parks, beaches, restaurants, and libraries. Although once an area in a public territory has been secured (e.g., a particular picnic table or a seat in a movie theater), it is thought of as "belonging" to the occupant; occupancy is generally determined on a first-come-first-serve basis. Further, ownership rights of areas in public territories are extremely limited and temporary. The familiar expression "move your feet, lose your seat" underscores the fact that one must be physically present to maintain possession of public territories. Nonetheless, unspoken rules and norms serve to regulate the usage of public territories in the same way that they do in secondary territories. That is, once a seat has been taken in the theater or a table occupied in a restaurant, others look for alternate locations, and if they do attempt to intrude, the occupants are likely to defend their spot. Further, occupants of public territories often *reserve* their locations by leaving territorial *markers* such as personal possessions, and these territorial claims are usually honored by others. For example, most people hesitate to sit on a chair that has a coat hung on the back, and they are not likely to sit down at a table that has books and personal notebooks on it, even when the owner is not present.

Although some of these observations of the regulation of territories may seem obvious to you, it is important to determine whether or not they are supported by empirical research. It is equally important to account for empirical verifications of our everyday observations in terms of unifying theories and concepts. In the remainder of this chapter we will review some of this research and will attempt to explain some of the findings in terms of the concepts of privacy and personal space.

TIME-OUT: Think back to the first TIME-OUT of this chapter. Classify the examples given in terms of the of the types of human territories discussed above. Analyze the differences among the examples in terms of the different feelings and behavioral reactions you experienced in each situation. Are there similarities in any of the examples? What is the "common thread" among these examples? Finally, are there any examples that do not fit neatly in any of the three types of territories? What features of the example make it difficult to classify? Can you think of other examples of territoriality in your daily life?

Research on Human Territoriality

The research on territoriality has primarily dealt with either the functions of territories in regulating social behavior, or the role of markers in preventing territorial intrusions. We will first consider research on territorial markers and then turn to research on the functions that territories serve in governing human behavior.

Territorial Markers.   As mentioned earlier, it is common for people to "personalize" their rooms or offices with decorations that reflect their personalities and that signify the area is uniquely theirs. In a very real sense, an individual's personal identity depends upon the ability to occupy and mark a territory as one's own. Researchers have noted a similar phenomenon with group territoriality and personal identity. Those who have seen the movie *West Side Story* have observed a classic example of group territoriality in New York street gangs. The personal lives of the characters in the film were very closely related to being a member of the "Sharks" or the "Jets," and being a member of one or the other groups was basically determined by ethnic background. The groups marked their territories by writing their names on the sides of buildings in the vicinity of their *turf.* Suttles (1968) reported clear evidence of such ethnically based territories in Chicago, and Ley and Cybriwsky (1974) have described the role of *gang graffiti* in establishing and maintaining territorial claims.

A number of researchers have sought to identify the various kinds of markers that people frequently employ, as well as to determine the relative effectiveness of different markers in preventing encroachments. For example, in a study of territoriality in public areas, Sommer (1969) investigated the effectiveness of various markers in a library under different levels of density. Under low levels of density it was found that practically any type of a marker left on a table (e.g., a newspaper or an open library book) served to prevent people from sitting at the table. Under conditions of high density, however, personal effects (e.g., a sweater or a notebook with a name on it) were more effective than nonpersonal items in preventing people from sitting at a table. Gal, Benedict, and Supinski (1986) also reported that personal markers on a library table created greater avoidance than did nonpersonal markers. They also reported that the only seat at a marked table that did not elicit high avoidance was the seat positioned diagonally from the marked seat.

In a study of primary territories, Edney (1972) reported interesting differences between homeowners who employed clear markers, (e.g., "No Trespassing" signs) and those who did not use such markers. Homeowners employing markers were either long-term residents or expected to live in the area longer than those who did not use such markers. The former group also displayed more behaviors indicating vigilance, such as answering the doorbell more quickly or exhibiting greater wariness of strangers. The idea that clear markers of ownership (e.g., "Private Property" signs) prevent territorial invasions is supported by research indicating that vandalism is less likely to occur in properties that are well marked than in properties that appear to be abandoned (Ley & Cybriwski, 1974; Newman, 1972).

Researchers have recently developed the concept of *defensible space* to account for differences between territories that are less likely to be invaded than others. Brower, Dockett, and Taylor (1983) suggest that people interpret the presence of defensible space features and territorial signs to mean that occupants have stronger territorial attitudes and behaviors. They reported that people do, indeed, interpret the presence of real barriers (e.g., fences and plantings) as a deterrent to intrusion and an indication of stronger occupant territorial attitudes. In a study comparing burglarized to nonburglarized houses, Brown and Altman (1983) reported that burglarized houses had salient "public" territorial qualities (e.g., cues of openness and an unoccupied appearance), whereas nonburglarized houses had salient "secondary" or "primary" territorial qualities (e.g., territorial markers communicating privacy and individuality).

Moran and Dolphin (1986) operationalized the concept of defensible space by developing 11 indicators, which included day visibility, opposite land use, light quality, traffic, quality of surveillance, and zone of influence. They reported that the meaning of these indicators varies according to the environmental context, and that prediction of the occurrence of crime or vandalism must take these variations into account. Thus, the effectiveness of territorial features depends not only on their inherent physical qualities and general symbolic meaning, but also on the social context in which they are perceived to exist. For example, Brower et al., (1983) split their sample between those who perceived that they lived in high- and low-problem neighborhoods. Residents of perceived high-problem neighborhoods viewed territorial displays as less effective deterrents to intrusion than did residents of perceived low-problem neighborhoods. Also, Brown and Altman (1983) reported that even when markers were present, nonburglarized homes had greater visual contact with neighboring houses than did burglarized houses. MacDonald and Gifford (1989) also reported that easily surveillable houses were rated by convicted burglars as the least vulnerable targets. Interestingly, they also reported that symbolic barriers (e.g., fences, decorations, good maintenance) actually increased rather than decreased the attractiveness of houses to burglars. They suggested that this may be because such cues indicate house value and evidence of long-term care.

Thus, the research conducted on territorial markers indicates that a variety of territorial markers serve to protect one's spot in public areas, with personal effects being more effective than nonpersonal items when the area is crowded. In primary territories, the presence of clear territorial markers enhances the perception that the area uniquely belongs to the owner, and serves as a signal to potential intruders that the area is "off limits," thereby preventing unwanted intrusions. However, the effectiveness of "defensible space" depends on the social and physical context of territorial markers.

Social Organization.   Much of research and theorizing concerning the functions of territoriality deals with the organization of social behavior. One example of social organization is the establishment and maintenance of status, or dominance, hierarchies in the social order of a group. You may recall that we discussed the role of dominance in Calhoun's study (see Chapter 9) of the effects of population density in animals—the dominant animals claimed the spacious areas of the manufactured universe, which resulted in behavioral sinks in the other areas of intensified population concentrations. Calhoun reported a breakdown of the social organization of animals in the latter areas.

While animals exhibit clear effects of dominance in the pecking order of social organization in the spatial regulation of territories, the relationship between dominance and territoriality in humans is less clear. Many of the early studies of this relationship revealed contradictory results. For example, Esser and his associates (Esser, 1968; Esser, Chamberlain, Chapple, & Kline, 1965) reported that more dominant adult psychiatric patients in a hospital ward exhibited less territoriality (i.e., they roamed the ward freely) than did less dominant patients. However, they found no relationship between dominance and territoriality in children in a psychiatric hospital, but reported that dominant children in a residential cottage for juvenile delinquents showed more territoriality than less dominant children.

Altman (1975) and Sundstrom (1976) suggested that these inconsistencies may have been due to differences in the availability of choice spots (areas clearly more desirable than others) in the different settings. Thus, in settings where no areas are clearly more desirable than others (such as a psychiatric ward in a hospital), dominance would not be expected to be consistently related to territoriality. However, in settings where some areas are more desirable than others (such as one-person rooms in a cottage for juvenile delinquents), dominance would be expected to be positively related to territoriality, with dominant individuals claiming choice areas for themselves.

Individual differences in territorial behavior among the elderly have also been reported. Kinney, Stephens, and Brockmann (1987) investigated the relationship between personal competence of residents of a facility for older adults and tendencies to demonstrate possession, control, and defense in private, public, and semipublic areas. Behavioral independence was related to territorial behavior in private spaces, while mental alertness was related to territoriality in public spaces.

Territorial behavior has been related to social organization in everyday settings as well as in the institutional settings discussed above. Altman, Nelson, and Lett (1972) have discussed the ways in which territoriality can aid in the smooth functioning of daily activities. For example, most families have clearly established territories, such as chairs at the dinner table, bedrooms, dresser drawers, and even the side of the bed that partners sleep on. Were it not for these territorial norms, family members would experience chaos everytime they sat down to eat, went to bed, or tried to get dressed in the morning! Sebba and Churchman (1983) examined territoriality within the home in terms of attitudes and behaviors in and toward given physical areas. Interviews of parents and children indicated that the home was described as a "sociospatial system" in which each area had a clear social classification: individual, shared, public, jurisdiction, and activity areas. These areas differed in the degree and nature of control possible, with control being related to the size of shared areas and the quality of boundaries of individual and shared areas.

On a more global level, territories also serve an important function. In his song *Imagine*, John Lennon asked us to envision "no countries, nothing to kill or die for." Although this exhortation certainly appeals to those of us who would like to see the world rid of unwarranted invasions of one nation on the territory of another, as well as the jealous vengeance with which nations defend their territories, it is an irony that while the territorial imperative can increase hostility and aggression, territoriality can also serve to prevent antisocial behavior. We noted earlier that clear territorial markers tend to prevent invasions. Research on animals has shown that aggression is more frequent when territories are not clearly defined (Eible-Eibesfeldt, 1970; Lorenz, 1966), and the dispute over territorial claims certainly seems to be a major reason for the conflict between Israel and Palestineans in the Mideast. Thus, while ambiguously defined territorial boundaries can lead to increased aggression, a number of researchers have reported that clearly defined demarcations of what is "ours" and "theirs" can serve to reduce hostility and aggression, thereby facilitating harmonious interpersonal relations (e.g., Ley & Cybriwsky, 1974; Mack, 1954; Marine, 1966; O'Neal & McDonald, 1976). This is not to suggest that John Lennon's vision of the eradication of an "ours" and "theirs" mentality would create international chaos instead of oneness, but rather, that as long as such a global mentality exists, clear and mutually agreed-upon territorial boundaries are perhaps the best preventions of mutual annihilation. However, the 1983 downing of a Korean commercial passenger plane by Soviet air-to-air missiles should lead one to have second thoughts. In discussing the political uses of territoriality, Merelman (1988) described the recurrent struggle between "authority" and "community." He suggested that authority prefers and requires expansion of territorial units, while community prefers and requires contraction of units.

Psychological Benefits. Another area of research regarding the functions of territoriality in humans concerns the psychological benefits to the individual or group as a consequence of occupying an area. We have alluded to this in our discussions of the sense of personal and group identity gained from the ability to establish and maintain an area that the individuals perceive as belonging uniquely to themselves or to their group. This has sometimes been referred to as the "home court advantage," and, in fact, Altman (1975) reported that an analysis of the record of the University of Utah's football team revealed that they won two-thirds of their "home" games versus only one-fourth of their "away" games over a three-year period. Apart from the obvious advantages of crowd support and familiarity with the (astro) "turf," there seems to be a sense of well-being, or security, that goes along with being "at home," as opposed to being on "foreign ground" when visiting someone else's territory. Other researchers (e.g., Edney, 1975; Martindale, 1971) have reported similar findings indicating that people on their "home turf" exhibit greater feelings of relaxation and control, in addition to feeling that the setting is more pleasant than do visitors.

The feeling of being on one's "home turf" can extend beyond the primary home territory to area surrounding the home (i.e., the neighborhood). The neighborhood is a secondary territory, and many of the behaviors and experiences of residents are similar to those of the home. Further, neighborhoods vary in the degree to which residents view them as "home ground." Taylor, Gottfredson, and Brower (1985) identified two dimensions of *attachment to place*: rooted/involved and acquaintanceship. Their research suggests that not only are some people more attached to place than others, but there are some places to which people become attached more easily. Brown and Werner (1985) explored the concept of *neighborhood attachment* by comparing interrelated behavior patterns and attitudes of residents of cul-de-sacs vs. through streets. Neighborhood ties were stronger on cul-de-sacs, and behavioral manifestation of this attachment was observed in the presence of holiday decorations, which tended to be a block phenomenon (i.e., if the target home was decorated, so were the neighbors' homes). Pinet (1988) related a "sense of belonging" to traffic patterns, reporting that calm streets generate a sense of belonging, while streets with heavy traffic undermine this sense by constraining space appropriation. Habe (1989) also reported that citizens opposed to community growth were motivated primarily to protect a family-oriented life style. Finally, Van Vliet (1983) described the importance of the local neighborhood as a developmental context for young children in their exploration of the "fourth environment" (i.e., the environment outside the home, playground, or specifically child-oriented institutions).

It is interesting to note that these studies fit well with the theoretical framework outlined in Chapter 2. That is, personal territories are likely to be settings where the configuration of physical and social stimuli are within the optimal range preferred by the individual. It seems that the psychological and behavioral advantages of being in one's own territory are mediated by the feelings of pleasantness, relaxation (i.e., low arousal), and control (dominance) experienced when one is on "home turf." We suggest that the explanation of such advantages lies mainly in the feeling that establishing a territory gives people control over their lives, in terms of regulating when and with whom one interacts. Such control over social inputs has been referred to as *privacy*, and it is to this important concept that we turn next.

PRIVACY

Privacy is clearly important to our daily functioning, and much of our territorial behavior is aimed at protecting our privacy. The relationship between privacy and territoriality was implied in our discussions regarding the functions and defense of primary territories. For example, this relationship is clearly illustrated in the use of territorial markers, such as PRIVATE PROPERTY signs, and the enacting of laws to protect our homes from uninvited intruders. In fact, the existence of these laws derives from a fundamental principle upon which our nation is based: the right to privacy (i.e., freedom from surveillance of and unwanted intrusions upon our "private life").

TIME OUT: Several of the examples given at the beginning of this chapter dealt with privacy. The NO BOYS/GIRLS ALLOWED sign you posted on your clubhouse was a means of restricting access to your private domain to only those members of your gender. The reaction you were asked that you would experience upon returning to your dorm room to find an uninvited "guest " there illustrates our likely outrage at blatant invasions of privacy. Your embarrassment upon interrupting your roommate in a lover's embrace exemplifies our respect for privacy as well as our discomfort when we accidentally intrude upon others' privacy.

Can you think of other examples in which you felt that your privacy was invaded? What were the circumstances of the "invasion"? Think of this in terms of the people involved, the place and feelings and needs at the time. Why do you think people seem to place such a high value on privacy? Is it possible to have *too* much privacy?

Although the above discussion demonstrates the importance of privacy in our daily lives, until recently this concept has been relatively ignored by environmental psychologists. In the following pages we will discuss some of the efforts to define and conceptualize the dimensions of privacy, the functions privacy serve, and some of the mechanisms by which privacy operates. In so doing we will discuss the relationship between privacy and territoriality. Finally, we will also see that privacy is also closely related to the one remaining topic of this chapter, the concept of personal space.

Privacy Defined

Irwin Altman (1975) was among the first to emphasize the importance of privacy in making it a central concept in his theory of environment-behavior relationships. In his extensive discussion of privacy, Altman identified eight features of privacy, including: (1) privacy as an *interpersonal boundary-control* process by which individuals regulate contacts coming from others and outputs they make to others; (2) privacy as a *dialectic* process involving a dynamic interplay between the opposing forces of seeking versus restricting interaction (i.e., different balances of *opening* and *closing* the self to others that vary over time and circumstances); and (3) privacy as an *optimizing* process, in which a deviation from an optimal degree of desired access of the self to others at a given time (a deviation in the direction of *either* too much or too little interaction) is perceived as unsatisfactory.

Privacy as an Optimizing Process. The above features are interrelated, and are subsumed in Altman's general definition of privacy as "the selective control of access to the self or to one's group" (p. 18). While this may seem to be a simple definition, closer analysis of its components reveals the complexity of privacy. First, Altman takes a broader view of privacy than is suggested by common use of the term (i.e., privacy does not simply involve "keeping to oneself" by avoiding interaction). On the contrary, the optimizing nature of privacy indicates that achieving *too much* privacy (i.e., being socially isolated) can be just as aversive as not having enough privacy. The various combinations of desired versus achieved privacy levels can be seen in the two extremes of mismatches between desired and achieved privacy levels: (1) where a person desires a great deal of social contact, but has achieved very little, and (2) the individual desires very little contact, but experiences a great amount. Put more simply, at any given moment, there is an optimum degree of privacy sought, with extremes in either direction producing "loneliness" on the one hand, and "crowding" on the other.

Wilmoth (1982) provided support for the above distinctions in a multidimensional scaling analysis of privacy situations. He reported that both *intimacy* (high interpersonal involvement) and *solitude* (low interpersonal involvement) were associated with high perceived privacy. However, while perceived privacy was high for *solitude* in low social density, privacy was low for anonymity in high social density. Also recall from Chapter 9 that Neil and Jones (1988) reported that the best predictor of mental health problem in remote "boom" communities in Australia was reported loneliness.

Privacy as Selective Control. The relationship between this optimizing process and the dialectical process of privacy is captured by Altman's use of the term *selective control*. This suggests we all experience forces in us that cause us to both approach and avoid others, and that the real goal of privacy is to control the balance between these forces at a particular point in time. That is, we want to be able to seek out others' company when we experience the need to be with others, but we also want to be able to prevent interaction when we would rather be alone. Of course, the preference to be with others or to be alone will vary over time and situations, and the key is to be able to choose the presence or absence of others according to our present needs. Thus, as I sit here writing, I would rather not have students or colleagues interrupt me to sit down and chat. On the other hand, when I venture to the local pub at 5:00 P.M., I will be very disappointed if those same people are not there to greet me.

Privacy as Interpersonal Boundary Control. The notion that privacy is an interpersonal boundary-control process is expressed in the phrase "selective access to the self or to one's group." Here "selective access" means more than merely whether or not others are permitted contact, but implies that the *nature* or content of the interaction is also relevant, in addition to with *whom* the interaction takes place. Thus, when I feel like talking to someone about the Monday night football game that I just saw, any of my acquaintances will do. However, I WILL NOT discuss my private fears and anxieties with just anybody (which is why an example is not provided!). Altman distinguishes among different social units in boundary control, such as that among individuals, families, neighbors, and racial groups. In a related vein, Westin (1970) distinguished among four types of privacy: (1) *solitude* (being alone and free of observation), (2) *intimacy* (two or more people separating themselves from others), (3) *anonymity* (being in a public setting in which one is not recognized), and (4) *reserve* (setting up "psychological barriers" when forced to be with others by "screening them out" of conscious awareness. Finally, Marshall (1972) identified two major orientations that people have toward privacy. The first involves *general withdrawal,* and includes the components of solitude, seclusion, and intimacy. The commonality of these components is that they relate to the desire to get away from others to be either alone or with a special person or group. Marshall identified the second orientation as *control of information,* involving the components of anonymity, reserve, and not-neighboring. These components have in common the general desire to avoid intimate self-disclosure to and involvement with casual acquaintances.

However, the above discussion implies that privacy can still be achieved in intimate contacts. In a study comparing "backpackers" to "car campers," Twight, Smith, and Wissinger (1981) report that backpackers avoid casual contacts with other campers, preferring physical settings that afforded opportunities for intimately shared confidences and experiences. Thus, privacy is more closely related to interpersonal relationships than to objective social density. This last statement may sound reminiscent of our discussion of crowding in Chapter 9. Indeed, Gormley and Aiello (1982) compared crowding stress of students living double vs. triple rooms, and reported that crowding stress and satisfaction with privacy were influenced not only by the number of people, but also by the positivity-negativity of interpersonal relationships. Walden, Nelson, and Smith (1981) reported gender differences in reactions to crowded dormitory living conditions: Women tended to increase values of privacy and spent more time in dense rooms while men decreased values of privacy and spent less time in dense rooms.

The above conceptualizations reveal the many and subtle distinctions that can be made in defining privacy, but they can be integrated in the theoretical framework discussed in Chapter 2. To begin with, people desire to maintain certain optimal levels of environmental inputs (in this case, social inputs). In addition to maintaining a particular *level* of social inputs at a given time (e.g., how many people are present), humans also have preferences for the *types* of social inputs they receive (e.g., who the people are, and what the activity is). People compare their perceptions of present conditions with these optimal levels. Given a desired breadth and depth of interaction in a particular situation, to the extent that the appropriate number of people (as well as the right kind of people) are present (or absent), then homeostasis exists, resulting in normal, or *steady-state* behavior. Perceived deviations from this optimal range are likely to lead to displeasure, increased arousal (in the case of excessive social inputs) or decreased arousal (in the case of inadequate social inputs), and feelings of lack of control over the level of social interaction. This situation will lead to a variety of coping behaviors aimed at restoring an optimal level and kind of social interaction. In the following section we will discuss some of these coping behaviors in the context of the functions of privacy and the mechanisms of achieving optimal privacy levels.

Research on Privacy

Functions of Privacy.   Some of the functions of privacy, as well as some privacy mechanisms, have already been alluded to in our discussion of territoriality
and in our consideration of approaches to defining privacy. In general, privacy
can be thought of as serving two basic functions: (1) the achievement of a self-
identity, and (2) the management of interactions between the self and the social
environment. The first of these is reflected in Westin's (1970) suggestion that privacy promotes *personal autonomy* (a sense of a central core of the self), *emotional
release* (a respite from social roles and expectations), and *self-evaluation* (the integration of experiences and planning for the future). Hammitt and Brown (1984)
provided support for this model and reported that *emotional release* was the most
important dimension for people who seek privacy in wilderness settings. Thus,
privacy permits us to maintain a self-image of being an individual who exists
independently of other people, and it allows us to distinguish between a public
self and a private, personal self. Privacy permits us to have times when we can
drop the *social mask* comprising our public self, free from concern about how we
look or behave in others' eyes. Finally, privacy allows us to reflect on our experiences, to take stock of our lives and relationships with others, and to formu-
late strategies for future events.

Altman (1975) suggests that the second function of privacy (interaction
management) is important largely because it facilitates the operation of the
first—defining and maintaining self-identity. He argues that the child's recognition that it is separate and distinct from other people is one of the first steps in
the control and regulation of interpersonal boundaries. Further, the ability to
define one's own boundaries contributes to what Altman calls the "interface of
self and nonself." This interface concerns how we relate to and interact with
other people. These interactions take place in the context of various role relationships, and privacy serves to help us assess our different roles, such as son,
daughter, brother, wife, husband, employee, etc. Again, Altman proposes that
the ability to reflect on our role relationships and to exert control over regulating our various role-related interactions are important privacy functions in the
ultimate service of establishing and maintaining a sense of self. Without the
interpersonal boundary-control and interaction management functions of privacy, we would feel vulnerable, and perhaps worthless as individuals.

Privacy Mechanisms.   There are a number of mechanisms by which people
maintain preferred levels of privacy. Altman (1975) presents a typology of the
various privacy mechanisms in terms of their verbal, nonverbal, environmental,
and cultural characteristics. We have all used or heard the *verbal mechanisms* such
as, "I want to be alone right now," "Please leave!" or the more forceful and
direct, "Get out or I'll throw you out!" The message is clear and usually successful in preventing contact, as are phrases such as "Come up and see me
sometime," "Come on in," and even the indirect, "Would you like to see my
etchings?" in achieving desired contact with others. In addition to the obvious

messages communicated by verbal content, we communicate privacy intentions by means of a variety of more subtle paraverbal cues, such as rate, pitch, and intensity of speech. Typically, verbal content and style correspond, but occasionally two different messages are sent by what we say and how we say it. In the latter instance, the paralinguistic cues often take precedence, as in the case of sarcasm. The phrase "Please, stay all day" can take on very different meanings as a function of the manner in which it is spoken! Apart from the approach/avoidance aspect of verbalizations, some researchers have studied the relationship between the depth and breadth of verbal self-disclosure and interpersonal variables such as attraction and intimacy, reporting that greater self-disclosure of private information is associated with greater attraction and intimacy between interactants (e.g., Altman & Taylor, 1973; Jourard, 1971; Mehrabian, 1968). Thus, verbal mechanisms of privacy not only determine whether or not and with whom we interact, but also the nature of the interaction.

A variety of *nonverbal privacy* mechanisms also serve to regulate interactions. Among the more obvious are gestures, such as fist-shaking versus outstretched arms, or facial expressions, such as smiling versus sneering. Less obvious cues such as body posture (rigid versus relaxed), body orientation (leaning toward versus away), and fidgeting, communicate the desire to be with someone or not. These cues also tend to be in agreement with verbal and paraverbal or nonverbal cues, with verbal content seeming to be less important. You can illustrate this to yourself sometime by extending your hand to your pet dog, smiling gently, and saying softly, "Come here, you rotten little mangy mutt." Your dog will undoubtedly come running with tail wagging, not between its legs!

Among the more interesting of nonverbal privacy mechanisms is eye contact, in that prolonged eye contact can communicate either intimacy or threat, depending on the circumstances. Thus, maintaining eye contact can signal both the desire to be with another person and the desire to intimidate another person into leaving. Eye contact can also serve to facilitate the optimizing function of privacy, in the sense of compensating for too much or too little intimacy in an interaction. The avoidance of eye contact is generally interpreted as communicating that the individual feels uncomfortable, or would like to terminate the interaction. For example, Exline, Gray, and Schuette (1965) reported that people reduced eye contact when disclosing intimate information about themselves, as if they were compensating for their discomfort at revealing personal information by symbolically decreasing intimacy via reduced eye contact. Similarly, Argyle and Dean (1965) proposed an "equilibrium model" by which eye contact compensates for interpersonal distances that are inappropriate for interaction. They reported that as the distance between two conversing individuals increased beyond a certain point, eye contact also increased, while as distance decreased beyond that point, eye contact also decreased. Thus, eye contact serves as a mechanism for symbolically decreasing or increasing interpersonal distance. We will have much more to say about interpersonal distancing as a privacy mechanism later. But in the use of eye contact we can see a clear example of the kinds of "coping behaviors" that result when perceptions of environmental conditions deviate from optimal ranges, as postulated by the model of environment-behavior relationships in Chapter 2.

Altman (1975) describes a variety of *environmental privacy mechanisms*, many of which are specific to our culture, and some of which we have already mentioned in our discussion of territoriality. In fact, it is in the use of the physical environment that we can see the clearest connection between privacy and territoriality. As we suggested earlier, probably one of the major functions of territoriality in humans is to faciliatate the maintenance of privacy. Thus, territorial markers such as fences, hedges, and signs serve to signal that a particular geographical area is ours, and is therefore excluded from entry unless by invitation. It is the ability to stake out a territory of our own that permits us to achieve the "selective access to the self or group" which is so necessary for optimizing privacy. The phrase "A man's home is his castle," although sexist, still illustrates that the home territory is the place where we do have ultimate control over social inputs, a place where we can retreat for reflection, introspection, or meditation, free of the demands and expectations of our social roles, as well as a place we can be with the people we choose. However, even within the home, territoriality continues to function in the service of privacy, especially in our culture. As mentioned earlier, family members reserve special chairs and rooms as *their place*, and doors and locks are particularly important privacy mechanisms. Finnighan (1980) discussed the importance of parental attitudes, attitudes toward bodily functions and use of rooms to be important determinants of residential privacy, with control of visibility being an important privacy goal. Keeley and Edney (1983) asked subjects to construct models of houses that would promote privacy or social interaction. Privacy models had more rooms, corridors, and external wall surfaces, while social-interaction houses had greater visibility among rooms and fewer external wall surfaces.

We also discussed earlier various physical environmental markers in public and secondary territories, areas that we do not own, but still claim for ourselves. For example, we described research on the role of personal effects, such as coats and notebooks, in preventing others from sitting at *our* library desk. Thus, while primary territories are probably the most important privacy mechanisms, people attempt to regulate privacy in public territories as well. Of course, there are limitations on our ability to prevent privacy invasions in public territories. Sometimes we have no personal effects but the clothes on our back. But, we do have the space immediately surrounding our body, which we consider to be ours, no matter where we are. This area, an *invisible bubble*, has been referred to as personal space, and is as important as territoriality as a privacy mechanism. In fact, a great deal more research has been devoted to this topic than to either that of territoriality or privacy. It is to this considerable volume of research that we turn next.

PERSONAL SPACE

In addition to territoriality, space regulation can be conceptualized by the use of the term *personal space*. Katz (1937) coined the term and compared it to a "shell of a snail," and others have employed the analogy of people surrounded by "soap-bubble worlds." In reference to this term, Stern (1938) spoke of an "aura" surrounding the person. More recently, Sommer (1969) defined personal space as an area with "invisible boundaries" surrounding a person. These boundaries are not at a fixed distance from the individual (i.e., the size of the personal space area expands or contracts in response to a host of individual, social, and situational variables).

Several of the examples given at the beginning of this chapter illustrate the varying distances that people attempt to maintain between themselves and others, as well as how they react to the distances that different people position themselves from the individual. Recall that you clung to your mother's coat in the shopping mall—a very close distance that gave you a feeling of security. Your attempt to keep away from your strange Aunt Mathilda, as well as your revulsion when she proceeded to smother you with kisses, illustrates our desire to maintain a "safe" distance from unknown others and our negative reaction to inappropriate intrusions on our personal space. Similarly, your disgust at the person with the bad breath behind you in line at the grocery store and your uneasiness when the stranger sat next to you in the bus station suggest that we do not want others to break into our "soap bubble world." Avoiding sitting in the front row in the classroom illustrates our attempts to maintain a "comfortable" distance between ourselves and authority figures.

That you could relate to most, if not all, of the above examples highlights the importance and pervasiveness of personal space in our everyday lives. While we may not give much conscious thought to the distancing between ourselves and others in our daily interactions, the importance of this "hidden dimension" (see Hall, 1966) can be seen in the spatial symbols of our language regarding interpersonal relationships. For example, we describe someone we really like as a "close" friend, and we attempt to keep a disliked other at "arm's length." Someone who is hard to get to know is described as "distant," whereas someone who is inappropriately intimate or dominant is thought of as "pushy." These linguistic metaphors suggest that while we may not "own" the space between ourselves and others, we often think of it in much the same way that we think of our territory. In a sense, we might think of personal space as "social territory."

Although at first the terms *territoriality* and *personal space* appear synonymous, they are entirely different concepts and can be distinguished in several ways. First, personal space is carried around while territory is relatively stationary. Second, territorial boundaries are usually marked such that they are visible to others, whereas the boundaries of personal space are invisible. Third, personal space has the body as its focal point whereas the center of a territory is usually the home of the animal or person. Fourth, animals will usually fight to maintain dominion over territory whereas withdrawal (where possible) is the characteristic response to intrusions of personal space by others. W.H. Auden (1965) has written:

> Some thirty inches from my nose
> The frontier of my person goes,
> And all the untilled air between
> Is private PAGUS or demesne.
> Stranger, unless with bedroom eyes
> I beckon you to fraternize,
> Beware of rudely crossing it:
> I have no gun, but I can spit.

Interpersonal Distance Zones

Anthropologist Edward Hall (1959) suggested that interpersonal distancing is an important form of nonverbal communication. On the basis of observational research in a variety of cultures, Hall enumerated eight distances in human regulation of space based on vocal shifts, but upon further observations and criteria other than just voice changes he has reduced this number to four (Hall, 1966). He has labelled these distances *intimate distance, personal distance, social distance,* and *public distance.* Additionally, he conceptualizes each as having a close and far phase and has gone to great lengths in an attempt to apply a physical metric to them. He cautions, however, that the measured distances vary, within limits, with differences in personality and environmental factors. This caveat is reminiscent of that of Stokols appearing in the last chapter regarding attempts to measure density and crowding.

The above distances communicate to participants and observers of an interaction both the nature of the relationship between interactants and the nature of the activity. Despite the fact that Hall's delimitation of space regulation in humans is based on a restricted and recognizedly biased sample and even by Hall seen as only a crude approximation to what proxemic observations are likely to discover, his general notions are intriguing enough to now outline them in some detail.

Intimate Distance. Intimate distance necessarily involves increased sensory inputs. In its close phase (0 to 6 inches) physical contact is inevitable and very much central to the perceptions of the individuals involved. Olfaction and the sensation of radiant heat is salient; vision is blurred and vocalization is essentially nonexistent. In its far phase (6 to 18 inches) physical contact except for the extremities is absent, vision is clear but distorted, heat and odor are still detectable, and vocalization is usually confined to a whisper.

Personal Distance. Personal distance in its close phase (one and one-half to two and one-half feet) involves the absence of physical contact except as desired and then involves only the extremities; visual distortion is no longer apparent, radiant heat is all but undetectable, whereas certain odors may still be perceived, and vocalization can be considered as modified conventional (neither a whisper nor the natural consultative style). In its far phase, personal distance (30 to 48 inches) is characterized by lack of physical contact, vision is unusually acute, radiant heat is undetectable, normal odors are imperceptible (however, breath odors, cologne or foot odors may be perceived), and the voice level is moderate.

Social Distance. The close phase of social distance constitutes an area of from 4 to 7 feet surrounding the individual. At this distance no one touches or expects to touch another. Visual acuity is good, olfaction is operative only for unusual odors, and voice level is social consultative. In its far phase (7 to 12 feet) social distance is characterized by a noticeably louder voice level, diminishing visual acuity, lack of odoriferous cues, no physical contact, and no stimulation of the thermal receptors via heat radiated from the other.

Public Distance. Public distance in its close (12 to 25 feet) and far (twenty-five feet or more) phase is characterized by changes in voice loudness, inflection, tempo, enunciation, by changes in the amount of peripheral stimuli entering the field of vision, and by the lack of acuity with which the peripheral stimuli are perceived.

Behavioral Correlates of Interpersonal Distance

With the use of anecdote and nonsystematically controlled observations, Hall (1966) has given a preliminary elucidation of the kinds of social behaviors which take place and are condoned at the various distances. He describes, for example, the close phase of intimate distances as the distance of "lovemaking and wrestling, comforting and protecting" (p. 117). The far phase of intimate distances, like the close phase, is not considered publicly proper for adult, middle-class Americans, although the young may be observed to be intimately involved in automobiles and on beaches and other public places.

The close phase of personal distances is reserved for very close relationships (spouses, relatives, etc.), whereas the far phase is open to others. Subjects of personal interest and involvement can be discussed at this distance. Impersonal business occurs at the boundaries of social distance with more involvement occurring in the close as compared to the far phase. Casual social gatherings and work relations are characterized by spatial regulations utilizing social distance at its close phase. Formal business and social discourse is carried on in the far phase especially when social or business status is to be maintained.

Public distance is well outside the individual's circle of involvement and occurs primarily in a speaker-audience situation. A person observing a mother calling for her child, an overheard argument at some distances, or perhaps a person watching television could possibly be considered within the domain of public distance. The primary characteristic of all these examples is that the individual is not directly interacting with other persons.

Functions of Personal Space

Social Learning Theory.   The above regularities in interpersonal distancing can be observed in most people with only minor variations. Why do such pervasive regularities in the use of space occur? It might be tempting to suggest that personal space is instinctively determined (cf. Evans and Howard, 1973) and is simply a specific instance of territorial behavior. However, as we saw in our discussion of territoriality, spatial behavior in humans is flexible and exhibits subtle gradations in response to a variety of individual, social, and situational variables. We will review some of the research on these variables in a later section of this chapter. Thus, although we may be genetically predisposed to use and respond to interpersonal distance in predictable ways, it is more likely that personal space regulation is a socially learned form of behavior (cf. Duke & Nowicki, 1972). For example, very young children do not employ personal space the way adults do, but through observation of adults' spatial behavior (e.g., Mommy and Daddy stand closer to each other than to other people) and in response to direct training (e.g., "Don't go near strangers") children as young as three years of age exhibit some regularities in interpersonal distance (Lomranz, Shapira, Choresh, & Gilat, 1975), and adult-like spatial behavior is manifested by puberty (Aiello & Cooper, 1979). In general, cultural norms regarding spatial behavior appear to be learned just as other behavioral norms. These norms serve the function of permitting the smooth functioning of society, and spatial norms specifically allow individuals to feel comfortable in their interactions with others.

Self-Protection.   Probably the most often-cited function of personal space is the avoidance of threat to the self. Obviously, it is difficult for another person to physically attack us if we maintain a safe distance between them and ourselves. In addition to protection from physical threat, Horowitz, Duff, and Stratton (1964) referred to personal space as a "body buffer zone" which protects the individual from undue stress or anxiety. We saw in our discussion of Hall's zones of interpersonal distance that other people provide a great deal of sensory information at close distances. Recall from Chapter 2 that we can only process a limited amount of information at any given time, and our information-processing system is easily overloaded. Information overload produces heightened arousal and stress. Thus, maintaining personal space prevents excessive stimulation from social sources (cf. Evans, 1974). Note that this explanation sounds very similar to our discussions of responses to high levels of population density, a point to which we will return. Finally, we mentioned in our discussion of privacy that personal space is a mechanism for protecting our privacy (Altman, 1975).

Communication.   In the previous section we noted that Hall considered personal space to be a form of nonverbal communication. Thus, the distance that people maintain between themselves communicates information regarding the relationship between the interactants (e.g., the degree of intimacy or attraction) as well as the nature of the activity (e.g., lovemaking or formal business contacts). In general, close distances communicate an interest in the other person and a desire to continue the interaction, whereas far distances communicate a lack of intimacy or a desire to avoid interacting with the other person. Although we usually do not give distancing much conscious thought, people do seem to respond at some level to these nonverbal cues, with this response most probably being either positive or negative affect.

All of the above explanations of the functions of personal space can be incorporated in the model of environment-behavior relations presented in Chapter 2. That is, the physical distance between people is one aspect of objective environmental conditions. Through learning, we come to develop expectations about comfortable interaction distances under different conditions. As long as the distance between people is within an optimal range, given the nature of the relationship and the type of activitiy, homeostasis exists and we do not give conscious attention to the distance. When the distance deviates from this optimal range, negative affective responses occur, we become aware of the inappropriate distance, and we make efforts to adapt or adjust in order to restore homeostasis. We will discuss these coping responses in a later section.

Measuring Personal Space

We noted that Hall's zones of interpersonal distance are only approximations and were derived primarily from his admittedly unsystematic observations. Since then a number of more psychometrically reliable and valid measures of personal space have been developed. These can be classified as the (1) observational method, (2) laboratory method, and (3) simulation method.

Observational Method. This approach involves systematically observing and measuring the distances that individuals maintain between themselves and others in natural settings. This method has the advantage of external validity, but it is difficult to control for other variables (e.g., the presence of other people) and some have raised the ethical question of informed consent.

Laboratory Method. This approach involves asking subjects to indicate comfortable distances in a room when being approached by an experimenter. Variables such as gender can be manipulated under highly controlled conditions, but this method has the disadvantage of lack of realism.

Simulation Method. This approach has been used a great deal by researchers. It usually involves a variety of methods asking subjects to respond as if they were actually in a simulated situation. For example, "paper-and-pencil" measures request people to mark off distances on a diagram, or people are asked to arrange felt or wooden figures according to the situation described by the experimenter. These methods have the advantage of permitting the manipulation of a large number of social/situational variables, but some have questioned the degree to which these measures correlate with those of the other methods described above (e.g., Jones & Aiello, 1979).

Despite the problems associated with these approaches, the above measures have allowed researchers to be more systematic than Hall in assessing space regulation in relation to a variety of individual and social/situational variables. We turn now to the research on the variables causing the "expanding" or "contracting" of the personal-space bubble discussed earlier.

Factors Influencing Personal Space

If Edward Hall is at all correct in his observations, it is possible to define at least three categories of variables that may act to influence our use of and reactions to interpersonal distance: (1) individual differences in the use of space, (2) social/situational variables affecting the size of personal space, and (3) responses to violation of personal space regulation with respect to either the physical metric or to social behaviors deemed appropriate for particular distances.

Individual Differences. Hall (1966) has noted cross-cultural differences in distance regulation, with people from Latin countries maintaining greater proximity than North Americans. Williams (1971) and Liepold (1963) have shown differences in spatial regulation among introverts and extroverts, with introverts maintaining more distance between themselves and others than extroverts. Additionally, a number of investigators have reported gender differences in spacing with male-male dyads interacting at greater distances than female-female dyads. Sommer (1969) has reported differences between normals and schizophrenics with respect to spatial regulations. Finally, Kinzel (1970) reported that violent prisoners have much larger personal space zones than do nonviolent prisoners.

Social/Situational Variables. A large number of studies have investigated a variety of factors in the circumstances of an interaction influencing the distance that individuals maintain between themselves. Perhaps one of the most important factors affecting personal space is the degree of attraction between interactants. In general, people maintain larger personal space zones from strangers than acquaintances (Little, 1965), and as attraction increases so does the proximity of interaction. Much of this research has focused on the well-known similarity-attraction relationship identified in social psychological research. For example, Byrne, Baskett, and Hodges (1971) "matched" couples for a blind date according to their responses on an attitude questionnaire. Couples whose attitudes were similar to one another reported greater liking for their partner than did those whose attitudes were dissimilar. Similar couples also stood closer to one another in front of the experimenter's desk when they returned from their date than did dissimilar partners. This proxemic relationship appears to be mainly due to females positioning themselves closer to the male partner, rather than vice versa (Edwards, 1972).

Other research (e.g., Heshka & Nelson, 1972) verified this assertion, indicating that female-female dyads exhibit the attraction-proximity relationship, but that male-male dyads tend to position themselves at the same distance, regardless of the degree of attraction. Other types of similarity-proximity relationships have also been reported, such as age (Willis, 1966), race (Campell, Kruskal, & Wallace, 1966) and status (Lott & Sommer, 1967).

The above research can be understood in terms of the positive affective state that individuals experience when with a liked other (cf. Byrne & Clore, 1970). We saw in Chapter 4 that we tend to approach situations (and people) that are associated with positive affect. Other research has indeed shown that negatively toned situations result in increased interpersonal distances (e.g., Dosey & Meisels, 1969). Finally, others have reported that people maintain greater distances when expecting to compete with someone than when cooperation is expected (Sommer, 1965).

Invasions of Personal Space.   Several investigators (Birdwhistell, 1952; Garfinkle, 1964; Goffman, 1963; Hall, 1966) have described the effects of physical intrusions into another's personal space. These descriptions, while insightful and intriguing, lack scientific validity in that the observations upon which they are based were not undertaken with scientific precision but were rather casual or founded in anecdote. In an attempt to be more systematic in defining the effects of inappropriate proximity, Baxter and Deanovich (1970) utilized the technique of attributive projection and found that crowded subjects projected more anxiety than did uncrowded subjects.

Perhaps more important to the present discussion are two studies by Felipe and Sommer (1966). The first study, conducted at Mendocino State Hospital, involved an experimenter's (E) invasion of a patient's (P) personal space. Patients meeting particular criteria were located, whereupon E would walk over and sit beside P without saying a word. If P moved his chair or sidled farther down the bench, E would move a like distance to keep the space between them about six inches. P's behavior was then observed. Control subjects were selected from other patients seated at some distance from E but still within E's visual field. To be eligible for the control group, a patient had to be sitting alone and not reading or otherwise engaged in an activity.

The second study took place in the study hall of a university library. Although there were five different conditions plus control subjects, all conditions involved the physical intrusion of personal space. An experimenter would walk up to an empty chair beside a person (seated at a table), pull the chair out at an angle, sit down, ignore that person's presence, and unobtrusively pull the chair up to the table within a specified distance of the person (1-foot shoulder separation; 2-foot shoulder separation; three-and-one-half-feet-shoulder separation with an empty chair between them; two empty seats between them with a resulting shoulder distance of about 5 feet; or directly across from them a distance of about 4 feet).

The results of the two studies are very similar, with the most obvious reaction to the intrusion being departure on the part of the subjects. There were, however, more subtle indications of discomfort. In the first study the persons would typically face away from the intruder immediately, pulling in their shoulders, and placing their elbows at their side. Mumbling, irrelevant laughter, and delusional talk was also used by subjects seemingly to keep the intruder at a distance. In the second study subjects frequently drew in their arms and head, turning away from the intruder and exposing the shoulder and back; they often placed the elbow on the table and rested the head in the hand. Additionally, subjects who chose not to flee would use objects including books, notebooks, purses, coats, and occasionally chairs in building a barricade between themselves and the intruder. These types of behavior were not observed in control subjects where personal space was not being intruded upon.

It would appear, then, that the physical intrusion of one's personal space is very annoying for the intruded upon, so much so that the typical reaction is one of flight. Even where subjects decided not to flee they are distrubed to the extent that they attempt to build barriers to the intrusion. Whether this annoyance can be construed as the experience of crowding is at this time undetermined, but it is not implausible that studies involving spatial limitations are merely setting up conditions of mutually intersecting personal spaces. Thus, the psychological experience of "crowding" may be due more to invasions of personal space than to a response to the absolute number of people present (cf. Arkkelin & Veitch, 1978).

With respect to this variable of physical intrusion, other possibilities beside proximity of bodies exist. For example, it is possible to invade another's personal space through visual contact. It is not an uncommon occurrence to feel the disconcerting effects of having someone stare at you while you are engaged in some activity. The perception of radiant heat or odors given off by another and penetrating the barrier of personal space are also likely to have irritating effects. Or imagine yourself living in an apartment. You are entertaining a guest. The lights are low, the music soft. You have mutually penetrated the concentric bubbles surrounding you until at last you have reached that sought after goal—intimate distance, close phase. "Where the hell have you been?" you hear in a shrill voice through the thinly uninsulated walls of your prefab-apartment, "I've been waitin' . . ." and so on. The shrieks, the retorts, the sound of a pan hitting the wall all intrude upon and vex your carefully planned tryst. The sounds have penetrated the domain of your personal space. Whether the anguish, anxiety, and uneasiness you feel under these circumstances can be considered the same as the experiential state of crowding is at this time undetermined.

Crowding and Personal Space

It is obvious that both more research and greater specification of the parameters of crowding are needed. Each of the above examples could be described as "the inability to control social interactions"; however, they are so different from each other that any attempt to group them under a single categorical heading would be futile. Nonetheless, it is quite possible that each of the above would lead to similar kinds of reactions in the individual: flee, if possible; set up barriers; do nothing but live with the uneasiness the situation has produced. The exact coping behavior would, of course, depend on the configuration of emotion aroused and the learned adaptive and adjustive mechanisms one has available.

Earlier it was noted that a third variable which may act to determine the experience of crowding was the behavior on the part of others that you deem inappropriate for the particular distance separating you. For example, Hall (1966) has observed that persons from Latin countries stand closer in social conversational situations than do North Americans, and that Arabs consider it rude not to breathe on someone with whom they are conversing. Americans talking with Latins or with Arabs feel very ill at ease. The American feels uncomfortable and moves to increase distance; the Latin then feels uncomfortable and moves to decrease the distance. The American feels crowded; the Latin feels put off. Thus, what appears to be appropriate behavior to one individual is perceived an inappropriate to another.

Finally, suppose that you are at a bank applying for a loan. You sit down on the opposite side of the desk and proceed to ask for a loan with the voice inflection, style, and loudness normally appropriate for public distances. Again the inappropriate behavior is likely to lead to uneasiness on the part of the loan officer. More examples, of course, could be given, but enough has been said to indicate that when the regularities with which space is usually utilized are ignored, behavior is likely to be disrupted. Again, owing to the paucity of research it is impossible to determine whether these kinds of violations are at all connected with the experience of crowding. It would appear that using such vague definitions of crowding as "excessive stimulation from social sources" or the "inability to adequately control interactions with others" leads to a great deal of semantic and theoretical confusion. A better approach might be to attempt to understand crowding in terms of the concepts of territoriality, privacy, and personal space discussed in this chapter. Instead of addressing the question of whether or not humans respond negatively to high density, this approach would utilize these concepts to answer the question of what are the particular conditions of density that lead to aversive consequences.

SUMMARY

Humans as well as other animals seem to have a penchant (if not a need) for establishing dominion over some aspect(s) of their life space. The most likely reason for territorial behavior is to gain control over social interactions (i.e., to maintain privacy). Some animals establish this control by marking out territories (many mammals by secreting chemicals with their urine, birds by means of the songs they sing), which is then defended from intrusion. Humans, it would seem, also tend to establish areas that are declared off limits to others. As a result of language capabilities of humans, though, this "marking off" of territory is far more sophisticated and extends beyond the primary hunting, gathering, and suckling boundaries. Also, unlike other animals, humans appear to maintain a portable boundary—an area around them which is carried from place to place but expands and contracts depending on the behavior being enacted, the characteristics of the interactants, and the available environmental props. This portable area has been labelled *personal space.*

These areas that are marked off have more than physical properties. They help to define the kind of behavior expected, by and with whom, and under what conditions. It is suggested that one of the effects of population density referred to in the previous chapter is that the likelihood of these expectations being violated is increased. If these violations do occur then the psychological condition of crowding results; if not, then the interactants merely find themselves in a densely populated area. Density is, therefore, a possible cause but not a necessary precondition for crowding; and as we saw in the previous chapter, it also is not a sufficient cause of crowding.

IMPORTANT CONCEPTS

proxemics
territoriality
interspecies distance
"flight" distance
"critical" distance
intraspecies distance
personal distance
social distance
fixed action patterns
human vs. animal territoriality
primary, secondary, public territories
territorial markers
defensible space
dominance and territoriality
sociospatial system
"home court advantage"

neighborhood attachment
privacy
interpersonal-boundary control
privacy as a dialectical process
privacy as an optimizing process
selective control
functions of privacy
privacy mechanisms
personal space
intimate, personal, social, public distance
functions of personal space
individual differences in personal space
social/situational influences on personal space
responses to personal space invasions
crowding and personal space

REFERENCES

Aiello, J.R., & Cooper, R.E. (1979). *Personal space and social affect: A developmental study.* Paper presented at the Meeting of the Society for Research in Child Development, San Francisco.

Altman, I. (1975). *The environment and social behavior.* Monterey, Calif: Brooks/Cole.

Altman, I., Nelson, P.A., & Lett, E.E. (1972). The ecology of home environments. *Catalog of selected documents in psychology.* Washington, D.C.: American Psychological Association.

Altman, I., & Taylor, D. (1973). *Social penetration: The development of interpersonal relationships.* New York: Holt, Rinehart and Winston.

Ardrey, R. (1966). *The territorial imperative.* New York: Atheneum.

Argyle, M., & Dean, J. (1965). Eye-contact, distance and affiliation. *Sociometry,* 289–304.

Arkkelin, D., & Veitch, R. (1978). *The effects of number, interpersonal distance, sex, and acquaintance level on affective reponses of males and females.* Paper presented at the Midwestern

Psychological Asssociation Annual Convention, Chicago.

Auden, W.H. (1965). Prologue: The birth of architecture: *About the house*. New York: Random House.

Baxter, W.C., & Deanovich, B.S. (1970). Anxiety-arousing effects of inappropriate crowding. *Journal of Counseling and Clinical Psychology*, 35, 174–178.

Birdwhistell, R.L. (1952). *Introduction to kinesics*. Louisville, Ky.: University of Louisville Press.

Brower, S., Dockett, K., & Taylor, R.B. (1983). Residents' perceptions of territorial features and perceived local threat. *Environment and Behavior*, 15(4), 419–437.

Brown, B.B., & Altman, I. (1983). Territoriality, defensible space and residential burglary: An environmental analysis. *Journal of Environmental Psychology*, 3(3), 203–220.

Brown, B.B., & Werner, C.M. (1985). Social cohesiveness, territoriality, and holiday decorations: The influence of cul-de-sacs. *Environment and Behavior*, 17(5), 539–565.

Burt, W.H. (1943). Territoriality and homerange concepts as applied to mammals. *Journal of Mammalogy*, 24, 346–352.

Byrne, D., Baskett, D.G., & Hodges, L. (1971). Behavioral indicators of interpersonal attraction. *Journal of Applied Social Psychology*, 1(2), 137–149.

Byrne, D., & Clore, G.L. (1970). A reinforcement model of evaluative responses. *Personality: An International Journal*, 1, 103–128.

Campbell, D.T., Kruskal, W.H., & Wallace, W.P. (1966). Seating aggregation as an index of attitude. *Sociometry*, 29, 1–15.

Dosey, M.A., & Meisels, M. (1969). Personal space and self-protection. *Journal of Personality and Social Psychology*, 11, 93–97.

Duke, M.P., & Nowicki, S., Jr. (1972). A new measure and social learning model for interpersonal distance. *Journal of Experimental Research in Personality*, 6, 1–16.

Edney, J.J. (1972). Property, possession, and permanence: A field study in human territoriality. *Journal of Applied Social Psychology*, 2, 275–282.

Edney, J.J. (1975). Territoriality and control: A field experiment. *Journal of Personality and Social Psychology*, 31, 1108–1115.

Edwards, D.J.A. (1972). Approaching the unfa-

miliar: A study of human interaction distances. *Journal of Behavioral Sciences*, 1(4), 249–250.

Eibl-Eibesfeldt, I. (1970). *Ethology: The biology of behavior*. New York: Holt, Rinehart & Winston.

Esser, A.H. (1968). Dominance heirarchy and clinical course of psychiatrically hospitalized boys. *Child Development*, 39(1), 147–157.

Esser, A.H., Chamberlain, A.S., Chapple, E.P., & Kline, N.S. (1965). Territoriality of patients on a research ward. In J. Wortis (Ed.), *Recent advances in biological psychiatry*. New York: Plenum.

Evans, G.W. (1974). An examination of the information overload mechanism of personal space. *Man-environment Systems*, 4, 61.

Evans, G.W., & Howard, R.B. (1973). Personal space. *Psychological Bulletin*, 80(4), 334–344.

Exline, R., Gray, D., & Schuette, D. (1965). Visual behavior in a dyad as affected by interview content and sex of respondent. *Journal of Personality and Social Psychology*, 5, 201–209.

Felipe, N.J., & Sommer, R. (1966). Invasions of personal space. *Social Problems*, 14, 206–214.

Finnighan, W.R. (1980). Some empirical observations on the role of privacy in the residential environment. *Man-Environment Systems*, 10(3–4), 153–159.

Gal, C.A., & Benedict, J.O., & Supinski, D.M. (1986). Territoriality and the use of library study tables. *Perceptual and Motor Skills*, 63(1), 567–574.

Garfinkle, H. (1964). Studies of the routine grounds of everyday activities. *Social Problems*, 11, 225–250.

Goffman, E. (1963). *Behavior in public places*. New York: Free Press.

Gormley, F.P., & Aiello, J.R. (1982). Social density, interpersonal relationships, and residential crowding stress. *Journal of Applied Social Psychology*, 12(3), 222–236.

Habe, R. (1989). Community growth gaming: A survey method. *Environment and Behavior*, 21(3), 298–322.

Hall, E.T. (1959). *The silent language*. New York: Doubleday.

Hall, E.T. (1966). *The hidden dimension*. New York: Doubleday.

Hammitt, W.E., & Brown (1984). Functions of privacy in widerness environment. *Leisure Sciences*, 6(2), 151–166.

Hediger, H. (1950). *Wild animals in captivity.* London: Butterworth.

Hediger, H.P. (1961). The evolution of territorial behavior. In S.L. Washburn (Ed.), *Social life of early man.* New York: Wennergren Foundation.

Heshka, S., & Nelson, Y. (1972). Interpersonal speaking distance as a function of age, sex, and relationship. *Sociometry, 35,* 491–498.

Horowitz, M.J., Duff, D.F., & Stratton, L.O. (1964). Body-buffer zone. *Archives of General Psychiatry, 11,* 651–656.

Howard, D. (1948). *Territory and bird life.* London: Cellen's Publication Co.

Jones, S.E., & Aiello, J.R. (1979). A Test of the validity of projective and quasi-projective measures of interpersonal distance. *Western Journal of Speech Communication, 43*(2), 143–152.

Jourard, S.M. (1971). The need for privacy. In S.M. Jourard (Ed.), *The transparent self.* New York: Van Nostrand.

Katz, P. (1937). *Animals and men.* New York: Longmans, Green.

Keeley, R.M., & Edney, J.J. (1983). Model house designs for privacy, security, and social interaction. *Journal of Social Psychology, 119*(2), 219–228.

Kinney, J.M., Stephens, M.P., & Brockmann, A.M. (1987). Personal and environmental correlates of territoriality and use of space: An illustration in congregate housing for older adults. *Environment and Behavior, 19*(6), 722–737.

Kinzel, A.S. (1970). Body buffer zone in violent prisoners. *American Journal of Psychiatry, 127,* 59–64.

Ley, D., & Cybriwsky, R. (1974). Urban graffiti as territorial markers. *Annals of Association of American Geographers, 64,* 491–505.

Liepold, W.E. (1963). *Psychological distance in dyadic interview.* Unpublished doctoral dissertation, University of North Dakota, Grand Forks, N.D.

Little, K.B. (1965). Personal space. *Journal of Experimental Social Psychology,* 237–247.

Lomranz, J., Shapira, A., Choresh, N., & Gilat, Y. (1975). Children's personal space as a function of age and sex. *Developmental Psychology, 11,* 541–545.

Lorenz, K. (1966). *On aggression.* New York: Harcourt Brace Jovanovich.

Lott, B.S., & Sommer, R. (1967). Seating arrangements and status. *Journal of Personality and Social Psychology, 7,* 90–95.

MacDonald, J.E., & Gifford, R. (1989). Territorial cues and defensible space theory: The burglar's point of view. *Journal of Environmental Psychology, 9*(3), 193–205.

Mack, R. (1954). Ecological patterns in an industrial ship. *Social Forces, 32,* 118–138.

Marine, G. (1966). I've got nothing against the colored, understand. *Ramparts, 5,* 13–18.

Marshall, M. (1972). Privacy and environment. *Human Ecology, 1,* 93–110.

Martindale, D.A. (1971). Territorial dominance behavior in dyadic verbal interactions. *Proceedings of the Annual Convention of American Psychological Association Division of Personality and Social Psychology, 6,* 305–306.

Mehrabian, A. (1968). Relationships of attitude to seated posture, orientation, and distance. *Journal of Personality and Social Psychology, 10,* 26–30.

Merelman, R.M. (1988). The political uses of territoriality. *Environment and Behavior, 20*(5), 576–600.

Moran, R., & Dolphin, C. (1986). The defensible space concept: Theoretical and operational explication. *Environment and Behavior, 18*(3), 396–416.

Neil, C.C., & Jones, J.A. (1988). Environmental stressors and mental health in remote resource boom communities. *Australian & New Zealand Journal of Sociology, 24*(3), 437–458.

Newman, O. (1972). *Defensible space.* New York: Macmillan.

O'Neal, E.C., & McDonald, P.J. (1976). The environmental psychology of aggression. In R.G. Geen & E.C. O'Neal (Eds.), *Perspectives on aggression.* New York: Academic Press.

Pinet, C. (1988). A "sense of belonging" in the neighborhood: The effect of traffic on space appropriation. *Environmental Design Research Association, 19,* 173–178.

Sebba, R., & Churchman, A. (1983). Territories and territoriality in the home. *Environment and Behavior, 15*(2), 191–210.

Sommer, R. (1965). Further studies of small group ecology. *Sociometry, 28,* 337–348.

Sommer, R. (1969). *Personal space.* Englewood Cliffs, N.J.: Prentice Hall.

Stern, W. (1938) *General psychology* (H.D. Spoerl, trans.). New York: Macmillan.

Sundstrom, E. (1976). Interpersonal behavior and the physical environment. In L.S. Wrightsman (Ed.), *Social psychology* (2nd ed). Monterey, Calif.: Brooks/Cole.

Suttles, G.D. (1968). *The social order of the slum: Ethnicity and territory in the inner city.* Chicago: University of Chicago Press.

Taylor R.B., Gottfredson, S.D., & Brower, S. (1985). Attachment to place: Discriminant validity, and impacts of disorder and diversity. *American Journal of Community Psychology, 13*(5), 525–542.

Twight, B.W., Smith, K.L., & Wissinger, G.H. (1981). Privacy and camping: Closeness to the self vs. closeness to others. *Leisure Sciences, 4*(4), 427–441.

Van Vliet, W. (1983). Exploring the fourth environment: An examination of the home range of city and suburban teenagers. *Environment and behavior, 15*(5) 567–588.

Walden, T.A., Nelson, P.A., & Smith, D.E. (1981). Crowding, privacy, and coping. *Environment and Behavior, 13*(2), 205–224.

Westin, A. (1970). *Privacy and freedom.* New York: Atheneum.

Williams, J.L. (1971). Personal space and its relation to extroversion-introversion. *Canadian Journal of Behavioral Science, 3*(2), 156–160.

Willis, F.N. (1966). Initial speaking distance as a function of the speaker's relationship. *Psychonomic Science, 5,* 221–222.

Wilmoth, G.H. (1982). Toward an empirical model of perceived privacy: A multidimensional scaling analysis and implications for design. *EDRA: Environmental Research Association, 13,* 85–99.

Wynne-Edwards, V.C. (1962). *Animal dispersion in relation to social behavior.* New York: Hafner Press.

Institutional Design

11

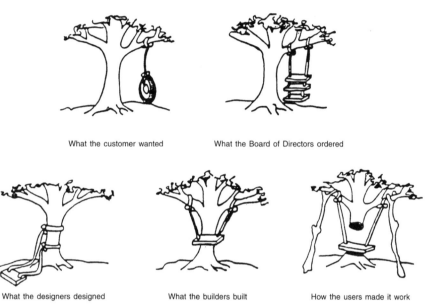

What the customer wanted

What the Board of Directors ordered

What the designers designed

What the builders built

How the users made it work

FIGURE 11-1 Designers and builders of environments are sometimes at odds with the users of these environments.

The line one of the authors gets in at the grocery store is always the slowest moving. The couple ahead of me can't find their checkbook; the clerk has to run a price check on the stewed prunes; a worm is discovered in the tomatoes necessitating another five minutes of squeezing and choosing; the roll of tape in the cash register is used up; or the cashier decides to take a break just as it's my turn to be checked out. My luck is no better at the bank, automobile registry, travel agent's counter, or fast-food restaurant. Someone nearly always spots a friend who just happens to be ahead of me, they exchange pleasantries, engage in conversation, and they both are served before I am. I am also a sucker for the "I'll only be a second and I've left my motor running—would you mind if I go ahead of you?" ploy.

Although these situations are presented from a first-person perspective, I'm sure that you could have written in a similar vein about *your* experiences with waiting in lines. Lines are a fact of life. We assume that there is nothing that can be done about them and that the time we spend in them will inevitably increase. In fact, John Hershey (1974) wrote a futuristic novel, *My Petition for More Space*, in which the entire story is carried out in a waiting line.

When I'm not waiting in line, I often seem to be just waiting—waiting at the bus depot for my predictably late bus, waiting in the reception area to see my dentist, waiting in the baggage claim section hoping that my luggage took the same plane I did. I seem to spend far too much time doing far too little in public places where I'd rather not be. I am not alone in this feeling. Fairfield (1977) claims that most public waiting spaces are "drab, cramped, unimaginative, anxiety provoking and dehumanizing" (p.43), and suggests that life is too short to cumulatively waste weeks, months, or years just waiting. I agree. But must waiting be a fact of life, and need it be so annoying? Is it possible it is merely the result of poor planning or oversights in design? Could these waiting annoyances be designed out of grocery stores, banks, fast-food restaurants, baggage claim areas, and similar situations?

Upon reflection it becomes obvious that the arrangement of our immediate surroundings create both opportunities and limitations. Supermarkets afford us the opportunity to purchase all of our food needs in one location, but they also place limits on our ability to get in and get out quickly. The realization that physical design limits human capabilities comes easily when we observe someone confined to a wheelchair attempting to negotiate a street curb, or someone who is visually impaired trying to read street signs. But, while these may be extraordinary yet poignant examples, it is nonetheless true that all of us are affected in varying degrees by the built environment. It is also true that while we are likely to blame the designer of curbs for the difficulty we perceive the person in the wheelchair as having, we are *not* likely to blame the designer of grocery stores for our own long wait, or the designer of street signs for the difficulty exhibited by the visually impaired. But is it possible the designer is equally blameworthy in all these instances? In the remainder of this chapter we will be examining a number of aspects of the designed environment and the impact of that design on our behaviors, and we will be returning to the question of who is to blame.

TIME-OUT: Consider the following known as Vile's Laws of Advanced Linesmanship (Bloch, 1983).

1. If you're running for a short line, it suddenly becomes a long line.
2. If you're waiting in a long line, people behind you are shunted to a new short line.
3. If you step out of a short line for a second, it becomes a long line.
4. If you're in a short line, the people ahead of you let in their friends and relatives and make it a long line.

5. A short line outside a building becomes a long line inside.
6. If you stand in one place long enough, you make a line.

Think of instances when each of these statements has been true for you. Now consider how the design of the location in which the incident occurred contributed to its occurrence. Finally, see if you can recommend design modifications that might render these statements moot.

C.M. Deasey (1974) quotes a leading architect as saying "good architecture is impossible until there is a change in the public attitude about architecture." A restatement in the context of the opening paragraphs is "Nothing will be done about the design of supermarkets, fast-food restaurants, airports, parks, and similar situations until the public demands that something be done." Deasey further claims that his colleague's comment is irrelevant and draws an analogy to the medical profession. The remark, he says,

> is something like a doctor saying that it is impossible to practice medicine well until the human physique is radically revised. No doubt surgery would be greatly simplified if we had a zipper in our sides so that internal inspections and rearrangements could be made more efficiently, but no doctor who still maintained touch with reality could argue that this was essential to proper treatment. The doctor works with the human body as he finds it; the designer must work with human nature as he finds it. (p. 39).

No doubt a sensible position is somewhere between these two extremes. The doctor need not require a zipper, but he (or she) certainly has to ask the patient where it hurts if the doctor is to remedy any ailments. The public need not change its attitudes about architecture, but must certainly let designers know what's wrong if they expect designers to serve them better.

When creating space, designers should to be aware of the needs of its intended users. For a supermarket designer, a valuable source of information is the shopper; when designing an airport terminal, architects should talk to travellers; for hospital design, patients (among others) may provide valuable input. Normative data (telling us what other shopping centers are like, how most airports are designed, or the standard way of utilizing space in hospitals) does little to minimize the hassle and maximize the potential of the users of that space. The best way to find out the influence of design is to ask those that are influenced by it. The best indicator of a designer's success is the comments of users, rather than a comparison with other (perhaps equally aberrant) designs.

At first this seems an elegantly simple way to evaluate the fit between the user of the designed environment and the environment itself. Users can tell designers what they don't like, what they do like, and how to get from the former to the latter. I, as a user of supermarkets, dislike waiting in checkout lines. More than that, however, I dislike the fact that others, by serendipitously choosing some other line, are able to queue up later and get out earlier than I. I want checkout lines to be equitable—"first ready, first out." Now design me a store that will provide for this.

Unfortunately for me, I am not the only user of grocery stores, and my exchanging of money for goods in the least amount of time is only one of the goals that the checkout space has to fulfill. For example, the needs of the cashiers, as well as the security guard, the baggers, the person who returns the carts to the cart stalls, the shelf-stockers, and the multitude of vendors who daily make drop-offs at the store, must be considered. Any prudent designer should incorporate the needs of all of these users in the design. Of course, in doing so, the solution is no longer "elegantly simple," and often the needs of one group of individuals are at odds with the needs of another group.

Further, as discussed in Chapter 4, self-reports of attitudes, perceptions, feelings, and even needs are subject to a number of biasing influences. So even if designers did ask users about their design needs, the user responses may or may not be reliable or valid. Furthermore, this assumes a willingness on the part of designers to gather information from potential users and then design space based on that information. Architects, however, have been reluctant to do this. In fact, Lang (1988) suggests that architectural theory, and thus architectural practice, consists primarily of normative positions espoused either by individual architects or by schools of architectural thought. And, Spreckelmeyer, Domer,

FIGURE 11-2   Waiting in lines has become a way of life in our modern society.

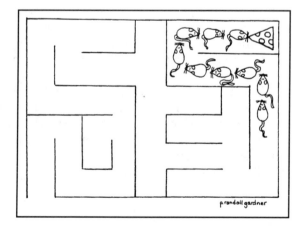

p. randall gardner

and Carswell (1985) conclude, on the basis of questionnaire information obtained from nearly 600 practicing architects, that consistent differences in perception exist among graduates of different schools, that these differences are manifested in their designs, and are a direct reflection of their respective schools. Thus, architects tend to rely predominantly on their own experiences, feelings, and ideas and tend to feel justified in doing so (Tzamir & Churchman, 1989), despite the fact that only the very wealthy seek environments that reflect the tastes of architects (Newman, 1980). Hence, our elegantly simple solution is fraught with difficulties—difficulties in getting reliable and valid information regarding user needs, difficulties in reconciling the varying needs of the various users, and difficulties in getting designers to use this information once it has been obtained.

Before attempting to develop a system of user-designer interaction that might alleviate some of these difficulties, it may be helpful to examine some aspects of the designed environment and note the impact on inhabitants. Thus, we will now turn to the effects of institutional design and, because they in many ways represent prototypical institutions and because more empirical work has been done with them, we will look specifically at hospital, prison, and school designs.

INSTITUTIONAL SPACE IN GENERAL

In an early but important paper, M. Powell Lawton (1974) reviewed a number of variables that influence the fit between individuals and their environments. To build environments that are in harmony with their users, each of these factors must be considered. Various aspects of the environment (e.g., site location, building type, design layout) as well as of the user (e.g., patient type, gender, owner/user) need to be carefully assessed and a match between them sought. As we look specifically at hospitals, prisons, and schools we will consider such factors as the inhabitants' adaptation to the institution, the location of the institution, the within-institution dispersion of space, the building type, each individual's personal (private) space, the individual's social space (e.g., lobbies, halls, cafeterias), the outdoor spaces surrounding the institution, the instrumental activity space, and staff space. We will also attempt to determine how the designs of these various spaces influence other environmental factors such as noise and illumination contribute to such psychological factors as privacy and control. We will also attempt to identify, where possible, the genesis of various design models.

HOSPITALS

The hospital is easily recognized as an institution in its own right. So firmly established is its image that the mere mention of one conjures up thoughts of long sterile hallways, stainless steel utensils, banks of life-monitoring equipment, people in white uniforms rushing to and fro, specialized rooms for specialized functions, wheelchairs lined up at elevators, and the smell of rubbing alcohol and disinfectant. The design of hospitals is so uniform that if you were blindfolded, taken inside of one, and then given back your sight, you would recognize immediately where you were. Indeed, by paying attention to changes in sounds and smells, you might even know before the blindfold was removed.

Given this uniformity in design, a paradoxical aspect of hospitals is the variety of people there. In a broad sense, they can be categorized as patients, medical staff, administrators, support personnel, and visitors, but within each of these a variety of subcategories could be enumerated. For example, the medical staff includes doctors, nurses, radiologists, X-ray technicians, and others, each of whom could be further classified with respect to his and her sundry specialties. Patients vary in terms of their age, gender, diagnosed ailment, therapeutic regimen, and thus in terms of their environmental needs. The environmental requirements of these various subgroups are not always the same and are occasionally in conflict. Visitors are occasionally "put off" by housekeepers, floor nurses by administrators, doctors by candy stripers, etc.

In fact, in some instances the needs of the patient and those of the staff are in direct conflict. For example, during surgery the patient requires a warm and moist atmosphere, whereas the surgical staff, who are under a great deal of stress, would ideally be submerged in dry, cool air. However, because the stress of the staff is of relatively short duration, and any added strain to the patient's system could be disastrous, the thermo-atmospheric environment of the operat-

FIGURE 11-3 The design of hospitals is so uniform that if you were blindfolded, taken inside of one, and then given your sight back, you'd recognize immediately where you were.

ing room is usually designed in favor of the patient. The staff momentarily suffers and recovers later.

Although the case cited above demonstrates a decision in favor of the patient, all too often the patient's psychological well-being suffers in favor of enhanced staff efficiency. In fact, if there has been an over-riding philosophy in hospital design, it has been to attempt to maximize medical personnel efficiency by manipulating the environment with the implication that by increasing efficiency of the medical staff the patients' well-being will also be enhanced. This is not always the case, however. Increased efficiency is sometimes obtained at the cost of depersonalization.

Robert Sommer (1969) describes a mental hospital that had decided to spend some pension funds on amenities for the elderly. New furniture, air conditioners and a TV were purchased for their ward. These purchases were to have a salutary effect on patients; however, Sommer described them thusly: "They were like strangers in a train station waiting for a train that never came" (p. 79). After some time on the ward, Sommer made a number of observations: (1) The patients had never been consulted prior to or even after the installation of the new furnishings; (2) the straight row, back-to-the-wall chair arrangement was *enjoyed* by the nurses because it made surveillance easier, by cafeteria help because it provided a wider corridor for their food carts, and by custodians because it left the appearance of orderliness; (3) the straight line arrangement was maintained by the patients themselves; (4) no attempt had been made to arrange the furnishings in any other fashion; (5) this arrangement was highly detrimental to promoting social interaction among the patients and, in fact, led to a greater degree of disengagement. Here is a good example of the physical design of the environment being created to satisfy the needs of the staff in deference to the needs of the patients. Incidentally, many of these physical design barriers to communication and effective functioning were later rectified, but not without some foot-dragging by the staff.

More recent documentation of the relationship between mental hospital design and psychiatric theory and practice (e.g., Cooksey, 1989; Luchins, 1988; St. Clair, 1987) suggests that experimentation in design and correlative experimentation in the treatment of mental illness has been going on for some time. Further, when the needs of the patients as well as the staff are considered, profound positive effects can be found on staff mood, staff absenteeism, patient self-image, and also decreases in patient violence (Christenfeld, Wagner, Pastva, & Acrish, 1989). Data from Devlin (1992), however, suggest that only staff who have initially high morale, and those who have to serve a less difficult patient population, tend to rate environmental variables higher after renovation than before.

Returning to Lawton's (1974) classification of design concerns we find that the institutional design of hospitals requires: "(1) permanent behavior-maintaining structures; (2) structures that will exercise latent healthy behavior that may be learned for permanent use (rehabilitation); and (3) structures that will allow for freedom of operation and expansion in scope of healthy aspects of the individual (self-realization)" p. 62. The hospital environment necessarily has to be designed to compensate for failures in individual performance (Lindsley,

1964) and where possible to raise the level of individual performance to the point where prosthesis is either unnecessary or minimized. The patient is in the hospital because the body was unable to fight off infection, because various anatomical or physiological structures or processes succumbed to environmental stressors, or because mental or psychological mechanisms have placed the individual at risk in the noninstitutional environment. The hospital environment must be designed to compensate for these individual failures. Not only do different people need different environmental solutions but even the same individual's differing and changing competencies may require, at different stages of confinement, prosthetic, therapeutic, and/or self-realizing environments.

Hospital Design and Its Effects

Most of what we know about the effect of hospital design on user behavior comes from descriptive, noninvestigative reports. Much of the literature is comprised of anecdotal accounts of patients or members of the medical profession who have been content to observe behavior (often their own) within a single setting and without attempting to validate their observations. This, of course, does not mean that their observations are wrong or that their accounts are without value. Rather, it means that additional, systematic research is required before any theory-based generalizations can be developed and before designers will be amenable to making changes in the standard floorplan of hospitals. A second difficulty with the information we have associated with hospital design and its effects is that a great deal of it is derived from patients in psychiatric hospitals. Clearly, this population should not be considered prototypical of all patients and their needs. Despite these caveats there are a number of interesting findings which are more or less generalizable to all hospitals and all patients independent of the particular reasons for being hospitalized.

One obvious reason for evaluating hospital design is the efficiency with which staff are able to provide medical care for patients. Lippert (1971) suggested the possibility that the location of nurses' stations relative to patients' rooms may be related to the efficiency of patient care. Using patient care stops as a measure of efficiency, Lippert was unable to report that design layout was a factor in nurse efficiency. Trites, Galbraith, Sturdavent, and Leckwart (1970), on the other hand, found evidence for greater efficiency and greater satisfaction in hospitals with radial ward design in comparison with both single and double corridor design. One solution to the problem of efficiency is to place the nurses in as close proximity to the patients as possible. Unfortunately, the outcome of this type of design is not always benign. Pill (1967) discusses the loss of privacy experienced by the nursing staff as a result of this arrangement. Clearly there are times when the discussion of patients and their needs require at least minimal privacy for the nurses; equally clear is the need for nurses simply to "get away" from their patients for short periods of time. Proximity in deference to privacy is probably not the design answer to efficiency.

Just as it is probably wise to design hospitals to ensure the privacy of nurses when needed, it is equally wise to design for the necessary privacy of the patient. Beckman (1974) suggests that appropriate hospital design encourages patients to leave their rooms and seek out others for social interaction. This interaction is seen as having therapeutic value. Your authors suggest that social interaction will be sought and be therapeutic only to the extent that it can be managed by the patient. Without some degree of privacy social interaction is likely to be thwarted and withdrawal behaviors are more likely to be exhibited. Finally, the issue of privacy for patients is directly related to the degree of control patients feel they have over their environment and perhaps over their own personal care, and as we saw in Chapter 5, the perception of control is very important to the way in which we deal with stressful situations.

People confined to hospitals for more than a few hours are apt to remark on, if not complain about, the number of rules and regulations they are asked to comply with and the regimentation that rapidly pervades their day and night. Patients are given very little control over the limited space that is available to them. Often the placement of flowers, or other gifts, the temperature of the room, whether the windows or drapes can be opened, the volume of the television set, the number and frequency of visitors, and the time of the day for both ingestion and egestion are controlled by hospital staff. This *low control* aspect of hospital designs has drawn the attention of researchers, leading Olsen (1978) to conclude that hospital design and its accompanying regimentation communicate the message that all patients are sick and dependent and should behave in a passive manner. Low control and expected passivity may contribute to patients becoming overdependent, and for some withdrawal from normal, healthful, rehabilitative activities, thus slowing the healing process and further delaying release.

Indirect evidence in support of this speculation comes from Wilson (1972), who has reported higher incidences of postoperative problems (physiological as well as psychological) among patients housed in windowless intensive care units compared to those in units with windows. Minckley (1968) has shown that surgical patients exposed to uncontrollable noise experienced greater postoperative pain and made greater use of painkillers than did those who were not exposed to the noise. Finally, Reizenstein (1976) has reported that patients' disclosures to physicians are more frequent in certain types of design settings than in others. All told, it can be safely said that providing patients with privacy as needed and control as desired within the hospital setting will lead, all other things being equal, to reductions in hospital confinement times. Incidentally, nurses are not immune to the effects of lack of control. Topf (1989) has shown that the inability to control noise produced by heart monitors, respirators, and other hospital equipment can influence the performance of nurses in critical care units. However, nurses who are less sensitive to noise, or who report a greater commitment to their work, experience less stress as a result of this lack of control than do those who are more sensitive to noise or less committed to their work.

Several studies, while acknowledging the rehabilitative qualities of social interaction, have nonetheless shown social and spatial density (see Chapter 10) to be negatively related to behavioral diversity within the room, to room utilization by the patient, and to overall satisfaction of the patient with the facility (Ittleson, Proshansky & Rivlin, 1970; Rivlin, Wolfe, & Beyda, 1972; Wolfe, 1975). Too much opportunity for social interaction it would seem can be as bad as too little.

RESIDENTIAL-CARE FACILITIES FOR THE ELDERLY: A SPECIAL KIND OF HOSPITAL

Among the population trends not mentioned in Chapter 10 is that a growing proportion of the population is living longer (National Center for Health Statistics, 1990). For example, in the United States the percent of people 65 and over in 1940 was 8 percent while in 1970 that proportion had climbed to nearly 10 percent (or approximately 19 million), and by the year 2000 individuals over age 65 are expected to represent nearly 20 percent of the population (approximately 53 million). Of the 19 million aged 65 or over in 1970, nearly 9 million had some activity limitations, and approximately 7 million had major activity limitations (United States Public Health Service, 1970). If we assume that these proportions will remain consistent, we can expect in excess of 20 million individuals age 65 and over to experience major activity limitations by the year 2000. Many of these activity limitations are imposed on the elderly because of specific physiological disorders (e.g., diabetes, emphysema, heart trouble, epilepsy, etc.). However, a great many impediments to activity and to mobility are the result of physical design barriers.

TIME-OUT: Spend some morning at a local hospital (make sure you get permission and avoid getting in the way). Especially observe the ways in which the physical design of the building influences behaviors. For example, are patients requiring X-rays kept waiting because their room and the radiology department are on different floors? Are food service and housekeeping employees vying for the same space at the same time? Does the location of the restroom relative to the patient's bed make it difficult to use for those requiring intravenous treatment? Are the window sills wide enough to accommodate plants sent by well-wishers? Are various out-patient facilities within the building clearly marked and easy to locate? Are they readily accessible from parking areas or public transportation drop-off areas?, etc.

Try this. When you get home draw the floor plan of the building for a friend. Can you do it? Is your friend able to find his or her way around the building given your sketch?

Finally, based on your obviously superficial observations, what kinds of changes in design might you suggest to make the hospital easier to find your way around in? to make it more efficient? Are these suggestions compatible?

Recall the person in the wheelchair in the example presented earlier in this chapter who was having difficulty negotiating a street curb. The street curb in that instance represented an impediment to activity but could hardly be considered insurmountable or as residing within the individual. Rather, the problem existed because of the lack of fit between the environment and its user. Minor modifications in design (e.g., curb ramps) would eliminate this difficulty. Likewise, a number of design modifications can be made to better serve individuals with a variety of physical impairments. In this regard it is conservatively estimated that over 30 million Americans suffer from a variety of deformities or orthopedic impairments including arthritis and/or rheumatism, diseases of muscles, bones and joints, and nonparalytic impairments of the back and spine or of the upper or lower extremities (Collins, 1991). Many of these individuals are at least potentially mobile (i.e., with appropriate prosthetic design and/or mechanical human aids many would be partially to totally self-reliant).

In addition to these impairments of mobility, the elderly are likely to have developed sensory disabilities, most notably of the visual and auditory systems. It has been estimated by the United States Public Health Service (Collins, 1991) that over 21 million Americans have audio impairments, and 8 million are visually impaired. A good number of these individuals are either able to cope successfully with their environments in spite of these handicaps or have available others who are willing to act as their buffer and provide the necessary aid for them to get along. However, a growing segment of the elderly population is finding that one result of living longer is that these physical limitations are often accompanied by various breakdowns of other health-related processes including diseases of the heart, circulatory system, and digestive tract. Many are finding that while constant care and surveillance is not necessary, some degree of hospitalization is. They are, therefore, seeking out permanent residential-care facilities within which to live out their lives.

In 1986 there were 16,388 nursing homes, 9,258 residential facilities, and 734 hospital-based facilities in the United States. These facilities could accommodate up to 1,767,497 people and showed 91.8 percent occupancy rates with over 90 percent of those occupants aged 65 or older (Sirrocco, 1989). There is no doubt that a growing segment of society requires the specialized environment that can be provided by these types of facilities. But what exactly should these facilities be like? Several commissions have been established, and in-house reports have been written that speak to the design of these residential-care facilities. What follows is a prescription for design based on a composite of the many suggestions from these earlier reports (United States Congress, Senate, 1971; United States Department of Housing and Urban Development, 1971a, 1971b; United States Veterans Administration, 1967). This prescription will be elucidated, incorporating those factors which Lawton (1974) suggested and were provided earlier in this chapter. Think of the following paragraphs as a verbal tour of a residential facility for the elderly in which various aspects of design will be noted and their *raison d'etre* provided.

Housing for the Elderly

Outside Areas. Adequate space surrounding the building should be planned for the parking and service area so that semi-trucks may back up and turn around. Because large trucks and vans are noisy, unsightly, and often malodorous, where possible the service entrance areas should be separate from and out of view of the visitor parking area. Visitor parking areas should be close enough to the main entrance of the building to allow for convenient pick-up and drop-off, and the walkway from the building door to the car door should be covered (to allow for inclement weather) and for obvious reasons should have handrails on both sides. The main entrance should be wide enough to allow the passage of wheelchairs. If possible, convenient access to public transportation should be made available and covered stalls should be provided for their parking.

Outside relaxation or recreational areas that are concrete should be paved in neutral, light-absorbing colors. Additionally, numerous wind screen and sun shades should be provided. One way to supply ample protection from the sun is to provide some seating areas with canopies. Outside areas should be attractively landscaped using different-sized trees and shrubs and a variety of flowers chosen to bloom at different times of the season to provide for continuous color. Finally, outside furniture should be easy to rearrange to allow for the vagaries of the weather, the changing of the shadows, and the confidentiality of conversation.

The selection of plant materials for these public areas should be made carefully and with a few basic rules in mind. Potentially dangerous plants such as those having large thorns or those with poisonous fruit should not be placed immediately adjacent to major walks where they may present a hazard. This is not to say that such plant materials should not be used near heavily travelled areas, but only that they should be used with discretion. Proper maintenance of plant material is necessary to assure that dangerous situations do not arise. Seed pods, berries, or fruit that may produce a slippery surface should be removed. Branches that overhang walks should be pruned to prevent eye or face injuries. Plant material is useful for providing shelter from the sun, and to an extent, from the wind. Plant materials can be used effectively as barriers in controlling the movements of people through public spaces or in keeping them away from hazardous areas. Planting materials where their shadows might prevent the effective melting of ice by the sun should be avoided (American Society of Landscape Architects Foundation, 1977).

Inside Areas. Inside public areas should be designed to provide a relaxing atmosphere for socializing. Often the main entrance can act as a solarium if the windows are large enough and situated at angles that do not allow the direct rays of the sun to shine through. With careful planning all outside activity can be observed by persons in the main building, making the task of surveillance easier as well as allowing those who are required to stay inside at least a *visual excursion* to the outdoors. Comfortable chairs should be placed for ease of viewing and for promoting social interaction. Chairs are an often overlooked commodity in nursing homes. Younger people tend to think that the same kind of overstuffed chairs they use are suitable for the elderly. However, such chairs are inappropriate, primarily because the chair arms are too low and often do not provide adequate support. That is to say, many old people need to push themselves out of chairs, and most chair arms are too low to allow them to do this. This seemingly trivial detail could lead some elderly persons to stay clear of public areas simply to avoid the embarrassment of not being able to extricate themselves from their seats.

When drinking fountains are provided in public areas there should be one regular-sized fountain and one shorter fountain (maximum height of 33 inches) for people in wheelchairs. Also, public telephones should be similarly adapted for use by the handicapped and the hard of hearing (American Society of Landscape Architects Foundation, 1977).

Hallways are a problem in all institutions, although there are myriad ways to make them seem less institutional. First, they should be five or more feet wide with handrails on both sides. Whenever handrails end they should turn in toward the wall and have some kind of tactile warning six inches before the end. Buildings with multiple halls should have each well-lit hall painted a different, easily distinguishable color. It is not uncommon for the elderly to become disoriented when faced with several halls of similar colors that can look the same. Color-coding of halls makes it much easier for them to comprehend their environment and to get around in it. "I live in the third room down the green hall" is much more descriptive than "I live in room 229." Halls and other public and private rooms should be carpeted; low pile rugs are better than shag because they are easier to maintain and to walk on.

Elevators also need some modification for use in these facilities. They should be big enough to transport a bed, and the controls should be low enough for a person sitting in a wheelchair to reach them. Institutional elevators should also be fixed so they move slower and stop more gradually than do regular elevators, and the doors should open and close more slowly. An audio intercom, connecting the elevator with the main nurses' station, is also a wise idea.

Stairways and ramps in nursing homes deserve careful design considerations. At first it might seem that making stairs wider and each step less high would be helpful to old people. However, changing stairs from the normal 9-inch step with a 7-inch riser only makes negotiating them more difficult for the elderly as they, and we, are used to a conventional step. Staircases should therefore be built with standard height and width steps so the elderly won't trip. Handrails should be provided on both sides of staircases, should be continuous around staircase turns, and should extend two feet beyond the last stair. A change in the texture of the handrail signalling its termination is desirable. Ramps should not be used in place of stairs, but should supplement them. All ramps should be at least five feet wide with double sets of handrails on both sides; one set of handrails should be about two and a half feet above the ramp and the other set around three feet above the surface. These handrails should also extend at least one foot beyond the ramp. There should also be a curb on the outside edge of the ramp to prevent wheelchairs from slipping off. All elevators, stairs, and ramps should be marked with signs that are clearly visible in the dark as well as in the light. Outside ramps should be heated in colder climates to prevent the accumulation of ice and snow.

One final comment regarding the design of extended-care facilities for the elderly. Many elderly, despite having to use prosthetic devices, remain relatively active, mobile, and in touch with the environment outside of the resident facility. Therefore, in choosing a site location, designers should be careful to assess the services of the community in and around the planned site to ensure that there are museums and other recreational facilities, public transportation, convenient shopping, and medical and pharmaceutical facilities nearby.

In summary, a significant and growing proportion of our population is or soon will be living in extended-care facilities. Many of these individuals do or will require prosthetic devices to successfully manage their environment. Design accommodations are possible and often easy to implement if foresight is allowed to be the brainchild of insight. By observing the interactions of the elderly with their environment and by surveying them regarding their needs, it is possible to design institutions that are not just tolerable but actually capable of promoting learning, enjoyment, health, and even life itself.

TIME-OUT: Take an afternoon off and visit a residential care facility for the elderly. Pay particular attention to design features which limit mobility. Are chairs easy to get in and out of? Are the doors wide enough to accommodate wheelchairs? persons on crutches? Do doors open easily enough, and when self-opening, do they give the elderly plenty of time to pass through?

Check out the drinking fountains, telephones, electrical outlets and switches. Are they all easily accessible by persons with restricted mobility? There is an old saying that "to really know someone walk in their shoes for a day." Put yourself in the position of one of the residents. What kinds of things are you able to do that they can't? Could they do these things if the environment were designed differently?

PRISONS

Robert Sommer (1976) succinctly draws attention to the conflicting goals of imprisonment by noting the words of a prominent corrections official: "We are trying to operate the prison to be both a junkyard and a salvage yard" (p. 17). In this light he remarks that corrections employees, judges, police, legislators, and inmates all have diverse, vague, and often conflicting ideas of what prisons are supposed to accomplish. It is perhaps because of these conflicting views that we see great sentencing disparity among judges, differential parole criteria, varying opportunities for vocational training and psychological counseling, and differences in time actually served by individuals imprisoned for the same offenses. Siegler and Osmond (1974) refer to this state of affairs as a "model muddle." What should be taken as the model for prisons? What should they attempt to accomplish? What is the best way to achieve those goals? What features of institutional design should be put into place to help reach those goals?

Sommer provides a list of models, each of which has its advocates and each of which is derived from a different philosophy vis-à-vis the goals of imprisonment (Sommer, 1976). These models are: deterrence, incapacitation, reform, rehabilitation, retribution, restitution, re-education, and integration.

Each of these philosophies represents a somewhat different problem to the designers of the physical facility of prisons. Very different "buildings" are required if a model of integration is being followed than if, for example, a model of incapacitation is being adhered to. The former, which aims at integrating the offender back into society, might include libraries, auto repair shops, truck-driving academies, food preparation laboratories, work cottages, facilities for conjugal visits, etc., whereas the latter, which requires only that the offender be physically removed from society, requires little more than cages. In the case of deportation or capital punishment even this minimum in design is not needed. We will now turn to empirical work on prison design features and will, where possible, link these features to the philosophy which spawned them.

The life of a prisoner is in many ways similar to the life of a hospital patient. Prisoners are subjected to control by others, to highly ritualized routines, and to a great many rules and regulations. They also have very little mobility, very little space, and virtually no privacy. The physical design of a hospital as we have seen is the symbolic representation of an "aseptic" container, and the massive fortress-like structure of the prison, with its stone walls and guard towers, is the symbolic representation of an "impermeable" container. Also, as hospitals are designed primarily with the hospital staff in mind, prisons are built to suit the needs of prison administrators. Cell blocks are often multitiered as a matter of convenience and security. In fact, a publication of the United States Bureau of Prisons (1949) comments that "the bars used in such prisons are usually twice as large, and more than twice as strong, as those used in zoos to restrain lions or giant Kodiak bears." This degree of control is so oppressive for some that it has been argued that inmates engage in self-destructive behavior as a means of regaining some degree of control. Punitive measures it is suggested only serve to increase the likelihood of more serious self-destructive behaviors (Holley & Arboleda-Florez, 1988).

Historically, the architecture of prisons has been in concordance with the deterrence/incapacitation/retribution philosophies of criminology. Prisoners must be detained, must be kept from doing harm to the general public, and must be made to pay for their misdeeds. Indeed, the penitentiary is a place for stark penitence. The result of traditional design is that prison life becomes impersonal, anonymous, and without choice. Even in the area where prisoners can exert the greatest degree of control over their lives (the cell) the space is very limited and the ability to personalize is minimal. However, Gilbert (1972) has found that restriction of movement is more important than cell size. Prisoners

FIGURE 11-4   The massive fortress-like structure of the prison is the symbolic representation of the "impermeable" container.

apparently can content themselves with small sleeping quarters if they are able to engage in a variety of activities in more than one setting during the rest of the day. Sommer (1972) adds crowding, lack of privacy, and sensory deprivation to the list beginning with the factors of confinement and restriction.

Sommer (1972) suggests that prison architecture should reflect the modern philosophies of re-education, reform, and integration. New Jersey's Leesburg prison has made an attempt in this respect by providing brightly decorated, larger, homelike cells that look out on a garden court and an attractive dining pavilion. Luxenberg (1977) has indicated that new prisons have attempted to avoid the unwanted consequences of designing for maximal security and have been successful in varying degrees.

Research by Paul Paulus and his associates has led to a number of very important conclusions regarding the effects of prison design on prisoners' behavior and health. For example, they have found, as might be expected, that single or double occupancy cells are judged as less crowded than are cells having larger numbers (Cox, Paulus, McCain, & Korlovac, 1982). Additionally, it has been shown that prisoners confined to cells of greater social density report more ailments and spend more time in the infirmary than do prisoners in single or double occupancy cells. Finally, Schaeffer, Baum, Paulus, and Gaes (1988) have shown that one form of expedient architectural intervention (cubicle partitioning) ameliorates one indicator of stress (urinary catecholamine level), even though Houston, Gibbons, and Jones (1988) have shown that physical attractiveness of institutional facilities has very little to do with prisoners' attitudes toward these places.

Wener and Keys (1988) have noted that perceived crowding, sick call rates, and isolated passive behavior all increase when the population density of prison cells increases. Given these findings, a number of corrections officials are now experimenting with designs that allow for more privacy, including conjugal visits, more mobility within the confines of the still-remaining fortress walls, and more personalizing of individual spaces by the prisoners themselves. Often in these prisons correctional officers remain in constant, direct contact with inmates (rather than in control booths), and communication and negotiation skills are fostered (Wener, Frazier, & Farbstein, 1987). However, Rutherford (1985) suggests that although architecture provides the context for these "new generation" prisons, the critical ingredient is staff commitment to run the prison as a cooperative venture.

Taking a very different perspective, Ekland (1986) provides data in support of the notion that the violence in prisons which has been linked with density is less a matter of cognitive confusion and tension (i.e., stress) as some have claimed than it is a matter of control. Adding support to this thinking, Goetting and Howsen (1986) provide data which show that rule-breaking behavior among inmates is associated with a number of parameters linked to low control including being young, black, male, having a relatively high number of prior convictions, having been unemployed prior to incarceration, and having been in prison a relatively long period of time. Only time and much needed research will tell us the impact of design changes on the behavior, attitudes, and values of the incarcerated (Ruback & Innes, 1988).

TIME-OUT: Charles, age 34, has been picked up and arrested for driving 41 mph in a 25-mph zone. His blood alcohol level indicated that he had not been drinking and he was drug-clean. He was, however, a known user of cocaine and two 1-gram packets were found in his car at the time of his arrest. He was additionally charged with possession of an illicit drug.

Brought before a municipal judge, Charles was given a two-year sentence in the city jail. His time was served in a single cell designed for two people where he had a series of cell-mates who had been given sentences ranging from three days for vagrancy to "lifers" who were waiting transfer. During his incarceration Charles was to learn the names of several new dealers, as well as methods of "mainlining" that he was not aware of before his incarceration.

Do you think the design of the city jail might have been related to the judge's philosophy regarding crime and punishment? Do you think the design of the prison may have had an effect on Charles's subsequent behavior?

EDUCATION ENVIRONMENTS

The Classroom

The image evoked by the term *educational environment* is one of students lined up in rows (perhaps in desks affixed to the floor) and facing an instructor (primarily a lecturer) at the front of the room. Not only does this image conform to the traditional classroom but it also represents the modal arrangement. There is probably a number of reasons why this arrangement is most typical, including ease of surveillance and attendance taking, ease of getting in and out of seats and in and out of classrooms, ease of maintaining control by the instructor, and others. Its genesis, however, is more likely the result of using outside light as the major source of illumination in lecture halls. Typically, classrooms are longer than they are wide, and on one of the long walls is usually a row of windows to let in light. Various investigators have studied the influence of this arrangement on the behaviors of individual students. Sommer (1969), for example, found that class participation was related to the student's placement in such a classroom, with those students seated in the front row participating more. Koneya (1976), however, found that while increases in participation as a function of seating in the front row was true for moderate verbalizers, low verbalizers tended not to participate in class discussion no matter where they sat. Along these same lines Schwebel and Cherlin (1972) found that students assigned front row seats are more attentive than those assigned anywhere else in the classroom, and Becker, Sommer, Bee, and Oxley (1973) have found that students who sit in the front and in the center of large lecture halls attain higher grades than those who sit in the back. This relationship between grades and seating position held in one study even when students were not allowed to choose their own seats (Stires, 1980). A review of this literature by Montello (1988) tends to support a consistent pattern for participation but fails to reveal any consistent relationship between seating arrangement and course achievement as measured by examinations.

Research in small classroom, seminar-type classes has also shown an effect for seating position. Sommer (1969), for example, has shown that students seated directly opposite the instructor participate the most, while those at the sides participate next most frequently. Those students directly adjacent to the instructor (shoulder to shoulder) tend not to participate at all. This finding is not unlike that of Steinzor (1950), who obtained the same results with groups arranged in circles. With this arrangement, interaction was greatest among those individuals who sat directly across from one another. Finally, in a free-choice seating situation, as well as when positions are assigned, those who sit at the ends of seminar tables are seen as participating more and as having more power. Such individuals more often emerge as leaders than do those sitting at any other location around the table. Is it any wonder that the Paris peace talks leading to a settlement of the Vietnam War were held up for months awaiting a decision on the shape of the table to be used and the positions of the delegates around it?

Before turning to recent design changes in classrooms, a number of other factors relating to design efficacy must be briefly mentioned. It should go without saying that classroom behavior, and thus performance, as well as learning will be influenced by such environmental conditions as temperature (see Chapter 6), noise (see Chapter 8), and crowding (see Chapters 9 and 10), and that the design of learning settings ought to take these variables into account. An additional factor (which has not as yet been dealt with) that may also affect learning is light. That is, both the intensity and the quality of the lighting provided in a classroom have an impact on students.

Obviously, minimal illumination is required to read a book or write a paper. And although it's entirely possible that Abraham Lincoln obtained much of his early education by the light of an open fireplace, recent evidence suggests that performance decrements can be expected if illumination is not sufficient or if it is greater than the general level to which we are adapted. Within the limits of these extremes, however, research reveals several facts: (1) As illumination increases, visual acuity increases; that is, with more light we are able to detect and recognize smaller visual details; (2) the effects of changes in illumination are more pronounced on difficult tasks than on easy tasks; (3) greater illumination allows for more accurate and quick discrimination; (4) at very high levels of illumination performance decrements are likely, because additional light can act to suppress some information cues, such as visual gradients (Boyce, 1975). If this additional light stems from a source closer to the direction in which we are looking and is sufficiently greater than the illumination to which our eyes have adapted, then we say there is visual glare. This glare can directly influence performance by rendering vision impossible (or at least less acute), and/or it can indirectly influence performance by creating discomfort or causing fatigue (Boyce, 1975; McCormick, 1976).

On the psychosocial side, illumination level has been shown to be directly related to conversational volume (Sanders, Gustanski, & Lawton, 1976), as well as to self-disclosure (Gifford, 1988). An exception to this latter finding occurs in situations involving sexual or romantic intimacy where both males and females prefer a lowered level of illumination (Biner, Butler, Fischer, & Westergren, 1989). A great deal more research is required to define proper illumination types and levels for learning and for socializing, for soothing and arousing, and for hurting, helping, and healing (see Chapter 6).

One final note regarding light involves not the light source (and thus its intensity) itself, but rather the reflecting surface and the lengths of light waves being absorbed and reflected. This, of course, relates to hue, commonly referred to as *color*. Speculation regarding the influence of color on psychological processes and psychomotor performance abounds, although very little empirical knowledge of the phenomenon is available. Despite this paucity of information, there is some evidence that color may affect people's moods and levels of arousal (Mehrabian & Russell, 1974) as well as their attitudes. Some colors are thought to induce feelings of security (blue), or to be stimulating or lead to excitement (red); others are thought to be soothing or comforting (Wexner, 1954). Acking and Kuller (1972) have shown that colors influence blood pressure and respiration rate, and Wilson (1966) has shown that color variations are related to galvanic skin response (GSR). The effect of color on physiological responding, on mood, and on attitudes may have some indirect effect on the way students view their classrooms, and thus on the amount and nature of learning that takes place.

Open-Space Classrooms. An open-space classroom is virtually a school without walls; that is, at least a school without permanent, inside, partitioning walls. The open classroom replaces the row-and-column seating arrangement of traditional classrooms. It is a large space broken only by portable partitions, desks, laboratory tables, bookshelves, plant dividers or the like. The central goal of the open classroom is to provide flexibility. Without permanent walls, space can be easily divided, arranged, and rearranged to meet the changing demands of the various classes housed in the area (Gump, 1975). It is felt that the open classroom encourages interaction between students and teachers and between teachers and other teachers. This increased interaction it is assumed has great educational value (EFL, 1965).

Research on the open classroom has resulted in a number of unsettling findings. Among these are that teachers and students alike are likely to report that this type of classroom is noisier and that the noise is more distracting (Brunetti, 1972; Burns, 1972; Rivlin & Rothenberg, 1976). Additionally, visual distractions are more common, and lack of privacy is likely to be seen as a problem by students and faculty alike. The effects of noise are more disruptive for those involved in study groups than those involved in laboratory experiences, and when the noise is conversational rather than study related (Brunetti, 1972). Thus, the open classroom has the potential to be more disorderly and for the students to be more disruptive than the traditional classroom.

In defense of the open classroom, it is cheaper to build and easier to maintain. Lighting and thermal conditions are better, and social interaction is increased. However, a number of design problems need to be dealt with before the open classroom will meet its economic and educational goals. In this regard,

---

TIME-OUT: Take a moment to consider the last classroom you were in. How well was it designed? For what purpose was it designed: to promote discussion? to promote note taking? Could the instructor be heard equally well from all locations? Could everyone see the chalkboard and read what was being written on it? Did the use of the chalkboard interfere with the smooth flow of information exchange or did it facilitate this exchange?

Having answered these questions (and others that I'm sure you have thought of), try to determine if the answers were influenced by design factors. For example, is it because of high ceilings, or lack of acoustical tiles, or noisy in-ceiling water pipes that everyone could not hear equally well? If you find that design has influenced your answers, how might changes in design change your answers? Specifically, how would changes make the environment more accommodating?

Evans and Lovell (1979) offer the following design modifications: (1) Visual and auditory distractions should be reduced; (2) activity boundaries need to have definite demarcations; (3) classroom materials need to be more unobtrusively accessible; (4) privacy areas for teachers as well as students need to be provided; and (5) some areas to which territorial claim can be laid need to be provided so students can develop a sense of personal control and efficacy.

It is felt that much of this can be established by such design changes as using sound-absorbing partitions, carpeted floors, establishing traffic routes away from heavily used study areas, providing for and allowing personal markers in certain areas, and establishing privacy islands where one can escape the direct surveillance of others.

The Dormitory

Much of the educational life of college students is spent in the dormitory. While it is true that a great deal of information is imparted in straight-row lecture halls and variously designed seminar rooms, the organizing, encoding, and committing to memory of this material often takes place in the dormitory rooms. The design of dormitories should therefore be of great interest to those concerned with providing educational settings that act to maximize learning potential. Research evidence from studies conducted by Baum and Valins and their associates (Baum, Aiello, & Calesnick, 1978; Baum, Harpin, & Valins, 1975; Baum & Valins, 1977; Valins & Baum, 1973) and by Holahan and Wilcox (Holahan & Wilcox, 1978; Wilcox & Holahan, 1976) indicates that high social density can have negative social and psychological effects on residents, particularly when the density leads to (as it often does) a lack of personal control. High-rise housing with rooms on either side of long corridors and small, common facilities (e.g., lounges, showers, bathrooms, laundries) are especially likely to lead to situations of social unmanageability and are therefore likely to be detrimental to learning and performance.

In addition to increasing loss of control, the socially dense environment may cause residents to experience louder noise levels that are intermittent, unpredictable, and often uncontrollable. This combination of characteristics is, of course, one shown to be most disruptive of performance and most likely to have residual aftereffects. Additionally, Lakey (1989) has reported that first-year students assigned to denser, corridor dormitories develop less social support by the end of their first term than do students living in less dense, suite dormitories. These findings argue against present dormitory design, which appears to be more the result of economic expedience than educational philosophy.

In a few instances college and university officials have been mindful of the possible consequences of these socially dense housing units and have allowed for some modifications such as giving students some control over their rooms (e.g. building lofts, changing floor patterns, rearranging furniture, and others) and by doing some remodeling to provide for shorter corridors and sound-absorbing partitions. Finally, at the University of California-Davis, students lived in dorms of polyurethane foam and fiberglass that housed two students apiece. The students (within limits) were able to design the interior of these dorms (Baum & Davis, 1980; Corbett, 1973). These innovative approaches to housing design have been shown to lead to greater feelings of control, less crowding, and greater group spirit than conventional design. No major effects on learning, however, have been reported.

In summary, the physical design of living and learning environments can affect the amount of learning that takes place. This influence can be the result of design features that allow for more or less illumination, more or less noise, differential ventilation, and of design features that preclude privacy or take away control. With careful planning, however, the deleterious effects of design can be minimized and the enhancing effects capitalized upon.

INSTITUTIONAL DESIGN RECONSIDERED

We began this chapter with some reflections on institutional design in general and suggested that planners, architects, and other designers pay attention to the wants, needs, desires, and behaviors of the users of the space that they are designing. Mindful of the oversimplified "question-answer-solution" paradigm for design, it was suggested that a more complex depiction awaits the perusal of existing data on selected institutional environments. If our ultimate goal is to design our built environments to promote human welfare, there are several lessons to be learned from the brief excursion we have taken into the world of institutional design. Among these are that (1) the performance of a given built environment depends not only on its physical characteristics, but on the interaction of these characteristics with the needs and requirements of the users of that environment; (2) most designed environments have multiple users and often their design needs and requirements are not the same; and (3) evaluation of a design requires more than comparing it with a "model" or prototype for that type of environment. With our admittedly cursory glance at hospitals, prisons, and schools now completed we return to reconsider the design process.

Because of their training, architects and designers are primarily concerned with the technical, mechanical, structural, and economical aspects of their designs. Has the best use been made of the selected site? Has the maximum space been attained at the lowest practical price? Does the building fit with its context? Does the building perform the functions dictated by the client? Is the building structurally sound? Because designers' knowledge limit their work, they are no different from anyone else, and it is unlikely that they know very much about the cultural idiosyncrasies of the users or of their ecological interrelatedness to the space that is being designed. It would be rare indeed if their knowledge encompassed an understanding of privacy needs, territoriality, habit, custom, interaction distances, adaptation levels, and other factors. Even if architects and planners were aware of these variables, it is unlikely that their understanding would extend to cross-cultural nuances among them which influence, and are influenced by, design and which interact with design characteristics to bring about social change (see, for example, Kent, 1991; Moghaddam, Taylor, & Lalonde, 1989, Soliman, 1991). Finally, even when individual and social needs are well understood, it is still possible that the inherent limitations of the design will preclude their fulfillment.

There are, however, a number of steps in the design process that, if followed systematically, could lead to a recognition of existing limitations and an amelioration of problems before they become incapacitating. In a very real sense, these steps are nothing more than the scientific method applied to problems of design. They are as follows:

1. Preparation (stating the problem).
2. Information (gathering relevant data).
3. Evaluation (defining desirable outcomes).
4. Creativity (determining cost-effective means of achieving desired outcomes).
5. Selection (deciding on one plan from the set of alternatives).
6. Implementation (transforming of the blueprint to a physical structure).
7. Reevaluation (determining how well the structure performs the desired function).

Wheeler (1967) has written:

> There are clearly healthy and unhealthy buildings in the medical sense, in the psychological sense and in the sociological sense. Our ability to adapt is probably why bad elements of architecture are so widely tolerated. After a while they cease to be noticed by those who are continuously exposed to them. This does not mean, however, that adaptation is without cost to humans. It requires energy to move to a new level of adaptation and it requires energy to stay there. Environmental factors that do not conform to some modal value on each of the perceptual dimensions are expensive to live with; we pay for tuning them out by using more energy or by being less effective in our work or play. (p. 4)

On the physical level, there must be some congruence between the environment and the user. A glove must have five fingers on it, and shirts must have sleeves of certain and equal lengths. Eyeglasses must fit the wearer and, more importantly, the lenses should be ground to accommodate visual defects. In all such relationships certain limits and ranges are set by humankind's physical and anatomical characteristics. The designed environment is no exception. The clearest examples, as we have seen, involve the use of prosthetic design by the disabled, but is no less true for those who are not disabled. Certain levels of illumination, certain intensities of sound, certain distances between machines, and others are prescriptions for design based on physical limitations of humans.

On the cultural level such prescriptions are not as easy to come by, and therefore the design process must proceed with greater caution. The realization that the "right answers" to design are very much dependent on the potential users of the design and on the functions to be served, as dictated by the paying clients of design, is crucial. Hall (1962) has specified a number of criteria utilized in setting performance standards for any system, including the interactive system of environment and environment inhabitant. These criteria and a brief description of each are outlined below.

> *Profit.* This criterion involves getting the best product at the lowest price. Of course, running costs (maintenance, insurance, and others) as well as start-up costs must be considered.
>
> *Quality.* In terms of design characteristics, this criterion relates to the way in which the design is judged by the user.
>
> *Performance.* This criterion relates to the design's ability to carry out its specified functions in a specified period of time. In a sense, we are talking about a system's reliability.
>
> *Competition.* What are the other design characteristics that are developed to carry out the same or similar functions?
>
> *Compatibility.* How well does this designed space fit into the space surrounding it? The concern here is with functional as well as physical proximity.
>
> *Flexibility.* How easily can the design be modified or adjusted to account for expansion or changing use?
>
> *Elegance.* Are the functions carried out in the simplest, least confusing fashion?
>
> *Safety.* Is the design not only structurally but user safe? (Recall the design of stairwells earlier in this chapter.)
>
> *Time.* How long does it take to get from the preparation to the reevaluation stage in the planning process?

To meet these criteria the designer must be adept at crystal-ball gazing; not only must the present needs and desires of users and clients be ascertained but the changing role of the design in light of the changing composition of the users must be ascertained as well. Contini (1965) has remarked that much contemporary design is for a population of 50 to 75 years ago when people were shorter, several pounds lighter, and a few years younger. And as Kennedy and Highlands (1964) have agreed, we often become trapped by forms which were designed and constructed to care for the needs of previous generations. Finally, as Rapoport (1969) notes, immigrants moving to the United States have often brought with them the architecture of their homeland, which is often unsuitable for the region to which they have brought it.

So what crystal ball do we gaze into? How do we predict the future? How can we know what to build today that will be functional in a changed tomorrow? Bross (1953) has outlined a series of prediction techniques, each of which is no doubt somewhat more accurate than the crystal-ball method, but each with its own limitations. It is, according to Bross, possible to engage in *persistence, trajectory, cyclic, associative, analog,* and/or *hindsight* prediction.

The last of these, *hindsight* prediction, if the least well understood, is certainly the most accurate. It involves prediction after the fact, and requires only a generalized "I told you so" attitude and the ability to make ambiguous (or even contradictory) remarks with an exalted degree of self-righteousness. All too often designers of our environment engage in this kind of prediction either as a means of self-congratulation or to derogate the work of others.

Equally potent, however, is the tendency to engage in *persistence* prediction. This type of prediction is based on the premise that certain things never change; consistencies are looked for over a short period of time and then are presumed to be invariant over a long period of time. It is this kind of prediction that led to Contini's remark concerning the inadequacies of design. On behalf of persistence prediction, it is true that there are a number of invariants in the use of space, and that these invariants need to be accounted for in environmental design (see, for example, Barker, 1968). Bross (1953) notes that if one is interested in predicting the weather and merely describes today's weather, approximately 75 percent accuracy will result. Persistence prediction in this instance, therefore, is relatively effective.

Trajectory prediction is a matter of observing trends and then extrapolating from those trends. Again, in predicting the weather, one might observe temperatures on three consecutive days and note that the temperatures were 76, 77, and 78 degrees, respectively. In the short run it might be a fairly good strategy to extrapolate from this data and predict that today's temperature would be 79 degrees. There are obvious disadvantages, however, for using this basis of prediction over longer periods of time. Certainly one wouldn't necessarily predict that in three weeks the temperature will reach 99 degrees. By the same token one might be able to make predictions regarding the use of the built environment over short periods of time based on present usage, but it would be much more difficult to extrapolate very far into the future using only present usage as a basis for determining trends.

Cyclic prediction depends on the lessons of history. It was first used in predicting astronomical events such as phases of the moon, eclipses of the sun, and others, and is highly practical today in, for example, the design of solar collectors, tidal turbines, expressways for inbound traffic during the morning hours and outbound traffic during the evening, etc.). Its application has not been as widespread in design as it might be, however—perhaps because natural human cycles have not been looked for as much as they could be.

Associative prediction is often used in science. It involves the observation that two events are related. Although this relatedness may certainly take the form of a causal relationship, it need not and often does not. Most predictions in ordinary life are also of the associative type, and are often oversimplified. That is, two events that occur simultaneously are often mistaken for cause and effect. All too often, however, the relationship is not causal. In fact, most events are multi-determined, so that a single association very often does not tell the whole story. Nonetheless, associative prediction is likely to be more accurate when applied to design problems than any of the others discussed, if for no other reason than the application of this method requires the careful observation and measurement of the events that are assumed to be related.

Analog prediction is based on the assumption that if two events are related with respect to certain properties, they are assumed to be alike on properties for which we know the values for one of the events but not for the others. Analog prediction depends on the richness and clarity of the particular metaphor being utilized. In design, if the aged are assumed to be like the physically ill, then the design for the elderly will be identical to the design for the physically ill. The advantage of this method, of course, relies on the veridicality of the analog, and the danger lies in its inexactitude.

Obviously, some methods of prediction are more useful and/or more efficient than others, depending on what is being predicted and the criticality of the fit between the environment and the user. Nonetheless, designers must engage in prognostication in the context of every stage of the design process. With this in mind, let us now return to the seven stages of the design process as outlined earlier in this section.

In the preparation stage of design, planners must determine exactly what they are to design. For example, in building for the elderly, are planners designing an intensive care unit, a general care hospital, a waiting room to death, small, individualized, but self-contained housing units, or what? The answer to this question will lead to additional questions about other users of the facility. In what capacity will others use the facility, and what are their special design needs? Having decided the specialties of the potential user, many facts must be gathered. Indeed, many of the empirical facts of the present chapter would be relevant to this stage of the design process. Having thus determined what designs lead to what behaviors, designers must engage in evaluation (what are the most desirable outcomes), and in creativity (what are the most cost-effective means of achieving the desired outcomes, and what are the necessary trade-offs that will have to be made). After consultation with clients, potential users, and contractors, the selection process begins, and the selected design is transformed into a physical structure. In all of the above stages the designer is engaged in prediction. In a sense, planners wager that the decision made will lead to the outcomes that were deemed desirable. Finally, in the reevaluation phase, the accuracy and the validity of the predictions are assessed. Is the structure carrying out the functions that it was designed to carry out, and is it doing so in a cost-effective and humane fashion? If flexibility was used as a design criterion, the planner will now be back at stage one and ready to proceed through the entire process once again, constantly refining the structure so that the best fit between the organism and environment can be obtained.

One final note before closing this chapter on institutional design. Much of this discussion has focused on the infirmities of design as related to user-client needs and desires. We have harshly criticized designers of the built environment for not fully considering the human element of design, or at the very least considering only those humans who have control over the purse strings. We have declared, as have others, that the fact that environments wreak relatively little havoc is a tribute to human adaptability. Without in any way backing down from these declarations, it is also true that users and clients have not fully exploited the potential of present designs, and behavioral scientists have only recently begun to examine the interdependency of humans and their envi-

FIGURE 11-5 The design process must begin and end with collection of information. Information first tells us what our objectives should be and later how well we have met them.

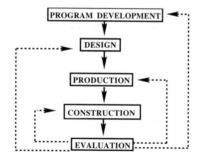

I. Program Development
  A. Problem Identification
     1. What is to be built? (entire community, large building, addition to building, renovation, etc.)
     2. For whom? (client, user, community)
     3. For what purpose? (functions to be served)
  B. Information collection
     1. Prototype identification
     2. Client/user needs and requirements
     3. Environmental and structural requirements
  C. Information organization
II. Design
  A. Develop alternative design solutions
     1. Drawings and models
     2. Evaluate
        a. Analogy: How is this design like other designs built for the same purpose
        b. Simulation: does the mock-up reveal design flaws
        c. Introspection: imagine what the effect of given design characteristics might be
        d. Experimentation: where possible, test out some of the parameters
  B. Develop the best alternative
     1. Maximize function
     2. Minimize costs
     3. Make necessary compromises
III. Production
  A. Develop detailed drawings
  B. Develop lists of materials and specifications
  C. Let out contracts
IV. Construction
  A. Build the design
  B. Involve users and designers to fine-tune the structure
V. Evaluation
  A. Structure
     1. Physical tests
     2. Simulations
     3. Panel of experts
  B. Function
     1. Questionnaires
     2. Behavior mapping
     3. Social sampling
     4. Activity logs, etc.
VI. Feedback: Evaluate information to redefine the problem, suggest alternative designs, refine production, and set construction specifications

TIME-OUT: Suppose you were appointed to a task force to determine the need for a new classroom building on your campus. What kinds of prediction strategies would likely be used in making this determination? What kind of data would be utilized to confirm these predictions? Assuming that your group decided that a new building was needed, what types of additional questions would have to be asked before designing could begin? Organize these questions with respect to user needs, structural requirements, environmental impact, institutional resources, etc.

Develop a strategy for determining answers to the questions you have just identified. What kinds of questions have to be answered first? How do the answers to one set of questions influence the answers (and perhaps even the questions) to another set?

ronments. With a clearer understanding of the uses to which the present environments are being put, accommodations in existing space-time-user relations could be made to provide for a better organism-environment fit. One obvious example is for clients to refrain from having sidewalks put in until traffic patterns among pedestrians is ascertained. Sidewalks should then be placed in parks, on campuses, and other areas to correspond to where people normally walk. Perhaps designs based on descriptions are more humane than those based on either prescription or proscription.

QUEUING THEORY

Let us return to some of the issues raised in the opening paragraphs of this chapter, and let us do so in light of queuing theory. *Queuing theory*, as the name implies, is concerned with waiting. This might involve waiting to be "checked out" at the grocery, waiting to have one's car serviced, waiting to have a telephone installed, or waiting for the delivery of a home computer. Queuing is obviously related to transportation problems: We wait in line at the bus stop; cars proceed along a highway in single file, their speed dependent on and limited by the slowest driver; planes are provided "landing patterns," and must await their turn to land. Sometimes queues are irritating (e.g., in the grocer's line, or in the cashier's booth) and sometimes they can be very costly (e.g., if workers are queued to obtain tools, or to have necessary repairs completed, or if the production line queue breaks down). Queuing theory, therefore, has a great deal to offer the designer who is concerned with planning for efficiency.

Duckworth (1965) provides a model for understanding queuing based on the concept of traffic intensity. The model takes into account the rate at which people join a queue and the average time it takes for one of them to be served. As an example, let us suppose that over a span of 113 minutes, 21 customers have lined up to be checked out at a grocery. Further, let us suppose that the succession of arrival intervals reads 2,5,8,4,6,3,7,5,6,8,7,4,3,2,6,7,5,6,5,8,4. By adding the first two intervals (2,5) and dividing by two we find that the average interval for the first two customers is 3.5, by adding the first three arrival intervals and dividing by three (i.e., 15 divided by 3) we find the average interval for the first three customers to be 5. If similar calculations are made for all 21 customers it can be shown that the average interval between arrivals would be 4.68. Similarly, the average service time could also be calculated. We might find, for example, that the average time to tally the bill, bag the purchases, and send the customer out to be 3.5 minutes. Traffic intensity in this example would thus be 3.50 divided by 4.68, or 0.748, and the average waiting time per customer could be calculated and would be found to equal to 13.85 minutes. Thus, although people are being checked out at the rate of one every 3.5 minutes and are arriving at the rate of one every 4.68 minutes, the average waiting time per customer is 13.85 minutes.

If store managers kept track of the arrival intervals of their customers and knew the average time required to shop at different times throughout the day, then they could anticipate the arrival intervals at the checkout counter and could open more registers as required, or close some of them and have the cashiers carry out other duties during slack times. The prevalent method of waiting until long lines are formed and then deploying cashiers is both inefficient and frustrating. Utilizing queuing theory would minimize the waiting time of customers and maximize the efficiency of the cashiers and, best of all, the animosity your author expressed at the beginning of this chapter would be minimized.

Incidentally, as noted earlier, queuing theory would also have application in other areas of concern to environmental psychologists, including the

FIGURE 11-6 One method of maximizing utilization of space is to restrict or control usage patterns.

anticipation of fluctuating power demands and the more efficient use of electrical generators and the more effective use of public transportation. Indeed, queuing theory has utility in any situation where all potential users of a facility cannot utilize the facility simultaneously, but rather must await their turn as specified by some procedure where service times, and arrival intervals, can be ascertained.

Obviously, queuing theory is not the only solution to waiting. Some places have adopted a "pick-a-number" system wherein the customer obtains from a consecutively numbered mechanism (ticket, token, etc.) a place in the queue and then obtains service based on that placement. Other establishments have one queue that feeds into a number of "service stations." Once you reach the head of the line, you know that you are the next to be served independent of which station is next to open up. Either of these solutions is more acceptable than the situation described in the opening paragraphs of this chapter.

SUMMARY

The efficiency with which humans function is determined in large part by the limitations and proscriptions of the designed environment. Good design, everyone agrees, is that which causes minimal human discomfort and maximum human functioning. In the present chapter we looked generally at several examples of designed environment: hospitals, prisons, and educational settings. And we developed a prescription for extended-care facilities for the aged.

A.D. Hall has set forth a number of criteria for setting performance standards involving designed human/environment interactions. These include profit, quality, performance, competition, compatibility, flexibility, elegance, safety, and time. To meet these criteria, we alleged, the designer must be adept at crystal-ball gazing (i.e., the designer must attempt to meet not only the needs of present users and clients, but must be aware of potential changes in users and therefore changes in needs). As we reviewed this literature, it became painfully apparent that the designers of institutional settings find themselves in a web of conflicting user/client needs and wishes. It is suggested, however, that they will remain in that web unless a couple of prediction strategies are utilized: cyclic and associative strategies. Each of these forms of prediction requires careful observation and data collection.

With greater data collection, empirically based design is possible at each stage of the design process. During the preparation stage the planners must find out exactly what it is they are supposed to design, and what the primary functions of that design are going to be. They must know what designs lead to what behaviors. After ascertaining the answers to these questions for client/users, they must engage in evaluation (what the most desirable outcomes are) and creativity (What are the most cost-effective means of achieving the desired ends, and what are the necessary trade-offs that will have to be made?). Finally, designers must engage in reevaluation. After the structure is built and functioning, it must be determined how well its primary functions are being served.

What is called for is data collection throughout the design and utilization processes. Too often, it was contended, designers of institutional environments merely turn out near carbon copies of what already exists, making the implicit assumption that because that's the way it's always been done, it must be the correct way.

IMPORTANT CONCEPTS

hospital design
  patient vs. staff needs
  individual differences
  efficiency and radial designs
  privacy and control
residential-care facilities
  single vs. multiple stories
  passive outdoor recreation
  landscape considerations
  table and fountain height
  dining area considerations
  multipurpose auditoriums
  color-coding
  stairway risers/handrails
  living quarters issues
philosophies of prison design
classroom position and participation

position and seminar participation
illumination and visual acuity
room color and emotion
open-space classrooms: noise, distraction,
  privacy
high-density dormitories and control
stages of the design cycle: preparation,
  information
creativity, selection, implementation,
  reevaluation
user-environment congruence
design criteria: profit, quality, performance,
  competition, compatibility, flexibility,
  elegance, safety, time
persistence, trajectory, cyclic, associative, analog
and hindsight prediction
queuing theory

REFERENCES

Acking, D.A., & Kuller, R. (1972). The perception of an interior as a function of its color. *Ergonomics, 15,* 645–654.

American Society of Landscape Architects Foundation. (1977). Washington, D.C.: U.S. Government Printing Office.

Barker, R.G. (1968). *Ecological psychology: Concepts and methods for studying the environment of human behavior.* Stanford, Calif.: Stanford University Press.

Baum, A., Aiello, J., & Calesnick, L.E. (1978). Crowding and personal control: Social density and the development of learned helplessness. *Journal of Personality and Social Psychology, 36,* 1000–1011.

Baum, A., & Davis, G.E. (1980). Reducing the stress of high-density living: An architectural intervention. *Journal of Personality and Social Psychology, 38,* 471–481.

Baum, A., Harpin, R.E., & Valins, S. (1975). The role of group phenomena in the experience of crowding. *Environment and Behavior, 7,* 185–197.

Baum, A., & Valins, S. (1977). *Architecture and social behavior: Psychological studies of social density.* Hillsdale, N.J.: Erlbaum.

Becker, F.D., Sommer, R., Bee, J., & Oxley, B. (1973). College classroom ecology. *Sociometry, 36,* 514–525.

Beckman, R. (1974, November). Getting up and getting out: Progressive patient care. *Progressive Architecture, 55,* 64.

Biner, P.M., Butler,, D.L., Fischer, A.R., & Westergren, A.J. (1989). An arousal optimization model of lighting level preferences: An interaction of social situation and task demands. *Environment and Behavior, 21,* 3–16.

Bloch, A. (1983). *Murphy's law, Book three: Wrong reasons why things go more.* Los Angeles: Price/Stern/Sloan Publishers.

Boyce, P.R. (1975). The luminous environment. In D. Canter & P. Stringer (Eds.), *Environmental interactions: Psychological approaches to our physical surroundings*. New York: International Universities Press.

Bross, I.D.J., (1953). *Design for decision*. New York: Macmillan.

Brunetti, F.A. (1972). Noise, distraction, and privacy in conventional and open school environments. In W.J. Mitchell (Ed.), *Environmental design: Research and practice*. Los Angeles: University of California Press.

Burns, J. (1972). Development and implementation of an environmental evaluation and redesign process for a high school science department. In W.J. Mitchell (Ed.), *Environmental design: Research and practice*. Los Angeles: University of California Press.

Christenfeld, R., Wagner, J., Pastva, G., & Acrish, W.P. (1989). How physical settings affect chronic mental patients. *Psychiatric Quarterly*, 60(3), 253–264.

Collins, S.G. (1991). Impairments due to injuries: United States, 1985–87. National Center for Health Statistics, Vital Health Stat. 10 (177).

Contini, R. (1965). Human behavior and building: An engineer's view. *Building Research*, 2, 15.

Cooksey, E.C. (1989). Contain the mad: Moral architecture and the nineteenth-century asylum. *Research in the Sociology of Health Care*, 8, 253–271.

Corbett, J.A. (1973). Are the suites the answer? *Environment and Behavior*, 5, 413–420.

Cox, V.C., Paulus, P.B., McCain, G., & Karlovac, M. (1982). The relationship between crowding and health. In A. Baum & J.E. Singer (Eds.), *Advances in environmental psychology* (Vol. 4). Hillsdale, N.J.: Erlbaum.

Deasey, C.M. (1974). *Design for human affairs*. New York: John Wiley.

Devlin, A.S. (1992). Psychiatric ward renovation: Staff perception and patient behavior. *Environment and Behavior*, 24(1), 66–84.

Duckworth, E. (1965). *A guide to operational research*. London: Methuen.

EFL. (1965). *Profiles of significant schools: Schools without walls*. New York: Educational Facilities Laboratories.

Ekland, O.S. (1986). Crowding, social control, and prison violence: Evidence from the post-Ruiz years in Texas. *Law and Society Review*, 20(3), 389–421.

Evans, G.W., & Lovell, B. (1979). Design modification in an open-plan school. *Journal of Educational Psychology*, 71, 41–49.

Fairfield, R.P. (1977). Humanizing the waiting spaces. *Humanist*, 37(4), 43.

Gifford, R. (1988). Light, decor, arousal, comfort, and communication. *Journal of Environmental Behavior*, 8, 177–189.

Gilbert, A. (1972). Observation and recent correctional architecture. In National Institute of Law Enforcement and Criminal Justice. *New environments for the incarcerated*. Washington, D.C.: National Institute of Law Enforcement and Criminal Justice.

Goetting, A., & Howsen, R.M. (1986). Correlates of prisoner misconduct. *Journal of Quantitative Criminology*, 2(1), 49–67.

Gump, P.V. (1975). Ecological psychology and children. In E.M. Heatherington et al. (Eds.), *Review of child development research*. Chicago: University of Chicago Press.

Hall, A.D. (1962). *A methodology for systems engineers*. Princeton, N.J.: Van Nostrand.

Hershey, J. (1974). *My petition for more space*. New York: Alfred A. Knopf.

Holahan, C.J., & Wilcox, B.L. (1978). Environmental satisfaction in high- and low-rise student housing: An interactional analysis. *Journal of Educational Psychology*, 70, 237–41.

Holley, H.L., & Arboleda-Florez, J.E. (1988). Hypernomia and self-destructiveness in penal settings. *International Journal of Law and Psychiatry*, 11(2), 167–178.

Houston, J.G., Gibbons, D.C., & Jones, J.F. (1988). Physical environment and jail social climate. *Crime and Delinquency*, 34(4), 449–466.

Ittleson, W.H., Proshansky, H.M., & Rivlin, L.G. (1970). Bedroom size and social interaction of the psychiatric ward. *Environment and Behavior*, 2, 255–270.

Kennedy, D., & Highlands, D. (1964, November). *Building and organizational effectiveness*. Paper presented at the 63rd annual meeting of the American Anthropological Association, Detroit.

Kent, S. (1991). Partitioning space: Cross-cultural factors influencing domestic spatial segmentation. *Environment and Behavior*, 23, 438–473.

Koneya, M. (1976). Location and interaction in row-and-column seating arrangements. *Environment and Behavior*, 8, 265–283.

Lakey, B. (1989). Personal and environmental antecedents of perceived social support developed at college. *American Journal of Community Psychology, 17,* 503–519.

Lang, J. (1988). Understanding normative theories of architecture: The potential role of the behavioral sciences. *Environment and Behavior, 20*(5), 601–632.

Lawton, M.P. (1974). The human being and the institutional building. In J. Lang, C. Burnette, W. Moluski, & D. Vachon (Eds.), *Designing for human behavior: Architecture and the behavioral sciences.* Stroudsberg, Pa.: Dowden, Hutchinson and Ross.

Lindsley, O.R. (1964). Geriatric behavioral prosthetics. In R. Kastenbaum (Ed.), *New thoughts in old age.* New York: Springer.

Lippert, S. (1971). Travel in nursing units. *Human Factors, 13,* 269–282.

Luchins, A.S. (1988). The rise and decline of the American asylum movement in the 19th century. *Journal of Psychology, 122,* 471–486.

Luxenberg, S. (1977). Crime pays: A prison boom. *The New York Times,* July 17, 1–5.

McCormick, E.J. (1976). *Human factors in engineering and design.* New York: McGraw-Hill.

Mehrabian, A., & Russell, J.A. (1974). *An approach to environmental psychology.* Cambridge, Mass.: MIT Press.

Minckley, B. (1968). A study of noise and its relationship to patient discomfort in the recovery room. *Nursing Research, 17,* 247–250.

Moghaddam, F.M., Taylor, D.M., & Lalonde, R.N. (1989). Integration strategies and attitudes toward the built environment: A study of Haitian and Indian immigrant women in Montreal. *Canadian Journal Of Behavioural Science, 21,* 2, 160–173.

Montello, D.R. (1988). Classroom seating location and its effect on course achievement, participation and attitudes. *Journal of Environmental Psychology, 8,* 149–157.

National Center for Health Statistics. (1990). Health, United States, 1989. Hyattsville, Md.: U.S. Public Health Service.

Newman, O. (1980). Community of interest. *Society, 18,* 1(129), 52–57.

Olsen, R. (1978). *The effect of the hospital environment.* Doctoral dissertation, City University of New York.

Pill, R. (1967). Space and social structure in two children's wards. *Sociological Review, 15,* 179–192.

Rapoport, A. (1969). The design professionals and the behavioral sciences. *Architectural Association Quarterly, 1,* 20–24.

Reizenstein, J.E. (1976). *Social research and design: Cambridge hospital social services offices.* Springfield, Va.: National Technical Information.

Rivlin, L.G., & Rothenberg, M. (1976). The use of space in open classrooms. In H.M. Proshansky, W.H. Ittelson, & L.G. Rivlin (Eds.), *Environmental psychology: People and their physical settings.* New York: Holt, Rinehart & Winston.

Rivlin, L.G., Wolfe, M., & Beyda, M. (1972). The early history of a psychiatric hospital for children: Expectations and reality. *Environment and Behavior, 4,* 33–72.

Ruback, R.B. & Innes, C.A. (1988). The relevance and irrelevance of psychological research: The example of prison crowding. *American Psychologist, 43*(9), 683–693.

Rutherford, A. (1985). The new generation of prisons. *New Society, 73,* 408–410.

Sanders, M., Gustanski, J., & Lawton, M. (1976) Effect of ambient illumination on noise levels of groups. *Journal of Applied Psychology, 59,* 527–528.

Schaeffer, M.A., Baum, A., Paulus, P.B., & Gaes, G.G. (1988). Architecturally mediated effects of social density in prison. *Environment and Behavior, 20*(1), 3–19.

Schwebel, A.I., & Cherlin, D.C. (1972). Physical and social distancing in teacher–pupil relationships. *Journal of Educational Psychology, 63,* 543–550.

Siegler, M., & Osmond, H. (1974). *Models of madness, models of medicine.* New York: Macmillan.

Sirrocco, A. (1989). Nursing home standards: 1986 inventory of long-term care places. National Center for Health Statistics, Vital Health Stat. 14 (33).

Soliman, T.M. (1991). Societal values and their effect on the built environment in Saudi Arabia: A recent account. *Journal of Architectural and Planning Research, 8,* 235–254.

Sommer, R. (1969). *Personal space.* Englewood Cliffs, N.J.: Prentice Hall.

Sommer, R. (1972). *Design awareness.* San Francisco: Rinehart Press.

Sommer, R. (1976). *The end of imprisonment.* New York: Oxford University Press.

Spreckelmeyer, K.F., Domer, D.E., & Carswell, J.W. (1985). Measuring curricular orientation in architectural education. *Journal of Architectural and Planning Research, 2*(2), 99–114.

St. Clair, R. (1987). Psychiatric hospital design. Special Issue: Architecture and design in private psychiatric hospitals. *Psychiatric Hospital*, 18, 1, 17–22.

Steinzor, B. (1950). The spatial factor in face-to-face discussion groups. *Journal of Abnormal and Social Psychology*, 45, 552–555.

Stires, L. (1980). Classroom seating location, student grades, and attitudes: Environment or selection? *Environment and Behavior*, 12, 241–254.

Topf, M. (1989). Sensitivity to noise, personality hardiness, and noise- induced stress in critical care patients. *Environment and Behavior*, 21, 717–733.

Trites, D., Galbraith, F.D., Sturdavent, M., & Leckwart, J.F. (1970). Influence of nursing unit design on the activities and subjective feelings of nursing personnel. *Environment and Behavior*, 2, 203–234.

Tzamir, Y., & Churchman, A. (1989). An ethical perspective on knowledge in architectural education. *Journal of Architectural and Planning Research*, 6(3), 227–239.

United States Bureau of Prisons. (1949). *Handbook of correctional institutional design and construction.* Washington, D.C.: U.S. Government Printing Office.

United States Congress, Senate (1971). A barrier-free environment for the elderly and handicapped. *Hearings before the Social Committee on Aging, 92nd Congress, 1st Sess.*, Oct. 18–20. U.S. Government Printing Office

United States Department of Housing and Urban Development (1971a). *The family environment for the elderly and handicapped.* Washington, D.C.: U.S. Government Printing Office.

United States Department of Housing and Urban Development. (1971b). *Housing for the physically impaired: A guide for planning and design.*

Washington, D.C.: U.S. Government Printing Office.

United States Public Health Service. National Center for Health Statistics. (1970). *Current estimates.* Series 10, No. 72. Washington, D.C.: U.S. Government Printing Office.

United States Veterans Administration, Department of Medicine and Surgery, (1967). *Bulletin of prosthetics research.* Washington, D.C.: U.S. Government Printing Office.

Valins, S., & Baum, A. (1973). Residential group size, social interaction and crowding. *Environment and Behavior*, 5, 421–440.

Wener, R., Frazier, W., & Farbstein, J. (1987, June). Building better jails. *Psychology Today*, 21(6), 40–49.

Wener, R.E., & Keys, C. (1988). The effects of changes in jail population densities on crowding, sick call, and spatial behavior. *Journal of Applied Social Psychology*, 18(10), 852–866.

Wexner, L.B. (1954). The degree to which colors (hues) are associated with mood-tones. *Journal of Applied Psychology*, 38, 432–435.

Wheeler, E. (1967). Architectural considerations in planning for handicapped children. *Rehabilitation and Physical Medicine*, Section XIX, March.

Wilcox, B.L., & Holahan, C.J. (1976). The social ecology of the megadorm in university student housing. *Journal of Educational Psychology*, 68, 453–458.

Wilson, G.D. (1966). Arousal properties of red versus green. *Perceptual Motor Skills*, 23, 947–949.

Wilson, S. (1972). Intensive care delirium. *Archives of Internal Medicine*, 130, 225.

Wolfe, M. (1975). Room size, group size and density: Behavior patterns in a children's psychiatric facility. *Environment and Behavior*, 7, 199–225.

Residential Design

12

FIGURE 12-1 Could this be the future of residential design?

TIME-OUT: Think about the house or building in which you spent all or most of your childhood years. Try to form a mental image of this structure—it might help to begin by counting the number of windows, doors, and rooms. Now walk through each room in your mind's eye, recalling as much detail as possible; consider such factors as furniture arrangements, appliances, wall and floor coverings, colors and lighting. Consider also the less obvious features: How many windows are on south-facing walls? Was your heating system forced air, hot water, electric baseboard? Were the floors tiled, carpeted, wood? What materials were used for the exterior walls (vinyl, wood, brick, aluminum, stucco)? How much insulation was there in the walls? in the attic?

Next, think about the typical behaviors that occurred in each room and try to recall the various feelings that you experienced as you engaged in these behaviors. Make a list of aspects of your home that you liked, as well as factors that you disliked. Try to think why you liked or disliked these things.

Now do the same thing with respect to a friend's house or the apartment you've recently moved into. Compare the complexity of your cognitive map, your feelings, your behaviors in these two places.

The above exercise was not meant to be just a nostalgic trip down memory lane. Rather, it illustrates a variety of issues to be discussed in the present chapter. First and foremost, the richness and detail of the image you were able to create regarding your own house relative to that of your friend's house or your current apartment can be understood in terms of the sheer amount of time you spent in your home (see our discussion of cognitive maps in Chapter 4). Indeed, humans spend the vast majority of their lives indoors, and most of this indoor life is spent at home. Given the amount of time spent in this structure, it is important to understand the relationships between the physical design of a residence and the experiences and behaviors that occur there. A second purpose of this exercise was to get you to think about the number and variety of design features that need to be considered in planning a residence and adapting to it once it has been occupied. These features range from seemingly minor factors such as the location of electrical outlets and light fixtures, through more obvious issues such as furniture arrangements, to critical issues such as the number, size, and location of rooms in a house. Many of these factors have previously been considered to be within the realm of architecture and interior design, but they recently have become the concern of environmental psychologists as well.

Another purpose of this example was to get you to think about design features of residential buildings that relate to energy usage. In Chapter 15 we will discuss the cavalier attitudes we have regarding energy (i.e., it's just there and we use it). In the present chapter we will see that this attitude is relatively new regarding residential buildings, developing hand in hand with mechanical technologies for mastering the environment; and, we will see that this attitude has serious repercussions regarding energy use. A final purpose of this exercise was to reemphasize a point made in the previous chapter: The ultimate measure of success of a building revolves around the extent to which that structure meets the needs of its inhabitants and facilitates desired behaviors there. Thus, many of the issues concerning institutional design also apply to residential design.

Environmental psychologists are concerned with design features that promote optimal adaptation and functioning of individuals and groups in the residence. This adaptation is, after all, what makes a house a home.

If you look back on your list of likes or dislikes regarding your home, they most probably concerned the facilitation or inhibition of desired feeling states and behaviors. You may have liked the kitchen because it was "bright and cheery"; the living room because it was "cozy"; the family room because of the pleasant interactions between you and your family that occurred there; or the bedroom because it was a "sanctuary" to be alone with your thoughts. On the other hand, you may have disliked the kitchen because the arrangement of appliances and cupboards was inconvenient for meal preparation and cleanup; the family room because you couldn't do homework with the noise and interruptions of other family members; or the bedroom because you had to share it with your little brother or sister!

The above examples all illustrate the ways in which the design of the living environment can have a beneficial or adverse impact on the experience and behavior of the occupants of a residence. Later in this chapter we will present an overview of this relatively new topic in environmental psychology. We will also look at physical design characteristics of residences as they relate to energy use. Before doing this, however, a brief history and cross-cultural look at residential design is necessary.

A BRIEF HISTORY OF RESIDENTIAL DESIGN

Animal Architecture

Long before the first humans bent some twigs about them to create shelter many animals were already accomplished builders. Mammals, birds, reptiles, and even some insects have shown an ingenuity and proclivity for engineering their homes. Among the more human-like animals, Darwin observed that the orangutan in the islands of the Far East and the chimpanzees in Africa built platforms on which they sleep. The orangutan is also known to cover itself at night with leaves from the trees in which it sleeps, and baboons have been known to protect themselves from the heat of the sun by throwing a straw mat over their heads. In these behaviors it is possible that we see the first steps toward human architecture. Unfortunately, we see similar behaviors among the urban homeless as they crawl into cardboard boxes or pull sections of the Sunday paper over their sleeping bodies to protect them from the cold and damp of the evening.

Primitive Human Architecture

From these rather inauspicious beginnings, humans have turned architecture and design into a discipline requiring an artist's eye and an engineer's precision. Builders in the past as well as today's primitive builders have demonstrated an

FIGURE 12-2   Many animals are accomplished architects

admirable talent for fitting their structures into the natural surroundings. Instead of trying to conquer nature, as we in the United States presently seem to do, they welcomed the vagaries of climate and the challenge of topography. Primitive people are attracted by rugged country; in fact, they do not hesitate to seek out the most complicated configurations in the landscape (see Rudofsky, 1964). This tendency to build on sites of difficult access can be traced, no doubt, to a desire for security but perhaps even more so to the need for confining a community's borders. In the Old World many towns were solidly enclosed by moats, lagoons, or walls that have long lost their defensive value, and although the walls present no hurdles to modern-day invaders, they do help prevent undesirable expansion.

In a pictorial essay entitled *Architecture without Architects*, Bernard Rudofsky (1964) introduces the reader to *communal architecture* (i.e., architecture produced not by specialists but by the spontaneous and continuing activity of people sharing a common heritage and acting in a community of experience). His essay takes us from troglodyte dwellings to grand castles, from houses carved from the baobob tree to imperial mansions. The wisdom to be derived from this primitive architecture, he feels, goes beyond economic and aesthetic considerations and touches the far tougher problem of how to keep peace with one's neighbors. The design of buildings, the materials from which they are built, and the layout of settlements were all designed, according to Rudofsky, to promote physical and social harmony.

Within this folk tradition, Amos Rapaport (1969) distinguishes between *primitive* and *vernacular* buildings, and he further bifurcates vernacular buildings into preindustrial and modern. Primitive buildings, according to Rapaport, are those produced by societies defined as primitive by anthropologists; primitive building refers largely to certain technological as well as economic levels of development but also includes aspects of social organization. In primitive societies, for example, there is a diffuse knowledge of everything by all, and every aspect of communal life is everybody's business. In terms of building, this implies that all members are capable of constructing their own dwelling, and usually do. The trades are little differentiated, and the average family has all the available technical knowledge that is required. Any member of the group can erect a building that is needed by the group, although in some cases for social (e.g., temples, or communal grain silos) as well as technical reasons (e.g., the need for additional manpower) the building may be done cooperatively by a larger group.

Because average members of the group build their own house, they understand very well their own personal needs and requirements; any problems that arise will affect them personally and will be dealt with. Users are not only the designers but also the builders. Compare this with modern architecture and design where, depending on the problem, one may have to rely on a plumber, electrician, painter, bricklayer, rough carpenter, finish carpenter, interior designer, landscape architect, carpet layer, or any of a number of other specialized artisans, in order to bring one's house to a state of livability. Primitive builders are in touch with life as it is to be lived in the home they are creating; modern builders are in touch with the structural and zoning requirements imposed upon them.

Preindustrial Vernacular Architecture

When building tradesmen are used for construction of most dwellings, the primitive building gives way to *preindustrial vernacular* (Rapaport, 1969). Even in preindustrial vernacular building, though, everyone within a particular society knows the building *types* and how to build them; the owner is still a participant in the design process. This change to the use of tradesmen, however, marks the beginning of the process of increasing specialization of trades. In fact, in preindustrial vernacular design the form of buildings does not change from the primitive; only the process does. Individual buildings are modified, but the type is kept intact. For example, when a tradesman builds a farmhouse for a peasant, they both know the type of house to be built, the form or model to be constructed, and even the materials to be used. What remains to be determined are the specifics (e.g., the family requirements, the size, the relation of site to the remaining microclimate, and so forth). The outline of the home is in the mind's eye (of both the peasant and the tradesman) at the start. Even the execution involves the use of principles applicable to every building. The major change from primitive to preindustrial vernacular design is in who actually does the building. Owner-builders are replaced by specialized tradespeople.

Rapaport (1969) sums up the characteristics of vernacular building in the following way: "lack of theoretical or aesthetic pretensions; working with the site and microclimate; respect for other people and their houses and hence for the total environment, man-made as well as natural; and working with an idiom with variations within a given order" (p. 5).

Because knowledge of the model and the values inherent in it is shared by all, there is no need for designers. A house is designed and built to be like all the other houses designed to serve similar purposes. Construction is typically simple. Tradition is honored by everyone. Rules for design and construction are thus accepted and obeyed since respect for tradition provides a kind of collective control. This approach works because there is a shared image of life, an accepted model of buildings,and a small number of building types. Individuals know their place in the greater society and therefore know the type of building available to them and its location in the community.

Modern Vernacular Architecture

According to Rapaport, tradition in the United States as a regulator of the building process has all but disappeared. This is so for a number of reasons. First, there is a greater number of building types in the United States, many of which are too complex to build in traditional fashion. Second, there is a loss of a common shared value system and image of the world and, thus, a consequent loss of an accepted and shared hierarchy and generally a loss of goals shared by designers and the public. The result is a disappearance of the spirit of cooperation that makes people respect the rights of adjoining people and their buildings and ultimately the right to the settlement as a whole. (Recently a number of municipalities have had to pass laws protecting home-owners' rights to sunlight by restricting heights of buildings on the southern sides of houses with solar collectors; with tradition and respect for the rights of others, such laws would not have been passed or needed.) The third reason for the disappearance of tradition as a regulator is the fact that our culture puts a premium on originality. In fact, we often strive for originality for its own sake. As a result, society becomes dissatisfied with traditional forms and the vernacular process no longer works. Dissatisfaction is often based on nonfunctional considerations and is linked to social and cultural factors. In most traditional cultures novelty is not sought, and indeed may be regarded as undesirable.

With the disappearance of tradition, the design of buildings and settlements became increasingly the concern of professional designers. Land developers began to determine the face of the landscape and to make decisions as to where buildings would be sited. Professional builders replaced owner-builders in construction. Tradition was replaced with laws and ordinances regarding building materials and their installation. In the United States today, we see many specialized structures, each designed and built by teams of specialists. Indeed, close to 80 percent of all residential housing is built in this fashion. This highly specialized, high-tech, architecture is what Rapaport refers to as *modern vernacular*.

Designing for Climate

A study of preindustrial vernacular design is a study in harmony; buildings are constructed with artificial, social, and especially natural environments carefully considered. R.G. Stein (1977) has gone so far as to say that the history of human buildings is a history of solar architecture. When we think of solar architecture today, we conjure up images of a rather complex and expensive series of collectors, pipes, pumps, switches, thermostats, and so forth (see Chapter 15). But while these systems are useful and do give greater versatility to us in our ability to capture, store, and redirect the sun's energy, they are not what Stein is referring to. Rather, he is referring to *passive solar* buildings (i.e., those buildings whose basic form and material were developed to introduce solar heat when advantageous and needed, to deflect or reflect the sun's energy when it was not needed, and to defer or store solar heat until it was required). Further inquiry into vernacular design shows that not only were buildings built in harmony with the sun but also with other weather conditions, including wind and rain.

Thus, as we view building design across time, culture and geographical location, we see that shelters traditionally were built to reduce the range of local climate and meteorological variations (i.e., to avoid some of the heat of the sun in hot climates, to hold more of the heat of the sun in cold climates, to take advantage of winds where they contribute to desired cooling, and to deflect or avoid winds where they exaggerate an already cold environment). These shelters were also designed to provide protection from drenching rains and chilling snows; to permit light to enter in sufficient amounts for the performance of work required in the shelter, and to keep out light that is excessive or unnecessary. Examples of such architecture may be old or contemporary. They have in common a responsiveness to the particulars of their location and to the development of nonmechanical ways to modify or ameliorate conditions. That houses in both the American Southwest and the Sahara in Africa characteristically use adobe, or clay bricks, in their walls is no accident. In these climates the day is very hot and the nights are cool. Because the buildings are made of adobe, individuals inside are protected from the hot rays of the daytime sun, while the walls simultaneously collect some of this heat. At night when the sun goes down and the night air cools, heat is given off by the adobe to warm the inside of the structure. Students interested in building performance have given a good deal of attention to the process involved here and have called it *thermal lag*. Thermal lag refers to the delay in passage of heat from one surface to another. A dense material will heat up slowly, and as it captures heat on the side facing the heat source it will slowly allow the heat to suffuse through the material until it can be felt on the other side. Adobe brick has good thermal lag characteristics.

Stein (1977) describes villages in the Republic of Cameroon on the West African savanna. These villages consist of clay structures that look like elongated beehives. The groupings respond to the social organization of their culture and provide protection from marauding animals. The layout of the buildings permits airflow through the entire complex with velocities intensifying as openings are restricted, and slowing in the larger courts used for family gatherings. Additionally, the surface of the beehives is covered with a network of projecting fins. These fins (similar to the metal fins we find on the head of a small gasoline motor) provide additional heat transfer surface to speed the cooling at night. The natives of the Cameroon utilize materials and design to take advantage of not only the sun but also the wind, and they do so in a manner that is consistent with family values and cultural mores.

Among the best examples of vernacular architecture taking advantage of the wind is the city of Hyderabad in Pakistan. The houses in this city have diamond-shaped air scoops on their roofs that utilize the wind to bring hot air from the innards of the building to atmospheres above. It is estimated that the temperature of these buildings are reduced by as much as 30°F by use of these wind scoops. These scoops are a nonenergy-consuming method of cooling the inside atmosphere (compare this with the costly mechanical air conditioning units in most American homes). While no one is sure of the exact origins of these contraptions, they have been in use for at least 500 years (Rudofsky, 1964). Additional examples could be provided showing how various cultures have used the materials available to them in creating residential buildings attuned to the greater environment of which they are a part. For additional information and examples the reader is referred to Rapaport (1969) *House Form and Culture*; to Turner and Fichter (1972) *Freedom to Build*; and to Richard Stein (1977) *Architecture and Energy*.

Present Architectural Design

In place of vernacular design, buildings in our culture today are often designed as though they were independent of environmental factors. Architects, designers, and planners are confident in the capability of mechanical systems to overcome any uneven or unsatisfactory internal conditions caused by excesses in environmental conditions. If the structure has too much heat loss, a larger furnace is added; if there is inadequate light, additional incandescent or fluorescent lighting is added; if the sun provides too much heat in the summer, air conditioning is added. Architects of the recent past thus considered buildings to be liberated from the local and specific demands of climate and meteorology that had shaped earlier architecture. Historically, as this idea became more prevalent, energy requirements climbed steadily year by year and the need for institutionalized laws and codes governing the design of buildings became urgent. Furthermore, as the building assumed a shape more and more divorced from the requirements of its environment, less concern was shown for elegance of solution and more with the critical building components (i.e., architects became more concerned with heating, cooling, lighting, and ventilation, and how these problems can be handled mechanically, than with the building being in harmony with its environment). Rudofsky (1964) claims that part of modern society's troubles results from a tendency to ascribe to architects, or for that matter to all specialists, exceptional insight into problems of living, when in truth most of them are concerned with business and prestige.

At the same time that this change in building design was being accepted, there were coincidental shifts in the use of building materials. Vinyl asbestos flooring replaced asphalt tile; sheet polyvinylchloride replaced linoleum; epoxy cements replaced sand cements, mortars and terrazzo; acrylic and other synthetic carpets replaced wool carpeting; fiberglass and polyester fabrics replaced cotton and wool for draperies, etc. Parallel with these developments was the large-scale desertion of the city by the upwardly mobile middle class and the growth of suburbia. The design and energy consequences of this shift are extensive, not only in terms of the material costs to erect a building but also in terms of the costs of maintaining them and in getting to and from the workplace, which very often remained in the city.

Despite restrictive codes, discriminatory federal mortgage insurance practices, and the general trend toward specialization of construction tasks, somewhere between 150,000 and 200,000 families in the United States build their own homes each year. To be more precise, they act as general contractors who oversee the designing and financing as well as the construction of their homes. Many of these owner-builders put in months of hard labor, including pouring the foundations and nailing on the shingles; selecting building materials and completing electrical and plumbing work; laying the carpets and hanging the drapes. Others work along with the people they have hired to help them, while still others merely supervise these people.

This brief overview of the history of architecture has shown a trend away from designing and building the residence with environmental characteristics in mind toward architecture of specialists who have relied on mechanical devices rather than design features to create comfortable living environments. More recently, however, there has been a growth in awareness of these issues among both designers and inhabitants of private dwellings. In addition to an increased consciousness of energy use in residential design, architects and designers have begun to recognize other important relationships between physical design features and adaptation to the residence. The remainder of this chapter will address these issues. We will begin by reviewing some of the research on factors related to residential satisfaction and space usage within the home. We will subsequently consider specific design features in different parts of a residence, and we will conclude by suggesting some future issues in residential design.

RESEARCH ON RESIDENTIAL SATISFACTION

The concept of *residential satisfaction* is becoming an important indicator for developers, analysts, and policymakers in a number of ways. Satisfaction has been used as an ad hoc device for measuring the success of housing developments constructed by the private sector (Lansing & Marans 1969; Zehner, 1972) and by the public sector (Cooper, 1976; Holahan & Wandersman, 1987; Rent & Rent 1978). The concept has also been used as an indicator of residential mobility and, hence, of changing housing demands (Varady, 1986). Finally, satisfaction has been used to assess perceptions of inadequacies in current housing so as to direct efforts to improve the status quo (Craik & Zube, 1976; Michelson, 1977).

What Makes a House a Home?

Sime (1986) has suggested that "space" be distinguished from "place." He argued that modern architecture has tended to concentrate on geometric space without regard for people, while psychology has focused on people without regard for their physical context. He offered the term *place* to integrate the two approaches, and he concluded that it is not possible to create a place for users simply by manipulating the physical environment on their behalf. In a similar vein, Pastalan and Polakow (1986) suggested that what "makes a house a home" is an affective bond between people and place. Their research suggests the importance of certain "life themes" in this bond, such as autonomy, privacy, and environmental mastery. Sixsmith (1986) stressed the multidimensional nature of the meaning of home, including personal, social, and physical dimensions, and Lawrence (1987) has emphasized the importance of identity, self-esteem, and personal values in the "psychology of home." Lindberg, Garling, Montgomery, and Waara (1986) reported that evaluations of aspects of housing quality were best predicted by their consequences for performing everyday activities, which in turn were highly correlated with beliefs about these activities and their role in the attainment of important life values. Finally, Pennartz (1986) identified themes of home "atmosphere," including the ability to communicate with others, the freedom to do what one wants, the ability to relax after work, and freedom from boredom by being suitably occupied.

There are two major conceptual underpinnings of this empirical work: the *purposive* approach and the *actual-aspirational gap* approach (Galster & Hesser, 1981). From the former perspective, people are seen as having certain goals, and they engage in activities directed toward achieving them. To the extent that the residential environment is seen as facilitating these goal-directed activities, incumbents will express satisfaction with their buildings; to the extent that the environment thwarts these behaviors, dissatisfaction will be expressed. From the perspective of the actual-aspiration gap approach, people view their present environment in comparison with some ideal that they believe they can reasonably aspire to. The extent to which the present environment coincides with the ideal provides the measure of satisfaction. The former approach can be thought of as *nomothetic* (i.e., there are features of design that have functional utility independent of the goals and aspirations of inhabitants) whereas the latter can be thought of as *ideographic* (i.e., design features will provide satisfaction only to the extent that they provide the utility, status, prestige, etc., that a given individual aspires to). What this means, of course, is that aggregated data are appropriate for assessing satisfaction from the former perspective but not from the latter. In the discussion to follow we will be looking at residential satisfaction from a purposive perspective. That is, we will be looking at design features of various aspects of our living space with an eye to how these features carry out their *raison d'etre*.

Residential Preference

Some research on residential satisfaction has dealt with preferences for one setting over another. Not surprisingly, this research has indicated that most people in the United States prefer single-unit suburban dwellings over multiple-unit urban residences (e.g., Cooper, 1976). The primary reason for this preference is that the single-family unit prevents unwanted excessive interaction with neighbors (Michelson, 1977). This preference can be easily understood in terms of our discussions of territoriality and privacy in Chapter 10. The home appears to be a critical physical mechanism for satisfying the need to establish a permanent spatial location that the individual considers as his or her private domain, and which serves as a base for regulating social interaction. Thus, the home physically separate from other buildings is most likely to facilitate this *interpersonal boundary control* (Altman, 1975). However, financial factors preclude the possibility of the single-unit residence for many, accounting for the increased popularity of the double-unit townhouse and multiple-unit condominiums.

Preference for dwelling types has been shown to vary as a function of age (Michelson, 1977) and socioeconomic status (Salling & Harvey, 1981). For example, younger families report a greater preference for the single-unit structure than do older couples, and neighborhood interaction has been shown to be a more important determinant of residential satisfaction for inner-city residents than for suburbanites. Again, these differences can be understood in terms of the differing needs and resources of the relevant individuals.

Space Use in the Home

A considerable amount of research on residential satisfaction has concerned the uses that various rooms in the house serve. For example, Black (1968) reported that leisure reading is most likely to occur in the living room, Mehrabian (1976) suggested that the kitchen is likely to be the hub of activity in the household, and Parsons (1972) pointed out that the bedroom is the place where the most time is spent in the house. Finally, Kira (1976) has conducted extensive studies of the use of bathrooms. As we shall see later, this knowledge can be very useful in designing residential environments to suit the behaviors most needed or desired in different parts of the home.

Although the above studies are helpful for their descriptive data, other research has dealt with prescriptive suggestions for residential design. For example, Altman, Nelson, and Lett (1972) emphasize the need to consider differences in family privacy regulation in residential design. They distinguish between *open* vs. *closed* families. The former tend to rely less on physical barriers (such as closed doors) than do the latter for maintaining privacy for individual family members. Also, Steidl (1972) has reported evidence that the size of rooms and the floor plan of a house are important determinants of residential satisfaction. This kind of research can be very helpful to the architect and interior designer in planning a home.

Actually, in some respects, these professionals are ahead of psychologists in recognizing the importance of these issues and in incorporating them into residential design. In the next section of this chapter we will review some of the insights that these professionals have contributed to residential design. We will begin by discussing important concepts in the interior design profession, then turn to their application in the context of specific design features of parts of the residence.

BASICS OF INTERIOR DESIGN

In his text, *Interior Design*, John F. Pile (1988) suggests that "excellent design satisfies three essential criteria: it works well, serving the needs and requirements of its users; it is well made of good, appropriate materials; it is aesthetically successful" (p. 27). He identifies a number of basic design concepts, including: (1) *size* (both absolute and relative), (2) *scale* (size in relation to other space), (3) *proportion* (relationship of parts to each other and the whole), (4) *harmony/unity* (design elements that relate to each other and an overall theme), and (5) *variety/contrast* (elements that are set apart from one another to relieve monotony), and he suggests that these concepts be simultaneously considered when designing living space.

Planning

While the above design concepts would seem to emphasize the aesthetics criterion, equally important to interior design is planning for function. John Pile discusses this process in the context of designing space. The process begins by evaluating the available space. Some important criteria he suggests are illustrated in Figure 12-3 on pages 236-237, which shows examples of poorly planned and well-planned houses. He uses the term *program* to mean a precise statement of the user's requirements and the problems to be surmounted in achieving these objectives. Programming typically involves diagramming the space after measurements have been made and drawing a plan to scale. After the initial programming and diagramming have been completed, the designer then begins to sketch possible space plans. Pile states that it is difficult to describe exactly how the planner arrives at a particular completed design, but there are some basic criteria to be borne in mind, such as traffic flow, furniture arrangement, the nature of the activities to take place in various spaces, and the positioning of spaces vis-à-vis one another.

Human Factors

Although it may not be possible to specify a formula for arriving at a completed design, interior designers are increasingly recognizing the value of research directed at enhancing the "fit" between humans and their built environment. The term *human factors* refers to an area of research concerned with bodily dimensions, comfort levels, sensory performance, and cognitive functioning. This research provides useful information in designing environments that promote optimal functioning by taking into account human limitations and expectations when interacting with technology. Examples of this type of information would include range top height for the typical homemaker, safe and visible upper cupboard heights, distances between the oven door when down and facing cabinets, etc. Without this type of data, the planning process could result in designs that are uncomfortable, inefficient, and even unsafe.

In addition to normative information regarding typical human characteristics, good interior design employs research regarding the specific needs and desires of the particular user. Thus, the interior designer needs to objectively assess characteristics of the future resident before planning the design, and should also systematically evaluate the adequacy of the resulting design. Of course, knowledge of research discussed in earlier chapters (e.g., regarding personal space, privacy, and territoriality) can also be useful in helping the resident clarify what his or her needs are.

The purpose of the exercise below is to counter a common response of individuals when introduced to the field of interior design (i.e., that most of this is self-evident and just represents good common sense). It is true that good

---

TIME-OUT: Take a few minutes to draw a floor plan of what you would consider to be an ideal home for yourself. Include sketches of arrangement and placement of furniture, appliances, and fixtures. Then make a list of specific factors that should be considered in the design of each room of the home. Include things such as design features that would promote particular activities, space use, building materials, lighting, and floor covering. Do this before reading the next section of this chapter. After you have completed your design plan, compare it to the design features discussed below.

FIGURE 12-3a This plan contains some serious problems

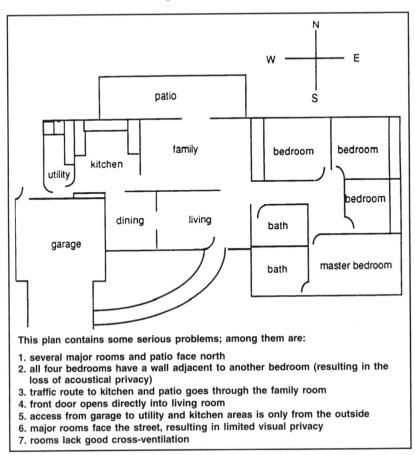

This plan contains some serious problems; among them are:

1. several major rooms and patio face north
2. all four bedrooms have a wall adjacent to another bedroom (resulting in the loss of acoustical privacy)
3. traffic route to kitchen and patio goes through the family room
4. front door opens directly into living room
5. access from garage to utility and kitchen areas is only from the outside
6. major rooms face the street, resulting in limited visual privacy
7. rooms lack good cross-ventilation

design does require common sense. It is also true that a well-designed residence is self-evident—indeed, a useful criterion of good design is that the user does not even think about it. However, as you read the following, it is likely that many of the design features discussed were not incorporated into your design plan. These discrepancies should convince you of the value of systematic study of interior design.

Much of what follows is taken from a book entitled *Inside Today's Home*, by Ray and Sarah Faulkner (1975). The Faulkners' book is a standard text employed in courses on interior design, and as such represents somewhat of a departure from a strictly researched-based approach to residential design. Interior designers view themselves as much artists as technicians, and the Faulkners' text is intended as a guide in training interior designers to practice their art according to the unique demands of any particular design problem. Thus, you should view the next sections in much the same way as those in the previ-

FIGURE 12-3b This plan is relatively problem-free.

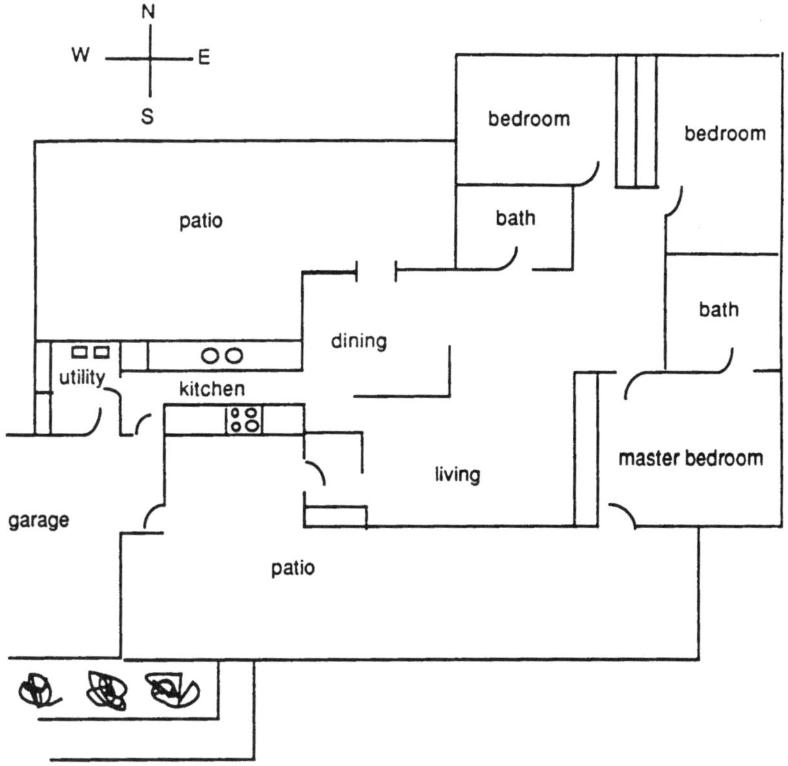

Good design should have all or most of these conditions:

1. the major rooms face south
2. no major rooms face the street
3. two outdoor living spaces
4. garage has direct access to utility room and kitchen
5. second bath is accessible to all living spaces
6. there is direct access to the patio from master bedroom
7. bedrooms do not share common partitions, thereby providing acoustical privacy
8. main entrance does not open into major living space

ous chapter concerning the residential-care facility (i.e., as a verbal tour through a well-designed home).

As we consider specific design issues in different parts of the residence, much of what will be said should sound familiar to you. The reason, of course, is that the same design principles discussed concerning institutional design apply to residential design. Thus, the stages of preparation, information gathering, evaluation of alternatives, creativity in achieving desired outcomes, selection, implementation, and reevaluation should be followed in designing (or redesigning) a home. Here, also, we will see an emphasis on sensitivity to user wants and needs through frequent and clear communication between the designer and the resident at each stage of the process. Finally, as illustrated in the example at the beginning of this chapter, a theme running throughout the following is that design decisions should be made with a primary consideration to the functional value of design alternatives in promoting optimal experience and functioning within the home.

Creating a Lifespace

In planning the design of a residence, various levels of analysis need to be employed. It is perhaps best to think of a house as a system, with the dynamic elements of the system beginning at the smallest level of analysis (e.g., the individual room), through intermediate levels (e.g., floor plan, exterior design, landscaping), to broader levels (e.g., neighborhood, community, geography, and even culture). Of course, existing in reciprocal relationships with these elements of the system is the individual person and/or family that inhabits the dwelling.

Faulkner and Faulkner chose the term *lifespace* to describe this system to engender an awareness of the importance of the human element in physical design systems. They invoke the concept of territoriality (see Chapter 10) as central to the idea of lifespace, emphasizing that the lifespace should promote feelings of belonging, safety, and comfortable familiarity. Territoriality is not only important for the house as a whole, but each member should also have some territory that is inviolate to other household members.

Factors in Planning the Lifespace. Several factors should be considered in planning the lifespace. For example, the lifespace can be designed to counteract climate (e.g., designing the interior in "warm" colors to create an atmosphere of "snugness" in a house in Minnesota) or location (e.g., employing mellow furniture, soft textures, and growing plants to offset the harshness of a basement apartment in the city). An optimal lifespace should be planned to provide appropriate degrees of both privacy and interaction with others. Planning the lifespace should also take into account the daily cycles of individual members, accommodating conflicting schedules and promoting harmonious relations between members. Issues such as the proportion of time spent in various activities in the home, as well as where these activities take place should also be considered. Finally, assessment should be made of individual differences in need for space, preferences for certain floor plans, and tastes in "atmosphere" and decor.

Goals in Planning the Lifespace. The Faulkners point out that it would be possible to design a dwelling that addresses all of the above issues, yet is still not a satisfying home. In discussing what constitutes good home design, they give an example of a well-designed chair meeting the criteria of: "Utility if it gives comfortable support, economy if it is worth the original cost, time, energy and money necessary for its maintenance, beauty if it gives pleasure when seen or touched, and character if it suits the individual or group so well that it 'belongs' in the home, yet at the same time has special qualities of its own" (p. 21). Thus, a well-designed house is one that serves its purposes (e.g., has adequate spaces for activities, storage, and effective lighting and plumbing), is economical (in terms of human, material, monetary, and environmental resources), pleases the senses of the inhabitants, and expresses the personality of its owners.

Creating the Lifespace.   A suggested system for applying the above principles is to follow five steps in the planning process: (1) inventory present possessions and list expected additions, (2) list preferred activities, (3) decide on the general character of the home, (4) learn ways and means of achieving the desired character, and (5) consider finances, both short and long term. This process is not dissimilar from the stages of the design process discussed previously, and this process necessarily involves clear and effective communication between designer and user.

Group and Private Spaces in the Residence

Two major categories of space in the residence concern the use of that space by solitary individuals and space that is shared by groups within the household. We will now discuss some of the Faulkners' recommendations for the design features promoting optimal functioning in each type of space, beginning with the latter.

Entertainment/Leisure.   Probably the most frequent shared use of space in the residence entails some form of entertainment or leisure. Design features facilitating several examples of these activities follow. Conversation is facilitated by comfortable chairs arranged in a circular or elliptical pattern with a total diameter of the seating area not exceeding 10 feet, but allowing at least 3 feet between chairs that are opposite to one another (see discussions of personal space in Chapter 10). Moderate intensity lighting should be used, and tables or shelves should be located near chairs for ease in placing objects such as coffee cups. Reading requires seating that gives adequate support to the back, neck and arms, light coming over the shoulder, and security from distracting sights, sounds, and traffic. Enjoyment of music is promoted by seating arrangements that permit a balanced projection from multiple speakers, rooms whose opposite surfaces are not parallel to each other or in which the space is broken up in some way, and by sound-reflecting acoustical materials. For television viewing, seats should be arranged within a 60 degree angle of the screen, the screen should be as near eye-level as possible, and low-intensity lighting should be used. Children's play areas should be large enough for toys and boisterous activities and in close proximity to bathrooms, kitchens, or outdoors. Consideration should also be given to sturdy surface materials and ease of adult supervision of play.

Dining. Eating is a special communal activity and is often the only time when the entire household is congregated in the same location. Convenience to kitchen access, freedom from excessive noise, and pleasant surroundings and table settings promote the enjoyment of this group activity. Surfaces should be 30 inches high, seats should provide upright support, and nonglaring lighting should be employed. A dining area with at least one side opening to another area of the house facilitates serving larger numbers on special occasions such as holidays. Snack and quick-meal areas should be designed with speed and economy of effort in mind, while minimizing interference with other activities. Counters and stools adjacent to the cooking area often serve this function well.

Sleeping and Dressing. Foremost among the private spaces in the residence is the bedroom. As noted earlier, this is the room where individuals spend the largest proportion of their time. A well-designed bedroom not only facilitates sleeping, but is also a place for relaxing, reading, study, or self-reflection. Minimal requirements for the bedroom are a bed or beds long and wide enough for occupants, a bedside table, a light source next to or over the bed, control of natural light by draperies, and quietness. Other design considerations concern space for standing, stretching, turning and bending, seating to facilitate dealing with hosiery and shoes, counters for cosmetics, and facial and full-length mirrors for grooming. The number, location, and layout of bedrooms will depend on the specific needs of the inhabitants.

Hygiene. Kira (1976) has argued that the bathroom is the one room of the residence that has been most-neglected in research, despite its obvious importance in our daily lives. The Faulkners have succinctly described this situation: "For several decades bathrooms were the home's most standardized utility, and until recently we took for granted the three unrelated white fixtures jutting conspicuously out into the smallest room of the house. Walls were invariably of plaster or tiles, timidly pastel in color. Small, hard-to-reach windows offered the only access to the outside world—if indeed they existed at all. Such bathrooms promised little beyond dispiriting efficiency and often failed to live up to even that minimum essential" (p. 54).

In recent years, however, the bathroom has come under scrutiny regarding design alternatives that might enhance the function that this space serves in the residence. Some basic requirements of bathroom design include a minimum size of 5½-by-6 feet (for single occupancy only), a door that, when opened will not hit a person at any of the fixtures and which will shield the toilet without giving a full view when left partially open, and lighting adequate for grooming. Other design considerations involve window placement, arrangement of fixtures, storage, and shape/size of fixtures.

In general, private spaces and group spaces should be located in separate parts of the house. This promotes the privacy function of the former by preventing unwanted noises and unnecessary intrusions by individuals engaged in leisure or support activities. It is to these support spaces that we turn next.

Support Spaces

Faulkner and Faulkner refer to support spaces as those areas of the residence responsible for the maintenance of daily living. Indeed, it would be very difficult to function in a home without support spaces. The smooth day-to-day functioning of the home depends on the ease with which the support spaces facilitate the accomplishment of mundane yet essential tasks such as food preparation and clothing cleaning and repair. In this section we will discuss design recommendations for promoting optimal functioning in these important spaces.

Kitchens.   The major support space in the residence is the kitchen. While not everyone can have a "dream kitchen," a great deal of research and effort has gone into planning the average kitchen to maximize its efficiency and attractiveness. Three major principles in kitchen design are (1) *Physical limitations* of the principal cook need to be considered to maximize comfort and effectiveness, (2) the kitchen is best organized around *work centers* arranged in logical sequence, and (3) the principle of *first use*—storage of items where needed rather than by category fosters efficiency.

The Faulkners suggest design features for several major work centers in the kitchen. The *refrigerator center* should be placed either first or last in the work sequence; it should have a counter at least 18 inches high by the latch side for holding supplies, wall cabinets for cold food storage containers and a base cabinet for refrigerator and freezer supplies. The *mixing center* should be placed either between the sink and the refrigerator or next to the cooking center. It should have a counter at least 3 feet wide, 32 inches high (in contrast to the typical height of 36 inches), and a stool and knee space should be provided. Sufficient electrical outlets for small appliances and wall and base cabinets for supplies should be located in close proximity to this center. The *sink center* should have counters on both sides at least 18 inches wide and 36 inches high. A dishwasher should be placed to the left of the sink and near dish-storage cabinets. Trash and garbage storage should be within easy reach of both the mixing and sink centers. The *cooking center* should have a heat-resistant counter 24 inches wide and 36 inches high on at least one side of the range. Built-in wall ovens are desirable because they avoid the need to stoop and they create more counter space. Here also cabinets for cooking utensils should be nearby, and adequate ventilation by a quiet exhaust fan should be provided. Finally, the *serving center* should be placed between the cooking center and the eating table. It also should have adequate counter and cabinet space.

All of the above design recommendations clearly facilitate ease of functioning and should minimize the tedium of performing daily tasks. Finally, a well-planned closet should be either in or near the kitchen for storing cleaning supplies. The arrangement of the work centers discussed above usually begins with the placement of the sink (since it is the most used), with the other centers located around it according to the busiest paths between them and the dining area. Arrangements should minimize traffic by others not involved in meal preparation or cleanup, and distances between centers should be short and the routes as direct as possible. Several standard arrangements are depicted in Figure 12-4.

Utility Rooms. Utility rooms generally can be classified as either laundry, sewing, or workshop. The laundry area should be designed to facilitate receiving, sorting, and preparing clothing, in addition to washing, drying, folding, and ironing. Sewing areas should include a sewing machine table, and upright chair, a cutting surface, adequate storage, an ironing board, and good lighting. Workshop areas should be isolated from the rest of the house to prevent noise, odors, and debris from reaching living areas. Sufficient tool storage, electrical outlets, and, if possible, a sink should be included.

FIGURE 12-4 Depending on one's personal needs and the design of the remainder of the house, a variety of kitchen layouts are possible.

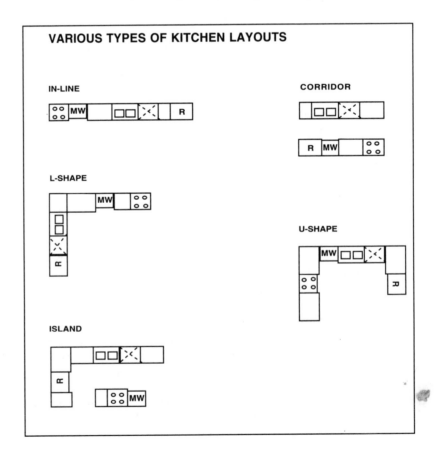

General Storage. Builders frequently give a much lower priority to spaces for general storage than to the spaces described in the preceding sections, and potential occupants of a residence often do not give these spaces much thought when examining the building. However, this inattention is often regretted when a family moves into a residence and members find that they have no convenient place to put their possessions. The Faulkners offer a few general guidelines for planning these spaces. They recommend a storage wall consisting of built-in shelves, drawers, and cupboards as a decorative and practical place to store a variety of objects from books and knickknacks to puzzles and games. These units can be placed either along a wall or at right angles from a wall, thereby functioning as room dividers as well. Larger spaces in closets should be designed for easy storage and access to bulky equipment such as vacuum cleaners, folding chairs, and sports equipment. Even larger empty spaces should be available for limited-use items such as suitcases, tents, out-of-season clothing and sports equipment, and furniture that is not currently used but is not ready for discard (e.g., baby cribs).

Support Systems

Support systems include things such as lighting, heating, and walls. Important issues such as different kinds of systems (e.g., incandescent vs. fluorescent lights or conduction vs. convection heating), the orientation of windows, and the materials used in constructing walls have typically been taken for granted by modern societies and have been left to the designer or builder to decide between alternatives. As we saw earlier in this chapter and will discuss in Chapter 15, these decisions have often been made without regard to factors such as climate or energy usage. While these issues can be quite complex and technical, in the following we will review some of the considerations the Faulkners recommend be taken into account in planning the lifespace. Many of the design considerations discussed in the previous sections apply here as well. All of these systems should be incorporated in the residence with the goal of facilitating efficiency, comfort, and optimal functioning.

Lighting. Two categories of illumination are relevant here: natural daylight and artificial light. With regard to the former, the amount of direct sunlight that comes into the home needs to be regulated to allow a desirable amount of natural light without overwhelming a room. This is especially important where large wall areas consist of glass. Factors such as the orientation of the house on the site, the presence or absence of sun-shielding trees, the possibilities for skylights, and the type of window covering can be brought to bear on the problem of allowing enough light to prevent a dim, gloomy atmosphere on the one hand, while preventing glare on the other. Some of these factors will be discussed in the context of wall design, and we turn next to a consideration of issues in artificial illumination.

Two major types of artificial lighting are employed in most residences: (1) incandescent light is produced by heating a metal (usually tungsten) via an electric current to a temperature at which it glows, and (2) fluorescent light (also called cold light), which is produced by activating gases (usually mercury and argon) via an electric current in a glass tube coated with fluorescent powder. Invisible ultraviolet rays produced by the gases cause the fluorescent coating to produce visible light. The advantages of incandescent lighting include inexpensive fixtures and bulbs, absence of a flicker or hum, and less likelihood of radio or television interference. Advantages of fluorescent lighting include a life up to 10 times as long as incandescent bulbs, absence of heat production and a considerably larger light source, which spreads the light more and produces less glare.

Apart from the decision to employ one of the above two types of illumination, Faulkner and Faulkner distinguish between the need to consider general lighting vs. local lighting. General lighting (e.g., ceiling fixtures) provides uniform lighting by shining either directly on objects or indirectly via reflectance off a surface such as the ceiling. General lighting is desirable in that it reduces shadows and harsh contrasts in lighting, but it is too diffuse for performing specific tasks or activities. Local lighting (e.g., lamps or wall fixtures) provides this kind of illumination. In addition, local lighting can be employed to create moods, emphasize objects, or simply create sensory variety in a room. If possible, both types of lighting should be available to facilitate any or all of these functions.

Some of the design considerations to keep in mind with lighting include: (1) brightness (to avoid both fatigue produced by glare or blandness from too much uniformity), (2) location and direction (which concerns the placement of fixtures at an optimal distance and orientation given a particular wattage), and (3) activities taking place in a particular area (e.g., providing general and local illumination to facilitate flexibility in living room use and spot lighting in baths and kitchens to facilitate grooming and cleaning). A final consideration is the placement of switches and outlets for light sources. Switches should be placed next to access doors, and ideally should be selective in providing current for general vs. local lighting. Switches should also be placed at both ends of hallways and stairs. An outlet should be present on each wall that is 3 or more feet wide and separated from other walls by a door or window.

Heating. Faulkner and Faulkner suggest that while many inhabitants of modern dwellings may express surprise at the lack of central heating in the homes of their great grandparents, our great grandchildren may be equally surprised at the inattention to important factors such as house orientation, design, and materials in current homes. As we discussed earlier in this chapter, recent designers and residents have tended to rely on mechanical devices to produce comfortable temperatures without regard to climate or to implications for energy use.

Environmental considerations to keep in mind regarding house orientation include sun, wind, slope of site, changes in elevation, the presence of trees or adjacent bodies of water. While these considerations will vary dramatically between geographical regions and even between sites in the same general area, two general rules of thumb should always be employed in planning a residence: (1) If possible, large glass areas should face the south or southeast, and (2) the opposite side of the house should be sheltered with opaque and insulated materials. If possible, the northwest side of the house should be partially submerged in a hillside to protect from cold winter winds and hot summer sun.

Next to orientation, a critical feature of climate control is insulation. Four standard insulation materials are available: (1) porous substances (e.g., fiberglass) available either loose or in battens nailed between studs in walls, (2) rigid panels installed between the roof decking and finished roofing, (3) thick panels (e.g., vinyl-faced fiberglass) on interior walls, and (4) foam (e.g., sprayed polyurethane) either between interior and exterior walls or as an interior finish. Wall materials also influence insulation value. For example, dense and uniform materials such as metal and glass permit a great deal of heat and cold conduction, whereas porous materials such as wood or concrete are better insulators. Other factors that should be considered are weatherstripping doors and windows to reduce drafts and the use of double-glazed windows and storm windows to reduce heat and cold conductance. In general, a properly insulated house uses only 50 percent of the energy to heat than a poorly insulated house, a fact that current and future homeowners would do well to remember.

The major types of heating systems include heating air in a warm-air furnace, heating water in a boiler, sending electricity through a resistant conductor, or extracting heat energy via a heat pump. Heat can be transmitted throughout the house by conduction through solid matter, by convection (i.e., moving air currents), or by radiation (where heat jumps from one object to another without heating the air in between). Faulkner and Faulkner discuss the merits and problems of three basic ways in which heat is brought into rooms: (1) Registers convect air warmed in a furnace, produce quick heat, and are relatively inexpensive (e.g., the same registers can be used for heating and cooling). Problems include interference in furniture arrangement and fluctuations in temperature. (2) Baseboard heaters generate heat by circulating hot water/steam or electricity through resistance coils. They provide uniform temperatures, but can be expensive to install and operate, and they are slow to heat or cool. (3) Radiant panels, located in ceilings or floors, heat these surfaces by water or air heated in a furnace or by wires converting electricity to heat. They heat by radiation, thereby warming objects while keeping the air relatively cool. These systems are quite expensive both to install and operate.

Wall Design. Faulkner and Faulkner point out that walls serve a variety of important functions besides simply supporting the roof. They provide protection and privacy, affect heat, light and sound, and govern the shape, size, and character of both the exterior and interior of a house. Traditional walls have been thick, opaque and fixed, and they provided vertical support of the roof. The Faulkners note recent trends, however, toward nonsupport walls that are sometimes thin or transparent, movable or include cutout views of adjacent rooms. As with the other support systems discussed above, walls have generally been taken for granted with little attention to important design features.

With respect to interior walls, important design considerations include: (1) the character of wall materials (e.g., *active materials* such as patterned wallpaper, tiles, or grained wood arouse sensory interest, while *passive materials*, such as smooth plaster or uniformly painted wallboards are less stimulating); (2) the degree of enclosure versus openness (e.g., opaque walls, dark colors, and small windows promote the former, while transparent or translucent surfaces promote the latter); (3) the degree of light absorption/reflection (e.g., lighter materials increase perceived room size); and (4) sound absorption/reflection (e.g., hard surfaces such as metal, plastic or glass reflect sound, while soft surfaces such as cork or fabric absorb sound). Additional factors to be considered are the durability and ease of maintenance of materials, as well as the specific uses for the room (e.g., a den versus child's playroom).

While typical materials for the interior walls of a house include plaster, plywood, gypsum board, and paneling, the structural frame of most houses consists of wood studs placed 16 inches apart (a useful fact to remember when hanging things!). Exterior layers of walls typically consist of brick, stone, protected wood, or metal.

The above discussions of lighting, heating, and walls represent only a few of the support systems that should be carefully considered in residential design. For example, similar design features should be considered in selecting and planning ceilings and floors, as well as floor-covering materials. This brief review was meant to give an understanding of some important issues concerning technical factors in the physical design of a residence. We turn next to a consideration of the broadest level of consideration of a home: the organization of space.

Organization of Space

Organization of space in the residence typically refers to the floor plan, and deals specifically with the arrangement of the various spaces discussed above in relation to one another. We have mentioned some issues in this regard at various points in the preceding discussion, but here we will briefly comment on some general factors that should be considered in floor plans.

Open versus Closed Plans. Faulkner and Faulkner define the *closed plan* as one which divides space into separate rooms for specific activities. It allows for maximal privacy and permits conflicting activities to occur simultaneously without interference. The closed plan does limit flexibility in the use of space, however. The *open plan* provides a minimum of fixed, opaque, floor-to-ceiling partitions, and a maximum of flexible group space. In this plan, space is organized as a continuous entity, flowing from one section to another, creating a sense of spaciousness. It has the disadvantages of noise transmission and lack of privacy.

Needless to say, the choice of one plan over the other depends on the individual family. Indeed, the research by Altman, Nelson, and Lett (1972) discussed earlier in this chapter concerning open vs. closed families has direct relevance here. For example, the latter would be well-advised to avoid the open floor plan. Here again we see the importance of considering the needs of the inhabitants in the organization of space in the residence.

Types of Living Plans. The two basic determinants of shaping a plan are the intended occupants and the available space. Recognizing that both of these must be kept in mind, the Faulkners describe two basic plans. The *one-story plan* is well suited to small houses as well as larger houses where there is plenty of land area. They avoid stairways, permit easy supervision of children, and give ready access to the out-of-doors. The *multiple-story plan* has the advantage of being less expensive to build than a one-story plan of equal square footage. Heating and cooling of the structure is also less expensive, and the vertical separation of rooms facilitates privacy.

Selecting a Plan. Finally, Faulkner and Faulkner suggest a series of questions to be asked in choosing a lifespace: (1) Is the total amount of enclosed space and the usable outdoor space suited to your needs? (2) Is the space appropriately allocated for your needs? (3) Is the enclosed space well-zoned and adjacent to outdoor areas? (4) Is the pattern of circulation satisfactory? (5) Are the rooms of suitable size? (6) Will the rooms take the required furniture gracefully and efficiently? (7) Is there adequate storage space? (8) Does the home lend itself to necessary or desired change? (9) Is the plan effectively oriented on the site? Anyone in the process of selecting a residence would do well to ask these questions. Such a decision is a major one, and given the amount of time spent in the residence, the choice of a particular setting can have profound influences, both short and long term, on one's daily life.

DESIGNING FOR THE SINGLE PARENT AND THE HOMELESS

Thus far in our discussion of residential design we have provided "models for family living," and have not considered possible variations in usage patterns among users. Our exposition notwithstanding, it should come as no surprise that different individuals within a family have quite different needs and therefore require quite different space designs. For example, Ahrentzen, Levine, and Michelson (1989) have shown that fully employed mothers co-occupy household rooms with their family members more than do working fathers. They are also more involved in housekeeping and child-care activities. As a result it is much more difficult for working mothers than working fathers to find spaces for privacy and solitude in conventionally designed homes. It also should come as no surprise that every family is not made up of mother, father, and two children. Yet, upon reflection, our earlier proscriptions of housing interiors seem to presuppose this familial configuration.

As a remedy to this seeming oversight we will, in the remainder of this chapter, discuss the need for understanding design requirements for single-parent families and for the homeless. Presently one out of every four American families is headed by a single parent (U.S. Bureau of the Census, 1984), one out of every five American children lives with a single parent (Bianchi & Seltzer, 1986), up to 3 million Americans are homeless (Greer, 1991), and approximately 30 percent of these homeless are families (i.e., they are not the single, detached, and disenfranchised wino or drug addict that has long been the stereotype of the homeless). To make matters worse, the number of single-parent families whose head is aged 25 to 34 has tripled in the last decade (Anthony, 1991) and their median yearly income is a paltry $4,688 (Apgar & Brown, 1988).

Single-parent families are ubiquitous and live in a variety of housing. Some are fortunate to live on their own and have the means to maintain a permanent residence, but a significant number of them find housing a cost burden. Birch (1985) estimates that 30 to 40 percent of income generated by single-parent families goes for housing. Very often these economic circumstances result in a series of downward spiraling moves often from single family dwelling, to apartment, to a public housing project (Bane & Weiss, 1980). A great many of these individuals even resort to subletting rooms in apartments or in other ways sharing accommodations in order to manage the costs of housing (Mulroy, 1988). Public housing projects contain a disproportionate number of households headed by single adults (National Low Income Housing Coalition, 1980), many of whom, having been homeowners during marriage, must now also adjust to the shift from middle- to low-income status (Mulroy, 1988).

In designing for this rapidly growing segment of contemporary society, distinctions must be made among inner-city, suburban, and rural residents, among those single parents who have never married, are separated, divorced or widowed, and among families with preschool, young school-age, or teenage children. Finally, large families experience a different set of housing needs than do smaller families (Anthony, Weidemann, & Chin, 1990). Several types of housing have been designed to meet the changing needs of these families. What is often required first is some sort of emergency shelter, a place to go when circumstances force them out of their immediate homes (e.g., foreclosure, fire, eviction, battering spouse, pregnant teenager, etc.). These shelters are set up to accommodate the temporarily homeless for limited periods of time, usually a few days to a few weeks. A second type of housing accommodation, transitional housing, is then required to provide shelter for more extended periods of time and until permanent housing can be located. Finally, permanent housing is needed to provide, as the name implies, permanent shelter.

Each of these types of housing has its own design requirements. Emergency shelters, because they house individuals for very short periods of time, require bare minimum home design (i.e., a place to eat, a place to sleep, and a place to toilet). Additional functional space, though, is desirable: Rooms for active as well as passive play, meeting rooms, temporary storage space, laundry rooms, staff office space, and a nursing station to be staffed 24 hours per day should be provided. In a nutshell, the basic requirements for an emergency shelter include sleeping accommodations, facilities for personal hygiene and health, an infirmary, and a laundry. Additionally, it should be easily accessible, welcoming and not demeaning; it should provide privacy, security, and a sense of dignity; and it should provide the opportunity for job and psychiatric counseling. Very often structures such as armories, churches, or schools are renovated to provide emergency shelter (Greer, 1991).

Transitional shelters can take a variety of forms, but these are usually more like permanent housing than emergency shelters. Often multi-apartment structures consisting of two bedroom units (though some may have as many as four), private kitchen, dining, and living areas are provided, though other arrangements include single-room units, group homes, and individual apartments with common shared recreational and living areas. Some of these shelters are designed and operated as cooperatives, giving residents the opportunity to share many activities including formal socializing, shared baby-sitting, preparing meals, and even managing the co-op (Wekerly, 1988).

Whatever form transitional housing takes, it must provide for a sense of community, security, and privacy. Common areas (dining, recreation, etc.) must be accessible from the inside for security as well as convenience; children's areas must be open to easy surveillance; and staffing space for private counseling, teaching, and self-improvement should be provided.

Permanent housing should have many of the design features of transitional housing. These are the accommodations that can rightfully be called *home*, the kind of accommodations that provide not only shelter and security but a sense of place and a sense of identity for their inhabitants. Siting is particularly important in the construction of permanent housing. Sites should be located with easy access to shopping, schools, and health-care facilities. Where possible, they should be located close to public transportation. Beyond these considerations, though, they must be affordable.

There is no doubt that the sheltering needs of American society are changing. No longer is the split-level home sited among the birch and oak of the suburbs within reach, or even desirable, for a growing segment of our society. Multi-unit structures to house a diversity of "family" living arrangements are becoming more common. Unfortunately, there is not enough data presently to determine the types of personal and sociocultural effects these types of living arrangements are likely to produce. There are those who fear that if temporary housing is built "too good" it will lead to an institutionalization of the homeless and further degradation of the human condition. The determination of whether this is true or not awaits further research.

What is currently known is that with respect to much of this type of housing a NIMBY ("not in my back yard") attitude is expressed by a significant segment of society. Fear of increased crime, decreased property values, higher costs to public education, and increased congestion all fuel opposition to this type of housing. Failures of the past only feed these concerns. But despite this opposition, the housing needs of our society will have to be met in new and innovative ways. The dilemma of meeting these needs while reconciling the fears of current homeowners, and doing so in a way that promotes human dignity and maximizes human functioning, may be one of the biggest problems facing our society in the next 20 years.

FUTURE ISSUES IN RESIDENTIAL DESIGN

In this chapter we have considered residential design from both a historical and present-day perspective. We conclude by suggesting a few issues likely to be of concern in residential planning for the future. We have already discussed some of these issues in other places. For example, the problems of population growth, urbanization, urban sprawl, and the flight to the suburbs discussed in Chapter 9 are likely to intensify in the future. The numbers of single-parent families and the homeless are both increasing at an accelerating rate. Problems of energy use will be discussed in a later chapter, and the need to seriously consider efforts to conserve energy as well as the need to develop alternative energy sources such as sun and wind will also be examined. None of these issues can be ignored in residential design considerations for the future.

Certainly the future is likely to see an increasing trend toward multiple housing units. Some prototypes of future units of this nature can be seen in the planned communities being attempted in some states such as New York and North Carolina. Called Planned Unit Developments (or PUD), these are designed as housing projects consisting of primarily residential apartments or townhouses that are grouped in clusters with large areas of open space between clusters. Some nonresidential spaces are also planned for shopping and employment. In the previous chapter we discussed extended care facilities for the elderly. An increase in this type of housing is likely in the future, and many retirement communities are already in existence in states such as Florida and Arizona. Finally, it is possible that the future will see an increase in mobile home communities that still maintain the single-family structure without the costs of a permanent home.

Faulkner and Faulkner describe two interesting examples of possible future trends in residential design: the *megastructure* and the *plug-in home*. A megastructure is seen as a single structure that incorporates the various functions of daily life, including private residences, shopping, and leisure facilities. The megastructure they envision is 21 stories and includes 1,000 apartments. In the center of this structure is an enclosed lake. Plug-in homes represent another version of the future of residential design. These are envisioned as self-contained one-person dwellings prefabricated at a factory that could literally be plugged into a central structural core that would provide utilities. These modules would be ready for occupancy as soon as they have been lifted into place. An advantage of this would be mobility, in that the same lifespace could be plugged into different structures if the occupant needed to move. We have seen this type of "plug-in" technology in the automobile and computer industries for some time now, and we have seen the development of modular life spaces and offices. It is not too much to assume that these two technologies will merge to provide plug-in residences in the future.

Finally, it is not impossible that future residential design will be considered in extraterrestrial contexts. Recent experiments with space labs orbiting the earth and current plans to develop more permanent "space stations" may pave the way for orbiting residential communities in the distant future. While perhaps more fiction than possibility, we may indeed find the need to develop such communities in the future as a means of alleviating some of the problems mentioned at the beginning of this section.

SUMMARY

This chapter began with an example illustrating the myriad aspects of residential design that need to be considered in understanding its effects on our experience and behavior and in facilitating our adaptation to the residence. After a brief review of the history of architecture and research on residential satisfaction and space use in the home, a detailed discussion of design feature considerations promoting optimal functioning in the residence was presented from the perspective of the interior designer. Issues in planning and creating a lifespace were discussed in the context of group spaces, private spaces, support spaces, energy use, and the floor plan. The recommendations presented represent ideals, and it is unlikely that many people will be able to occupy a residence that meets all of the criteria suggested. Ultimately, the choice of a residence will have to be based on the needs and resources of the specific individual or group, and trade-offs will be inevitable. Nonetheless, this chapter and the preceding chapter both suggest several important issues in architectural design related to human experience and behavior that have been relatively ignored in the past, but should play a greater role in future design processes.

IMPORTANT CONCEPTS

primitive architecture
preindustrial vernacular architecture
modern vernacular architecture
passive solar design
thermal lag
residential satisfaction
"space" vs. "place"
life themes: autonomy, privacy, mastery
home "atmosphere"
purposive vs. actual-aspirational gap approaches
nomothetic vs. ideographic approaches
residential preference
space use in the home
"open" vs. "closed" families
size, scale, proportion, harmony, contrast
planning program

lifespace goals
design features of group and private spaces
relative location of group and private spaces
design features of support spaces
kitchen work centers
support system considerations
incadenscent vs. fluorescent lighting
general vs. local lighting
house orientation on site
convection vs. conduction heating
active vs. passive wall design
wall/light sound absorption/reflection
organization of space: open vs. closed plans
single vs. multistory plans
future design issues: population trends and
   energy depletion

human factors
functional value of design alternatives

megastructures
plug-in homes

REFERENCES

Ahrentzen, S., Levine, D.W., & Michelson, W. (1989). Space, time, and activity in the home: A gender analysis. *Journal of Environmental Psychology, 9*(2), 89–101.

Altman, I. (1975). *The environment and social behavior.* Monterey, Calif.: Brooks/Cole.

Altman, I., Nelson, P.A., & Lett, E.E. (1972). The ecology of home environments. *Catalog of selected documents in psychology* (No. 150).

Anthony, K.H. (1991). Housing the single parent family. In W.F.E. Preiser, J.C. Vischer, & E.T. White (Eds.), *Design intervention: Toward a more humane architecture.* New York: Van Nostrand Reinhold.

Anthony, K.H., Weidemann, S., & Chin, Y. (1990). Housing perceptions of low-income single parents. *Environment and Behavior, 22*(2), 147–182.

Apgar, W.C. Jr., & Brown, H.J. (1988). *The state of the nation's housing: 1988.* Cambridge, Mass.: Joint Center for Housing Studies of Harvard University.

Bane, M.J., & Weiss, R.S. (1980). Alone together: The world of single-parent families. *American Demographics, 11*(5), 11–12.

Bianchi, S.M., & Seltzer, J.A. (1986). Life without father. *American Demographics, 8*(12), 43–47.

Birch, E.L. (1985). *The unsheltered woman: Women and housing in the 80's.* New Brunswick, N.J.: Center for Urban Policy Research.

Black, J.C. (1968). *Uses made of spaces in owner-occupied houses.* Doctoral dissertation, University of Utah, Salt Lake City.

Cooper, C. (1976). The house as symbol of the self. In H.M. Proshansky, W.H. Ittleson, & L.G. Rivlin (Eds.), *Environmental psychology: People and their physical settings.* New York: Holt, Rinehart & Winston.

Craik, K.H., & Zube, E.H. (1976). *Perceiving environmental quality.* New York: Plenum.

Faulkner, R., & Faulkner, S. (1975). *Inside today's home.* New York: Holt, Rinehart & Winston.

Galster, G., & Hesser, G. (1981). Residential satisfaction: Compositional and contextual correlates. *Environment and Behavior, 13,* 735–759.

Greer, N.R. (1991). Design for the homeless. In W.F.E. Preiser, J.C. Vischer, & E.T. White (Eds.), *Design intervention: Toward a more humane architecture.* New York: Van Nostrand Reinhold.

Holahan, C.J., & Wandersman, A. (1987). The community psychology perspective in environmental psychology. In D.L. Stokols & I. Altman (Eds.), *Handbook of environmental psychology* (Vol. 1). New York: John Wiley.

Kira, A. (1976). *The Bathroom.* New York: Viking.

Lansing, J.B., & Marans, R.W. (1969). Evaluation of neighborhood quality. *Journal of the American Institute of Planners, 35,* 195–199.

Lawrence, R.J. (1987). What makes a house a home? *Environment and Behavior, 19*(2), 154–168.

Lindberg, E., Garling, T., Montgomery, H., & Waara, R. (1986). Preferences for housing aspects: A study of underlying beliefs and values. *UMMEA Psychological Reports, 184,* 29.

Mehrabian, A. (1976). *Public places and private spaces.* NY: Basic Books.

Michelson, W. (1977). *Environmental choice, human behavior, and residential satisfaction.* New York: Oxford University Press.

Mulroy, E.A. (1988). Who are single-parent families and where do they live? In *Women as single parents: Confronting institutional barriers in the courts, the workplace, and the housing market.* Dover, Mass.: Auburn House.

National Low Income Housing Coalition (1980). *Triple jeopardy: A report on low income women and their housing problems.* Washington, D.C.: National Low Income Housing Coalition.

Parsons, H.M. (1972). The bedroom. *Human Factors, 14,* 421–450.

Pastalan, L.A., & Polakow, V. (1986). Life space over the life span. *Journal of Housing for the Elderly, 4*(1), 73–85.

Pennartz, P.J. (1986). Atmosphere at home: A qualitative approach. *Journal of Environmental Psychology, 6*(2), 135–153.

Pile, J.F. (1988). *Interior design.* Englewood Cliffs, N.J.: Prentice Hall.

Rapaport, A. (1969). *House form and culture.* Englewood Cliffs, NJ: Prentice Hall.

Rent, G.S., & Rent, C.S. (1978). Low-income housing factors related to residential satisfaction. *Environment and Behavior, 10*, 459–488.

Rudofsky, B. (1964). *Architecture without architects.* Garden City, N.Y.: Doubleday.

Salling, M., & Harvey, M. E. (1981). Poverty, personality and sensitivity to residential stressors. *Environment and Behavior, 13*, 131–163.

Sime, J.D. (1986). Creating places or designing spaces? *Journal of Environmental Psychology, 6*(1), 49–63.

Sixsmith, J. (1986). The meaning of home: An exploratory study of environmental experience. *Journal of Environmental Psychology, 6*(4), 281–298.

Steidl, R.E. (1972). Difficult factors in homemaking tasks: Implications for environmental design. *Human Factors, 14*, 472–482.

Stein, R.G. (1977). *Architecture and energy: Conserving energy through residential design.* Garden City, N.Y.: Anchor Press/Doubleday.

Turner, J.T.C., & Fichter, R. (1972). *Freedom to build.* New York: Macmillan.

U.S. Bureau of the Census (1984). *Current population reports: Divorce, child custody, and child support.* Series P-23, No. 84. Washington, D.C.: U.S. Government Printing Office.

Varady, D.P. (1986). Neighborhood confidence: A critical factor in neighborhood revitalization? *Environment and Behavior, 18*(4), 480–501.

Wekerly, G.R. (1988). Women's housing projects in eight Canadian cities. Report prepared for the Research Division; Policy, Research and Program Sector; Canada Mortgage and Housing Corporation. Toronto, Canada: Faculty of Environmental Studies, York University.

Zehner, R.B. (1972). Neighborhood and community satisfaction: A report on new towns and less planned suburbs. In J.F. Wpohlwill & D.H. Carson (Eds.), *Environment and the social sciences: Perspectives and applications.* Washington, D. C.: American Psychological Association.

Environmental Disaster and Technological Catastrophe

13

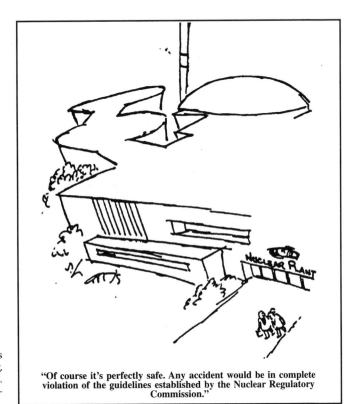

"Of course it's perfectly safe. Any accident would be in complete violation of the guidelines established by the Nuclear Regulatory Commission."

FIGURE 13-1 Technological devices are designed never to fail unpredictably, and to warn us when they are worn out. (©1980 by Sidney Harris, *American Scientific Magazine.*)

On a global scale, 1988 brought enormous human suffering at the hands of natural and human-made events. In September, Hurricane Gilbert wreaked havoc in Jamaica, killing 35 people and damaging up to 80 percent of all housing. It also caused the displacement of 12,000 people in the Dominican Republic, 5,000 in Haiti, and 30,000 in Mexico. In October, Hurricane Joan left her mark, destroying 90 to 95 percent of all buildings in the towns of Rama and Bluefields on the Corn Islands; Costa Rica reported $65 million in damages. On the other side of the globe, Typhoon Ruby hit the Philippines killing 41 and causing the evacuation of 37,000.

Raging waters in Bangladesh left 25 million people homeless when 90 percent of the country was flooded in September. As cleanup and repair was going on (at an estimated cost of $9 billion), a cyclone hit, delaying relief efforts and killing an additional 2,000. The African countries of Chad and the Sudan were similarly hit by floods, destroying much of the crops required to stave off starvation. But as water raged in some areas, in other parts of the world shamans and rain dancers were brought in to bring relief from droughts. The United States, Ethiopia, the People's Republic of China, India, and Vietnam were all short on rain, reducing crop yields to 60 percent and below.

Earthquakes of major proportion hit Nepal (resulting in 52,000 inhabitants losing their homes and millions of dollars in damages) and Armenia (where the homes of over 500,000 people were destroyed and up to 50,000 people were killed). Insect invasions occurred in Burkino Faso, Cameroons, Chad, Ethiopia, Mali, Mauritania, Niger, and Sudan. Adding to these calamities is the fact that during 1988, twenty-two wars were being waged worldwide, leaving an estimated 416,000 dead (most of whom were civilians), toxic wastes were being dumped into questionably safe landfills at increasing rates, safe methods for disposal of atomic waste were still being sought, and debate raged over the size and the meaning of holes in the ozone layer.

Hurricane Andrew, massive flooding of the Mississippi River and its tributaries, political unrest in Bosnia, starvation in Somalia, and a failed war on drugs are more recent, yet no less disquieting, reminders of the uneasy balance that exists among humans and between humans and their natural environment. Thus, we are left with a number of burning questions regarding the resiliency of Mother Earth and her inhabitants. It is hoped, through careful and systematic study of natural disasters and technological catastrophes, that we will gain optimistic answers to some of these questions and we will act on available knowledge to diminish the negative effects brought on by those natural forces that are inevitable.

In this chapter we will attempt to define more precisely the concept *environmental disaster* and we will show how, as humans, we deal with nature's calamities (and with some of our own making). We will address these issues from the perspective that disasters are stressful. The reader is, therefore, referred to Chapter 5 for an extensive consideration of the concept of stress.

FIGURE 13-2   A disaster is easier to recognize than it is to define.

ENVIRONMENTAL DISASTER

At a conceptual level, it seems easy to say what constitutes a disaster: A disaster *is something that has extreme negative consequences for those affected by it and is brought about as the result of the interaction of natural events and social systems.* However easy this definition is to declare, properly operationalizing it is far more complicated than first appears. Part of the problem is that some events, like a lightning bolt or a flood, may be a productive resource and a hazard at the same time. For example, lightning may kill an animal but also start a fire essential to burn-off and to the preservation of the ecosystem. Or a flood may destroy a farmer's crops, while simultaneously fertilizing the fields. Heavy snows in the Rockies may place human lives at risk while providing the necessary water to fill reservoirs for the summer's drinking water. The blazing sun that bakes the soil is the same sun necessary for the process of photosynthesis that is essential to life. It is unfair, then, and of little practical use, to label these natural events as disasters. If not for the presence of people, lightning, floods, heavy snows, and sunshine would be considered beneficial and not hazardous. It is fair to say that it is people who transform the environment to resources (and hazards) by using natural features for economic, social, and aesthetic purposes. Surface liquids seeping into underground aquifers do not in and of themselves represent a hazard. This seepage is needed to maintain a healthy supply of drinking water. If, however, these surface waters are contaminated by PCB, or dioxin, or some other harmful chemical, then the process becomes dangerous to humans and may be considered hazardous.

Quarantelli (1985) provides an example to illustrate the point that there is no *self-evident* definition of disaster. He states that in June 1983, flooding occurred along the banks of the Colorado River after the Federal Bureau of Land Reclamation released water from swollen reservoirs. Millions of dollars in property damage, contamination of underground wells, a fear of the spread of disease due to the extensive breeding grounds that were afforded mosquitos, and several deaths occurred as a result of these events. Argument over whether this event was "an act of God" or was caused by human action ensued. The Bureau of Land Reclamation was faulted for having waited too long to lower water levels. Federal engineers responded that there was no choice but to release the waters given the additional amounts that came into the system in late spring. Others thought that the flooding was a recognized trade-off between flood control and water storage. Was there a disaster, and if there was, who or what was responsible for it? Who should pay for the resulting damages, and who should be responsible for recovery? Quarantelli goes on to say that the debate over this event illustrates the difficulties in trying to define the nature of disasters and in understanding the implications of such definitions. Barkun (1974), whose position is similar, says that "disaster is easier to recognize than it is to define." Much of the difficulty in settling on a definition of what constitutes as disaster has very little to do with actual physical impact, but rather has to do with who is responsible for the costs of recovery.

Whatever the definition, it should be obvious by now that disaster can be a psychological, economic, and even a political construct, in addition to being a physical one. It should also be clear that while a disaster results from the interface of natural physical forces with human social forces, many of these same interfaces lead to the development of resources. To highlight the difficulty in providing a definition of disaster that would be satisfactory to everyone, Quarantelli (1985) has recounted the ways in which it has been defined in the past. The term *disaster* has referred to (1) physical agents, (2) the physical impact of such physical agents, (3) an assessment of physical impacts, (4) the social destruction resulting from an event with physical impacts, (5) the social construction of reality in perceived crisis situations which may or may not involve physical impacts, (6) the political definition of certain crisis situations, and (7) an imbalance in the demand-capability ratio in a crisis occasion. Each will be briefly discussed below.

The first three of these formulations emphasize physical referents, whereas the latter four consider psychological, social and political implications of crisis situations. For example, the word *disaster* has been equated with certain kinds of physical agents such as earthquakes, fires, floods, tornados, and hurricanes. Persons working within such a definition often make a distinction between natural agents, or "acts of God" and "humanmade" agents. Thus, natural land movement of a certain kind (e.g., an earthquake) is an act of God. On the other hand, the accidental transformation of land (as, for example, a mud slide resulting from the over-logging of a hillside) is humanmade. Theorists have often differentiated these events by labelling them *natural disasters and technological catastrophes*, respectively (Berren, Beigel, & Ghertner, 1980; Beigel & Berren, 1985; Berren, Santiago, Beigel, & Timmons, 1989). The key feature in these definitions, though, is the event itself (i.e., a hurricane is a disaster independent of its impact, as is a tornado, flood, airplane crash, etc.). In this formulation, the focus is on *antecedent conditions* responsible for the impact, regardless of the extent of that impact.

In the second and third formulation listed above, actual physical impact becomes the distinguishing feature. In the second, something is considered a disaster when that something has a *discernible impact*, and in the third, that something is considered a disaster only when the impact is assessed as *notable*. Thus, these two notions of disaster differ only with respect to the degree of impact. Within the former, a disaster has occurred when there has been any kind of noticeable impact on the environment: A forest or grassland has been burned, land or water has been moved, etc. In the latter, this change in the environment has to be categorized as disastrous by some criterion or set of criteria, (e.g., number of homes destroyed, acres of crops ravaged, lives lost, etc.).

Conceptions of disasters that involve social aspects appear in the fourth view. Here a physical impact is a *disaster* if the magnitude of the impact, as indicated by property damage and casualties, is assessed to be high enough to result in *disruption of social life*. Events become disasters not because of their physical impact, per se, but because of the social consequences of that impact. Thus, a hurricane out in the ocean does not become a disaster until it hits coastal towns or ships at sea, and even then only if it brings about a disruption of social life in the towns or on the ships. Likewise, a fire in a remote uninhabited part of the planet would not be a disaster as there is no "social life" to disrupt.

From the above discussion it can be seen that there is neither an automatic nor a linear relationship between visible physical impact and social impact. The former can occur without the latter, and the latter can occur without the former, as for example when chemical pollutants seep into the groundwater supply or when invisible pollutants such as carbon monoxide are discharged into the atmosphere. It is even possible for there to be large-scale social disruption in anticipation of physical destruction which may never occur. A fifth view of disaster, therefore, involves a *socially constructed perception of a crisis situation* (Quarantelli, 1985). For example, the widespread evacuation of people from an area, given that an explosion has occurred, would be defined as a disaster, but so would the widespread evacuation of an area, given that there was a rumored explosion, even though none may have occurred. Either situation results in a socially constructed perception of a crisis situation that necessitates collective action. Likewise, seepage from a toxic-waste-disposal site may affect the physical and personal health of those living nearby, but so might a rumored seepage, even if none occurs. The key to definitions of this sort is that there need not be any physical impact nor, for that matter, even a physical agent present to apply the term *disaster*; there need only be a social construction of impact which is disruptive of the social order.

Some have argued that disasters are basically *political phenomena* (Quarantelli, 1985). Thus, whether crisis situations are defined as *disasters* depends upon political decisions. Governmental declarations of disasters often carry with them an obligation to do something, to provide resources, to mobilize help and sometimes to adjudicate existing laws or legislate new ones. These considerations can take precedence over physical and social impact as criteria for defining disaster. But while political definitions may have a bearing on the resources made available in the aftermath of a crisis, they have little immediate impact on the way in which people prepare for and cope with crises.

Finally, there are those who argue that a disaster has occurred only when the *demands for action exceed the capabilities for response in a crisis occasion*. Thus, an earthquake, tornado, or flood is a disaster only if individually and/or collectively people are unable to deal with the situation. Emphasis in this formulation is not on social disorganization, perceptual beliefs of danger, or on political labelling, but rather on the individual and collective efforts to terminate a crisis by restoring capabilities to the level of demands (Quarantelli, 1985). This definition of a disaster comes closest to the definition used for pathological environments presented in Chapter 2, and in a very real sense a disaster can be considered pathological.

Obviously the definition of an event as a disaster or catastrophe carries a hidden agenda. This agenda may involve economic considerations, political expediency, and/or moral culpability, among others. At some level, though, a definition is required so that systematic research on "unusual events" can be conducted to ascertain their effects on physiological, psycholological, sociological, and economic systems.

In an attempt to define disaster broadly enough to encompass these various considerations McCaughey (1984) defines disaster as "an event that occurs suddenly, unexpectedly, and uncontrollably, that is catastrophic in nature, involves threatened or actual loss of life or property, disrupts the sense of community, and often results in adverse psychological consequences for the survivors" (p. 8). And, Shah (1985) has described a disaster as "an external force capable of destroying human life or its resources for survival, on a scale wide enough to excite public attention, to disrupt normal patterns of behavior ..." and which "overload any of the central services necessary to conduct normal affairs or for the prevention or alleviation of suffering and loss" (p. 462).

While these definitions have intuitive appeal it is possible to think of some events as disasters that (1) do not occur suddenly, (2) are, in fact, expected, and/or (3) are at least theoretically controllable. The insidious seepage of toxic waste into underground aquifers and the depletion of the ozone layer are but two examples (i.e., both are occurring gradually, are no longer unexpected, and are not beyond our control). Furthermore, it is possible to think of disasters as injuring only small numbers of people and not necessarily destroying large communities. A car accident or house fire comes to mind.

In general, it is safe to say that in a disaster situation there is a relative concensus that things have to be done, but the wherewithal is not enough to meet the demands. Thus, depending on whether one is a researcher studying the effects of disaster on the physiological, psychological, and behavioral outcomes of victims, or one is a bureaucrat trying to obtain funds (or attempting to avoid allocating funds), or one is making an effort to cope with a natural system run amok, the interface of a social system and that of a natural system may or may not be labelled a disaster.

Labelling aside, the behaviors of ranchers in Kansas responding to an impending tornado, of occupants of land abutting a toxic-waste-disposal site, or of survivors of a devastating earthquake can be understood by examining the ways in which (1) they recognize and describe their respective situations (i.e., primary appraisal), (2) the ways in which they think they might deal with it (i.e., secondary appraisal), and (3) how and when they make their choices among the actions that seem available to them (i.e., coping behaviors; see Chapter 5).

It is these factors applied to all societal levels that lead to the following definition to be followed in the remainder of this chapter: A disaster is "any event that stresses a society, a portion of that society, or even an individual family beyond the normal limits of daily living" (Berren, et al., 1989). The key word in this definition is "stresses" (i.e., a disaster, by definition, taxes the adaptive resources of the individual, its tissue system, and/or the social system of which one is a part). The process by which this taxation occurs is known as the *stress response* and begins with an appraisal of the environment and ends with either successful or unsuccessful coping. Between these two events a number of cognitive, physiological, behavioral, and emotional responses occur, and various resources (psychic, monetary, social, etc.) are tapped. The nature of the appraisal and the responses that are likely to occur, as well as the resources that are called into play, are all linked to various aspects of the disaster. It is for this reason that researchers and theorists have attempted to identify those characteristics or dimensions of disasters which influence the various stages of the stress response.

TIME-OUT: Assume that you have been vacationing and have arrived at a small town through which a tornado has gone just the night before. The friend you have been travelling with surveys the physical destruction and exclaims, "What a disaster!" Not wishing to be insensitive, but certainly trying to see if the situation conforms to any of the definitions given in this chapter, you withhold your labelling of the situation until you get more information.

What informatioin would you need to have to fulfill the requirements for each of the definitiions of disaster given? Where and how would you get this information? Discuss both the reliability and the validity of this information.

DIMENSIONS OF DISASTER

There have been a number of attempts to classify disasters in multidimensional terms. To be useful, however, classification systems must at least be able to differentiate among disasters qualitatively; they must contain dimensions which are measureable, they have to be made up of dimensions that are predictive of social/psychological impact, and, finally, they should have roots in a larger conceptual framework for understanding human behavior.

Quarantelli's Dimensions

Quarantelli (1985) has argued forcefully and convincingly for a generic (as opposed to an agent-specific) approach to disasters. That is, he feels that the mental health and psychosocial effects of various disaster situations have more in common than they have at variance with one another, and that all disaster situations can be described along a small number of dimensions useful in predicting community and individual reactions to them. The implication here is that tornadoes, earthquakes, floods, etc., while clearly differing in their physical characteristics, vary only in scale value on a number of other dimensions. Having made this argument he singles out several characteristics of disaster occasions that have an impact on social life and either create or exacerbate mental health problems. Among these characteristics are (1) the proportion of the population involved, (2) the social centrality of the affected population, (3) the length of the involvement, (4) the rapidity of the involvement, (5) the predictability of the involvement, (6) the unfamiliarity of the crisis, (7) the depth of the involvement, and (8) the recurrency of the involvement. Each of these characteristics will be elaborated below. (See Table 13-1.)

The *proportion of the population involved* relative to some base is probably more important than absolute numbers when dealing with disasters. The same absolute numbers might mean a catastrophe in some communities but only a bigger-than-usual emergency in others. A nursing home fire is a bigger disaster if it is the only nursing home in town than if it is merely one of 50. The derailment of a train carrying liquid chemicals in a small town my call forth the sum total of the town's resources to manage cleanup, whereas the same derailment in a large city may go unnoticed by most of the community. Thus, the degree of community involvement has to be identified in social terms relative to the total population base. Twenty displaced octogenerians in a town of 300 people is more socially disruptive than the same number in a town of 50,000, and a $100,000 cleanup bill from a total budget of $100,000 is more devastating than that same bill deducted from a multimillion-dollar budget.

Green (1982) has suggested considering whether the affected population is central or peripheral to the larger geographic community. A tornado destroying a local migrant worker camp and killing seven probably will not have the

TABLE 13-1 Summary Characteristics of Disasters that Impact on Social Life and Either Create or Exacerbate Mental Health Problems

---

The type of disaster
The size of the disaster
The proportion of the population affected
The social centrality of the population affected
The visibility of the effects
The rapidity of the involvement
The length of involvement
The depth of involvement
The predictability of the disaster
The unfamiliarity of the crisis
The existence of an identifiable low point
The recurrency of involvement
The perception of control

---

same community impact as a tornado touching down on a high school soccer practice field and killing seven players. The high schoolers have their roots in the community and therefore the affected polpulation is central; the migrant workers do not, and therefore the affected population is peripheral. Thus, the *degree of social centrality of the involved population* appears to be an important characteristic of disasters. This dimension is critical to understanding both the mental and physical health problems that are likely to result and in the difficulties and willingness of the community in providing mental and physical health services.

There is certainly some relationship between *length of involvement in crisis occasions* and possible mental health effects. It is probably true that after some initial period of time, the longer a population is involved with a threat, the more its members will be able to make adjustments to it (i.e., the relationship may be curvilinear with things getting worse and worse up to a point, at which time they start getting better). But while this curvilinear relationship may hold in situations where coping (even if only palliative) is successful, there are probably a number of situations where effective coping strategies are not available (e.g., living near a toxic-waste-disposal site, or near the site of a nuclear accident). In these instances we might expect mental health deterioration to vary directly with the length of time of involvement.

In some disaster occasions, the population becomes slowly involved in the crisis, whereas on other occasions the general population takes over very quickly. Short-term adjustment seems to be much more difficult in cases where there is *rapid involvement*. Acute mental health effects stem not from how long, in some chronological sense, people have available to act, but rather from whether they perceive themselves as having to hurry. A tornado, for example, calls for a rapid mobilization of forces to salvage threatened homes, water supplies, etc. A rumored leak in a toxic waste lagoon does not call forth the same urgency to get something done. We might, therefore, expect short-term adjustment to be more difficult in the aftermath of a tornado than in the aftermath of a rumored waste leakage. Long-term adjustment to these same two situations, however, might take a quite different course. Chronic forms of psychological disturbance such as free-floating anxiety and various psychosomatic difficulties are apt to occur as the result of a rumored toxic waste leak.

There are times when populations can *predict* their possible involvement in disasters. For example, an impending hurricane is usually forecast by meteorologists, and warnings are issued by the media. In other cases the crises are unexpected—for example, a train derailment. Evidence exists that the unexpected is much more psychologically disturbing than the expected. Of course there are circumstances where the event expected is slow to arrive (i.e., you *know* that something bad is going to happen, you just don't know when). In these circumstances the stress of anticipation can be just as disturbing as the stress resulting from totally unexpected events. We will return to this notion of predictability later in this chapter.

Other features which might influence people's response to disaster include the *unfamiliarity of the crisis*, the *depth of involvement of the population*, and the *recurrency of involvement*. Generally, the more unfamiliar we are with a stressful situation, the fewer resources we have available to deal with it, and therefore the greater the stress. Additionally, we generally have a fear of the unknown, and therefore unfamiliar situations generate more stress. Finally, unfamiliarity is associated with controllability—the less familiar, the less control. As we saw in Chapter 5, control (or at least the perception of it) is a strong moderator of the stress response.

Depth of involvement refers to either the absolute or relative loss created by disaster situations. Generally, the greater the loss incurred (more money lost, more crops devastated, more people dead), the greater the stress. However, one's own losses in the context of what others have lost can moderate stress. For example, a farmer who loses 50 percent of his crops to a drought would stand to lose a great deal of money, but not as much as his neighbor who has lost his entire crop. Knowing that you are better off than you might have been (as witnessed by your neighbor's losses) eases the stress somewhat.

Finally, disasters can be classified in terms of *recurrency*. Has it happened before? Will it happen again? Has its occurrence in any way readied victims for its recurrence? What little data exists suggests that if victims "learn from their experience" and use this knowledge to prepare themselves for the future, some disaster effects can be ameliorated. Unfortunately, as we will see later, people do not always learn from their experiences.

These dimensions of disasters formulated by Quarantelli (1985) have been useful in that they direct the attention of researchers to important antecedents of the stress response. They allow for comparison of consequences given disasters with varying physical properties, and they point the way for potential amelioration of disaster effects.

The Berren et al. Dimensions

Berren, Beigel, and Ghertner (1980) have developed a somewhat different yet overlapping model for distinguishing disasters from one another. Their classification system involves five primary factors: (1) type of disaster (natural vs. human type), (2) duration, (3) degree of personal impact, (4) potential for recurrence, and (5) control over future impact. More recently, Berren, et al. (1989) have modified this model to make it more appropriate for the inclusion of high-technology disasters. Accordingly, factor three has been expanded to include both personal and geographic dimensions of disaster. The fourth factor now refers to whether the disaster has an identifiable low point (see Baum, 1985), and the fifth variable now refers to the size of the disaster.

This revised conceptualization like the Quarantelli dimensions described above considers both personal and geographic implications, the duration of involvement in the disaster situation, and its predictability (either in terms of "When is it going to happen?" or When is the worst over?"). And, of course, predictability is a precursor of potential control.

NATURAL DISASTERS AND TECHNOLOGICAL CATASTROPHES

The remainder of this chapter will deal specifically with two related types of stressors: natural disasters and technological catastrophes. Earlier, in describing cataclysmic events, reference was made to natural disasters, and various geologic and meterological examples were presented as falling within this category of stressor. Technological catastrophes (including such events as dams breaking, mine disasters, airplanes crashing, nuclear accidents, and water and air contamination as a result of disposal failures) share a number of characteristics with natural disasters (see Table 13-1). Their main similarity is that they both create a dramatic change from a "steady-state" environment, thereby requiring coping efforts to return to normal functioning.

However, there are a number of dimensions on which they differ. First, natural disasters, as their name implies, include those cataclysmic events which are the result of abnormally intense natural events, whereas technological catastrophes (again as the name implies) are the result of breakdowns in our technological environment. Second, natural disasters are almost always abrupt in onset and usually acute in their effects; technological catastrophes may or may not be abrupt in their onset and are usually more chronic in their effects. Third, natural disasters typically have a recognizable low point, whereas technological catastrophes do not. Finally, technological catastrophes and their subsequent stress are more likely to threaten our feelings of perceived control than are natural disasters.

TABLE 13-2   A Thumbnail Comparison of Natural Disasters and Technological Catastrophes

	TYPE OF EVENT	
Characteristic of Event	Natural Disaster	Technological Catastrophe
Size	Often large geographical area directly affected; response from remote geographical locales is that it probably won't happen here	Often only small geographical areas directly affected; response from remote locales is, When will it happen here?
Proportion of Population Affected	Nearly everyone in immediate locale, only some in more remote locales	Nearly everyone directly in immediate locale; many others indirectly from afar
Visibility	Usually environment is disfigured, with homes, businesses, etc., visually destroyed	There may be some visible destruction (e.g., airplane crashes), but often invisible (e.g., illnesses related to radiation or other toxic exposure)
Rapidity of Involvement	Often abrupt, though some hurricanes, tornadoes, etc., are forecast with some lead lead time	May be sudden (e.g., dam busts, nuclear power plant failure) or more insidious (e.g., toxic waste leakage, asbestos exposure)
Length of Involvement	Often short duration, identifiable low point after which things get better; effectsappear to be relatively short-lived	May be relatively short or, in the case of toxic disasters, involvement lasts over long periods of time; effects may be acute or chronic, especially with toxic disasters
Perception	Not usually viewed as controllable	Usually perceived as a loss or usurpation of control

RESEARCH ON THE HUMAN IMPACT OF DISASTERS AND CATASTROPHES

These various classification schemes have been useful in that they have provided a framework for research in the area. Investigators studying the human impact of disasters need to be aware of the fact that small changes in any of the antecedent dimensions have the potential for developing large changes in terms of human impact. Before looking at the research in which disaster effects have been studied, it is necessary to note a number of methodological issues regarding crisis research. These considerations not only determine what we know about the effects of disaster, but also dictate the questions remaining unanswered.

First, as we have seen, the determination of whether a disaster has occurred is dependent on how one chooses to define disaster. Second, investigators from different disciplines vary in the aspects of disaster events in which they are interested. Third, because the various studies conducted on disasters have differing goals and purposes (to say nothing of differing methodologies), comparisons across disaster settings are difficult, if not impossible, to make. For these and addditional reasons, most disaster research has been done without aid of a formal guiding theory. Key concerns in developing, conducting, and evaluating this research center on the reliability, generalizabilty (external validity), and internal validity of the various impact measures used. Also of concern is the issue of the use to which the data will be put (i.e., What question or questions is the research trying to answer? What is the goal or purpose of the study?).

In the psychological realm three general types of studies have been conducted: (1) the clinical description, (2) the study of individual differences in response to disaster, and (3) studies of the extent of impairment (Green, 1985). Each of these research strategies has a different focus and a different purpose. In *clinical descriptions*, the primary goal is to understand the constellation of symptoms exhibited by survivors in terms of how they go together, their meaning, and the mechanisms by which they develop. The focus of such studies is the individual response to disasters as aggregated across individuals, with the hope of developing and refining theories and developing specific treatment interventions. The assumption underlying this research is that all individuals will be affected similarly by specific disaster agents.

The second type of study focuses on *individual differences* in response to disaster events based on the person's particular experience or dispositional makeup. These studies are designed to provide information regarding who among the population might be more susceptible to (or immune from) the psychological repercussions of disasters, and as such, permit prior identification of individuals who are most at risk. This approach also allows for planning of treatment once the event has occurred, and contributes to the typologies of disasters that have psychological implications.

The third type of study focuses on impact. What is the *extent of the effect* produced by the disaster? How many people were affected? These studies are often referred to as *epidemiological*. They are useful because they can help in planning strategies for dealing with disaster events. They are also useful in the development of typologies dealing with the extent of stressful impact. It is possible that any given study could address all of the above implicit goals (i.e., allow us to build conceptual and theoretical models of psychological response to stress; develop disaster typologies; design intervention strategies; estimate the need for mental health services; and, determine which survivors are most at risk for mental health problems). But, while it is possible, it is unlikely.

In developing research strategies for studying the psychological effects of disaster events, it is important to have firmly in mind the questions to be answered by the research. Having determined the questions, the answers that are admissible and germane to the questions need to be explicated and a method of assessment needs to be developed. This assessment must provide reliable and valid measurements (see Chapter 2), and the outcomes of the assessment must be relevant to existing data and theorizing. Finally, the researcher should keep in mind that no study ever stands alone in answering a question, and that the issues of generalizability and comparability of findings must also be carefully considered.

Research of any type on natural disasters is difficult to conduct for a number of reasons. First, the events can only be studied after they have occurred. It is impossible to know where a natural disaster is going to occur, and therefore one cannot get information about people before or as they are exposed to the disaster, and again after they have been exposed. It is, therefore, difficult, if not impossible, to demonstrate changes in mood and/or behavior as a result of the cataclysmic event. A second problem, actually stemming from the first, is the choice of an appropriate control group: With whom should the findings be compared? And finally, the choice of measures is difficult. Since research in disaster areas must often be conducted in recently devastated and highly chaotic conditions, the kinds of measures that can be taken are restricted. However, in-depth testing has occurred in some research (Madakasira & OBrien, 1987; Solomon & Canino, 1990). Obtaining samples is also problematic, since recruitment must be done quickly. Often the sample cannot be random and is chosen in a manner that is convenient to the researcher and is least disruptive of efforts to cope with the disaster at hand. Subject samples are therefore always subject to charges of being nonrepresentative of the entire area affected by the mishap.

THE EFFECTS OF NATURAL DISASTERS

Natural disasters were described earlier as abnormally intense natural events. This definition would allow for the inclusion of extreme weather of any kind (extreme heat or cold, hurricanes, blizzards, tornadoes, ice storms, windstorms, monsoons, and others). Earthquakes, volcanic eruptions, mudslides, and avalanches are also natural disasters; however, the effects of these disasters may be influenced by human alteration of the earth. Floods are often caused by a combination of natural and human-influenced events (for example, abnormal rain and the improper use of riverbanks), but some floods are caused almost entirely by humans—for example, dam failure. Flooding resulting from dam failure would, therefore, be more appropriately considered a technological catastrophe.

Partly because of the research problems outlined in the previous section, our understanding of natural disasters is not complete. Despite these problems, many studies have been done, and we now know a great deal about the impact of natural disasters. Because they occur seldomly, they are usually *unpredictable*. Depending upon the event, we have more or less warning. Although living near a fault tells us there is the possibility of an earthquake, it does not tell us when it will occur. Being in a tornado belt tells us there is the possibility of tornadoes, but again, exactly where and when one is going to hit is unknown. Often we receive adequate warning of storms or floods, but just as often we do not. Natural disasters, then, are generally not well-predicted and are also typically viewed as *uncontrollable*.

The destructive power of a natural disaster is sometimes enormous and usually substantial. The sheer magnitude of the impact of some disasters makes them unique among stressors. But while the magnitude is great, the *duration* is typically short. Natural disasters last as little as a few seconds (as in the case of an earthquake) or sometimes minutes, and with the exceptions of heat waves and cold spells, they generally do not persist more than a few days. Once the crisis has passed, environmental conditions return to normal, and coping can proceed, rebuilding can occur, and recovery can be achieved. Usually this coping requires a great deal of physical effort, the expenditure of much psychological energy, and a great deal of money.

Mental health impacts, when they occur, result from the interaction of physical, psychological, social, and material forces (Bolin, 1989). Natural disasters, thus, are environmental events which place demands on persons, individually and collectively, in terms of their ability to respond efficaciously. Continued attempts to cope create stress, which can result in psychological distress. This distress can take many forms, some of which have been studied by disaster researchers. It is to these manifestations of distress that we now turn.

More than any other symptom, researchers report a stunned, numb response to the immediate impact of disaster (Burger, Van Staden, & Nieuwoudt, 1989; Crashaw 1963; Erikson, 1976; Lifton & Olson, 1976; Rangell, 1976). Quarantelli and Dynes (1977) note that panic is rare among survivors, and that most individuals act calmly and rationally. It appears that disbelief of warnings is more common than is panic (Perry, Lindell, & Green, 1981), perhaps because of the well-documented fact that people tend to underestimate the hazardous features of their physical environment (Covello, 1983).

Most studies of the effects of disasters have used the psychiatric interview. As a result, findings are expressed as frequency of psychiatric problems. For the most part, anxiety, depression, and other stress-related disturbances have been found among the victims of floods, tornadoes, hurricanes, and other natural disasters (Canino, Bravo, Rubio-Stipec, & Woodbury, 1990; de la Fuente, 1990; Lima, Santacruz, Lozano, Chavez, et al., 1990; Logue, Hansen, & Struening, 1979; Milne, 1977; Moore, 1958; Penick, Powell, & Sieck, 1976; Phifer & Norris, 1989; Taylor, Ross, & Quarantelli, 1976). These effects have been found to last up to one year, but are not nearly as widespread among victims as one might expect. Studies generally show 25 to 30 percent of the victims suffering psychological effects when tested months after a disaster. It also appears that those individuals who have lost more in the disaster are those who continue to suffer. Roca and Ivaldi (1986) suggest that a particular type of traumatic neurosis that occurs in victims of earthquakes (*seismic neurosis*) persists for longer periods of time and may become an enduring feature of the local culture. Thus, there are individual differences in the magnitude and duration of psychological impairment following a disaster, with some of these differences accounted for by differences in the extent of the loss experienced.

Some researchers have looked at the effects of disasters on child victims. Children, it would seem, take their cues from their parents (Crashaw, 1963) and

respond to their parents' fear or lack of it. When they are exposed more directly to environmental disruption, they react strongly to scenes of death and muti-
lation (Newman, 1976). They may also regress to earlier stages of behavior or
have recurring sleeplessness, sometimes accompanied by nightmares (Seroka,
Knapp, Knight, & Siemon, 1986). Further, the number of children at risk following a disaster seems to be related to the length of time needed for the community to reorganize following the disaster (Galante & Foa, 1986). The elderly, too,
have been shown to be at special risk (Bolin & Klenow, 1988; Krause, 1987).
Those suffering rheumatoid arthritis display an increase in disease activity and
report greater pain (Grady, Reisine, Fifield, & Lee, 1991), and evacuation problems are exacerbated with aged victims (Mangum, Kosberg, & McDonald, 1989).

Natural disasters, then, can affect people in a number of ways. They are
psychologically stressful, they limit freedom, and they may lead to a breakdown
or disruption of a community. Unfortunately, nearly all relief efforts, when they
are available at all, are aimed at physical reconstruction, at getting the physical
environment to approximate what it was before the disaster hit. Minimal attention has been paid to "psychological reconstruction." It is hoped that with additional research this glaring error of omission will be rectified.

Research suggests that the ability to externalize losses to higher systems
is an important coping mechanism for responding to natural disasters (Bolin &
Bolton, 1986; Drabek & Key, 1984). Thus, individuals turn to families (spouses,
children) first. If familial support is inadequate, external interpersonal networks
may be drawn upon (e.g., friends and neighbors) and finally formal aid givers
such as the Red Cross and disaster relief agencies are sought (Drabek, 1986).
Finally, some may draw on religious beliefs and religious leaders as a means of
support and as a way of assigning meaning to such events (North, Smith,
McCoal, & Lightcap, 1989), although this is not always effective, particularly in
the case of technological catastrophes (Kroll-Smith & Couch, 1987). Also, clergy
are not always comfortable approaching people as counselors in the aftermath
of natural disasters (Chinnici, 1985). Other coping mechanisms include talking
about the experience, humor, and altruism (Weinrich, Hardin, & Johnson, 1990).

Research further suggests that informal social networks offer several
advantages over professional intervention. First, the informal network provides
personal and reciprocal interaction. Second, members of the informal network
are typically more geographically accessible. Third, they are more likely to be
available prior to or soon after the disaster, and their help is less costly, less stig-
matizing, more familiar, and more consistently available (Solomon, 1985). This
social support, whatever its origins, in addition to providing victims with additional resources also appears to have a stress-buffering effect (Bolin, 1983; Lindy
& Grace, 1985).

In determining whether demands exceed response capacities (our definition of disaster), it is important to view the environmental event as it unfolds.
Typically this unfolding begins with warnings (when possible), followed by the
actual event and the emergency responses required, a period of immediate rehabilitation, and finally, recovery. We will briefly discuss each of these stages
below.

Warning. Depending on the type of environmental event, warnings can be fairly timely, as in the case of hurricanes and some floods, of relatively short duration, as in the case of tornadoes and hail storms, or nonexistent, as with the onset of most earthquakes and lightning strikes (cf. Apostol, 1985; Mattsson & Persinger, 1986; Persinger, 1988). Research has shown that when adequate warnings are provided, disasters create much less in the way of significant psychological disturbance unless destruction is very high (Bolin, 1985). One possible reason for this is that warnings provide an opportunity for *anticipatory socialization* to occur, which, in turn, has the potential for reducing stress, should it occur (Drabek, 1986). Additionally, there is evidence that the ability to predict and prepare for a hurricane allows for a greater sense of mastery over the experience (Austin, 1991). If, however, warning information is ambiguous or contradictory, stress levels may increase (cf. Baum & Davidson, 1985; Drabek, 1986). In most natural disasters this is not a problem, as they can often be described in terms of knowable dimensions such as speed of onset, scope, intensity, and possible duration. Along these same lines, the ambiguity surrounding threat of recurrence (as with earthquakes or volcanoes) may also contribute to increased stress levels.

Warnings often come in the form of base rate information. The weather forecaster tells us, for example, that there is a 70 percent chance of rain, or that up to 8 inches of snow will fall overnight. Aside from these daily forecasts, it is safe to say that if you live on a floodplain, there is a greater likelihood of being in a flood than if you live on a mountain top, simply because more floods occur on the former than on the latter. This, and similar information, however, is not universally used by the public in estimating the risk of being exposed to disaster. Lave and Lave (1991) suggest that even people who have recently been flooded have little knowledge of what causes floods. They further claim that current government publications about flood risks are not likely to be understood by those at risk, and only those people who work and are better educated are likely to have flood insurance. Likewise, the major factor in the perception of tornado hazard (deMan & Simpson-Housley, 1987a), and of earthquake hazard (deMan & Simpson-Housley, 1987b) is the educational level of the individual. Thus, sometimes warnings may be ineffective in preparing for the natural event, and in coping with it once it occurs, simply because those warnings are not understood by those likely to be affected.

Agent Impact. Bolin (1989) summarizes the characteristics of agent impact that influence psychological stress as follows: (1) Life-threatening situations are more likely to produce psychological stress than situations which are not life threatening; (2) postimpact threat of recurrence is more stressful than preimpact stress; (3) disasters with a high ratio of damaged to undamaged community are more likely to have mental health effects; (4) a sudden and unanticipated onset of a disaster is more stressful than one that is gradual or anticipated; and (5) unfamiliar events are more stressful than are familiar ones (Norris & Murrell, 1988).

Postimpact Effects. Thus far we have looked at the impact of the impending agent as well as the agent itself, but other factors involve those stresses that are generated by individual and collective responses to the disaster rather than the agent characteristics per se. These factors involve such behaviors as evacuation, temporary sheltering, temporary housing, and recovery activities (Bolin & Bolton, 1986). Generally, it can be said that evacuation and emergency sheltering do not lead to extensive psychological distress. For the most part, families evacuate as a unit and, more often than not, seek temporary shelter and support from kin or friends (North et al., 1989). The more affluent families may evacuate to motels or perhaps even to second homes outside the impact area (Bolin, 1986b). Poorer families are more likely to use mass shelters such as those established by the Red Cross or other disaster relief agencies. When families are not able to evacuate as a whole or are not able to stay together, then some mental health stresses can be expected to occur as a result of evacuation (Drabek & Boggs, 1968). However, much of this stress seems to be the result of ambiguous threats rather than the separation per se (Bromet, Schulberg, Dunn, & Gondek, 1980). Parker (1977) has indicated that distress from evacuation and temporary sheltering can be expected when the departure from one's home is protracted.

When frequent residential changes are required as a result of evacuation, more stress seems to be placed on the individual (Bolin & Bolton, 1986; Gleser, Green, & Winget, 1981). The effects of relocation which appear to influence the type and amount of social distress developed include (1) the disruption of social support, (2) loss of home, (3) personal injury, and (4) financial burdens (Bolin, 1989). These effects are compounded when the victims do not feel in control of the relocation process (Garrison, 1985). Because poorer victims face uncertainties as to where they are going to eventually live, the incidence of depression and heightened anxiety appears to be greater among them (Bolin, 1986b). By contrast, middle-income families tend to have more extensive support networks. Because they own their homes, they qualify for more extensive government aid and face fewer of the uncertainties regarding their long-term prospects in the community (Bolin, 1986a; Bolin & Klenow, 1988). The extent of stress in middle-income families appears, therefore, to be much less than stress among poorer families.

Recovery. The major factor influencing stress in the recovery phase appears to be utilization of state and federal aid (Bolin, 1986a). Bolin (1989) reported that victims who either could not or did not receive financial, housing, or material aid were consistently slower to recover and more likely to report emotional strains persisting 15 months after the disaster occurred. Again, as would be expected, poorer, older, and black victims were less likely to receive adequate aid and were thus slower to recover. In extreme disasters, such as earthquakes, it is very likely that there will be major changes in the community from pre- to postdisaster. If the community is transformed to a great extent, this may create additional adjustment problems for persons in the community.

Summary. When considering the psychosocial impact of natural disasters it is important to understand the interactions of a number of factors. One set of factors would be found under the rubric *victim characteristics,* and such things as age, sex, race, and socioeconomic status would be included. *Agent characteristics* such as scope, speed of onset, duration, and severity also influence the amount of stress felt by an individual or the society at large. Finally, there are *response-generated variables,* such as evacuation, relocation, and temporary sheltering.

Each of these sets of variables will influence perceptual and cognitive processses (What is the likelihood of danger? How will it affect me? What can I do about it? How well have I done so far?) and physiological, psychological, and behavioral processes, and will impact on social, economic, and political systems. Therefore, the perception and definition of disaster, the effects of disaster, and the means of coping with disaster, all need to be assessed at a number of interacting levels. The more we know and the broader the perspective from which that knowledge is derived, the easier it is to minimize disharmony between natural physical forces and human social systems.

THE EFFECTS OF TECHNOLOGICAL CATASTROPHES

Improvements in the quality of life and in its prolongation resulting from human mastery over disease, and a similar conquering of the environment, are based on the creation of a broad technological network. Machines, devices, new chemicals, and physical structures share increasing responsibility for supporting our lives. For the most part, they accomplish this goal and work well under human control. Planes get us to and from distant places at unprecedented speeds; new and improved chemicals keep us alive longer and living more comfortably; nuclear power plants provide us with all the energy we could ever want at the push of a button. However, this network occasionally fails. Hence, we have electrical blackouts, dam failures, bridge collapses, airliner crashes, and toxic chemical leakage from waste dumps. Thus, technology is a two-edged sword, simultaneously improving the quality of life while posing potentially disastrous threats not only to the quality of life but to life itself. Further, it has been suggested that, as a species, we neither share equally in the technological harvest nor in its bur-

---

TIME-OUT: Assume that the town you came upon earlier in this chapter while vacationing had sustained heavy damages to permanent residences, leading to the displacement of 10 percent of the population of 20,000. Assume further that there had been no advanced warning, and that there had not been a tornado within 200 miles of this town in the last 100 years. Victims were described as young (average age of 34), well-educaated (most having a college degree), with on average 2.2 dependent children at home. Moreover, this population was quite stable, and most victims had family living nearby.

What kind of short-term mental health effects might you expect to occur as a result of this tornado? Why? What about long-term effects? What kind of action plan might be instituted to hasten recovery?

FIGURE 13-3 Since technological devices are designed never to fail unpredictably, when they do fail we are left with a sense of having been betrayed.

dens. For example, blacks in the United States are more likely to be involved in high-risk and hazardous occupations than are whites, and they are exposed to greater health risks in their neighborhoods (Bullard & Wright, 1987).

Technological catastrophes share many of the same characteristics as natural disasters (see Table 13-2, p. 366). Perhaps the biggest difference between the two, however, is the threat to our feelings of perceived control resulting from technological catastrophes. Chemical or radioactive leaks, dam failures, airliner crashes, and similar happenings *are never supposed to happen.* Technological devices, we are told, never fail unpredictably, and they warn us when they are worn out. Airplanes are not supposed to lose engines in midflight, nuclear power plants are not supposed to have accidents, and toxic waste dumps are not supposed to leak. But these things do happen, often appearing to strike at random. Instead of saying "No accidents will happen," we often find ourselves wondering "Where will the next explosion occur?" "Which plane will crash?" "Which waste dump will leak?" These kinds of events can reduce general perceptions of control and lead to stress (Davidson, Baum, & Collins, 1982). This increased fear of technological hazards appears to afflict more vulnerable groups (i.e., women, blacks, uneducated) to a greater extent than their affluent male counterparts (Pilisuk & Acredolo, 1988).

The effect of "lost control" is not confined to the area surrounding the failure, however, nor to those individuals directly affected. The malfunctioning of nuclear power plants at Three Mile Island and at Chernobyl has made us all more aware that there are very dangerous forces in the world over which we have no personal control. Likewise, toxic chemical leakage at Bhopal, India, and seepages at Love Canal and Times Beach in the United States tend to make us all feel a bit more vulnerable. Dramatic scenes of airliner crashes add to those feelings, and the shifting of blame from technology to terrorists does litttle to restore our sense of personal efficacy. Each event, in its own way, contibutes to a growing sense of vulnerability and to an uneasy anticipation of events that may or may not be forthcoming. Persons living near power plants, toxic-waste-disposal sites, and large dams that have had no problems are more than a little concerned about what their future has in store.

Research at Buffalo Creek, West Virginia in the aftermath of a flood that was at least partly attributable to human mismanagement, has identified a number of psychological problems. Among these are (1) *anxiety* (Gleser, Green, & Winget, 1981; Lifton & Olson, 1976; Titchener & Kapp, 1976); (2) *withdrawal or numbness* (Lifton & Olson, 1976; Erikson, 1976; Rangell, 1976); (3) *depression* (Titchener & Kapp, 1976; Kilijanek & Drabek, 1979); (4) *stress-related physical symptoms* including gastrointestinal distress, aches and pains, and similar symptoms (Titchener & Kapp, 1976); (5) *unfocused anger* (Lifton & Olson, 1976; Gleser, et al., 1981); (6) *regression* (Newman, 1976; Titchener & Kapp, 1976); (7) *nightmares* and other sleep disturbances (Gleser, et al., 1981; Newman, 1976).

Anxiety, depression, character, and life style changes and maladjustments and developmental problems in children occurred in more than 90 percent of the cases studied. Anxiety, grief, despair, sleep disturbances, disorganization, problems in temper control, obsessions, and phobias about survival guilt, a sense of loss, and rage were some of the other commonly reported symptoms. Lifton and Olson (1976) list several characteristics of the flood at Buffalo Creek that may have influenced their reactions to it. Suddenness, the human cause factor, the isolation of the area, and the destruction of the community were among them. Survivors were aware of the symptoms; they were surprised at how long they had lasted and were afraid that recovery was impossible.

Research on the nuclear accident at Three Mile Island (TMI) also illustrates the kinds of effects that can occur over a long period of time following a technological catastrophe. Several sets of investigations were conducted which concerned themselves with the mental health effects of the accident. There was a Presidential Commission which included a Task Force on Behavioral Effects; there was research sponsored by the Department of Health of the Commonwealth of Pennsylvania; there was research sponsored by the Nuclear Regulatory Commission; and, there was epidemiologic research funded by the National Institute of Mental Health (Bromet, 1989).

During the crisis, which lasted several days, there were a number of scares. Some people feared a nuclear explosion, others a meltdown, and still others feared massive radiation releases. Information intended to reduce fears often increased them because it was contradictory or inconsistent with other information that had been released. Evacuation was advised, and this may have contributed to the chaos of the moment. There is little doubt that the accident at TMI caused distress. Research suggests that most people living near the plant were threatened and concerned about it (Flynn, 1979; Houts et al., 1980). Immediately after the accident, studies found greater psychological and emotional stress among nearby residents than among people living elsewhere (Bromet, 1980; Flynn, 1979; Houts et al., 1980).

Research on the chronic effects of living near TMI is still going on, but there is evidence that stress effects persisted among some area residents up to two years after the accident. Bromet (1989), for example, has reported evidence of emotional distress among young mothers living near TMI. Several studies have also identified stress effects among some TMI area residents 15 to 22 months after the accident (Baum, Gatchel, & Schaeffer, 1983).

In general, these studies found that some residents of an area within five miles of Three Mile Island reported more emotional and psychological distress, more somatic distress, showed greater stress-related task performance problems, and exhibited higher levels of physiological arousal than did control subjects. Though levels of these variables did not indicate severe stress, they did suggest chronic difficulties of moderate magnitude.

Summary.   General conclusions to be reached from this and other research is that elevations in psychological stress promulgated by the accident at TMI have persisted, but that these levels of distress are subclinical and functioning appears not to have been impaired (Bromet, 1989). A second conclusion is that while most people reestablished normal life patterns, adaptation was slower for some groups. Finally, it should be noted that at present it is unknown if the persistent low level symptomology will eventuate in a full-blown clinical episode.

Clearly, not all technological catastrophes are like the Buffalo Creek flood or the accident at Three Mile Island. For a number of reasons, each accident or failure has its unique aspects. These studies do illustrate the potential for acute and chronic consequences of technological catastrophe. In many other instances (for example, power blackouts) the problem is far less serious and the effects are likely to be much more transient. Still other types of technological catastrophes are more insidious, slow developing and continuing. Webb (1989) describes the introduction of the fire-retardant polybrominated biphenyl (PBB) into the food chain in Michigan in just such terms, and Vyner (1988) has provided a penetrating and illuminating look at the psychosocial effects of such invisible environmental contaminants. After having provided an historical analysis of the great plague, a review of the studies regarding Love Canal, a summation of the Michigan PBB case as well as his own work on the effects of ionizing radiation, Vyner proposes a model for the development of traumatic neurosis. This model is presented in Figure 13-4.

Successful adaptation to a stressor or threatening situation, including many technological disasters and natural catastrophes, involves (1) gathering

FIGURE 13-4 A model fashioned after Vyner (1988) for understanding the development of traumatic neurosis.

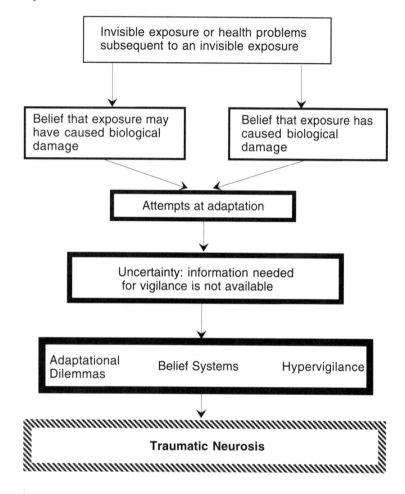

information that permits effective adaptation to that threat, and (2) mastering the situation by responding to it in a manner suggested by the acquired information. Adaptation to technological catastrophes and natural disasters will always be hindered by the fact that all of the necessary information to adapt successfully is not available. We have seen that individuals who are victims of an environmental event are very often concerned with protecting themselves from further exposure (from a recurrence) and are often consumed by the uncertainties they experience as a result of trying to recover from that event. This uncertainty, according to Vyner, becomes the breeding ground for a number of psychological effects.

Uncertainty gives rise to adaptation dilemmas because the individual is unable to obtain the information needed to adapt successfully. Uncertainty also gives rise to nonempirical belief systems because adaptation must go on in the absence of empirical information. As a result, persons exposed to an environmental threat often construct appraisals, which may or may not be veridical with the degree of actual threat. They do this as a means of providing themselves with some basis of information upon which they can mount an adaptation. Uncertainty also can give rise to hypervigilance. Because of the uncertainty of the environment and its possible consequences, individuals are on guard for changes in themselves or in the environment in which they find themselves. As these effects converge and intensify, traumatic neurosis occurs. Anything that would add to the uncertainty exacerbates this neurosis, just as information which clears up the uncertainty tends to ameliorate some of these effects.

The remainder of this chapter will deal specifically with uncertain environmental events. In fact, our concern will be with a "nonevent" (i.e., we will be concerned with environments that have the potential for catastrophe but where that potential has not yet been realized). In particular, we will focus on individuals living near toxic-waste-disposal sites. A study involving residents who live in an area surrounding a toxic-waste-disposal site will be reviewed (Stang & Veitch, 1985) and the ubiquity of such environments will be documented. These situations fit the description of environments which Vyner (1988) suggests lead to states of hypervigilance.

Subjects in the study to be reviewed (Stang & Veitch, 1985) all lived within five miles of a toxic-waste-disposal site in which various liquid chemicals, including PCB, are first stored and then infused in deep underground wells. The disposal site was managed by persons not directly from the community and therfore the best interests of the indigenous population may not have been served. Over the course of several years, operators of the site withheld information, provided misinformation, retracted previous information, denied any wrongdoing, and then in the face of intractable evidence, subsequently admitted some wrongdoing with respect to the operation and safety of the facility. All of this conspired to leave the local people in a state of uncertainty.

It can be said, therefore, that citizens of this area live in an environment which might be considered as outside the "normal bounds" of living and working environments, an environment that is exacting a toll on their physiological and psychological well-being. As discussed earlier, the stress response is triggered by the perception of a stressor in the environment. This stressor can be real or imagined, present or anticipated; to the organism it makes no difference. Whether, in reality, the atmospheric or groundwater chemical composition in this area represents a biological or physiological danger to the inhabitants is not the only question to be asked. Data regarding the perceptions, expectations, values, and fears of the area residents also need to be taken into consideration. Nonempirical belief systems are as powerful as actual knowledge (see Vyner, 1988).

As previously discussed, perception of control (or the lack of it) and the extent of predictability are two important psychological factors in the stress process. The greater the degree of control (real or perceived) the less exacting is the stress response; likewise, the greater the degree of predictability, the less is the likelihood of stress-related damages. Given the breach of trust by operators in this study it is little wonder that subjects reported feeling low levels of control over their environment. These feelings of uncertainty and lack of (or usurped) control manifested themselves in personal and insidious ways. For example, some citizens report being unable to sell property (if considering that option), others report that former visitors to their homes now refuse or make excuses not to visit, some guests visit, but refuse to dine or drink household water, etc. This uncertainty has also had a number of psychological ramifications to be discussed below.

Recall that regarding natural disasters, the recognition of a clearly distinguishable low point was found to be important in the amelioration of the stressor as a threat or danger. If the "threat" imposed by an environmental event reaches its maximum, the point where individuals can say that the worst is over and things will now begin to get better, stress typically begins to ameliorate. The situation near the toxic waste site, at the time of the study, had not yet developed to such a point. In fact, Pijawka, Cuthbertson, and Olson (1988) suggest that the disaster may never end for technological disaster victims because of the long latency period between exposure and disease manifestation.

The situation confronting the people of this study fits that category of environments herein labelled *technological catastrophe*. What makes this situation especially intriguing, however, is that a *catastrophe* in the usual sense of the word has not yet occurred. There has been no event the equivalent of a burst dam, nuclear accident, or airliner crash, yet the situation is reminiscent of that existing in the aftermath of other technological catastrophes discussed in this chapter.

The people who live in the area surrounding the waste-disposal site experience stress above and beyond what one would expect in the course of everyday living. Indeed, in many ways their experience is similar to that of individuals who have undergone extreme duress (residents near TMI, residents of the Buffalo Creek area). As a group, when compared with an appropriate control group, they showed elevated demoralization scores, higher anxiety, greater concern with health and bodily functions, less derived pleasure from their environment and a greater subservience to it, and a greater distrust of authorities in charge of waste management (Stang & Veitch, 1985). These results are consistent with those of other researchers (e.g., Horowitz & Stefanko, 1989; Stefanko & Horowitz, 1989). Fitchen (1989) suggests that toxic contamination, in addition to being a health and financial risk, represents an attack on the cultural institutions of home and home ownership and is therefore especially distressing. It should be noted that in the Stang and Veitch sample there were those who felt there was much ado being made about nothing; there were those who felt that the authorities in charge would not let any harmful actions occur; there were those who saw the waste-disposal site as an economic asset to the community. These latter individuals, however, were in the minority.

These findings are especially important when we realize that the Environmental Protection Agency (EPA) suggests that there are as many as 29,000 waste sites that are known to be dangerous enough to qualify for the Superfund cleanup program (Caplan, 1990). Furthermore, it is estimated that our nation may have as many as 300,000 additional hazardous waste dumps, at least 180,000 pits, ponds, and lagoons that contain chemical poisons, approximately 16,000 municipal and private landfills that contain toxins, and thousands of deep-well injection facilities operating with dubious safety (Caplan, 1990). Many of these are leaking poisons into underground drinking water supplies that serve over 120 million people including 95 percent of rural America.

Is it any wonder that people are becoming concerned regarding the safety of current chemical disposal methods? The stress experienced by those living near these sites is real (even if current conditions contain no imminent danger). The real stress comes from the uncertainty resulting from unpredictability and the loss of felt control people have over their lives. Who would have predicted a valve breaking at Bhopal, India, releasing 30 tons of methyl isocyanate gas? Who would have predicted that at least 2,500 people would be killed and that another 17,000 would be permanently disabled? The EPA has documented over 6,900 accidental chemical releases in the United States between 1980 and 1985. These releases resulted in 138 deaths, 4,717 injuries, and the evacuation of 200,000 people (Caplan, 1990). When will the next accident occur? Who knows? What can we do to prevent it? Probably nothing. Lack of predictablity and lack of control thus lead to the stress of anticipation and make areas surrounding chemical manufacturing and disposal sites pathological. This uncertainty is likely to lead to states of hypervigilance, and thus to stress often above and beyond what the physical environmental conditions actually warrant.

SUMMARY

Although primarily within the limits of normal human adaptability, natural systems occasionally stretch those limits. Unusually high temperatures, hurricanes, tornadoes, earthquakes, and the like call for out of the ordinary responding on the part of those affected. Likewise, technology is primarily under control; planes and trains don't often crash; nuclear power plants don't often malfunction; toxic wastes are usually disposed of in a safe and efficient manner. But sometimes planes do crash, sometimes trains carrying explosive or toxic cargo do derail, sometimes nuclear power plants do malfunction, and sometimes toxic wastes seep into our drinking water and evaporate into our atmosphere. These conditions can be labelled as disastrous or even catastrophic. What is important from the present perspective is that they call upon the human organism to respond in something other than a "steady-state" fashion; they call forth the human stress response.

Stress is the process through which the organism interacts with changes in its environment. It involves the organism's perception and evaluation of the environment, its selection of strategies for interaction, the mobilization of psychological and physiological counterforces to energize the interaction, and the behavior itself. This is a normal process ensuring the organism's reaction to meet the demands of the environment of which it is a part. Within the normal bounds of environmental hazard this process is an adaptive one. When the environment falls outside these "normal bounds," however, the stress response can take its toll. Various physiological as well as psychological aberrations are likely to result, some manifesting themselves immediately, with others being more insidious and delayed in their onset. Natural disasters and technological catastrophes represent two similar categories of environments which exceed these "normal bounds." There is growing evidence that these environmental hazards exact a toll from residents, and that while some of the effects are similar, other effects apppear to be unique to technological catastrophies. In particular, catastrophes create much greater threat to perceived control.

IMPORTANT CONCEPTS

disaster
natural/social system interaction
social disruption/crisis
anticipatory stress
demand/capability imbalance
social centrality
predictability/familiarity
technological catastrophes
similarities/differences between
   disasters and catastrophes
TMI
trust in authorities
hazard

physical agents impact/assessment
social construction of disaster
political dimensions of disaster
proportion of population
length/rapidity of involvement
research strategies
effects of disasters
psychological reconstruction
Buffalo Creek
hazards as stressful "nonevents"
demoralization
life satisfaction

REFERENCES

Apostol, A. (1985). Dowsing and earthquake prediction. *PSI Research, 4*(3–4), 212–218.

Austin, L.S. (1991). In the wake of Hugo: The role of the psychiatrist. *Psychiatric Annals, 21*(9), 520–524.

Barkun, M. (1974). *Disaster and the millennium.* New Haven, Conn.: Yale University Press.

Baum, A.S. (Speaker). (1985). Toxins, technology, and natural disaster (Cassette Recording No. 154-297-86A). Washington, D.C.: American Psychological Association.

Baum, A., & Davidson, L. (1985). A suggested framework for studying factors that contribute to trauma in disaster. In B. Sowder (Ed.), *Disasters and mental health: Selected contemporary perspectives* (DHHS Publication No. ADM 85-1421, pp. 29–40). Washington, D.C.: U.S. Government Printing Office.

Baum, A., Gatchel, R.J., & Schaeffer, M.A. (1982). Emotional, behavioral, and physiological effects of chronic stress at Three Mile Island. *Journal of Consulting and Clinical Psychology, 51*(4), 565–572.

Beigel, A., & Berren, M.R. (1985). Human-induced disasters. *Psychiatric Annals, 15,* 143–150.

Berren, M.R., Beigel, A., & Ghertner, S. (1980). A typology for the classfication of disasters: Implications for intervention. *Community Mental Health Journal, 16*(2), 103–111.

Berren, M.R., Santiago, J.M., Beigel, A., & Timmons, S. (1989). A classification schema for disasters. In R. Gist & B. Lubin (Eds.), *Psychosocial aspects of disaster.* New York: John Wiley.

Bolin, R. (1989). Natural disasters. In R. Gist & B.

Lubin (Eds.), *Psychosocial aspects of disaster.* New York: John Wiley.

Bolin, R. (1983, April 21–23). *Social support and psychosocial stress in disaster.* Paper presented at the meeting of the Western Social Science Association, Albuquerque, New Mexico.

Bolin, R. (1985). Disaster characteristics and psychosocial impacts. In B. Sowder (Ed.), *Disasters and mental health: Selected contemporary perspectives* (DHHS Publication No. 85-1421, pp. 3–28). Washington, D.C.: U.S. Government Printing Office.

Bolin, R. (1986a). Impact and recovery: A comparison of black and white disaster victims. *Mass Emergencies and Disasters, 4,* 35–50.

Bolin, R. (1986b). A quick response study of the 1986 California floods. *Report to the Natural Hazards Information Center.* University of Colorado, Boulder.

Bolin, R., & Bolton, P. (1986). *Race, religion, and ethnicity in disaster recovery.* Boulder: University of Colorado, Institute of Behavioral Science.

Bolin, R., & Klenow, D.J. (1988) Older people in disaster: A comparison of black and white victims. *International Journal of Aging and Human Development, 26*(1), 29–43.

Bromet, E. (1989). The nature and effects of technological failures. In R. Gist & B. Lubin (Eds.) *Psychosocial aspects of disaster.* New York: John Wiley.

Bromet, E., Schulberg, H.C., Dunn, L., & Gondek, P. (1980). *Three Mile Island: Mental health findings.* Rockville, Md.: National Institute of Mental Health.

Bullard, R.D., & Wright, B.H. (1987). Blacks and the environment. Special Issue: Black America in the 1980's. *Humboldt Journal of Social Relations, 14*(1–2), 165–184.

Burger, L., Van Staden, F., & Nieuwoudt, J. (1989). The Free State floods: A case study. *South African Journal of Psychology, 19*(4), 205–209.

Canino, G.J., Bravo, M., Rubio-Stipec, M., & Woodbury, M. (1990). The impact of disaster on mental health: Prospective and retrospective analyses. *International Journal of Mental Health, 19*(1), 51–69.

Caplan, R. (1990). *Our earth, ourselves.* New York: Bantam.

Chinnici, R. (1985). Pastoral care following a natural disaster. *Pastoral Psychology, 33*(4), 245–254.

Covello, V. (1983). The perception of technological risk: A literature review. *Technological Forecasting and Social Change, 23,* 285–297.

Crawshaw, R. Reactions to disaster. (1963). *Archives of General Psychiatry, 9*(2), 157–162.

Davidson, L.M., Baum, A., & Collins, D.L. (1982). Stress and control-related problems at Three Mile Island. *Journal of Applied Social Psychology, 12*(5), 349–359.

de la Fuente, R. (1990). The mental health consequences of the 1985 earthquakes in Mexico. *International Journal of Mental Health, 19*(2), 21–29.

de Man, A.F., & Simpson-Housley, P. (1987a). Factors in perception of tornado hazard: An exploratory study. *Social Behavior and Personality, 15*(1), 13–19.

de Man, A.F., & Simpson-Housley, P. (1987b). Factors in perception of earthquake hazard. *Perceptual and Motor Skills, 64*(3), 815–820.

Drabek, T. (1986). *Human system responses to disaster.* New York: Springer-Verlag.

Drabek, T., & Boggs, K. (1968). Families in disaster: Reactions and relatives. *Journal of Marriage and the Family, 30,* 443–451.

Drabek, T., & Key, W. (1984). *Conquering disaster: Family recovery and long-term consequence.* New York: Irvington.

Erikson, K. (1976). *Everything in its path.* New York: Simon & Schuster.

Fitchen, J.M. (1989). When toxic chemicals pollute residential environments: The cultural meanings of home and homeownership. *Human Organization, 48*(4), 313–324.

Flynn, C. *Three Mile Island telephone survey: Preliminary report on procedures and findings.* (1979). Tempe, Ariz.: Mountain West Research.

Galante, R., & Foa, D. (1986). An epidemiological study of psychic trauma and treatment effectiveness for children after a natural disaster. *Journal of the American Academy of Child Psychiatry, 25*(3), 357–363.

Garrison, J. (1985). Mental health implication of disaster relocation in the United States. *Journal of Mass Emergencies and Disasters, 3*(2), 49–66.

Gleser, G., Green, B., & Winget, C. (1981). *Prolonged psychosocial effects of disaster: A study of Buffalo Creek.* New York: Academic Press.

Grady, K.E., Reisine, S.T., Fifield, J., & Lee, N. (1991). The impact of Huricane Hugo and the San Francisco earthquake on a sample of people with rheumatoid arthritis. *Arthritis Care and Research, 4*(2), 106–110.

Green, B. (1985). Conceptual and methodological issues in assessing the psychological impact of disaster. In B. Sowder (Ed.), *Mental health and disaster: Selected contemporary perspectives* (DHHS Publication No. ADM 85-1421). Washington, D.C.: U.S. Government Printing Office.

Green, B.L. (1982). Assessing levels of psychological impairment following disaster: Consideration of actual and methodological dimensions. *Journal of Nervous and Mental Disease, 170*(9), 544–552.

Horowitz, J., & Stefanko, M. (1989). Toxic waste: Behavioral effects of an environmental stressor. *Behavioral Medicine, 15*(1), 23–28.

Houts, P.S., Miller, R.W., Tokuhata, G., & Ham, K.S. Health-related behavioral impact of the Three Mile Island nuclear incident, Part I (1980). Report submitted to the TMI Advisory Panel on Health Research Studies of the Pennsylvania Department of Health. Hershey: Pennsylvania State University, College of Medicine.

Kilijanek, T.S., & Drabek, T.E. (1979). Assessing long-term impacts of a natural disaster: A focus on the elderly. *The Gerontologist, 19*(6), 555–566.

Krause, N. (1987). Exploring the impact of a natural disaster on the health and psychological well-being of older adults. *Journal of Human Stress, 13*(2), 61–69.

Kroll-Smith, J.S., & Couch, S.R. (1987). A chronic technical disaster and the irrelevance of religious meaning: The case of Centralia, Pennsylvania. *Journal for the Scientific Study of Religion, 26*(1), 25–37.

Lave, T.R., & Lave, L.B. (1991). Public perception of risks of floods: Implications for comunication. *Risk Analysis, 11*(2), 255–267.

Lifton, R.J., & Olson, E. (1976). The human meaning of total disaster. *Psychiatry, 39*, 1–18.

Lima, B.R., Santacruz, H., Lozano, J., Chavez, H., et al. (1990). Disasters and mental health: Experience in Colombia and Ecuador and its relevance for primary care in mental health in Latin America. *International Journal of Mental Health, 19*(2), 3–20.

Lindy, J.D., & Grace, M. (1985). The recovery environment: Continuing stressor versus a healing psychosocial space. In B. Sowder (Ed.), *Disasters and mental health: Selected contemporary perspectives* (DHHS Publication No. ADM 85-1421, pp. 137–149). Washington, D.C.: U.S. Government Printing Office.

Logue, J.N., Hansen, H., & Struening, D. (1979). Some indications of the long-term effects of a natural disaster. *Public Health Reports, 96*(1), 67–69.

Madakasira, S., & O'Brien, K.F. (1987). Acute posttraumatic stress disorder in victims of natural disaster. *Journal of Nervous and Mental Disease, 175*(5), 286–290.

Mangum, W.P., Kosberg, J.I., & McDonald, P. (1989). Hurricane Elena and Pinellas County, Florida: Some lessons learned from the largest evacuation of nursing home patients in history. *Gerontologist, 29*(3), 388–392.

Mattsson, D., & Persinger, M. A. (1986). Geophysical variables and behavior: XXXV. Positive correlations between numbers of UFO reports and earthquake activity in Sweden. *Perceptual and Motor Skills, 63*(2, Pt. 2), 921–922.

McCaughey, B.G. (1984). U.S. naval disaster: The psychological symptomatology. *U.S. Naval Research Center Report, 84*(2), 8.

Milne, G. (1977). Cyclone Tracy: Some consequences of the evacuation for adult victims. *Australian Psychologist, 12*, 39–54.

Moore, H.E. (1958). *Tornadoes over Texas: A study of Waco and San Angelo in disaster.* Austin: University of Texas Press

Newman, C.J. (1976). Children of disaster: Clinical observations at Buffalo Creek. *American Journal of Psychiatry, 133*(3), 306–312.

Norris, F.H., & Murrell, S.A. (1988). Prior experience as a moderator of disaster impact on anxiety symptoms in older adults. *American Journal of Community Psychology, 16*(5), 665–683.

North, C.S., Smith, E.M., McCool, R.E., & Lightcap, P.E. (1989) Acute postdisaster coping and adjustment. *Journal of Traumatic Stress, 2*(3), 353–360.

Parker, G. (1977). Cyclone Tracy and Darwin evacuees: On the restoration of the species. *British Journal of Psychiatry, 130*, 548–555.

Penick, E.C., Powell, B.J., & Sieck, W.A. (1976). Mental health problems and natural disasters: Tornado victims. *Journal of Community Psychology, 4*, 64–67.

Perry, R.W., Lindell, M.K., & Green, M.R. (1981). *The implications of natural hazard evacuation warning studies for crisis relocation planning.* Seattle, Wash.: Battelle Human Affairs Research Centers.

Persinger, M.A. (1988). Geophysical variables and behavior: Indications of a tectonic strain factor in the Rutledge (UFO) observations during 1973 in southwestern Missouri. *Perceptual and Motor Skills, 67*(2), 571–575.

Phifer, J.F., & Norris, F.H. (1989). Psychological symptoms in older adults following natural disaster: Nature, timing, duration, and course. *Journals of Gerontology, 44*(6), S207–S217.

Pijawka, K.D., Cuthbertson, B.A., & Olson, R.S. (1988). Coping with extreme hazard events: Emerging themes in natural and technological disaster research. Special Issue: Research in thanatology: A critical appraisal. *Omega: Journal of Death & Dying. 18*(4), 281–297.

Pilisuk, M., & Acredolo, C. (1988). Fear of technological hazards: One concern or many? *Social Behavior, 3*(1), 17–24.

Quarantelli, E. (1985). Social support systems: Some behavioral patterns in the context of mass evacuation activities. In B. Sowder (Ed.), *Disasters and mental health: Selected contemporary perspectives* (DHHS Publication No. ADM 85-1421, pp. 122–136). Washington, D.C.: U.S. Government Printing Office.

Quarantelli, E.L., & Dynes, R.R. (1977). Response to social crisis and disaster. *Annual Review of Sociology, 3*, 23–49.

Rangell, L. (1976). Discussion of the Buffalo Creek disaster: The course of psychic trauma. *American Journal of Psychiatry, 133*(3), 313–316.

Roca, F.J., & Ivaldi, M.E. (1986). Seismic neurosis: Traumatic neurosis and daily life. *Psicologic Medica, 8*(2), 213–231.

Seroka, C.M., Knapp, C., Knight, S., & Siemon, C.R. (1986). A comprehensive program for postdisaster counseling. *Social Casework, 67*(1), 37–44.

Shah, G. (1985). Social work in disaster. *Indian Journal of Social Work, 45*, 462–471.

Solomon, S. (1985). Enhancing social support for disaster victims. In B. Sowder (Ed.), *Disasters and mental health: Selected contemporary perspectives* (DHHS Publication No. 14-8521, pp. 107–121). Washington, D.C.: U.S. Government Printing Office.

Solomon, S., & Canino, G. (1990). Approriateness of DSM-III-R criteria for posttraumatic stress disorder. *Comprehensive Psychiatry, 31*(3) 227–237.

Sowder, B. (1985). Some mental health impacts of loss and injury: A look outside the disaster field. In B. Sowder (Ed.), *Disasters and mental health: Selected contemporary perspectives* (DHHS Publication No. ADM 14-8521, pp. 74–106). Washington, D.C.: U.S. Government Printing Office.

Stang, S. & Veitch, R. (1985, May). Anticipatory stress in a potentially toxic environment. Paper presented at the annual meeting of the Midwestern Psychological Association.

Stefanko, M., & Horowitz, J. (1989). Attitudinal effects associated with an environmental hazard. *Population & Environment: A Journal of Interdisciplinary Studies, 11*(1), 43–57.

Taylor, V., Ross, G.A., & Quarantelli, E. (1976). *Delivery of mental health services in disasters: The Xenia tornado and some applications* (Book and Monograph Series, Vol. 11). Columbus: Ohio State University, Disaster Research Center.

Titchener, J.L., & Kapp, F.T. (1976). Family and character change at Buffalo Creek. *American Journal of Psychiatry, 133*(3), 295–299.

Vyner, H.M. (1988). *Invisible trauma: The psychosocial effects of the invisible contaminants.* Lexington, Mass.: D.C. Heath.

Webb, D.B. (1989). PBB: An environmental contaminant in Michigan. *Journal of Community Psychology, 17*(1), 30–46.

Weinrich, S., Hardin, S.B., & Johnson, M. (1990). Nurses respond to hurricane Hugo victims' disaster stress. *Archives of Psychiatric Nursing, 4*(3), 195–205.

People, Environment, and the Future

14

"Slaying the dragons is the easy part—the part I hate is filling out the environmental-impact statements!"

FIGURE 14-1 Will preserving the environment become institutionalized?

In 1974, economist Robert Heilbroner wrote a provocative and controversial book entitled *An Inquiry Into the Human Prospect*, in which he posed a *terrible question*: "Is there hope for man?" In posing this question, Heibroner was attempting to project the future for humanity. After a sobering review of the challenges confronting humans and our capabilities for meeting those challenges, Heibroner came to the depressing conclusion that the answer to this question was a resounding no. This book stimulated a great deal of debate regarding the premises of Heilbroner's terrible question, the urgency of the challenges, the accuracy of his projections, and the validity of his arguments and conclusions about the human prospect. Many concluded his analysis was overly pessimistic, and that his doomsday answer to the question was not supported by adequate evidence. Regardless of the potential refutation of his arguments or doubts about the inevitability of his conclusion, the book was important for raising a question that forced people to take stock of the present situation and think seriously about the future of humanity. In the first section of this chapter, we will review Heilbroner's analysis. This will be followed by a more detailed consideration of the economic and political implications of the issues posed by Heilbroner. Incorporated in these sections will be an analysis of ethical and values issues relevant to decision making and future planning in attempts to preserve our environment for the future. Alternatives will be suggested that might lead to a more optimistic answer to Heilbroner's *terrible question*. Finally, this chapter will conclude with a consideration of legal implications of environmental issues.

THE EXTERNAL CHALLENGES: OVERPOPULATION, ENVIRONMENTAL PROBLEMS, AND WAR

Heilbroner begins his analysis by suggesting that the overriding challenges to the human prospect are overpopulation and the environmental problems that inevitably accompany increasing world population. We need not elaborate on these issues, since the problem of overpopulation was discussed in Chapter 9, and Chapters 6, 7, and 8 enumerate the specific environmental problems to which Heilbroner refers. While we alluded to war as a consequence of territoriality in Chapter 10 and discussed the potential for conflict over diminishing freshwater supplies in Chapter 1, Heilbroner emphasizes war as an inescapable consequence of the first two problems, should current trends continue. He argues that the propensity of the developed industrialized nations to deplete natural resources (many of which are obtained from *underdeveloped* countries) in overwhelming disproportion to their relative population will simply not be tolerated by underdeveloped countries for much longer.

This, of course, is a variation of other writers' predictions of the conflicts between the *haves* and the *have-nots*. As the have-nots become increasingly aware of the exploitation of their natural resources by developed countries (the haves), they will begin to demand a share of the rewards. Specifically, the inequities in the standard of living between the developed and underdeveloped nations will become increasingly obvious in the future, and the latter countries will aspire to the same standard of living as the developed countries. However, the attainment of these aspirations is unlikely to occur, since the finite resources of the earth simply could not sustain such a situation. The result will be war brought on by a combination of the superpowers' struggle for control of these third world countries and the resistance of these countries to domination by the superpowers.

The reader of the above scenario might be tempted to conclude that this is just speculation supported more by imagination and fiction than by fact. Before you adopt this reassuring position, however, we suggest that recent events in the Middle East and current events in Central America could be construed as conforming to this model. Heilbroner adds an ominous dimension to this challenge by suggesting that conventional warfare (which would not favor the undeveloped nations) may not be the means by which the third world countries would attempt to create equity in resource use and standard of living. He believes that this goal will be accomplished by *nuclear blackmail*, where a third world country will eventually acquire access to a nuclear weapon and will threaten to use the weapon unless the developed countries agree to its demands.

There is no question that at least some third world nations are trying to develop nuclear weapons (e.g., Iraq, Iran, and Syria), although the degree of progress and the intended use of these weapons is not yet clear. Another recent phenomenon, however, also seems to support Heilbroner's analysis: terrorism. The bombings of civilian targets occurring with frightful regularity and the frequent taking of hostages by terrorist groups both exemplify the type of *blackmail* that Heilbroner predicted in 1974. The means of blackmail may not be as dramatic as a nuclear threat, but they are more insidious and difficult to prevent than the availability of nuclear weapons. Furthermore, there is still the possibility that Heilbroner's nuclear blackmail hypothesis may yet be borne out.

Humanity's Capabilities of Response

If you found the above description of the challenges confronting humanity depressing, you are not likely to be cheered by Heilbroner's analysis of humankind's abilities to respond to these challenges. Heilbroner assesses what he calls a *civilizational malaise* as both a symptom of the problems confronting humanity and a barrier to effective solutions to these problems. He argues that a plethora of maladies of modern society are a result of the problems posed above. Racial conflicts, international tensions, mental and physical illness, family disruption, unemployment, inflation, homicide and suicide, substance abuse, and violence are just a few of the many consequences of a world attempting to do too much with too little.

Heilbroner suggests that the above problems have roots in both economic and political features of the dominant nations in the world today, in addition to fundamental characteristics of human nature. He argues that both capitalist and socialist political ideologies share a common economic value: *Growth is good*, and is the ultimate criterion of success. Much more will be said of this later, but the important point in Heilbroner's analysis is that the earth is simply not capable of sustaining unlimited growth. Given that the major industrialized

FIGURE 14-2   A synopsis of Heilbroner's analysis.

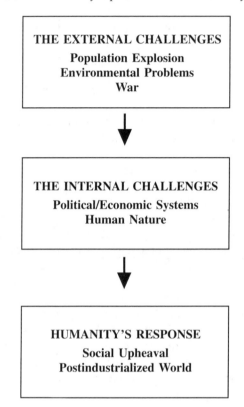

nations of the world are unlikely to give up this mentality, Heilbroner believes that current unrestrained growth will eventually be brought to a jarring halt. This will precipitate a crisis situation, leading to the third of his *external challenges*: war. Thus, Heilbroner suggests that none of the major ideological orientations in the world today are capable of effectively responding to the challenges confronting humanity, and the result will be a total breakdown in the social order.

But why is neither political system capable of meeting these external challenges? Heilbroner believes the answer to this question lies in what he calls the *internal challenges*—the fundamental flaws in human nature that transcend political ideologies and preclude a willingness to make the sacrifices that would be needed to avert the disaster he predicts. The thrust of Heilbroner's argument is that we are simply not willing to make the drastic changes in our individual and collective actions that are a prerequisite for avoiding an apocalyptic upheaval.

Projections of the Future

Given that humans living in the major industrialized societies as well as the third world countries are unwilling to alter the current direction that we are heading,

Heilbroner initially predicted that the environment would be able to sustain our growth mentality for another 30 years. At that point, we would enter a period of transition, in which governments would be forced to take drastic steps to avoid social upheaval. He believes that socialist governments, because of their greater centralized authority and control, will be better able to deal with this initial period of crisis than will democratic societies. However, since socialist societies share the same unwillingness to give up immediate personal goals in the service of long-range global goals that capitalistic societies have, they are doomed to the same ultimate fate. The third world nations will not be in any better position, and, in fact, they will be contributing to societal instability in the ways outlined above.

Thus, Heilbroner concludes his analysis with the assertion that there is, indeed, "no hope for man." He projects a bleak future, in which all of humankind will be beset with an environment that is not only incapable of sustaining life as we currently know it, but which will also exact its revenge by leaving society in a no-win position. In a reprint of his book published in 1980, Heilbroner revised his projections in light of efforts that have been taken to preserve the environment, and even qualified his answer to the *terrible question*: "There is no hope for man to maintain a standard of living comparable to that which is currently experienced by industrialized societies." He projected a future which he described as a *post-industrialized* society, in which humans may be able to survive in an environment which affords a standard of living comparable to that experienced by societies before the Industrial Revolution.

The remainder of this chapter will present a more detailed analysis of some of the implications of Heilbroner's arguments, as well as alternatives that could prevent the bleak future that he predicts. Much of what follows is taken from a book entitled *Environmental Science: A Framework for Decision Making*, by Daniel Chiras (1985). In this book, Chiras addresses many of the issues discussed in the present text. In addition, Chiras offers an analysis of some of the broader

TIME-OUT: Do you agree with Heilbroner's dismal analysis of the human prospect? What do others think? Develop a questionnaire in which you ask others to provide you with their assessment of what are the current greatest challenges to "life, as we know it" (see Chapter 3 on research methods to help you in developing this questionnaire). Be sure to include questions designed to tap into Heilbroner's external challenges as well as his internal challenges. You might also ask questions regarding their perceptions of humanity's current response to these challenges and whether they see these responses as adequate. If they are perceived as inadequate, you might try to determine what they think should be done.

Administer this questionnaire to several different samples. You might, for example, obtain a sampling of older adults, another of college students, and a third of middle-school children. Do these samples differ in their perceptions and opinions? How might you account for these differences, or the lack of them? Finally, spend some time considering the validity and reliability of your questionnaire. How might you attempt to revise it to get "better" answers to the questions you're asking?

FIGURE 14-3   A comparison of the severity and probability of hazard.

SEVERITY

		Low	High
PROBABILITY	**Low**	Acceptable Risk	?
	High	?	Unacceptable Risk

public policy implications of environmental issues. Thus, we will review his pre-sentation in light of Heilbroner's analysis of the human prospect.

ENVIRONMENTAL DECISION MAKING:
RISK ASSESSMENT AND MANAGEMENT

In Chapter 13, we distinguished between *natural disasters* and *technological cata-strophes*, noting that one of the most important differences between the two is that natural disasters are generally perceived as unavoidable but, since technol-ogy is a human development and under human control, technological catastro-phes are "never supposed to happen." We pointed out though that they can and do occur, and we presented several well-known examples. Given that there is at least the potential for problems when a new technology or process is introduced, the fledgling discipline of *risk assessment* (Kates, 1978) has emerged as an attempt to identify potential hazards of technology. In addition, attempts are made to ascertain the *probability* and *severity* of these hazards, as a basis for decision mak-ing (see Figure 14-3). Clearly, if a hazard has a low probability of occurring and its severity should it occur is also low, there is not much reason for concern. On the other hand, if a hazard is both very probable and severe, it is best to try to avoid it. Indeed, Weinstein, Sandman, and Roberts (1990) reported that both risk probability and severity information were strongly correlated with orders for a $20 home radon test kit. But what if the values of these two variables are quite different? Specifically, how are we to assess the risk of a low probability–high severity hazard? For example, the probability of a core meltdown of a nuclear reactor may be extremely small, but as we saw with Chernobyl, the severity of its effects can, indeed, be catastrophic locally and even significant on a global scale. Also problematic are assessments of high-probability-low-severity haz-ards, such as exposure to carbon monoxide in rush-hour traffic.

It is for these reasons that the concept of *risk acceptability* has been pro-posed. This concept implies a cost-benefit analysis, in which the potential costs of a technology are weighed against potential benefits. Generally, if the benefits outweigh costs, then a risk is considered acceptable. While the policy implica-tions of this procedure may seem straightforward, the determination of costs and benefits is an imprecise process, and there are no universally agreed-upon criteria for making this determination. For example, should benefits include economic growth, increased business investments, more jobs, and a higher standard of living? Even more troublesome can be the criteria for costs. For example, should costs be determined by immediate environmental effects, such as increases in the pollution emissions in an area, or should long-range effects that are not immediately observable (such as cumulative effects on health) also be considered?

Public perceptions of risk acceptability have also been studied. Napier, Carter, and Bryant (1986) tested a "vested interest" model derived from utilitarian orientations of social exchange theory in a reservoir-disrupted community. Vested interests in the reservoir were predictive of the extent of change of perceived risk acceptibility for long-term, but not for short-term, residents. Van der Pligt, Eister, and Spears (1986) examined risk acceptability of nuclear power stations, and also reported that attitudes toward the building of such a station in one's own locality were not only related to differential evaluations of potential benefits and costs, but also to differences in perceived importance of the various consequences. Interestingly, these researchers also reported greater and more extreme opposition to building a station in one's own locality than to building a station elsewhere. Presumably, greater benefits and lower costs were perceived to result from building nuclear power stations elsewhere. Kunreuther, Easterling, Desvousges, and Slovic (1990) compared a cost-benefit model and a risk perception model of the willingness of Nevada residents to accept a high-level nuclear waste depository, and found that acceptance depended on subjective risk factors, especially the perceived seriousness of risk to future generations and the level of trust placed in the Department of Energy to manage a repository safely. An offer of annual monetary compensation did not significantly decrease opposition to the repository.

Chiras points out that assessment of perceived harm can also be confounded by the public's perception that the introduction of the risk is voluntary or involuntary. Voluntary risk is seen as more acceptable, and as we discussed in Chapter 13, the potential adverse effects of hazards are also mediated by this perception of control. Researchers have recently conducted surveys of residents affected by actual or potential hazards. For example, Baird (1986) surveyed residents at a hearing for an arsenic emitting copper smelter. Informal risk estimates and risk tolerance were associated with judged benefits of the hazard source, judgments of exposure voluntariness, and environmental attitudes. The importance of attitudes was also demonstrated by Levi and Holder (1986), who reported that acceptance of nuclear power plants was negatively correlated with environmentalism and positively correlated with belief in experts' evaluations of the safety of nuclear power plants.

Other researchers have studied the role of information in risk perceptions. Pedigo (1986) investigated awareness of risks of nuclear radiation by providing residents information regarding their own radiation dosage levels. Overall only 20 percent of residents would consider changing their life style as a result of this information; however, 87 percent would do so if informed that their dosage level was above the median. Cvetkovich and Earle (1988) investigated the relationship between risk judgments and information seeking. They reported that people who judged a high probability of water contamination in a area were more knowledgeable about steps that could be taken to reduce the risks of the hazard than were people who made low risk estimates. Fathaddin (1986) studied risk perceptions and decision making in the context of technological innovations in water reuse. A large segment of the population was uninformed regarding the consequences of prolonged water shortages or the possibilities of extending existing water supplies through reuse. The population was evenly divided regarding the relative risks of shortages versus reuse. This researcher concluded that reuse is psychologically feasible, but contingent upon perceptions of reliable technology, professional management, and quality control. Other studies (e.g., Cvetkovich & Earle, 1988; Kunreuther, Easterling, Desvousges, & Slovic, 1990) have also indicated the importance of trust and public confidence in experts' ability to control a hazard in risk acceptability.

Most risk studies have been correlational in nature; however, Vaughan (1986) used an experimental approach manipulating high and low levels of relevant variables, and demonstrated complex interaction effects on perceived risk and risk acceptability. For example, "vividness of exposure pathway" only had an effect if other dangerous characteristics were also present. Also, high control did not always lead to greater acceptability; for some cancer-causing substances, involuntary exposure led to a "denial of threat." Clearly, the psychological processes involved in risk perceptions and acceptability decisions are exceedingly complex. In this regard, Kraus and Slovic (1988) have argued for a taxonomic analysis of perceived risk, which accounts for a variety of risk characteristics across individuals and across hazards, and Johnson and Fisher (1989) suggest that communication of risk information should consider the specific perceptual tasks the programs require people to perform. Finally, Larrain and Simpson (1990) reported differential responses to predictions of earthquakes versus volcanic hazards as a function of the episodic versus continuing nature of the two threats.

To complicate matters even further, environmental policy-making often involves the difficult process of attempting to achieve a "match" between *actual*

FIGURE 14-4 Adequacy of protection given high and low levels of actual and perceived risk.

| | **ACTUAL RISK** | |
	Low	High
PERCEIVED RISK Low	Adequate Protection	Underprotection
PERCEIVED RISK High	Overprotection	Adequate Protection

risk and *perceived* risk (see Figure 14-4) in order to provide cost-effective protection from environmental risks. That is, lawmakers try to avoid *overprotection* (where perceived risk exceeds actual risk) as well as *underprotection* (where perceived risk is below actual risk). In this regard, McClelland, Schulze, and Hurd (1990) reported sharp disagreement between homeowners and experts in health risk beliefs about the hazards of a landfill site, and Shem (1990) suggested that variation in risk perception is a barrier to the implementation of control policies. Deitz, Stern, and Rycroft (1989) identified four prevalent characteristics of conflicts over environmental threats: differential knowledge, vested interest, value conflict, and mistrust of expert knowledge, and suggested that environmental conflict is defined in ways that parallel the values and political interests of different actors in the conflicts. Anandalingam (1989) suggested a multiagent–multiattribute approach for conflict resolution in acid rain mitigation.

Chiras argues that an understanding of such decisions among the trade-offs described above ultimately requires an ethical analysis. This, in turn, involves a consideration of values. As we discussed in Chapter 4, values involve higher-level cognitive judgments about desirable end states (i.e., our thoughts about what is inherently "good/bad" or "right/wrong"). These cognitions then get translated into attitudes about environmental issues and decisions regarding risk acceptability. In particular, these overriding values often tip the balance in weighing costs and benefits of technology.

Values are typically arranged in our cognitive structures according to priorities. For example, when a decision has to be made by a community regarding the introduction (or elimination) of a pollution-causing technology, conflicts of interest can often be described in terms of differences in value priorities. Which is more important: providing (or preserving) jobs for community members, or the protection of their children from the potential long-term effects of the pollutants? If a public utility in an area of high unemployment argues that drastic rate increases will result from installing scrubbers to decrease sulfur dioxide emissions, how do citizens decide which is more important—keeping rates down, or keeping pollution down? If these sulfur dioxide emissions do not have an impact on the local environment, but may adversely affect that of Canada, where does the responsibility lie?

The above questions can only be answered by a consideration of *value priorities*. Although the issues do not lend themselves to easy decisions, it can nonetheless be argued (as we have at various points in this text) that individual citizens and lawmakers alike have tended to resolve these problems in terms of self-interest. That is, there is profound tendency of humans to give immediate, individual goals a higher priority than future, collective goals. Thus, for example, Lynne and Rola (1988) measured farmers' beliefs about soil conservation in relation to responsibility and profit-related values. They suggested that the comfortable life value, which leads to more income, may have been traded off against the value of being environmentally responsible. This is a point to which we shall return in Chapter 15, and Chiras makes the same point in his "time-space" characterization of most people's values orientation (see Figure 14-5).

Heilbroner comes to the same conclusion by suggesting that the present generation has no sense of or concern for posterity. In fact, it is this conclusion

FIGURE 14-5   Time-space characterization of peoples' values orientation. (From *Environmental Science*, Third Edition by Daniel D. Chiras [p. 461]. Copyright ©1991 by Benjamin/Cummings Publishing Company. Reprinted by permission.)

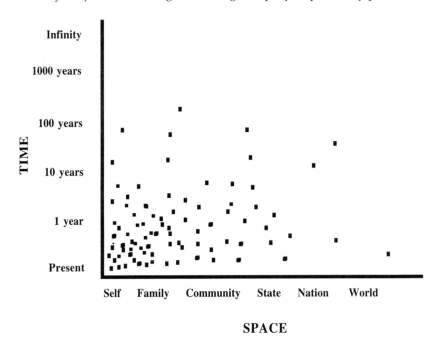

that serves as the primary basis for his reluctant negative answer to the question "Is there hope for man?" In essence, Heilbroner believes that rather than make the drastic changes in life style that would be required to preserve the environment for posterity, humans will opt, instead, to make decisions that will promote the longest possible maintenance of the current standard of living. In the postscript to his 1980 reprinting of the book, Heilbroner poses this question: "What has posterity ever done for me?" The obvious answer to this present, self-oriented question is "nothing," and it is this value priority that Heilbroner sees as the ultimate cause of the future downfall of humanity. Thus far our consideration of the bases of environmental decision making seems to support Heilbroner's answer to the *terrible question*. In the following section we will discuss some of the sociological and psychological roots of the barriers to a more optimistic answer to the question. We will then turn to a consideration of the changes that would permit an affirmative answer to the question.

ROOTS OF THE "FRONTIER MENTALITY" REGARDING THE ENVIRONMENT

Chiras suggests that an important determinant of values priorities regarding the environment and the future is the "frontier mentality," an ethic that is characterized by three assumptions: (1) Humans view the environment as an unlimited supply of resources, (2) we see ourselves as separate from, rather than a part of, the environment, and (3) nature is seen as something to be overcome. We have also discussed this mentality, suggesting that humans have historically seen the environment as being at our disposal to satisfy our never-ending search for comfort and leisure. Chiras similarly suggests that the frontier mentality leads us to see the world as simply a means for fulfilling human needs, and is the basis of our commitment to maximum material output and consumption. He argues that these values subordinate long-term environmental costs to immediate, short-term costs, such as the materials, energy, and labor required for manufacturing products to satisfy our needs and desires. He identifies three major roots of this unrestrained pursuit of materialism: theological, biological, and psychological theories of the relationship between humans and their environment.

Judeo-Christian Teachings

The principle that has been promoted in this predominantly Western religious tradition is that we are directed by God to "be fruitful, multiply, and subdue the earth." Thus, the exploitation of nature for our own purposes has been not only viewed as sanctioned by God, but is actually regarded as His will. This belief has been adopted without much concern for other Gospel writings that direct us to be "good stewards" of God's gift to us. In this regard, Eckberg and Blocker (1989) provided evidence suggesting that the disenchantment of nature in the first chapter of Genesis led to reduced concern for the environment in the West, and they reported that belief in the Bible predicted scores on all indices of environmental concern.

Biological Imperialism

This theory proposes that each organism naturally seeks to convert as much of the environment as possible into itself and its offspring. Chiras argues that humans also inherit this drive, but unlike other species and earlier societies (who lived within the limits imposed on them by the environment), modern technology has permitted our species to exploit the environment to a greater extent than have other species or previous societies. The implication, of course, is that this biological advantage could work to the eventual destruction of our own and other species.

The Skin-Encapsulated Ego

This psychological theory assumes that humans are predisposed to develop a sense of an "I" (what is inside the skin) and a "Not I" (what is outside of the skin). Of course, this psychological tendency contributes to the false dichotomy between humans and their environment. As seen in Chapter 1, environmental psychologists emphasize a "holistic" perspective on person–environment relations, regarding the two as a unit. Nonetheless, the degradation of our environment that is prevalent in current society suggests that humans do perceive themselves as separate and apart from the environment, and we seem to believe that *we* won't be harmed by damaging *it*.

WHAT HAVE WE EVER DONE FOR POSTERITY? TOWARD AN "ENVIRONMENTAL ETHIC"

We suggest that Heilbroner's question, "What has posterity ever done for me?" needs to be turned around and reasked as "What have we ever done for posterity?" If asked in this fashion we would find that progress has been made toward environmental preservation for future generations. Energy use in our country has declined somewhat, partly because people are driving more fuel-efficient automobiles, and are more energy conscious in their homes, installing increased insulation and turning down thermostats. Laws have been passed to protect the environment, agencies have been created to regulate pollution levels, and funds have been allocated for cleaning up toxic waste dumps. Population growth in our country has also slowed, and some have suggested that we are moving from an industry-based to an information- and service-oriented economy.

All of these events are encouraging, and might lead one to an affirmative answer to Heilbroner's *terrible question*. But are these changes enough? We will see in Chapter 15 that energy use and abuse still occurs to an alarming degree in our country, and population growth still remains unchecked in many parts of the world. More importantly, one could argue that the changes noted above have been motivated by a present, self-oriented concern, rather than by a genuine desire to preserve the environment for posterity. In the next section of this chapter we will discuss economic issues that might shed some light on this point, but for now we are suggesting that dramatic changes in attitudes and values may be needed more than some of the changes that have just been outlined. This is what is meant by an "environmental ethic," and we turn next to some of the precepts of this ethic.

Chiras suggests that real progress toward a sustainable society must first, and foremost, involve abandoning the frontier mentality. Humans must come to the realization that the earth has a limited supply of resources, some of which are nonrenewable. Thus, we need to recognize the stark fact that there is not always more, and must adopt strategies of *conservation, recycling*, and use of *renewable resources*. Second, we must recognize that we and nature are one. This involves changing the belief that the earth is an object to that of the earth as a living organism. This notion was proposed by Lovelock (1979) as the GAIA hypothesis. This theory proposes that the earth is a giant self-regulatory system, a superorganism, and that all living and nonliving matter interacts in a dynamic fashion. Russell (1982) extended this notion by suggesting that humans are the nervous system of the earth superorganism. These suggestions are in complete agreement with the holistic perspective of environment–people relationships discussed earlier.

The above shifts in perspective would lead to an awareness that the ethics of materialism and consumption characterizing modern society are just as much a threat to humanity itself as to the environment (see Swearingen, 1990). Put more directly, according to the GAIA hypothesis, the frontier mentality will have the ultimate result of killing ourselves in the same way that the brain dies if the body is killed. Thus, a more optimistic answer to Heilbroner's question requires a major change in attitudes and values regarding humans, the environment, and the future. These changes would involve a recognition of the interconnectedness between the environment and ourselves, leading to ethics of restraint rather than growth, conservation instead on consumption, and an orientation to the future rather than the present. These ethics would also entail values that give greater priority to the environment and posterity than to the needs and desires of the present generation. Some have referred to such a shift as a new environmental paradigm or postmaterial values (see Noe & Snow, 1990; Steger, Pierce, Steel, & Lovrich, 1989), and have suggested that positive nature experiences such as visiting national parks may promote indirect value shift toward such an ethic.

The above discussion essentially agrees with the changes that Heilbroner proposes are needed for an affirmative answer to the question "Is there hope for man?" Now that we have addressed these changes directly, the question really becomes: "Are we willing and able to make these changes?" That is are we willing and able to make the necessary changes to be able to say yes to the question "Is there hope for mankind?" Clearly, Heilbroner believes that we are not. Before you decide your answer, let us first consider some economic and political issues that are relevant to such projections.

TIME-OUT: On the title page of this text we quote an old Amish proverb: "We do not own the land, we are only borrowing it from our children." A quick glance at Chiras's time-space characterization of people's values orientations, however, suggests that most individuals think primarily of themselves (in the present) and not of others nor of the future. Psychologists have referred to this latter position as an inability to delay gratification and have shown it to be quite prevalent among children.

Design a study in which subjects can receive some relatively attractive immediate reward for their efforts, or can wait and receive a more attractive reward. Try to determine how much more attractive the reward has to be for individuals to wait one week, one month, one year. See if you can determine the nature of the relationship between incremental changes in reward and time. Now change the conditions such that subjects will receive an immediate punishment of moderate intensity, or they can choose to delay the punishment but in doing so the punishment will intensify with the passage of time. Now what is the relationship between time and punishment increments?

How do these two functions differ? Can we learn anything from these propensities to help establish environmental policy?

ECONOMIC IMPLICATIONS OF ENVIRONMENTAL ISSUES

Many of the issues discussed above can be formulated in economic terms. For example, we noted that an important basis for Heilbroner's negative assessment of the human prospect is his argument that both the major capitalist and socialist societies of the world share the same economic value (i.e., "growth is good" and is the criterion against which progress is measured). The cost-benefit analysis in risk assessment is essentially an economic judgment. We alluded to economic features of decision making regarding the trade-off between jobs and potential health effects of industry. Finally, the frontier mentality is firmly rooted in the belief in unrestrained growth. In this section we will discuss relevant theories and research regarding economic behavior and the environment.

Some have called economics the "science of growth," in that most economic theories assume that growth is the ultimate goal of all economic activities. Economic growth depends on increased consumption, which in turn depends on either increased population or an increased market. The most common measure of economic growth is the GNP (Gross National Product), defined as the total national output of goods and services. Chiras argues that the use of the GNP as a measure of standard of living can be misleading in that it does not take into account the wide variation in the costs of equivalent goods and services across different countries, nor does it incorporate variables such a population growth, accumulated wealth, and, most importantly, the environmental costs of the production of goods and services. Thus, he suggests that a true measure of standard of living would adjust for the effects of these variables on the *quality of life*.

Chiras also criticizes the chief doctrine of economic theory—the *law of supply and demand*. Basically, this law proposes a predictable relationship between the supply of a product, the demand for the product, and its price. The law proposes that increases in demand result in increased prices and decreased supply. Higher prices (and resulting profits) will stimulate greater production, thereby increasing the supply. The basic flaw is the assumption of unlimited availability of resources to perpetually permit increases in supply: with the rapid depletion of non-renewable resources, this assumption is simply false.

This analysis suggests that neither traditional economic indicators nor economic theory is compatible with the kinds of economic behaviors that would characterize the *environmental ethic* discussed in the previous section of this chapter. Thus, perspectives from economics also seem to support Heilbroner's conclusion that people by nature are unwilling—indeed, unable—to respond effectively to the external challenges confronting humanity. Once again, however, we ask that you withhold judgment until we have considered alternative models and behaviors. Specifically, in the following paragraph, we will discuss the economics of resource management, pollution control, and the notion of a steady-state economy.

An important determinant of economic behavior is *rate of time preference*, which refers to an individual's willingness to give up current income or goods for future income or goods (Heyne, 1976). Economists suggest that most people have a positive rate of time preference—that is, they place a higher value on goods presently held than on goods held in the future. Thus, other things being equal, if a person has a dollar, he or she is more likely to spend it today than to save it for tomorrow. This implies that an individual requires a return on the investment to be induced to give up current income or goods. In other words, for an individual to be willing to give up a dollar today, that person will want more than a dollar tomorrow. Rate of time preference will vary in relation to several factors, such as immediate needs, the magnitude of potential return, the certainty of return, and the length of time between investment and return. For example, a person will exhibit a high rate of time preference if there are immediate needs to fulfill, a small and uncertain return, and a long time delay before a return is experienced.

Chiras illustrates the role of time preference in resource management by contrasting different farming strategies. A *depletion strategy* attempts to maximize short-term production, leading to practices such as multiple cropping and using fertilizers, herbicides, and pesticides. A *conservation strategy* attempts to prevent topsoil erosion, involving practices such as crop rotation. A high rate of time preference would cause the farmer to adopt the depletion strategy, while a low rate of time preference would lead to a conservation strategy. As discussed in the preceding paragraph, time preference itself will be determined by factors such as market prices, interest rates, and profit margins. Thus, conservation or depletion of resources can be understood in terms of economic consequences of these strategies to the farmer (see Lynne & Rola, 1988).

But time preference will also vary according to ethical considerations. A frontier ethic is likely to be associated with a high rate of time preference, with little regard to the future. An environmental ethic would result in a lower rate of time preference, with the goal of preserving the environment for the future rather than satisfying immediate needs. Note that the depletion strategy will have the end result of higher costs in the future, while the conservation strategy will result in long-term profits that would eventually exceed the short-term profits of a depletion strategy. As more individuals come to this realization, the adoption of an environmental ethic becomes more likely. Specifically, it may be self-interest which eventually will result in the displacement of the frontier mentality with an environmental ethic. For example, Arcury and Christianson (1990) interviewed Kentucky residents in 1984 and 1988, reporting that the only county to show a significant increase in the level of an environmentalist world view during that time was one that had significant water restrictions in 1988.

Economic factors also play an important role in pollution control. Chiras suggests that until very recently, pollution was considered an *economic externality*. That is, the potential costs of pollution were not internal to traditional computations of the cost of manufacturing products, such as costs for materials, labor, and transportation. It was only when the government began enacting pollution regulations that the cost of installing pollution-control devices became internalized to economic calculations. Needless to say, this internalization has the effect of increasing the overall costs of production, so it is not surprising that pollution control has become a controversial economic and political issue.

The controversy revolves not around whether pollution control is desirable (one would be hard put to find an individual who would argue that it is not a desirable goal), but rather who will pay the costs and what the effects of these costs will be on the economy. Many industries have been reluctant to bear the cost of pollution control, with some arguing that it is the consumers using the product who should pay. Others argue that since it is the government that should bear the costs, because government has imposed new regulations that were not present when the industries were established. Still others argue that the imposition of laws requiring installation of costly pollution control devices hurts everyone by creating a drag on the economy. That is, the higher costs of production lead to higher prices, resulting in less consumption and lower profits. This is seen as leading to a downward spiral of decreased production, increased unemployment, and further reductions in consumption.

As we discussed earlier with risk assessment and management, however, this is not a simple, one-sided issue. That is, there are certainly costs of pollution control, but there are also certainly costs of the harmful health effects of pollution. Examples of costs include coping with the mental and physical health effects of pollution, cleaning up toxic-waste dumps, and repairing environmental damage from technological catastrophes. Thus, Chiras argues for a cost-benefits analysis of pollution control. The problem with this approach, however, is that the true costs of pollution are sometimes difficult to assess, and it is equally difficult to demonstrate the benefits of a clean environment. What is needed is a criterion for balancing the costs and benefits of pollution control.

Some (e.g., Daly, 1973; Peters, 1990) have argued that a major economic transformation is needed to restore and maintain the balance between humans and their environment. This would entail changing from an economy based on maximum growth via continual increases in production and consumption to a *steady-state economy*. This type of economy would depend on conservation, recycling, use of renewable resources, and global population control. A steady-state economy would be possible only through a change in value priorities favoring a better environment over economic growth. Enjoyment of nature would be sought more than material pleasures. Major changes in governmental structure and operation would be needed. Some critics argue that these suggestions are utopian and unlikely to be realized, and we saw earlier that this is the major thrust of Heilbroner's thesis. However, government has taken important steps in this direction in the past, and at least the potential for the role of the political process should be considered before we address these criticisms.

POLITICAL IMPLICATIONS OF ENVIRONMENTAL ISSUES

In the last chapter of his book, Chiras outlines some characteristics of the American political process that are obstacles to a sustainable society, and he recommends some changes that might help remove these obstacles. First and foremost among these obstacles is the lack of consensus about what the future should be like and which policies should or should not be enacted to preserve the environment. The tremendous diversity of the American public is reflected in Congress and influences elected officials in many ways. For example, industrial lobbyists attempt to sway decisions regarding pollution control (see above discussion). Other special interest groups have begun organizing on a large scale in the form of PAC's (political action committees), which contribute huge sums of money to political campaigns in the hope of electing representatives who will be sympathetic to their views. Public opinion polls influence officials also, but public opinion frequently changes dramatically over short periods of time. Public opinion itself can be influenced by charismatic leaders. For example, public concern over environmental matters, a major political issue in the 1970s, receded into the background in the 1980s. This change can be seen as at least partly due to the popularity of Ronald Reagan, who put economic growth and defense at the top of his political agenda. Needless to say, effective legislation to deal with environmental issues is difficult to enact and enforce when there is no long-term consensus over the importance of these issues, much less what should be done to preserve the environment.

Other obstacles to change identified by Chiras include *crisis politics*, in which long-range planning and critical decisions are put aside in order to deal with more urgent issues occupying the immediate attention of lawmakers; *single-issue politics*, in which issues are approached individually, with no effort to integrate separate issues into a cohesive environmental policy; *budgetary constraints*, in which huge deficits make it difficult to spread money around, resulting in environmental issues taking a "back seat" to more visible programs; *limited planning horizon*, in which politicians are concerned with only politically "hot" issues relevant to the "next election," and *lack of a focal point* regarding what environmental issues should be addressed in the first place. All of these problems are complicated by the bureaucratic inefficiency of government, bogged down by myriad agencies, inept management, and infighting within and between agencies.

Foremost among the changes that Chiras suggests is striving for a *proactive* rather than a *reactive* government. He describes a reactive government as largely retrospective, attempting to patch up problems in response to political pressures. He cites the Clean Air Act as legislation passed only after a public outcry over air pollution, and the Superfund to clean up toxic waste dumps that have been permitted to proliferate in the past. By contrast, proactive government attempts to prevent problems from occurring in the first place. The Toxic Substance Control Act is an example of proactive legislation; it requires screening of new chemicals before they are permitted to be introduced. Chiras cites other examples of proactive government anticipating problems before they occur, including the Water Resources Planning Act, the Resources Planning Act, the Resource Conservation and Recovery Act, and the National Environmental Policy Act. The last piece of legislation will be described in detail in the last section of this chapter.

The focus of these examples is on future planning, and an important part of this involves education of the public regarding environmental issues. This text is seen as one step in this direction. Thus, farsighted and wise environmental planning and policy-making relies on an educated public. Finally,

Chiras also proposes the enactment of a "Future Security and Sustainable Earth Society Act," a law that would require the government to take responsibility for promoting a society that lives within the limits imposed by nature. We agree with these proposals—indeed, we assert that these and other changes are the key ingredient to mobilizing an effective response to the external challenges posed by Heilbroner. Further, it is our belief that such major changes are the only alternative to the dismal analysis of the human prospect suggested by Heilbroner. In the next section of this chapter, we elaborate on the National Environmental Policy Act (NEPA) as an example of just what a proactive government should be like. As mentioned above, this will be done in the context of the legal implications of environmental issues. The concluding chapter of this book will present ideas about how the dramatic attitude changes alluded to in the present chapter could be brought about to save the environment for ourselves and for posterity.

LEGAL IMPLICATIONS OF ENVIRONMENTAL ISSUES

Environmental law has become a regular part of the curriculum in American law schools. This reflects not only the growing awareness of the public of environmental issues, but also the increasing number of lawsuits regarding personal and property damage heard by state and federal courts. This has been a result of the gradual increase in the number of laws that have been passed in the interest of protecting the health and welfare of the public. The basic issue of legal debate has been the conflict between the rights of corporations to pursue economic activities and the rights of private citizens to be protected from harmful effects of these activities. However, these issues have not been resolved easily. For example, the courts must often make difficult decisions among the rights of the individual citizen to protection from harm, the legitimate rights of the corporation to do business, the economic interests of the community, and broader issues, such as the long-term environmental effects of the industrial activity.

The two major principles upon which legal disputes are usually decided are nuisance and negligence. A *nuisance* is defined as arising from an unreasonable, unwarranted, or unlawful activity that results in injury to the public or an individual. Nuisance is difficult to demonstrate, in that courts will often consider defenses such as "good faith" efforts to reduce the nuisance, availability of technology to limit the nuisance, and the existence of the nuisance before the plaintiff moved to the area. *Negligence* is defined as acting in an "unreasonable" manner leading to personal or property damage. To demonstrate negligence, it is necessary to show that an individual or company has acted or failed to act in a way that a "reasonable" person or entity would to prevent harm to others. For example, if a company fails to employ commonly used technologies to reduce pollution, it could be found negligent. However, negligence is even more difficult to prove than is nuisance. Specifically, it is often difficult to demonstrate what a "reasonable" entity could or would have done to prevent damage. Thus, both nuisance and negligence carry with them the "burden of proof" that significant damage has been done and that the defendant knowingly produced the damage. Weait (1989) has suggested that unlawful behavior of organizations be examined in terms of organizational structure, ideology, and objectives in addition to external influences that relate to the qualitative aspects of unlawful behavior.

Another problem in resolving legal disputes is that the damage produced by the manufacture of a product may not influence individuals in the immediate proximity of the corporation. For example, a company that dumps toxic chemicals into a river may cause problems for a city downstream, or even to individuals in a different state. As discussed earlier in this chapter, sulfur dioxide emissions from power plants in the Midwest can produce acid rain in the Northeast. Thus, local and state courts often have difficulty resolving these types of disputes.

Many environmental issues are increasingly being decided at the federal level. In the previous section of this chapter we mentioned an example of a federal law enacted that has played an increasingly important role in dealing with issues of environmental law: The National Environmental Policy Act. We present next a detailed description of the provisions and implementation of this law.

THE NATIONAL ENVIRONMENTAL POLICY ACT (NEPA)

On January 1, 1970, President Richard Nixon of the United States signed the National Environmental Policy Act (NEPA) into law. This law encourages productive harmony between people and their environment. In essence, the federal government had at long last recognized the reciprocal, fragile and homeostatic relationship between humans and their habitats. The Congress also recognized that humans do not always act in their own best (long-term) inter-

---

TIME-OUT: Consider for a moment how your health and welfare may be influenced (perhaps even jeopardized) by environmental events occurring at some distance from you. Where does the drinking water in your city, town, or country home come from? A nearby river or lake? How clean is it? Who's dumping in what and how much? A reservoir? What types of airborne contaminants might it contain? An underground well? Are there any toxic chemicals seeping into the aquifer from chemical disposal sites some distance from you?

What about the food you eat? The air you breathe? Are they free from harmful pollutants? How can you be sure?

A little reflection on these questions should lead you to the conclusion that local surveillance of our environment is insufficient, that regional, national, and even international safeguards are required if we are to maintain even minimal environmental safety standards.

---

ests, and that it was incumbent upon the government to provide the means for maintaining conditions in which humans and their environment can coexist in productive harmony.

The act has had a resounding impact on actions affecting the environment by requiring environmental considerations to be included in decision-making processes concerning federal projects and activities. Specifically, NEPA requires each federal public agency to prepare a detailed statement of environmental impact before proceeding with any major action, recommendations, or report on proposals for legislation that may significantly affect the quality of the human environment. Major actions may range from dredging operations to new highway construction or from recommendation on legislation to major water resource projects. With the passage of NEPA, many state governments have enacted analogous legislation and have thus increased the number of projects requiring some sort of pre-action impact assessment.

Environmental impact assessment has become an increasingly important vehicle for curbing pollution and for minimizing environmental disruption. In principle, and by law, any federal action which may influence the relationships of humans to their environments in a detrimental fashion has to be fully researched and described before the action can take place. Additionally, alternatives to the action must be sought and mitigation measures implemented where feasible. There are really two titles under this act. Title I is a declaration of a national environmental policy and Title II, to be explained later, mandates the development of the Council on Environmental Quality (CEQ).

Title I: The Policies and Procedures of NEPA

Title I sets forth national policy on restoration and protection of environmental quality. Section 101 of the law is substantive in nature. Under this section the federal government has a continuing responsibility "consistent with other essential considerations of national policy ... to minimize adverse environmental impact and enhance the environment as a result of implementing federal plans and programs." Section 102 is procedural in nature. Under this section the proponent federal agency is required to make full and adequate analyses of all environmental effects of implementing its programs or actions. The Congress stipulates that policies, regulations, and public laws shall be interpreted and administered in accordance with the policies of NEPA. Further, Section 102 directs all federal agencies to follow a series of steps to ensure that the goals of the act will be met.

The first requirement is that "a systematic and interdisciplinary approach be used to insure the integrated use of social, natural and environmental sciences in planning and decision making." The environment encompasses not only the more obvious areas of air and water quality and ecology, which are in and of themselves highly complex, but less tangible areas as well, such as sociological relationships, economics, land use, aesthetics, and psychological impact. No single individual possesses the range and depth of knowledge to address adequately all aspects of the environment in an environmental impact analysis. The sociologist simply does not know the effect of a proposed housing project on groundwater sedimentation, on air pollution, or on the flight patterns of migratory birds. By the same token, the geologist should not be expected to anticipate the changes in friendship patterns, family governance, and crime that might occur as a result of this same housing project. Civil engineers, foresters, psychologists, and economists, along with a host of other professionals, all have their special acumen to be applied to an understanding of the environment/human relationship.

The second requirement of Section 102 is that federal agencies shall in consultation with the CEQ identify and develop procedures and methods such that presently unquantified environmental amenities and values may be given appropriate consideration in decision making along with traditional economic and technical considerations. This section is of particular importance in that it recognizes our inability, at this time, to define the parametric values of certain aspects of human life (i.e., aesthetic considerations, historical preservation, the value of the wilderness experience, and so forth). How does one compare the "beauty" of the Rocky Mountains with the oil that might be extracted from its shale? How does one compare the extinction of a species with the beauty and warmth provided by a fur coat? What is the equation that tell us the degree of anxiety produced by living near a toxic-waste-disposal site that is equal to the convenience and economics of having the site near high-population-density areas? The Congress recognizes that these questions are not presently, and may never be, answerable. They are problems that need to be dealt with, however, and latitude is provided in an environmental assessment for doing so.

Section 102 also sets forth the requirements and guidelines for preparing *Environmental Impact Statements* (EIS). This section requires all federal agencies evaluating plans that could significantly affect the environment to include a detailed statement by the responsible official covering the following elements: (1) the environmental impact of the proposed actions; (2) any adverse environmental effects which cannot be avoided should the proposal be implemented; (3) the alternatives to the proposed actions; (4) the relationship between local short-term uses of the environment and the maintenance and enhancement of long-term productivity; and (5) any irreversible and irretrievable commitment of resources which would be involved in the proposed action should it be implemented.

Section 103 of the law states that all federal agencies are required to review their regulations and procedures for the purpose of determining whether there are any deficiencies or inconsistencies therein which prohibit full compliance with the purposes and provisions of the act and shall propose to the President such measures as may be necessary to bring their authority and policies into conformity with the law. Basically, this section of the act states that it is incumbent on each agency of the federal government to ensure that it is complying with the intent of NEPA, and that where it finds impediments to compliance, it should make recommendations for rectifying them to the President through the Council on Environmental Quality.

Title II: The Council on Environmental Quality

Title II of the act establishes the Council on Environmental Quality as an environmental advisory board for the Executive Office. In addition, by law, the President is required to submit to the Congress an annual "Environmental Quality Report." This yearly summary sets forth (1) the status and conditions of the major natural, artificial, or altered environmental quality of the nation; (2) current and foreseeable trends in the quality management and utilization of such environments and socioeconomic impact of these trends; (3) the adequacy of the available natural resources; (4) a review of governmental and nongovernmental activities on the environment and natural resources; and (5) a program for remedying the deficiencies and recommending appropriate legislation.

Specifically, the Council on Environmental Quality has a number of duties and functions that can be summarized as follows: (1) assist and advise the President in the preparation of the Environmental Quality Report; (2) review and appraise the various programs and activities of the federal government in light of the policy of environmental protection and enhancement; (3) develop and recommend to the President national policies to foster and promote improvement of environmental quality; (4) conduct research related to ecological systems and a continuing analysis of changes in environmental quality; (5) report at least once a year to the President on the state and condition of the environment; and (6) conduct such studies and furnish such reports and recommendations that the President may request.

The Environmental Impact Statement (EIS)

The Environmental Impact Statement (EIS) can be thought of as serving a four-fold purpose. It should be thought of as (1) part of the planning process, (2) a "full disclosure" document, (3) a decision-making tool, and (4) an environmental management tool (Corwin, Heffeman, Johnston, Remy, Roberts, & Tyler, 1975). The purpose of an EIS is to report the potential impact of a proposed change in land use before the change is actually made. To meet this objective, an EIS can be, and is sometimes required to be, prepared as part of the planning process. This planning process requires two primary steps: (1) identification of present land use and (2) identification or development of alternative uses. The logical point for preparation of an EIS is immediately after completion of these two steps, but before a decision is made on a specific alternative. If done at this time, an EIS can become a tool for planning, not merely a device to be used to oppose or justify a proposed plan. It can then be used in concert with economic, engineering, and aesthetic factors to determine the overall feasibility of a project.

The planning process mandated by law is shown in Figure 14-6. The initial step identifies the condition of a given parcel of land prior to development, whereas the second step develops alternative land uses. The first step takes inventory of the natural resources found on or affecting the property or

FIGURE 14-6 EIS in the planning process.

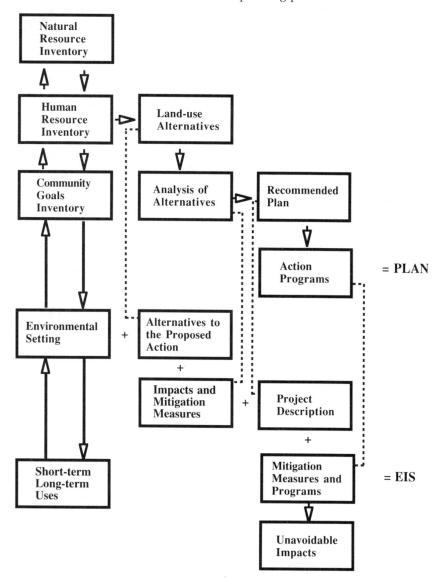

resources under question. *Physical conditions* include such fundamental categories as geology, soils, vegetation, hydrology, groundwater, climate, wildlife, and so forth. *Human resources* include present use of the land, transportation systems, recreation facilities, agriculture, historic factors, and utilities. A final cultural factor is represented by the goals of the given area. Such goals can take the form of a master plan but may be no more than a loosely defined expression of what people in the community feel their community is or ought to be.

Most land users have at least a general range of uses in mind before they fix their sights on a given area. However, within certain bounds they usually are open to evaluation of alternative uses. These alternatives are considered by the Council on Environmental Quality to be the *heart* of the EIS. Alternatives are determined by the natural resource inventory, human resource inventory, and community goals. In essence, the alternatives are developed from all the available facts coupled with economic reality. Once the alternatives have been developed, it is possible to evaluate the effect of each one on the natural and human environment and to determine how well this fits in with the community goals. The results of this evaluation can be presented as a set of environmental impact statements, one for each alternative use. After each alternative has been considered, a recommended land use can be selected and action programs developed for its implementation.

As an example, a small city might have at its disposal a 300- to 400-acre plot of land adjacent to its present boundaries. Present use of the land is agricultural, and on alternate years wheat, soybeans, and corn are cash-cropped. The community benefits from this use of the land directly through property taxes that are paid and indirectly through the additional money brought to the community from the sale of these commodities. Suppose further that a group of developers would like to see this land utilized to construct a small airport, or perhaps to build a shopping mall. An environmental impact statement would then be implemented as part of the planning process. Questions regarding the overall plans for the growth of the city would have to be answered. What is the present drainage like on this land? How might these changes affect other parts of the city and its suburbs? What future uses of this and adjacent land would be precluded if one of these actions were to be implemented? Would the quality of the air or water be adversely affected? A host of environmental attributes need to be considered when contemplating the impact of cer-

TIME-OUT: Assume that you live in a relatively small town with a population of 50,000. A group of local entrepreneurs are looking into the feasibility of purchasing 200 acres on the edge of town and building an airport large enough to handle small propellor-driven aircraft. The land has a small creek cutting diagonally across one corner of the parcel and is lined with primarily deciduous trees to a width of 60 feet. The only portion of the land abutting the current boundaries of the city is a one-quarter-mile long road running east to west. On the south side of this road are two small homes, but a builder has plans to construct an eight-unit apartment complex, as well.

What kinds of questions would you like to see answered before the okay is given to go ahead with the plans? What are the environmental implications of the answers to some of these questions? See if you can develop a questionnaire where the answers would provide you with the information necessary to develop an environmental impact statement. Where would you have to go to get some of your answers? What kinds of experts might you have to call in?

tain projects on the quality of the environment and the quality of life in that environment.

NEPA and the Future

The federal government, with the passage of NEPA, has laid the groundwork whereby humans can enjoy a peaceful and productive coexistence with their environment. There are those who argue that the passage of this law represents a big step forward. Others argue that it has created a bureaucratic impediment to the salvation of the environment and acts as a brake to human progress. Still others argue that the law provides "too little, too late."

By establishing the Council on Environmental Quality and by specifying the particulars of its functions, NEPA guarantees a yearly assessment of the state of the environment. It also establishes, in principle, an informal watchdog of the environment over all federal agencies, and reiterates the need for further data collection, collation, and interpretation. Unfortunately, while the law has established a watchdog, it has given it no teeth, and a "bark" which more closely resembles a "meow." Many legal impediments exist even in the triggering of an EIS. For example, recent decisions by the United States Supreme Court have ruled that psychological stress cannot be considered as an environmental attribute that would require an EIS. Environmental lawyers complain that even when an EIS suggests potential environmental damage, the land user is not required to change his or her plans. Finally, although the EPA has been elevated to cabinet-level status, the Council on Environmental Quality has been eliminated as a result of budget cutting. Partly because of these problems, environmental psychologists have explored a more "grass-roots" approach to solving environmental problems. Some of these efforts are described in our concluding chapter.

SUMMARY

If we are to maintain a habitable planet a number of external challenges to the health of Mother Earth must be thwarted. Robert Heilbroner makes a cogent argument that these external threats can be categorized as overpopulation, environmental problems, and war. He sees these external challenges as being highly interdependent and inevitable. Furthermore, he argues that, given present value systems and ethical outlooks, these challenges inexorably spell the death of humankind.

Other writers, while adhering to the notion that these challenges are real, are reluctant to say that they are insurmountable. The development of an environmental ethic and the passage of pertinent legislation, they claim, will do much to alleviate the problems posed by these challenges. We have seen how the passage of the National Environmental Policy Act provides some hope, and in the final chapter we will look at some individual strategies for lessening the burdens of overpopulation and environmental degradation.

IMPORTANT CONCEPTS

external challenges
industrialized societies
underdeveloped countries
nuclear blackmail/terrorism
postindustrial society
internal challenges
hazard probability/severity
cost-benefit analysis
risk assessment
risk acceptability
voluntary risk
vested interest model
actual vs. perceived risk
values & value priorities
frontier mentality
time-space continuum
biological imperialism
Judeo-Christian teachings
skin-encapsulated ego
environmental ethic
nonrenewable resources

GAIA hypothesis
economics and growth
GNP
supply and demand
rate of time preference
depletion strategy
conservation strategy
steady-state economy
economic externality
crisis politics
PACs
limited planning horizon
single-issue politics
proactive vs. reactive government
toxic substance control act
individual vs. corporate rights
nuisance and negligence
NEPA
Title I policies/procedures
Council on Environmental Quality
EIS components

REFERENCES

Anandalingam, G. (1989). A multiagent, multi-attribute approach for conflict resolution in acid rain impact mitigation. *IEEE Transactions on Systems, Man, and Cybernetics, 19*(5), 1142–1153.

Arcury, T.A., & Christianson, E. H. (1990). Environmental worldview in response to environmental problems: Kentucky 1984 to 1988 compared. *Environment and Behavior, 22*(3), 387–407.

Baird, B.N. (1986). Tolerance for environmental health risks: The influence of knowledge, benefits, voluntariness, and environmental attitudes. *Risk Analysis, 6*(4), 425–435.

Chiras, D.D. (1985). *Environmental science: A framework for decision making.* Menlo Park, Calif.: Benjamin/Cummings.

Corwin, R., Heffeman, P.H., Johnston, R.A., Remy, M., Roberts, J.A., Tyler, D.B. (1975). *Environmental impact assessment.* San Francisco: Freeman, Cooper & Company.

Cvetkovich, G., & Earle, T.C. (1988). Judgment and hazard adaptation: A longitudinal study of responses to the risks of water contamination. *Acta Psychologica, 68*(1), 343–353.

Daly, H.E. (Ed.). (1973). *Toward a steady-state economy.* San Francisco: Freeman.

Deitz, T., Stern, P.C., & Rycroft, R.W. (1989). Definitions of conflict and the legitimation of resources: The case of environmental risk. *Sociological Forum, 4*(1), 47–70.

Eckberg, D.L., & Blocker, T.J. (1989). Varieties of religious involvement and environmental concerns: Testing the Lynn White thesis. *Journal of the Scientific Study of Religion, 28*(4), 509–517.

Fathaddin, A.A. (1986). Risk perceptions and decision making in the management of technological innovations: The case of water reuse. *Dissertation Abstracts International, 46*(11-B), 4051.

Heilbroner, R.L. (1974). *An inquiry into the human prospect.* New York: W.W. Norton & Co., Inc.

Heyne, P. (1976). *The economic way of thinking* (2nd ed.). Chicago: University of Washington Science Research Assoc., Inc.

Johnson, F.R., & Fisher, A. (1989). Conventional wisdom on risk communication and evidence from a field experiment. *Risk Analysis, 9*(2), 209–213.

Kates, R.W. (1978). *Risk assessment of environmental hazards.* New York: John Wiley.

Kraus, N.N., & Slovic, P. (1988). Taxonomic analysis of perceived risk: Modeling individual and group perceptions within homogeneous hazard domains. *Risk Analysis, 8*(3) , 435–455.

Kunreuther, H., Easterling, D., Desvousges, W., & Slovic, P. (1990). Public attitudes toward siting a high-level nuclear waste respository in Nevada. *Risk Analysis, 10*(4), 469–484.

Larrain, P., & Simpson, H.P. (1990). Geophysical variables and behavior: Lonquimay and Alhue, Chile: Tension from volcanic and earthquake hazard. *Perceptual and Motor Skills, 70*(1), 296–298.

Levi, D.J., & Holder, E.E. (1986). Nuclear Power: The dynamics of acceptability. *Environment and Behavior, 18*(3), 385–395.

Lovelock, J.E. (1979). *Gaia: A new look at life on earth.* Oxford: Oxford University Press.

Lynne, G.D., & Rola, L.R. (1988). Improving attitude-behavior prediction models with economic variables: Farmer actions toward soil conservation. *Journal of Social Psychology, 128*(1), 19–28.

McClelland, G.H., Schulze, W.D., & Hurd, B. (1990). The effect of risk beliefs on property values: A case study of a hazardous waste site. *Risk Analysis, 10*(4) , 485–497.

Napier, T.L., Carter, M.V., & Bryant, E.G. (1986). Local perceptions of reservoir impacts: A test of vested interests. *American Journal of Community Psychology, 14*(1), 17–37.

Noe, F.P., & Snow, R. (1990). The new environmental paradigm and further scale analysis. *Journal of Environmental Education, 21*(4), 20–26.

Pedigo, S.K. (1986). The risks of radiation: A study of the attitudes of a select sample of residents of southeast Tennessee. *Dissertation Abstracts International, 47*(3-B), 1016.

Peters, J.S. (1990). Integrating psychological and economic perspectives on energy consumption: The determinants of thermostat setting behavior. *Dissertation Abstracts International, 51*(4-B), 2116–2117.

Russell, P. (1982). *The global brain.* Los Angeles: Tarcher.

Steger, M.A., Pierce, J.C., Steel, B.S., & Lovrich, N.P. (1989). Political culture, postmaterial values, and the new environmental paradigm: A comparative analysis of Canada and the United States. *Political Behavior, 11*(3), 233–254.

Swearingen, T.C. (1990). Moral development and environmental ethics. *Dissertation Abstracts International, 50*(12-B), 5905.

van der Pligh, J., Eister, J.R., & Spears, R. (1986). Construction of a nuclear power station in one's locality: Attitudes and salience. *Basic and applied social psychology, 7*(1), 1–15.

Vaughan, E. (1986). Some factors influencing the nonexpert's perception and evaluation of environmental risks. *Dissertation Abstracts International, 47*(3-B), 1332.

Vining, J. (1987). Environmental decisions: The interaction of emotions, information, and decision context. *Journal of Environmental Psychology, 7*(1), 13–30.

Weait, M. (1989). The letter of the law? An enquiry into reasoning and formal enforcement in the Industrial Air Pollution Inspectkorate. *British Journal of Criminology, 29*(1), 57–70.

Weinstein, N.D., Sandman, P.M., & Roberts, N.E. (1990). Determinants of self-protective behavior: Home radon testing. *Journal of Applied Social Psychology, 20*(10), 783–801.

Applying Psychology to Preserve the Environment

15

FIGURE 15-1 A possible scenario of our energy future.

As noted in the previous chapter, dissatisfaction with the potential for political, economic, or legal changes to preserve the environment has resulted in "grassroots" efforts to effect behavioral change. These efforts range from neighborhood recycling programs to community-based plans to produce voluntary reductions in resource use. To have a significant effect on environmental preservation, though, such efforts must elicit the cooperation of individual members of society on a broad scale. Changing individual behavior falls within the professional domain of psychologists, and therefore some applications of behavioral technology to preserve the environment are discussed in this chapter. Before planning change programs, though, it is important to know something about the behaviors we may wish to change. Thus, we will first discuss one critical type of environmental behavior: energy consumption.

ENERGY USE AND ABUSE

Neither the multipurpose utilization nor the casual use of energy is new. Since early times, humans have attempted to make their lives easier by converting energy from the environment to their own use. This energy conversion in the beginning was quite unsophisticated by today's standards, but probably involved the harnessing of wind, fire, and gravity to move materials, heat domociles, and to aid in hunting and gathering. Modern people have added to

---

TIME-OUT: At precisely 5:45 A.M. every morning I (one of the authors) awake to the sound of music, followed by voices relaying the late-breaking events of the world. I arise, turn on the necessary lights, stumble to the bathroom, and prop myself up under a chrome-plated nozzle where I subject myself to a stream of aerated warm water. My blow dryer and coffee-maker await some 15 minutes of this self-indulgence. From the refrigerator a breakfast tart, soon to be made a tolerable brown, is thrown into the innards of the toaster. By 6:45 I am in my pick-up truck and headed for the office five miles away. Because of my early arrival, I am able to get a parking space near the psychology building where I abandon the truck, walk to the building, enter the elevator, and proceed to the second floor where my office is located.

I could go on boring you with the chronology of my day (it doesn't get any more exciting) but enough has been said to make my point, which is, of course, the cavalier, almost contemptuous, way in which I, and nearly everyone else, treat energy consumption. My clock radio, water heater, blow dryer, coffee-maker, refrigerator, toaster, pick-up truck, and elevator all use energy, not to mention the electric lights in my home and office and the heating and the cooling apparati that keep my built environments at a near constant 72°F year-round.

As an exercise, you might try keeping a daily log for a week of each time you engage in an activity that utilizes energy. Then go back and mark out activities that you really could have done without. Would you be willing to give up these conveniences to preserve the environment? How difficult would these changes be (i.e., would your life style be dramatically affected by them?).

these uses and have found an incredible number of new ones to which energy can be applied. So ubiquitous is the use of energy that the American public consumes approximately 85 quadrillion Btu's (British thermal units) per year (Prugh, 1993). In fact, if we include our Canadian neighbors to the north we account for nearly 28 percent of total global energy consumption (British Petroleum, 1992).

In a study for the National Science Foundation conducted by the Stanford Research Institute (1972) a broad-based, trifold breakdown regarding energy consumption was established. Researchers found that in the United States the transportation industry is responsible for approximately 25 percent of all energy consumed; industrial and manufacturing sources account for about 42 percent of energy utilization; and *home* and *commercial* buildings (including heating and cooling, lighting, cooking, water heating) account for the remaining 33 percent.

Energy Use in Transportation

George Pierson (1973) has persuasively argued that Descartes' dictum "I think, therefore I am" has been changed by and adapted to the American philosophy regarding mobility to read: "I move, so I'm alive." Without doubt the movement of people and goods is one of the most identifiable features of modern American life. One has only to drive in any major city in the country about 5:00 in the afternoon to be painfully reminded of this penchant for mobility. This movement accounts for the largest single block of energy usage in the United States. Even without considering the enormous amounts of energy required to manufacture cars, airplanes, trucks, buses, and other vehicles, and considering only the energy required to fuel them, the transportation industry still consumes one-fourth of all the energy utilized in this country. Approximately 55 percent of this energy fuels the movement of people and materials in automobiles, and total highway transportation (including automobiles, trucks, buses, motorcycles, etc.) accounts for 76.48 percent of all transportation energy utilization (The U.S. Department of Transportation, 1972). The average household in the United States operates 1.8 vehicles and, in the aggregate, we drive more thean 1.5 trillion miles annually. In doing so we use 82.4 billion gallons of fuel at a cost of over $81 billion (Prugh, 1993).

Automobiles actually represent the second most inefficient means of transportation. When we add to this the energy costs of manufacuring, autos become even more inefficient. Clark (1975) provides data showing that 60 percent of all synthetic rubber manufactured in the United States is devoted to the automobile industry; additional resources used by the auto industry and their percentages are: aluminum (10), steel (20), zinc (35), and lead (50). Each of these components of the automobile also requires a great deal of energy to get them to a usable form. So, not only are automobiles energy-costly to operate, they are energy costly to produce.

Hirst (1973) provides data on the energy intensiveness of several modes of transportation, noting that the airplane is the most energy intensive (least efficient) means of transportation, being approximately 60 times more energy costly for moving freight and about 3 times more costly for moving passengers than are railroads. Yet this least efficient of all modes of transportation is growing with respect to utilization. For example, the extent of intercity passenger traffic electing to use airlines increased by a factor of 5 during the period of 1950 to 1970, and the airplane's share of the freight traffic increased by a factor of 7.

Among the most efficient means of transport are the railroads in that they require only 670 Btu's of energy for each ton of freight transported each mile (Hirst, 1973). Compare this with the 42,000 Btu's required by airplanes to perform the same function. Additionally, trains carry large loads where most of the fuel used is consumed in pulling the load and not in moving the vehicle carrying the load— that is, automobiles and trucks utilize a great deal of fuel simply to move the vehicle, while most of the energy used on trains goes to move the cargo. Despite the obvious advantages, trains are carrying less and less of the transportation load. The American consumer, it seems, wants not only mobility but wants it fast and convenient.

If we stand back to look at the trends in transportation over the past three decades, several things become apparent: (1) We are using an increasing amount of energy in transporting people and materials; (2) we are forsaking energy efficiency in moving these materials for speed and convenience; (3) we are using modes of transport that are not only energy-intense with respect to fuel costs for transport but in material costs in initial manufacturing; and (4) our entire transportation system is built on fossil fuels as the one and only fuel source.

Energy Use in Industry

As stated earlier, approximately 42 percent of all energy consumption in the United States is accounted for by the industrial sector. Almost two-thirds of this amount is required for processes within six major industries. Much of the industrial energy consumption takes place in the metals, chemicals, and energy industries themselves. In fact, these three groups account for over half of all the energy consumed by the industrial sector of our economy.

To provide the reader with some idea of the costs in terms of energy for various basic materials, comparisons show that the production of steel requires about one-sixth the amount of energy as does the production of aluminum, and that the production of glass is less energy-intensive than the production of steel. Two major consumer lessons can be deduced from such comparisons: (1) If at all possible one should choose less energy-intensive materials over more energy-intensive materials; (2) because the energy costs of manufacture and transport are so high, materials should be used as long as possible and reused or recycled where appropriate.

Energy Use in Homes

Over the centuries one of the greatest tributes to human ingenuity has been the ability to develop housing that was minimally dependent on outside energy. Bernard Rudofsky (1964) provides an excellent pictorial account of what he calls anonymous architecture, or "architecture without architects." In this book humans' incredible capacity for construction of homes which mesh not only with the geography and topography but also with the prevailing climates of their sites is revealed. And in a rather ingenious book entitled *Tents: Architecture of the Nomads*, Torvald Faegre (1979) shows how the nomads have adapted the use of the tent to such diverse climates as the Sahara Desert and the Himalayan Mountains. Clark (1975) laments the loss of this ingenuity as he claims that with each passing year the American home becomes not only more uniform but now bears no relationship to the geography or to climate in which it is sited. The same home built in exactly the same way can be found on any street in Atlanta, Georgia; Bangor, Maine; Houston, Texas; or Bimidji, Minnesota. As we will see, this uniformity in design is true not only of homes but also of commercial buildings, and it leads to buildings that are energy-wasteful.

One of the three major determinants of how energy is likely to be consumed by residential homes is the type of heating/cooling system installed. In determining the energy costs of heating and cooling, consideration should be given to the number of energy conversions required to get the job done. In this respect heating with a natural gas furnace is more energy efficient than electrical baseboard heating because energy is lost in the conversion of the primary energy source (e.g. coal, fuel oil, or natural gas) to the secondary source: electricity. Electric homes use almost twice as much energy even though they are built with better insulation. The same is true of heating water: It is cheaper to heat water for home use with natural gas than it is with electricity.

Other than the choice of heating and cooling equipment, the next major determinant of energy utilization is the life style of the inhabitants. The extent to which a home is filled with electrical appliances and the extent to which these appliances are used will determine the amount of energy utilized. Color TVs are more energy intensive than are black-and-white ones, self-cleaning ovens use more energy than do conventional methods of cleaning, frost-free refrigerators consume more energy than do conventional refrigerators, air conditioners consume more power than window fans, and incandescent lights require more electricity than do fluorescent lights.

The real savings to consumers who purchase and use more energy-efficient appliances are substantial. For example, Clark (1975) reports on a study done by Neely (1972) in which he extrapolates from the sale of 6.6 million refrigerators/freezers in 1970. If all purchasers had chosen the more efficient units, he contends that the economic savings (based on one dollar per month reduction in monthly use costs) would equal $80 million at the end of the first year, and by the time 100 million new refrigerator-freezers were sold the economic savings would equal $1.2 billion dollars annually. He goes on to assume that the fuel burned to create the electricity to operate the refrigerators was coal, and that it was burned at a modern electric power plant. Given the assumption that the savings in electricity would equal 40 billion kilowatt hours, the savings in coal would be 17 million tons. Additionally, buying the more efficient appliance would prevent the introduction into the atmosphere 690,000 tons of sulfur dioxide, 25,000 tons of particulate, and 147,500 tons of nitrogen oxides. Finally, the more judicious purchase would result in saving 26,000 acres from being strip-mined and 10,000 acres from being claimed for the use of power plants and transmission lines. All these savings accrue by merely choosing a more efficient over a less efficient refrigerator; think of the savings if the same choices were made over a variety of energy-consuming goods.

As alluded to earlier, perhaps the most important determinant of the amount of energy a household will consume is the construction of the home itself; the major factor in construction is the wise use of insulation coupled with shading in the summer and utilizing the sun's rays in the winter. The National Mineral Wool Insulation Association (1972) claims that if 75 percent of all new construction used good insulation techniques, if 25 percent of all older homes were upgraded with better insulation, and if 12 percent of all older homes were equipped with storm doors and windows, then the nation's energy bill would be reduced by $3.1 billion each year. Incidentally, the costs of insulating are minimal compared with the costs of heating uninsulated or poorly insulated spaces. Using wool as an insulator, for example, results in a 15 Btu savings for each Btu required in processing. In summary, anything that will capture the heat indoors in the winter and keep the heat out in the summer will result in substantial savings with no reduction in comfort.

Energy Use in Commercial Buildings

If the energy waste in homes can be considered obscene, then the energy waste in commercial buildings should be considered outright criminal. Our affinity for using glass and our love affair with tallness contribute to this waste. The Sears Tower in Chicago, for example, requires more electricity than the city of Rockford, Illinois, with its population of 147,000 people. This same building, incidentally, has 80 miles of elevator cables hidden somewhere in its viscera and enough concrete for 78 football fields (*Time*, 1973). It has been estimated that commercial buildings use up to one-fourth of the nation's electricity just in lighting and over 50 percent of all the electricity produced (Clark, 1975). Because a great deal of the material used in modern commercial building is glass, great expenditures of energy are required for heating and cooling.

Enough has been said about residential and commercial energy usage to conclude that the structures themselves are not built with energy conservation in mind, and that the users of these spaces are not particularly energy conscious. With slight modifications in design and in appliance usage, substantial savings in the amount of energy consumed could be realized. But energy use and abuse is not the whole story. One must also consider such by-products of energy use as air pollution, water pollution, and other forms of environmental degradation. It is to these effects that we now turn.

ENVIRONMENTAL COSTS OF ENERGY AND MATERIALS USAGE

The use of energy and materials influences environmental quality throughout the extracting, processing, transporting, and usage stages. For example, it was once common for blow-outs to occur at drilling sites. These uncontrolled bursts of crude oil ascending the well shaft under great pressure and eventually being ejected into the surrounding area were particularly consequential when they occurred at offshore drilling sites. Before the use of more modern techniques was instituted, these uncontrolled bursts of oil dumped thousands of barrels of crude oil into the environment before the well could be capped. The resulting oil slick killed much marine life and endangered the lives of many more. But blow-outs aren't the only kind of environmental disaster that can occur at drilling sites. The drilling platform can ignite, as occurred in the Gulf of Mexico in 1970. Chevron Oil lost over a thousand barrels of oil a day to the sea, eventually destroying $100 million in shrimp and oyster beds. In the prior year a spill near Santa Barbara, California, destroyed a number of shore birds, shellfish, and an unknown quantity of other marine life. Because many effects of an oil slick (no matter what the cause) are not fully determined for years after the initial event, the environmental costs of an oil slick are difficult to calculate. And the story continues. The massive Exxon oil spill in Prince William Sound in Alaska serves as a constant reminder of the ongoing environmental degradation resulting from our never-ending appetite for energy.

Although blow-outs, blow-ups, undersea pipeline breaks, and tanker accidents are dramatic and well-publicized, the amount of oil released into the sea by such incidents represents less than one-fifth of the total spillage (SCEP, 1970). By far the largest spillage of oil into the sea occurs as a result of normal operations—cleaning the tanks and ballasting of oil tankers, bilge pumping and cleaning of non-tankers, exhaust from ship's engines, and normal offshore production procedures. Baldwin (1971) estimates that as much as 4 million metric tons of oil per year spill into the world's waterways. Refining operations not only pollute the seas through spillage and seepage of oil but also through the release of other chemical effluents. For example, the National Wildlife Federation (1970) reports that one refinery dumped up to two and one-half tons of toxic lead per day into the Mississippi River in Louisiana. Other waste products of the refining industry include heat, phenols, hydrogen sulfide, heavy metals, etc. (Dewling, 1970).

Without doubt the use of fossil fuels as a major source of energy is not without problems, and these problems need to be addressed immediately. This is brought home not only as a result of concern over the detrimental side effects produced by the use of fossil fuels but also by looking at the reserves of these resources and other high energy minerals that are known to be available. Several conclusions have recently become apparent in this regard: (1) The world's supply of natural resources is in serious jeopardy (mercury, gold, and tin are likely to be depleted very soon); (2) the United States will become increasingly dependent on other nations not only for its energy but also for other natural resources; (3) the United States is the prime consumer of a number of nonrenewable resources; and (4) the United States with only 5¼ percent of the world's population accounts for from 14 percent (manganese) to 65 percent (natural gas) of the world's consumption of various resources (Makhijani & Lichtenberg, 1971). The carrying capacity of current American civilization is precariously perched on an enormous subsidy of fossil fuel and on resources which are likely to be more difficult to attain.

STRATEGIES FOR SAVING ENERGY

Arthur Purcell (1980) in a very provocative and informative book, *The Waste Watchers*, provides us with some very simple strategies for saving energy and materials and for reducing environmental degradation. Rule or strategy number one is simply to use and produce less. For every pound of aluminum, paper, steel, or other product that is not made we will save energy and avoid polluting. What Purcell says we can do without using is "convenience." The convenience of owning two cars, the convenience of a radio in every room of the house, the convenience of a "weed eater" relative to getting down on one's hands and knees and pulling out weeds all represent areas where energy is forsaken for convenience. In summarizing this particular strategy Purcell cautions: If you don't need it, don't buy it; if you need only one, don't buy two.

But there are other strategies available as well, and a second is to use products longer. How often, for example, have you seen someone throw away clothes because they were not longer "in style," or a toaster because it looked old-fashioned, or a lamp because it was the wrong color? How often have 19-inch TV sets been thrown out, because a 25-inch model has just been purchased? How often have you thrown away a sheet of paper after having made only a few scribbles on it, or more likely, how often have you thrown away paper which has one unused side? Purcell (1980) estimates that if we were to use a product for its usable lifetime we could save in the neighborhood of a million barrels of oil per day.

Other strategies for trimming waste include reusing discarded products, making and using more durable and repairable products, and making and using simpler products. These various strategies include recycling, as well as being innovative (using materials for several generations of uses; e.g., an empty milk carton can become a pot for starting tomato plants, pop bottle tops attached to a board can become a shoe sole cleaner to be placed at outside entrances, etc.); they involve letting others use your discards, and repairing your own goods rather than discarding them. Finally, these strategies involve avoiding throwaway goods, buying energy-efficient products, and avoiding articles made from energy-intensive materials.

It is abundantly clear that as consumers and users of materials we are wasteful beyond credence. We spend far too much to have our goods packaged (approximately 9 percent of our total food budget) and then have to find some way of disposing of the packaging. We throw away enough materials in the United States to fill from floor to ceiling the New Orleans Superdome twice a day, 365 days per year. The direct cost of this disposal is around $4 billion annually (as a basis of comparison this represents a figure totaling more than the yearly budget of the Environmental Protection Agency and four times the budget of the American Cancer Institute). In energy costs, disposal represents approximately 10 percent of our total energy consumption, or enough to run the entire country for 36 days each year. Finally, in material costs we see that almost 30 percent of all materials produced each year end up in the discard pile. These figures make the strategies outlined by Purcell (1980) even more important, and their adoption even more critical.

OUR ENERGY FUTURE

The last two decades have dramatically changed the way most people think about energy. In fact, 20 years ago most of us probably didn't think much about it at all. It was abundant and cheap, and we used lots of it. Then came a series of "energy crises" that changed our awareness and understanding of energy use. We had to face the implications of being dependent on limited supplies of non-renewable fuels, fuels that would never be cheap again.

A very important turning point came in 1970 when America's surplus capacity vanished and production reached what proved to be its peak (approximately 11.3 million barrels per day). From that point on, oil production declined but demand continued to increase and cheap imported oil took a greater share of the U.S. market. In response to sporadic shortages that began to develop around the country, the Nixon administration abandoned oil import quotas in 1973 and imported oil poured in. Our decline in production was interrupted briefly in 1978 by an on-rush of Alaskan oil, but in 1979 domestic output turned down once again. In the two decades from 1960 to 1980 American consumption of oil doubled from approximately 9.7 to 17.9 million barrels a day (Stobaugh, 1979). In this same period, production increased from approximately 8 million barrels a day to only 10.2 million, and imports went from 1.8 million barrels a day in 1960 to 8.4 million barrels a day in 1979.

On what kind of nation has the world become so dependent? We have become highly dependent on the oil empires of the Middle East including Saudi Arabia, Iran, South Yemen, Iraq, Syria, Egypt, and Libya. But political unrest is rampant in these countries. The numerous succession of crises occurring there represents not only an internal threat to these nations but also an external one. In 1977 and 1978 political assassinations occurred in Syria, South Yemen, and North Yemen, and in the past 30 years dissidents have overthrown ruling groups in Libya, Egypt, Iraq, Syria, South Yemen, and Iran. The press has also reported attempted coups in Saudi Arabia. Too little is known about the internal relations in Saudi Arabia, however, to make solid predictions about that country's political stability.

Without doubt we are highly dependent on sources of oil which are in a state of turmoil and for which no stability can be predicted. It is necessary for us, as a nation and as a world, to try to develop alternate energy sources. While a number of energy sources are possible including wind, coal, natural and synthetic gases, and nuclear, the remainder of this chapter will deal with two major sources—solar energy and conservation. We will look at these two because they are the ones over which we as individuals are able to exert the most control. The others are more likely to be influenced by technologies and politics, which we as individuals lack the expertise or the power to influence. Furthermore, Richard Stein (1978) suggests that as much as 43.5 percent of all energy used for all purposes is directly related to the relationship between architecture and energy. Architectural and energy decisions, he says, are affected by conflicting and partisan attitudes, cultural, financial, political, psychological, and aesthetic factors reflecting a diverse cast of characters who are involved in the process. The individual (or corporate or government) client, the source of the financing of the construction, the producers of the building materials, the building tradespeople who assemble and erect buildings, the contractors who hire them, the newspapers, magazines, TV and radio that influence public opinion, the professional journals and, of course, all members of the building design professions (i.e., the various engineers as well as the architects) all influence the energy consumption of our built environments and energy-consuming technology.

ALTERNATE ENERGY RESOURCES

Solar Energy

In the broadest sense, nearly all fuel systems in use today are based on solar energy. Fossil fuels store solar energy over millions of years. Natural gas, coal, and petroleum are stored reserves that cannot be renewed in our planet's lifetime. Wood fuels store solar energy for hundreds of years and can be a renewable energy resource if used with careful reforestation. Solar energy is also stored in plants and crop residue and can be released into biomass energy generation systems and renewed in periods as short as months or years. Systems which make direct use of solar radiation are using energy that is renewed daily, hourly, or instantaneously. The term *renewable energy system* generally refers to the use of these last energy alternatives, and it is to these systems that we now turn.

Renewable energy systems can take many forms. Wind energy conversion systems use airflow patterns generated by solar radiation. This energy is usually used to perform mechanical work or is converted into electricity. Systems which use the sun's rays directly for heat are usually referred to as either active or passive solar systems. These systems can be used either to heat or cool a home, to heat domestic hot water, or to maintain comfortable swimming pool temperatures. The sun's energy is well suited to these relatively low temperature tasks.

Passive solar systems.   These systems have no solar panels; instead, part of the building collects, stores, and distributes solar energy. Passive solar buildings or additions are designed and built with materials that enable the structure to perform these functions. South-facing windows, doorways, greenhouses or skylights serve as solar collectors, while floors or walls contain the thermal storage mass necessary to store excess heat until it is needed. A variety of energy-conserving techniques are incorporated into the building to help keep heat in. These systems rely on natural processes of heat transfer (i.e. radiation, convection, and conduction) to distribute collected heat.

Active solar systems.   Active solar systems use solar panels for heat collection and electrically driven pumps or fans to transport the heat to the living area or to storage. Electronic devices regulate the collection, storage, and distribution of heat within the system. Hybrid systems contain features of both passive and active systems. The successful performance of any solar system depends upon good design, the proper balance among various components of the system, and quality construction and installation.

Active solar heating begins with the collector panel, which captures and converts the sun's energy to heat. Basically, this panel is a glazed, weather-tight box that contains a black metal absorber plate. In colder climates double glazing is generally recommended, and the panel must be well insulated to prevent heat loss. Materials in the panel must be able to withstand extreme weather conditions; for example, freezing, thawing, snow, ice, rain, high winds, exposure to ultraviolet light and summer stagnation temperatures of 400°F. Roof-mounted collectors are most common because they are out of the way and generally have fewer shading problems. However, wall or ground mounts may be desirable in some instances.

Why hasn't the use of solar energy become more widespread, given this renewed interest? One reason has already been referred to: A public misunderstanding of solar technology has people awaiting some giant (but unlikely) technological breakthrough. Other reasons include the fact that oil and natural gas are still relatively cheap; solar installation requires a large one-time investment, whereas other sources of energy can be bought in lower-priced packages usually by the month; landlords typically pass energy costs onto tenants, a system which works easier when the utilities are collecting the debts; and, people seem to want a two- or three-year payback for their investment and the usual payback period for solar installation is five years. One thing for certain is that with increased shortages of energy those individuals with solar installations will be less at the mercy of forces over which they have no control. When the oil, gas, and coal reserves have run out, the sun will still be shining.

Conservation as an Energy Source

There is a source of energy that produces no radioactive waste, nothing in the way of start-up dollars and very little, if any, pollution. Moreover, the source can provide the energy that conventional sources may not be able to furnish (Yergin,

1979). Unhappily, however, it does not receive the emphasis and attention that it deserves to receive. The source of this energy might be called *energy efficiency* but is generally known by the term *conservation*. To be semantically accurate, the source should be called *conservation energy* to remind us of a reality that conservation is no less an energy alternative than oil, gas, coal, or nuclear. If the United States were to make a serious commitment to conservation, it might well consume 30 to 40 percent less energy than it now does and still enjoy the same or an even higher standard of living. These savings would not hinge on any major technological breakthroughs and would require only modest adjustments in the way people live. The possible energy savings would be the equivalent of the elimination of all imported oil and then some.

Three types of conservation are possible. The first is *curtailment*. This is what happened when interstate natural gas ran short in 1976 and 1977, during the coal strike of 1977 and 1978, and during the gasoline lines of 1979. A second category of conservation is *overhaul* (i.e., dramatically changing the way in which Americans live and work). An extreme example might be outlawing of further suburbanization, forcing people to move into the urban center and live in tall buildings not equipped with places to park a car. A third way to think about conservation is a form of *adjustment*. This entails such things as insulating the house, or making automobiles, industrial processes, and home appliances more efficient, or capturing waste heat. Conservation, therefore, is not a theoretical or ideological issue. It should be pursued not as an end in itself but as a means toward greater social and economic welfare.

Voluntary reduction in energy consumption through conservation (coupled with penalties for noncompliance) represents a viable means of saving energy. These strategies seem to make sense, but why have we not adopted them? Some of the answers to this question were discussed in the previous chapter. For pragmatic reasons, perhaps the better question is *how* to get people to adopt these strategies. Some solutions are the subject of the remainder of this book.

TIME-OUT: Take a few minutes to reflect on what you would like your life to be like 40 to 50 years from now. Rather than thinking of the typical things such as what your family, friends, or job will be like, focus on where you would live—the ideal environment to live out the remainder of your life. Think about the geographic area in which you would live as well as your specific place of residence. Try to imagine what the quality of life would be like in this setting.

It doesn't matter whether the environment you just imagined consisted of a grass hut on a warm tropical island, a condominium in a large city on the coast, a single-resident wood-frame house in a small rural town in the country, or a cabin snugly nestled in a range of pristine mountains. It is likely that your image included things such as fresh air, clean water, ample food, and comfortable living quarters—these are, after all, the basics of the "good life." In your imagination you probably had enough "space" you could call your own and the means of comfortably travelling from your "space" to that of friends and relatives. It is equally likely that your ideal environment did not include images of smog, polluted water, fuel rationing, unsafe food, or unheated and crowded living quarters!

The question we would like to put to you now is which of the above two scenarios is most likely to occur in the future given past and current trends? The one you imagined, or the one you didn't? Will the world in which you live out your life afford you the opportunities of the "good life" or will it be beset with shortages and calamity? Will there be clean air to breathe or will it be filled with photochemicals and particulates? Will the water be pure or will it be contaminated with seepage from toxic chemical disposal sites and agricultural run-off? Will you enjoy geographical mobility or will energy shortages and rationing force you to remain relatively immobile? Will your visual vistas be clear and uncluttered or filled with the discards of a throw-away society? Before you give the reassuring answer, "probably something in between the extremes," we submit that that is a description of the present environment, and the answer is therefore disallowed! The earth's carrying capacity has already been reached in some places on the globe and is being approached in many others. In scanning the issues covered in this text, there seems to be ample support for the likelihood of the more dismal of the two scenarios occurring.

The purpose of the above exercise, however, was not to convince you that your authors are "doomsday prophets" who have joined the likes of Robert Heilbroner (see Chapter 14). We do, indeed, have grave concerns about the future of the environment and the quality of life for humanity in the years to come. We have at times felt overwhelmed by the immensity and complexity of environmental problems and disheartened by the woefully little progress that has been made toward their alleviation. We have watched with no little concern the resources of the earth diminish while simultaneously observing the increasing demands placed on them. Thus, it is safe to say that we are not optimists with respect to such projections of the future. However, we are not pessimists either. Indeed, if the latter were true, we would not have made the effort to write this book. On the contrary, it is our hope that this book will stimulate readers to think critically about environmental issues and motivate some of them to work toward solutions to environmental problems.

A REVIEW AND PREVIEW

Of course the preceding paragraph begs the question of what can be done to preserve the quality of life in the future. We have already touched on a number of recommendations at various places in this text in answer to this question. For example, we discussed noise abatement procedures in Chapter 8; we described energy-efficient institutional and residential design features in Chapters 11 and 12; we outlined alternative energy sources as well as specific ways to conserve energy and reduce waste in the present chapter; and we reviewed economic, political and legal prescriptions for preserving the environment in chapter 14. But many of these suggestions may have seemed to be beyond the reach of any given individual. As an individual, you probably felt that there is very little you can do to increase significantly the use of mass transit systems while simultaneously cutting back on the use of the automobile, or to require owners of commercial buildings to curtail on electrical usage, or to halt the dumping of toxic wastes into our waters, land, and atmosphere. You may have found yourself saying: The contribution I can make is so small, what difference will it make if I use public transportation (and inconvenience myself) when so many others continue to drive their automobiles? What effect will turning down my thermostat in the winter (and being somewhat uncomfortable) have on world energy consumption?

Further, while you as an individual may be prepared to engage in environmentally constructive behavior, you may question how it could be possible to convince millions of other individuals to make similar changes in their behavior. You may have already decided to retrofit your home to solar usage (or to build a new solar home). But what effect, you may legitimately ask, will your behavior have on the total energy picture in the world. The answer, of course, is very little, unless others join you in your effort. Recall from earlier in the chapter the example provided by Neely (1972) in which 100 million people buy a refrigerator/freezer each of which represents only a one dollar per month energy savings. Summing across all of them, however, leads to a net savings of $1.2 billion annually, prevents the introduction to the environment of 690,000 tons of sulfur dioxide, 25,000 tons of particulate, 147,500 tons of nitrogen oxides, plus other ancillary savings. So, while you are aware that your effort singly will have a minuscule effect, you should also be aware that aggregated across many individuals, the impact can be great. So how can you convince others to follow your lead?

Another question that may have crossed your mind in reading the last three chapters is, Where has the "psychology" gone in environmental psychology? Indeed, much of the material in those chapters suggest phrases such as environmental engineering or environmental law. In fact, these are recognized fields of study in their own right, and there are others (e.g., environmental biology). We have drawn heavily from these and other disciplines purposefully. We emphasized in the first chapter of this book and at several other points that environmental psychology is an inherently interdisciplinary field, and that some knowledge of and ability to communicate with others from related disciplines is essential to realistic solutions to environmental problems. However, the discipline of psychology has its own unique concerns and contributions to make. These are the subject of the remainder of this chapter.

BEHAVIORAL SOLUTIONS TO ENVIRONMENTAL PROBLEMS

In Chapter 1 it was argued that technology is a two-edged sword: Technological advances have yielded incredible improvements in the quality of life, yet many of these same technologies threaten not only the quality of life, but life itself. Despite these threats, many people still look to technology for solutions to environmental problems. There are any number of possible reasons for this apparent contradiction. Perhaps it is simply too difficult or too unsettling to imagine that technology—the very tool that has served humanity so well over the centuries—could ultimately become the mechanism of our undoing. Perhaps it is due to a belief that new technologies will be discovered as soon as it becomes economically profitable or politically popular to pursue their development. Whatever the reason, many people cling desperately to the notion that increased technology is the solution to environmental problems. We believe that such reasoning is based on a false sense of security in the power of technology, and that it would be a mistake to place all of our hopes in a *deus ex machina* (translated as "god out of machine," a convenient means of resolving many problems in Greek myths).

To be sure, physical technology (e.g., designing more fuel-efficient transportation systems, developing means of eliminating industrial pollution) will play a critical role in solving some problems. However, it is our belief that technology alone will not be enough, or that these discoveries will not be made soon enough to reverse the serious environmental deterioration that has already occurred. What many people overlook is the important—and perhaps overriding—need to produce changes in human behavior to preserve the environment and the quality of life. This social technology entails knowledge of individual human behavior (e.g., techniques to promote use of public transportation, or to encourage energy conservation in the home). The science of psychology has been devoted to understanding human behavior and developing technologies for changing behavior. Such change must always occur at the level of the individual, and this is the unique contribution that psychology has to offer in solving environmental problems.

In the following pages the concept of *social dilemma* will be described, a concept which sheds light on human tendencies that inhibit environmentally constructive behavior. We will then discuss techniques for altering environmental attitudes, and methods for promoting a variety of specific pro-environmental behaviors will be presented.

The Tragedy of the Commons

During the early years of our country it was frequently the practice of settlers to create a "commons," an area shared by all members of a settlement and set aside for their individual animals to graze. Often these areas would consist of a green, or cleared pastureland, surrounded by the buildings of the settlement. By posturing land and buildings in this way, the animals could graze while under the watchful and protective eyes of the various members of the community. Because of this arrangement a commons did not have unlimited resources, but as long as each settler maintained the size of his or her herd at an appropriate limit, there was enough food for all the animals.

While this may seem like a reasonable arrangement, according to Garrett Hardin (1968) most commons are destined to fail. The reason is that as long as individuals are free to pursue their own interests, they will do so at the expense of the public good. Thus, Farmer Jones desires to build a new barn and determines that he could finance this by increasing the size of his herd. Farmer Smith desires to purchase some new harvesting equipment and decides to finance this in the same fashion. While each farmer reasons that the small increase in his herd is negligible relative to the size of the commons, the tragedy is that eventually the commons will be depleted to the point that it cannot sustain anyone's herd. Imagine, for example, that there are 50 farmers surrounding and utilizing a commons that will sustain 100 head of cattle (i.e., if 100 cattle are left to graze on the grasses the commons will replenish itself as rapidly as it is being consumed). Farmer Smith assumes that the addition of one more cow (representing a 50 percent increase in his herd's milk-producing capability) will have a negligible effect on the commons (an increase of only 1 percent). Farmer Jones thinks similarly.

The difficulty occurs when all of the settlers think the same way. Each is only increasing the demand for the resources of the commons by 1 percent while simultaneously increasing their individual output by 50 percent. If everyone follows his individual interests, the commons, which is capable of supporting only 100 cows, will now be asked to provide for 150. The net effect is that Farmer Smith, and all of the others, will now be getting less milk from three cows than they originally obtained from two. The only logical thing to do is to add a fourth cow. Of course, Farmer Jones is in the same predicament as Farmer Smith and all the other herdsmen. So they too add to their herds. And so on, further depleting the resources of the commons. They will have quickly gone beyond the point of diminishing returns to the point of negative returns.

Hardin postulates that the tragedy of the commons occurs as a result of the fact that the commons by definition is owned by everyone and no one. No single person feels responsible for the ultimate fate of the commons, and thus disregards the impact of his or her individual acts. Hence, it is the accumulation of individual actions in pursuing self-interests that brings about the destruction of the commons.

J.R. Platt (1973) describes similar problems as "social traps" where individuals caught up in satisfying immediate needs lose sight of long-term costs. These future costs ultimately are much greater than the benefits derived from satisfying present needs and desires. Thus, it is the conflict between immediate, self-interest and future, public-interest that constitutes a *social dilemma* (Dawes, 1980). The analogy to environmental problems should be obvious. For example, nobody owns the atmosphere and we all use its air. Individual actions (e.g., driving to work instead of walking) that serve our needs (having a few extra minutes for a cup of coffee) will be taken without regard to their impact on the environment. My one car isn't going to ruin the atmosphere. My throwing one bottle out of may car along the highway will have very little impact on litter, unless everyone does it. My disconnecting the pollution control devices on my car will have very little impact on air pollution, unless everyone does it. My harvesting one additional whale (beyond legal limits) will have very little impact on the whale population, unless all whalers do it. The long-term accumulation of these individual behaviors can entail extremely high costs to reverse their negative effects. Thus, we see that our individual efforts to protect and preserve the environment have little consequence unless others follow our lead, and our behaviors that degrade the environment have very powerful impact if others do follow our lead.

In Chapter 14 we discussed the need to promote an "environmental ethic" as a means of preserving the environment for posterity. This might seem to offer a possible solution to the commons dilemma. But it is one thing to call for an environmental ethic and quite another to produce requisite changes in attitudes. What psychological processes are involved in influencing how we manage our "commons"? Samuelson and Messick (1986) presented subjects with a resource management task in which they were to harvest "points" from a regenerating resource pool. They were told to maximize their individual points while maintaining the pool. Subjects were given information indicating that the pool was being used optimally or being overused. Subjects in the overuse condition were more willing to give up free access to the pool. Does this mean that given information about environmental problems, people will change their behaviors? Not necessarily, for other research shows that how people react depends on the way information is presented. For example, Vining (1987) gave subjects a resource management problem in which a pro-development versus a preservation emphasis was presented. Overuse decisions were more likely in the former condition. However, simulations have been reported to be successful in promoting favorable attitudes toward energy conservation (Dresner, 1990) and cooperative behavior among group members in situations involving social interdependence (Loomis, 1989; Naseth, 1990).

Such simulations could be useful in promoting pro-environmental attitudes. In the following sections we will discuss other educational efforts to promote environmentally constructive attitudes, as well as presenting social psychological research on factors promoting attitude change. First, however, one might ask whether some people are more predisposed toward environmentally constructive behavior than others. Thus, we will begin by discussing some of the research that has been conducted on this question.

ENVIRONMENTAL ATTITUDES AND BEHAVIORS

Recent investigations have demonstrated relationships between individual characteristics and environmental attitudes and behaviors. For example, Stout-Wiegand (1986) reported relationships among environmental concern, respondent characteristics, and environmental organization memberships. Among the variables reported to relate to environmental attitudes are age (Schreckengost, 1986), education (Conover, 1986), and socioeconomic status (Griffin, Glynn, & McLeod, 1986; Stephens, 1986). In general, these researchers report that pro-environmental attitudes/behaviors occur with greater frequency among older, more educated, and higher-status respondents. However, Griffin (1989) reported that younger homeowners adopted actions to save energy in the home at a faster rate than did older homeowners. Schahn and Holzer (1990) reported that women are more concerned than men in areas relating to household behavior, whereas men knew more about environmental problems. Others have recently investigated environmental concern among blacks (Taylor, 1989), Hispanics (Noe & Snow, 1990), and people in other countries (Thornton, McMillan, & Romanovsky, 1989).

But why would these people (or others, for that matter) be more likely to engage in environmentally constructive behavior? Some researchers have suggested the importance of motivational factors as determinants of environmentally relevant behaviors. For example, De Young (1986) reported that recycling was associated with a series of specific satisfactions, such as frugality and participation. Goitein and Weinstein (1986) concluded from their research that although satisfaction with a residential energy audit was only weakly correlated with subsequent energy conservation, satisfaction may be important in secondary recruitment and public attitudes. Vining and Ebreo (1990) reported that recyclers were more aware of publicity about recycling and more knowledgeable about materials and means of recycling than were nonrecyclers, while the latter were more concerned with financial incentives to recycle and personal convenience. Sivek and Hungerford (1990) reported that the best predictors of environmentally responsible behaviors were perceived skill in using environmental action strategies and level of environmental sensitivity. Van Houwelingen and Van Raaij (1989) demonstrated that households with a stated conservation goal saved more energy than did those simply provided monthly feedback on energy use or those asked to monitor their energy use. Thus, increased understanding of the motivations and personal satisfactions of individuals for engaging in pro-environmental behaviors may enhance efforts to promote these behaviors. In the next section of this chapter we will discuss ways in which education and attitude change campaigns might influence such personal determinants of behavior.

Education to Preserve the Environment

It might seem that an important first step in changing attitudes would be to provide realistic information about environmental problems. The assumption here is that rational people will alter their attitudes appropriately when they are informed of the negative environmental consequences of their actions. Environmental education can take many forms, such as media campaigns (e.g., Keep America Beautiful), distributing informational leaflets, or introducing environmental issues into formal educational curricula. Research has shown that educational efforts can significantly increase awareness of and improve attitudes toward the environment (Cohen, 1973). Education is particularly important when individuals are simply lacking in relevant knowledge about environmental issues (Ditton & Goodale, 1974), and is more likely to be effective in changing attitudes of children and young adults than of older adults (Asch & Shore, 1975; Williams, 1991). Finally, educational efforts are likely to be effective if they emphasize solutions as well as awareness of environmental problems (Rankin, 1969). In this regard, Dennis and Soderstrom (1988) concluded that the ideal dissemination of energy information involves specific feedback to consumers who are already seeking answers to existing problems. Burrus, Bammel, and Kopitsky (1988) suggested ways of increasing the effectiveness of informational brochures, such as depicting more people engaged in wilderness recreation, undomesticated animals, and using a lower reading level.

FIGURE 15-2   Will this prompt be sufficient to encourage non-littering or will it be necessary to add incentives?

Various recent studies have demonstrated the importance of these factors as determinants of environmental behaviors. For example, Jeppesen (1986) argued that the increased cost of utilities has not been sufficient to motivate energy conservation, but that the public needs clear, concise information of what to do. He presented one group of consumers with residential heat-loss pictures ("thermograms"), a second group with thermograms and a weatherization workshop and a third group with the thermograms, workshop, and a follow-up of mailed information. The latter two groups showed significantly more subsequent conservation behaviors than did the first or a control group receiving no information. Conover (1986) reported that individuals who were offered an audit and an interest-free loan in a retrofitting program were more likely to participate than individuals who did not receive this information. Finally, Jordan, Hungerford, and Tomera (1986) conducted a six-day workshop on residential conservation in which groups received either instruction on issue awareness only or instruction plus action strategies. The second group subsequently demonstrated a significantly greater participation in pro-environmental behaviors.

Changing Attitudes to Protect the Environment

Temple (1986) has suggested that a 30 to 50 percent reduction in home energy use could be achieved with current technology and without major disruption in life styles. He argued for a need to address the effective promotion of pro-environmental attitudes and actions. Parthasarathy (1989) suggested exploitation of mass communication and electronic media as the best possible way to achieve significant energy savings, and Winett (1987) concluded that there are growing indications that the media can be effective in changing relatively simple behaviors, including energy conservation. Protess, Cook, Curtin, and Gordon (1987) suggested that the impact of news media investigative journalism has greater impact on policymakers than on the general public and argued that changes in public policy could be facilitated by collaboration between journalists and government officials. Costanzo, Archer, Aronson, and Pettigrew (1986) argued that informational appeals should emphasize convincing the consumer of the payoff in energy conservation. Rockwell, Dickey, and Jasa (1990) suggest capitalizing on the personal factor by using a team approach to conservation. All of these articles indicate the importance of the processes of attitude change in efforts to preserve the environment. In the following section we review some of the research demonstrating how these processes might be facilitated.

Social psychologists have exerted considerable effort to understanding the processes of persuasion and investigating factors that can promote attitude change. Carl Hovland and his associates conducted one of the most systematic programs of research in this area (Hovland, Janis, & Kelley, 1953). They identified three major categories of variables that should be considered in attitude change: the communicator (variables related to the individual delivering a persuasive message), the message (variables related to the communication itself), and the audience (variables related to the recipients of a persuasive communication).

Examples of communicator variables include expertness (Aronson, Turner, & Carlsmith, 1963) and trustworthiness (Walster, Aronson, & Abrahams, 1966). As you might expect, individuals who are perceived as experts (i.e., having some relevant knowledge that the audience does not) and as trustworthy (i.e., having nothing personal to gain by persuading the audience) are more influential than are nonexpert or untrustworthy communicators. Both of these variables can be thought of as related to the credibility of the communicator (i.e., is this a person I should bother listening to in the first place?). This suggests that persuasive appeals to save the environment should be delivered by people who are recognized as experts on the particular issue (e.g., the Surgeon General discussing health effects of air pollution) and as having nothing to gain by persuading the audience (e.g., Lee Iacocca arguing for walking rather than driving to work). Gonzales, Aronson, and Costanzo (1988) suggested a variety of strategies to increase communicator effectiveness, emphasizing training home-energy auditors to communicate vividly, to personalize their recommendations, to induce commitment, and to frame recommendations in terms of loss rather than gain.

Two major variables related to the message are the discrepancy between the communication and the audience's initial position (Hovland & Pritzker, 1957) and the degree of fear arousal created by the message (Janis, 1967). For both variables, an intermediate level seems to produce the greatest attitude change. That is, for a message to produce attitude change, it must deviate from the target's initial position, but extremely discrepant communications can result in a boomerang effect leading to a strengthening of the original position by either derogating the source or rejecting the argument outright. Also, messages need to arouse the audience, but extremely frightening scenarios could result in a defensive repression of the message to prevent anxiety. Thus, communications designed to promote environmentally constructive attitudes should not be too radical (e.g., arguing that people should not drive their cars at all) nor too pessimistic (you may have noted that your authors have not adopted Robert Heilbroner's dismal analysis of the human prospect).

A major variable related to the audience, or recipient(s), of a persuasive communication is the degree of commitment to the original position (Petty & Cacioppo, 1979). People who are very committed to their attitudes are extremely resistant to change, whereas people who do not feel more strongly one way or the other about an issue are more likely to be persuaded. Thus, efforts to produce changes in environmental attitudes are best directed at individuals who do not hold extreme positions. Also, commitment interacts with message discrepancy (i.e., the higher the commitment, the less discrepancy is required to produce the boomerang effect). The lesson here is that smaller attitude changes should be attempted for extremely committed individuals, whereas greater changes can be expected from middle-of-the-road audiences.

One of the problems with educational and attitude-change campaigns is the tenuous link between attitudes and behavior. As we discussed in Chapter 4, studies attempting to predict behavior from attitudes have generally reported a disconcerting inconsistency between the two. Similar findings have been reported by investigators of environmental attitudes and behavior (Cone & Hayes, 1980; Lingwood, 1971), while others (Arcury, 1990; Heberlein, 1989) have argued for the utility of attitude studies in promoting environmentally responsible behavior. It may be that attitude-behavior inconsistency is due to a real absence of a causal relationship between general environmental attitudes and specific environmental behaviors, or to methodological problems in assessing attitude-behavior relationships. A number of researchers have recently identified specific issues in the evaluation of the effectiveness of change programs (Bennett, 1989; Hanna, 1989; Heilman, 1989; Keating, 1989; Kushler, 1989). Whatever the reason for the lack of consistency, educational and attitude-change programs are worth pursuing—it may be that not enough time has elapsed since serious efforts to educate the public about environmental issues began in order to see an improvement in environmentally constructive behavior. Nonetheless, a great deal of research has taken the more direct approach of changing behavior vis-à-vis the environment. Indeed, some researchers and theoreticians have argued that an effective way to change attitudes is to first change behaviors (Bem, 1972).

We turn now to this application of behavioral technology to solving environmental problems.

Changing Behavior to Preserve the Environment

Earlier in this chapter it was suggested that conservation should actually be considered as a source of energy. The variability in energy use within the home is quite large, with researchers reporting that some families use as much as two or three times the energy as other families living in identical houses (Socolow, 1978). This difference can be traced to specific conservation behaviors in some homes that do not occur in others. Finding ways to encourage people on a large-scale basis to engage in behaviors to conserve energy in the home could result in a substantial energy savings. We also discussed the enormous energy cost involved in disposing of trash in our country. Thus, finding ways to reduce specific behaviors (e.g., littering) and to increase other behaviors (e.g., recycling) could also result in a major energy savings. Finally, we also discussed the immense difference in energy required for private versus public transportation. Here, also, encouraging individuals to choose public transportation could contribute to energy conservation.

     All of the above examples represent specific behaviors of individual people, which if modified could take us a long way toward preserving the environment for posterity. As mentioned earlier in this chapter, behavior modification lies within the domain of expertise of psychologists, and this is one contribution that psychology can make toward solving environmental problems. A number of environmental psychologists have already conducted much research on this issue. Perhaps most impressive among these efforts has been the work of E. Scott Geller and his associates (Geller, Winett, & Everett, 1982). Much of what follows is described in greater detail in their book *Preserving the Environment: New Strategies for Behavior Change.* The serious student of environment-behavior relationships and the future is urged to read this book.

Applied Behavior Analysis and Intervention

Geller and colleagues begin with the assumption that environmentally relevant behaviors, just as any other behaviors, can be increased or decreased in frequency by applying the principles of behavior modification. This approach is relatively simple and straightforward. One begins by defining in objective and specific terms the target behaviors to be increased or decreased. For example, we might be concerned with conserving energy via turning off lights when they are not needed or with decreasing litter by having refuse placed in appropriate receptacles. The next step is to make careful observations of the naturally occurring incidence of these behaviors, known as the *baseline period*. We might observe the frequency of lights being turned off in restrooms, offices, closets, etc., when they are not being used, or the frequency of individuals disposing of litter in trash cans and those dropping it indiscriminately. This phase is necessary to evaluate the efficacy of the subsequent phase, the *treatment period*. The treatment phase involves the manipulation of environmental stimuli or events preceding and/or following the target behavior. This phase might involve giving rewards for engaging in the desired target behavior (e.g., turning off lights), meting out punishments for engaging in nontarget behavior (leaving the lights on), providing models exhibiting "appropriate" behavior, etc. Behavioral observations are continued during this phase and are compared with their frequencies during baseline. The final phase is the *follow-up period* during which the experimental treatment is removed and observations are continued. This is often called an ABA design (see Figure 15-3), and a successful program is one in which the frequency of target behaviors increases (or decreases) from baseline to treatment

FIGURE 15-3 The proportion of cans sold in a cold drink vending machine that were placed in a nearby recycling bin under baseline, treatment (prompting), and follow up (no prompt . . . three weeks later) conditions.

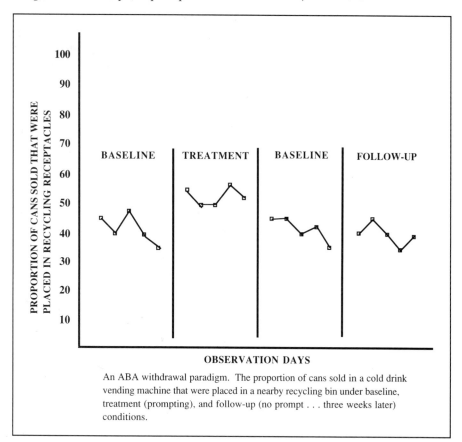

An ABA withdrawal paradigm. The proportion of cans sold in a cold drink vending machine that were placed in a nearby recycling bin under baseline, treatment (prompting), and follow-up (no prompt . . . three weeks later) conditions.

periods, and at least remains above (or below) the original baseline level during the posttreatment follow-up period.

The above design is appropriate for a single target group, but sometimes the behavior of a control group (individuals not receiving the treatment) is also observed during the three phases to rule out extraneous variables as explanations of frequency changes observed during the treatment and/or follow-up periods. Also, it should be clear that a critical feature of applied behavior analysis and intervention is the treatment period. Environmental psychologists have employed a wide variety of intervention strategies in this regard, and in the following section we will review some of these techniques. These can be generally classified as either antecedent strategies (stimuli or events presented before the target behaviors designed to either prompt or prevent their occurrence) or consequence strategies (stimuli or events presented after the target behaviors designed to either increase or decrease the probability of their recurrence). We will discuss these separately, although both strategies can (and in many instances should) be employed in combination.

Antecedent Strategies.   This intervention typically involves the use of either a written message (such as a "Please don't litter" sign) or a verbal statement (such as a radio or TV spot reminding people to turn off the lights in unoccupied rooms). These techniques are often referred to as *prompts* in that they are designed to trigger the occurrence or nonoccurrence of a particular response that may not have been performed without the reminder. As we shall see, prompts are relatively easy and inexpensive to employ, and they can be effective as well. A recent demonstration of their effectiveness was provided by Yu and Martin (1987). Golfers were given an explanation and photograph of ballmarks (i.e., damage to the putting green resulting from balls landing on the green hit from a distance) and recommended steps to repair them. This simple prompt produced a significant decrease in the number of unrepaired ballmarks at the course. The effectiveness of a prompt has been related to features of the prompt itself as well as aspects of the behaviors it is designed to encourage or discourage.

Prompts can be general (e.g., "Don't be a litterbug") or specific (e.g., "Please deposit litter in receptacle in back of room"). Specific prompts tend to be more effective, especially if they are close to where the desired behavior is to occur. For example, Winett (1978) was able to increase significantly the response of shutting off lights in public buildings by placing signs next to switches indicating that lights should be turned off when leaving the room. Prompts that are attractive or unusual are more effective than unattractive or unobtrusive prompts. For example, Geller, Brasted, and Mann (1980) found people much more likely to employ decorated trash receptacles than a standard trash can, and O'Neill, Blanck, and Joyner (1980) reported that on the Clemson University campus twice as much litter was deposited in a receptacle that looked like a hat students at Clemson typically wore to football games than in a standard container.

Finally, prompts that are polite rather than demanding are less likely to trigger psychological reactance (Brehm, 1972). For example, Reich and Robert-

FIGURE 15-4　Some parks encourage non-littering in children by using eye-catching role models.

son (1979) handed out flyers at a public swimming pool with the message, "Help Keep Your Pool Clean," "Don't Litter," or "Don't you DARE litter." The first message produced the least littering and the last produced the greatest amount. In general, prompting strategies are most effective for responses that are easy and convenient to make. Responses that require more effort—that is, are either inconvenient or time-consuming, tend not to be very amenable to prompting strategies (Geller, 1982). These types of behaviors are more likely to be responsive to consequence strategies.

Consequence Strategies.　These strategies involve the presentation/removal of a pleasant/unpleasant consequence after a behavior has occurred. These consequences can be generally categorized as *reinforcement* (consequences which increase the frequency of a behavior) or *punishment* (consequences which decrease the frequency of a behavior). Further, these consequences can be either *presented* (e.g., giving a tax rebate for installing additional installation in the residence, known as *positive reinforcement* because it presents a pleasant consequence for desirable behavior; applying a fine for littering, known as *positive punishment* because it presents an unpleasant consequence for undesirable behavior) or *removed* (e.g., lifting a ban on federal highway subsidies when a community lowers its pollution levels, known as *negative reinforcement* because it removes an unpleasant event; cancelling federal contracts with a corporation that has contaminated area water supplies, known as *negative punishment* because it removes a pleasant event). Finally, consequences can be either response-based (i.e., contingent upon the performance of a specific behavior, such as carpooling) or they can be outcome-based (i.e., contingent upon a specified standard of performance, such as sulfur dioxide emission levels). These relationships are summarized in Figure 15-5).

Geller and colleagues (1982) note that while psychologists have consistently demonstrated that positive reinforcement is more effective than either negative reinforcement or punishment, it is ironic that government has tended to rely on the latter methods in passing laws applying sanctions for undesirable behaviors rather than incentives for desirable behaviors. A problem with the control of behavior through aversive means is the lack of internal acceptance of the behavioral change. In other words, people perceive a greater threat to their freedom by aversive contingencies, resulting in psychological reactance and, at best, overt compliance in their behavior in order to avoid aversive consequences. People are more apt to internalize behavioral change when they perceive that they are working toward pleasant consequences. Thus, we will focus on positive reinforcement for response-based and outcome-based contingencies.

A great many studies have reported success in encouraging environmentally constructive behavior through positive reinforcement. Witmer and Geller (1976) were able to promote recycling paper by awarding raffle tickets to people who brought a specified amount of paper to a recycling center. Walker (1979) demonstrated that apartment renters were willing to set their room temperature at 74°F in the summer and keep windows and doors closed when the air conditioner was running in return for a $5.00 reduction in their rent. Kohlenberg and Phillips (1973) decreased littering by offering a coupon redeemable for a soft drink for depositing litter in a particular receptacle. Everett, Haywood, and Meyers (1974) were able to increase bus ridership by offering tokens redeemable at local businesses. Hake and Foxx (1978) produced a 10 percent reduction in miles of travel over a month by a $5.00 incentive, and Winett and Nietzel (1975) were able to produce reductions in home-heating energy through a similar incentive program. More recently, Levitt and Leventhal (1986) reported the effectiveness of the New York State "Bottle Bill" (requiring a five-cent deposit on returnable containers) on littering. They reported a significant difference in the number of returnable containers (but not nonreturnable containers) between New York and New Jersey (which did not have such legislation) as much as a year later. Clearly, even the consequence of only five cents can influence environmental behavior.

The above examples of reinforcement procedures represent only a small sampling of programs that have been shown to be effective in producing at least temporary changes in a wide range of environmentally relevant behaviors. The applications of consequence strategies are limited only by imagination and cre-

FIGURE 15-5 Four types of strategies for promoting the preservation of the environment.

| | | NATURE OF CONSEQUENCES | |
		PLEASANT	UNPLEASANT
ACTION	**APPLY**	**POSITIVE REINFORCEMENT** Provide "50% off pizza coupons" for each bag of litter picked up on roadside. $25 rebate on insurance premium for a 5,000-mile per year reduction in driving.	**POSITIVE PUNISHMENT** Post a list of people who continue to smoke in their offices. Patrons in restaurant call smoker the worst kind of polluter as smoke reaches their table.
	REMOVE	**NEGATIVE PUNISHMENT** City park pass taken away for two weeks for littering. Electric rates per kilowatt hour increase a specified amount as a result of exceeding some level of consumption.	**NEGATIVE REINFORCEMENT** City park pass reinstated on condition of picking up litter within park for specified period of time. Per pound surcharge on household garbage avoided by separating trash and recycling.

Four types of consequence strategies for promoting the preservation of the environment. The first example in each cell has the consequence dependent on some particular response, whereas the second example has the consequence dependent on a specified outcome.

ativity. A serious problem with these approaches, however, is the high costs of implementation on a large scale. Another problem characteristic of behavior modification programs in general is the maintenance of the desired behavior after the treatment period is over. A potential alternative that would alleviate these problems is simply to provide feedback to the individual regarding his or her behavior vis-à-vis the environment. Such information is useful in self-monitoring of behavior and can yield a sense of self-efficacy and satisfaction as a result of self-control. Examples of such methods include sending a special feedback card monthly regarding residential energy use (Seaver & Patterson, 1976), installing a device that illuminates a light when electricity use exceeds a particular criterion (Blakely, Lloyd, & Alferink, 1977), and teaching people how to read their own electric meters (Winett, Neale, & Grier, 1979). These are relatively inexpensive techniques suitable for widespread use, and they can be helpful in promoting long-term behavioral change.

AN INTEGRATION AND A LOOK TO THE FUTURE

We have reviewed a number of psychological approaches to altering the behavior of individuals to preserve the environment. These approaches include educational programs to inform the public about environmental problems and possible solutions, media campaigns to promote pro-environmental attitudes and values, and applied behavior analysis employing antecedent and consequence strategies. There are problems with each approach, but each has some value in encouraging environmentally constructive behavior. Optimally, all strategies would be employed on a large-scale basis, but the approach taken will depend on the particular problem being studied.

The point is that collectively our behaviors do make a difference either for better or worse for the future of the "commons." In this chapter and others we have considered a large variety of environmentally relevant behaviors, including expanding industry and transportation, and the polluting by-products of all these activities. All of these behaviors (as well as many others) contribute to environmental degradation and threaten the quality of life. On the other hand, we have also discussed behaviors such as litter control, energy conservation through less waste, and recycling as means of preserving the environment and future quality of life. As individuals we must choose between environmentally constructive or destructive behaviors, and our children's children will have to live with the consequences of those choices.

To return to the commons dilemma, this choice basically comes down to that between immediate self-interest and long-term public interest. We have outlined approaches favoring the latter choice. As we saw with social traps, choosing the former may have short-term benefits to the individual but long-range costs that could be tragic for humanity. Of course, there are short-term costs in taking steps to preserve the environment, but surely they are less than the costs likely to be incurred by posterity if they are not taken. Also, as Geller, Winett, and Everett (1982) have argued, there is nothing incompatible with pro-environmental behaviors and the "good life," and, indeed, wastefulness is incompatible with maintaining a high standard of living.

The approaches described in this chapter can have a major impact on environmental preservation. However, these represent only a part of the solutions to environmental problems. Geller and colleagues refer to these as "first-order change," in that they promote change in the behaviors of individuals within in a social system. Certainly, these changes will be more effective if they occur in the context of "system-level change" on the order of those described in Chapter 14. Thus, we are not arguing that changing the behavior of individuals is all that is required to be effective in the context of system-level changes in political and economic policies.

In the beginning of this chapter we argue that there is a false sense of security in the power of technology to solve environmental problems. We also pointed out that this is not to suggest that technology has no role to play in developing solutions. At many points in this text we have emphasized the need for an interdisciplinary approach to understanding environment–behavior relationships. Geller (1982) has proposed a model of "experimental social innovation" for integrating behavioral, physical, and system-level expertise that would focus on the individual, commercial, and governmental sectors that would target five areas of conservation for the future: heating/cooling, solid waste management, equipment efficiency, and water consumption. This model is inherently interdisciplinary and requires cooperation on the part of individuals and groups at all levels of society. We believe that this model represents a realistic and comprehensive approach for dealing with the complex problems facing society in order to preserve the environment for posterity.

SUMMARY

This chapter began with a discussion of the cavalier way in which we employ energy, a presentation of various uses of energy, and a discussion of how energy could be conserved. You were then asked to perform an exercise in which you were to imagine what your life would be like in the future. We suggested that the setting in which you imagined yourself probably included a clean, comfortable, and safe environment, but that this idyllic image is not likely to become a reality given past and current trends. It was argued that a reliance on physical technology alone to solve present and future environmental problems was not likely to be enough, and that changes in individual and collective behavior would also be needed to preserve it for posterity. After discussing barriers to such changes in the context of "social dilemmas," a number of approaches for producing individual behavioral change were reviewed, including educational and attitude change programs, prompting strategies, and reinforcement programs for encouraging environmentally constructive behavior. The chapter concluded with a call for an interdisciplinary approach to preserving the environment involving the private, commercial, and public sectors of society and integrating knowledge from the physical, social, and behavioral sciences. It is hoped that this text in some small way has served to further the cause of preserving the environment for posterity. Finally, we hope that you have, in the context of our Time-Outs, thought about the various issues and problems we have addressed and have added to the information we need to solve some of them.

IMPORTANT CONCEPTS

major energy consumers
energy intensiveness
energy conversions
fossils fuels
nonrenewable resources
passive solar
active solar
conservative as an "energy source"
social dilemma
tragedy of the commons
social traps
environmental education
changing environmental attitudes

communicator variables: expertise,
   trustworthiness
message variables: discrepancy, emotional
   arousal
audience variables: commitment, initial position
applied behavior analysis: baseline, intervention,
   follow-up
antecedent strategies: prompts
consequence strategies: positive/negative
   reinforcement/punishment
first-order change
system-level change
experimental social innovation

REFERENCES

Arcury, T.A. (1990). Environmental attitude and environmental knowledge. *Human Organization, 49*(4), 300–304.

Aronson, E., Turner, J.A., & Carlsmith, J.M. (1963). Communicator credibility and communicator descrepancy as determinants of opinion change. *Journal of Personality and Social Psychology, 67*, 31–36.

Asch, J., & Shore, B. M. (1975). Conservation behavior and the outcome of environmental education. *Journal of Environmental Education, 6*, 25–33.

Baldwin, M.F. (1971). Public policy on oil—An ecological perspective. *Ecology Law Quarterly, I*(2), 265.

Bem, D.J. (1972). Self-perception theory. In L. Berkowitz (Ed.), *Advances in experimental social psychology* (Vol. 6). New York: Academic Press.

Bennett, D.B. (1989). Four steps to evaluating environmental education learning experiences. *Journal of Environmental Education, 20*(2), 14–21.

Blakely, E.Q., Lloyd, K.E., & Alferink, L.A. (1977). *The effects of feedback on residential electrical peaking and hourly kilowatt consumption.* Unpublished manuscript, Department of Psychology, Drake University, Des Moines, Iowa.

Brehm, J. (1972). *Responses to loss of freedom: A theory of psychological reactance.* New York: General Learning Press.

British Petroleum. (1992). *Statistical review of world energy.* London: Author.

Burrus, B.L.L., Bammel, G., & Kopitsky, K. (1988). Content analysis: A technique for measuring attitudes expressed in environmental education literature. *Journal of Environmental Education, 19*(4), 32–37.

Clark, W. (1975). *Energy for survival: The alternative to extinction.* Garden City, N.Y.: Anchor Books.

Cohen, M.R. (1973). Environmental information vs. environmental attitudes. *Journal of Environmental Education, 5*, 5–8.

Cone, J.D., & Hayes, S.C. (1980). *Environmental problems–behavioral solutions.* Monterey, Calif.: Brooks/Cole.

Conover, M.E. (1986). Differences and relationships between selected characteristics of participants and nonparticipants in an interest-free retrofitting loan program. *Dissertation Abstracts International, 46*(9-A), 2593.

Costanzo, M., Archer, D., Aronson, E., & Pettigrew, T. (1986). Energy conservation behavior: The difficult path from information to action. *American Psychologist, 41*(5), 521–528.

Dawes, R.M. (1980). Social dilemmas. *Annual Review of Psychology, 31*, 169–193.

Dennis, M.L., & Soderstrom, J.E. (1988). Application of social psychological and evaluation research: Lessions from energy information programs. *Evaluation and Program Planning, 11*(1), 77–84.

Dewling, R.T. (1970). *Statement before the subcom-*

mittee on air and water pollution of the U.S. Senate Committee on Public Works, Machias, Maine.

DeYoung, R. (1986). Some psychological aspects of recycling: The structure of conservation satisfactions. *Environment and Behavior, 18*(4), 435–449.

Ditton, R.B., & Goodale, T.C. (1974). Water quality perceptions and attitudes. *Journal of Environmental Education, 6,* 21.

Dresner, M.H. (1990). Changing energy end-use patterns as a means of reducing global-warming trends. *Journal of Environmental Education, 21*(2), 41–46.

Everett, P.B., Haywood, S.C., & Meyers, A.W. (1974). Effects of a token reinforcement procedure on bus ridership. *Journal of Applied Behavior Analysis, 7,* 1–9.

Faegre, T. (1979). *Tents: Architecture of the Nomads.* Garden City, N.Y.: Anchor Books.

Geller, E.S. (1982). The energy crisis and behavioral science: A conceptual framework for large-scale intervention. In A.W. Childs & G.B. Melten (Eds.), *Rural psychology.* New York: Plenum.

Geller, E.S., Brasted, W., & Mann, M. (1980). Waste receptacle designs as interventions for litter control. *Journal of Environment Systems, 9,* 145–160.

Geller, E.S., Winett, R.A., & Everett, P.B. (1982). *Preserving the environment: New strategies for behavior change.* Elmsford, N.Y.: Pergamon Press.

Geller, E.S., Wylie, R.C., & Farris, J.C. (1971). An attempt at applying prompting and reinforcement toward pollution control. *Proceedings of the 79th Annual Convention of the American Psychological Association, 6,* 701–702.

Goitein, B., & Weinstein, B. (1986). The consequences of participant satisfaction with energy conservation programs. *Evaluation Review, 10*(3), 377–384.

Gonzales, M.H., Aronson, E., & Costanzo, M.A. (1988). Using social cognition and persuasion to promote energy conservation: A quasi-experiment. *Journal of Applied Social Psychology, 18*(12), 1049–1066.

Griffin, R.J. (1989). Communication and the adoption of energy conservation measures by the elderly. *Journal of Environmental Education, 20*(4), 19–28.

Griffin, R.J., Glynn, C.J., & McLeod, J.M. (1986). Energy and communication: Social status in a tale of two cities. *Man Environment Systems, 16*(1), 34–44.

Hake, D.F., & Foxx, R.M. (1978). Promoting gasoline conservation: The effects of reinforcement schedules, a leader and self-recording. *Behavior Modification, 2,* 339–369.

Hanna, G.M. (1989). The effects of adventure and ecology education programming on participants' wilderness knowledge, attitude, intentions and behavior. *Dissertation Abstracts International, 50*(2-A), 386.

Hardin, G. (1968). The tragedy of the commons. *Science, 162,* 1243–1248.

Heberlein, T.A. (1989). Attitudes and environmental management. *Journal of Social Issues, 45*(1), 37–57.

Heilman, J.G. (1989). Theory-driven evaluation: How conceptions of personal choice and organizational process can inform studies of energy conservation. *Evaluation and Program Planning, 12*(2), 113–120.

Hirst, E. (1973). Energy intensiveness of passenger and freight transport modes, 1950–1970. *ORNL Report NSF-EP-44.* Oak Ridge, Tenn.: Oak Ridge National Laboratory.

Hovland, C., Janis, I., & Kelley, (1953). *Communication and persuasion.* New Haven, Conn.: Yale University Press.

Hovland, C.I., & Pritzker, H.A. (1957). Extent of opinion change as a function of amount of change advocated. *Journal of Abnormal and Social Psychology, 54,* 257–261.

Janis, I.L. (1967). Effects of fear arousal on attitude change: Recent developments in theory and experimental research. In L. Berkowitz (Ed.), *Advances in experimental social psychology* (Vol. 3). New York: Academic Press.

Jeppesen, J.C. (1986). Residential energy conservation: Do follow-up programs make a difference? *Dissertation Abstracts International, 46*(7-B), 2498–2499.

Jordan, J.R., Hungerford, H.R., & Tomera, A.N. (1986). Effects of two residential environmental workshops on high school students. *Journal of Environmental Education, 18*(1), 15–22.

Keating, K.M. (1989). Self-selection: Are we beating a dead horse? *Evaluation and Program Planning, 12*(2), 137–142.

Kohlenberg, R.J., & Phillips, T. (1973). Reinforcement and rate of litter depositing. *Journal of Applied Behavior Analysis, 6,* 391–396.

Kushler, M.G. (1989). Use of evaluation to

improve energy conservation programs: A review and case study. *Journal of Social Issues, 45*(1), 153–168.

Levitt, L., & Leventhal, G. (1986). Litter reduction: How effective is the New York state bottle bill? *Environment and Behavior, 18*(4), 467–479.

Lingwood, D.A. (1971). Environmental education through information seeking: The case of an environmental teach-in. *Environment and Behavior, 3,* 220–262.

Loomis, D.K. (1989). Common property natural resources and outcome interdependence: Effects of motivational orientation, information and resource characteristics. *Dissertation Abstracts International, 49*(11-A), 3504.

Makhijani, A.B., & Lichtenberg, A.J. (1971). *An assessment of energy and materials utilization in the USA: Memorandum No. ERL-M310.* Berkeley: College of Engineering, University of California.

Naseth, G.J. (1990). The effects of warnings of impending resource depletion, resource control and environmental attitudes on behavior in a social dilemma. *Dissertation Abstracts International, 51*(3-B), 1549.

National Mineral Wool Insulation Association, Inc. (1972). *Impact of improved thermal performance in conserving energy.* New York: Author.

National Wildlife Federation (1970). *Conservation News.*

Neely, J. (1972). *Thesis in energy utilization.* Cambridge, Mass.: Harvard University Press, pp. 111–12.

Noe, F.P., & Snow, R. (1990). Hispanic cultural influence on environmental concern. *Journal of Environmental Education, 21*(2), 27–34.

O'Neill, G.W., Blanck, L.S., & Joyner, M.A. (1980). The use of stimulus control over littering in a natural setting. *Journal of Applied Behavior Analysis, 13,* 379–381.

Parthasarathy, R. (1989, Fall). Psychological or attitudinal factors which influence the introduction of energy conservation technologies. *Abhigyan,* 36–47.

Petty, R.E., & Cacioppo, J.T. (1979). Effects of forewarning of persuasive intent and involvement on cognitive response and persuasion. *Personality and Social Psychology Bulletin, 5,* 173–176.

Pierson, G.W. (1973). *The moving American.* New York: Knopf.

Platt, J.R (1973). Social traps. *American Psychologist, 28,* 641–651.

Protess, D.L., Cook, F.L., Curtin, T.R., & Gordon, M.T. (1987). The impact of investigative reporting on public opinion and policymaking: Targeting toxic waste. *Public Opinion Quarterly, 51*(2), 166–185.

Prugh, T. (1993). Energy (in the *1993 Information Please Environmental Almanac*). Boston: Houghton Mifflin.

Purcell, A.H. (1980). *The waste watchers: A citizen's handbook for conserving energy and resources.* Garden City, N.Y.: Anchor Books.

Rankin, R.E. (1969). Air pollution control and public apathy. *Journal of the Air Pollution Control Association, 19,* 565–569.

Reich, J.W., & Robertson, J.L. (1979). Reactance and norm appeal in antilittering messages. *Journal of Applied Social Psychology, 9,* 91–101.

Rockwell, K.S., Dickey, E.C., & Jasa, P.J. (1990). The personal factor in evaluation use: A case study of a steering committee's use of a conservation tillage survey. *Evaluation and Program Planning, 13*(4), 389–394.

Rudofsky, B. (1964). *Architecture without architects.* Garden City, N.Y.: Doubleday.

Samuelson, C.D. (1990). Energy conservation: A social dilemma approach. *Social Behaviour, 5*(4), 207–230.

Samuelson, C.D., & Messick, D.M. (1986). Alternative structural solutions to resource dilemmas. *Organizational Behavior and Human Decision Processes, 37*(1), 139–155.

Schahn, J., & Holzer, E. (1990). Studies of individual environmental concern: The role of knowledge, gender, and background variables. *Environment and Behavior, 22*(6), 767–786.

Schreckengost, R.L. (1986). Energy-efficient housing alternatives: A predictive model of factors affecting household perceptions. *Dissertation Abstracts International, 47*(1-B), 160.

Seaver, W.B., & Patterson, A.H. (1976). Decreasing fuel oil consumption through feedback and social consumption. *Journal of Applied Behavior Analysis, 9,* 147–152.

Sivek, D.J., & Hungerford, H. (1990). Predictors of responsible behavior in members of three Wisconsin conservation organizations. *Journal of Environmental Education, 21*(2), 35–40.

Socolow, R.H. (1978). *Saving energy in the home.* Cambridge, Mass.: Ballinger.

Stanford Research Institute (1972). *Patterns of energy consumption in the United States, prepared for Office of Science and Technology, Executive Office of the President.* Washington, D.C.: U.S. Government Printing Office.

Stein, R. (1978). *Architecture and energy.* Garden City, N.Y.: Anchor Books.

Stephens, S.H. (1986). Attitudes toward socially responsible consumption: Development and validation of a scale and investigation of relationships to clothing acquisition and discard bahaviors. *Dissertation Abstracts International,* 47(1-B), 160–161.

Stobaugh, R. (1979). After the peak: The threat of hostile oil. In R. Stobaugh & D. Yergin (Eds.), *Energy future: Report of the energy project at the Harvard Business School.* New York: Ballantine.

Stout-Wiegand, N. (1986). Development of the short scale of environmental concern. *Dissertation Abstracts International,* 46(8-A), 2241–2242.

Study of Critical Environmental Problems (SCEP). (1970). *Man's impact on the global environment: Assessment and recommendations for action.* Cambridge, Mass.: MIT Press.

Taylor, D.E. (1989). Blacks and the environment: Toward an explanation of the concern and action gap between blacks and whites. *Environment and Behavior,* 21(2), 175–205.

Temple, J.A. (1986). Three interactive processes of social influence: Facilitation changes in energy conservation attitudes and actions as a function of exposure to five types of communication strategies. *Dissertation Abstracts International,* 46(7-B), 2502.

Thornton, J.A., McMillan, P.H., & Romanovsky, P. (1989). Perceptions of water pollution in South Africa: Case studies from two water bodies. *South African Journal of Psychology,* 19(4), 199–204.

Time (1973). *The tallest skyscraper,* June 11, pp. 54–59.

United States Department of Transportation (1972). *Summary of National Transportation Statistics.* Washington, D.C.: U.S. Department of Transportation.

Van Houwelingen, J.H., & Van Raaij, W.F. (1989). The effect of goal-setting and daily electronic feedback on in-home energy use. *Journal of Consumer Research,* 16, 98–105.

Vining. (1987). Environmental decisions: The interactions of emotions, information, and decision context. *Journal of Environmental Psychology,* 7(1), 13–30.

Vining, J., & Ebreo, A. (1990). What makes a recycler? A comparison of recyclers and nonrecyclers. *Environment and Behavior,* 22(1), 55–73.

Walker, J.M. (1979). Energy demand behavior in a master-meter apartment complex: An experimental analysis. *Journal of Applied Psychology,* 64, 190–196.

Walster, E., Aronson, E., & Abrahams, D. (1966). On increasing the persuasiveness of a low prestige communicator. *Journal of Experimental Social Psychology,* 2, 325–342.

Williams, E. (1991). College students and recycling: Their attitudes and behaviors. *Journal of College Student Development,* 32(1), 86–88.

Winett, R.A. (1978). Prompting turning-out lights in unoccupied rooms. *Journal of Environmental Systems,* 6, 237–241.

Winett, R.A. (1987). Comment on Costanzo et al.'s "Energy concervation behavior: The difficult path from information to action." *American Psychologist,* 42(10), 957–958.

Winett, R.A., Neale, M.S., & Grier, H.C. (1979). The effects of self-monitoring and feedback on residential electricity consumption. *Journal of Applied Behavior Analysis,* 12, 173–184.

Winett, R.A., & Nietzel, M. (1975). Behavioral ecology: Contingency management of residential use. *American Journal of Community Psychology,* 3, 123–133.

Witmer, J.F., & Geller, E.S. (1976). Facilitating paper recycling: Effects of prompts, raffles, and contests. *Journal of Applied Behavior Analysis,* 9, 315–322.

Yergin, D. (1979). Conservation: The key energy source. In R. Stobaugh & D. Yergin (Eds.), *Energy future: Report of the energy project at the Harvard Business School.* New York: Ballantine.

Yu, D., & Martin, G.L. (1987). Low-cost procedures to conserve a public sport environment. *Behavior Modification,* 11(2), 241–250.

INDEX

Name Index

Subject Index

law and, 226
  in living environment, 216–19
  predictability, 214–16
  in schools/hospitals, 221–22
  social behavior and, 219–20
  sources of, 208
  stress and, 138
  task performance and, 40–43, 69
  in workplace, 208–14; comfort effects, 211; health effects, 209–10; hearing loss, 210–11; productivity effects, 211–12; reduction of, 212–14
Nomothetic approach, 331
Norwegian lemmings, population density and, 136–37
Nuclear blackmail, 385
Nuisance, defined, 400–401

Object perception, 35
Observation, 58
Observational learning, 103
Observational measurement techniques, 65–68
One-story plan, 345
Open plan, for organizing space, 344–45
Open-space classrooms, 306–7
Operant conditioning, 103, 106–7
Optimizing process, privacy as, 267–68
Organism-environment relationships
  causal links, 27–31
  example of, 40–43
  framework for understanding, 31–38
  model of, 38–40
Orientation, to new environments, 88–89
Osteoporosis, 165
Outside density, 240
Overpopulation, 124, 384
Overstaffing, 25
  urbanization and, 234
Ozone (O$_3$), 189

Particulates, 193–95
Passive solar
  design, 327
  systems, 421
Passive wall design, 344
Paths, cognitive maps and, 90
Perceived risk, actual risk *vs.*, 390–91
Perception, 76–87. *See also* Environmental perception
  cognitive bases of, 80–81
  complexity of, 82–83
  contextual/social bases of, 81–82
  psychophysics and, 76–79
Persistence prediction, 310, 311
Personal distance, 257–58, 274–75
Personal space. *See also* Privacy; Territoriality
  crowding and, 280–81
  factors influencing, 278–79
  functions of, 276–77
  interpersonal distance zones, 274–75; behavioral correlates of, 275
  invasions of, 279–80
  measuring, 277–78
Personal space invasion, 20
Phons, 207
Physical milieu, standing patterns of behavior and, 24–25
Pineal gland, 163–64
Pitch, 206, 207
Place-specificity of behavior, 27–31
Planned Unit Developments (PUD), 348
Plug-in homes, 348
Political action committees (PACs), 399
Pollution. *See* Chemical pollution; Noise pollution
Pollution control, economic factors in, 397–98
Polychlorinated biphenyls (PCBs), 2

Population density, 10, 69. *See also* Crowding; Urbanization
  density/crowding distinction, 240–42
  difficulties in defining, 239–40
  inside, 240
  outside, 240
  social, 242
  spatial, 242
Population trends, 10, 230–32. *See also* Urbanization
Positive punishment, 435–38
Positive reinforcement, 106, 435–38
Post-impact effects, of natural disasters, 369–70
Postindustrialized society, 387
Prediction, as goal of science, 49–50
Preindustrial vernacular architecture, 325–26
Preserving the Environment: New Strategies for Behavior Change (Geller, et al.), 418
Primary appraisal, 124–26
Primary territories, 260
Primitive architecture, 323–25
Primitive beliefs, 103–4
Prison design, 300–303
Privacy. *See also* Personal space; Territoriality
  defined, 267–69
  hospital design and, 294–95
  research, 270–72; functions, 270; nonverbal mechanisms, 271–72; physical mechanisms, 272; verbal mechanisms, 270–71, 271–72
Private spaces, residential design and, 337–38
Proactive government, 399
Probabilistic functionalism, perception and, 85–87
Problem solving, cognitive maps and, 96
Productivity effects, workplace noise and, 211–12
Prompts, 434–35
Prosocial behavior, rural-urban differences in, 235
Proxemics, 256
Psychologic, concept of, 104
Psychological reactance, 22
Psychological reconstruction, after natural disasters, 368
Psychophysics, 76–79
  stimulus detection, 76–77
  stimulus discrimination, 78–79
  stimulus recognition, 77–78
  stimulus scaling, 79
Public distance, 274, 275
Public policy, environmental psychology and, 11
Public territories, 260, 261, 272
Punishment
  environmental behavior change and, 435–37
  operant conditioning and, 106
Purposive approach, 330–31

Questionnaires, 62–63
Queuing theory, 314–15

Random assignment, 59
Rate of time preference, 396–97
Rating scales, 63–64
Reactance, 62, 64–65
Reactive government, 399
Reasoned action model, 108–10
Recreational areas, density effects in, 248–49
Refrigerator center, in kitchen design, 339
Reinforcement-affect model, 35, 104–5
Reinforcement procedures, 435–38
Relative humidity
  cardiovascular systems and, 161
  respiratory illnesses and, 160–62
  thermal comfort and, 155
Relaxation response, 141
Reliability, 54–55
Renewable energy systems, 420–21
Research methods

Research methods *(cont.)*
  criteria for evaluating, 53–58; reliability, 54–55; validity,
    55–58
  in environmental psychology, 58–71
  goals of science and, 48–53, 58
Reserve, privacy and, 269
Residential-care facilities, design of, 296–300
Residential density, effects of, 247–48
Residential design, 322–49
  basics, 332–45; group/private spaces, 337–38; human factors,
    333–36; lifespace concept, 336–37; planning program,
    332–33; space organization, 344–45; support spaces,
    339–41; support systems, 341–44
  energy use and, 416
  future issues, 348–49
  history of, 323–29; animal architecture, 323; climatic aspects
    in, 327–28; modern vernacular architecture, 326–27;
    preindustrial vernacular architecture, 325–26; present-day,
    328–29; primitive human architecture, 323–25
  residential satisfaction, research on, 330–32; conceptual
    approaches, 330–31; residential preference, 331; space use,
    331–32
  for single parents/homeless, 345–48
Resistance stage, of GAS, 123, 124
Resource Conservation and Recovery Act, 399
Resource depletion, environmental psychology and, 11
Resource management, economics of, 396–97
  risk assessment and, 388–92
Resources Planning Act, 399
Respiratory illnesses, indoor atmosphere and, 159–61. *See also*
    Chemical pollutants, urbanization, particulates, smoking
Response set, 64
Reticular activating system (RAS), 20, 122–23
Reticular formation, 122
Rickets, 165
Risk
  acceptability, 388–89; vested interest model, 389
  actual *vs.* perceived, 390–91
  assessment, 388
  perception, 389–90
Running records, 68
Rural-urban comparisons, 234

Santa Anas, 169, 171
Schema discrepancy model, 102
Schools. *See* Education environments
Science
  goals of, 48–53, 58; control, 48–49; prediction, 49–50;
    understanding, 50–53
  meanings of, 48, 58
Scientific method, 48, 58
Seasonal affective disorder (SAD), 164
Secondary appraisals, 122
Secondary territories, 260–61
Seismic neurosis, 367
Selective control, privacy as, 268
Self-fulfilling prophecies, 56
Self-protection, personal space and, 276
Self-report measures, 62–64
  reactive nature of, 64–65
Self-serving subject, 64
Serving center, in kitchen design, 339
Sharavs, 169, 171
Shared symbols, cognitive maps and, 96, 97
Sidestream smoke, 190
  mainstream smoke *vs.*, 191–92
Sika deer die-off, 236, 237–38
Single-issue politics, 399
Single parents, residential design for, 345–48
Size constancy, 81, 83
Skin-encapsulated ego, frontier mentality and, 393–94

Social acceptability set, 64
Social density, 242
Social dilemma, 425–26
Social distance, 257–58, 274, 275
Social learning, 107
Social/situational variables
  personal space and, 278–79
Social support, as stress moderator, 140–41
Social traps, 426
Sociospatial system, 264
Solar
  architecture, 327–28
  energy, 420–21
Solitude, privacy and, 268
Sound, physical components of, 205–7. *See also* Noise pollution
Space organization
  living plan types, 345
  open *vs.* closed plans, 344–45
  plan selection, 345
Space *vs.* place, in residential design, 330
Spatial density, 242
Specific *vs.* diversive exploration, 99
Split-half reliability, 54
Standing patterns of behavior, physical milieu and, 24–25
State-Trait Anxiety Inventory, 136
Steady-state economy, 398
Steady-state influence
  of environment, 33–34; disruptions from, 34–35
  goal-directed behavior and, 37–38
Stimulus
  detection, 76–77
  discrimination, 78–79
  generalization, 106
  recognition, 77–78
  scaling, 76, 79
Stimulus load theories, 18, 20–22, 26
  urbanization and, 234
Stress-strain hypothesis, 133, 134
Stress/stressors. *See* Environmental stress
Subjective norm, 109
Sulfur oxide (SO_2), 187–89
Sunlight, 162–67
  beneficial/harmful effects of, 165–67
  human rhythms and, 164
  light dimensions and, 162–63
  pineal gland and, 163–64
Supply and demand, law of, 396
Support spaces, design features of, 339–41
  general storage, 341
  kitchens, 339–40
  utility rooms, 340
Support systems, in residential design, 341–44
  heating, 342–43
  lighting, 341–42
  wall design, 343–44
Suprachiasmatic nucleus (SCN), 163–64
Surprisingness, 99
Symmetry, of sound waves, 206, 207
Systemization, in new environments, 88, 89
System-level change, 439

Task performance. *See also* Arousal, Yerkes-Dodson Law
  ambient temperature and, 156–57
  noise and, 40–43, 69
Technological catastrophes, 357
  effects of, 371–78
  natural disasters and, similarities/differences, 363–64
Temperature. *See* Ambient temperature
Territorial Imperative, The (Ardrey), 257
Territoriality, 256–66. *See also* Crowding; Personal space;
    Privacy

animal, 257–58
human: animal *vs.*, 258–60; research on, 262–66; types, 260–61
Terrorism, as blackmail, 385
Test-retest reliability, 54–55
Theory, interrelationship of data and, 50–53
Thermal comfort, 154–56
Thermal lag, 327–28
Threat appraisals, 121
Three Mile Island, 2, 125, 138, 373–74
Timbre, 206, 207
Tinnitus, 217
Tobacco smoke, 189–93
restrictive legislation, 190
sidestream *vs.* mainstream, 191–92
social effects, 192
Toxic Substance Control Act, 399
Toxic waste, 2
disposal sites, 376–78
Tragedy of the commons, 425–27
Trajectory prediction, 310, 311
Transportation, energy use in, 413–14
Treatment period, in applied behavior analysis, 433–34

Unconditioned response, 105
Unconditioned stimulus, 105
Understaffing, 25
Understanding, as goal of science, 50–53
Unobtrusive measurement techniques, 67
Urbanization
accelerating trend toward, 230–32
beneficial effects, 235–36
physical effects, 232–33; theories of, 233–34
social-behavioral effects, 234–35
urban-rural comparisons, 234
Urban sprawl, 232
User-designer
congruence, 308–9

interaction, 288–91
Utility rooms, design features of, 340

Validity, 55–58
Values, attitude formation and, 103–4
Values/value priorities, environmental decision making and, 391–92
Variables
control of, 48–49
dependent, 49
independent, 49
Vernacular architecture
modern, 326–27
preindustrial, 325–26
Vested interest model, 389
Vicarious conditioning, 107
Victimization hypothesis, 133, 134
Vitamin D, 165
Voluntary risk, 389
Vulnerability hypothesis, 133, 134

Wall design, 343–44
Walsh-Healy Public Contracts Act (1968), 223
War
as external challenge to humanity, 384, 386
territoriality and, 265
Waste Watchers, The (Purcell), 418
Water Resources Planning Act, 399
Weather. *See* Atmospheric environment
Weber's law, 78
White noise, 206
Wide band sounds, 206
Wind, as behavioral determinant, 168–70
Work centers, in kitchen design, 339–40

Yerkes-Dodson law, 19